People Resourcing

PEARSON
Education

We work with leading authors to develop the strongest educational materials in human resources, bringing cutting-edge thinking and best learning practice to a global market.

Under a range of well-known imprints, including Financial Times Prentice Hall, we craft high quality print and electronic publications which help readers to understand and apply their content, whether studying or at work.

To find out more about the complete range of our publishing, please visit us on the World Wide Web at: www.pearsoned.co.uk

PEOPLE RESOURCING

HRM in Practice

Second edition

Stephen Pilbeam
Marjorie Corbridge

 Prentice Hall
FINANCIAL TIMES

An imprint of **Pearson Education**

Harlow, England • London • New York • Boston • San Francisco • Toronto • Sydney • Singapore • Hong Kong
Tokyo • Seoul • Taipei • New Delhi • Cape Town • Madrid • Mexico City • Amsterdam • Munich • Paris • Milan

Pearson Education Limited
Edinburgh Gate
Harlow
Essex CM20 2JE
England

and Associated Companies throughout the world

Visit us on the World Wide Web at:
www.pearsoned.co.uk

First published 1998
Second edition 2002

ISBN 0 273 65580 9

British Library Cataloguing-in-Publication Data
A catalogue record for this book is available from the British Library

Library of Congress Cataloging-in-Publication Data
Pilbeam, Stephen.
   People resourcing : HRM in practice / Stephen Pilbeam, Marjorie Corbridge.—2nd ed.
      p. cm.
   Rev. ed. of: Employment resourcing / Marjorie Corbridge. 1998.
   Includes bibliographical references and index.
   ISBN 0–273–65580–9 (pbk.)
      1. Personnel management.   I. Corbridge, Marjorie.   II. Corbridge, Marjorie.
   Employment resourcing.   III. Title.
   HF5549 .C7262 2002
   658.3—dc21   2002022247

10 9 8 7 6 5
07 06 05

Typeset in 10/12.5pt Sabon by 35
Printed and bound in Malaysia

CONTENTS

LIST OF FIGURES

LIST OF EXHIBITS

PREFACE

Title of the book and relationship to the CIPD Professional Standards

The first edition of this book was titled *Employment Resourcing*, rather than the Chartered Institute of Personnel and Development's *Employee Resourcing*, quite simply because not all those who work in organisations are employees. Therefore employment resourcing was considered by us to be a more holistic and contemporary term. The 2002 revision of the CIPD Professional Standards has produced the title *People Resourcing* and we are quite comfortable with this. We have, however, stretched the title of the book to *People Resourcing – HRM in Practice* to reflect the applied nature of our approach and also the growing use of the term HRM. People resourcing is a highly contextual and contingent activity and this is recognised throughout the book. We do not believe that there is 'one right way' to resource organisations with people, as it all depends on the contingent characteristics of the organisation and the people. The contextual nature of people resourcing makes it necessary for managers to be aware of influences in the internal and external environments. This is recognised throughout the book and given particular attention in Chapters 1, 2, 15 and 21.

People resourcing is often treated in a narrow way with a focus principally upon human resource planning, recruitment and termination of employment. This ignores the breadth of activity necessary for the management and retention of people. This book therefore addresses the **breadth** of resourcing issues and includes all the activities essential for the acquisition, management and retention of people from HR planning through to release from employment.

Therefore the aim of the book is:

> **to describe and to analyse current practice and developments in people resourcing with full regard to context.**

This people resourcing text meets the knowledge and understanding requirements of the CIPD Professional Standards for the People Resourcing module, and the CIPD performance indicators/learning outcomes have been matched against the chapters in this book (see below). The primary focus of the book is on the effective resourcing of organisations with people, but we have **horizontally integrated** Employee Reward, Employee Relations and Learning and Development to enable this book to be used as a text for the CIPD People Management and Development (PM and D) field. This provides an opportunity to integrate this field with the People Resourcing module, and the PM and D performance indicators/learning outcomes are also mapped against the chapters in this book (see below). In addition, the chapters on reward, relations and development offer a useful summary for the CIPD generalist modules. It is therefore intended to be a multi-purpose CIPD text.

As well as serving the needs of CIPD students, the book is sufficiently comprehensive in scope to be attractive to tutors and students on other management or business related programmes who are seeking an applied and integrated text to contribute to the exploration of fundamental aspects of managing people in contemporary organisations. Units of HRM study, particularly on HND, degree and postgraduate programmes, invariably have a high people resourcing element. We were encouraged by the reviewers' comments on the first edition and it was evident from these that the book was being used not only on professional programmes but also on Level 3 undergraduate units and on Masters programmes. We are also aware that the book is used as underpinning knowledge for personnel and development NVQs and it has also claimed a place on the bookshelf of HR practitioners.

Changes in the 2002 edition

This text has been fully updated to reflect:

- Changes in the developing body of HR knowledge.
- The 2002 CIPD Professional Standards, which place increased emphasis on the HR practitioner as a Business Partner who is not only professionally competent but seeks an added-value contribution through strategic awareness and an identification with the ideology of his or her managerial colleagues.
- Significant changes in employment and related law since the book was first published in 1998.
- A greater acknowledgement of the value of computerised HR information systems and the rapid development of e-enabled HR (Chapters 2 and 5).

In addition to updating and adding new material to existing chapters we have included three new chapters – **The changing world of work and the changing role of the HR professional, Human resource strategy** and, to reflect the proliferation in the use of competencies in HR activity, **Competencies in people resourcing.**

Style and approach

- The functions of effective people resourcing are examined whilst seeking a balance between academic rigour and practitioner relevance.
- Prescriptive solutions are avoided and critical evaluation is encouraged to enable HR practitioners and line managers to make informed choices from available resourcing options – in other words there is a need to be 'a thinking performer'.
- Resourcing questions are raised but 'pre-packaged' answers are not provided.
- The study programme progresses logically, and whilst necessarily having to divide the book into topic areas we aim to avoid the disintegration of what we see as an integrated subject.

Each chapter begins with clear objectives and ends with a summary of the main learning points. Other pedagogical features include illustrative exhibits, discussion topics, assignments, in-class activities, coursework opportunities and short cases. Relevant references enable the reader to pursue lines of enquiry. In this preliminary section we also include a list of websites which may be useful to students of people resourcing.

Our overall approach reflects our experience as HR practitioners as well as HR teachers, and we are evidently straddling the practitioner/academic 'divide' – we get compliments and criticisms from both camps. This encourages us to continue with this approach in the hope that we offer something distinctly different.

CIPD PROFESSIONAL STANDARDS

The content of this book is mapped against both the operational (to be able to) and the knowledge (to understand and explain) performance indicators and learning outcomes of the CIPD Professional Standards for the People Resourcing module and for the PM and D field. Relevant chapters are indicated against each performance indicator or learning outcome for the reader's benefit.

People Resourcing Professional Standards: performance indicators

Operational indicators – practitioners must be able to:

1. Make constructive contributions to the development or enhancement of people resourcing policies.   All

2. Evaluate existing people resourcing processes, systems and procedures, and propose cost-effective improvements.   All

3. Optimise the use of available tools and techniques in the field of IT (including the Internet) for all aspects of people resourcing.   2 and 5

4. Assist with the design, development, implementation and review of people resourcing methods to resolve specific corporate scenarios; representative examples are geographical relocation, new business development, management of an acquisition, corporate restructuring, graduate/expatriate appointments, delayering, devolution, decentralisation, retrenchment, and using an outsourcing partner such as a recruitment agency.   All

5. Undertake the full range of day-to-day functions for which a people resourcing professional generally is accountable, for example: All
    Recruitment   6 and 7
    Performance   11, 20 and 21
    Reward   9 and 10
    Retention   All
    Release   18 and 19

6. Contribute to the development of human resource plans that relate to and help achieve business/corporate goals.   3 and 4

7. Critically evaluate existing people resourcing systems and new approaches or methodologies.   Thematic

8. Co-operate positively with executive/managerial stakeholders – 'customers' – in the design and implementation of resourcing processes.   2

9. Advocate and secure compliance with all appropriate ethical and legal obligations associated with people resourcing.   6, 7, 8, 13, 17, 19 and 20

10. Apply the principles and practice of Continuing Professional Development for their own personal development.   12 and 21

Knowledge indicators – practitioners must understand and be able to explain:

1. The underpinning rationale for people resourcing as a means for accomplishing corporate purposes, strategies and goals through people.	1, 2 and 3
2. The environmental context in which people resourcing is designed, operated, reviewed and improved.	1, 2 and 15
3. The benefits, limitations and potential of existing and emerging methodologies in the generic field of people resourcing.	All
4. The legal obligations governing the creation and use of all people resourcing strategies, policies, procedures and systems.	6, 7, 8, 13, 14, 17, 19 and 20
5. Ethical criteria for all key aspects of people resourcing, including the benefits of compliance and the risk associated with its neglect.	1 and thematic
6. The systematic approach to people resourcing, from the creation of a cost-effective human resource plan, through recruitment, selection, socialisation, training/development, performance management, retention and review, to eventual employee release.	3–14 and 17–20
7. The nature, purposes, features, applications, benefits and disadvantages of the principal techniques for human resource planning, selection, corporate socialisation and people performance.	3–7, 11 and 20
8. The operational need for pragmatic people resourcing programmes, in circumstances of organisational turbulence, crisis, closure or apocalyptic change.	1, 2 and 3
9. New developments in people resourcing and their application potential.	2, 20 and 21
10. Contingency factors that influence the principles and practice of people resourcing across and within various employment sectors.	1, 2, 3, 15 and 21

People Management and Development Professional Standards

Operational indicators – practitioners must be able to:

1. Implement appropriate people management and development policies that maximise the contribution of people to organisational objectives and wider societal needs.	Thematic
2. Supply accurate and timely advice on the rights and obligations of employers and employees arising from the contract of employment and associated legislation, bearing in mind conflicts of interest and issues of confidentiality.	7, 13, 14, 17, 18 and 19
3. Access, use and interpret data from a range of internal and published sources in preparing and presenting reports.	1, 5 and 15
4. Contribute effectively to the planning, design and implementation of projects.	All
5. Manipulate people management and development databases, and provide advice on how to interpret the information and results they produce.	2 and 5
6. Demonstrate an ethical approach to people management and development.	1 and thematic
7. Contribute to the effective implementation of appropriate people management and development policies in different types of organisations.	1, 2, 3, 15 and 21

8. Work in partnership with other stakeholders to help overcome   2, 3 and thematic
   blockages and barriers to change.
9. Make recommendations about the advantages and disadvantages   2
   of outsourcing some or all elements of people management and
   development.
10. Provide and use benchmarks and other measures to assess the   2 and 21
    contribution of people management and development to
    organisational success.
11. Implement and operate cost-effective processes for recruiting and   6, 7 and 8
    retaining the right calibre of staff for their organisation.
12. Contribute to the design, development and delivery of learning   12, 20 and 21
    and training, and utilise measures to evaluate their effectiveness
    in supporting organisational goals.
13. Work in partnership with other stakeholders to develop procedures   14–17
    and processes that enhance the commitment of employees and
    resolve conflict at work.
14. Provide advice about how to motivate and reward people so as to   9 and 10
    maximise employee contributions to organisational performance.

Knowledge indicators – practitioners must understand and be able to explain:

1. The implications for the effective management and development of   1, 2 and 15
   people that arise from the changing nature of work and employment.
2. The context within which people management and development   1, 2, 13, 14 and 15
   takes place in terms of government actions, legal requirements and
   wider societal needs.
3. The relationship between employing organisations and the   1 and 15
   economic and institutional framework within which they operate.
4. The role of research and change management skills in organisations.   21 and thematic
5. The role of information technology in supporting people   2 and 5
   management and development.
6. The nature and importance of ethics, professionalism, equal   1 and 8
   opportunities and managing diversity.
7. The meaning of strategic management and its implications for   3 and 4
   people management and development.
8. How different aspects of personnel and development are integrated   1, 2, 3, 20 and 21
   with each other, with business strategy and with organisational
   structures and cultures.
9. The ways in which people management and development is   1 and 2
   implemented by line managers, functional specialists and
   consultants, and how these interact with each other.
10. The contribution that people management and development can   2 and thematic
    make to organisational success.
11. How effective recruitment, selection and performance management   6, 7, 8 and 11
    can contribute to organisational effectiveness.
12. How effective learning and training processes can contribute to   12, 20 and 21
    enhanced employee skills and organisational performance.
13. How effective employment relations can contribute to increased   15, 16 and 17
    employee potential and commitment.
14. How effective reward management practices can contribute to   9 and 10
    enhanced employee motivation and satisfaction at work.

GENERAL INTERNET REFERENCES

Innovation in technology has increased access to relevant information and research outputs through the Internet. HR publications and research, employment statistics and government papers, as well as international information, are easily available to those with access to the Internet and provide interesting and useful supplementary and complementary material for both the practitioner and the student. The dynamic nature of the Internet makes it impossible to identify all but a few interesting websites, as the sites and pages are constantly updated. It is, however, a way of searching for additional material. Much of the HR Internet material originates in the USA but continuing expansion of the Internet will deliver an increasingly diverse collection of reference material to libraries, the workplace and the home. The following websites provide an interesting starting point.

HR and related websites

ACAS: www.acas.org.uk
AEEU: www.aeeu.org.uk
American Compensation Association: www.acaonline.org/
American Management Association: www.amanet.org
American Society for Training and Development: www.astd.org
Association of British Insurers: www.abi.org.uk
Australian Human Resources Institute: www.ahri.com.au
BBC business news: http://news.bbc.co.uk/hi/english/business/default.htm
British Chambers of Commerce: www.britishchambers.org.uk
Bureau of National Affairs: www.bna.com
CBI: www.cbi.org.uk
Centre for Economic Performance: Cep.lse.ac.uk/
Chartered Institute of Personnel and Development: www.cipd.co.uk
Commission for Racial Equality: www.cre.gov.uk
Company Annual Reports Online: www.carol.co.uk
Corporate Life (Dilbert): www.dilbert.com
Croner's HR webcentre: www.human-resourcescentre.net
Daily Telegraph: www.telegraph.co.uk
Data Protection: www.dataprotection.gov.uk
Data Protection Registrar: www.open.gov.uk/dpr/dprhome.htm
Department for Education and Employment: www.dfee.gov.uk
Department for Education and Skills: www.dfes.gov.uk
Department of Social Security: www.dss.gov.uk
Department of Trade and Industry: www.dti.gov.uk
Disability on the Agenda: www.disability.gov.uk

Discrimination issues and the law: www.equalitydirect.org.uk

DTI Employment Relations pages: www.dti.gov.uk/IR/index.htm

Employee Relations: www.dti.gov.uk/er/

Employers Forum on Age: www.efa.org.uk

Employment Appeal Tribunal: www.open.gov.uk/employmentappeals/index.htm

Employment Law: www.compactlaw.co.uk

Employment Law: www.lawzone.co.uk

Employment Service: www.employmentservice.gov.uk

Engineering Employers' Federation: www.eef.org.uk

Equal Opportunities Commission: www.eoc.org.uk

euro: www.euro.gov.uk

European Court of Justice: www.europa.eu.int/cj/en/index.htm

European Industrial Relations Observatory: www.eiro.eurofound.ie/

European Management Case Studies: www.ecch.cranfield.ac.uk

European Telework Online: www.eto.org.uk/

European Trade Union Confederation: www.etuc.org

European Union: http://europa.eu.int/index-en.htm

Federation of European Employers: www.euen.co.uk

FIET: www.fiet.org

Financial Times (ft.com): www.ft.com

Futurestep: www.futurestep.co.uk

Government Statistical Service – The Source: www.statistics.gov.uk

Gradunet: www.gradunet.co.uk

Harvard Business Review: www.hbr.org

Hay Paynet: www.haypaynet.com

Health and Safety Executive: www.open.org.uk/hse/hsehome.htm

Healthy Workplace Initiative: www.doh.gov.uk/workp/index.htm

Her Majesty's Stationery Office: www.hmso.gov.uk/

HM Treasury: www.hm-treasury.gov.uk

HR Global Network: www.mcb.co.uk/hr

HRnet Web Centre: http://195.188.37.131/

HRNetwork: www.hrnetwork.co.uk

HRZone: www.hrzone.com

Inland Revenue: www.inlandrevenue.gov.uk

Institute for Employment Research: www.warwick.ac.uk/ier

Institute for Employment Studies: www.employment-studies.co.uk/

Institute for Fiscal Studies: www.ifs.org.uk

Institute of Management: www.inst-mgt.org.uk

Institution of Occupational Safety and Health: www.iosh.co.uk

International Labour Organisation: www.ilo.org

International Telework Association and Council: www.telecommute.org/

Investors in People, UK: www.iipuk.co.uk

Japan Institute of Labour: www.jil.go.jp/index-e.htm

Jobsite: www.jobsite.co.uk

JobsUnlimited: www.jobsunlimited.co.uk

Learning and Skills Council: www.lsc.gov.uk

Lifelong Learning: www.lifelonglearning.co.uk/
Low Pay Commission: www.lowpay.gov.uk
Mentors Forum: www.mentorsforum.co.uk
Milkround Online: www.milkround.co.uk
Modern apprenticeships: www.dfee.gov.uk/mapintro.htm
Monster: www.monster.co.uk
MSF: www.msf.org.uk
National Aids Trust: www.nat.org.uk
National Association of Pension Funds: www.napf.co.uk
National Training Awards: www.dfee.gov.uk/nta/index.htm
National Training Organisations: www.nto-nc.org/newsite99/learning&skills/nvqs.htm
New Deal: www.newdeal.gov.uk/
Occupational Pensions Regulatory Authority: www.opra.co.uk
Office for National Statistics: www.ons.gov.uk
Opportunity Now: www.bitc.org.uk/opportunitynow/
Pensions Institute: www.econ.bbk.ac.uk/pi
Pensions World Online: www.pensionsworld.co.uk/
People Management: www.peoplemanagement.co.uk
Personnel Today: www.personneltoday.net
Policy Studies Institute: www.psi.org.uk
Qualifications and Curriculum Authority: www.qca.org.uk
Race for Opportunity: www.bitc.org.uk/rfo/
Redundancy Advice Network: www.ran-advice.co.uk/employer_help/html
Redundancy: www.redundancyhelp.co.uk
Reward: www.e-reward.co.uk
Society for Human Resources: Management: www.shrm.org/
Stationery Office: www.tso-online.co.uk
Suzy Lamplugh Trust: www.suzylamplugh.org
T&G Online: www.tgwu.org.uk
Taps: www.taps.com
Technologies for Training: www.tft.co.uk/
Telework, Telecottage and Telecentre Association: www.tca.org.uk/home.htm
Top Jobs on the Net: www.topjobs.co.uk
TUC: www.tuc.org.uk
UK Official Publications: www.official-documents.co.uk
UK Parliament: www.parliament.uk
UNISON: www.unison.org.uk
University for Industry: www.ufiltd.co.uk/
Work and Family: www.workfamily.com
Workforce Online: www.workforceonline.com
Working from Home www.wfh.co.uk/wfh/homepage.htm

ACKNOWLEDGEMENTS

We owe a debt to our families for their continued support and encouragement. We acknowledge the invaluable contributions of our colleagues Amal El-Sawad, Sylvia Horton, David Farnham and Derek Adam-Smith. We owe a special thanks to Marcus Corbridge for the design of most of the figures.

CHAPTER 1

People resourcing in context

INTRODUCTION

This introductory chapter sets the scene for the rest of the book. It introduces the people resourcing philosophy, explains the approach and provides a framework for study. The context of people resourcing is examined and tensions, conflicts and ambiguities in the practice of personnel and development are exposed. People resourcing is defined as 'that part of personnel and development which focuses on the recruitment and release of individuals from organisations, as well as the management of their performance and potential whilst employed by the organisation'. The path through the book is intended to be logical and integrated and is based on three practical questions – How do I resource people into the organisation? How do I manage them effectively? How do I exit them from the organisation? People resourcing, rather than employee resourcing, is used as a more inclusive term because not all people at work have employee status. Academic textbooks are not always read from cover to cover and therefore each chapter is largely freestanding within the integrated framework. The constituent elements, or activities, of people resourcing are referred to as functions and this book takes a functional approach whilst recognising that resourcing activities need to be integrated with corporate strategy.

CHAPTER OBJECTIVES

- To examine the contingent nature of people resourcing.
- To explore the external context of people resourcing.
- To introduce the concept of the psychological contract in employment.
- To expose the debate about personnel management and human resource management.
- To discuss concepts of professionalism and ethics in people management practice.
- To identify conflicts and ambiguities in personnel and development.

A CONTINGENT APPROACH

A fundamental contention is that the functions of people resourcing, and the relative relationship between these functions, are contingent upon particular organisational circumstances and the organisational context. A specific type of personnel management and development practice or a particular approach to the management of people is not assumed. It is recognised that people resourcing is enacted by specialist personnel management or human resource practitioners and by line managers. The precise role of a personnel management function within an organisation, and the distribution of personnel or human resource responsibilities and activities, is influenced by a wide range of factors. These contingency factors include:

- the ownership, sector, size, tradition and stage of development of an organisation
- the degree of turbulence or dynamism in the competitive or task environment and the influence of the contexts external to the organisation
- the attitude and imagination of the chief executive, or the most senior person, towards the management of people
- the enactment of a unitary, neo-unitary or pluralistic approach to the employment relationship (*see* Chapter 15)
- the competence, reputation and track record of personnel and development jobholders and the existence or absence of the skills and capacity to resource people effectively.

A contingent approach to people resourcing is therefore proposed with the aim of enabling managers to make informed choices about people resourcing activities. This is in accord with the CIPD's notion of '*a thinking performer*'. Opportunities are provided by this text for managers to select and apply people resourcing techniques in the specific organisational context within which they operate. For example, in recruitment and selection the appropriateness of standard recruitment and selection procedures is questioned, as the professional recruiter needs to be aware of the strengths, weaknesses and implications of recruitment methods and selection devices so that they can be chosen and utilised appropriately and effectively. In employee reward systems a contingent attitude is neatly summarised by Murlis who suggests that there is no 'Holy Grail' in pay and reward, only 'horses for courses'. A knowledge of reward components, an awareness of the often conflicting aims of a reward policy, recognising the need to integrate reward strategy with other personnel and development policies, and also with corporate objectives, and the ability to be critically evaluative about pay and reward alternatives will allow informed choice, which is based on the understanding and interpretation of organisational contingencies. Sisson and Storey (2000: 252) make this point well: 'policies and practices configured or tailored to the organisation's specific circumstances are likely to be much more effective than those plucked off the shelf or bought from a consultant. HR is not a technological area where there is an automatic best practice solution.' There are no simple solutions or universal right answers and it all depends on organisational circumstances.

The functions of people resourcing are exposed in Fig. 1.1. A horizontally integrated approach to people resourcing incorporates human resource and organisational development, the employment relationship and reward. Figure 1.1 demonstrates this integrated and holistic approach to the effective resourcing of the organisation with people and provides a framework for this book. In short, to effectively resource the organisation with people HR activities need to be complementary to each other and with the strategy, if one exists, of the organisation.

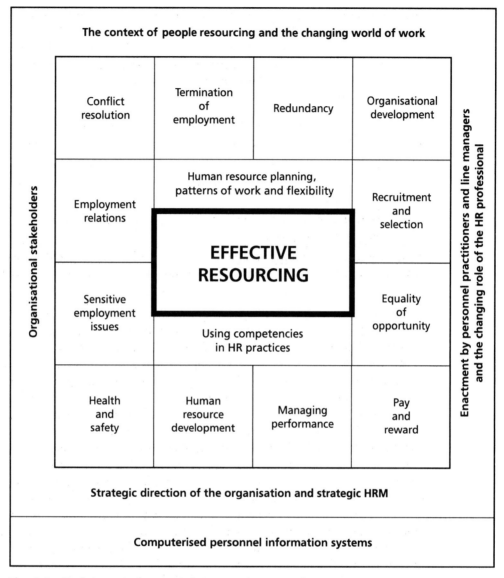

Fig. 1.1 An integrated approach to people resourcing

A critical perspective

A critically evaluative approach to people resourcing decisions, including a healthy scepticism towards evangelical rhetoric and the latest jargon, is encouraged. Caution is urged in relation to energetic, assertive and overused terminology. Examples are provided with some hesitation, but they are provided because these issues need to be confronted. The aim is to stimulate debate and prompt a healthy questioning of the concepts. Some indicative illustrations of this language include quality and excellence, vision, empowerment, people are our most valuable resource, world class, delighting our customers, the customer is king, business process re-engineering, and so on. The fundamental question is – What do these words mean and how is the worthy rhetoric translated into reality and practice? Moss Kanter (1996), Harvard Professor of Business Administration, exhibits this healthy scepticism, particularly in relation to management gurus, in indicating that she does not like:

> glib, easy answers and popular fads of the moment; trying to create social movements around ideas as opposed to providing information and enabling people to make up their own minds . . . there is a whole lucrative realm of business and management books with billboard jackets and shouty titles that offer more miracle cures than a television evangelist.

(Moss Kanter, 1996)

Peters and Waterman's *In Search of Excellence* (1982) triggered interest in the 'big idea'; they distilled 12 golden rules of management from research into 40 organisations with outstanding corporate performance. The reality is that two-thirds of these organisations have gone bankrupt or been taken over, which does cast some doubt on the efficacy of the golden rules. Marchington (1995) also appears to be critical of obedience to recent management fads when he argues that 'we are fed a diet of simplistic solutions that are based on assumptions of happiness and peace where conflict is and organisational politics are aberrations instead of being the norm'. He also argues that conclusions are frequently based on an unrepresentative sample of case study organisations.

Management terms of the new millennium are used conservatively in this text and attention is drawn to the need for a reflective engagement with contemporary language. Engage contemporary ideas, but make up your own mind about how effective they might be in your organisation. A critical approach need not be negative or cynical, because in the search for excellence new HR ideas need to withstand robust scrutiny if there is a genuine interest in effective people management.

Strategy and people resourcing

The contribution of strategic people management to corporate strategy is the subject of considerable debate. At the very least the strategic direction of an organisation will be influenced to some degree by the functional members of the organisation, and those engaged in people resourcing play a part in shaping strategy. Managers of people need to focus on the functional elements of people resourcing, but also need to keep an eye on strategy.

Strategy in this sense is adopting a strategic state of mind, rather than necessarily being extensively engaged in strategic activities.

Managers need to undertake environmental scanning (*see* page 10) and develop a sensitivity to the external contexts within which organisations operate in order to inform a strategic state of mind. In this way people resourcing strategy can be vertically integrated with corporate strategy.

The strategy thing can be enacted at different levels in the context of the position and the potential of the individual:

Level 1   Strategic awareness
Level 2   Strategic thinking
Level 3   Strategic decision-making
Level 4   Strategic planning

Strategic awareness is actively seeking knowledge of the corporate strategy, and HR strategy if it exists; strategic thinking is building this acquired knowledge into day-to-day HR activities; and strategic decision-making is actively incorporating strategic knowledge into making HR decisions. Strategic planning is thinking ahead and predicting the strategic consequences of any HR action. Torrington and Hall (1998) are quite revealing on HR strategy:

> The influence of business need was also apparent in the nature of the strategy that was produced. Few organisations looked towards the personnel function to produce an integrated HR strategy in response to business needs, but looked towards a strategic response to identified key business issues. HR strategy thus tended to be in many cases reactive rather than proactive, and was built up in a piecemeal rather than holistic way. None of our interviewees identified HR strategy as driving business strategy, but many identified business strategy as driving HR strategy. This demonstrates the personnel function being responsive to business need, and moves us on from the situation of the personnel manager hankering after a nicely-packaged HR strategy driven by lofty ideals distinct from commercial imperatives. The internally integrated, proactive HR strategy seems no more than an ideal to dream of. A stream of strategic decisions is needed rather than a strategy. We found evidence of strategic thinking rather than written HR strategy. The critical issue is whether what constitutes the HR strategy, piecemeal as it is, is simply directed by the business strategy or whether other influences are recognised and incorporated, so that a distinct, authoritative line of thinking on HR issues is integrated with business strategy.

Clearly, strategy is an important concern, and in this second edition we have included a specific chapter on Human Resource Strategy, by David Farnham, which examines perspectives and theories in order to provide a strategic context for readers of this primarily practical text. In addition, we have included a chapter on Competencies in Human Resourcing because, as Sylvia Horton puts it:

> Competencies have become one of the 'big ideas' in HRM on a par with management by objectives (MBO) and total quality management (TQM), and competency management is fast becoming a prominent HR strategy.

People make the difference

At the risk of invoking political debate about the precise meaning of the term 'stakeholding', particularly in the context of a government that aligns itself with ethical stakeholding, it is a firm contention that successful organisations appreciate and value the rights and responsibilities of all organisational stakeholders.

> Firms which show commitment to employees, adopt an egalitarian and open style of management, build long term relationships with suppliers and customers, and are actively involved in their local communities will deliver higher profits and create more and better jobs. However, business responsibility to stakeholders must never become an excuse for cosiness at the expense of the consumer.

(Mandelson and Liddle, 1996)

Therefore resourcing the organisation with effective people requires the mutual satisfaction of the providers of work (the employers) and the providers of skills (the employees), whilst recognising the need for customer orientation. It is through the process of reciprocal commitment between employers and employees, and this may be dependent upon a reasonable balance of power between the two parties, that business objectives and individual objectives at work can be accurately defined and successfully achieved. A healthy psychological contract (*see* page 15) needs to underpin a healthy legal contract if the benefits of a healthy employment relationship are to accrue. People may then actually make the difference in terms of organisational performance.

> The increasing importance of people as the primary sustainable source of competitive advantage makes it even more important that dedicated resources and thinking time are applied to the strategies through which people are developed and managed.
>
> (*People Make the Difference*: CIPD)

The creation and development of a healthy psychological contract, whilst being desirable and aspirational, may be constrained by the current conjunction of social, political, economic and global factors. Organisations are demanding greater employee involvement, commitment and flexibility coupled with loyalty to the corporate vision, whilst concurrently decreasing job security, reducing promotion opportunities and dampening down expectations about progressive increases in reward. This paradox makes the reality of a healthy psychological contract more difficult to achieve, but does not expunge the concept itself. Innovative approaches to the pursuit of mutuality of satisfaction in the employment relationship will be necessary. Research into the nature of the contemporary employment relationship exposes something of a divide between the rhetoric and the reality in relation to the health of the psychological contract (*see* page 15).

No right answers!

This book aims to provide insight into the functional areas of people resourcing, as identified in Fig. 1.1, without attempting to provide the 'right' answers or seeking to determine 'the one best way'. This approach can be disturbing for some students and managers who may be more comfortable with, or accustomed to, more prescriptive and assertive approaches. Practitioner and academic experience leads the authors to the inevitable conclusion that people resourcing is characterised by uncertainty and diversity. Embracing this uncertainty, adopting a critical perspective and seeking a fit with particular organisational circumstances appears to be a much more practical and productive approach to effectively resourcing the organisation with people.

THE EXTERNAL CONTEXTS OF PEOPLE RESOURCING

Organisations do not exist in a vacuum; they are subject to an avalanche of external influences, or environments, which shape the way the business is organised and managed. Competition, levels of funding, the economic climate, government policy, technological developments and social change are illustrations of these external influences and provide a context for people resourcing. Effective people resourcing is dependent on scanning the external environments, seeking to interpret the implications and planning or responding accordingly. An appreciation of the context of people resourcing is therefore a prerequisite to effective people resourcing action.

A book of this nature cannot provide a comprehensive map of the external environments within which organisations operate, not least because the map is subject to dynamic influences and continuous change. Some analytical tools are introduced to promote the development of a sensitivity to the environment and to help identify contemporary influences. These analytical tools include the representation of the organisation as an open system subject to environmental influences, the partitioning of the environments through PESTEL, SWOT analysis, and an explanation of the process of environmental scanning. There are many competing approaches, from a wide range of academic disciplines, to conceptualising the external context of organisations and only a limited treatment can be provided here. Universality and certainty, epitomised by the human search for answers that are true at all times in all circumstances, are conspicuously absent in the art of understanding the external environment. There are debates, for example, about the degree of stability and turbulence in the external environments, about the degree to which organisations are subject to constraints or can influence environmental forces, and about the extent to which conceptualising the external environments is an objective-based process or an individual, social construction (Morris and Willey, 1996). Add to this the problems associated with obtaining accurate data about economic, political and social factors and then predicting how these factors interact with each other, and reading the impact of external environmental influences becomes a formidable challenge. Reading the external environment is therefore an imperfect process because:

1 Accurate information is elusive, and information is invariably historical, casting doubt on the integrity of any extrapolation and prediction.

2 Human skills, sensory apparatus and preconceptions filter information to produce an individual perceptual map of the external environment.

3 In order to provide a complete picture every variable within the organisation and every interrelated influence in the external environment would need to be conceptualised as an holistic whole.

These factors combine to produce an individual rationalisation of the external environment – 'a bounded rationality'. Conceptualising the whole external environment is beyond normal human ability and the best that can be done is some limited and rationalised attempt at perceiving it. It is through a process of challenging personal assumptions and beliefs about the political, economic, social, technological, European and legal environments (PESTEL) that conflicts and ambiguities can be exposed and confronted. If it is accepted that environmental reality is constructed and perspectival, a whole range of alternative interpretations become available to the environmental scanner and these demand a critical approach. External environmental influences cannot be discounted because of the difficulty of mapping or of interpretation, as managerial decision-making cannot occur within an internal organisational vacuum. Organisations are inevitably an element within a much wider economic, political and societal system, and there is a need to be sensitive to this wider system to contribute to more informed and responsive people resourcing decisions. There is a tendency in the more assertive and unitary management literature to suggest prescriptive, or universal, organisational solutions in relation to environmental influences. This can be beguiling, but does not reflect the fact that organisations are different in terms of size, ownership and accountability, nature of the task, tradition, stage of development, management style, employment relations philosophy and so on. These organisational factors will be influenced by the external environments in different ways. Prescriptive answers to complex questions require extreme caution, and managers are encouraged to adopt a contingent approach to reading the external environment and to seeking effective people resourcing responses.

Therefore, whilst it is possible to collect information on the context of people resourcing and seek to identify trends and influences, it is important to do this in the knowledge of human 'bounded rationality' and within a contingent management approach. This does not compromise the value of scanning the external environments for useful information.

> Since the environments in which organisations operate cannot be predicted other than for the short term, what really matters is that managers are **sensitive** to signals in their environment and **flexible** and **intuitive** to such signals; and that they build organisations capable of such responses. Analysis is here much more concerned with helping sensitise managers to the environment than arriving at precise explanations or bases of prediction.
>
> (Johnson and Scholes, 1999, emphasis added)

The organisation as system and the PESTEL partitioning of the external environments

One approach to the analysis of the organisation and its interaction with the external environment is to view the organisation as a system (Fig. 1.2) – socio-technical systems theory (*see also* Chapter 21). The organisation system consists of inputs, a processing or transformation unit and outputs; and the system is open to influences from the external environments.

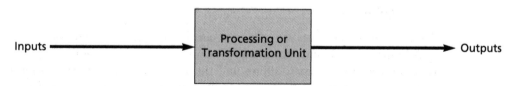

Inputs ⟶ Processing or Transformation Unit ⟶ Outputs

Fig. 1.2 The organisation as a system

The input elements are people, finance, expertise, other resources, and demands and pressures from other organisations. The outputs are products, services and demands on other organisations. The processing unit consists of a social sub-system, a technical sub-system and a managerial techno-structure.

Social sub-system – people behaviour; attitudes and expectations; skills; motivation; reward.

Technical sub-system – organisation structure and design, nature of the task, systems, processes and procedures and technology.

Managerial techno-structure – technical expertise and managerial skills applied by managers to organise activities in the pursuit of organisational objectives.

The organisation system does not function in a vacuum and is subject to an array of environmental influences. These can be categorised into the task and the wider environments. The task environment consists of the competitive and market forces, whilst the wider environment can be partitioned into political, economic, social, technological, European and legal contexts (PESTEL), as well as including international factors. A representation of this is provided in Fig. 1.3.

Fig. 1.3 The organisation as a system open to influences from the external contexts

This systems representation identifies the organisation as an organism seeking to adapt to external environmental influences; a biological analogy is of a living organism seeking to maintain metabolic equilibrium by compensating for changes in environmental conditions (homeostasis). It provides a framework for identifying environmental influences and for seeking to assess the implications for the sub-systems of the organisation and it provides a way of viewing the external contexts within which people resourcing takes place. The partitioning of the wider environment into political, economic, social, technological, European and legal factors provides a convenient framework for analysis. The method of identifying PESTEL influences is environmental scanning.

Environmental scanning

A brief explanation of environmental scanning is provided to stimulate interest in doing it and to 'pump prime' personal environmental scanning. A collection of current trends, which have implications for people resourcing, are included as an illustrative snapshot of PESTEL influences (*see* Fig. 1.5 on page 13). To a large extent environmental scanning is a state of mind and is achieved through:

1 Developing a general mental map of the environmental influences through adopting a framework such as PESTEL.
2 Actively collecting information through the media, publications and professional networking.
3 Developing a sensitivity to environmental signals.

Environmental scanning is not a new concept and was well defined as:

> That part of the strategic management process in which emerging trends, changes and issues are regularly monitored and evaluated as to their likely impact on corporate decisions. Scanning usually entails . . . collecting data by monitoring and forecasting changes in key variables . . . and . . . the interpretation and integration of these informal inputs into an organisation's strategic planning process.
>
> (Preble *et al.*, 1988)

Environmental scanning is therefore about a sensitivity to the external environment within which organisations operate, and the need for it increases in dynamic and turbulent environmental conditions. Environmental scanning is a process through which managers, as the organisation's strategists, use tools and perceptions to constantly gather and feed back information about the environment to inform decision making. 'The complexity of the environment is such that everyone in the organisation has valuable information and key relationships with external systems. Scanning the environment is not just a job of specialists and directors' (Large, 1992). Organisations which achieve greater perceptual 'accuracy' in environmental scanning tend to do better, signifying some correlation between scanning behaviour and above-average organisational performance. Environmental scanning as a process is an important step in the change in perceptions and actions that can lead to an organisation's environmented adaptation.

Cognitive mapping can be used to examine individual perceptions, subjective views and enacted environments. Cognitive mapping is:

> A method which enables managers to draw on their own resources and, through self awareness of their own bias and blind spots, to liberate themselves from the old way of seeing and responding to the environment. Through action research methods, managers and the researcher are able to continually reflect on his or her interrelationships with the environment and each other and to respond in a way that allows them to own their **own** solution.
>
> (Rutter, 1994)

Cognitive mapping can produce a more holistic and intuitive representation of the environment and also develop greater environmental sensitivity amongst the cognitive mapping participants as it encourages the challenging of beliefs and assumptions.

Sensitivity to environmental influences is necessary for the effective application of people resourcing skills. Changes in both the task environment and the wider environment will have organisational implications and impact upon the quantity and quality of people required. The development of a sensitivity to environmental influences through scanning the media and other information networks is therefore a skill worth developing. The collection, synthesis and actioning of environmental data is a prerequisite to human resource planning (*see* Chapter 4) and organisational development (*see* Chapter 21).

> Effective managers accept the uncertainty of their environment because they realise that they cannot do away with this uncertainty by trying to 'know' factually about how the environment will change; rather they seek to become highly sensitive to environmental signals through constant environmental scanning and by testing changes in strategy in small-scale steps.
>
> (Johnson and Scholes, 1999)

SWOT analysis

Strengths, weaknesses, opportunities and threats, or SWOT, is a strategic analysis technique where the influences in the external environments are categorised as opportunities or threats and assessed against organisational strengths and weaknesses, and normally summarised and represented in the form of a four-quadrant grid – Fig. 1.4. Strengths are internal, positive attributes of organisations that give advantage in the pursuit of strategic objectives. Some organisations define their strengths through benchmarking and comparing their processes, product, services or activities with those of effective practice organisations. Weaknesses are internal, negative attributes of organisations that hinder the achievement of strategic objectives. Weaknesses, too, can be identified and possibly remedied by benchmarking and excavating effective practice. Opportunities are external

STRENGTHS	WEAKNESSES
OPPORTUNITIES	THREATS

Fig. 1.4 SWOT quadrants

factors that substantially assist organisations in achieving strategic objectives, whilst threats are external factors that inhibit organisations from achieving strategic objectives. Opportunities need to be seized and threats need to be countered (Farnham, 1999).

SWOT analysis provides a systematic mechanism for thinking through the implications of environmental forces, focuses managerial attention on priorities for action and facilitates strategic choice.

Trends and influences in the external environments

The abstract discussion so far about the concept of the external environments and the process of scanning for information can usefully be illustrated so that the people resourcing implications can be identified more specifically. Three representations are provided:

1 An exhibit of labour market and skill trends – Exhibit 1.1.

Exhibit 1.1 Labour market and skill trends which have implications for people resourcing

- Increasing competitive challenge through technological advances, customer aspirations and power and globalisation of markets, causing skill changes.
- Female participation in the labour market increasing from 57 per cent of women in 1971 to 72 per cent in 1998.
- Seventy-five per cent of jobs are in distribution, hospitality, public services and financial services with only 17 per cent in manufacturing.
- Self-employment remained steady in the 1990s at around 12 per cent.
- Ninety-nine per cent of all enterprises have fewer than 50 employees, employing around 45 per cent of all UK workers.
- Part-time employment increased from 21 per cent to 25 per cent of all employment in the period 1981 to 1999; 80 per cent of all part-time workers are female; part-time jobs have been created at a faster rate than full-time jobs; increased female participation in the labour market coincided with an increase in part-time jobs (which came first?).
- The workforce is ageing – those aged 45 years and over are predicted to increase by 16 per cent by 2011 whilst those under 35 years of age are decreasing (–7 per cent from 1996 to 2001), raising questions about age diversity and also skill shortages, because older workers tend to have fewer and more outdated qualifications.
- The participation rate for women with dependent children is 60 per cent, with implications for childcare provision and work/life balance initiatives; only 11 per cent of women have contracts with flexible arrangements.
- Male and female occupational segregation continues to exist.
- Ethnic minorities account for 6 per cent of the UK population, have lower labour market participation rates and have higher unemployment rates; participation rates vary between different ethnic minority groupings.
- The labour market participation rate for people with disabilities is 50 per cent of the rate for the whole population.

Source: DfEE, 2000

2 An illustrative snapshot – Fig. 1.5.

International Context
Globalisation of communications, distribution of knowledge and intelligence, internationalisation of trade and increasing competitive challenge.

Political	Economic
• social partnership in the employment relationship • constitutional reform and regional devolution • sovereignty debate in relation to the EU • welfare state reform • ethical socialism in a market economy • balance between private and public sector provision • deregulation of labour markets • direct action pressure groups	• tensions between economic objectives and concerns with social values • recession and recovery and monitoring the impact of inflation, growth, public spending and borrowing, balance of payments and exchange rates • funding of LSCs, training and employment initiatives

Social	Technological
• redistribution of wealth and the emergence of an underclass • ageing population • increasing female participation in the labour market • changing views of marriage and the disintegration of family life • challenges to traditional authority structures and class distinctions • concern with environmentalism and morality • post-modernism and the threat to social consensus • improvements in maternity, paternity and parental leave	• the information revolution • diffusion of IT competence • teleworking • developments in artificial intelligence • the substitution of human work by technology • facilitation of a learning society • continuing dialectic about technological determinism and strategic choice • e-commerce, e-recruitment and e-HR

European	Legal
• acceptance of Social Charter principles • parental leave, protection for atypical workers, works councils, working time directive • economic and monetary union and the single currency • enlargement of the European Union • further political integration and 'threats' to the nation state • cross-cultural management teams	• exponential growth in employment tribunal claims • the Disability Discrimination Act, the Human Rights Act, the Data Protection Act and the Code of Practice on age diversity • new interpretations of equality rights • resolution of individual and employment disputes through arbitration • statutory trade union recognition • minimum wage regulation

Fig. 1.5 An illustrative snapshot of UK PESTEL influences as a map of the external environments

3 An indicative list of the implications of current environmental influences for work organisations.

The conjunction of PESTEL influences and labour market trends impacts on the management of people and in the structure of organisations. An indicative list of organisational implications is provided:

1 An emphasis on efficiency, effectiveness, quality and continuous improvement.
2 Leaner, more complex organisations emphasising a corporate vision and mission statements.
3 A reconstruction of organisations as a collection of quasi-independent, smaller business units with specific objectives, linked to other business units in flexible networks.
4 A sharpening of customer focus to respond to the escalating demands of external and internal customers.
5 The pursuit of teamworking, 'empowered' individuals and a 'learning organisation'.
6 Unrelenting demand for flexibility from employees, accompanied by the intensification of each person's work, and accompanied also by concern for work/life balance.
7 Resourcing strategies which incorporate a variety of contractual relationships from core employees to portfolio workers and the purchase of externalised services.
8 A concern with managing and valuing diversity.
9 The emergence of human resource management as a collection of assumptions and beliefs about people management, including a business and customer orientation for the personnel function.
10 Downsizing and delayering may have contributed to corporate anorexia and corporate amnesia – too lean and lacking in corporate memory.
11 The marketisation of the public sector and the emergence of the 'new public manager' (NPM).
12 A reduction in collective employment disputes, but an exponential growth in individual disputes.
13 A changing employment relationship and 'a new psychological contract'.

The intention of this section has been to increase the reader's awareness of the influences in the external context and to encourage contextual thinking, for as Beardwell and Holden (2001: 57) put it:

> . . . ultimately awareness of context is empowering. One of the outcomes may well be greater knowledge but less certainty, the recognition that there may be competing interpretations, that the several perspectives may yield different conclusions. Attention to context, therefore, encourages us not to be taken in by our initial impressions, nor to accept unquestioningly the definitions of reality others would have us adopt. There are, however, no easy answers and we have to make a choice between alternatives.

THE PSYCHOLOGICAL CONTRACT

In addition to the legal contract, the employment relationship can be viewed as having a psychological contract.

The psychological contract can be defined as a series of expectations which characterise the relationship between employers and employees.

The psychological contract consists of behaviour, relationships and treatment at work, with the expectations generally unstated and undefined. Where the expectations of both parties are largely met a sense of mutuality prevails in the employment relationship and this is generally beneficial to the achievement of organisational objectives and corporate performance. A good psychological contract provides a sense of identity, offers recognition for employee contribution and conveys a feeling of security. A breach of the terms of the psychological contract can provoke a loss of trust and a sense of betrayal. The psychological contract is the glue which holds together the employment relationship. Environmental influences and the consequent implications for organisational change have had a significant impact on the psychological contract.

IPD research (1996) into the employment relationship revealed that effectively the psychological contract had been violated:

- a process of work intensification was taking place;
- the extent of organisational change, often coupled with redundancies, was having a negative impact;
- although loyalty to colleagues was strong, there was a diminution in loyalty to the organisation;
- the employee and employer relationship was characterised by low trust;
- there was a sense of employee powerlessness, because of a perceived lack of ability to influence organisation strategy and operations.

The old psychological contract consisted of elements such as a fair day's pay for a fair day's work, high job security, career possibilities and development, mutuality of loyalty and to some extent an illusion of comfort: in short, 'a secure job for dedicated service'. In the new psychological contract the elements are an individual basis to the employment relationship, employee loyalty to personal competence or to a profession, employee acceptance of responsibility for self-development but with a primary concern for employability, and a psychological contract based on transaction and exchange rather than one which is sustained by a familial relationship, in other words a movement from a relational contract to a transactional one: in short, 'I will commit to what you want for as long as the financial and other rewards are sufficiently attractive'.

If the new psychological contract is to be healthy then people need to be treated as an asset and not just as a resource and there needs to be sufficient security of employment to satisfy human needs, a sense of identity and purpose at work and the provision of recognition, as these remain important to individuals. People still seek security, support and structure and not everyone is a natural portfolio worker. If these human needs are denied there is a danger of 'me plc' being created, where employees become primarily committed to what they can get rather than to what they can offer. There is an underlying unease in the employment relationship, but this may reflect a wider societal shift towards individual responsibility for life management, not only in employment, but also in education, health, pensions and so on. Employment unease may therefore be part of a general societal unease. As the labour market has tightened a general reduction in feelings of insecurity at work may be occurring, and even more recent CIPD research suggests this might be the case, although there is contradictory research from the Rowntree Foundation (1999), but the underlying problem remains – increased demand on employees with reduced reward.

Although employment has become more unstable, many employees maintain traditional employment values and attempts need to be made to reconcile the expectations embodied in the psychological contract. It is ultimately in the interests of employers to achieve a healthy psychological contract as employers, as well as employees, need security of employment relationships. Further information can be found in *Organisational Change and the Psychological Contract* (CIPD, 2001). The basic premise of that research is that progressive HR practices contribute to a healthy psychological contract which in turn leads to higher employee commitment. There are, of course, those who argue that the psychological contract is no more than a myth, and that the interest of workers cannot be reconciled in psychological terms because of conflicting perspectives on the purpose of work and the primacy of the economic contract. Nonetheless, understanding the concept of the psychological contract may cast further light on the employment relationship in contemporary organisations and is therefore useful in making appropriate people resourcing decisions.

PERSONNEL MANAGEMENT AND HUMAN RESOURCE MANAGEMENT (HRM)

In considering the context of people resourcing it is important and useful to expose the personnel management and human resource management debate. The debate is about the extent to which HRM is a new and distinct form of people management, the extent to which it is practised and whether it actually works. The aim is to illuminate rather than resolve this largely academic debate by discussing:

1 The origins of HRM

2 The characteristics and key elements of HRM

3 Policies, practices and 'levers' which support HRM

4 Is HRM different from personnel management?

5 The rhetoric versus reality argument.

The origins of HRM

Elements of HRM can be traced back to the human relations movement of the 1930s and the discovery of the social needs of workers, and also the developments in the body of knowledge associated with job satisfaction, motivation and leadership in the 1950s and 1960s in pursuit of increased human performance at work. HRM as a term and an approach to managing people originated in the USA in response to global competitive pressure. In particular, the impressive performance of Japanese organisations stimulated management interest in the ideas of employee commitment and loyalty and their impact on productivity (Hendry and Pettigrew, 1990). UK organisations also came under competitive pressures from developed and emerging countries and one response was to import American and Japanese ideas associated with 'human resource management'. These global competitive factors and the rise of the Conservative 'New Right' in the UK in the 1980s contributed to the emergence of HRM through creating an employment climate based on hostility to collectivism, the deregulation of labour markets and the reassertion of the 'right to manage'. This climate was conducive to the individualist and unitary emphasis of the HRM philosophy. Managerial aspiration became effective human resource utilisation and HRM claimed to put people at the heart of the business, which was something of an indictment, and suggestive of failure, for personnel management. The emergence of HRM provoked a debate about whether HRM is a new and distinct, and more effective, form of managing people, and it is useful to examine HRM and the juxtaposed construct of TPM (Traditional Personnel Management).

Personnel management has long been the source of role conflicts and ambiguities and there are many models which provide an analysis of the personnel and development role. Tyson and Fell (1986) draw attention to different operational levels of personnel management (*see also* Tyson, 1995).

Clerk of works – reactive, administrative role with little or no involvement in business planning; principal activities are recruitment, record keeping and welfare.

Contracts Manager – mainly reactive, based on professional skills and the development of personnel procedures and policies to support management activity.

Architect – creative and proactive in the development of integrated strategic policies and practices which give effect to corporate aims and objectives.

There are many other models (Storey, 1992; Thomason, 1991; Guest, 1989), but a common theme is a continuum of personnel management activity in which TPM is associated with short-term, tactical practices and HRM emphasises strategic issues (Fig. 1.6). Ulrich (1996) argues that the successful HR manager must embrace four roles,

Bureaucratic and reactive	Tactical	Strategic/managing change
TPM ——————————————————————————— **HRM**		

Fig. 1.6 A continuum of personnel management activity

categorised as strategic partner, change agent, administrative expert and employee champion. The first two roles are associated more with HRM and the latter two with TPM. The difference in Ulrich's argument is that each of the four roles may need to be enacted by the HR manager in order to be successful. Advocates of HRM argue that it represents a paradigm shift in the personnel and development contribution to the business. This continuum is largely an academic construction because strategic personnel management (SPM) could substitute for HRM, so what is the difference, if any, between HRM and personnel management?

HRM and TPM differences are often represented as extremes, or ideal (stereo)types, and may not reflect the reality of organisational life, but they do provide a framework for analysis. Guest's model is typical of these comparative frameworks which serve to emphasise the differences (Fig. 1.7). The purpose of these frameworks is for useful investigation rather than a prescription of HRM as the best way of maximising people potential. Guest (1998a), in *HRM – the New Agenda*, argues the case for and against HRM as the current and dominant orthodoxy. There is no consensus as to whether HRM represents a fundamentally different approach to the management of people or whether in reality it is more hyped than real.

	TPM	HRM
Time and planning	Short-term/reactive *ad hoc* and marginal	Long-term/proactive strategic and integrated
Psychological contract	Compliance	Commitment
Control systems	External	Self-control
Employee relations perspective	Pluralist, collective, low-trust	Unitarist, individualist, high-trust
Preferred structures	Bureaucratic, mechanistic, centralised, formal defined roles	Organic, devolved, flexible roles
Roles	Specialist/professional	Largely integrated into line management
Evaluation criteria	Cost minimisation	Maximum utilisation (human asset accounting)

Fig. 1.7 Stereotypes of TPM and HRM

Source: From 'Stereotypes of TPM and HRM' by D. Guest (1987), *Journal of Management Studies*, Vol. 24, p. 507. © Blackwell Publishers Ltd. Reproduced by permission of the publishers.

The characteristics and key elements of HRM

HRM exhibits philosophical characteristics which may include:

- the belief that investment in people is good business, because *people* make the difference to organisational performance
- an emphasis on the alignment of the objectives of the individual employee with those of the organisation
- the right to manage is legitimised by the need for organisations to survive in competitive environments
- a unitary or neo-unitary employment relations frame of reference consisting of harmony, consensus, commitment and shared employer and employee interests
- the alignment of the HR function firmly with managerial interests and aims requiring the enactment of a 'business partner' role.

There is clearly a contrast here with pluralistic frames of reference which are based more on the inherent nature and inevitability of conflict in the employment relationship and focus on how conflict can be productively reconciled.

Five key elements emanate from the HRM philosophy:

1 The strategic integration of personnel management with corporate strategy
2 The devolution of HR activities to line managers
3 Employee commitment
4 Worker flexibility
5 The management of corporate culture.

The strategic integration of personnel management is often identified as the key distinction between new HRM and old-style personnel management (Hendry and Pettigrew, 1990). The aim of strategic integration is to achieve a close relationship between business strategy and people management strategy (vertical integration) and also to ensure that personnel and development activities are mutually reinforcing (horizontal integration) – in other words, the pursuit of a business focus to people management which creates and sustains competitive advantage (Fig. 1.8). HRM is therefore directly concerned with the needs of management and not directly with the needs of employees. The HRM argument is that the benefits of corporate success based on employee alignment with managerial interests 'trickle down' to employees, so creating a mutuality of interests and benefits. Strategic integration can elevate the standing and influence of the personnel and development function, spice up the image and provide a stark contrast to perceptions of personnel as a 'trash can', administrative and welfare function which hinders line managers through procedural control. The extent to which the aspiration of strategic integration is achievable remains a matter of debate.

The devolution of HR activities to line managers is the second key HRM element. The devolution rationale is that people management is critical to effective business performance and therefore needs to be enacted by empowered line managers who are responsible

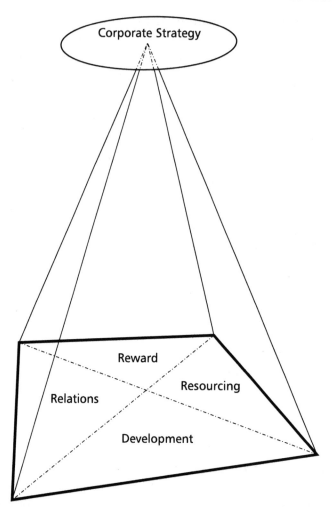

Fig. 1.8 Vertical and horizontal integration of corporate strategy and personnel and development

for coordinating and directing all resources, including human resources, towards organ-isational success. Responsibilities for HR activities such as recruitment and selection, reward, grievance and discipline, managing diversity and so on, are devolved to line managers who exercise greater autonomy and authority. This clearly has implications for personnel practitioners. It can be perceived as a threat to the personnel function by removing a *raison d'être*, with negative consequences in terms of power and influence, or it can be viewed as liberating by freeing up personnel practitioners to adopt an expert advisory and consultancy role and a strategic people management focus (Storey, 1995). Hall and Torrington (1998) report that HR managers tended to be enthusiastic about the transfer of activities to line managers, although some concerns were expressed about letting go of familiar and enjoyable tasks only to be faced with the vulnerability and uncertainties of the advisory and consultancy role. Nor are all HR professionals enthusiastic about the demands of the strategic role. Line manager perspectives can also be mixed, with devolution of HR activities being perceived as either empowering or merely unwelcome extra work. Flood (1998) points out that devolution to line managers can have dysfunctional HR consequences, such as a lack of opportunity to learn from HR specialists, inefficiency and duplication as each line manager invents new methods of HR management, lack of consistency in employee treatment and working conditions, and unstructured *ad hoc* HR policies. Successful devolution therefore requires competent and confident line managers, advisory support from HR professionals and continuous management development. Devolution to the line is unlikely ever to be total in anything but very small organisations and the extent of devolution will be contingent upon organisational circumstances. HR activities have always been devolved to some degree and it remains a question of achieving an appropriate balance. Some corporate level HR activity is always necessary in order to ensure compliance with the law, fairness and consistency in treatment and the dissemination of effective practice (Hendry and Pettigrew, 1990). The demise of the personnel profession is not an inevitable consequence of devolution; in fact it may bring personnel specialists and line managers closer together through having to work in partnership.

Exhibit 1.2 Personnel trends in strategy and devolution

- The term 'Personnel' is used in 70 per cent, and 'Human Resources' in 24 per cent, of people management positions, but 'Human Resources' is increasing.
- Clear evidence of strategic personnel roles exists, with board membership in around 60 per cent of organisations.
- The extent of the strategic role is influenced by factors such as the rate of organisational change, the mindset of the chief executive and the expertise of the personnel professional.
- Devolution of personnel and development activities is common, but more *ad hoc* than based on a clearly articulated devolution philosophy.
- It is not yet clear whether devolution is a result of personnel professionals seeking a more strategic role or the consequence of 'leaner and meaner' personnel functions.
- The success of devolution is influenced by the extent of support and training for line managers; do line managers perceive devolution as 'dumping' or 'liberating'?
- Devolution may inhibit the updating process for personnel professionals.

Source: Hall and Torrington (1996)

Employee commitment, the third key element of HRM, is pursued on the assumption that committed employees will willingly identify with corporate goals and work flexibly to achieve them. HRM seeks employee commitment through a psychological contract which is nurtured through individualistic involvement practices, increasingly given a positive spin and referred to as modern human resource practices or progressive people management practices (Caulkin, 2001), and based on shared values which incorporate the internalisation of organisational objectives. The performance lever of management is therefore the commitment rather than the control of employees. However, because employee commitment is consciously secured through managerial interventions, HRM faces the charge of being more controlling than is at first apparent – is it really 'employee manipulation dressed up as mutuality'? (Fowler, 1987). The requirement for committed employees is also evident in the quality movement with its emphasis on employee identi-fication with corporate values, the pursuit of continuous improvement and excellence and the need for high individual performance levels.

Worker flexibility is the fourth key HRM element and is based on the idea that adapt-ive organisations need adaptive workers. This requires workers to be flexible about the 'what', 'how', 'when' and 'why' of performing work in order that activity can be managerially directed towards the achievement of organisational objectives. Flexibility occurs in many interrelated forms, including functional, numerical, temporal and finan-cial, and these together with concepts of core, periphery and tertiary workers are dis-cussed in Chapter 4. Flexibility has the potential to be an important HRM lever for the effective utilisation of human resources, but the extent to which it is a strategic response or a collation of reactive, *ad hoc* and cost-driven measures is problematic to estab-lish. There are inherent tensions and problems associated with the pursuit of flexibility. Flexible workforces and flexible working may actually contribute to instability, discon-tinuity and fragmentation by creating status divides between groups of workers, who may be contracted on different arrangements, and also by demanding a flexibility com-mitment from employees which is perceived as excessive and therefore dysfunctional to the employment relationship. Sparrow and Marchington (1998) refer to the pursuit of worker flexibility as being 'associated with different types of battles or struggle between the interested parties'. In other words, flexibility can damage the psychological contract. This is not to say that flexibility is a bad thing, but just to draw attention to the possib-ility that it could undermine the organisational cohesion which may be necessary for optimum quality and performance.

The management of corporate culture is a central HRM activity and the fifth key ele-ment. Culture is 'taken for granted assumptions, beliefs, meanings and values enacted and shared by organisational members' (Gowler and Legge, 1986). Culture is the cement which holds together the HRM approach and therefore needs to be actively managed to secure the identification of employee interests with those of the organisation. Managing corporate culture means creating shared values and a sense of purpose. The creation of these shared values and the communication of the corporate vision are invariably dependent on strong, often charismatic leadership and hence the HRM emphasis on the quality, and the reward, of senior managers. The adherence to corporate values by employees is encouraged through the reward system and supported by personnel policies which communicate the cultural values desired by management, and indeed seek to limit 'deviant' worker behaviour. This fifth HRM element also harbours tensions. There are doubts about the extent to which culture can actually be managed. Whilst *corporate culture* and the associated values can be projected by management, the *organisational culture* is created and sustained by individuals and groups working in the organisation. Organisational cultures are not necessarily homogeneous and in reality there may be a collection of sub-cultures with some exhibiting 'resigned behavioural compliance' to projected corporate values, because the alternative is unemployment or diminished rewards (Legge, 1995). A second cultural tension is between a strong culture and the adaptive organisation – a strong corporate culture may militate against responsiveness to environmental influences through being resistant to change. Nonetheless the management of corporate culture is a strong plank of an HRM philosophy.

Policies, practices and 'levers' which support HRM

There is a collection of personnel and development policies and practices, or levers, which support an HRM approach, seek to shape a new employment relationship and aid the pursuit of the horizontal and vertical integration referred to above. These include:

- Sophisticated selection based on proactive human resource planning
  - psychometric measurement
  - assessment centres
  - socialisation and induction processes.
- Involvement and commitment of human resources
  - employee communication and participation techniques
  - quality initiatives
  - team working
  - profit sharing
  - training, development and education.
- Performance management
  - cascading of corporate objectives and definition of individual objectives with the aim of focusing employee effort
  - appraising, developing and rewarding performance.
- Reward management
  - rewarding achievement of personal and corporate objectives
  - rewarding conformity of behaviour
  - performance-related pay systems.
- Training and development
  - seeking a rate of learning at least equal to the rate of change required by the adaptive organisation
  - equipping employees with the right skills, knowledge and competence to maximise performance
  - a focus on flexibility.

HRM – different or not?

This question is difficult to answer as opinions continue to vary about whether HRM is different from personnel management. There is the 'old wine in new bottles' (with a sexier title) view and 'differences which are largely a matter of opinion rather than fact', with similarities much greater than differences (Torrington and Hall, 1995). HRM in this sense is not revolutionary, but an evolutionary dimension to a multifaceted personnel function. Fowler (1987) suggests that HRM simply represents 'the discovery of personnel management by chief executives'. Keenoy (1990) sees the primary purpose of HRM as legitimising managerial ideology and thereby enhancing control, intensifying work and extracting maximum added value from people. To others HRM represents a paradigm shift in the way that people are managed and is embodied in a new 'constellation of beliefs and assumptions' (critically exposed in Storey, 1992, 1995, 2001 and in Guest, 1987, 1989, 1990, 1998b).

There are further dimensions to HRM – is it hard or soft, tight or loose, open or closed? Hard (business-centred) HRM focuses on maximising (exploiting) the economic return of human resources through managerial control, whilst soft (people-centred) HRM seeks to release the potential of resourceful people through engaging the hearts and minds of employees (Storey, 1995). Tight HRM involves the rigorous integration of HRM policies and corporate strategy, whereas loose HRM may just represent the adoption of some more proactive personnel and development practices and the use of a more contemporary title (Guest, 1987). Closed HRM is prescriptive and advocates the one best way, whilst open HRM is a contingent approach which seeks compatibility between a bundle of high performance HR practices and the organisational context.

Personnel and HRM – rhetoric, reality and the future

Even accepting an assumption that there is something different about HRM leaves a residual question about the extent to which it is practised. There is limited empirical evidence to confirm a paradigm shift to HRM in its fullest sense in the UK. HRM appears to be much 'talked up', hence the rhetoric, whilst the available evidence reveals considerable diversity in practice (Sparrow and Marchington, 1998). The assumption that HRM practices lead inexorably to competitive advantage is more aspirational than proven; whether this is due to a failure of HRM practices themselves or misapplication is not clear. There is, however, a growing body of evidence promoted and presented by the CIPD that good HR practices do equal good business (Caulkin, 2001).

What conclusions can be drawn about personnel management and HRM? The debate about whether HRM is truly a new people management paradigm may actually be sterile (Tyson, 1995). The fact of the matter is that personnel management as a function and a collection of practices, along with other 'professions', needs to adapt to its context – survival depends on achieving homeostasis. The historical development of the personnel profession provides evidence that personnel management thrives on contextual adversity, witnessed by a large and successful professional institute, huge interest in the subject of people management and improving financial rewards for personnel and development expertise. The personnel and development profession is adaptable and continues to evolve in response to its environment, and whilst HRM may represent a new model there will continue to be a variety of models according to internal and external organisational factors. The personnel profession is often accused, and indeed accuses itself, of being in crisis. This is nothing new and, as Torrington (1998) puts it, 'the personnel profession has been in crisis for at least a century, so it would be very strange if things were not that way now'.

This personnel and HRM discussion is not introduced to tempt the reader to come down on one side (HRM cynic) or the other (HRM evangelist), but to expose some of the contemporary tensions, conflicts and ambiguities in personnel and development. This should lead to a more informed awareness of the context of people resourcing and promote a critical re-examination of personnel and development practice without suggesting that all that has gone before should be disposed of, to be replaced by HRM. It is possible to embrace change and engage the 'great HR issues of the moment' whilst recognising that there is much that is good about the practice of personnel and development, not least of which is professionalism and ethics, where personnel and development faces the challenge of reconciling the needs of the organisation for efficiency and effectiveness with the people needs of fairness and justice in employment. Ethics and professionalism are the focus of attention in the final section of this scene-setting chapter.

ETHICS AND PROFESSIONALISM

Ethical questions arise from 'the HRM debate', particularly from the hard dimension of HRM which gives pre-eminence to the business over respect for the employee. A 'hard' approach may threaten the lawful, fair and transparent management of people and it may promote unethical managerial behaviour. A number of difficult ethical questions are posed in this section to demonstrate some of the conflicts and ambiguities associated with people management generally – answers are more elusive.

Ethics can be broadly defined as the moral principles and values that govern behaviour. This definition, because it is so broad, may not be helpful in assessing the ethics of personnel policies and practices. Although there may be a general acceptance of broad societal values, there are differences in the individual view of societal values in practice. Winstanley, Woodall and Heery (1996) provide alternative ethical frameworks for judging personnel practices.

Basic rights – The right to be consulted on matters affecting the individual at work and the right of all employees to see and understand how employment decisions are taken.

Organisational justice – Fairness in treatment, equality of opportunity and equity in reward and performance decisions.

Universalism – 'Do as you would be done by', acknowledging respect for the individual.

Community of purpose – A stakeholder view which accepts that there are different groups or stakeholders who are potentially advantaged or disadvantaged by organisational decisions and actions; there should not be extreme disparities of benefit in these groups.

There are advantages to the HR practitioner in appreciating theoretical ethical frameworks, as they help in the investigation and interpretation of the employment relationship and allow managers to develop and implement sound personnel procedures and practices. The current focus on business success and the obsession with market principles may threaten ethical standards in personnel management. The thoughtful development of people management strategy which acknowledges ethical principles should ensure that business risks are not only taken by the employees, but shared by other organisational stakeholders. If employees are treated just as a disposable resource, they will not necessarily be contributing to their full potential and people will not 'make the difference' to organisational performance. Is it reasonable for a disproportionate amount of the economic risk to be borne by the employee to protect the profits of the business?

Ethical dilemmas

All areas of people management need to be exposed to ethical scrutiny to open up the debate, and a number of employment issues may present ethical dilemmas for the personnel practitioner.

Flexibility – A much-used 'buzz word' that may, for many workers, merely be a euphemism for job insecurity or increased work demands. Demands for employee flexibility have escalated as organisations seek tighter control of headcount, markets and finance. Financial benefits may accrue to the employer from the ability to acquire and shed labour 'on demand', but what measurement has there been of the long-term cost in terms of employee performance and commitment? How is the opportunity cost of a reduced organisational ability to attract and retain high-calibre employees actually assessed? The flexible firm model (*see* Chapter 4) includes core employees, peripheral workers and sub-contractors and incorporates differential treatment between the groups – should not the ethical employer be giving equal consideration to the employment standards of all workers?

Work intensification – Relentless pressure to 'do more with less' is a factor in increasing stress levels. The pressure to work harder and for longer may be dysfunctional, as productivity can decrease in proportion to the number of working hours, actually increasing overall costs. Work pressure, coupled with job insecurity, may reduce the employees' power to fulfil family, community or societal responsibilities – is this ethical?

Sophisticated managerial techniques – Performance management systems, performance-related pay, orientation and socialisation programmes allow close managerial monitoring, measurement and control of employees and raise issues about equity and respect for the individual. Many of these systems recognise and reward conformity to managerially acceptable rules and behaviour, exerting a strong control over employees – when does the exercise of this power in the employment relationship (a form of social engineering) become ethically questionable?

There are also many day-to-day issues which expose the tension between business needs and ethical actions. Should a pregnant woman be recruited? How will the genuine whistleblower be treated? Will the organisation 'pay off' the senior executive who has behaved unacceptably, rather than risk adverse publicity, when in the same circumstances a less senior employee would be dismissed? Personnel policies, procedures and practices provide the framework for managerial action in these circumstances and they should incorporate an ethical dimension, unless of course the organisation is content to be unethical. Ethical principles, values and standards are accessible in legal precepts, codes of practice and natural justice. If work organisations are to be excused from ethical behaviour, it would be the only area of human endeavour that is exempted.

Ethical leadership

Ethical considerations are important not only in managing people, but also in doing business generally. Organisational leaders should recognise that the high profile of issues related to, for example, the natural environment and animal rights, are a public expression of dissatisfaction with the 'profits first philosophy' and indicative of a public desire for more ethical actions in business. Top management needs to take a lead in promoting ethical behaviour and developing a business ethics policy. The pursuit of good business ethics should not be based on short-term competitive advantage, or managerial concern with ethics may just attract the charge of being instrumental and therefore unethical. Connock and Johns (1995) assert that 'managers adopting an ethical stance on the grounds of principle rather than expediency will seek to avoid the short-term fix'. Ethics should be embedded in organisational culture rather than a fashionable add-on or because it results in short-term gain.

Some organisations have ethics as a cornerstone of their business, but the ethical path is not easy because open and public statements expose an organisation to scrutiny and challenge from all directions. The introduction of a social audit (The Bodyshop, for example) gives a voice to all organisational stakeholders and enables internal ethical accounting and also the benchmarking of ethical standards with other organisations. Arkin (1996) contends that:

> Business will only be legitimate in the eyes of stakeholders if it behaves in an accountable way. So companies cannot continue to behave as if they operate in a vacuum.

This transparent way of working not only extends to external dealings with customers and suppliers, but also includes internal people management policies and practices.

Business leaders have a responsibility to appreciate that, ultimately, ethical business is good business. The need to establish the Cadbury and Greenbury Committees to examine executive reward and the allegations of 'sleaze' that engulfed the 1992–1997 Major government suggests that an ethical void was perceived in the leadership of business and in public life. A public perception of this nature is unlikely to encourage ethical behaviour in society generally and amongst employees in particular. There is increasing interest in organisational policies on business ethics – who should have the responsibility for developing, implementing and monitoring these policies? There may be a role for personnel practitioners in what Winstanley and Stuart-Smith (1996) term 'ethical stewardship', which has the objectives of:

- raising awareness of ethical issues
- promoting ethical behaviour
- disseminating ethical leadership practices
- communicating codes of ethical conduct
- devising and providing training to enable employees to uphold these codes
- managing compliance and monitoring arrangements
- taking a lead in enforcement proceedings.

This stewardship role will only be credible, as will the ethical policy, if the personnel function has sufficient status to drive it through successfully. This will normally require personnel representation at director level on the Board. The role of the 'conscience of the organisation' must not be exclusive to the personnel function, or it will lead to the accusation of not having 'a business focus'; ethical behaviour and actions must be the concern of all organisational members.

Professionalism in personnel management

Whether personnel management is a 'profession' is the subject of debate. A profession exhibits certain occupational characteristics, including:

- the ownership of a specialist body of knowledge
- the control of access to the occupation through regulation of the education required to obtain employment – a licence to practise
- the setting and monitoring of the professional and ethical standards of members
- the right to withdraw entitlement to work in the profession
- the requirement of members to continuously update knowledge and expertise to ensure professional standards are maintained – continuing professional development (CPD)
- the pursuit of professional closure
- the professional autonomy of members, who have a primary allegiance to the profession.

The existence of a well-regarded professional institute, the Chartered Institute of Personnel and Development (CIPD), is illustrative of the importance of professional standards in the management of people. Entry to CIPD membership is controlled through practitioners needing to demonstrate professional standards and expertise, through examination or through verified competence, in relation to 'the people management body of knowledge'. Although CIPD membership requires the meeting of professional standards, entry to personnel management work is not exclusive to CIPD members. Therefore, this test of professional status is not one that personnel management would strictly pass; however, most personnel and development jobs require candidates who are CIPD qualified. The CIPD claims professional status by describing itself as a 'professional resource' and as 'providing a passport to professionalism'. CIPD membership has increased considerably since its foundation in 1913 and it is the largest professional body devoted to the management and development of people in Europe, with membership exceeding 100 000 in 2000. There is a specialist 'body of knowledge' associated with personnel and development on which practitioners base their professional and ethical behaviour. This includes:

- published research
- CIPD position papers
- CIPD, ACAS, CRE, EOC, DRC and HSE codes of practice
- employment law and associated principles
- sociological and psychological theory.

CIPD members are required to update their knowledge through continuing professional development (CPD). There are, therefore, many characteristics of personnel management which are supportive of claims to be a profession.

The role of the personnel professional is to resource the organisation with people effectively; to plan, recruit, develop, reward and manage the employment relationship fairly and lawfully. The personnel professional is an enabler who strives to develop people management strategy alongside business strategy and puts in place policies, procedures and practices to enable the organisation to succeed through the efforts of all employees. If people are to 'make the difference', people management activity has to be professional, ethical and reflect an understanding of the organisational environment. The balancing act between making a positive contribution to organisational success and acting as guardian of fairness in the treatment of employees is a central conflict in personnel management practice. A criticism of personnel practitioners is that of acting in a policing (of line managers) role, rather than facilitating business success. This may be the case if the personnel function operates in an administrative way, becomes preoccupied with welfare, seeks to interfere with legitimate line manager responsibilities for people, or lacks ethics, professionalism or expertise. The professional personnel function should be at the heart of the business, have board representation and develop people strategies in line with organisational development. The rapidly changing nature of many businesses requires that the HR function demonstrates business leadership and facilitates organisational change and restructuring. For example, the finance sector has been characterised by an increase in mergers and acquisitions; this brings its own tensions in having to manage the organisational restructuring while coping with the merger of different HR functions with their different personnel policies, procedures and practices. The mergers of General Accident and Provident Mutual, followed by a merger with Commercial Union to form CGU, occurred between 1996 and 1999. When the third merger with Norwich Union to form CGNU occurred in 2000, the HR Director decided that the merger of the HR functions should take place before any attempt was made to harmonise the other business functions. As Malin *et al.* (2000) say: 'This enabled the new HR function to establish itself as the unified leader of the merger process. It also permitted the immediate allocation of HR managers to each of the newly formed divisions of the merged business.'

Personnel practitioners can also experience a tension between being managerialistic and being professional. The HRM approach to managing people levers the personnel professional firmly into the managerial camp. An exclusive concentration on value-added activities and profit-making may threaten some aspects of professionalism, and personnel specialists may come under pressure to make decisions and take actions that are in conflict with their professional and ethical standards. Part of the personnel role is to ensure that legal requirements in employment are observed, but the professional role also seeks to be proactive in the management of the employment relationship. Altruistic concern for employee well-being may not be fashionable, but there are organisational benefits because employees who feel valued and who have their health, safety and welfare needs protected may demonstrate a commitment to work that gains competitive advantage. Understanding and investing in the personal development needs and the work/life balance of employees in the context of organisational needs is likely to benefit both employee and employer.

Ambiguities and tensions in personnel management can be reduced, but they first need to be recognised. The personnel professional needs to be proactive rather than content just to react to managerial decisions which are made without due regard for the people management dimension.

SUMMARY LEARNING POINTS

The perspective of this book encompasses the following contentions:

1 People resourcing consists of a set of integrated HR activities or functions.

2 People resourcing functions are enacted by personnel management practitioners and by line managers.

3 Those responsible for people resourcing need to focus on effective functional activity, whilst keeping an eye on strategy and adopting a strategic state of mind.

4 People resourcing decisions and activities are contingent upon particular organisational circumstances, and prescriptive and universal people management solutions are to be treated with caution.

5 People resourcing is enacted within a turbulent and dynamic environment, and scanning the external organisational contexts is necessary to inform resourcing decisions.

6 Effective people resourcing is underpinned by the aspiration of a healthy psychological contract in employment.

7 Whilst it may be unfashionable to think of employers and employees as being on different sides, there is scope for incongruence in the employment objectives of employers and employees and this needs to be accommodated.

8 Opinions continue to vary about whether HRM is different from personnel management and the extent to which it merely reflects an adaptation of 'the profession' to a changing environment.

9 There can be conflict between the business drive for profit and ethical behaviour. Leaders who develop ethical standards as a matter of principle rather than for short-term expediency may derive benefits from both employee commitment and customer loyalty.

10 Personnel professionals have a responsibility to behave ethically in the management of people. This may include raising awareness of ethical issues, communicating codes of conduct and providing training in upholding these codes.

11 Personnel management exhibits certain professional characteristics, but it is also characterised by conflicts, ambiguities and ethical tensions.

REFERENCES AND FURTHER READING

Arkin, A. (1996) 'Open business is good for business', *People Management*, January, 24–7.

Beardwell, I. and Holden, L. (2001) *Human Resource Management: A contemporary approach*. Harlow: Financial Times Prentice Hall.

Caulkin, S. (2001) *Performance through People, the New People Management – the Change Agenda*. CIPD.

CIPD (2001) *Organisational Change and the Psychological Contract*. London: CIPD.

Connock, S. and Johns, T. (1995) *Ethical Leadership*. London: IPD.

DfEE (2000) 'Labour market and skill trends', *Skills and Enterprise Network*.

Farnham, D. (1995) *The Corporate Environment*. London: IPD.

Farnham, D. (1999) *Managing in a Business Context*. London: CIPD.

Flood, P. (1998) 'Is HRM dead?', in Sparrow, P. and Marchington, M. (eds) *HRM – the New Agenda*. London: FT Pitman Publishing.

Fowler, A. (1987) 'When chief executives discover HRM', *Personnel Management*, 19(1).

Gowler, D. and Legge, K. (1986) 'Images of employees in company reports: do company chairmen view their most valuable asset as valuable?', *Personnel Review*, 15(5), 9–18.

Guest, D. (1987) 'HRM and industrial relations', *Journal of Management Studies*, 24(5).

Guest, D. (1989) Personnel and HRM: can you tell the difference? *Personnel Management*, January.

Guest, D. (1990) 'HRM and the American dream', *Journal of Management Studies*, 27(4), 377–97.

Guest, D. (1998a) 'Beyond HRM: commitment and the contract culture', in Sparrow, P. and Marchington, M. (eds) *HRM: The New Agenda*. London: FT Pitman Publishing.

Guest, D. (1998b) 'Is the psychological contract worth taking seriously?', *Journal of Organisational Behaviour*, 19, 649–64.

Hall, L. and Torrington, D. (1996) Paper on *Developments in the Personnel Management Function – summary of research results*.

Hall, L. and Torrington, D. (1998) *The Human Resource Function: The dynamics of change and development*. London: FT Pitman Publishing.

Hendry, C. and Pettigrew, A. (1990) 'HRM: an agenda for the 1990s', *International Journal of HRM*, 1(1).

Hutton, W. (1995) *The State We're In*. London: Vintage.

Hutton, W. (1997) *The State to Come*. London: Vintage.

IPD Statement on Employment Relations, July 1996. London: IPD.

Johns, T. (1995) 'Don't be afraid of the moral maze', *People Management*, October.

Johnson, G. and Scholes, K. (1999) *Exploring Corporate Strategy*, 5th edition. Hemel Hempstead: Prentice Hall.

Keenoy, T. (1990) 'HRM: reality, rhetoric and contradiction', *International Journal of HRM*, 1(3).

Large, M. (1992) 'Eco-mapping', *Management Education and Development*, 23.

Legge, K. (1995) *Human Resource Management: Rhetorics and Realities*. Basingstoke: Macmillan.

Legge, K. (1996) 'Morality bound', *People Management*, December.

Malin, G., Wright, J. and Hessey, P. (2000) 'Three point turn', *People Management*, 20 July.

Managing the People Dimension: The lean organisation (1996). IPD consultative document.

Mandelson, P. and Liddle, R. (1996) *The Blair Revolution*. London: Faber.

Marchington, M. (1995) 'Fairytales and magic wands: new employment practices in perspective', *Employee Relations*, 17(1), 51–66.

Morris, H. and Willey, B. (1996) *The Corporate Environment: A guide for human resource managers*. London: Pitman Publishing.

Moss Kanter, R. (1996) *World Class: Thriving locally in global economy*. London: Simon and Schuster.

Murlis, H. (1991) *The Future for Total Remuneration Packages*. IPM Conference, October.

Olsen, M. and West, J. (1989) 'Environmental scanning in the hospitality industry', *International Journal of Hospitality Management*, 8, 283–98.

People Make the Difference (1994). IPD Position Paper.

Peters, T.J. and Waterman, R.H., Jr (1982) *In Search of Excellence: Lessons from America's best-run companies*. New York: Warner.

Pickard, J. (1995) 'Prepare to make a moral judgement', *People Management*, May.

Preble, J., Rau, P. and Reichel, A. (1988) 'The environmental scanning practices of US multinationals in the late 1980s', *Management International Review*, 28.

Rowntree Foundation (1999) *Job Insecurity, Work Intensification, Flexibility and the Changing Boundaries of Work*.

Rutter, A. (1994) 'Finding your way', in Peacock, A. and Adam-Smith, D. (eds) *Cases in Organisational Behaviour*. London: Pitman Publishing.

Sissons, K. (1994) *Personnel Management: A comprehensive guide to theory and practice*. Oxford: Blackwell.

Sissons, K. and Storey, J. (2000) *The Realities of HRM*. Oxford: Oxford University Press.

Sparrow, P. and Marchington, M. (1998) *HRM – the New Agenda*. London: FT Pitman Publishing.

Stanworth, C. and Moon, C. (1997) 'Ethical issues of teleworking', *Business Ethics: A European Review*, 6(1), 35–45.

Storey, J. (1992) 'HRM in action: the truth is out at last', *Personnel Management*, April.

Storey, J. (1995) *Human Resource Management: A critical text*. Oxford: Blackwell.

Storey, J. (2001) *Human Resource Management: A critical text*. London: Thomson Learning.

Subramanian, R., Fernandes, N. and Harper, E. (1993) 'Current practices in environmental scanning by Fortune 500 corporations', *Journal of International Business*, 33, 272–85.

Thomason, G. (1991) 'The management of personnel', *Personnel Review*, 20(2).

Torrington, D. (1998) 'Crisis and opportunity in HRM', in Sparrow, P. and Marchington, M. (eds) *HRM – the New Agenda*. London: FT Pitman Publishing.

Torrington, D. and Hall, L. (1995) *Personnel Management: HRM in Action*. Hemel Hempstead: Prentice Hall.

Torrington, D. and Hall, L. (1998) 'How human resource strategy is put into practice', *Employee Relations Review*, Issue 4. Croners.

Tyson, S. (1995) *Strategic Prospects for HRM*. London: IPD.

Tyson, S. and Fell, A. (1986) *Evaluating the Personnel Function*. London: Hutchinson.

Ulrich, D. (1996) 'Transforming the HR function', *Journal of Gemini Consulting Group*, Spring.

Winstanley, D. and Stuart-Smith, K. (1996) 'Policing performance: the ethics of performance management', *Personnel Review*, 25(6), 66–83.

Winstanley, D., Woodall, J. and Heery, E. (1996) 'Business ethics and human resource management', *Personnel Review*, 25(6), 5–12.

ASSIGNMENTS AND DISCUSSION TOPICS

1 In small groups brainstorm ten contemporary HRM or people management terms which are in common usage and discuss what they mean in practice.

2 Using socio-technical systems theory consider the inputs, the processing unit sub-systems and the outputs of your organisation and prepare a diagrammatic representation along the lines of Fig. 1.3. Explain the representation of your organisation to a small group.

3 Discuss the extent to which the external environments within which organisations operate can be described and interpreted with any degree of certainty.

4 Discuss the value of environmental scanning for people resourcing decisions and suggest how scanning can be undertaken.

5 Using the PESTEL model (*see* Fig. 1.5) identify the principal environmental influences currently impacting on your organisation in particular or on work organisations in general.

6 Analyse and list the employee and employer expectations of the psychological contract in your organisation. Discuss the extent to which they are changing and establish whether the psychological contract is healthy or not.

7 What is HRM and is it different from personnel management? How is it driving the personnel/HR profession?

8 Examine personnel and development practices in your organisation and discuss the extent to which the five key elements of an HRM approach to people management are exhibited.

9 Is the devolution of HR activities to line managers a good or a bad thing, first, for the HR profession, and second, for organisational effectiveness?

10 Examine the way that personnel and development activity has developed within your organisation. Where do personnel and development activities take place and who does them?

11 What justification is there for personnel/HR calling itself a profession? Are you a member of a profession or 'a professional' or both?

12 Why is there is currently a greater concern with business ethics? What ethical tensions exist for personnel/HR specialists in the professional management of people? How should the personnel/HR professional respond to ethical tensions?

13 In small groups identify and discuss examples of ethical issues affecting the workforce in your organisations. What role is played by the HR or personnel function in anticipating and responding to these issues?

14 Discuss the extent to which conflicts, ambiguities and ethical tensions occur in the professional personnel and development role in your organisation. How can they be accommodated or reduced?

CHAPTER 2

The changing world of work and the changing role of the HR professional

INTRODUCTION

The importance of the context of people resourcing has been emphasised in Chapter 1, and it is useful now to consider more broadly current changes in so far as they affect organisations, management activity and HR practitioners. The aim is to highlight some of the features of these changes whilst, in the spirit of contextuality and the exercising of informed managerial or practitioner choice, leaving it to the reader to assess the extent of the changes and the impact on their role within the current or future organisational context. This approach also seeks to recognise that whilst we are bombarded with stories of organisational turbulence and change, the state of play may be subject to exaggeration. We may live in a dynamic organisational world, but there are degrees of stability too and we need to recognise that change is evolutionary as well as revolutionary.

Changes in the world of work have implications for HR practitioners and the role and competencies expected of them in organisations, and in particular the expectation that they should demonstrably add value. Add to this the potential of e-enabled HR and it is evident that HR professionals, and line managers with responsibility for people, are experiencing change. Whether HR practitioners are entering a new era or merely contending with traditional professional adaptation is worthy of some debate. Traditionalists will underplay the rate of change and the impact on the HR profession, and conversely the plethora of excitable commentators will trespass into exaggeration – the thinking practitioner or manager will make their own informed judgements.

CHAPTER OBJECTIVES

- To highlight trends in the changing world of work.
- To provide additional contextualisation for people resourcing activities.
- To explore how these changes may be impacting on the role of HR practitioners.
- To consider the advent of e-HR and the potential this has for the restructuring of HR activities.

THE DRIVERS FOR CHANGE IN THE WORLD OF WORK

It would appear that the competitive environment is a major driver of change in the world of work:

> The pressures on organisations to add value, achieve sustained competitive advantage, and respond and adapt quickly and flexibly to new challenges and opportunities are relentless. The responses to these pressures have taken many forms, including new types of organisation, lean, delayered, flexible, process- or project-based, increasing reliance on information technology, and an emphasis on continuous improvement in terms of performance, quality and customer service. The quality of the human or intellectual capital possessed by organisations is seen generally as the key factor in differentiating them from their rivals and achieving superior results. The focus is on the development of business strategies to achieve longer-term goals, and the part played by human resource strategies in general, and reward strategies in particular, in supporting their achievement is now well recognised.
>
> (Armstrong and Brown, 2001)

Clearly some organisations can survive 'quite nicely thank you' on fairly traditional hierarchical structures to deliver standardised ranges of products and service, but increasingly customer orientation, product differentiation and service support require new forms of organisation. This is requiring no more than 'horses for courses' but it does draw attention to the fact that there is no guarantee that today's organisations will exist indefinitely in their present form, or indeed exist at all. Therefore there is a case for organisational strategists to recognise drivers for change and for managers to diagnose and be able to act upon the implications of these drivers, because organisational survival may depend on it. This impacts on approaches to managing people and the demands made on people managers, whether they are line managers or HR professionals. Armstrong (2000) contends that it is the context within which people are managed that is changing and HR managers have had to reposition themselves 'in the ever-changing environment of global competition, new technology, and new methods of working and organising work'. Armstrong identifies the private sector mantras as sustainable competitive advantage, added value, core competencies and strategic capability, whilst in the public sector the driving force is 'best value'.

Organisational transience, employability and the transactional psychological contract

Organisational fluidity and transience, the 'here today gone tomorrow' perspective, has impacted on feelings of job security. Whilst it may be statistically possible to prove that in many cases jobs are more secure than they have ever been, the expression of organisational and environmental uncertainty, together with the managerially projected imperative of adaptation and change, has impacted upon employee perceptions of job permanence. It has also impacted upon the mutuality of obligation between employer and employee with regard to traditional career patterns. The end of the job for life may have been subject to hyperbole, but career patterns are different and twenty-first century workers may need to engage in continuous development in order to maintain employability. This promotes a loyalty to self rather than intensifying loyalty to the organisation. Worker loyalty may have to be bought by the employer through the currency of self-development opportunities. Promoting self-development is not just about offering training courses but encompasses lateral career moves, development appraisal and employer responsiveness to worker employability needs. These ideas have links to the concept of the 'war for talent' where employers compete with each other to recruit and retain valuable employees. This competition involves offering not only appropriate financial rewards but also non-financial rewards. Armstrong and Brown (2001) contend that managers should not underestimate the significance of pay as a means of attracting, retaining and providing tangible rewards to people, because it is essential to get this right since much damage can be done if it is wrong. But as a means of generating long-term commitment and motivation they argue that pay has to be regarded as only part of a whole and that it is the non-financial rewards that will ultimately make the difference. For Armstrong and Brown non-financial rewards include 'recognition, scope to achieve and exercise responsibility, opportunities for growth and development, the intrinsic motivation provided by the work itself and the quality of working life provided by the organisation'.

This refocusing of the employer–employee relationship can create the transactional psychological whereby both parties sustain the employment relationship all the time there is 'something in it for them'.

Customer aspirations and power

Although phrases like 'the customer is king' and 'delighting our customers' can be accused of being trite, there is little doubt that, amongst other things, organisations have had to become more customer-focused in order to survive and prosper in competitive environments. Excellence in customer service has always been a differentiating factor, but perhaps what is different now is that customers have had their expectations fuelled and are encouraged to feel empowered to demand quality products and good service. Customers are also more inclined to exercise their power through either the withdrawal of custom or the pursuit of compensation or restitution. Philpott (2001) sums up this customer power: 'intense competition in global and domestic markets forces businesses to keep labour costs in check and/or raise their game in terms of product quality, because empowered consumers want ever-better goods at ever-lower prices.'

This rise in customer aspirations is not only a private sector phenomenon, because citizen consumers of public services have also been encouraged, principally through public policy, to perceive themselves as fully fledged customers. It is not for this section to debate the legitimacy of the customer-driven organisation, nor to say how it should be achieved, but merely to draw attention to an issue which has implications for the world of work. Customer aspirations and power are influencing the way organisations are structured and managed and have significant implications for workers who have to contend with the increased emphasis on satisfying customer needs through being more responsive and more flexible and providing emotional labour.

The war for talent and the new paternalism

Shortage labour markets confer power to workers, as sellers of their labour, and enable a greater degree of choice to be exercised over whom to work for and on what terms.

This is one element of the war for talent – employers having to compete with each other to secure their human resource needs. The war for talent goes beyond this, as the name suggests, and it is argued that in order to survive in competitive product and service markets employers need to attract and retain the most talented workers. It is through securing the expertise, creativity and innovation of talented people that the organisation will prosper. In service-based and knowledge economies employees are not only the major operating cost but also the source of competitive advantage. Studies by Goleman in the USA, reported by Brown (2001), found that in low-skill work the highest performing workers contributed twice to three times as much as average workers, whilst in professional jobs top performers were capable of adding ten times as much value as their co-workers. Kets de Vries, in summing up the competition for talent (Williams, 2000), creates an interesting metaphor: 'Today's high performers are like frogs in a wheelbarrow, they can jump out at any time'. The implication is that organisations need to prevent talented employees from escaping. To extend the metaphor, this does not mean putting a lid on the wheelbarrow, it means making the wheelbarrow a sufficiently attractive place to stay. This attractiveness cannot be defined in any generic way because this rather depends on what the frogs want. Williams argues that the answer resides in talent management processes which go beyond ensuring that financial rewards are market competitive and encompasses the whole range of non-financial and environmental rewards. The work environment, depending on the type of work, might include opportunities to exercise discretion, to engage in innovative work, to have opportunities for self-development, to work with interesting people and to be able to share in success in the broadest sense. These features would be in addition to what might be considered more traditional non-financial rewards such as recognition, responsibility and being treated with respect. The role of managers in talent management is to exercise empowering leadership and deploy competencies related to coaching, mentoring and feedback.

In the war for talent the aim of the organisation is to become the employer of choice and seek to project the employer brand to the labour market. Some employers seem to be going to extraordinary lengths to retain people and this can be termed the 'new paternalism'. Examples of this include schemes for accumulating supermarket-style reward points, leisure zones at the office, 'duvet days' and concierge services. Concierge services might involve collecting dry cleaning, renewing road tax and buying birthday cards and presents (Cooper, 2000b). Chaudhuri (2000) quotes a new economy organisation as saying:

> If you want to keep staff then you have to look after them. That is why we try and create a campus atmosphere at our office. We have top quality gourmet food available and in the evenings we run cookery classes. You also get Waitrose Direct, a grocery shopping service – who wants to waste their spare time by pushing a supermarket trolley? Every morning workers are offered free fruit with breakfast.

The new paternalism and the war for talent may be fought principally in the dot.com or new economy sectors, despite the recent travails of those sectors. However, the underlying principle is that in today's world of work employers need to offer an attractive financial and non-financial rewards package, which incorporates personal choice and flexibility, if they are to compete effectively in the labour market and secure and retain the services of good people.

We have endeavoured to draw attention, no more than that, to a number of contextual features in the changing world of work and by way of summary these are listed, with others, in Exhibit 2.1. These have been given limited treatment in this chapter principally because further changes in the world of work might render them obsolete. It is up to the informed practitioner or manager to keep up to date and be able to analyse changes in the world of work and anticipate the implications for organisations, for managers and for workers.

Exhibit 2.1   Changes in the world of work

- Job insecurity perceptions and organisational transience
- New career patterns, concern with employability and the transactional psychological contract
- New HR techniques of commitment and involvement
- The war for talent, employer branding and the new paternalism
- Globalisation and internationalisation of goods, service, finance, information and workers
- The 'new public services', best value and the Third Way
- Continuing demographic and labour market change
- Customer aspirations and power
- ICT exploitation and diffusion, including e-commerce
- Continuing corporate restructuring, take-overs and mergers

THE CHANGING ROLE OF THE HR PROFESSIONAL

In examining the changing role of the HR professional it is useful to explore the notion of 'the business partner' together with the competencies required, the pursuit of an added value contribution and the impact of e-HR which, when combined with other influences in the world of work, can result in a reconfiguration of the HR function, and may extend to the outsourcing of HR activities.

The rise of the business partner role

Armstrong (2000) is helpful in articulating the notion of the business partner:

Another concept often associated with HRM is that of the HR director as a business partner or manager. This idea is generally attributed to Ulrich (1998) but was advanced many years before by Tyson who suggested that: 'Personnel specialists as business managers integrate their activities with top management and ensure that they serve a long term strategic purpose and have the capacity to see the broad picture and to see how their role can help to achieve the company's business objectives'. In 1993 the HR director of Motorola stated that, 'I have agreed with my teams that we will be business partners in each business; we will have the understanding of what is going on to converse knowledgeably with any of the business people'.

Armstrong is making the point that the notion of being a business partner is not brand new, but it does appear to be receiving greater attention. In essence the philosophy of the business partner role concerns being a business manager first and a functional HR specialist second. From this perspective there is no intrinsic value in HR activities *per se*; it is in supporting business objectives that the HR specialist establishes a *raison d'être*. Clearly a prerequisite of the business partner role is to ensure that HR policies and processes are characterised by effective administration, fairness and equity, compliance with the law and effective practice, all of which requires high levels of professional competence; but, in order to add real value, it is argued, the HR business partner is expected to appreciate and understand corporate strategy, identify with the objectives of their managerial colleagues and contribute to the optimisation of people performance, and thereby organisational performance. Business results are therefore the dominant concern of the HR business partner. Within its Professional Standards the CIPD has articulated an aspirational vision of the ten competencies required of the effective HR business partner at the start of the twenty-first century. These are as follows.

Personal drive and effectiveness – The existence of a positive, 'can-do' mentality, anxious to find ways round obstacles and willing to exploit all of the available resources in order to accomplish objectives.

People management and leadership – The motivation of others, whether subordinates, colleagues, seniors or project team members, towards the achievement of shared goals, not only through the application of formal authority but also by personal role-modelling, a collaborative approach, the establishment of professional credibility and the creation of reciprocal trust.

Business understanding – Adoption of a corporate, not merely functional, perspective, including awareness of financial issues and accountabilities of business processes and operations, of 'customer' priorities, and of the necessity for cost/benefit calculations when contemplating continuous improvement or transformational change.

Professional and ethical behaviour – Possession of the professional skills and technical capabilities, specialist subject, especially legal knowledge, and the integrity in decision-making and operational activity that are required for effective achievement in the personnel and development arena.

Added-value result achievement – A desire not to concentrate solely on tasks, but rather to select meaningful accountabilities – to achieve goals which deliver added-value outcomes for the organisation, but simultaneously to comply with relevant legal and ethical obligations.

Continuing learning – Commitment to continuing improvement and change by the application of self-managed learning techniques, supplemented where appropriate by deliberate, planned exposure to external learning sources.

Analytical, intuitive and creative thinking – Application of a systematic approach to situational analysis, development of convincing, business-focused action plans, and the deployment of intuitive and creative thinking in order to generate innovative solutions and proactively seize opportunities.

Customer focus – Concern for the perceptions of personnel and development's customers, including the central directorate of the organisation; a willingness to solicit and act upon customer feedback as one of the foundations for performance improvement.

Strategic thinking – The capacity to create an achievable vision for the future, to foresee longer-term developments, to envisage options and their probable consequences, to select sound courses of action, to rise above the day-to-day detail, to challenge the status quo.

Communication, persuasion and interpersonal skills – The ability to transmit information to others, especially in written report form, both persuasively and cogently, display of listening, comprehension and understanding skills, plus sensitivity to the emotional, attitudinal and political aspects of corporate life.

The extent to which all of these competencies can be developed through professional education is debatable. Professional education can provide a base on which competencies can be exhibited and developed in the real world. This is, of course, no different from other professions. Hall and Torrington (1998) refer to 'the need to develop consultancy and coaching skills, political, networking and business skills, and marketing skills. We argue that these skills are most appropriately developed within the job rather than by a professional qualification, which may form the foundation for them.'

Within the business partner model, line managers and senior managers become the internal customers of the HR practitioner and the HR function, and managerial needs therefore take precedence over the needs of other stakeholders. The business partner role for HR practitioners therefore requires the adoption of a managerial ideology and the HR practitioner firmly plants his or her feet in the managerial camp, and consequently needs to demonstrate added value to the business. This tends to intensify some of the ambiguities of the HR role, because being a business partner is potentially in conflict with ideas associated with being an employee champion (as often perceived by employees) and is not entirely compatible with notions of professional status since the HR business partner's allegiance is primarily to the employing organisation rather than to the profession. The business partner role may enable the HR practitioner to jettison some of the functional activities, such as recruitment, training and discipline, through devolving them to line managers. This may create space to be a key player in performance management, quality and continuous improvement, reward strategy, organisational development and driving change, and in pursuing a place on the Board. The business partner role is frequently projected as best practice, whilst many would argue that it is best fit that counts (see also Chapter 3 for 'best practice' and 'best fit' human resource strategies). The business partner role may therefore be appropriate for the HR function within some organisations but not in others, but there is little doubt that it is becoming more pervasive. Extracts from recent job advertisements illustrate this (emphasis added):

HR Manager – You will work in **partnership with the business managers** to develop and implement a proactive HR function. This is a highly challenging role which will test your ability to deliver best in class HR solutions that **add value** to a demanding and **quality focused** business.

Human Resources Associate – Reporting to the HR Group Leader and **working closely with line management,** you will provide **value added support to the business.**

Human Resources Manager – You will ensure that HRM initiatives **complement the company's strategies and business plans.**

Adding value through HR practices

HR practitioners may have always known intuitively that well-managed people will work better and thereby influence the financial performance of the organisations in which they are employed, but HR practitioners are under increasing pressure to demonstrate that they add value and contribute to the bottom line. Nirvana for the HR profession must therefore be evidence of a demonstrable and causal link between people management and organisational performance. The search for proof is being pursued with energy and vigour. There is a distinction between people management by line managers and functional activity by HR specialists; as Guest and King (2001) put it, 'good people management was as much about the way front line supervisors, team leaders and middle managers engaged with their staff as it was about implementing particular HR practices'. Clearly the right balance of HR activity between the line and a specialist HR function is an additional dimension in the added-value debate, but whilst acknowledging this let us examine some of the research so far.

The CIPD, through their President Don Beattie, is convinced of a positive link: 'The business case for good people management is now proven. We have developed evidence that there is a strong correlation between people management practices and business performance' (CIPD Annual Report, 2001). Guest and Baron (2000) reported mounting evidence that it was beneficial to organisations to pursue progressive people management practices. These 18 key progressive practices are exposed in Exhibit 2.2.

The main findings from the Guest and Baron (2000) research were:

- Chief executives are waking up to the importance of good people management and most acknowledge that there is a link between HR practices and business performance. But, despite asserting that people are their greatest asset, most businesses still fail to prioritise employee issues. Only 10 per cent of chief executives agree that people are a top priority ahead of finance or marketing.

- Most businesses fail to make full use of modern HR practices. From a list of 18 key progressive HR practices, only 1 per cent of firms use more than three-quarters, 25 per cent use more than half and 20 per cent use fewer than a quarter.

- Chief executives and personnel managers both give a low rating to the performance of the HR department and the effectiveness of HR practices in their company. The areas whose performance is most highly rated are practices relating to the labour market

Exhibit 2.2   Key progressive people management practices

```
 1  Realistic job previews
 2  Use of psychometric tests for selection
 3  Well-developed induction training
 4  Provision of extensive training for experienced employees
 5  Regular appraisals
 6  Regular feedback on performance from many sources
 7  Individual performance-related pay
 8  Profit-related bonuses
 9  Flexible job descriptions
10  Multi-skilling
11  Presence of work-improvement teams
12  Presence of problem-solving groups
13  Information provided on firm's business plan
14  Information provided on the firm's performance targets
15  No compulsory redundancies
16  Avoidance of voluntary redundancies
17  Commitment to single status
18  Harmonised holiday entitlement.
```

and employment security, with job design and financial flexibility seen as only slightly effective.

- HR managers in firms using the most key HR practices have the most positive perceptions of employee attitudes and behaviour, which are linked to higher productivity and improved financial results.

- The researchers conclude that those who embrace progressive HR practices with enthusiasm can gain a competitive advantage.

It would appear that, whilst the research is quite compelling, business leaders still remain to be convinced. The second stage of the research seeks to articulate statistical correlations between people management practices and business performance measures, and the third stage must be to examine practical applications in the workplace. Purcell *et al.* (2000) are also assertive about the link: 'The existence of a link between the way people are managed and business performance is now well established.' Guest and King (2001) agree: 'There is a link between all types of financially successful UK firms and the presence of an HR function.' Having said that, Guest and King go on to say that despite this finding, chief executives perceive line managers as the key to effective people management. This casts HR practitioners firmly in the role of supporting the line.

What do we make of this research so far? First, that the profession is even more convinced that effective HR practices and a professional HR function add value and contribute to bottom-line performance. Second, others, including senior managers, are still to be convinced. Third, we are some way from articulating the bundle of HR practices that will lift corporate performance – but the search goes on enthusiastically and there are opportunities for HR professionals to seize opportunities.

e-HR, e-enabled HR and self-service HR

e-HR is difficult to define because of a multiplicity of models depending on organisational circumstances. Clearly, for small to medium-sized businesses the potential of e-HR is constrained, whereas in multi-site, multi-national organisations (the ones we tend to hear about in relation to e-HR) the potential for exploitation of the technology is much greater. Basically e-HR is about using e-mail, the World Wide Web, the Internet and organisational intranets to facilitate and mediate HR activities, as well as providing a new learning and development medium. e-HR tends to be linked to a restructuring of HR activities and in this case it may be better to use the term e-enabled HR. e-enabled HR incorporates e-HR, self-service HR and the potential separation of HR activity into three tiers or levels.

Basic level e-enabled HR – This might incorporate the intranet provision of, first, live information on training courses, vacancies, employee benefits entitlement and the staff handbook; second, the publication of HR policies and procedures such as discipline, grievance and health and safety; and third, interactive facilities such as changes in employee details, management reporting and requests for information on staff turnover or pay rates. This self-service activity is termed disintermediation, whereby there is no personal intermediary between the information and its recipient. The benefits being sought are quick and easy access to information and a reduction in the resources required to provide it. Employers would be seeking productivity gains, reduction in HR costs in the provision of HR services, and a freeing-up of HR capacity to focus more on advisory and strategic roles. These basic-level HR transactions could alternatively be provided through a call centre supported with intranet provision.

Intermediate level e-enabled HR – With routine HR transactions, estimated by some commentators as 60 to 80 per cent of the HR load, handled in real time by e-HR, the more important HR activities are escalated to the intermediate level. This may comprise business unit level HR practitioners in the field or in a shared services centre. These HR staff are subject experts able to provide advisory and consultancy services to line managers in specialist areas such as employment law, compensation and benefits, and performance management.

Top level e-enabled HR – This level will consist of strategic business partners working with line managers to provide business solutions through people.

There are clearly similarities between these three levels and Tyson and Fell's clerk of works, estates manager and architects (*see* Chapter 1), in this case facilitated by the technology. There are implications for line managers, who by definition will have to accept even more responsibility for managing their people. Goodge (2001) identifies this as a huge shift of responsibility from the HR department to line managers with 'the intelligent IT systems underpinning e-HR removing routine transactional processes from the HR function by providing line managers with the information, advice and help they once received from personnel'. There are also implications for the employees, who to a greater extent are disintermediated from HR professionals. Whilst e-HR facilitates the redefinition of HR roles and capacity, there are links also with the added-value, business orientation and strategic aspirations for the HR function introduced earlier in this chapter. Key findings from *IRS Employment Trends 721* (2001) included the following.

- The electronic revolution is well under way in the HR world, although not quite to the extent that its proponents believe.

- The systems that organisations have put in place – both internally developed and externally sourced – are generally effective in meeting their objectives, with a multitude of benefits reported.

- The majority of practitioners believe that e-HR will enable the profession to develop more of a strategic role within organisations, by reducing administrative work and improving the quality of information available to the function; and all the indications are that the use of e-HR systems will continue to grow.

- This potential for the redesign of HR services does also lend itself to the outsourcing of HR activity.

Outsourcing of HR activities

Outsourcing as a term means no more than resourcing an HR activity outside the organisation. There has always been outsourcing, prime examples being the use of recruitment agencies and training consultants. The reasons for outsourcing are generally related to cost efficiency or to the buying-in of expertise not available within the organisation. The current emphasis on the strategic role of the HR function provides another driver, and that is to outsource a range of HR activities in order to liberate the HR function to operate as a strategic business partner unencumbered with routine HR work. Whilst there are several high profile cases of this strategic rationale, such as BP Amoco, Unisys and Bank of America, other research suggests that the outsourcing of HR activities is more *ad hoc* and reactive (Pickard, 2000a, b, c). This is borne out by outsourcing trends in Europe: 'Organisations across Europe made extensive use of external providers, particularly for training and development and recruitment and selection. . . . In all countries it tended to be used opportunistically rather than as the result of deliberate strategy' (Pickard, 2000c). Hall and Torrington (1998) report that training, management development and recruitment are most likely to be outsourced, followed by outplacement, health and safety, quality initiatives and job evaluation. In this study there was less incidence of the outsourcing of reward, performance management and redundancy (*see* Assignment 7 at the end of this chapter).

Within the changing world of work and the hunger for economic efficiency the outsourcing of activities to bring corporate advantage has become a normal managerial pursuit. Organisations outsource cleaning, catering, security, IT support, accounting, legal advice and marketing *inter alia* – HR activity is no different. HR outsourcing is an opportunity rather than a universal solution and constitutes a part of the ongoing evaluation of the HR role and contribution to the business. In any case the in-house HR team needs to maintain professional expertise in order to manage and retain jurisdiction over external HR providers.

BRAVE NEW WORLD OR MORE OF THE SAME?

This chapter builds on some of the contextual ideas introduced in Chapter 1 by exposing changes in the world of work and the influences on the HR role within contemporary organisations. Whilst recognising that change is taking place, it is important not to become too excitable and suggest that we are entering some kind of brave new HRM world. Armstrong (2000) sums this up:

> The notion that personnel practitioners became involved in strategy formulation and implementation after HRM was invented is a travesty of the facts. Perhaps the word 'strategy' was not bandied around as much then as now but personnel specialists could not deliver effective services unless they understood the business context within which they were operating – where the business was going, what its needs were. To imply that until they travelled along the road to Damascus in the mid-1980s they were unaware of the need to innovate and think ahead is an insult to the many able personnel practitioners who were doing just that before the 1980s.

This is not meant to suggest that there is no change, but to encourage a balanced perspective. It is all a question of degree – line managers have always undertaken the management of human resources, but they may be doing more of it; the personnel practitioner has always had to have a business orientation, but perhaps it is sharper now; the personnel professional has always had to be aware of strategy, perhaps there is now a greater emphasis on this. Perhaps the personnel profession is in crisis, perhaps it is not: 'What we see is a variety of approach rather than a clear consensus about the appropriate way to organise the (personnel) function. Personnel specialists have a propensity for navel-gazing and neurosis about their role but on this occasion it seems ill founded. No doubt, however, observers will continue to tell the healthy patient that he or she is ill' (Torrington, 1998). Armstrong (2000), in concluding his analysis in 'The name has changed but has the game remained the same?', states:

> This means that practitioners must be aware of evolving business needs and how new ideas and good practice might fit those needs, however they are described. In its essentials the game has remained the same but the way it is being played has altered. Whether or not the name has changed is immaterial. New (HR) practices are developed and operated individually or 'joined up' because they meet the needs of the situation. What matters is what works.

We conclude that we may be in a new era but not a brave new world, but make up your own mind.

SUMMARY LEARNING POINTS

1 The world of work is changing, and whilst the rate of change may be exaggerated it is important for informed practitioners and managers to be aware of and able to react to the changes.

2 Organisational fluidity and transience coupled with exhortations to self-manage careers can result in workers giving primacy to their own employability concerns.

3 There is no doubt that customer aspirations and power are increasing and resulting in customer-driven organisations. This has significant implications for workers and for managers.

4 Employers may have to compete for good workers through offering competitive financial rewards and attractive non-financial rewards, and through deploying the art of talent management.

5 There are changes in the role of the HR professional encompassing business partnership, e-enabled HR, the restructuring of HR services and the potential for outsourcing HR activities. These influences should not be perceived as universal, because the role of the HR practitioner will be dependent on organisational circumstances and arguably it is 'best fit' that counts.

REFERENCES AND FURTHER READING

Armstrong, M. (2000) 'The name has changed but has the game remained the same?', *Employee Relations*, 22(6), 576–93.

Armstrong, M. and Brown, D. (2001) *New Dimensions in Pay Management*. London: CIPD.

Baron, A. and Collard, R. (1999) 'HR and the bottom line: realising our assets', *People Management*, 14 October, 30–8.

Beattie, D. (2001) *CIPD Annual Report*.

Brewster, C., Harris, H. and Sparrow, P. (2001) 'On top of the world', *People Management*, 25 October, 37–42.

Brown, D. (2001) 'Lopsided view', *People Management*, 22 November, 36–7.

Carter, M. (2000) 'e-Procurement: control shift', *People Management*, 23 November, 26–30.

Chaudhuri, A. (2000) 'Perk practice', *The Guardian: Management*, 30 August, 10–11.

CIPD (2001) *CIPD Professional Standards*. London: CIPD.

Cooper, C. (2000a) 'HR and the bottom line: in for the count', *People Management*, 12 October, 28–34.

Cooper, C. (2000b) 'Concierge services: chore competency', *People Management*, 7 December, 22–5.

Futures: the Industrial Society (2000) 'Most wanted: the quiet birth of the free worker'.

Glover, C. (2000) 'Time to show chief executives that HR makes the difference', *People Management*, 9 November, 20–1.

Glynn, C. (2000) 'Put people first on the balance sheet', *The Guardian: Management*, 16 September, 29.

Goodge, P. (2001) 'e-HR pure and simple', *People Management*, 8 March, 51.

Guest, D. and Baron, A. (2000) 'HR and the bottom line: piece by piece', *People Management*, 20 July, 26–31.

Guest, D. and King, Z. (2001) 'HR and the bottom line: personnel's paradox', *People Management*, 14 October, 30–8.

Hall, L. and Torrington, D. (1998) *The Human Resource Function: Dynamics of change and development*. London: FT Pitman Publishing.

Higginbottom, K. (2001) 'BP learns outsourcing lesson', *People Management*, 8 November, 8.

IPD (1994) 'People make the difference'. IPD Position Paper.

IRS Employment Trends 721 (2001) 'e-HR: personnel tomorrow', February, 6–13.

Kaplan, R. and Norton, D. (2001) 'Marked impact: business strategy', *People Management*, 25 October, 52–7.

Lecky-Thompson, R. (1997) 'Tales of the city: HR in the square mile'. *People Management*, 23 January, 22–7.

Lewis, A. (2000) 'Self-service HR: you've got to hand it to them', *People Management*, 28 September, 47.

Lewis, J. (2001) 'Out is back in: outsourcing HR's new skills', *Personnel Today*, 18 April, 24–33.

Littlefield, D. and Merrick, N. (2000) 'HR benchmarking: the realm of the peers', *People Management*, 7 December, 30–4.

Morgan, S. (2001) 'How to manage outsourcing', *People Management*, 3 May, 44–5.

People Management and Business Performance (2001) 'Performance through people: the new people management – the change agenda'. London: CIPD.

People Management and Business Performance (2001) 'The case for good people management: a summary of the research'. London: CIPD.

Philpott, J. (2001) 'The informed vote: the emerging political economy of work', *People Management*, 11 January, 42–3.

Pickard, J. (1998) 'Externally yours: outsourcing', *People Management*, 23 July, 34–7.

Pickard, J. (2000a) 'A sell-out strategy: outsourcing', *People Management*, 20 November, 32–6.

Pickard, J. (2000b) 'HR outsourcing: the truth is out there', *People Management*, 3 February, 48–50.

Pickard, J. (2000c) 'Study casts doubt on boom in outsourcing', *People Management*, 6 July, 16.

Purcell, J., Kinnie, N., Hutchison, S. and Rayton, B. (2000) 'HR and the bottom line: inside the box', *People Management*, 26 October, 30–8.

Richardson, R. and Thompson, M. (1999) *The Impact of People Management Practices on Business Performance: A review of the literature*. London: CIPD.

Schuler, R. and Jackson, S. (1999) *Strategic HRM*. Oxford: Blackwell.

Sisson, K. and Storey, J. (2000) *The Realities of HRM*. Oxford: Oxford University Press.

Sparrow, P. and Marchington, M. (1998) *HRM: The new agenda*. London: FT Pitman Publishing.

Tamkin, P., Barber, L. and Dench, S. (1997) 'From admin to strategy: the changing face of the HR function', *Institute for Employment Studies*: 332.

Thompson, M. (1998) 'HR and the bottom line: jet setters', *People Management*, 16 April, 38–41.

Torrington, D. (1998) 'Crisis and opportunity in HRM', in Sparrow, P. and Marchington, M. (eds) *HRM: The new agenda*. London: FT Pitman Publishing.

Turner, P. (2001) 'Professional development into the new millennium', *CIPD Professional Standards Conference*, July.

Tyler, E. (2001) 'Intranets: self service HR', *People Management*, 19 April, 51–2.

Ulrich, D. (1998) 'A new mandate for human resources', *Harvard Business Review*, January/ February, 124–34.

Williams, M. (2000) 'Retention strategies: transfixed assets', *People Management*, 3 August, 29–33.

Woodruffe, C. (2000) 'Keep X on the files', *People Management*, 20 July, 53.

ASSIGNMENTS AND DISCUSSION TOPICS

1 The changing world of work: in groups, discuss the following two questions and be prepared to feed back into a whole-class discussion. First, in what way is the world of work changing compared to 10–15 years ago and what changes do you anticipate in the next decade? You can refer to Exhibit 2.1 if this is helpful. Second, what are the implications of the changing world of work for employees and for the HR professional?

2 What is meant by 'added value' and 'business partnership' in relation to the HR role? How should personnel/HR professionals respond to the demands of their internal customers, normally line management colleagues?

3 To what extent is it possible to measure the contribution of HR activities to organisational success and what measures should be used?

4 Analyse the ten CIPD competencies required by HR professionals and comment on how they can be developed. To what extent does the specific organisational role of the HR practitioner determine the mix of competencies required? Illustrate your answer with practical examples, using your own role and that of other students.

5 Consider Guest's 18 key progressive people management practices listed in Exhibit 2.2. Identify which practices are present in your workplace and discuss how effective they are.

6 Is e-enabled HR a threat or an opportunity for the HR profession? Justify your point of view with practical examples.

7 The outsourcing (or externalisation) of HR activities can be defined as the use of consultants or specialist providers to supply HR activities or services previously undertaken by the organisation's own HR specialists. It can be viewed as the HR equivalent of facilities management – the facility in this case is 'the human resource'. Using the taxonomy of HR activities below, or one of your choice, analyse a number of organisations and identify which HR activities are currently outsourced. You should make some quantitative assessment of the extent of the outsourcing of each category.

HR strategy development	Human resource planning
Work and job design	Recruitment
Selection	Reward strategies and systems
Job evaluation	Payroll administration
Performance management	Internal communications
Quality initiatives	Diversity initiatives
Employee relations	Health and safety
Counselling/employee assistance programmes	Training
Management development	Careers advice and planning
Redundancy and/or dismissal	Outplacement
Employment law advice	HR advisory service to line managers
Organisation development	

In relation to your findings consider the following questions. What are the reasons for the outsourcing? What are the challenges associated with outsourcing? What evidence is there for an increase in HR outsourcing in the next three years? If so, which areas do think will increase and why? Write a report and/or give a presentation on the state of play in HR outsourcing which reflects your research.

CHAPTER 3

Human Resource Strategy – perspectives and theories

by David Farnham

INTRODUCTION

Both academics and practitioners have shown increasing interest in Human Resource Strategy (HRS) recently and in its relationship to corporate performance. But there is no generic definition of the term. Put simply, HRS has been explained as 'the intentions' of an organisation 'toward its employees, expressed through philosophies, policies and practices' (Tyson, 1995). Hendry and Pettigrew (1986) in turn have provided a wider definition, claiming that the strategic aspect of Human Resource Management (HRM) within organisations consists of four key elements. These are the use of planning, a coherent approach to the managing of people underpinned by a core 'philosophy', matching HRM activities and policies to some explicit strategy, and seeing people as a 'strategic resource' for achieving 'competitive advantage'. The framework of Hendry and Pettigrew suggests that those responsible for developing effective HR strategies, and linking these to business strategy, have to adopt a conceptual and reflective approach to the task. Determining an appropriate HRS in organisations is not simply about applying set techniques or simplified rules to the process, since there are no generally agreed tools of analysis or 'magic bullets' for action in this area of people management. Indeed, both research and practice point in a number of different and conflicting directions. This chapter outlines some of the contemporary debates and ambiguities in this area of HRM and explores the role of human resources strategy in contributing to organisational effectiveness.

CHAPTER OBJECTIVES

- To provide a typology of strategic management perspectives.
- To demonstrate the relationships between strategy, business performance and human resources.
- To outline the main models of HRS.
- To describe how an emergent HRS can be developed.

STRATEGY: MISCONCEPTIONS, CONCEPTS AND TYPOLOGIES

The noun 'strategy' and the adjective 'strategic' are used extensively in business literature, business education and 'management speak' today. Thus we have 'corporate strategy', 'strategic planning', 'business strategy', 'strategic management', 'strategic thinking', 'strategic analysis', 'strategic objectives', 'strategic human resource management', 'human resource strategy' and many other expressions of strategy and strategic intent. Yet while we intuitively understand that 'strategy' is something about 'setting one's goals and finding ways of achieving them', there is no universally agreed definition or conceptualisation of the term, despite the claims of some self-professed management gurus. Indeed, as Whittington (2000: 1f) has pointed out, 'there is not much agreement about strategy' and 'strategy isn't easy', while Markides (2000: vii) has concluded that 'we simply do not know what strategy is or how to develop a good one'.

Clearly, business strategy has always existed but was traditionally assumed to be a rational, logical, self-evident and profit-centred process. As the former President of General Motors confidently asserted in his autobiography some 40 years ago (Sloan, 1963: 49): 'The strategic aim of a business is to earn a return on capital, and if in any particular case the return in the long run is not satisfactory, the deficiency should be corrected or the activity abandoned.' But recent studies have shown conclusively that 'strategy' is not as simplistic as this (De Wit and Meyer, 1999). So why is there such interest, even obsession, with the strategic dimensions of organisational life in the business, public service and voluntary sectors today? And what sense can be made of 'strategy', in an increasingly post-modern age that is sceptical of rationality, receptive to individualism and values local contexts?

The answer to the first question lies in the 'new' globalisation and changing nature of the world economy, emergence of large, transnational business corporations and impact of information and communication technologies on the world of work and organisational systems over the past 20 years. The answer to the second question can be found in the search for 'strategy' by top managers in response to the increasing complexity of the contemporary business environment. This includes the pursuit of growth and reduction of market insecurity in an increasingly dynamic free-market, international economy (Farnham, 1999).

There is, then, no single model of 'strategy' but, because of intensified competition in product markets in the private sector, and greater accountability and competition in the public sector, top managers are now looking for appropriate strategic responses likely to ensure organisational survival and enterprise success in conditions of change, market turbulence and rising customer expectations. There are different approaches to this task. Whittington (2000) has summarised the contemporary debate, neatly and convincingly. He has argued that those creating strategy do so from two dimensions. They have to consider the *outcomes* of strategy and the *processes* by which it is made. The outcomes are either 'profit-maximising' or 'pluralist' ones (i.e. other than profit-making alone such as ethical choices, social goals or stakeholder interests); the processes are either 'deliberate' (i.e. planned) or 'emergent' (i.e. they come about by accident, muddle or inertia). This results in four 'idealised' perspectives of strategy, although in the practical world there can be hybrid, overlapping systems which interact and merge one into another:

- deliberate and profit-maximising (classical)
- emergent and profit-maximising (evolutionary)
- emergent and pluralist (processual)
- deliberate and pluralist (systemic).

These perspectives, or theories of strategy, are often neither explicit nor formalised but are short cuts to managerial action and getting things done in organisations in the search for market success, efficiency and profitability.

Where strategic emphasis is on profit-making outcomes and deliberate processes, we have the 'classical' approach to business strategy. This focuses on analysing, planning and commanding from the top and is typically found in mature, capital-intensive industries tending to monopoly or oligopoly in the UK, United States and Australasia. The 'evolutionary' approach to strategy is based on profit-making outcomes and emergent processes and is rooted in keeping production costs low and business options open. It is commonly found in small firms, new industries and Anglo-Saxon conglomerates. The 'processual' approach to strategy aims at pluralist outcomes and uses emergent processes. It stays 'close to the ground', goes 'with the flow' and is typically found in protected bureaucracies and knowledge-based firms. The 'systemic' approach to strategy is based on pluralist outcomes and deliberate processes and plays by 'local rules'. It is typically found in non-Anglo-Saxon businesses and family firms and state enterprises in France, Germany and parts of the Far East (Whittington, 2000).

The heyday of classical school thinking was the 1960s, where strategic success or failure was determined internally through managerial planning, rational analysis and rigorous calculation (Ansoff, 1965; Chandler, 1962). The influence of the processual perspective was strongest during the 1970s. It too was inward looking but its concerns were with political bargaining and the building of core managerial skills and competences within organisations (Cyert and March, 1963; Mintzberg, 1979; Pettigrew, 1973). The evolutionary school of strategy typified the 1980s and emphasised the external demands on organisations such as the impact of markets and economic factors on business decisions, as well as survival of the fittest in the marketplace (Williamson, 1985). And, most recently, the systemic school of theory, which came to the fore during the 1990s, has argued that to understand what is happening in organisations, and among business competitors, requires corporate strategists to be socially sensitive to the diversity of contemporary economic and business practices.

To sum up, each of these four perspectives of strategy is based on differing assumptions about its outcomes and processes, which leave managerial strategists with hard choices to make in practice. Certainty is replaced by uncertainty, simplicity by complexity, and prescription by contingency. As Whittington (2000: 118) concludes:

> Classical confidence in analysis, order and control is undermined by Processual scepticism about human cognition, rationality and flexibility. The incrementalist learning of Processualists is challenged in turn by the impatient markets of Evolutionists. But even Evolutionary markets can be bucked if, as Systemic analysts of social systems allege, the state is persuaded to intervene.

STRATEGY, BUSINESS PERFORMANCE AND HUMAN RESOURCES

Establishing measurable links between corporate strategy and HRS is problematic. In the small and medium-sized enterprise sector, for example, there may be no effective connection between corporate strategy and HRS, simply because corporate strategy might be essentially reactive and there may be no explicit HRS at all. In other sectors, corporate strategy may drive HRS or, less likely, HRS may drive corporate strategy. In yet other cases corporate strategy and HRS may be integrated in that a holistic strategy incorporates a number of sub-strategies, including HR issues. Such an approach is rooted in the belief that HRS is critical to business profitability and efficiency and is an organisational end in itself (Boxall, 1996).

Establishing measurable links between HRS and effective business performance is also problematic. However, as Torrington, Hall and Taylor (2002: 30) have pointed out, 'there is a strong lobby propounding the view that human resources are *the* source of competitive advantage for the business, rather than, say, access to capital or use of technology'. Also Boxall and Steeneveld (1999) have claimed it is self-evident that the quality of HRM is a critical influence on the performance of firms and managing people. Their study, for example, concluded, first, that successful firms enact those HR strategies enabling them to survive as credible members of their industry or sector. The fundamental strategic priority of those leading HRM activities should be to ensure that management takes a lead in those HR actions that are vital for supporting the viability of the firm, as it faces challenges of change and competition in its sector. They view alignment of organisational and employee interests as the basic congruence problem in managing employment relations. The second, more difficult task is to perceive and enact those HR strategies that might generate some kind of competitive advantage for the business.

There are a number of approaches attempting to link strategy, business performance and HRS. Although there are some overlaps, the three general categories are the 'resource-based' model, 'best-practice' models and 'best-fit' models, each of which is examined below.

THE RESOURCE-BASED MODEL

The origins of the resource-based model of HRS emerged out of the new business strategy literature, which has been influential in initiating developments in pay systems, training and development and other HR issues. The essence of the 'resource-based' argument is that organisations comprise unique bundles of assets (including 'human assets') and that access to these, and the firm's ability to make effective use of them, provides the source of its competitive advantage in the marketplace. The resource-based view of the firm concentrates on its internal resources, strategy and business performance, where the contribution of a firm's human resources is to promote competitive advantage through developing 'human capital' rather than just aligning human resources to the firm's strategic goals. The focus is not just on the behaviour of human resources but on the skills, knowledge, attitudes and competencies which people bring into the organisation, thus promoting sustained competitive advantage and corporate growth. As Sisson and Storey (2000: 34) have argued: 'such an approach to understanding strategy places managers' role in identifying, utilizing and renewing such assets centre-stage'.

The resource-based view of the firm is rooted in the business economics literature, where theories of profit and competition have identified the internal resources of the firm as the major determinants of competitive success (Penrose, 1958). Proponents of this model, such as Barney (1991), define 'resources' as 'all assets, capabilities, organizational processes, firm attributes, information, knowledge etc. controlled by a firm that enable the firm to conceive of and implement strategies that improve its efficiency and effectiveness'. He classifies them into three categories: physical capital, organisational capital and human capital, where 'human capital resources' include the experience, judgement and intelligence of individual managers and workers in the firm.

In the resource-based view of the firm, competitive advantage occurs when a firm implements a value-creating strategy that is not being simultaneously implemented by its competitors. But this only occurs in situations of 'resource heterogeneity' (i.e. where resources vary across firms) and 'resource immobility' (i.e. where competing firms are unable to obtain resources from other firms).

Sustained competitive advantage, in turn, only exists when other firms are incapable of duplicating the benefits of competitive advantage. Hence a competitive advantage is not considered sustained until all efforts by competitors to duplicate the advantage have ceased. According to Barney (1991), four criteria indicate whether the resource is getting a sustained advantage. The resource must: (1) add positive value to the firm, (2) be unique or rare among competitors, (3) be inimitable and (4) not be substituted with another resource by competing firms. He concludes that 'the resource-based model of strategic management suggests that organization theory and organizational behavior may be a rich source of findings and theories concerning rare, non-imitable, and non-substitutable resources in firms' (ibid: 116).

Wright et al. (1994: 308), building on this, have discussed how human resources meet the above criteria for sustained competitive advantage. First, by drawing on 'utility analysis' literature, they conclude that human capital resources do provide value to firms, as well as providing methods for estimating this value. Second, since cognitive ability is normally distributed in populations, they argue that human resources with high ability are rare. Thus 'it is safe to say that firms with high average levels of cognitive ability relative to their competitors possess more valuable human capital resources than those of their competitors.' Third, they also argue that, since HR advantages are most frequently characterised by unique historical conditions, causal ambiguity and social complexity, human capital is almost always inimitable. A potential problem with this is the notion that human resources are highly mobile. But Wright and his colleagues conclude that this is not the case, because of the high transaction costs in moving from one employer to another. Fourth, whilst accepting that it might be possible to substitute other resources in the short term, they suggest that it is very unlikely that such substitution could result in sustained competitive advantage. This is because, to the extent that the resource offsetting the advantage of human resources is not itself rare, inimitable or non-substitutable, it will not be imitated and human resources will again constitute a competitive advantage.

The role of human resources in sustained competitive advantage

Turning to the role of human resources in sustained competitive advantage, it is asserted, first, that firms with high levels of human capital have relative productivity advantages over their competitors. This is because they develop more efficient means of accomplishing their tasks. Such firms also have greater capacity to respond to external changes, through sensing the need for change and developing strategies to adapt to it. Second, HR practices help in developing human resources as a source of sustained competitive advantage by creating and developing a pool of high quality human capital. Third, those firms in an industry developing effective mixes of selection and reward systems have strategic advantage because human resources are not perfectly mobile. Fourth, having the correct mix of HR practices is a necessary condition for maximising the effectiveness of the human resource capital pool. Thus although HR practices are not themselves sources of sustained competitive advantage, they play an important role in developing sustained capital advantage through developing the human capital pool. Also by affecting HR behaviour, HR practices moderate the relationship between this pool and sustained capital advantage.

In summary, the resource-based view of the firm suggests the need to integrate human resources in the formulation stage of a firm's strategy. This approach also provides a framework for examining the potential for a given pool of human capital to carry out a given strategy. It is claimed that the resource-based view of HRS demonstrates that strategies are not universally applicable but are contingent on having a HR base necessary to implement them (Grant, 1991). The view of human resources as a pool of capital implies a change in treating the costs incurred in HR interventions. If human resources are a source of sustained capital advantage, then they are better viewed as investment in a capital asset rather than as an outgoing expense.

BEST-PRACTICE MODELS

Supporters of 'best-practice' models of HRS argue that there are certain HR practices which help organisations achieve competitive advantage in the marketplace. They suggest there is a positive link between HRS and business performance but argue that the effect is only optimised where 'best' HR policies are used. All of them suggest that the same basic HR policies and practices universally enhance business performance in every organisation, irrespective of particular product markets, business goals and organisational circumstances. This optimisation, they argue, takes place through a variety of mechanisms such as enhancing the competence of employees, gaining their commitment, motivating them and adopting appropriate methods of job design. According to Guest (2000: 2), for example, best practice borrows from expectancy theory and implies that all the above – competence, commitment, motivation and effective job design – need to be present to ensure the best organisational outcomes. 'Positive employee behaviour should in turn impact upon establishment level outcomes such as low absence, quit rates and wastage, as well as high quality and productivity.'

In another paper Guest (1989) has proposed four sets of HR policy goals: strategic integration, commitment, flexibility and quality. These relate to specific HRM policies, such as managing change, that are expected to result in desirable outcomes for organisations. Strategic integration means making sure that HRM is fully integrated into strategic planning (vertical integration), that HR policies are consistent with one another (horizontal integration) and that line managers use appropriate HR practices in their daily work. Commitment aims to ensure that employees feel bound to the organisation and are committed to high performance. Flexibility requires an adaptable organisational structure and functional flexibility based on multi-skilling. Quality is expected to result in high quality products or services delivered through high quality flexible employees.

The HR policies claimed to facilitate this are linked with organisational and job design, the management of change, recruitment, selection and internal socialisation, appraisal, training and development, rewards and communication. Expected organisational outcomes include high levels of job performance, problem solving, innovation, change and cost-effectiveness, matched by low levels of labour turnover, absence and grievances.

The Harvard model

One well-known 'best-practice' approach is the Harvard model, proposed by Beer, Spector, Lawrence, Quinn Mills and Walton (1984). They suggest that managerial HR policy choices are influenced by stakeholder interests and the particular situational factors interacting on them. The strategic task of management is to take policy choices in the light of these circumstances. Such choices result in certain HR outcomes and long-term consequences for individuals, organisations and society at large.

The stakeholder interests identified by Beer *et al.* include shareholders, management, employees, government, the community and trade unions. The situational factors impacting upon the organisation's stakeholders are workforce characteristics, business strategy, management philosophy, the labour market, task technology, laws and societal values. Four clusters of HRM policy choices are seen to be critical and these relate to the degree and nature of influence that employees are likely to have. These are 'employee influence', 'human resource flow', 'reward systems' and 'work systems'. Perceived HR outcomes are the four 'Cs': 'commitment', 'competence', 'congruence' and 'cost-effectiveness'. The long-term consequences are identified as individual well-being, organisational effectiveness and societal well-being.

Superficially, the Harvard model seems to allow for some variation of HR strategies and choices, thus appearing to contrast itself with situational determinism. But, in reality, its analysis of strategic choice has strong prescriptive overtones. For example, the specified desirable outcomes – the four 'Cs' – are attempting to elevate one particular type of strategic approach over others. Indeed, the Harvard approach appears to suggest that there is one preferred set of HR policy choices which are superior to all others – those incorporated within its own framework.

Many of the policies and practices typically associated with the Harvard model, as with other best-practice approaches, though not explicitly stated, are rooted in neo-human relations theory (Maslow, 1943; Herzberg *et al.*, 1957; McGregor, 1960). Thus some of their underlying beliefs and ideas include widespread use of the 'team' analogy in the models, assumptions about high levels of trust within enterprises, and perceptions of HRM as central to business strategy. Top managers are presumed to be highly visible and able to provide a 'vision' for the future of their organisations that employees can identify with and share, while middle managers are seen as inspiring, encouraging and facilitating change by harnessing the commitment and cooperation of employees. Best-practice models also assume federal, decentralised corporate structures, where job design is congruent with organisation structure, technology and HR policies and where work teams enjoy large measures of autonomy, with a great deal of task flexibility.

The implicit HR policies incorporated within the Harvard model and best-practice approach comprise six key elements. The first is numerical flexibility, temporal flexibility and single status. The second is selection processes emphasising attitudes as well as skills. Third, appraisal is assumed to be open and participative, with two-way feedback between managers and employees. Fourth, training and development of core employees are central to this model, with lateral as well as upward career advancement and an emphasis on general as well as specific employability. Fifth, reward systems utilise individual and group performance related pay, skill-based pay, profit and gain sharing, share ownership and flexible benefits packages. Sixth, participation and employee involvement are based on extensive use of two-way communication and problem-solving groups. Trade union organisation, whilst not necessarily excluded from best-practice models, is not central to this approach to HRS.

The partnership approach

Unions do have some legitimacy in another best-practice model, however. This is the 'partnership' approach, which has been on the HRS agenda for some years. The partnership model has been extolled by a variety of interests such as the Industrial Partnership Association (1992), the Department of Trade and Industry (1997) and the Trades Union Congress (1999). Even here, though, the union role is somewhat ambiguous. Indeed, as Sisson and Storey (2000: 38) have commented, it is especially controversial 'whether partnership is in essence about the relationship between the organization and the individual or the organization and the trade union'. There is no agreed definition of partnership but six key principles appear to underpin it:

1 Shared commitment to the success of the organisation, including support for flexibility and replacement of adversarial employment relations by cooperative ones.

2 Recognition that the interests of the partners (employer and union; employer and staff) may legitimately differ.

3 Employment security, including measures to improve the employability of staff, as well as limiting compulsory redundancy.

4 Focus on quality of working life.

5 Commitment to managerial transparency, openness to discussing future plans, genuine consultation and willingness to listen to the business case for alternative strategies.

6 Adding value, by drawing on resources not previously accessed.

The partnership best-practice model, in short, is HRM combined with some form of collective representation or employee voice, with or without trade unions.

There are three main sources of the partnership model. First, there was the 'new industrial relations' literature in the United States during the 1980s, which emphasised the common interests of employers and unions in the employment relationship in contrast to adversarialism (Kochan *et al.*, 1986). A second source was mainland Europe, with its version of 'social partnership' or 'concertation' amongst employers, unions and governments at national level in many EU countries. This was complemented by 'social dialogue' at EU level, involving employer and union confederations, public employers and EU institutions, so as to promote both social policy for citizens and modernisation of work organisations to advance competitive success (European Commission, 1997). Third, in the UK, debates over the 'new realism' during the 1990s suggested that unions should develop a joint approach with employers, thereby creating the conditions for both economic success and social cohesion (Farnham, 1994).

There is some evidence to show that partnership works. Both survey and case study evidence points to there being some positive links between partnership arrangements and business performance (Industrial Partnership Association, 1997). Both management and unions have had to adapt to the partnership model. Management has had to change its style from one of 'doing' to 'facilitating', to act more openly and change its approach to the unions by adopting a problem-solving methodology. Unions, in turn, have had to accept the need for joint communication and recognise that the long-term interests of their members are best served by helping organisations be successful and not by opposing change for its own sake. They have also had to give away collective bargaining power (Thomas and Wallis, 1998).

BEST-FIT MODELS

'Best-fit' models are based on the proposition that different types of HRS are suitable for different types of business conditions. The best-fit approach claims that there is a link between HRS and competitive advantage but that HRS is contingent upon the particular circumstances of each enterprise. Organisations need to identify the HR strategies which 'fit' their enterprises in terms of their product markets, labour markets, size, structures, strategies and other factors. What is 'right' for one organisation is not appropriate for others.

Three types of best-fit models

There are three main types of best-fit models. One links HR strategic choices to different stages in a firm's business cycle. Another relates them to the different strategic and structural configurations of organisations. And the third matches HR strategies to different business strategies.

The first of these, the business life cycle model, tries to link HR policy choices with the varying needs of firms at different stages in their life cycles from start-up, through growth, maturity and decline. At each stage, it is claimed, a firm has different business priorities which, in turn, demand different HR strategies. According to Kochan and Barrocci (1985), the recruitment, selection and staffing, compensation and benefits, training and development, and employee relations functions need to make different responses at different stages in an organisation's business cycle. During a firm's start-up stage, for instance, the training and development (T and D) function needs to define the company's future skill requirements and begin establishing career ladders for staff. During a firm's period of growth, however, T and D needs to maintain an effective management team through appropriate management development and organisational development activities. In a firm's maturity, T and D focuses on maintaining flexibility and the skills of an ageing workforce. And finally, in a firm's decline the T and D function has to focus on retraining and providing career consulting services to its staff.

The second best-fit model, linking HRS to the strategy and structure of firms, is exemplified by Fombrun, Tichy and Devanna (1984: 37), in their basic model for analysing strategic HRM. In their view, effective systems for managing human resources lead to increased effectiveness within organisations and these HR systems can be internally 'fitted' to business strategy. Their model provides a set of frameworks for conceptualising HRM and explores the link between HRM and the formulation and implementation of strategic and business objectives. They have elaborated the traditional view of how managers should think about strategic management by including HRM as an integral tool which they can use in strategy determination. For Fombrun and his colleagues (*ibid*: 37), 'the critical managerial task is to align the formal structure and human resource systems so that they drive the strategic objectives of the organization'.

The model of Fombrun *et al.* identifies a range of appropriate HR strategic choices, in terms of selection, appraisal, rewards and development, that are dependent upon an organisation's strategic/structural configurations. These configurations range from single product strategies with functional structures, through diversified product strategies linked to multi-divisional structures and multiple product strategies operating globally. Thus a business depending on a single product strategy and a functional structure is likely to pursue basic HR policies, which are largely functional, subjective and unsystematic. Businesses following a diversification strategy within a multi-divisional structure, in contrast, are likely to be characterised by a HRS driven by impersonal, systematic HR processes adaptable to different parts of the organisation. In terms of selection, for example, this is likely to be functionally and generalist oriented, with systematic criteria being used. Appraisal will be impersonal and based on returns on investment and productivity, with subjective assessments of contribution to the business. Rewards, in turn, could incorporate large pay bonuses based on profitability, linked with subjective assessments of contribution to business performance. Finally, T and D would be cross-functional, cross-divisional and cross-business.

Once management has articulated a philosophy about managing people, Fombrun *et al.* argue, it can then focus on designing the HR system. They identify four generic functions performed by HR managers, which they call the 'Human Resource Cycle', with performance being a function of all HR components. These are:

- selecting the people best able to perform the jobs defined by the structure
- appraising their performance to ensure equitable distribution of rewards
- motivating employees by linking rewards to high level performance
- developing employees to enhance their performance at work.

They argue that success in implementing strategic objectives depends on how well organisations carry out the human resource cycle. This means selecting the right people, measuring appropriate behaviours, rewarding progress against strategic objectives and developing skills to ensure success of the strategy.

The strength of this approach is that it provides a basic framework showing how selection, appraisal, rewards and development can be mutually linked to encourage appropriate employee behaviour. However, this 'internal fit' model, whilst useful, raises questions about the model's simplistic responses to organisational strategy. Further, the model has also been criticised because of its dependence on a rational, deliberate approach to strategy formulation, its unitary assumptions about the employment relationship and its lack of recognition of employee interests in the equation.

The third best-fit model matches business strategy with HRS. These theories draw on Porter's distinction amongst innovation, quality enhancement and cost-reduction strategies (Porter, 1985). Typical of this group is the work of Schuler and Jackson (1987), who have attempted to link the competitive strategies of firms with HRM practices. They have done this by conceiving HRS in terms of generating the kinds of desired employee 'role' behaviours required to fulfil given business strategies and then identifying HR policies and practices to achieve and reinforce such behaviours. Where the strategy goal is 'quality enhancement', for example, they argue that high concern for quality by employees can be generated by relatively egalitarian treatment of staff and some guarantees of employment security. Quality enhancement also requires a moderate amount of cooperative, interdependent employee behaviour. The sorts of HRM policies encouraging this are likely to incorporate mixes of individual and group criteria for performance appraisal, which is mainly short-term and results-oriented.

Where 'cost reduction' is a strategy goal, however, desired employee behaviour demands moderate concern for quality of output but high concern for quantity. The HRM policies supporting these behaviours are close monitoring of market pay levels when making payment decisions and minimal levels of training and development. Whilst agreeing that success or failure of firms does not turn entirely on their HRM practices, the authors conclude that 'HRM practices are likely to be critical' (*ibid*: 217).

DEVELOPING AN EMERGENT HUMAN RESOURCE STRATEGY

Because many managers view the above models as somewhat abstract and unreal, as well as being very time-intensive to operate, they are more attracted to developing HRS pragmatically and incrementally. Where they do this, HR managers, in association with senior managers, are more likely to do so by relying on a human resource planning (HRP) approach (see Chapter 4). This enables them to take account of organisational circumstances and the firm's unique human resources, rather than drawing on any of the particular models outlined above. This suggests that they are likely to adopt a more contingent approach, so as to configure or tailor HRS to particular corporate conditions.

Sisson and Storey (2000) argue that the first step in developing a HRS is identifying the strengths and weaknesses of the current strategy, if one exists. Sources of such information are the organisation's managers, employees and customers. Collins (1991) has provided a detailed framework questionnaire for managers when conducting an internal strategic HRM audit, which can be adapted to and used in individual cases. The five main questions raised by Collins, each of which has a number of sub-questions, are:

- Is there a clearly understood HRM strategy?
- Are people seen as a strategic resource by senior management?
- Are there clearly understood strategies for the main elements of HRM?
- Does human resource planning take account of internal and external environmental factors?
- Does the personnel function have a strategic role in HRM?

HRS and HRP

Since employing the right people in the right place at the right time is essential for any organisation, the second step in developing a HRS is applying HRP techniques to the task. This involves calculating the demand for human resources, starting with the organisation's business plan (however short-term and limited it might be) and using a range of forecasting techniques. This is followed by planning human resource supply through auditing the current structure of the workforce. This requires tracking those employed, transferring internally and leaving the organisation. The matching process seeks to link the demand and supply processes together. From this an HR gap analysis can be derived and policy options reviewed. This quantitative data needs supplementing by qualitative data about staff competencies, career preferences and performance ratings obtained from internal documentation where this is available.

Subsequent stages of HR strategic planning are less clear-cut, less easy to articulate and less easy to operationalise. But several observers stress the importance of organisational 'vision' and 'mission' in establishing the values underpinning strategic choices in HR policy and practice (Connock, 1991). These seek to link the direction in which the organisation is heading with its key business objectives, HR objectives, HRS and HR policies. It is sometimes argued that managing culture change is also an essential element in developing a new HRS. Culture change is associated with the attempted reconstructing of employee behavioural patterns built around the interlocking concepts of organisational vision, mission, values, customer-orientation and quality and performance management.

The final element that has to be considered in developing an emergent HRS is integration. This requires horizontal (or internal) integration of the resultant HR policies and practices. There is also the need for vertical (or external) integration to ensure that HR strategies are compatible with business strategy in turn.

SUMMARY LEARNING POINTS

1 There is no single model of strategy, but four perspectives can be identified based on the outcomes of strategy and the processes by which it is made.

2 Although it is difficult to establish measurable links between strategy, business performance and HRS, there is growing evidence that HRS is critical in ensuring organisational success and effectiveness.

3 The resource-based model of HRS focuses on promoting sustained competitive advantage through developing human capital resources rather than just aligning human resources to corporate strategy.

4 Best-practice models of HRS assume that a universal set of HR policies and practices (including the partnership model) are conducive to high organisational performance, irrespective of the competitive strategy of organisations.

5 Best-fit models of HRS focus on the need to align HR policies and practices with the requirements of business strategy and assume that different HR strategies are suited to different business strategies.

6 Developing an emergent HRS is more likely to be a pragmatic activity and can be processed by identifying the strengths and weaknesses of existing strategy, data collecting for HRP purposes, while taking account of corporate vision, culture and horizontal and vertical integration.

REFERENCES AND FURTHER READING

Ansoff, H. (1965) *Corporate Strategy*. Harmondsworth: Penguin.

Barney, J. (1991) 'Firm resources and sustained competitive advantage', *Journal of Management*, 17(1), 99–120.

Beer, M., Spector, B., Lawrence, P., Quinn Mills, D. and Walton, R. (1984) *Managing Human Assets*. New York: Free Press.

Boxall, P. (1996) 'The strategic HRM debate and the resource-based view of the firm', *Human Resource Management Journal*, 6(3), 59–75.

Boxall, P. and Steeneveld, M. (1999) 'Human resource strategy and competitive advantage: a longitudinal study of engineering consultancies', *Journal of Management*, 36(4), 443–63.

Chandler, A. (1962) *Strategy and Structure: Chapters in the history of American industrial enterprise*. Cambridge, MA: MIT Press.

Collins, M. (ed.) (1991) *Human Resource Management Audit*. Birmingham: North Western and West Midlands Regional Health Authority.

Connock, S. (1991) *HR Vision*. London: Institute of Personnel Management.

Cyert, R. and March, J. (1963) *A Behavioral Theory of the Firm*. Englewood Cliffs, NJ: Prentice-Hall.

De Wit, B. and Meyer, R. (1999) *Strategy Synthesis*. London: Thomson.

Department of Trade and Industry (1997) *Partnerships with People*. London: DTI.

European Commission (1997) *Green Paper: Partnership for a New Organisation of Work*. Luxembourg: Office for the Official Publications of the European Communities.

Farnham, D. (1994) *Employment Relations and the Rebirth of History*. University of Portsmouth Inaugural Lectures.

Farnham, D. (1999) *Managing in a Business Context*. London: CIPD.

Fombrun, C., Tichy, N. and Devanna, M. (1984) *Strategic Human Resource Management*. New York: Wiley.

Grant, R. (1991) 'The resource-based theory of competitive advantage: implications for competitive advantage', *California Management Review*, Summer, 114–35.

Guest, D. (1987) 'Human resource management and industrial relations', *Journal of Management Studies*, 24(5).

Guest, D. (1989) 'Personnel management and HRM: can you tell the difference?', *Personnel Management*, January.

Guest, D. (2000) 'Human resource management, employee well-being and organisational performance', paper presented at CIPD Professional Standards Conference, University of Warwick.

Hendry, C. and Pettigrew, A. (1986) 'The practice of human resource management', *Personnel Review*, 15(5), 3–8.

Herzberg, F., Mausner, B. and Snyderman, B. (1957) *The Motivation to Work*. New York: Wiley.

Industrial Partnership Association (1992) *Towards Industrial Partnership*. London: IPA.

Industrial Partnership Association (1997) *Towards Industrial Partnership: New ways of working in British companies*. London: IPA.

Kochan, T. and Barrocci, T. (1985) *Human Resource Management and Industrial Relations*. Boston, MA: Little Brown.

Kochan, T., Katz, H. and McKersie, R. (1986) *The Transformation of American Industrial Relations*. New York: Basic Books.

Markides, C. (2000) *All the Right Moves: A guide to crafting breakthrough strategy*. Boston, MA: Harvard Business School Press.

Maslow, A. (1943) 'A theory of human motivation', *Psychological Review*, May.

McGregor, D. (1960) *The Human Side of Enterprise*. New York: McGraw-Hill.

Mintzberg, H. (1979) *The Structuring of Organizations*. Englewood Cliffs, NJ: Prentice-Hall.

Penrose, E. (1958) *The Theory of the Growth of the Firm*. New York: Wiley.

Pettigrew, A. (1973) *The Politics of Organisational Decision-Making*. London: Tavistock.

Porter, M. (1985) *Competitive Advantage: Creating and sustaining superior performance*. New York: Free Press.

Schuler, R.S. and Jackson, S.E. (1987) 'Linking competitive strategies with human resource management', *The Academy of Management Executive*, 1(3), 207–19.

Sisson, K. and Storey, J. (2000) *The Realities of Human Resource Management*. Buckingham: Open University Press.

Sloan, A. (1963) *My Years with General Motors*. London: Sedgewick and Jackson.

Thomas, C. and Wallis, B. (1998) 'Welsh Water: a case study in partnership', in Sparrow, P. and Marchington, M. (eds) *HRM: The new agenda*. London: FT Pitman Publishing.

Torrington, D., Hall, L. and Taylor, S. (2002) *Human Resource Management*, 5th edition Harlow: Financial Times Prentice Hall.

Trades Union Congress (1999) *Partnerships for Progress*. London: TUC.

Tyson, S. (1995) *Human Resource Strategy*. London: Pitman.

Whittington, R. (2000) *What is Strategy – and does it matter?* London: Thomson Learning.

Williamson, O. (1985) *The Economic Institutions of Capitalism*. New York: Free Press.

Wright, P., McMahan, G. and McWilliams, A. (1994) 'Human resources and sustained competitive advantage: a resource-led perspective', *International Journal of Human Resource Management*, 5(2), 301–26.

ASSIGNMENTS AND DISCUSSION TOPICS

1 What is business strategy? Why has business strategy become so important for organisations in recent years? Why is it so difficult to provide a universal model of business strategy to guide strategists in undertaking a strategic review in their own organisation?

2 Identify and discuss the necessary conditions for determining a business strategy in an organisation (you may relate this to the organisation you work for or one with which you are familiar). What is the case for including HR issues within a business strategy?

3 What are the strengths and weaknesses of (a) the resource-based model of HRS, (b) the Harvard model and (c) the partnership model?

4 Distinguish between the 'business-life cycle' model, the 'strategic and structural configuration' model and the 'matching' model of HRS.

5 Drawing upon the models discussed in this chapter, what sort of HRS (or mix of them) does the organisation you work for have (or an organisation with which you are familiar)? Critically review it, indicating how it might be changed to achieve the organisation's business goals more effectively.

6 Get a copy of either Beer *et al.* (1984) or Fombrun *et al.* (1984) or the Industrial Partnership Association (1997) and write a short critical review of the text which could be useful to students studying HRS.

7 A new chief executive has been appointed to an organisation where people management has traditionally had a low priority and weak influence. She has asked you to provide an outline paper justifying the introduction of a new HRS. Do this, indicating the sort of issues that the HRS might address and how this might be done.

8 Identify, assess and evaluate the competencies and skills needed by an HR strategist.

CHAPTER 4

Human resource planning, patterns of work and flexibility

INTRODUCTION

The effective resourcing of the organisation with workers relies on the identification and definition of human resource requirements. For this to be achieved the organisation needs to know first, where it is now in terms of market position or service provision, second, its objectives in the medium and long term and third, have a clear vision of its future development – in other words it needs a strategic plan. The strategic plan should take account of the workers already in the organisation, or available to the organisation, and the workforce behaviour in terms of length of stay and progression through the organisation. Human resource planning is a strategic opportunity, contributes to strategic decisions and shapes the development of the organisation. There are many ways of 'getting the work done', not only through the direct employment of workers, but also through outsourcing of activities and using contract labour. A variety of patterns of work and various forms of workforce flexibility can be utilised to meet the strategic requirements of the organisation and these are important elements of human resource planning.

CHAPTER OBJECTIVES

- To consider what is meant by human resource planning.
- To discuss the forecasting of human resource supply and demand.
- To identify different labour markets.
- To expose alternative patterns of work and the increase in non-standard contracts.
- To examine different forms of worker flexibility.
- To explore the concept of the flexible firm.

HUMAN RESOURCE PLANNING

Human resource planning (HRP) seeks to ensure that organisational objectives are achieved by developing and implementing a human resource strategy. When considering HRP it is important to be clear what is meant by the term. The numerical, extrapolative approach, usually referred to as workforce planning, is often termed a *'hard'* approach and focuses primarily on the number of staff in the organisation. Numerical indicators, such as staff grades, labour turnover, stability, cohort analysis and a precise definition of the manpower system are used to create a numerical picture of the organisation. This can be developed into a sophisticated mathematical model, but however sophisticated it becomes it remains a mechanistic approach which seeks to identify numerical shortfalls or excesses, or 'gaps', and seeks quantitative corrective action. It is probably best viewed as a sub-set of the broader HRP approach. HRP is more strategic, less focused on numbers and takes account of the people resourcing policies, procedures and practices needed to meet strategic objectives. This is termed the *'soft'* approach. The IPM Statement on Human Resource Planning (1992) stands the test of time and reflects this broad view of HRP:

> Human resource planning is the systematic and continuing process of analysing an organisation's human resource needs under changing conditions and integrating this analysis with the development of personnel policies appropriate to meet those needs. It goes beyond the development of policies on an individual basis by embracing as many aspects of managing people as possible with a key emphasis on planning to meet the skill and development needs of the future.

This definition exposes the holistic, strategic focus of HRP. This is not to deny the value of *'hard'* workforce planning, but to identify that it may be too narrow a perspective in dynamic organisational contexts and environments. HRP is also a logical and convenient starting point for examining people resourcing in practice. It provides the necessary signposts and a rational framework for the broad range of people issues to be considered when seeking to resource the organisation effectively.

THE PROCESS OF HUMAN RESOURCE PLANNING

There is a need for good, accurate and up-to-date information for the quantitative and qualitative analysis of people needs and this is undoubtedly assisted through the use of a computerised HR information system (*see* Chapter 5). Bramham (1994) provides a framework for this analysis (Fig. 4.1). The model has been adapted to give an increased profile to the resourcing dimension and identifies four main components of HRP activity:

1 Investigation and analysis – internal and external.
2 Forecasting to determine an HR imbalance or 'people gap'.
3 Planning, resourcing and retention activities.
4 Utilisation and control through HR techniques, policies and IT.

Investigation and analysis

Investigation and analysis are time consuming, detailed and fundamental activities involving the accumulation of organisational and external information. Data are required

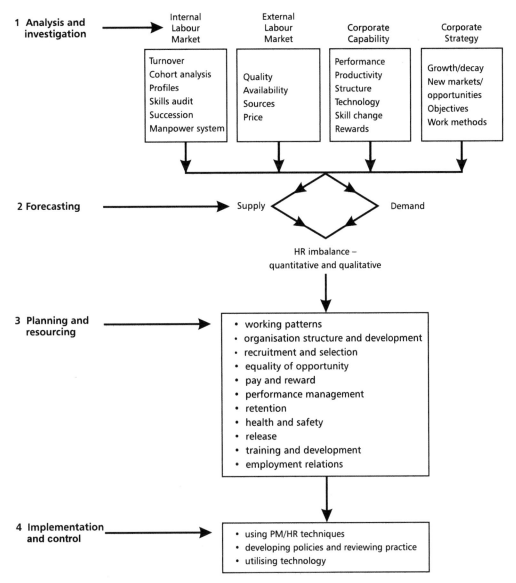

Fig. 4.1 The process of human resource planning

Source: Adapted from *Human Resource Planning* by Bramham (1994), Institute of Personnel Development. Reproduced by permission of the publisher.

from internal and external stocktakes of labour availability, and the organisation needs to be assessed in terms of *what* work needs to be done and *how* it should be done to achieve corporate objectives efficiently and effectively. The analysis focuses on determining the *supply* of labour available from internal and external sources and the *demand* for labour based on assessment of internal organisational needs and external competition or constraints. This knowledge of labour supply and labour demand enables the identification of the quantitative and the qualitative HR imbalance, or *people gap*. Knowledge of the 'people gap' informs people resourcing decisions and shapes the planning and resourcing activities needed for determining contractual arrangements for employment, for recruitment and selection, for managing, motivating, training and rewarding performance and for achieving employee release from the organisation. HR techniques, employment policies and IT are the tools for the implementation and control of the resourcing plans.

The internal labour market

In order to develop a sound understanding of how the internal labour market operates, it is important that the organisation considers not only the quantitative measures, such as labour turnover, workforce profiles and cohort analysis, which will provide indicators of the behaviour of the workforce; but also the more qualitative measures such as skills audits and succession planning.

Labour turnover or wastage – This is a measure of the rate at which employees leave the organisation. It is needed not only as a measure of organisational wastage as a whole, but also, and more significantly, to identify areas of concern. A total wastage figure may be meaningless as it can conceal significant differences in departments or occupational groupings. To be of value in the planning process different measures of labour turnover are needed to enable the HR planner to identify areas in the organisation with high or low turnover. High labour turnover can be costly and result in a poorly skilled workforce because employees may leave once they are trained and consequently more valuable. Investment in training will not pay off if employees do not remain long enough to return the investment. Low labour turnover can also be dysfunctional since it may lead to a static or depressed internal labour market and inhibit the entry of new blood into the organisation. Some departure from the organisation, such as retirement, can be planned, but it is the unplanned and unforeseen departure that is often problematic.

Different measures of labour turnover are available and it is important to be consistent in the measures used. It is also necessary to know what measures other organisations are using if benchmarking comparisons are to be made. Two common measures of wastage are the *transition method* and the *central method*. The transition method is a useful forecasting measure and compares the number of employees in post at the start of a period and the number of that group that leave during the period. It does not take account of other staff who start and leave during the period.

$$\text{Transition Rate (\%)} = \frac{\text{leavers from the group in post at the start}}{\text{total employees in the group at the start}} \times 100$$

The central method includes employees who join in the period and relates the total leavers to the average number of employees in a given period.

$$\text{Central Rate (\%)} = \frac{\text{total leavers from the group}}{\text{average number of employees in the group}} \times 100$$

These two measures give different results and when compared can indicate if employees are leaving within a short time of being recruited. Workforce stability can also be measured through calculating the percentage of employees with certain lengths of service – one, two or five years, for example. This is a reflection of accumulated knowledge, skill and experience.

$$\text{Stability Rate (\%)} = \frac{\text{Number of employees with service of one year}}{\text{Average number of employees in the group}} \times 100$$

In calculating labour turnover or stability it is important to use employee groupings that are meaningful such as occupational group, department or other logical grouping. Group size needs to be sufficient to give a meaningful result as small numbers distort the measure.

Cohort analysis – This describes the observation and recording of the behaviour and movement of a similar group of employees who join the organisation together. Wastage, transfer and promotion measures of this group provide information about the pathway through the organisation of those who stay and when and where the leavers go. Cohort analysis is a useful measure for those organisations which recruit relatively large numbers of the same type of employees at one time, for example new graduates. A thorough understanding of the rate at which individual members of the cohort leave, transfer or are promoted helps the planner to understand the organisation's need for employees of this type to meet future requirements.

Staff profiles – These provide additional indicators such as:

- age distribution – useful in planning retirements, identifying age clusters and generally recognising and anticipating problems associated with imbalances in the age profile
- gender or ethnic distribution – useful in monitoring the effectiveness of equal opportunity initiatives and in identifying gender and ethnic segregation
- skills audits – provide clear indications of shortages or surpluses of key skills within the organisation. The collection and recording of skills is a complex and challenging activity as skills have to be defined clearly in terms of both content and level if the information is to be useful for planning purposes.

The manpower system – This is another element in quantitative workforce planning. In broad terms it involves the detailed identification of the different manpower systems operating in the organisation, the measurement of people stocks at the different levels and the flows through the organisation. It is essential to know the main entry points into the organisation and the main outflow points.

Analysis involves looking at promotion and transfer rates and the wastage from the system. This provides useful information on progression and bottlenecks that lead to employees leaving the organisation and also on the behaviour and movement within the groups. The Institute of Employment Studies has developed sophisticated models to enable the detailed measurement of the manpower system.

The external labour market

The external labour market has to be investigated to assess the availability of labour outside the organisation. The external labour market includes all those working or actively seeking work. Labour markets are dynamic. People usually enter the market from full-time education, or they may return to the labour market after a period of non-participation, for example following a period of caring or travelling. People may leave the market through retirement, illness or injury or a decision to no longer participate in the labour force. Referring to the external labour market implies there is only one external labour market, whilst in reality there are many. The managerial skill is in knowing the specific labour markets which need to be accessed by the organisation. The number and quality of people externally is dependent on the nature, size, sector and geographical location of the organisation. External labour markets are defined by factors such as the nature of the work, the level of pay and the number of hours for the job.

The local labour market – or travel to work area, is influenced by the attractiveness or otherwise of these pay, work and contractual factors, and other external issues such as transport and infrastructure. All of these define the distance an individual is prepared to travel to work and will shape the boundaries of the local labour market.

The international, national or regional labour market – This is delineated by geographical boundaries. The jobs included in an international, national or regional labour market are normally higher paid and more specialised. They usually require national qualifications or significant high-level experience which command higher status and higher rewards. The more specialised the job requirements and the higher the job level the wider the geographical boundaries of the labour market.

Occupational or professional labour markets – These are defined by the qualifications required to practise or participate in a particular occupation.

Gender labour market – There are different views on the desirability of this as a concept, but in practice the individual experiences of both sexes tend to confirm the existence of a gendered labour market. This is becoming less defined, but part-time work is still more closely linked to female participation.

It is important for the organisation to know the labour market for the different jobs, to know how the markets behave and to recognise that these markets are different and have different features over time. Scanning the labour markets for information is done through job advertisement analysis, professional networking and benchmarking, exit interviews with employees who are leaving (*see* Chapter 7) and accessing labour market information generated by government agencies and other specialist providers.

The nature and structure of labour markets

The participation rate – This is a measurement of 'who' is in a particular labour market. The recruiter needs to know which people are in the relevant labour market and how they can be attracted. The DfES, the Careers Service, the Offices of Population, Censuses and Surveys and the Employment Service have information on participation rates for different groups, for example by age, educational attainment, gender and socio-economic grouping.

Flows from education – These measure the profile of those leaving education. It is important for the HR planner to have a clear picture of the skills and qualifications of labour market entrants from all stages of education. Quantitative and qualitative changes in those exiting at different points in the education system will be significant to the organisation and influence decisions relating to recruitment, rewards and investment in training.

Competition in the labour market – This also affects the nature and structure of the labour market. A large number of organisations in a particular location seeking a workforce with similar skills will lead to a seller's market or a shortage labour market where competition for labour is high and the power in the employment relationship may move more towards the employee. This situation will affect some resourcing policies such as family-friendly policies, reward strategies and worker flexibility as organisations look for a competitive edge in the recruitment and retention of labour. A small number of organisational competitors may lead to a surplus or buyer's market where there are many applicants for jobs and the balance of power returns to the employer.

Several other issues influence the nature of labour markets. The level of unemployment affects labour mobility. High unemployment may make individuals more concerned for job security and more fearful of the reduction in statutory employment protection when starting a new job. This influences job change decisions and contributes to a more static labour market. It cannot be assumed that all labour markets will react to high levels of unemployment in the same way as there will still be areas of skill shortage. Whether there exists a shortage (labour demand exceeds supply) or a surplus (labour supply exceeds demand), the labour market has a bearing on the balance of power in employment relationship between the sellers of labour (employees) and the buyers of labour (employers). Demographic changes influence labour markets because age and gender profiles and ethnic composition change over time. Demographic indicators and information on social trends increase the information available to the HR planner.

An analysis of the internal and external labour markets therefore generates considerable information about the supply, availability and cost of labour. The next stage of analysis and investigation is to consider the demand for labour within the organisation.

Corporate capability

Overall corporate performance needs to be disaggregated to highlight areas of strength and weakness. Targets and indicators are needed to identify how well the organisation is performing. Comparative techniques such as benchmarking can be used both internally and externally to compare activities and functions and to assess overall performance. Useful indicators include market share, profitability, financial turnover and other measures such as total output, product or service quality, employee productivity, staff retention and environmental auditing. The type of technology used within the organisation should be assessed. Investment in new technology may affect the demand for labour. It may increase demand by enabling the organisation to produce a higher quality product, to increase the market share and increase output. Alternatively the introduction of new technology may change the skills profile required and create the need for more investment in training the current workforce, or a need to release those without the required skills and replace them with employees with the 'right' skills. New technology can also result in labour substitution and reduce the number of employees needed.

The organisational structure should be examined for appropriateness for future developments. Are any alternative structures available that may increase effectiveness? Scope for delayering the organisational hierarchy, increasing employee empowerment, re-engineering business processes, and centralisation versus decentralisation are indicative of the range of issues that might feature in the organisational assessment which informs the human resource plan. The assessment of corporate capability is primarily concerned with the way that things are done within the organisation. Any change which affects organisational output must be taken into account in HRP as it will impact on the demand for labour. In times of labour shortage, organisations should be looking for ways to reduce their demand for labour by working more effectively.

Corporate strategy

All organisations need a clear vision of their development in the medium to long term. The pace of change in many business sectors is high; nonetheless, even in dynamic times organisations must seek to retain control over their strategic development. A significant change in retailing has been an increase in 24-hour opening in the supermarket sector. Key participants in this sector will have had to decide whether they compete or not and to have made an assessment of the impact of that decision on their market share. The introduction of telephone insurance and the extension of on-line banking are further examples of changes in the strategic direction of these sectors. These decisions have significant HR implications and demonstrate the importance of understanding the links between the corporate strategy and the human resource plans. Although the HR function is unlikely to change the overall corporate strategy, early involvement in the planning process identifies the HR issues and allows for more effective human resource planning.

Forecasting

The forecasting stage of the HRP process involves the comparison between the identified supply of labour and the quantified demand for labour in terms of the skills and competencies needed to achieve the corporate aims. This stage is often an iterative process with a bottom-up forecast, from the line manager, often different from the top-down forecast, from the senior team, and questions of affordability are raised. There is almost inevitably an imbalance at this stage with an HR surplus or a shortfall identified. The mechanism for restoring the HR balance is the development and effective deployment of a range of people-resourcing policies, procedures and practices – the planning and resourcing stage.

Planning and resourcing

The development of a range of people-resourcing policies and procedures enables the human resource plan to be effectively achieved. This means having a clear vision of direction and ensuring that the people-resourcing policies are integrated with the corporate strategy to secure 'best fit'. These HR policies determine how the organisation is to be resourced with people and include not only recruitment and release policies to achieve numerical balance but also a range of policies related to the effective management of people at work. These policies are significant retention tools and include patterns of work and flexibility, reward strategies, performance management, training and development and the effective management of the employment relationship – all of these are addressed in this text.

Implementation and control

The final stage in the HRP model is the approach to implementation and control. This focuses on both the skills and competencies as well as internal HR expertise to ensure that the management of the organisation is both competent and confident in the design and operation of the resourcing policies. Policies need to be appropriately applied and regularly reviewed to ensure compatibility with the corporate strategy coupled with a maximum exploitation of technology to enable the integration of the corporate plan and the human resource plan. If people really are to make a difference and to contribute fully to corporate success, human resource planning is a vital and integrative element of people-resourcing strategy.

PATTERNS OF WORK

In the last 25 years UK labour markets have undergone significant change. In the post-war era employment was not regulated and employers had the power to 'hire or fire' at will. Employment contracts were normally full time and the standard pattern of work was 40 to 48 hours a week from Monday to Friday; in the early part of that period, Saturday working was also included. Some industries worked in shifts, but this was mainly in the continuous production or the personal service industries. The contractual options for 'getting the work done' were relatively few and simple. This is no longer the case and an array of patterns of work are available to employers and, by definition, to employees, 'Patterns of work have always been subject to change but the pace of change is now more rapid than ever' (ACAS, 1999).

First, there is a choice between contracts of employment, where the worker has employed status and associated employment rights, and contracts for services, which enable the organisation to get the work done without having direct employees. Workers with contracts for services contribute to numerical flexibility for the organisation and have limited but increasing employment rights (*see* page 81). Second, there are a significant number of variations to the standard, full-time contract; these are termed non-standard or atypical arrangements. However, as less than 50 per cent of the working population has a traditional full-time, 'permanent' job with an employment contract, perhaps this arrangement should no longer be termed standard (Exhibit 4.1). Cully (1999), reporting on the most recent WERS, identifies changes in patterns of work. The percentage of managers in the survey reporting increases in the use of different forms of labour was for part-time employees 40%, contractors 26%, fixed term contract workers 20% and temporary agency workers 17%. A plethora of atypical contracts and patterns of work have developed primarily in response to concerns for competitiveness and the need to control costs by resourcing people in line with demand. Diverse working arrangements produce diverse employment challenges and the human resource planner needs to be aware of these.

Exhibit 4.1   Changing patterns of work

	1970s	1990s
Full-time tenured employee	55%	36%
Full-time self-employed	6%	8%
Full-time employee, either temporary or without tenure	4%	13%
Part-time	12%	15%
Government schemes	–	1%
Unemployed	5%	8%
Economically inactive	19%	20%

Source: Employment status of the working age population, *Oxford Review of Economic Policy* (rounded figures).

Temporary work

The most extensive atypical contract is the temporary or fixed-term contract. Institute of Employment Studies research (Atkinson, 1996) found that 58 per cent of organisations surveyed employed temporary workers, that temporary working arrangements were much more prevalent in larger organisations and that the majority of organisations showed an increase in the use of temporary workers. A temporary employment contract is for a limited time and the expectation of both the employer and the employee is that the employment will cease. A temporary contract can be terminated by either side giving notice, although statutory employment protection rights accrue to the employee at various points (*see* Chapters 8 and 18). A fixed-term contract is also temporary, but the period of employment is normally defined and the contract expires at a fixed point in time without a need for notice.

Temporary contracts have been common in organisations to cover specific requirements such as maternity leave or long-term sick absence, but the significant increase in use is largely attributable to the need to match staffing to workload demand to achieve numerical and financial flexibility. Temporary working amongst graduates has increased and there is evidence that a substantial number of temporary workers have a university degree. The popular image of temporary work being concentrated in the unskilled and unqualified population is therefore not entirely accurate, but it is concentrated in the 'young' and 'old' working population and amongst women.

There are challenges on both sides of the contract. Employers may perceive temporary workers as less reliable and characterised by high labour turnover. This may not be surprising, as reliability and stability can be correlated with employee commitment and it is more difficult for an employee to commit to an organisation where the organisational commitment is temporary. Workers accept temporary work for a number of reasons. The choice may be between temporary work or no work or it may offer an entry point to the organisation with the potential to become more permanent.

Part-time work

A part-time worker is anyone contracted to work less than the normal full-time hours. Some government bodies regard 30 hours as the qualifying figure. The majority of part-time workers are in the service sectors and in the public sector. The service sector, including retailing, banking, finance, tourism and catering, has been the fastest-growing sector of the UK economy with a consequential increase in part-time workers. The largest group of part-time workers is women and there are increasing numbers of part-time workers from the 'retired population', perhaps a function of the opportunities for early retirement in the 1980s and 1990s. Increasingly evident in the part-time labour market are students and this is partially attributable to the abolition of grants and the introduction of loans in higher education. Students need to work not only to live, but also to constrain debt.

The use of part-time staff has benefits for the employer. It enables the organisation to have workers available for busy periods and to avoid paying staff when the demand for work is slack. This is very evident in the retail sector where an increase in out-of-town shopping, the introduction of Sunday trading and longer opening hours each day has significantly increased the total staffing hours in each week and produced more slack periods overall. The managerial response to fluctuating, but predictable, work demands is to staff the stores with workers on a variety of part-time contracts appropriate to the staffing need. There are some disadvantages to the employer. The use of more part-time staff increases the total number of workers employed, pushing up training, administrative and recruitment costs. Managerial challenges are presented in relation to staffing continuity, holiday arrangements, and communicating with, managing and motivating employees who come to work at different times. In order to raise the perceived status of part-time workers they are sometimes referred to as key-time workers.

Ethically and legally, part-time workers are entitled, on a *pro rata* basis, to the same pay and benefits as full-time workers. The Part-time Workers (Prevention of Less Favourable Treatment) Regulations, 2000, prohibit employers from treating part-time workers, not just employees, less favourably than full-time workers unless such treatment can be objectively justified. The right not to be treated less favourably is based on the *pro rata* principle in comparison to a full-time worker working for the same employer and having the same type of contract. The employer is obliged to provide pro-rated equality for pay and benefits, promotion and training opportunities, pensions and holiday entitlement and equal treatment in relation to discipline, grievance, redeployment and redundancy selection. The employer has only two defences against a claim of less favourable treatment: first, that the unfavourable treatment was not connected to a worker's part-time status, or second, that there is a valid and objective business reason which justifies less favourable treatment. Like the sex discrimination legislation, part-time workers must be able to identify a comparator and this comparator must be a full-time worker (Aikin, 2000). A failure to pay the same rate may also constitute unlawful indirect discrimination as a greater proportion of women work part-time hours.

Variations on the part-time working theme are core hours contracts and term-time contracts. Core hours contracts guarantee a minimum numbers of hours per week, or none in the case of the infamous zero hours contracts, with the implicit right of the employer to flex the hours upwards in order to secure appropriate staffing levels for the business. In this case the employee is something of a 'beck and call' worker and is only likely to be sustained by this type of contract if it meets work/life balance needs as well as financial needs. Ethically the core hours worker should receive appropriate notice and be able to reasonably refuse the offer of extra hours. Term-time contracts are aimed at those workers who have caring responsibilities for school-age children and enable workers to be at home during school holidays. The holiday periods will either be covered by other workers, perhaps extending their hours, or require the recruitment of short-term workers, frequently from the student labour market.

Job sharing

Job sharing is a specific form of part-time work where two people share a full-time job. The tasks, duties and responsibilities of the job are divided in a way that meets the needs of the two individuals and the organisation. The pay and benefits of the full-time job are shared. The division can be:

- split days – one employee works mornings and the other works afternoons
- split weeks – the two employees work one week on and one week off, with a change-over in the middle of the week
- alternate weeks – the two employees work whole weeks, one week on and one week off.

An advantage of a job share is the opportunity for built-in cover for leave which provides continuity of work. It is also a way of retaining trained and committed employees who wish to reduce their working hours. One disadvantage is that training and administration costs are increased through some duplication in these areas and it can be problematic to replace one member of the job share duo if he or she leaves. Effective communication between the job-sharing employees is essential and this can be facilitated through a handover period or the logging of significant events. It is also essential to match the two workers to ensure compatibility and complementary skills.

Annualised hours

Annualised working involves specifying the contractual hours to be worked as an annual rather than a weekly figure and is a method of matching staffing to fluctuating work demands. An advantage of annualised hours is the control of overtime costs because employees work longer hours at peak times and shorter hours when demand is low, without adjustments in pay. Employee pay is unaffected by the fluctuation in hours worked and is stabilised over the year as a whole. Employers need to take the nominal full-time hours per week and compute an annual equivalent which allows for annual leave and bank holidays. A specific challenge of annual hours' contracts is complexity of management and administration, including, for example, absence payment calculations, training days allowance, the implications of unplanned leave and the hours and pay of workers who leave or join part way through the contractual year. Whitehead (1999) reports that annualised hours contracts, previously confined to manufacturing and transport, are becoming more attractive to banks and retailers in order to cover extended opening hours. Examples include the National Westminster Bank and Tesco. The National Westminster Bank scheme rosters 1595 hours per year after holidays have been accommodated. Hall and Torrington (1998) found that one respondent in ten reported some form of annualised hours working.

A change to annualised hours will have to be introduced carefully and sensitively as employees may be suspicious of managerial motives and feel they will lose out. The productivity advantages of annual hours to the organisation may mean that employees can be offered compensatory benefits; for example, an overall reduction in total contractual hours or increased job security due to an increase in competitive advantage for the organisation.

Remote working

Variously referred to as teleworking, home working or 'cottage-working', the essence of remote working is that a worker does not necessarily report to a corporate place of work on a daily basis. Most frequently this involves working at home for some or all of the time. Clearly remote working is only possible for certain types of job and depends on the worker having suitable facilities in terms of space and technology in the home. The primary benefits that employers gain are a reduction in office space costs and the recruitment and retention of workers who are unable or do not wish to take up standard office employment because of either personal preference or personal circumstances. The benefits for the worker are increased flexibility over working times and a reduction in travel times and costs. It can therefore be argued that remote working enhances work/life balance but this can be countered by the potential for physical and psychological intrusion into home life.

Fowler (1996) raises a number of issues for managerial consideration in relation to remote working. First, the remote working decision should be based on the suitability of the job and not just on potential cost savings or the availability of technology. Second, the suitability of the home environment needs to be assessed and audited in terms of space, equipment and health and safety. Third, technology requirements in the form of facsimile, telephone, e-mail, Internet access and computing need to be determined and, if necessary, supplied. Fourth, normal managerial concerns relating to supervision, performance management, rewards, communication and integration mechanisms, the social needs of workers and training will need close scrutiny in relation to the job and the individual – the art of remote management. It is important to recognise that in principle remote workers retain the employment rights associated with their contract regardless of where the work is located, and also that remote working requires high trust relationships between managers and workers. Remote working need not be all or nothing because it can be used in combination with office-based working, on either a specified or an *ad hoc* basis. The Labour Force Survey (Huws, 1999) reports that one worker in 20 was a teleworker, in this case defined as people working from home at least one day per week, and the incidence of remote working is growing.

A flexible approach to employee working patterns

A flexible approach to working patterns may manifest itself in empowering employees to exercise some discretion over when, where and how they work. It can be defined as 'the exercise of employee choice in relation to personal circumstances and work demands but compatible with the achievement of business objectives'. The employer benefits are the potential for improved employee effectiveness and performance and the recruitment and retention of talented workers. This can be an element in being perceived an employer of choice through offering scope for individual talent to prosper and opportunities for work/life balance. Like remote working it requires high trust, output-driven performance management and the overcoming of traditional cultural and managerial barriers.

Which patterns of work?

Each pattern of work has advantages and disadvantages for the employer and the employee. The pattern of work and the associated contractual arrangements are determined by considering factors such as:

- complexity of administration and relative cost
- attractiveness of the work and the contractual arrangements to quality recruits
- surpluses or shortages in the labour market
- the degree of worker commitment required for and associated with the type of work
- organisational concerns for equity and fairness
- acceptability to employee representatives.

Employers seek workforce flexibility through these different working patterns and flexibility comes in a variety of forms.

FLEXIBILITY AT WORK

The changing political, economic, social and global contexts of organisations are stimulating changes in the way in which work is organised. One adaptive response to these influences can be identified in the changing patterns of work. The argument for continuous and broad human resource planning, in contrast to the numerically focused manpower planning described earlier, is also a response to more turbulent organisational contexts. Traditional approaches to work organisation based on hierarchy, formalised structures, job definition, demarcation of activities and bureaucratic control may be less suitable for uncertain and unpredictable environments. Dynamic environments require more organic responses and the pursuit of flexibility at work, in all its forms, can be viewed as another functional adaptation by the organisation to environmental influences.

Stimulants to the development of wider organisational flexibility include:

- the pursuit of competitive advantage through organisational differentiation on people performance, hence the concept of the lean organisation
- a shift from Fordist mass production techniques to flexible specialisation in production processes (Horton, 2000)
- demographic and social changes, such as a changing age profile in UK employment, increasing female participation in the labour market, concern with work/life balance and the thrust towards 24-hour societies
- the deregulation of labour markets and the reassertion of the right to manage by managers to include managing employee flexibility
- the emergence of human resource management as an approach to people management which emphasises the flexible utilisation of human resources and illustrated by Guest's (1987) 'big four' tenets of HRM – strategic integration, commitment, quality and flexibility
- changes in technology, particularly Information Communications Technology (ICT)
- the search for economic efficiency and the satisfaction of shareholder financial demands
- increasing number of service sector jobs and escalating customer aspirations and power.

Employee flexibility has a number of forms, has given birth to a flexible firm concept and is subject to limitations.

Forms of flexibility from the employer perspective

Flexibility at work can be defined as:

The ability of the organisation to adapt the size, composition, responsiveness and cost of the people inputs required to achieve organisational objectives.

Fig. 4.2 Overlapping forms of flexibility

Various forms of flexibility exist and common categories include functional, numerical and financial (Blyton and Morris, 1992; Atkinson, 1984; Bramham, 1994; Sparrow and Marchington, 1998). Categorisation should not suggest that the forms of flexibility are mutually exclusive and many forms of overlapping flexibility exist (Fig. 4.2). Managers need to be able to distinguish between these forms of flexibility in order to be able to seize opportunities for increasing organisational flexibility, but they should also be aware of the problems.

Functional flexibility – This relates to the employer's ability to deploy people in response to work priorities and demands. It can be either horizontal or vertical. Horizontal implies a reduction in demarcation between activities and tasks at the same level as the job-holder. Vertical functional flexibility involves the acceptance and per-formance of tasks and activities by employees at either a lower or a higher job level. Functional flexibility is closely associated with skills flexibility (in order that employees are capable of performing the required tasks), with attitudinal flexibility and the redesign of work processes, equipment and layout. Consideration needs to be given to harmonising terms and conditions of employment as disharmony in these will inhibit functional flexibility. Reward systems need to be compatible with functional flexibil-ity objectives so that task demarcations are not perpetuated or reinforced. Working practices which incorporate elements of functional flexibility include teamworking, empowerment, multiskilling, re-skilling and project working.

Numerical flexibility – This is the scope to expand or contract labour supply through altering the number of people employed in proportion to product or service demand. It relies on the quick and easy engagement and release of people through rapid recruitment responses and the use of fixed, short-term or temporary contracts. Numerical flexibility also involves the increased use of agency staff and the sub-contracting of work. It requires a managerial predisposition for using employee redundancy as a human resource practice.

Temporal flexibility – This is concerned with restructuring working hours to increase organisational responsiveness to work demands. It has the aim of maximising productive time and minimising unproductive time and may be formal or informal. Formal temporal flexibility can be achieved through the use of annualised hours arrangements and through zero or core hours contracts. Flexi-time arrangements constitute temporal flexibility, but in this case they are primarily responsive to employee, rather than employer, needs. Informal temporal flexibility includes employee discretion to adapt working hours to work demands and also the growing expectation that employees should work 'beyond contract' when necessary (the concept of elastic working hours).

Financial flexibility – This increases the ability of the organisation to control employment expenditure. It is pursued in a number of ways. First, through the use of local market rates to determine the commercial worth and the reward package of employees to ensure that no more than necessary is paid. Second, through the use of individual pay arrangements instead of collectively regulated and uniform pay levels; for example, performance-related pay and profit-related pay. Third, through shifting from national or central bargaining to local bargaining arrangements to intensify the linkage between employment costs and local affordability. Fourth, through the use of non-consolidated bonus pay and non-pensionable payments to avoid consolidated payments which relentlessly and permanently increase the pay bill.

Skills flexibility – This incorporates not only skills development and acquisition, but also employee receptiveness to the updating and extension of the skills necessary to reduce job demarcation and promote employee versatility. Skills flexibility may be vertical or horizontal through a deepening or a widening of the employee's skill base. Skills flexibility can be promoted through the use of competencies which emphasise what people actually have to do.

Attitudinal flexibility – This infers a specific focus on the encouragement of flexible employee attitudes characterised by a receptiveness to learning new skills, a willingness to engage in functional flexibility and a responsiveness to changes in working practices or management approaches. Flexible attitudes and behaviour can be recognised, rewarded and reinforced through integrated human resource practices and the management of corporate values.

Learning flexibility – This has links to the concept of the learning organisation, broadly defined as an organisation which continuously transforms itself through the ability of its members to learn. The development of learning flexibility by employees includes a willingness to unlearn familiar and comfortable ways of working. Learning flexibility is associated with contemporary HRD philosophies, quality management and Investor in People standards (*see* Chapters 12 and 21).

Structural flexibility – As an objective, this is a response to concern that organisational hierarchy may reinforce job specialisation and restrictive working practices and consequently inhibit flexible working and organisational responsiveness. Teamworking, matrix organisation, project working, lateral job moves, delayering, empowerment and process re-engineering offer opportunities for increasing flexibility through fluidity of organisation structure.

Distance flexibility – This is achieved through utilising technology. Work may be undertaken in locations remote to the work organisation through teleworking and the exploitation of electronic mail, facsimile transmissions, telephone links and video conferencing – effectively making distance irrelevant.

The flexible firm

Many of the forms of flexibility can be identified within the model of the flexible firm, reproduced in Fig. 4.3. Old though it is, the flexible firm model is still valuable in bringing together different forms and dimensions of flexibility and in allowing a penetration of some of the implications of the flexible workforce. The flexible firm concept broadly divides the workforce into a core group, a first peripheral group and a second peripheral group. Alternative labels, in the context of the labour market, are primary, secondary and tertiary.

The primary group – This group is ascribed core status and tends to comprise full-time, permanent, career employees. It normally includes knowledge workers, managers and other professional and technical staff. This group can be considered critical to organisational success through the possession of the essential skills and knowledge which differentiate the organisation in competitive environments. Primary workers are insulated, or offered some protection, against market fluctuations in demand for their labour. This group of employees will normally be well rewarded and relatively secure and tend to have development and career opportunities in order to secure their long-term commitment to the organisation. In return, core status implies an employee willingness and an ability to engage in multi-forms of flexibility in order to contribute significantly to the achievement of organisational success. Core workers have careers.

The secondary group – These people are ascribed first peripheral status and have a skills and knowledge profile which is general rather than specific to the core business of the organisation. Secondary employees are important, but not critical, to organisational success, as their skills and knowledge will normally be readily available in the external labour market. Examples include administrative, secretarial, sales, production and supervisory staff. This secondary group of employees can be employed on permanent

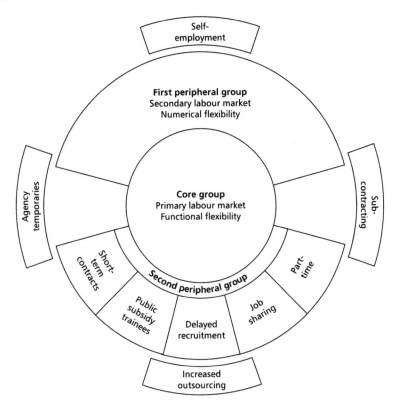

Fig. 4.3 The flexible firm

Source: Atkinson (1984), Institute of Manpower Studies, University of Sussex.

contracts, but with a lower level of job security than core employees, or on longer-term fixed or temporary contractual arrangements. Patterns of work tend to be non-standard, and this group contributes to numerical flexibility through being subject to release and re-engagement as required. They effectively buffer the core against insecurity. Secondary employees tend to have jobs rather than careers.

The tertiary group – These people are ascribed second peripheral or external status and consist of 'beck and call' workers, exemplified by casual, zero hours or core hours contracts of employment. This tertiary group also includes labour provided through contracts for services and the sub-contracting of work to other organisations or to self-employed individuals. Workers supplied through agencies can also be part of this group. Tertiary workers provide dynamic forms of numerical and financial flexibility. Examples of tertiary work include catering, cleaning, maintenance and assembly work. Tertiary employment arrangements are characterised by minimal job security, a relatively restricted reward package and worker disposability. People in this group can be said to have work rather than jobs or careers. In stark contrast it is possible to recognise also in this tertiary group those élite portfolio workers who possess skills for which there is high demand, who provide work on a paid-for-results or a consultancy basis, and where the correspondingly high rewards compensate for any lack of employment security or regularity. Perhaps this élite group are best described as core externals and include specialist providers of information technology support, change process consultants, interim managers and even chief executives.

The flexible firm model is only a model and not a prescription or a blueprint for the structuring of organisations. There is no rigid definition of the types of work which constitute each segment, nor is there guidance on the relative size of the segments in relation to organisational contingency factors. The model is a visual, analytical tool and allows a probing of the different forms of flexibility, an analysis of the varying patterns of work and employment packages, and a consideration of the relative size and managerial implications of the primary, secondary and tertiary elements. Handy (1989) proposes an alternative, but parallel flexible model consisting of a professional core, a flexible labour force and a contractual fringe to form what he terms 'a shamrock organisation'. This trinity of organisational 'leaves' are distinct groups and are managed, organised and rewarded differently based on their differing expectations of and commitment to the employment relationship. In common with Atkinson's model (1984) the shamrock concept is silent on the most appropriate distribution of work between the three groups, but it does provoke further critical evaluation of organisational activity and consideration of how it can most effectively be resourced.

There is a debate about whether the ideas associated with the flexible firm and shamrock organisation represent a strategic human resource response or merely a pragmatic reaction to the intensification of competitive pressures and the managerial opportunities presented by the deregulation of labour markets. The positive flexibility thesis is that it provides shock absorption in turbulent organisational environments, increases the strategic responses available to competitive pressure, and enables the optimum utilisation of people in the pursuit of corporate objectives. The negative flexibility thesis is that it capitalises on or exploits the labour market vulnerability of employees, is a managerial lever to intensify work demands, reintroduces disharmony in terms and conditions between different groups of workers which results in tensions and disintegration into sub-cultures, and inhibits the development of the committed employment relationships and healthy psychological contracts which are essential to organisational success. Legge (1998) expresses the view that 'flexible employment largely benefits the employer at the expense of the employee' by giving primacy to the need of the organisation to survive in competitive environments through the satisfaction of escalating customer demands and the financial demands of shareholders. This exposes a potential contradiction, which is expressed by Geary (1992) as:

> The peripheralisation of a significant element of the labour force would seem to have little in common with one of the main dictums of HRM – to value and develop employees as an organisation's key resource.

A balanced view of flexibility at work, rather than the evangelistic pursuit of 'full blown flexibility', is advocated and this needs to be based on first, an awareness of the different forms of flexibility, and second, an appreciation of the potential for positive and negative consequences of flexibility initiatives. Ultimately the complexity and inherent contradictions in the flexible firm approach require active management and demand a diverse range of human resource and employment relations skills.

SUMMARY LEARNING POINTS

1 Planning for the future requirements of the organisation in terms of workers is not a 'one off' annual activity, it is a systematic, holistic, proactive and continuing process which needs constant review. Human resource planning is a strategic HR opportunity.

2 Hard workforce planning is best considered as a sub-set of holistic human resource planning. HRP contributes to the achievement of strategic organisational objectives through planning the acquisition of an appropriately skilled workforce. Acquiring the right number of workers is only one factor and the ability to resource the organisation qualitatively with people is of equal importance.

3 Knowledge of the diverse nature of labour markets is fundamental to the HRP process and to understanding the labour supply.

4 A strategic corporate plan contributes to a common understanding of organisational direction and informs human resource planning.

5 There has been a significant increase in atypical workers. The full-time, Monday to Friday employee is declining and a variety of contractual arrangements and patterns of work are available to the employer.

6 Changes in the external environments within which work organisations operate are stimulating flexible responses to the structuring of work. Flexibility initiatives can take many forms and these forms overlap.

7 The concepts of the flexible firm and the shamrock organisation provide opportunities to analyse flexible approaches to work organisation, but they do not prescribe the 'one best way'. People flexibility can have positive and negative consequences and requires proactive and skilled management.

REFERENCES AND FURTHER READING

Advisory, Conciliation and Arbitration Service (1999) *Changing Patterns of Work: Advisory booklet* (periodically revised).

Aikin, O. (2000) 'Everyday rights for part-time staff', *People Management*, 25 May, 23–4.

Atkinson, J. (1984) 'Manpower strategies for flexible organisations', *Personnel Management*, August, 28–31.

Atkinson, J. (1996) *Temporary Work and the Labour Market*. London: IES.

Blyton, E. and Morris, J. (1992) 'HRM and the limits on flexibility', in Blyton, P. and Turnbull, P. (eds) *Reassessing HRM*. London: Sage.

Bramham, J. (1994) *Human Resource Planning*. London: IPD.

Cully, M. (1999) *Britain at Work as Depicted by WERS*. London: Routledge.

Fowler, A. (1996) 'How to: benefit from teleworking', *People Management*, March, 34–5.

Geary, J. (1992) 'Employment flexibility and HRM: the case of three American electronics plants', *Work, Employment and Society*, 6(2), 250–70.

Goss, D. (1997) *Principles of Human Resource Management*. London: Routledge.

Guest, D. (1987) 'Human resource management and industrial relations', *Journal of Management Studies*, 24(5), 503–21.

Hall, L. and Torrington, D. (1998) *The Human Resource Function: The dynamics and change and development*. London: FT Pitman Publishing.

Handy, C.B. (1989) *The Age of Unreason*. London: Business Books.

Horton, S. (2000) 'The changing context of employee relations', in Farnham, D. (ed.) *Employee Relations in Context*. London: CIPD.

Hutchinson, S. (1993) *Annual Hours Working in the UK*. London: IPM.

Huws, U. (1999) 'Wired in the country', *People Management*, 25 November, 46–7.

Huws, U., Jagger, N. and O'Regan, S. (1999) 'Teleworking and globalisation', *IES Report 358*.

Incomes Data Services (1993) *Annual Hours*. IDS Study 544.

IPM Statement on Human Resource Planning (1992).

Legge, K. (1998) 'Flexibility: the gift wrapping of employment degradation', in Sparrow, P. and Marchington, M. (eds) *HRM: The new agenda*. London: FT Pitman Publishing.

Oxford Review of Economic Policy (1994–95) *Employment status of working age population*.

Purcell, J. and Hutchinson, S. (1996) 'Lean and mean?', *People Management*, October, 27–33.

Skills and Enterprise Executive – SEN 263 (1996) 'Flexible working set to grow'. DfEE.

Sparrow, P. and Marchington, M. (1998) *HRM: The new agenda*. London: FT Pitman Publishing.

White, M. (1996) 'Flexible response', *People Management*, March, 33.

Whitehead, M. (1999) 'Nat West to put all branch staff on annualised hours', *People Management*, 28 January, 14.

ASSIGNMENTS AND DISCUSSION TOPICS

1 What information would you collect in order to assess the demand for labour within your organisation? What problems might you encounter in collecting this information?

2 Identify the labour markets within which your organisation operates. Select one of these labour markets and discuss its defining characteristics.

3 Outline the process of human resource planning within your organisation – who does HRP, what is involved and what difficulties are there to be overcome?

4 The external environments of organisations are characterised by turbulence, change and volatility. Is there any place for human resource planning when there is so much uncertainty?

5 What patterns of work are used in your organisation, and why? Where and how are the decisions made about the form of contract to be offered?

6 Consider the suitability of a job in your organisation for remote working. What conditions will be necessary for it to be a successful pattern of work for the employer and for the employee? Are there any cultural and managerial barriers to be overcome?

7 Using the overlapping forms of flexibility identified in Fig. 4.2, analyse the extent to which your organisation displays the characteristics associated with each form. Discuss the advantages and limitations of flexibility initiatives in your organisation.

8 To what degree does your organisation correspond to the model of the flexible firm? Using the three categories of primary, secondary and tertiary workers, discuss the characteristics of the workers in each category and comment on the nature of intrinsic and extrinsic rewards that are appropriate for each.

9 What constraints are there on organisational and employee flexibility and is there a limit to the flexibility that can be achieved in practice?

CHAPTER 5

Computerised HR information systems and people resourcing

INTRODUCTION

There has been exponential growth in the quantity and quality of information that is needed by all functions of the business in order to survive in and respond to the dynamics of change that are features of modern organisations. The information explosion is evident in all parts of our lives and instant access to 'what we want to know, when we want to know it' invades many things that we do. People resourcing is no exception. Chapters 1 (the changing organisational context), 2 (The changing world of work) and 4 (human resource planning) highlight some of the challenges facing organisations, and accurate and timely information is an essential requirement if those challenges are to be met. People are the most complex 'resource' to manage and the variety of employee contractual terms, attendance patterns, skills and experience demand increasingly sophisticated HR information systems in order to capture, store and retrieve useful information. Manual systems are severely challenged to meet these demands for accurate and timely information, resulting in a significant expansion in computerised systems.

CHAPTER OBJECTIVES

- To examine the role of information in the management of people and to identify the data requirements.
- To analyse the development, the advantages and the criticisms of computerised HR information systems.
- To highlight system choices.
- To illustrate the benefits of computerised systems in people resourcing.
- To consider the legal framework associated with holding and processing personal data.
- To expose challenges and changes confronting HR information systems.

INFORMATION NEEDS

The pressure on organisations for increased efficiency and effectiveness demands that all organisational resources are used to maximum effect. A mechanistic managerial approach may be appropriate for physical or financial resources, but human resources have a view of what they want from work and bring attitudes, beliefs and aspirations to the workplace. Decisions about people use cannot, or should not, normally be taken without consultation and individual agreement. Data collected and held on computerised HR information systems should include not only factual data about the organisation and the employee together with the managerial view on ability and potential, but also the expectations, ambitions and opinions of the employee. Planning for the effective utilisation of human resources requires employee acknowledgement and agreement if the plan is to be realised. Planning takes place at different organisational levels and these levels of planning and managerial activity have different information needs. Effective planning requires effective management information systems.

An information system should be designed, developed or chosen to meet particular organisational needs – a standard system cannot be prescribed. Provided the right data is collected and stored, modern computerised systems are able to provide the right information at the right time in response to a variety of managerial needs. The structure and culture of the organisation will have an impact on which management information system is the most suitable. Managerial choice needs to be exercised in deciding upon the 'right' information system. The only certainty is that manual information systems are unlikely to fulfil the needs of all but very small organisations.

In the early days of computers their full potential was hardly recognised. Computers were used for no more than streamlining clerical tasks or as electronic filing cabinets and were seen merely as a way of saving on increasing employment costs. Today computers are used in many different and increasingly complex ways, from electronic point of sale and stock control systems in retail organisations to missile guidance systems. Computerised information systems are used to assist in the management of the business through the collection, storage and manipulation of data in a huge variety of ways in order to provide meaningful management information. Accurate and timely information is essential to the effective management of people, and managing in rapidly changing environments demands information that is available at the touch of a button. Managers and planners cannot and will not wait for information to be made available. If the HR information system is slow, inaccurate or limited, the status and influence of a personnel function, and of professional people management practices generally, will be reduced and perceived as having little contribution to make to the future direction of the business. There is therefore a fundamental need for an appropriate computerised solution for the HR information needs of the organisation.

In addition to information needs for managing the organisation there is also an increase in the need for good information and communication systems for all employees. The e-revolution has increased expectations with regard to access to information. Increased accessibility to the Internet and on-line information has, in some instances, led to a change in the way that HR services are provided within organisations (*see* Chapter 2: e-enabled HR).

HR information needs for HR information systems

There is a temptation in the development of computerised HR systems to collect every piece of data about every worker as any and every information need can then be met. However, there are costs associated with the collection, storage and processing of large amounts of data, and information needs must be carefully assessed to maximise cost-effectiveness – the information needs of the business define the data requirements. A thorough analysis of information needs should be undertaken to ensure that all needs are considered and fully understood, and data needs should be identified *in detail* so that an appropriate database is produced or acquired.

Data will be required from the individual employee and about the organisation to provide information for the different levels of managerial decision making. Individual employee data may include:

- personal details
- contractual arrangements
- pay and pensions
- benefits
- education and qualifications
- skills and competencies
- appraisal records and ratings
- job details and employee progression (history)
- attendance records
- disciplinary details
- health records
- termination details, including reasons for leaving.

Organisational data may include:

- organisational structure
- departmental details
- job details
- grade, pay and reward structures and arrangements
- cost centres
- range of contracts and patterns of work.

Support systems should be developed and responsibilities assigned for the collection, input and maintenance of the data and these should be regularly reviewed to ensure that the potentially large task of data capture and data input is effectively managed. Data should ideally be captured and input into the system as close to the point of capture as possible. This will reduce the need for extensive systems for the manual transfer of data and also reduce the potential for error. The feasibility of devolving the capture, input and maintenance responsibility is dependent on the degree of centralisation or decentralisation of the computerised system. In a decentralised system the line manager, as the most likely person to know of a change to the personal or contract details of the employee, can be responsible.

For example, employees who change their marital status or who change from part-time to full-time working will need to have their personnel record updated to reflect this change. If this can be done by the line manager at the point of the change it will simplify the system and will need limited supporting manual systems. If the HR information system is centralised there will be a need for a manual system for notifying a central function, often the personnel department, of the change, and responsibility for updating the record will have to be assigned within the central department. There is the potential for tension between the line manager and the personnel function on the assignment of responsibility for system update. The successful resolution of this tension will ensure that both parties have a clear understanding of the aims and objectives of the HR information system and the benefits to decision making of ensuring an up-to-date management tool. Differences in practice of HR devolution versus centralisation are at the heart of this debate, and the outcome of any discussion will undoubtedly reflect the relationship between line management and HR practitioners and also the positioning of the HR function within the organisation.

Information needs for the provision of HR services

Many organisations have now developed organisational intranets, which allow different departments to provide information to all members of the organisation. This is a useful means of communication for the HR function and provides easy access to HR policies and procedures as well as internal vacancies, the availability of training courses and so on. The information requirements for an HR intranet may include policies and other documents relating to:

- recruitment and selection, with on-line application
- flexible working
- equal opportunities
- holidays and other leave
- maternity, paternity and parental entitlements
- absence reporting and management
- dignity at work
- performance management, staff development and promotion
- health and safety
- employee reward, including payment systems and benefits entitlements
- grievance, disciplinary and capability
- redundancy
- TU recognition agreements
- contractual terms and the staff handbook.

This is not an exhaustive list but merely an indication of the potential of an HR intranet for the delivery of HR information to employees and managers.

MANAGERIAL DECISION MAKING

The collection and storage of data allows information to be produced to meet the needs of the different levels of managerial decision making within the organisation – strategic, functional/tactical and operational (Fig. 5.1).

Strategic level – Information is needed in aggregated form about the whole organisation for medium- and long-term corporate planning. This includes, for example:

- age profiles of employees for human resource planning
- gender, ethnic, disability and other profiling to monitor trends for policy review
- skills and competencies profiling for product or service planning (Exhibit 5.1).

Tactical level – Information provides middle managers with analysis of trends, indications of where the organisation is going and how it is doing. Managerial need is for

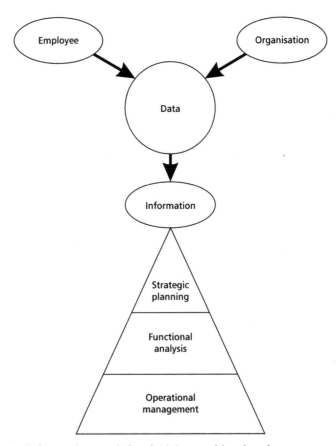

Fig. 5.1   Data to information and the decision making levels

Exhibit 5.1   Strategic decision making

Following the merger of two large financial services organisations, the senior management team need to see the employee profile of the new organisation to match this against the business needs for the skills and competencies that will be required to build a successful company. This may present a challenge in that information may be on two HR systems with different data and different structures. However, it may be the role of the new HR function to provide that information in a useful and easily accessible form.

summary reports, limited to totals and aggregations, and exception reports, which high-light unusual events or deviations from the norm. Examples include:

- employee absence reports by function or unit for trend analysis and comparisons
- analysis of accidents at work for health and safety monitoring or risk assessment
- training activity and costs for the function (Exhibit 5.2).

Exhibit 5.2   Tactical decision making

An organisation is considering applying for Investors in People status and a working party is undertaking an analysis of organisational training and development. It is reviewing policies on staff development and performance appraisal, but information is needed on where, what and when training activity is taking place.

A computerised HR system that captures data on training activities and events can produce comparative data by function, department or other grouping to identify the extent, nature, clustering or cost of training. By 'cutting' and presenting the data in different ways and through generating comparative information a realistic picture will emerge of what is happening in the organisation and this will inform the tactical decision-making process.

Operational level – Information provides detail for the day-to-day management of a department or unit. Examples include:

- diary reports of due appraisals
- skills and competencies analysis for staffing a departmental project
- individual employee attendance record for counselling (Exhibit 5.3).

Exhibit 5.3   Operational decision making

An organisation has introduced a new policy on the management of absence. Line managers are tasked with managing absence and attendance within their department and therefore need to be able to extract a variety of reports to assist in this managerial task. Aggregated reports on numbers of employees absent in a period, numbers and patterns of days absent and lists of individual staff with the number and frequency of days absent will provide the manager with an overview of the situation in the department, identify problem areas and inform plans to manage the employee absence at an operational level.

Although illustrations of information needs have been provided, specific information needs will be diverse and dependent on organisational contingencies. However, a good HR information system will contribute to effective people resourcing decisions on issues such as selection, reward, progression, development, patterns of work and performance, and will be invaluable in the review of personnel and development policies to ensure that human resources are effectively utilised.

DEVELOPMENT OF A COMPUTERISED HR INFORMATION SYSTEM (HRIS)

The involvement of system users is fundamental to the success of any new system. Failure to involve the users in any system development process will mean that ownership of the system will reside with the designers and not the users, thereby reducing the likelihood of successful implementation. Users are the people who will have regular contact with the system and are defined by the structure of the organisation. Users of an HRIS include:

- line managers
- trainers
- payroll staff
- occupational health professionals
- personnel specialists
- IT support staff.

Where responsibility for personnel management activities, and therefore access to the HRIS, has been devolved to line managers it is critical that the managers have a say in systems development. Not only will they have particular information needs, but also useful ideas about the day-to-day operation of the system. Training department staff need information from training needs analysis in order to plan the overall organisational training activity. Payroll staff must have up-to-date and accurate data to ensure that employees are paid the correct amount and at the right time. Increasingly the computerised HR and payroll systems are integrated and share data. An advantage of the payroll system being driven by data from the HR system is the priority which is then given to keeping the system updated – an out-of-date HR system may just provide 'bad' information, but an out-of-date HR system that drives the payroll system will pay employees incorrectly. Occupational health staff need information for monitoring accidents at work, risk assessment and individual sickness absence records. Personnel specialists will have different information needs and may be involved as commissioners of the system as well as users. IT support staff have a role to play in systems development which includes not only a user role, but also a strategic role to ensure that HRIS development is complementary to the corporate plan for information systems. An HRIS which is out of line with other information systems will be difficult to integrate and maintain.

Those who use the system therefore need to have their diverse needs fully taken into account and the HRIS must be developed to use all the expertise available in order to provide the most effective and appropriate solution for the organisation. Existing computerised and manual systems need to be critically reviewed to avoid replicating what is currently done, and future organisational developments and changes should be incorporated into systems development decisions. The implementation of new systems can also be a catalyst for change, with the business analyst and system developer fulfilling the role of a change agent – the persuader who seeks to overcome resistance to organisational change.

THE ADVANTAGES OF AN HRIS

An HRIS has several advantages over labour intensive manual systems.

Speed – Computers can handle a large amount of complex data very quickly. In a rapidly changing business environment the ability to interrogate the database and produce worthwhile information is very important. Information available from a personnel function without an HRIS is constrained in scope and the time required to produce it.

Reliability and accuracy – Humans are fallible and manually produced information has a high potential for error. Computers are often 'blamed' for inaccuracy and unreliability of information, but most computer errors are attributable to human error in inputting data or defining reports. If data is input accurately it tends to stay that way.

Storage and retrieval – Storing large quantities of data is expensive and the manual storage of data consumes physical space and time for filing. Computer data also occupies space in the form of computer memory and consumes time for input and updating, but the costs of physical space and labour to process manual data are increasing whilst the costs of computer memory and processing are reducing.

Consolidation – Manual personnel files are often located in several places with no complete picture of the individual employee available in one record. As many as five manual files may exist for one employee. For example:

- *The personnel department* may have a master file of personal details, the application form, references, contract details and other information passed to the department for holding.
- *The manager* may hold a file with basic personal details, appraisal record, disciplinary records or any other information the manager chooses to keep 'on file'.
- *The training department* may hold employee training records.
- *The payroll department* will have data related to the employee payment, including job contract and salary details.
- *The occupational health department* may hold details of accidents, sickness absence and health monitoring data.

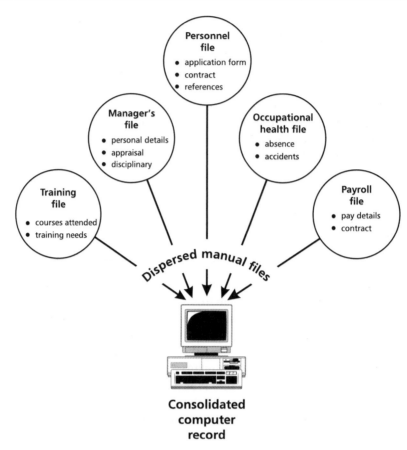

Fig. 5.2   Consolidation of manual files to a single computer record

This segmentation of employee records can be dysfunctional, inhibit decision making and be expensive, as data is inevitably duplicated. Costs of storage and maintenance are high. A single database to which all of these users have access, restricted on the basis of 'need to know', can reduce both storage and maintenance costs. Consolidation and integration of personnel information aids managerial decision making (Fig. 5.2).

Decision making – A principal reason for holding personnel data is to contribute to organisational decision making. Strategic decisions about the direction of the organisation need to be based on the availability and the profile of human resources and an HRIS can provide accurate and timely information. A human resource plan can be developed to reflect corporate strategy and ensure that the skills, experience and availability of employees are taken into account and plans are made for the acquisition of additional resources when necessary.

The role and influence of the personnel function – A good HRIS can promote the inclusion and participation of a personnel specialist in the strategic planning process and raise the profile of the personnel function from an administrative role to one of business partner. Personnel administration is time consuming and this can be managed and streamlined with the appropriate development and use of an HRIS. The cost of systems, particularly with regard to processing power, has reduced considerably in recent years, and systems are available that can liberate the personnel function from a tedious and routine administration role to a more strategic partnership role.

THE CHOICE OF SYSTEMS

There are two basic choices of hardware.

1 Mainframe computer.
2 PC based – networked or stand alone.

In the early days most HRISs were mainframe with a reputation for having out-of-date information and being difficult to access by the user (usually the personnel specialist). Information required by managers needed to be specified in advance and often several days were required to make it available. The operator of a mainframe system is normally a technical expert and the system may even be geographically remote from the user. The Richards-Carpenter (1996) analysis of the CIPD/IES survey revealed that mainframes accounted for only 10 per cent of HRISs, with mainframe systems most commonly found in large organisations, particularly large multi-site organisations which invested heavily in systems in the 1970s, and likely to have several complex business or resource management systems. The predominant HRIS is now PC-based (85 per cent) and has advantages which include:

- on-line update
- ease of reporting
- user accessibility
- familiarity – 'looking like' other Windows-based business packages.

HR software packages are complex, making them relatively expensive to purchase. There are two basic choices of software.

1 In-house developed.
2 Off-the-shelf purchased package.

In-house developed software occurs at the extreme ends of the organisational spectrum. It is a common feature of mainframe systems, because large organisations have the technical expertise and the financial resources to develop sophisticated applications in-house; these also tend to be complex organisations with very specific requirements. In-house developed software has relatively high development costs, takes considerable time to develop and will only be undertaken when there is no commercially available alternative which is feasible. At the other extreme, an in-house package can be developed by a small organisation with few employees using generic database software. The rationale for in-house development in this situation is that off-the-shelf packages are too expensive and offer features small organisations do not need. A skilled personnel practitioner with minimal technical knowledge may have the expertise to develop a simple database that meets the organisational information needs.

Off-the-shelf packages are most commonly used as a PC application and can offer good value for money. The choice of system will be driven by the business analysis and the identified information needs. Up to 95 per cent of many organisational information needs are likely to be met by a commercial package and many commercial packages can be customised to match the purchaser's requirements more closely. The increased availability of personal computers and the more widespread use of management information systems and business packages in all managerial functions mean that many managers have access to a wide range of business applications on their desks and the personnel information system should not be an exception. Increasingly sophisticated HRIS and off-the-shelf packages mean that many systems in use are relatively new. Robinson *et al.* (1999) point out in a survey by the CIPD and the Institute of Employment Studies that 30 per cent of HR information systems are less than two years old.

A key factor in determining the nature of the HRIS is the organisational culture and structure. Hardware and software are important but so too is the extent of centralisation or decentralisation of HR activities. Managers with devolved responsibility for people management will expect to have accurate personnel information available when it is needed. Devolution of HR activity does not appear to have been accompanied by decentralisation of the HRIS.

An HR information system arguably belongs to line managers: it is a general management information system, not just a system for the personnel function. There is evidence of organisational reluctance to devolve the HRIS to the line manager, but tight central control of the system is illogical and increases the administrative burden for the personnel function (although information can be power). It comes back to the question of ownership; managers who are responsible for the employees, collect and input the employee data and produce the employee information are more likely to take ownership of the system and make it work. Concerns about devolving HR information systems can relate to security and confidentiality, but these need not be an issue because sophisticated technology can provide a secure data environment. Another concern may relate to the manager's skill in using the system and keeping it updated and reliable; the remedy is available in training managers to make full use of the system and trusting them to keep it accurate. There is therefore an element of organisational maturity associated with how an HRIS is viewed and used. The advantages of this transfer of HRIS ownership to line managers are as follows.

- Cost savings through devolved updating.

- The technology can act as a catalyst for change.

- It frees the personnel function from an administration burden.

- The interaction of the managers with the system increases the managers' knowledge of the people management issues and allows the data to be communicated with those who make the decisions; for example, managers cannot fail to notice an increase in labour turnover and the reasons for it if they are inputting the data into the system themselves.

A devolved HRIS changes the specialist personnel role from choosing and administering computerised systems to contributing to a more sophisticated system design. This includes:

- being proactive in the development and production of more sophisticated information
- recognising that security of data will become increasingly important as the use of the Internet increases
- anticipating information needs and ensuring that the needs are met.

For most organisations an HRIS is not an option, but an essential requirement. The development of fully integrated business systems will continue to be a primary aim. Integrated systems using a common database to provide a range of resource management information are the systems of the future.

CRITICISMS OF THE USE OF HRIS

Kinnie and Arthurs (1996) found that IT potential in HR activity was still largely untapped. Although the incidence of HRIS ownership is extensive, the way in which it is being used remains disappointingly basic. HRIS usage can be considered at three levels of maturity.

Transaction applications – normally operational reports such as absence management and payroll.

Expert systems – the search for 'good decisions' based on previously identified rules for decision making.

Decision support systems – which look to improve decisions, but the rules are not well defined and alternative models are developed and evaluated.

Most personnel functions use systems which remain in the transaction application level, being largely administrative and focused on labour saving. Few organisations would appear to have developed expert systems or decision support systems and this is where the enhancements to the business and the personnel function can be achieved; organisations which are moving in this direction typically have a high profile personnel function normally with board representation.

This lack of interest in and recognition of the contribution that sophisticated computerised systems can make to the organisation is usefully exposed by Kinnie and Arthurs (1996) who argue that the structure of the personnel department, the knowledge, skills and attitudes of the personnel staff and the power and politics are the most important influences on the use of IT. The positive influences on the exploitation of IT are:

- the interest and involvement of personnel specialists who use their influence to specify and manage the developments of the system

- the existence of extensive knowledge and skills, effective training and the sophisticated use of expert systems and decision support systems elsewhere in the organisation
- an acknowledgement that IT will extend the opportunity to influence decisions in the organisation.

There are influences that act negatively on the exploitation of IT:

- no personnel specialists at head office or plant level and an emphasis on improvement of existing procedures
- low expectations and a lack of creativity and innovation
- concern over devolved access to employee data to line managers which is seen to threaten the personnel function.

The Kinnie and Arthurs research (1996) concludes that personnel specialists may be balancing the role between 'soft' and 'hard' HRM (*see* Chapter 1) and be striving to retain their influence by combining their inter-personal skills, personal judgement and specialised knowledge with a limited use of IT systems to support the role.

Robinson *et al.* (1999) show that while the extent of use of HRIS has not changed significantly in recent years there has been an increase in smaller organisations (fewer than 300 employees) using an HRIS from 24 per cent in 1998 to 27 per cent in 1999. Over half of the organisations (55 per cent) using an HRIS had fewer than 700 employees. The main uses of the system remain consistent with the Kinnie and Arthurs (1996) findings, with employee records identified by 95 per cent of users – clearly a *transactional application* – and less than 20 per cent using their system for more complex reporting such as succession planning and salary modelling. Robinson identifies a widespread dissatisfaction with reporting and also some dissatisfaction with such uses as psychometric profiling and ability/aptitude testing. He also observes that 'it is very unlikely that personnel (information) systems will be seen as business or management tools until they receive high ratings in these crucially important areas'.

THE BENEFITS OF AN HRIS IN PEOPLE RESOURCING

The benefits of an HRIS are derived from the effective application of HR information to the resourcing challenges facing the organisation. These challenges change over time and vary between organisations. The important requirement is to identify the relevant issues and be mindful of the fact that accurate HR information assists the decision-making process allowing options to be investigated, compared and costed. The following examination of specific people resourcing functions is illustrative and indicative of the benefits that can accrue from effective computerised HR information systems.

Human resource planning

Planning for the effective resourcing of the organisation with people requires information from inside the organisation, about the strategic direction and corporate goals and about the human resources available to achieve these goals, and from outside the organisation about the available resources in the external labour market. An HRIS can be used to provide information to assist in the planning and decision-making process. The information includes:

A skills audit of the workforce – This requires data on identified key skills, specialist skills and skill levels (appropriately coded for ease of reporting) and data on the current employee skills in order to provide reports which identify the skills gap and shape plans to close the gap, either through employee development or through recruiting the skills externally.

Labour turnover – Data on employee headcount and leavers will provide a figure for labour turnover and identify trends and areas of the organisation where it is difficult to retain staff; this can be analysed to identify causes of turnover and appropriate responses developed.

Workforce profiling – Profiling can identify, for example, potential problems with age clusters which may mean a large number of skilled staff leaving in a short time or alternatively reduced opportunities for challenge or promotion. Internal information can be combined with external information such as the number of school or university leavers, major competitors in the area and the local and national employment levels to enable options to be identified and included in the planning process.

Recruitment and selection

The implementation of a specialist recruitment package allows the recruitment and selection process to be streamlined and managed more effectively. An organisation which undertakes a substantial amount of recruitment or receives many speculative applications may gain significant benefits from computerising the process. Recruitment and selection administration is labour intensive and costs may be reduced and a higher quality service provided by a good computerised system. Information to be generated and processed includes:

- vacancy details
- recruitment sources
- advertising costs
- dates – including date of advertising, closing date, date of interview, start date of selected employee
- personal details for monitoring – age, sex, ethnic origin and disability
- tracking of candidates through 'the recruitment and selection system' (*see* Chapter 6)
- key skills database
- candidate travel costs
- relocation costs.

Reports can be produced to monitor recruitment and selection activity:

- numbers of applications from each recruitment source
- equal opportunity reporting to provide a profile of applicants by age, sex, ethnic origin and disability
- total cost of recruitment.

The recruitment process is streamlined through the production of standard letters to applicants and candidates with copies to the interviewing manager. This not only speeds up the process but can also be good public relations in projecting an efficient organisational image. The availability of information allows recruitment and selection activity to be targeted and increases cost-effectiveness. Electronic CVs can be scanned and matched against predetermined criteria to reduce the time spent on short-listing candidates.

Equal opportunities

The regular review of an Equal Opportunities Policy is needed to monitor policy effectiveness. The HRIS can provide information to identify trends and to highlight areas for more detailed investigation. Information to be generated and processed includes:

- age, sex, ethnic origin and disability profile of the organisation
- training undertaken – to monitor access to training for part-time staff or identify the need for positive action for under-represented staff
- promotion information – to observe trends and assess transparency of decisions
- appraisal ratings – to monitor distributions and ensure fairness.

The information can be combined in different ways and used to review the operation of the policy. Barriers to entry and progression in the organisation can be identified and appropriate adjustments made to the policy or training given to staff. The advantage of having good information is that action can be targeted on identified problems with some confidence because action is not based solely on assumptions being made about problems. Policies are more likely to be reviewed and action taken when good quality information is used to inform policy making.

Pay and reward

Reward systems are becoming increasingly complex and constant review is necessary to ensure that reward objectives are being achieved. Information from market surveys needs to be analysed and stored. HRIS reports can be used for reward comparisons, to monitor the operation of the reward policy and to assess value for money. The impact of pay increases can be projected to determine affordability. Equal pay can be scrutinised by looking for clusters of male and female jobs to ensure that any difference in pay is defendable in terms of the demands of the job. Internal pay comparisons can be undertaken to identify and investigate any potential problem areas and adjustments made. It is also easy for individual pay increases to be accessed to ensure fair treatment in pay decisions.

Reward reporting may include:

- salary profile of employees
- percentage increase profile to examine distribution of pay increases
- salary profile by sex for equal pay comparison
- impact of different percentage increases on the total pay bill.

Computerised job evaluation packages incorporating competence based or points rating schemes can accelerate the process of job evaluation and dispense with the need for individual calculation of job scores. The preparation of information to inform pay negotiations can identify a range of options and a variety of combinations of pay, hours and benefits to form the basis of the negotiating position.

Performance management

Benefits derive from monitoring the performance management system. The HRIS can store individual objectives and measures of performance following performance appraisal. Under- and over-achievers can be identified and development opportunities, such as mentors or challenging projects, assigned to support personal development. Performance management information to be processed consists of:

- individual objectives
- team objectives
- competencies required
- performance indicators
- departmental targets
- development needs
- individual potential
- individual ambitions – identified by the employee
- succession planning.

Information can be produced which identifies individual, team and departmental performance trends. Objectives can be analysed for fairness and assessed to see if they are achievable, with agreed adjustments made where necessary. Individual ambitions and organisational opinions of potential can be evaluated and expectations of both parties managed. Expert systems can be used to combine data for promotion (performance, salary and development) and identify those employees 'ready' for promotion.

Training and development

The development of employees is costly and needs to be focused and managed effectively. Training and development needs should be identified and can be input and stored within the HRIS, and these can then be assessed against strategic objectives. Training and development can then be provided to meet individual and organisational needs. Centralised access and aggregation of the data will identify collective development needs. Training information for processing includes:

- individual training needs
- team training requirements
- actual training undertaken
- training costs
- allocation of training
- forward planning in terms of competencies
- information for comparison with the strategic plan.

The data combinations are extensive and innovation is needed to recognise the potential for the information on employee training and development, and to combine it in creative ways.

Health and safety

An HRIS can contribute to the effective management of health and safety in the storage and analysis of data on individual employee health and on accidents at work, and also through recording the findings and outcomes of risk assessment. Analysis of employee health and absence records can identify health issues before they develop into major attendance problems and effective risk assessment can prevent injuries and ill health. Information to be processed includes:

- volume, pattern and distribution of employee sick absence
- reasons for absence
- actions taken to manage attendance
- accidents and injuries
- hazardous occurrences at work.

Recurring health and safety problems can be identified through HRIS reports, or clusters of sick absence may emerge from the analysis. Investigations can then focus on causes rather than just on symptoms.

Employment relations and conflict management

An HRIS also offers benefits in the management of the employment relationship. The analysis of aggregated data on disciplinary occurrences may identify common problems that point to poor communication, particularly relating to the communication of organisational rules. Through providing clearer statements on regulations and managerial expectations, the induction of new employees and the training of existing employees can be improved and should result in a reduction in disciplinary offences and action. Similarly, the analysis of formal employee grievance expressions and the identification of common problems that give rise to employee dissatisfactions can be identified through the HRIS and should result in clearer policy statements and reduce the potential for conflict in the employment relationship.

Redundancy

A redundancy situation is potentially emotional and traumatic for employees and for managers. The increased objectivity and transparency which computer listings give to redundancy selection can ease the situation. Alternative redundancy options can be modelled, investigated and costed by an HRIS in pursuit of the most appropriate solution. Information to be processed includes:

- age and length of service
- redundancy payments
- pension entitlement
- skills profile
- performance rating
- absence record.

Alternative selection criteria can be defined and costed prior to consultation with employees so that the impact on the organisation can be projected. Early retirement, 'last in first out', or a matrix of performance and skills indicators can be considered, weightings produced and calculations performed to produce a rank order of redundancy action; this may appear impersonal and uncaring, but the depersonalisation of the redundancy activity may be a strength.

The potential benefits of computerised HR information systems are extensive; they cover all areas of people resourcing and, in order to be realised, require commitment, innovation, knowledge, expertise and IT skills. Many of the benefits are what Kinnie and Arthurs (1996) refer to as 'transaction applications', but the potential is there for significantly more creativity in the exploitation of IT to the benefit of the individual, the organisation and the personnel function.

The HRIS and e-enabled HR

Chapter 2 incorporates discussion about e-enabled HR and it is useful within this HRIS chapter to examine some contemporary developments.

e-HR – The delivery of some HR services on-line has led to the development of what may be termed e-HR. Some organisations are seeking to exploit the benefits of technology by providing access to HR advice and information through what is, in effect, an HR service centre. Trapp (2001) describes how the exploitation of Web technology can 'liberate the HR function from its administrative chores and allow it to focus on more strategic matters'. A move to providing HR services in this way can bring considerable benefits through economies of scale, but not without considerable investment. For example, IBM have introduced 'Ask HR', which is an HR advisory and information service for Europe, the Middle East and Africa, from their UK headquarters in Hampshire. The benefits of this service is that all managers (and employees) throughout this extensive region have access to the same information from the same source, which they hope will lead to more harmonisation of the working processes and more effective use of HR expertise. It also can act as an agent of change in facilitating cross-cultural awareness and international worker exchange. This is an interesting development of the HR role and a different and imaginative way to provide access to HR services. It is not without some risk for, as Trapp observes, quoting Kettley from the IES, 'Perhaps the biggest problem for HR professionals, though, is the danger that e-HR will as Kettley puts it: start dehumanising people management at a time when technology is supposed to be freeing practitioners up.' The use of Web technology allows the development of different HR roles, from the generalist who provides the on-line advice and support to the HR specialist who develops policies, procedures and the on-line solutions. This is, however, one aspect of the HR service provision; there is still a role for the business partner, for the HR expert who works alongside the business manager to get to know the business needs and who provides sound HR strategies and solutions to enable the business to flourish.

e-recruitment – There is exponential growth in on-line recruitment, that is, the use of the Internet as a source of recruitment (see also Chapter 6). Web technology allows easy posting of vacancies either through specialist recruitment agency Web pages or through organisation Web pages – it is now common to see a 'current vacancies' button on many company Web pages. The main advantage of e-recruitment is speed of access to potential recruits. Recruitment agencies, in particular, who need a rapid turn-round of applicants for placement, find this a quick and relatively cheap way to do business. However, it is not suitable for everyone and it is important to be mindful of the characteristics of the labour market you are seeking to access and also equal opportunity issues, in particular the issues of access and the potential for exclusion.

e-learning – Employers and employees are looking for flexibility in access to learning, and changes in technology allow learning opportunities to be provided on-line. Learning can be available anywhere and at any time to meet the needs of the organisation and the employee. Interactivity enables learning design to incorporate not only knowledge provision but also learner testing.

In conclusion, computerised HR information systems are no longer limited to simple databases but are expanding to include expert systems, decision support systems, intranets and Web technology. All of this requires the HR professional to be skilled in the exploitation of the technology, creative and innovative in the development of the technology and prepared to use the technology to enhance their role within the business.

SECURITY OF PERSONAL DATA

Two significant and interrelated issues are associated with the security of personal data, whether it is kept manually or processed electronically by an HRIS: first, assuring confidentiality in possession and use of data; and second, determining who should have access to data. This concern for confidentiality is often heightened when the records are kept electronically, but the safe keeping of manual employee files is a legal requirement and should also be of intense concern to all managers and personnel practitioners. There are significant organisational variations in how and where manual files are kept, with some organisations permitting employee files to be left on desks unattended even overnight – how secure is that data? Other organisations have a 'clear desk' policy which requires that all files are returned to safe keeping when the desk is unattended, potentially making the data more secure.

All personally identifiable information is required by law to be secure. Commercial software normally has sophisticated security systems which allow individual user profiling to ensure that access is on a 'need to know' basis. The system developer should be looking for a system that features:

- a password

- user control defined for every user

- individual profiling to the level of the field – meaning that fields such as those relating to pay would appear blank on the screen, and whilst extensive access to the system to the data-inputter for purposes of updating remains possible, sight of sensitive data is denied

- log-on to the system to be tracked through an audit trail to record every change to the data for every user, enabling an auditable record to be kept.

The management of decentralised systems which have many users is complex, and responsibility for this task has to be clearly defined and assigned to ensure confidence in the security of the system. Disclosure of passwords and leaving an HRIS 'logged-on' while away from the workstation may need to be a disciplinary offence, as these actions impact adversely on the security of the data.

DATA PROTECTION – RIGHTS, ACCESS AND SECURITY

A raft of recent legislation provides protection for individuals and ensures that information given in confidence remains confidential and cannot be disclosed without consent unless it is in the public interest. The legislation includes:

- Human Rights Act, 1998

- Public Interest Disclosure Act, 1998

- Data Protection Act, 1998

- Freedom of Information Act, 2000.

Human Rights Act, 1998

The Human Rights Act brought into UK law, from October 2000, the European Convention on Human Rights. Among other things the convention states that everyone has the right to respect for private and family life and correspondence. Aspects of this are important both to the actions of employers and for the protection of employees, particularly with regard to confidentiality and the holding of information. Many organisations use e-mail systems as mainstream communication systems and the Human Rights Act requires organisations to respect the privacy of employees with regard to interception of e-mail and of telephone conversations.

Public Interest Disclosure Act, 1998

The Public Interest Disclosure Act is designed to give greater protection to whistle-blowers and protects employees against being treated unfairly because of the disclosure of information which is in the public interest. The Act applies only to protected disclosures, which include health and safety issues, employers' legal obligations, environmental damage and criminal offences. The Act requires that in order to obtain protection the employee must first disclose the information to the employer. If the employee fears either that the employer will not take appropriate action in the light of the disclosure or that they will be victimised by the employer, then the employees may go public with the information. Employers should make sure that they have in place processes and routes for disclosure that protect employees and provide mechanisms for action and for feedback to the employee.

Data Protection Act, 1998

The Data Protection Act (DPA) regulates all individually identifiable data relating to a living person and contained in a readily accessible filing system. This includes employment files and any individual 'informal' files kept by line managers. The DPA covers not just electronically held data but also manually held data. There are eight enforceable principles for the obtaining, holding and disclosing of personal data. These principles state that the data must be:

- lawfully and fairly processed
- processed for specified purposes
- adequate, relevant and not excessive
- accurate and kept up to date
- not be kept for longer than is necessary
- processed within the rights of the data subject
- held securely
- not transferred outside the EU to countries without adequate protection.

The DPA established the Data Protection Commissioner, now the Information Commissioner, and all organisations holding data are required to notify the Information Commission. The Information Commissioner reports directly to Parliament and is responsible for the dissemination of information, promotion of good practice and ensuring compliance with both the Data Protection Act and the Freedom of Information Act.

The DPA requires the identification of the designated data controller with responsibility for ensuring compliance. In the event of a breach of the legislation the data controller will be personally responsible unless he or she can demonstrate that reasonable steps have been taken to ensure compliance. Reasonable steps might include:

- an audit of systems
- a data policy and relevant procedures
- appropriate training
- well-documented communication
- clear links with disciplinary and grievance procedures.

The data subject, that is the identifiable person about whom data is held, has the right to know:

- what data is held
- where data is being processed
- the purpose of holding the data
- who might receive the data
- that decisions relating to that individual will not be taken solely on processed data.

Any request for information must be in writing and must give sufficient information to the employer to enable the identification and provision of the information. The information requested must be supplied within 42 days and the employer may charge a fee of £10.

The DPA identifies sensitive data, which can only be held with the explicit consent of the individual. Employers may seek this consent from new employees within the contract of employment and existing employees may be asked to give their explicit consent. Sensitive data includes:

- racial origin
- religious beliefs
- Trade Union membership
- sexual life
- physical or mental health.

An area of concern to employers is the provision of confidential information by a third party. The most common information of this type in the employment relationship is a reference, which may be requested and provided prior to employment. The key factor is whether the employee has the right of access to this information, which is held in the employment record. The most important factor in this instance is the status of the reference and thus hinges on whether the reference was requested and provided **in confidence**. The referee can withhold disclosure by supplying the reference to the employer in confidence. The employer must ensure compliance and therefore ensure that there are procedures in place that protect the confidential status of the reference. Alternatively, the employer should state that the individual may have access to the reference and as a consequence the referee supplies the reference in the full knowledge that it may be seen by the individual. Whatever approach is taken by the employer, appropriate systems must be in place to protect the supplier of the reference and the rights of access of the individual.

The DPA was effective from October 2001 when all computerised records, and manual information held after 24 October 2001, can be accessed by employees. However, information held manually before 24 October 2001 can be accessed by employees but claims in relation to breaches of the legislation cannot be brought until October 2007.

Freedom of Information Act, 2000

The Freedom of Information Act gives a general right of access to all types of recorded information held by public authorities and must be brought into force by November 2005 at the latest. The timescale for implementation is still under discussion and is likely to start with central government. This extends the right of access to information under the DPA from individual data to all types of information held by public bodies, including information supplied by third parties, although public authorities will have to be mindful of the DPA before disclosing individual data. The Freedom of Information Act will be enforced by the Information Commissioner under a newly defined responsibility which includes both the Freedom of Information Act and the DPA.

Data protection policies and procedures

The far-reaching data protection legislation raises a number of issues for the organisation. In order to ensure compliance with this extensive raft of legislation employers should devise and implement new policies and procedures, which both communicate to employees and guide employers' actions. Areas for consideration include:

- The appointment of an information controller
- A full audit of information systems which identifies who holds what information and why
- A full check of data security
- Ensuring compliance of data collection and data transmission outside the EU
- A review of policies and procedures regarding the requesting and filing of references
- A policy statement on the use of telephones and e-mail
- A policy statement and procedure on reporting under the Public Disclosure Act
- A statement on staff access to information procedures.

It is essential to ensure that managers understand the extent of the legislation, the rights of employees and the need to have a controlled and disciplined approach to the recording and use of information about employees. Organisations need to decide where information is held. If all information is to be held centrally, it may be easier to control if it is held in computer records rather than on extensive, dispersed manual files where security may be a high risk, from the point of view of both data collection and security of access to the data.

SUMMARY LEARNING POINTS

1 Accurate and timely information informs strategic planning and encourages the effective deployment of staff. The information explosion increases managerial expectations about the availability of information, and the personnel function can enhance its status and influence through utilising the potential of a computerised HR information system (HRIS) to contribute to the strategic planning process.

2 Different combinations of data provide information for all levels of decision making:

- strategic decision making and planning
- tactical decision making and monitoring
- operational decision making and control.

3 An effective HRIS will increase the speed of analysis, improve reliability and accuracy, simplify storage and retrieval, consolidate data and enhance decision making.

4 Organisational structure and culture together with the degree of centralisation or devolution of personnel and development activities will influence the type of HRIS implemented and the extent of user access. Line manager HRIS access can facilitate organisational change and promote line manager ownership of the system.

5 The personnel profession has been slow to exploit technology and the major use of an HRIS is for operational management, with limited strategic application. The effectiveness and scope of systems is determined by the interest and knowledge of personnel specialists, whether the personnel function has board level representation and managerial recognition of the potential for influence that good information provides.

6 Effective HR information systems have a role in all areas of people resourcing, and personnel practitioners are encouraged to be innovative in exposing managers to the more sophisticated analysis that enhances decision making.

7 The security of all individual data is regulated by the Data Protection Act 1998, which requires organisations to appoint an information controller, notify the Information Commission and comply with the eight enforceable principles.

8 There is a raft of legislation protecting the rights of individuals with respect to privacy and access to information, and employers must develop appropriate policies and procedures to inform employees and guide employers' actions.

REFERENCES AND FURTHER READING

ACAS (2000) *Personnel Records*.

Aiken, O. (1996) 'Be prepared for a data remember', *People Management*, May, 2(11), 38–40.

Angel, J. and Evans, A. (1987) 'Data protection and the subject of access', *Personnel Management*, October.

IPD (1995) *IPD Guide on Employee Data*. London: IPD.

IPD Key Facts (2000) *Employee Data*. London: IPD.

Kinnie, N. and Arthurs, A. (1993) 'Will personnel people ever learn to love the computer?', *Personnel Management*, June.

Kinnie, N. and Arthurs, A. (1996) 'Personnel specialists' advanced use of information technology', *Personnel Review*, 25.

Legge, K. (1989) 'Information technology: personnel management's lost opportunity?', *Personnel Review*, 18(5), 1–61.

Richards-Carpenter, C. (1996) 'Making a difference by doing IT better', *People Management*, June, 2(12), 39–40.

Richards-Carpenter, C. (1997) 'Systems overload', *People Management*, June, 3(13), 42–4.

Robinson, D., Hayday, S. and Edward, A. (1999) *Computers in Personnel 1999 Annual Survey Results*, Institute of Employment Studies.

Torrington, D. and Hall, L. (1989) 'How personnel managers come to terms with the computer', *Personnel Review*, 18(6), 26–31.

Trapp, R. (2001) 'Of mice and men', *People Management*, 28 June, 24–32.

ASSIGNMENTS AND DISCUSSION TOPICS

1 What type of computerised HR information systems are used in your organisation? Where does ownership lie and how does this affect use of the system?

2 What enhancements to your HRIS would you like to see and how might these changes impact on the personnel role?

3 Make a case to your chief executive for enhancements (or a total change) to the HRIS. Include reference to the benefits that the new system would provide and reference to the elements that will contribute to the costs.

4 What contribution does HR information make to the decision-making processes in your organisation? Identify the different levels of decision making and the way that information is developed and presented to meet these different requirements.

5 How well does the HRIS meet the needs of the 'users' in your organisation? Identify the barriers to effective use of information and examine ways to overcome these barriers.

6 How secure is personal data in your organisation? What systems are in place to ensure security of data and how are these systems monitored and reviewed?

7 Review the impact of the 1998 Data Protection Act on the obtaining, holding and disclosing of individual data in your organisation. What policies and procedures have been developed to ensure that the rights of individuals to access and the rights of individuals to privacy are protected?

CHAPTER 6

Recruitment: attracting the right people

INTRODUCTION

The recruitment and selection process is a matching activity between applicant and job, which is dependent first, on the organisation clearly defining and specifying a need; second, on utilising appropriate recruitment methods and selection techniques effectively; and third, on reviewing, evaluating and modifying the recruitment and selection system in the light of experience. Recruitment is addressed in this chapter and selection in the next chapter. The recruitment and selection of workers is fundamental to the functioning of an organisation. Inappropriate selection decisions reduce organisational effectiveness, invalidate reward and development strategies, are frequently unfair on the individual recruit and can be distressing for managers who have to deal with unsuitable employees. Inappropriate recruitment is also expensive. If the overall costs of leaving, including payroll and administration, recruitment and selection time and fees, induction, training, unproductive time and any indirect loss of business or customer satisfaction, are taken into account, the estimated cost per leaver can be around £4000, and £6000 for managers and professionals (CIPD Labour Turnover Survey: 2001). There is a compelling argument for trying to get it right.

CHAPTER OBJECTIVES

- To distinguish between recruitment and selection.
- To analyse the recruitment and selection process as a system with inputs, outputs and interrelated sub-systems.
- To recognise the importance of job analysis and the identification of labour market characteristics.
- To examine alternative methods of recruitment in order to facilitate informed choice of method.

CONTINGENCY IN RECRUITMENT AND SELECTION METHODS

Good recruitment and selection is important because well thought out, agreed and communicated policies, procedures and practices can significantly contribute to effective organisational performance, to good employee relations and to a positive public image. Ineffectiveness in recruitment and selection may lead to poor work performance, unacceptable conduct, internal conflict, low morale and job satisfaction and dysfunctional labour turnover. Recruitment and selection is therefore an essential part of people resourcing strategy. Recruitment and selection processes should be effective, efficient and fair – effective in generating candidates of appropriate quality and quantity and distinguishing between the suitable and the unsuitable; efficient in being timely and resource effective; fair by dealing equitably, honestly and courteously with all applicants and providing a positive framework within which diverse candidates can demonstrate their abilities. A contingent approach to recruitment and selection is advocated, whilst recognising that this may be constrained in practice by standard organisational procedures. Standard procedures will contribute to fairness and consistency, but some flexibility is desirable. Recruiters should be aware of the range, strengths and limitations of recruitment methods and selection techniques as this enables informed choices to be made.

The extent to which the functional elements of recruitment and selection are distributed between line managers and personnel practitioners will be contingent upon organisational circumstances. The division of recruitment and selection responsibilities will be determined by factors such as organisational size, administrative resources, locus of professional expertise and the human resource policy on devolution. A policy to devolve recruitment and selection to line managers will invariably be a question of **the degree of devolution** and rarely result in absolute decentralisation of recruitment and selection functions. Whether increased devolution is perceived by line managers as liberating or merely an abdication by personnel specialists, and extra unsolicited work, is subject to continuing debate. Regardless of the division of responsibilities, a manager who is not closely involved in the recruitment process and the selection decision is less likely to be committed to the outcome or accept full responsibility for the performance of the recruit. In the CIPD Recruitment Survey (2000) 50 per cent of organisations involved line managers in recruitment on the basis of equal partners, 37 per cent attributed a leading role to line managers, and the remainder 'played some part'. All involved in recruitment and selection, whether as a direct participant or as an advisor, will benefit from a knowledge and understanding of the range of options and also from an exposure to effective practice and professional principles. Whilst there may be effective practice and professional principles in recruitment and selection, there is no one best way and prescriptions are to be avoided. These recruitment and selection chapters adopt a systems approach, emphasise choice and flexibility, identify and discuss the functional elements in recruitment and selection, and stress the importance of critical review and evaluation of the recruitment and selection processes in the pursuit of continuous improvement.

RECRUITMENT, SELECTION AND THE SYSTEMS APPROACH

It is useful for analytical purposes to distinguish between recruitment and selection.

- *Recruitment* is a process which aims to attract appropriately qualified candidates for a particular position from which it is possible and practical to select and appoint a competent person or persons.
- *Selection* is a process which involves the application of appropriate techniques and methods with the aim of selecting, appointing and inducting a competent person or persons.

Recruitment and selection are components of the same system or process and can be considered separately, but they are not mutually exclusive functions. A systems approach to recruitment and selection (Fig. 6.1) is based on the idea that a system

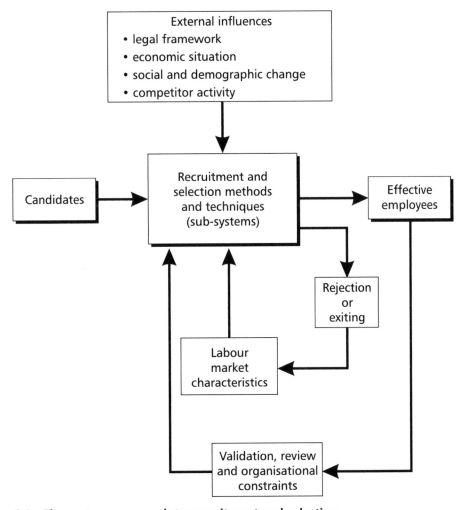

Fig. 6.1 The systems approach to recruitment and selection

has inputs, a processing unit and outputs. The processing unit contains the recruitment and selection sub-systems. The inputs are the candidates, the processing unit consists of various methods and techniques, and the outputs are either effective employees or candidates who return to the labour market. The candidates who return to the labour market are either rejected by the organisation or choose to exit from the recruitment and selection process. The system is subject to considerable external influence. The systems approach provides a convenient analytical framework and permits the penetration of the recruitment and selection sub-systems. It is also possible to recognise the inter-dependence of the sub-systems with the changes in one sub-system having implications for another and also for the quality of the outputs. For example, the most sophisticated selection methods will be rendered impotent by recruitment activity which fails to attract qualified candidates, and highly effective recruitment activity which generates appropriate candidates will be neutered by selection methods which fail to predict performance in the job.

RECRUITMENT AND SELECTION SUB-SYSTEMS

The sub-systems can be categorised as:

1 *Attraction*: attracting suitable candidates.

2 *Reduction*: eliminating unsuitable candidates.

3 *Selection*: assessing, choosing and appointing a suitable candidate.

4 *Transition*: converting the successful candidate to an effective employee.

The components and activities of each sub-system are exposed in Exhibit 6.1.

Exhibit 6.1 The recruitment and selection sub-systems

Sub-systems	Activities
1 *Attraction*	• Pre-recruitment activity – establishing a *prima facie* case for recruitment; job analysis; consideration of the labour market • Use of recruitment methods • Responding to enquiries.
2 *Reduction*	• Filtering, screening and shortlisting.
3 *Selection*	• Use of selection methods and techniques • Making the appointment – offer and acceptance.
4 *Transition*	• Pre-engagement process • Induction and appraisal.

The activities within each sub-system can be scrutinised to assess the contribution that each makes to the overall recruitment and selection process. The remainder of this chapter is concerned with **attraction**, whilst Chapter 7 focuses on the activities associated with **reduction, selection** and **transition**.

In advocating a contingency approach to recruitment and selection activities it is recognised that rarely does the recruiter have a free hand. Organisational constraints and influences on choice in recruitment and selection activities, methods and techniques include the:

- degree of flexibility within organisational recruitment and selection procedures and the potential for conflict with procedural standardisation necessary to achieve equality of opportunity objectives
- previous experience of organisational recruiters, and whether it is positive or negative, in relation to different methods and techniques
- physical and human resources available
- timescale and time constraints
- skill and expertise of the recruiters
- relative costs
- nature of the employment contract, hours of work and relative importance of the vacancy.

Some commentators argue that the recruitment and selection philosophy should be 'select for attitude and train for skill'. What this means is focusing the recruitment and selection process on behavioural competencies such as customer focus, team-working skills, responsiveness to change, willingness to conform with dominant corporate values and so on. Any deficiencies in technical skill can then be remedied through training needs analysis and the provision of learning opportunities. This philosophy in no way undermines the validity of a systematic recruitment and selection process; it merely refocuses it.

PRE-RECRUITMENT

The pre-recruitment process combines the three interdependent elements of establishing a *prima facie* case for recruitment, job analysis and labour market assessment (Fig. 6.2).

Establishing a *prima facie* case for recruitment

When a vacancy occurs, whether through resignation, dismissal, increased workload or reorganisation, there is only the **opportunity** for recruitment and a *prima facie* case should be established before proceeding.

> Every vacancy presents management with an opportunity to rethink the structure of the organisation and the allocation of duties.
>
> (Plumbley, 1991)

117

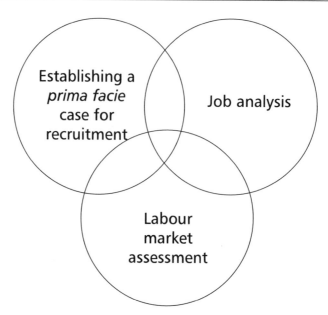

Fig. 6.2 Pre-recruitment activity

There are alternatives to recruitment when a vacancy occurs, and several questions can usefully be addressed.

- Is there actually a job to be done or can elements be distributed, eliminated or achieved through alternative means, for example by utilising technology or contracting it out?
- What constraints are placed on recruitment by the staffing budget?
- Do the workload predictions justify recruitment?
- Does the filling of the vacancy integrate with the human resource plan?
- How does the recruitment proposal fit with diversity objectives?
- Is the impact of the vacancy short-, medium- or long-term?

Job analysis

Once a *prima facie* case for recruitment has been established, job analysis provides the opportunity for assessing whether the job has changed and for reviewing the knowledge, skills, qualities and competencies required; for a newly created position the job analysis is a predictive activity. Job analysis is the systematic **process** of collecting information about the tasks, responsibilities and contexts of a job. The **outputs** of the job analysis process are job descriptions and person specifications. In addition to recruitment and selection, job analysis information is fundamental to many other people management activities, including:

- establishing the job requirements for appraising performance and identifying development needs
- making reward comparisons between jobs
- considering the implications of legislation relating to health and safety, unfair discrimination and the working time directive
- contributing to a common understanding of the job in grievances, disciplinary matters or the negotiation of job changes.

Job analysis is an information-gathering process and decisions need to be made about who does the job analysis, what information collection methods are appropriate and which sources of information are the most useful. The job analysis can be undertaken solely or jointly by the line manager or the personnel specialist depending upon the techniques being used, the expertise of the analyst and the complexity of the job. The sources of information include the line manager, the supervisor, the existing job-holder and other members of the team. A triangulation of these sources will generate the most balanced data as different perspectives will be provided by each of the contributors. Informal and formal job analysis methods are available and include questionnaires, interviews, observation, critical incident techniques, the use of standard checklists and the keeping of work logs and diaries (Pearn and Kandola, 1993). The information to be collected includes:

- data which identifies the job and locates it within the organisational structure
- job objectives and performance measures
- accountabilities, responsibilities and organisational relationships
- job duties and content
- terms of employment and work conditions
- skills, knowledge, qualities and competencies required
- other distinctive job characteristics.

The job analysis process generates information which is converted into the tangible outputs of a job description and a person specification and it is important to distinguish between these two outputs. A job description specifies the purpose, the task and the scope of the job, and the person specification profiles the people characteristics required to do the job effectively – the job description is the 'what' (has to be done) and the person specification is the 'who' (does it). The job description and person specification may be combined in one document and the complexity will vary according to the nature of the job. It is not possible to be prescriptive about format or content, but the objectives of the job description and the person specification in recruitment and selection include:

- to provide an objective focus for the matching of applicants to the job requirements
- to communicate a clear idea of the job to the applicant – a realistic job preview (RJP)
- to provide a basis for appraising performance and identifying training needs during the transition from candidate to effective employee.

Without wishing to undermine the contributions made by Rodger's seven-point plan and Munro's five-fold grading system (ACAS Advisory Booklet No. 6 *inter alia*) in providing systematic templates for the design of person specifications, a death knell has effectively been sounded by the evolving framework for unlawful discrimination, intrusion into private life, labour market changes and changing patterns of work and also increasing concern over workforce diversity. This raises questions about the appropriateness of using, for example, assessment categories relating to 'bearing', 'interests', 'disposition' and 'circumstances'.

> Although the broad framework may still be valid, it is now unethical, inappropriate and potentially discriminatory to probe too deeply into some of these areas of the person specification.
>
> (Marchington and Wilkinson, 2000)

This does not eliminate the need for a systematic approach in determining person specifications, but the approach needs to be founded on two concepts – *job relevance and measurability*. There are two fundamental questions. First, am I satisfied that the specified skills, knowledge and characteristics are necessary for the effective performance of the job? Second, can I systematically measure, or assess, them as part of the recruitment and selection process? The six-factor formula is offered as an alternative model for a person specification (Exhibit 6.2).

Exhibit 6.2   A six-factor formula for a person specification (Pilbeam)

The '**relevance and measurability**' of the following six factors in relation to a specific job.

1 Skills, knowledge and competencies.

2 Personality characteristics.

3 Level of experience.

4 Certificated qualifications.

5 Physical characteristics.

6 Development potential.

Job requirements may need to exceed those which are essential for a particular job when candidates are assessed on the basis of potential and career development. Further guidance on compiling person specifications includes:

1 Skills and knowledge should be specifically related to job needs.

2 Preconditions on length and type of experience should be restricted to what is necessary for effective job performance.

3 Training to enable candidates to achieve satisfactory job performance should be identified.

4 Education and training preconditions should not exceed the minimum requirements for satisfactory job performance.

5 Criteria covering personal qualities and circumstances should be directly related to the job and applied equally to all groups regardless of age, sex, race, ethnic origin, disability and trade union membership or non-membership.

Person specifications provide fertile ground for the introduction of personal prejudices, subjectivity and arbitrary criteria and this is not in the interests of the organisation or the applicants. There is also a tendency to over-specify in person specifications by seeking the super-human candidate or demanding characteristics which disbar perfectly competent people. There needs to be a balance between idealism and reality in person specifications. Characteristics can be divided into those which are **essential** and those which are **desirable,** or in the case of competencies, the threshold level of competence and a superior level of competence. This will introduce a necessary degree of person specification flexibility. It is salutary to test each element of the person specification against whether it can be measured or assessed in a consistent, valid and reliable way; if it cannot, it probably needs to be discarded. Despite these 'health warnings', the job description and person specification have invaluable parts to play in creating a systematic approach to recruitment and selection and in focusing the minds of the participants. It is good practice to begin all recruitment and selection activity with a job description and a person specification.

Attention is drawn to four contemporary, interrelated issues which justify reflection. First, there is a debate about the value of comprehensive and detailed job descriptions in rapidly changing organisations, which increasingly emphasise flexibility. Conventional job descriptions are criticised for focusing too heavily on tasks and processes and for being inflexible. It is suggested by some commentators that accountability profiles which concentrate on outputs, such as the results, purposes and added-value dimensions of the job, rather than job inputs are more versatile and complementary to HR strategies relating to empowerment, worker flexibility and autonomy in job design. This has implications for the design, rather than the concept, of job descriptions and person specifications. It raises also the question of the extent to which the person fits the job or the job is fitted to the person. Second, the job analysis information only provides a snapshot of a job at one point in time. Job descriptions and person specifications decay from inception and they need regular review to ensure currency and relevance. Third, there is a tension between the need for record keeping and evidence of job descriptions and person specifications for organisational purposes or as a requirement of validating and auditing bodies, such as Learning and Skills Councils (LSCs) or Investor in People (IiP) assessors, and the need for the job description and person specification to be organic documents, with a rate of change which is at least equal to the rate of change of the organisation. Fourth, the issue of corporate culture is difficult to address in formal job descriptions and person specifications. If the organisation is highly organic and having to adapt continuously to turbulent environments, a candidate with a career to date in a more mechanistic or steady-state organisation may not represent the best fit. But how is culture measured and how is cultural fit objectively and fairly assessed? Is cultural fit essential at recruitment or is it 'acquired' during the transition phase? Is cultural fit merely the cloning of conformity of behaviour? Is there any conflict between cultural fit and diversity objectives? Chapter 7 argues that the pursuit of equal opportunities is a social responsibility and a legal requirement and makes sound business sense, and it is in the interests of every organisation to ensure that it does not reduce the pool of talent from which it can draw employees by allowing unfounded prejudices to influence the decision. How legitimate is it to reduce the pool of talent through applying corporate culture criteria?

Analysing the labour market

The third element of pre-recruitment activity is labour market assessment. This is fundamentally about establishing the availability of candidates who meet the person specification and the ease or difficulty with which they can be attracted. It also involves consideration of the appropriateness of the terms, conditions and rewards being offered, as an incongruence with candidate expectations will have adverse implications for the recruitment and selection process.

It is necessary to consider the specific labour market and its characteristics as a prerequisite to designing and applying recruitment and selection methods. As a working definition, 'a labour market is the identified pool of potential employees from which it is possible to attract candidates of the required calibre for a specified job'. The organisation has access to the internal labour market (ILM) and the external labour market (ELM). The ILM describes arrangements whereby existing staff can apply and be considered for vacancies which occur, resulting in the promotion or transfer of current employees. The ILM has positive potential in terms of motivation, continuity and retention, but the organisation is effectively constraining access to a wider pool of talent. In addition, it may be more difficult to orchestrate a desired change in culture if relying on ILMs. The ILM cannot be relied upon indefinitely unless the rate of staff turnover exactly equals any planned or necessary adjustments in head count. Reasons for accessing the ILM include:

- the provision of opportunities for training and development
- enabling employees to pursue reward through internal promotion
- the retention of the investment in the organisation's human capital
- the lower cost of recruitment
- scarcity in the ELM
- the reinforcement of corporate culture.

The external labour market is segmented and stratified by occupation, industry, geography, gender, race and age. It is dynamic in nature and subject to many influences including demographic change; for example, the ageing UK population and a smaller pool of young people, emerging and declining skills, changing patterns of work and increasing female participation (*see* Exhibit 1.1). The ELM can also be considered in terms of primary, secondary and tertiary sectors, reflecting the flexible firm divisions (*see* Chapter 4).

A critical factor in recruitment and selection is the establishment of whether there is likely to be a shortage or surplus of candidates.

A shortage labour market is characterised by demand exceeding labour supply, giving more power to potential candidates and highlighting the two-way nature of the recruitment relationship. A surplus labour market is characterised by labour supply exceeding demand, giving more power and control to the employing organisation. In terms of strategy a shortage labour market needs a more **nurturing** recruitment and selection system, and a surplus labour market needs a more **targeted** approach (Walsh, 1992).

The job-seeking habits of the applicants in the identified labour market also need consideration. For example, and at the risk of being stereotypical, a chief executive candidate may expect the employing organisation to adopt the role of suitor within a sophisticated and considerate recruitment and selection process, whilst a casual kitchen porter may expect a minimum of bureaucracy and form filling, an interview with a very realistic job preview and an immediate start. The task for the recruiter is to anticipate the expectations of potential candidates in relation to the methods of application and treatment during the selection process.

In summary, the analysis of the labour market needs to take account of:

- the factors associated with ILM and ELM recruitment
- the stratification, segmentation and characteristics of ELMs
- the implications of recruiting and selecting within primary, secondary and tertiary labour markets
- whether the identified labour market reflects a shortage or surplus of labour in relation to demand
- the job-seeking habits and expectations of potential candidates.

Labour market assessment also involves the critical evaluation of the recruitment and selection process for each vacancy; record keeping of numbers, quality and expectations of applicants; market research through accessing the employment service, employment agencies and advertising media; and networking with other employers. Labour market intelligence is essential to determining appropriate recruitment and selection methods. Labour market analysis will also be influential in determining the nature of the contract, the pattern of work and the terms and conditions of employment.

RECRUITMENT METHODS – ATTRACTING APPLICATIONS

This section introduces a range of recruitment methods, identifies the characteristics of each method and discusses potential advantages and disadvantages.

The objective of a recruitment method is to attract an appropriate number of suitable candidates, at a reasonable cost. There is no ideal number of applications and there is no intrinsic value in attracting a high volume of candidates. Is the epitome of recruitment effectiveness the attraction of one well-qualified candidate for each vacancy? This would clearly have advantages in terms of time, effort and cost, but it is unrealistic. It does, however, provoke a useful mental discipline by focusing attention on attracting quality candidates rather than quantity of applications. There is a tension between a desire to ensure that sufficient applications are attracted and a sharp 'targeting' of the relevant labour market; this tension is reconciled by a knowledge of alternative recruitment methods and the exercise of informed judgement. There are many ways of attracting applications. They are listed in Exhibit 6.3 to demonstrate the range and to emphasise that advertising, often the first managerial response, is only one approach within a battery of potential methods. They can be used exclusively or in combination.

Exhibit 6.3   Recruitment methods

- Press advertising including:
  - local, regional and national newspapers;
  - professional and trade journals, and other specialist publications.
- Internet recruitment
- Other advertising:
  - television and radio;
  - vacancy boards – internal and external;
  - leaflet drops, posters and recruitment caravans.
- Waiting lists
- Employment agencies and recruitment consultants
- Job centres
- Careers service
- Direct access to schools and colleges
- Government training schemes
- University milkround
- Open days, recruitment fairs and careers conventions.

Press advertising

Scanning job vacancy advertisements will inevitably reveal wide ranges of style, opinion and skill in recruitment advertising. Although there is no one best way, and prescriptions are ill advised, good practice guidance is available from bodies such as the CIPD, the EOC, the CRE and ACAS (Exhibit 6.4).

Exhibit 6.4   Good practice in recruitment advertising

- Recruitment advertising should be genuine in that either a vacant job actually exists or recruiters seriously intend to consider applicants for employment.
- A person specification should be the basis for outlining the job requirements.
- The description of the employing organisation should be realistic, factual and clear.
- Job location, pay and allowances should normally be specified.
- Clear application procedure instructions should be given – whether a CV should be sent or whether to request an application form.
- Advertisements should not discriminate on the grounds of sex, race, disability, age and membership or non-membership of a trade union, except in specific statutory circumstances.

Effectiveness in recruitment advertising involves considering the following elements:

- the budget freedom or constraint
- media choice
- the compilation of advertising copy
- the opportunity to give a realistic job preview
- equality of opportunity or diversity objectives
- the resource requirements to deal with the anticipated response.

Most of these elements can be applied to other recruitment methods as well as press advertising. The recruiting organisation may elect to undertake these activities independently or with the advice and support of an advertising agency. An advertising agency will advise on labour markets, media choice and copy design. The compilation and production of the advert and also the purchasing of the advertising space will normally be undertaken by the agency. The agency covers its costs and makes a profit from the revenue received from the media in which the advertisements are placed, and the larger and more expensive the advertisement the greater the revenue for the advertising agency. Multi-site or national organisations with a house style will find the services of an advertising agency of value in ensuring consistency and professionalism, and also in the construction of a brand image for recruitment.

The budget constraints will need to be applied in the context of a cost – benefit analysis, but ultimately the advertisement has to achieve the objective of attracting candidates of a suitable calibre. The professional recruiter should develop a portfolio of advertisement costs in relation to size, style and media location to inform decision making.

The choice of media should be determined by labour market characteristics of the job being advertised. The local, regional and national press segment the labour market by geography, travel to work considerations and the practicality of relocation. Professional and trade journals and other specialist publications segment the labour market by skills and occupation. Newspapers segment the labour market by socio-economic group.

The compilation of the advertising copy needs to take account of the type of advertisement. The three types are, in descending order of size and potential impact, full display, semi-display and lineage. Big, bold and beautiful is the conventional wisdom, but the budget available and the expectations of the likely applicants will temper this. Clearly the bigger the advertisement the greater the cost. Three principal components of an advertisement provide a structure for copy design.

1 A strategy for gaining attention – headings, messages and illustrations.
2 Information about the position – to develop applicant interest and to enable the application decision.
3 The action message – how and when to apply and what information to supply.

An important consideration is the balance between the volume of wording and the 'white space'. There is a temptation to seek the greatest value from the advertisement by packing it with words and information, whereas in terms of impact the 'white space' provides a powerful window for the message. The astute recruiter should come to terms with paying for the correct amount of white space in order to enhance visual appeal.

A realistic job preview opportunity is presented by the advertisement. The greater the information which is communicated effectively and the more realistically the job is previewed the greater the probability that an informed application decision can be made by the applicant. The advertisement is potentially a filter for the recruitment and selection system by allowing unsuitable applicants to self-select out, and all advertisements should be overviewed from the perspective of potential applicants.

Equality of opportunity and diversity objectives can be pursued through recruitment advertising. This should go beyond the rhetorical statements of being an equal opportunities employer. The absence of criteria which constitute direct or indirect discrimination will send a more powerful message. Gender-neutral job titles, although giving succour to politically correct sceptics, provide one means of seeking to redress gender segregation in employment. The CIPD endorses the positive use of advertising in order to re-balance situations where particular groups may be under-represented, and the use of appropriate visual images can contribute to the reinforcement of non-discriminatory practices (Paddison, 1990). The overt welcoming of applications from disadvantaged groups sends a firm equal opportunities message.

The resource requirements necessary to deal with applicant response also need consideration. The choice is between a 'mail box' approach, which just receives applications, and the personal contact approach where applicants respond by calling in or telephoning. The personal contact approach is more resource intensive, but it is an opportunity to filter applications through objective and predetermined pre-selection criteria.

Internet recruitment

The Internet provides limited access to labour markets and relies on the positive efforts of the individual to visit the job vacancy and initiate the job search, but increasing use of Internet recruitment by employers, recruitment consultants and job seekers is predicted. One recruitment agency claimed 40 000 Internet visits per month as far back as 1995 (*People Management*, October, p. 18) and it is estimated that the on-line recruitment industry in Europe will have soared in value from £50 million in 1999 to £3.8 billion by 2005 (Taylor, 2001).

The use of the Internet for advertising jobs needs to be based on the likelihood of net surfers being within the target labour market. Currently this may include jobs in information technology, marketing, multimedia, computer-literate graduates and HR professionals, but Internet job search is broadening its base in terms of the job-seeking habits of applicants. In a survey of 150 senior HR professionals (Reed, 2000) the Internet was perceived as being most effective in recruiting graduates (cited by 47 per cent of respondents), IT staff (33 per cent), technical staff (30 per cent), professional staff (28 per cent) and middle managers (23 per cent). As the incidence of Internet access increases, *The Guardian* (1999) reported that 25 million people in the UK will have access by 2001, and as familiarity with on-line job search grows it is probable that Internet recruitment will enter mainstream recruitment practice. The CIPD Recruitment Survey (2000) suggests that Internet recruitment has already arrived, with nearly one half of all employers in the survey, up from 36 per cent in 1999, now using the Internet for recruitment. However, according to the CIPD survey the Internet is not replacing more traditional methods of advertising, with only a small minority of recruiters seeing the Internet as the *most* effective way of recruiting. Advertising on the Internet for six months costs approximately the same as one full display advertisement in a broadsheet newspaper.

The basic differences between traditional advertising and using the Internet for recruitment are that job details are viewed electronically and the application form can be completed and sent on-line, or a CV can be sent as an attachment to an e-mail. There are three principal ways an employer can use the Internet for recruitment (CIPD, 1998: *Recruitment on the Internet*). First, a recruitment zone may be added to an existing organisational website. This may be a good starting point because it is relatively quick and inexpensive, but it has limitations, because other than for well-known or high-profile organisations there is little reason for the job seeker to visit the site. The extent to which visitors to the corporate website will migrate to the recruitment pages will be significantly influenced by the clarity of the signposting and the user-friendliness of the hyperlinks. The second way is to design a separate recruitment website. This is more expensive than the first option, but it can be actively promoted and is likely to reach more job seekers. It can provide a direct access point for all vacancies and project a strong corporate identity through incorporating information about the company and the training and career opportunities. The third method is by advertising jobs on a specialist media site. Used like traditional press advertising, this may feature just a job advertisement or it could incorporate an extended description of the vacancy and have a link to a company website. Key players, amongst 300+ providers, include Monster, Stepstone, Top Jobs on the Net, Jobline, Jobpilot and Jobs Unlimited. It is, as yet, difficult for the HR professional to verify the claims of these service providers in terms of the size of their databases, the volume of job search hits and the relative costs and success rates.

The potential advantages of using the Internet include a shortening of the recruitment cycle, accommodating the job-seeking habits of an increasing proportion of the labour market, reducing the volume of paperwork associated with recruitment, projecting a technologically progressive corporate image and providing job search availability 24 hours a day. The potential disadvantages are associated with the possibility of generating high volume but not necessarily high quality or genuine job seekers (termed electronic time wasters) and limiting access to some labour markets.

The Internet can also be used as a pre-selection technique and a preliminary stage in the matching of applicants to the job. Banks of curriculum vitae (CV) and personal profile questionnaires are constructed on the system by specialist providers and can be accessed by employers. The level of sophistication is developing rapidly and job seekers can enter CVs directly onto the system; the CVs are scanned and artificial intelligence software recognises skills, knowledge and qualifications regardless of how they are presented within the CV. The candidate profile is appraised against the employer's selection criteria and a candidate shortlist. Candidate confidentiality can be maintained through the use of identity numbers. These developments would appear to herald the age of the multimedia curriculum vitae (Theaker, 1995). The 1998 Data Protection Act gives applicants a limited right to access the criteria and method of selection.

Other advertising

Vacancy boards may be either internal, and only seen by current employees, or external – located in a public place. They are a low-cost way of advertising jobs, but will only access a limited pool of applicants. Internal vacancy boards enable existing employees to apply for a job change, personal development or promotion. Employees may also bring vacancies to the attention of family members and friends. External vacancy boards are often used by restaurants and retail shops and are utilising the customer base as the labour market. These window boards need to be professionally designed and strategically positioned to maximise the impact upon the flow of customers and other members of the public. Some retailers take the concept further by advertising jobs on shelf labels and at checkouts. Employers should be aware of the possibility of unlawful indirect discrimination if access to the notice board makes it more difficult for one sex or for members of ethnic groups to apply for the advertised job. They may need to be used as a supplementary rather than the only method of recruitment.

Television and radio offer innovative ways of attracting applicants. The use of television is normally confined to teletext services. A judgement is required about the extent to which the job-seeking habits of the target population include accessing teletext. Local radio advertising is relatively low cost and functions by listener intrusion and message repetition. A limited amount of job and organisational information can be communicated by radio, but it can spark interest.

Leaflet drops, posters and recruitment caravans, as well as being recruitment methods, can function as promotional activities to raise the organisation's profile. Leaflets are relatively cheap to produce and deliver, but are poor at targeting a particular labour market. Leaflet drops may be a useful supplementary method within a recruitment campaign aimed at filling a substantial number of vacancies. They are often associated with the opening of new businesses, particularly retail or personal services outlets, where the need is for a high volume of low-skilled or semi-skilled applicants. The public suffer from unsolicited mail fatigue and leaflets may not trigger interest or action. Posters are another adjunct to wider recruitment activity; the issues are first, deciding upon and accessing appropriate locations, and second, how to stimulate applicant attention. A recruitment caravan is a mobile recruiting centre. The mobile unit can be located in a public place for a specified period of time and is more suited to multi-site national recruitment. The investment and maintenance cost is considerable, but this method has been used effectively by the armed services and by retailers to staff new supermarkets. Although not employment recruitment, the mobile recruitment centre is used by the AA and the RAC to recruit members and by further education colleges to recruit students.

Waiting lists

A waiting list consists of speculative enquiries and applications retained from previous recruitment activity, and a bank of suitable applicants can be accessed when a vacancy occurs. The advantages are low costs, resource efficiency and a shortened recruitment timescale, but waiting lists are problematic to manage and demand efficient and effective recording, filing and retrieval systems. A personnel information system will target the search of waiting lists in relation to a person specification.

There are three factors which militate against waiting lists. First, they have a tendency to decay quickly. Applications have a limited life, as candidate interest may wane over time or personal and occupational circumstances may change. Second, the resurrection of an application and the contacting of a candidate by the employer has implications for the psychological contract. The approach to the applicant by the employer, a reversal of normal roles, raises expectations about the likelihood of job success, with subsequent employer rejection being less acceptable to the candidate. This role reversal may also increase candidate perceptions of strength in negotiating the contract of employment and heighten the expectations of the successful candidate in respect of more positive or favourable treatment during the employment itself. Third, the exclusive use of waiting lists does not help the pursuit of equality of opportunity and diversity, because they may restrict access to jobs and may constitute unlawful indirect discrimination.

Employment agencies and recruitment consultants

Employment agencies and recruitment consultancies have a profit motive and provide a wide range of services in return for fees. Their services include:

- supplying temporary workers (agency staff) to accommodate peaks and troughs in work or to cover employee absence
- attracting, pre-selecting and referring candidates for 'permanent' positions
- seeking out candidates (head-hunting) and maintaining a register for specialist, professional, management, executive or technical positions
- providing training and development opportunities for individuals to make them more attractive to employers, for example updating on current word-processing packages.

The use of employment agencies is the externalisation of elements of the recruitment and selection system, including some administrative tasks, candidate attraction and applying pre-selection criteria. Success depends on a precise specification of requirements by the employer and the professionalism and ability of the agency.

The Employment Agencies Act, 1973, regulates the conduct of employment agencies by:

- specifying record-keeping requirements, principles of confidentiality and disclosure of fees
- specifying qualifications for those running agencies
- regulating advertisements to include the nature and place of work and the pay rates
- investigating complaints through an inspectorate.

Since 1995, employment agencies have not required a licence, but the Secretary of State can prohibit individuals from running employment agencies. New regulations governing the private recruitment industry were drafted in 2001 (Aikin, 2001) and these will regulate activities in areas such as constraints on work-seekers' future employment, the payments demanded when a work-seeker supplied by an agency is offered permanent employment, the payment of wages direct to the worker by the hirer and not by the agency, the advertising of work only where a genuine job exists, and ensuring that adverts contain details of pay rates and also the qualifications required. The Employment Consultants Institute provides a code of professional conduct, membership services, and professional training and accreditation for employment consultants.

The costs of services to employers can be high in relation to other recruitment methods. Where the agency can meet recruitment needs more quickly, efficiently or effectively through the availability of resources, contacts or recruitment expertise, these are a desirable option. Certain categories of employment, for example executive secretaries or information technology specialists, have a tradition of being recruited through agencies or consultants. Head-hunting of senior executives is frequently undertaken by executive search agencies or consultants through a network of contacts. Using executive search is rather like recourse to a dating agency, 'selling the job to the potential candidate and then trying to sell the candidate to the employer' (Taylor, 2002). The advantage to the employer is the opportunity to instigate confidential dialogue with talented executives from competitor organisations. It also enables approaches to be made to candidates who may not be actively seeking employment and would therefore be unlikely to respond to press advertisements. In this executive labour market many individuals may not have realised they were in the labour market until they were contacted by an executive search agency. Although executive search is initially expensive, the benefit of securing an influential executive can make it worthwhile. There are clearly ethical, confidential and professional boundaries that should not be breached. Employment agencies and recruitment consultancies, by having greater access to persons in employment, have certain advantages over job centres.

Job centres

Job centre applicants are more likely to be unemployed, although job centres offer services to employed people seeking a job change. Databases of candidates are maintained which facilitate a speedy search on the basis of employer requirements. A professional and executive recruitment service is also provided and, in addition to local services, job centres can access national and European Union labour markets. A proactive and cooperative job centre can respond quickly and effectively and may also advise on the development of the job description, the person specification and the terms and conditions of employment. The provision of a job description and a person specification will enable job centre staff to match candidates with employer requirements more objectively, in effect offering a screening service. However, a job centre refusal to refer a candidate to an employer may be perceived by the candidate as an inappropriate role for the job centre and raises questions about the responsibilities of job centre staff as agents of the employer or as agents of job seekers, although clearly it is not in the interest of any of the parties to refer to employers those candidates who do not match the job criteria.

Job centres may be able to provide promotional and marketing opportunities, interviewing arrangements, form-filling facilities and interview rooms. Job centres represent a responsive and economical recruitment opportunity. The extent of cooperation and the range of services will be influenced by local factors, and employers wishing to maximise the recruitment potential of a job centre should seek a positive and mutually beneficial relationship with job centre staff. The profit motive may be absent in job centres, but efficiency measures and performance targets increasingly drive job centre activity.

Careers service

The careers service is subject to value testing and externalisation. It provides advice for young people on career options and acts as a facilitator between the young person and the employing organisation. It is a suitable recruitment method for trainee positions or where limited experience is needed for the job. The advantages are low cost to the employer and the targeting of a particular labour market. The careers advisor, whilst recognising the realities of youth employment opportunities, will be confronted with an expectation of providing advice on career choices rather than just exposing the young person to 'jobs of work'. In addition to advice, some testing and search facilities are available.

Direct access to schools and colleges

This recruitment method requires the organisation to establish mutually beneficial relationships with schools and colleges with the aim of encouraging a flow of suitable applicants. The employer can establish professional networks with teachers, lecturers and careers advisors, attend careers fairs, make careers presentations, advise on job search and provide work experience. In return the school or college will distribute and make available the employer's careers literature and will be in a position to give knowledgeable advice to students about specific job opportunities. This requires a balancing of the school or college responsibility to the student and the responsibility to the employer, and, as with the careers service, there is a potential tension between the student, or parent, expectation of the promotion of career choice and the reality of exposure to 'jobs of work'. The employer should recognise this tension. The advantages to the employer are relatively low cost and also access to careers advisors, who will have some knowledge of the potential applicants. Restricting the development of school or college relationships to one or two institutions may, depending upon institutional characteristics and location, be perceived as élitist or even constitute unlawful indirect discrimination.

Government training schemes

Government training schemes, including The New Deal, aim to broker a marriage between employer and potential employee through the provision of training, financial support and work opportunities. Schemes are available for young people and adult workers and provide the opportunity for a trial period and a realistic job preview, often at relatively low risk to the employer. A contemporary characteristic of government training schemes is the provision and accreditation of vocational training, often NVQ related. The employer may view subsidies as an incentive, but managers should be clear about the training commitment and the degree of bureaucracy associated with administering the schemes; LSC audit requirements may act as disincentives. The training schemes suffer from a low-status reputation and concerns about the quality of the trainees. The development of a positive relationship with accredited training providers can contribute to the effectiveness of government schemes as a source of recruitment.

University milkround

The 'milkround' is the process of promoting employment opportunities through employer attendance at careers and other recruitment events at universities. This may involve the employer in responding to student enquiries, the initial screening of candidates and the formal presentation of organisational information. It is clearly targeted at the graduate and postgraduate labour market. Facilities are provided by the institution, but the milkround is resource intensive in terms of organisational representatives, travel, accommodation and the quality of display stands and supporting literature. The degree of milkround participation by an employer depends upon the number of graduate vacancies and the need to maintain or increase the profile of the organisation. It is useful to involve previous trainees, who have been converted into successful employees, not only to provide evidence of progression, but also to exemplify the desired characteristics of the graduate recruit.

It is difficult to measure directly the effectiveness of the milkround, and employers should be prepared for student enquiries which seek to gather information rather than demonstrate suitability for employment. The milkround is also used by undergraduates to search out 'sandwich' placements and employers should be ready for these enquiries as well. The milkround is probably best viewed as a component of overall graduate recruitment strategy. It is also an opportunity to find out what other employers are offering.

Open days, recruitment fairs and careers conventions

The innovative, aware organisation will take its product, namely the company, image and jobs package, to the potential employee rather than wait for the candidates to respond to them.

(Curnow, 1989)

Attracting applicants through open days, recruitment fairs and careers conventions is a proactive response to competitive labour markets or recruitment difficulties. They may also form part of an overall recruitment strategy by promoting organisational image and job opportunities and maintaining an overt presence in labour markets where the job-seeking habits of the candidates expect it. The open day format may range from informal drop-in sessions to highly structured events which incorporate presentations, guided tours, sophisticated hospitality and work sampling.

Recruitment fairs and careers conventions are normally organised by educational institutions, training providers, LSCs or Chambers of Commerce. They require employer participation in what is effectively 'a shop window of opportunities'. In common with the university milkround, quality representation and supporting material is essential. Open days, recruitment fairs and careers conventions can be labour intensive and fatiguing for representatives and demand professional organisation. Careful planning and effective resourcing are necessary to ensure that a positive message is communicated. These promotional activities offer opportunities for potential applicants to find out more about the organisation and the job without necessarily making a commitment to apply.

Offering incentives to employees for introductions

Organisations can use employee incentives to recruit qualified applicants. An employee recommending a candidate who is offered employment, and achieves a satisfactory performance level, can be rewarded for the introduction. This is not a new idea, with the *John Lewis Partnership Gazette* reporting in 1918 that 'We will pay an employee who introduces us to someone who we do actually employ a fee of one guinea'. In 1996, because of recruitment difficulties in the Army, soldiers were being paid £250 for every successful recruit introduced. Not only is this a way of utilising employees as search consultants, but also the applicant is likely to receive a more realistic job preview than would be the case with less personal recruitment sources. The *caveat* about the potential for indirect discrimination applies.

RECRUITMENT METHODS – ANALYSIS AND TRENDS

It is essential to analyse and evaluate the recruitment process and the methods of recruitment. First, this may be done through the capture of data relating to the number of responses, the number of applications received, the number of candidates interviewed and the number of candidates appointed and relating this data to the direct and indirect costs of the recruitment process. Second, it may be achieved by asking applicants to state on the application form the particular recruitment source that initially attracted their attention. Third, the coding of each recruitment method (*see* Exhibit 6.3) will identify the sources of successful candidates.

Trends in recruitment methods respond to labour market changes and the relative costs of the methods. Shortage labour markets and recruitment difficulties will encourage bigger and better advertisements and the use of innovative recruitment methods. There is a trend away from traditional announcement advertisements towards job advertisements which are creative in nature and visually striking:

- The quality of applicant response can be positively influenced by the appropriate use of humour, a more conversational style and a people-friendly approach.
- The most effective advertisements are informative, enticing, persuasive and include a clear and distinct proposition to the target audience (Exhibit 6.5).

133

Exhibit 6.5   Criteria for judging excellence in recruitment advertising

- Visual impact
- Typography and balance
- Clarity of message to the target audience
- Promotion of the job vacancy
- Projection of a professional organisational image
- Focus on workplace diversity.

Source: CIPD and IPA recruitment advertising industry awards 1996

RESPONDING TO ENQUIRIES AND THE CANDIDATE'S VIEW

Recruitment and selection is a two-way process.

> **Applicants have considerable control because they can, at any stage, decide to exit from the process.**

They are empowered not to respond to advertisements, not to return application forms, to decline the invitation of an interview, to reject an offer of employment, not to turn up on the first day, and ultimately to resign from a position which fails to meet their expectations. A comparison of the number of enquiries with the number of applications received, the conversion rate, will quickly reveal the exercise of choice by applicants. The recruiter must recognise these multiple opportunities for the candidate to exit.

> In recruitment the element of choice applies to the recruiter and the applicant. The discerning candidate is more likely to choose an employer who applies a professional approach to recruitment.

(CIPD Code)

The objective in responding to enquiries is to influence positively the conversion rate from enquiry to application by inhibiting the exiting of suitably qualified candidates. Professionalism in responding to enquiries includes:

- the speed and the courtesy of the employer response
- the provision and style of information about the job, the organisation and how to apply – a recruitment pack (Exhibit 6.6)
- the reasonableness of the effort and time expected from the applicant
- the availability of informed and skilled staff to deal with job enquiries.

Enquiries and applications should be recorded to ensure that good candidates are not lost, that applications are acknowledged and that unsuccessful applicants are informed of the outcome of their application. A computerised personnel information system with a recruitment database will facilitate the tracking of applications, the generation of correspondence and the provision of data for analysis and evaluation of the recruitment and selection process.

Exhibit 6.6 The recruitment pack

The style and content of the recruitment pack depend on the nature of the position and the culture and resources of the employing organisation. It may include the following:

- a letter of thanks and instructions on what happens next

- an application form or a request for a CV or a request to contact the employing organisation to arrange an interview

- a job description and a person specification

- an information booklet which includes wider organisational information

- reference to appropriate personnel policies, for example equal opportunities, training, promotion and reward systems.

The objective is to create the right impression and solicit appropriate applications. The recruitment pack is an opportunity to offer a realistic job preview.

CRIMINAL CERTIFICATES – POLICE ACT 1997

Recruiters may need to check the criminal record of an applicant. Three types of certificate are available from the Criminal Records Bureau:

1 A Criminal Conviction Certificate (CCC) – details convictions which are not legally spent, is issued to individuals at a small cost and needs to be produced on application for employment, if requested.

2 A Criminal Record Certificate (CRC) – details spent and unspent convictions and police cautions and is issued to individuals and registered employers at a small cost in excepted occupations, for example the teaching, health, legal and caring professions.

3 An Enhanced Criminal Record Certificate (ECRC) – comprises a full criminal check of convictions, cautions, acquittals and police intelligence and is available to individuals and registered employers (exceptionally to the employer only) in special occupations, for example judges and magistrates, those working unsupervised with children and where a betting or gaming licence is required.

ASYLUM AND IMMIGRATION ACT 1996

This Act imposes an obligation on employers to ensure that they do not employ anyone who is not legally entitled to live and work in the UK. Employers need to obtain documented evidence of an applicant's legal right to work and retain it for six months after the employee's contract has ended. Failure to do so is punishable by prosecution and a fine of up to £5000. The main sources of evidence are national insurance numbers, birth certificates, passports and work permits. The duty of the employer is to inspect and copy the relevant documents; it is not necessary to routinely investigate the validity of the documentation, although a prudent employer with reasonable suspicions may elect to do so. British citizens and EU citizens, including those of the European Economic Area, normally have the right to live and work in the UK, but there is more uncertainty associated with Commonwealth citizens.

To avoid unlawful discrimination individual applicants should not be singled out for different treatment. A policy of making recruitment more difficult for ethnic minorities or those with foreign-sounding names through demanding documentation not asked of other applicants may constitute a breach of the Race Relations Act. The obvious policy is to treat all applicants the same at every stage of the recruitment and selection process (*see* Chapter 8).

SUMMARY LEARNING POINTS

1 Whilst organisations need agreed, written and communicated policies and procedures for recruitment and selection, a contingent and flexible approach to recruitment and selection processes and methods is advocated.

2 Recruitment and selection can be viewed as a system with interrelated sub-systems. The first sub-system is **attraction** and this involves pre-recruitment activity, the use of recruitment methods and responding effectively to enquiries.

3 Pre-recruitment activity includes establishing a *prima facie* case for recruitment, undertaking job analysis as a prerequisite to focused recruitment, and an assessment of the labour market.

4 A wide range of recruitment methods can be used exclusively or in combination and the professional recruiter should be able to evaluate each method critically and to exercise informed choice.

5 Responding effectively to employment enquiries requires an acknowledgement that the potential applicant can exit from the recruitment and selection process at any time.

6 Non-discriminatory recruitment practices are legally required and socially responsible and make sound business sense.

REFERENCES AND FURTHER READING

Advisory, Conciliation and Arbitration Service (ACAS) (1983) *Recruitment and Selection: Advisory Handbook*, 6.

Aikin, O. (2001) 'The new seekers', *People Management*, 22 February, 18–19.

Anderson, N. and Shackleton, V. (1993) *Successful Selection Interviewing*. Oxford: Blackwell.

Annual Review of the Advertising Industry (1996) Published with *People Management*, June. IPD.

CIPD (1998) *Recruitment on the Internet*. CIPD Information Note.

CIPD (2000) *Recruitment Survey*.

CIPD (2001) *Labour Turnover Survey*.

Courtis, J. (1994) *Recruitment Advertising: Right first time*. London: IPD.

Curnow, B. (1989) 'Recruit, retrain, retain: personnel management and the three Rs', *Personnel Management*, November, 40–7.

Herriot, P. (1989) *Recruitment in the 90s*. London: IPM.

IPD (1995) *The IPM Code on Recruitment*.

Kiceluk, A. (1996) 'The net that helps you fill vacancies', *People Management*, May, 34–6.

Longmore-Etheridge, A. (1995) 'Personnel purgatory', *Security Management*, 39(7), 19–20.

Marchington, M. and Wilkinson, A. (2000) *Core Personnel and Development*. London: CIPD.

Overell, S. (1995) 'Agency woos big firms to recruit on the Internet', *People Management*, October, 18.

Paddison, L. (1990) 'The targeted approach to recruitment', *Personnel Management*, November, 54–8.

Pearn, M. and Kandola, R. (1993) *Job Analysis: A manager's guide*. London: IPD.

Plumbley, P. (1991) *Recruitment and Selection*. London: IPD.

Reed, J. (2000) 'The scatter-gun approach', *People Management*, 26 October, 69.

Taylor, C. (2001) 'Windows of opportunity', *People Management*, 8 March, 32–6.

Taylor, S. (2002) *People Resourcing*. London: CIPD.

Theaker, M. (1995) 'Entering the era of the electronic CVs', *People Management*, August, 34–7.

Walsh, D. (1992) in Winstanley, D. and Woodall, J. (eds) *Case Studies in Personnel: ABZee*. London: IPD.

ASSIGNMENTS AND DISCUSSION TOPICS

1 Describe and explain the distribution of recruitment and selection activities between the personnel specialist and the line manager in your organisation. Is the distribution appropriate? In addition, argue the case for and against the devolution of recruitment and selection responsibilities to line managers.

2 Identify and discuss the elements and activities of the recruitment and selection system within your organisation. Comment critically upon how the system might be improved, taking account of organisational constraints.

3 Identify a recent vacancy in your organisation. What alternatives to recruitment were possible?

4 Why is it valuable to undertake job analysis activity? What organisational purposes can it serve? For a specified job decide how job analysis information can be collected.

5 Obtain a job description (or an accountability profile) and a person specification for a job in your organisation. How effective are they in achieving each of the following:

- providing a focus for recruitment and selection?
- communicating a realistic job preview?
- providing a basis for appraising performance and identifying training needs during the transition phase of the recruitment and selection process?

6 For a vacancy in your organisation determine the characteristics of the labour market and comment upon the implications of these characteristics for the choice of recruitment and selection methods.

7 Identify shortage and surplus labour markets and consider the reasons for them.

8 Scan recruitment advertisements in the local or regional press. Select and critically evaluate three advertisements and prepare a checklist of learning points, both positive and negative, to share with colleagues at work or in class.

9 Which **recruitment** methods are appropriate for these vacancies?

- A university lecturer
- Fifty seasonal fruit pickers
- Twenty retail management graduate trainees
- A secretary to a managing director
- Maternity cover for a word processing operator
- An electrician
- A head chef
- Eighty part-time sales assistants for a new supermarket
- The manager of a security services firm
- One hundred call centre workers.

10 Evaluate critically the potential of the Internet to contribute to more effective recruitment.

11 Research the cost of recruitment advertisements in various sizes and styles in the local, regional and national press and in professional journals. Compile a portfolio of examples and costs and make a short presentation to your class.

CHAPTER 7

Selection: choosing the right people

INTRODUCTION

The attraction of applications is succeeded by efforts to eliminate and reject unsuitable applicants, the aim being to reduce the number of candidates to that which can be managed effectively in the selection stage of the process. Many selection methods are available and managers who select employees need to be aware of the strengths and limitations of the various techniques. The selection decision is not the end of the process, as the transition from successful candidate to successful employee requires further effort, skill and attention.

CHAPTER OBJECTIVES

- To distinguish between the elimination of applicants and the selection of candidates.
- To discuss the concepts of validity, reliability and popularity in selection methods.
- To introduce and comment critically upon alternative methods of selection.
- To consider the transition from applicant to employee.

SUBJECTIVITY, DISCRIMINATION, PROFESSIONALISM AND ETHICS

Although the recruitment and selection process can be made more methodical and systematic, it will inevitably remain subjective. A structured recruitment and selection system with rigour and consistency in the application of selection methods is highly desirable, but the appointment decision remains a matter of human judgement. It is important not to be beguiled by pseudo-scientific selection techniques.

The selection decision is a discrimination decision, as the employer discriminates between applicants on the basis of ability and suitability. This discrimination should be based on criteria which are valid and related to the requirements of the job. Unlawful direct or indirect discrimination should be avoided and all candidates should be able to demonstrate abilities for the job regardless of race, ethnic origin, gender, marital or family circumstances, sexual preference, age, spent convictions and disability, except in exempted statutory circumstances. This fair approach to discrimination is professional and ethical and also makes sound business sense (*see* Chapter 8).

A contract of employment includes an implied duty of mutual respect. As every candidate for a job is a potential employee, and whilst recognising that the contract of employment is not legally formed until there is offer, acceptance and consideration, it is a simple ethical principle to:

incorporate the duty of mutual respect into the recruitment and selection process.

A psychological contract (*see* Chapter 1) is developed during recruitment and selection, and the transition from candidate to employee is the realisation of the psychological contract. The recruitment and selection process, whether through the advertising material, a job description, the application form or personal contact, creates expectations for employers and for employees. The creation of these expectations and the development of the employment relationship should be based on mutual trust and should ensure that both parties have realistic expectations. Mutual respect and mutual trust are therefore desirable aims in recruitment and selection (Exhibit 7.1). Applicants have ethical responsibilities as well.

Exhibit 7.1 Employer ethics in recruitment and selection

- Advertising only genuine jobs
- Not abusing the power position
- Soliciting only the information that is necessary
- Not asking loaded questions or seeking to entrap candidates
- Assessing suitability on the basis of ability
- Maintaining confidentiality in the use and storage of candidate information
- Informing candidates appropriately of the selection decision.

ELIMINATION AND REDUCTION

As identified in the previous chapter, the second recruitment and selection sub-system is **reduction**. This has the objective of reducing the pool of applicants to a manageable number by eliminating and rejecting unsuitable candidates. This can be done indirectly, through the characteristics of the recruitment activity, and directly, through using pre-determined job criteria. The processes involved are filtering, screening and shortlisting. Recruitment activity filters applications not only through specifying job requirements, but also, indirectly, through factors such as whether a realistic preview of the job is communicated, the ease or difficulty of application, the timescale for applicant response and the quality of the recruitment pack information. These factors need critical evaluation as they contribute to ensuring that suitable candidates are retained within the recruitment and selection system and unsuitable candidates are eliminated.

Surplus labour markets generate a high volume of applicants and candidates are often screened through the written information they provide, and sometimes through telephone or personal contact. Effective screening involves using job criteria which are predetermined and applied consistently. For example, telephone screening should consist of set questions asked of each candidate and the systematic recording of responses. This enables more effective candidate and job comparisons to be made and will also help to prevent the use of unlawful criteria. Simple grading or scoring sheets are easy to develop and will contribute to a methodical approach. For example, candidates can be graded high, medium or low in relation to the essential and desirable criteria in the person specification. A grid can be created using the six-factor formula (Exhibit 7.2). Further sophistication may be needed in order to develop and weight the different factors according to their importance.

Exhibit 7.2 Shortlisting and the six-factor formula

Factor – where **relevant** and **measurable**	High 3 points	Medium 2 points	Low 1 point
Skills, knowledge and competencies			
Personality characteristics			
Level of experience			
Certificated qualifications			
Physical characteristics			
Development potential			
Overall rating and recommendation:			

The removal of personal information, such as age, gender, ethnic origin and family or marital circumstances, from the application form prior to screening will reduce the opportunity for personal prejudice, perceptual error and unwarranted assumptions. There are arguments for and against this detachment of information (Courtis, 1995).

Once applicants have been screened and unsuitable candidates eliminated, a shorter list remains. There are a number of simple principles to guide the construction of the final shortlist. First, only candidates who match the person specification should be considered for the shortlist, as making up the number with unsuitable candidates will be unproductive. The shortlisting of candidates will raise their individual expectations and create time, effort and stress demands; in keeping with the mutual respect ethic, only candidates who are genuinely going to be considered should be shortlisted. Second, the time spent on screening and shortlisting presents an opportunity for applicants to exit from the recruitment and selection process. Employers should not only be mindful of this, but also have a contingency arrangement to compensate for withdrawals. Third, a shortlist should be manageable in number in relation to the resources of the organisation and the selection methods being used.

The point was made previously that each element of each sub-system is interdependent and effectively the recruitment and selection system is only as strong as the weakest link. The screening and shortlisting process is another example of this, as insufficient attention at this stage will undermine the overall effectiveness of the recruitment and selection activity. As Napoleon said, 'time spent on reconnaissance is rarely, if ever, wasted', and this is particularly true in the context of shortlisting and screening.

The reduction and selection sub-systems merge at this point, but before discussing selection methods the concepts of validity, reliability and popularity are introduced.

VALIDITY, RELIABILITY AND POPULARITY OF SELECTION METHODS

The important concepts of validity, reliability and popularity provide dimensions for probing the potential and the limitations of different selection methods. The validity of a selection method is the extent to which it measures what it intends to measure. The main concern of recruiters is the predictive validity of selection methods – how effective is an interview, a test or an assessment centre in predicting the eventual job performance of a candidate? Predicting job performance through the selection process is a challenging task and should not be underestimated. The predictive validity of selection methods can be compared by using a correlation coefficient to measure the **probability** that a selection method will predict performance in a job. A correlation coefficient of 1.0 represents certain prediction, a correlation coefficient of 0.5 approximates to a 50 per cent chance that the selection method will predict performance, and a correlation coefficient of 0.0 indicates no connection between the selection method rating and job performance. There can also be negative correlations, meaning that positive candidate performance in a selection process correlates with poor job performance!

A number of studies have attempted to provide a comparison of predictive validities in selection methods. Exhibit 7.3 contains a summary of rounded figures (Smith and Robertson, 1993; Shackleton and Newell, 1991; Smith, 1994; Arnold, Cooper and Robertson, 1998; Conway, Jako and Goodman, 1995; Fowler, 1997, 1998; CIPD, 2001).

The predictive validity correlations listed are of limited value because they cannot be generalised to particular organisational situations, as any validity study will be constrained by the people sample chosen, the job performance measures used and the way in which the selection methods were applied. The summary of predictive validities therefore needs to be treated with caution, but important messages remain. First, faith in the ability of selection methods to predict job performance should be circumscribed, and second, some methods may be better than others. The search for appropriate methods can proceed accordingly. It is generally accepted that an appropriate combination of selection techniques improves predictive validity. Of particular note is the evidence to suggest that the interview, although almost universal in use, is frequently a poor performer in the selection process.

Exhibit 7.3 Predictive validity of selection methods: a summary of correlations

1.0	Certain prediction
0.9	
0.8	
0.7	Assessment centres for development
0.6	Skilful and structured interviews
0.5	Work sampling
	Ability tests
0.4	Assessment centres for job performance
	Biodata
	Personality assessment
0.3	Unstructured interviews
0.2	
0.1	References
0.0	Graphology
	Astrology

In an ideal world each organisation should attempt to validate its own selection methods for each type of job. This would involve comparing the information used in selection, for example test results or interview scores, with work performance criteria, for example output measurement or appraisal grading, of the candidates appointed, perhaps over variable time periods. Figure 7.1 identifies the elements in validating selection methods.

There is a significant problem with the validation of selection methods, because candidates who fail the selection process, usually because good performance is not predicted, are denied the opportunity to attempt the job to demonstrate that they are not good performers. It would therefore be necessary to appoint candidates with both high and low ratings in the selection process and conduct a validation study, as only then could it be determined that poor performers in the selection process are also poor performers at work. These issues are discussed, not because it is expected that organisations will be prepared, or able, to commit resources to the routine and rigorous validation of the selection methods used, but to expose the difficulties of predicting performance.

Other validity 'types' include face validity and construct validity. A selection method has face validity if, on the 'face of it', there appears to be a connection between the method and the job. For example, a word-processing test for a secretarial job has reasonably high face validity. A biodata questionnaire which seeks information about relationships with brothers, sisters and parents, or an assessment centre activity which involves making a raft out of planks and oil drums, may appear to have much less face validity. A selection technique with low face validity can still have high predictive validity, but it is important to be aware of the potential impact on the candidate if low face validity is perceived. As Fowler (1997) puts it, 'Will it be acceptable to candidates

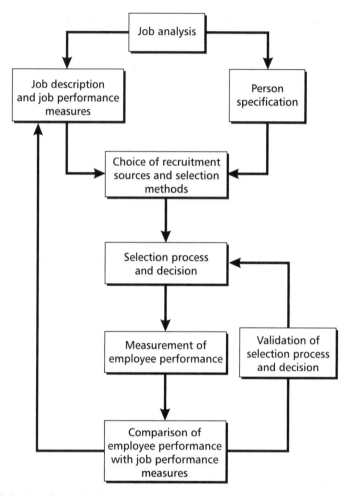

Fig. 7.1 Validating the selection process and decision

who may lack confidence in, or resent, a test that seems to ask irrelevant or intrusive questions?' Construct validity refers to whether or not a selection technique is based on sound evidence or underpinning theory. This is particularly important in psychometric assessment. It is frequently easier to demonstrate low construct validity than the reverse. For example, although biodata has reasonable predictive validity, the theory, or construct, which explains why it works is empirically fragile.

Reliability in selection methods is a consistency measure. To be considered reliable a method, such as an interview or test, should be able to ensure the same candidate result regardless of the person using the selection method. A further reliability measure would be the extent to which a selection method consistently produced the same outcome when used for the same candidate at different times. It is interesting to reflect on whether a consistent judgement would emerge if the same candidate group was interviewed by different interviewers – the inter-individual reliability of the interview as a selection method. There are also intra-individual reliability issues – the extent to which the same interviewer will be consistent in judgement at different points in time.

The popularity of selection methods in UK organisations provides another comparative dimension, with three broad groupings identifiable. Interviews, references and application forms, the classic trio, have almost universal popularity despite evidence of low predictive validity and lack of reliability in practice. Ability tests, personality assessment and assessment centres have medium popularity, and biodata, graphology and astrology have low popularity (Shackleton and Newell, 1991; CIPD Recruitment Survey, 2000). The most predictive methods are not the most popular.

SELECTION METHODS

Personnel specialists and line managers should be aware of the main selection techniques and recognise the extent and limits of their professional expertise. In this section selection methods are described, relevant issues and debates exposed and the fit within the overall recruitment and selection system discussed. The pursuit of a perfect selection method is unrealistic as there exists only a variety of less than perfect techniques. A critical perspective, which recognises that selectors need to exercise informed choice between and within selection methods, is the most constructive approach. Understanding the potential and the limitations of selection methods is essential to using them effectively and appropriately.

The application form

The application form has an important part to play in recruitment and selection, and attention to form design and use is warranted. Attention is drawn to three interrelated application form issues – duality of purpose, ease or difficulty of completion, and standard or flexible design.

Duality of purpose – Typically, the application form is designed to capture personal information which becomes part of the personnel record, should the applicant become an employee. The application form also has the purpose of providing job-related information which is used for shortlisting decisions and to structure the interview. There may be a tension between these two purposes, and application forms should be evaluated critically for usefulness in employee selection. Personal information which is not relevant to a selection decision can be collected later, and only for those candidates who are offered employment. The collection of personal information on applicants may also be necessary for monitoring objectives, but this can be collected separately from the application form.

The collection of personal information has become significantly constrained by law, and as the application form is the first collection point it useful at this stage to consider some of the constraints on the employer. The Data Protection Act, 1998, places an obligation on employers to ensure that the information asked for on an application form, and throughout the recruitment and selection process, is 'adequate, relevant and not excessive'. The application form should not therefore seek information which is irrelevant to the applicant's ability to do the job. Particular care must be taken in the collection of sensitive personal data, such as ethnic origin, political opinions, religious beliefs, health, sexuality, family or marital circumstances, and trade union affiliation. Basically, such data can only be collected if they are relevant to the entering into of an employment contract and with the applicant's consent. The application form will also need to make it clear that the information may be used as a basis for the personnel record and that it may also be used for monitoring purposes. The application form may need to incorporate a phrase such as: 'by signing this application form you are giving permission for your personal information to be stored and processed for the purpose of arriving at a selection decision, for it to be used as a basis for a personnel record and for sensitive data to be used for the purpose of equal opportunities monitoring'. Anti-discrimination legislation has promoted the withdrawal of questions on marital status and children, and questions on nationality or racial and ethnic origins have been similarly affected, or are asked only for monitoring purposes. The Disability Discrimination Act, 1995, has increased sensitivity to questions about health and sick absence (Leighton, 2000). Key clauses in the Human Rights Act, 1998, guarantee the right to privacy in family life and beliefs and the right to freedom of expression. The latter has implications for requiring employees to conform with organisational rules and corporate values. The implementation of EU Directives on equal treatment will outlaw discrimination based on age, sexual orientation and religious belief. Clearly, these principles relating to data protection, equal treatment and human rights need to be borne in mind throughout the recruitment and selection process, but they are introduced here to raise awareness (*see also* Chapters 5 and 8).

Application forms can be developed to generate more useful data by asking applicants to respond to extended questions or statements. For example, where a particular competency is required, an applicant could be asked to describe an instance where a competency was developed or exhibited. Exhibit 7.4 provides one example of how this approach is used in graduate recruitment. Used in this way, the application form becomes 'a correspondence interview' and is developing into a biodata approach. An application form which contains this type of extended statement is much more difficult to complete and will not be suitable for all types of job.

Exhibit 7.4 Extended application form statements for behavioural competencies

1 Provide an example of where you had to persuade others to accept an unpopular course of action.

2 Describe how you provided leadership for a team and how you set about achieving the team's objectives.

3 Evaluate an occasion when you needed to assert yourself.

4 Describe the most difficult non-academic problem you have solved, indicating why it was difficult.

5 Evaluate a piece of your own work, which may be practical, academic or artistic, to demonstrate your personal creativity.

6 Describe a situation where your planning skills made a significant contribution to the successful achievement of individual or team objectives.

7 Identify three personal standards which you consider are important for a manager to have.

Ease or difficulty of completion – The desire to collect useful candidate information needs to be balanced against the deterrent effect on the applicant of a lengthy and complex application form. In a surplus labour market the deterrent effect may be a useful way of eliminating less strong applicants. In a shortage labour market, or where the job-seeking habits of applicants do not expect a difficult application form, the deterrent effect may cause a low rate of return and the exclusion of good candidates because applicants exercise their right to deselect the employer.

Standard or flexible design – A standard application form is administratively attractive and less expensive, but there is a case for flexibility in design. Flexibility may not extend to individual forms for each job, but ought to reflect the varying requirements of different job categories. A range of form styles will improve the contribution of application form information to the recruitment and selection process. Application form information should be compared systematically to the job description and person specification to reduce personal bias and to avoid the use of arbitrary criteria. There are arguments for and against the acceptance of CVs in place of, or to supplement, the application form. Information presented in a standard format on an application form facilitates candidate and job comparison and contributes to a common interview structure. Conversely a CV is an opportunity for candidates to demonstrate individual capacity for providing evidence of achievement and suitability for the job (or demonstrating they have been coached in preparing CVs).

References

Despite low validity and reliability, and the reluctance of referees to express negative views, most organisations continue to seek references. Choices exist over the use of references in recruitment and selection and it is not possible to prescribe 'the one best way'. The first choice relates to the **stage** at which references are obtained and used – before shortlisting, before the interview or after the offer of employment. There should be a sensitivity to the impact on the applicant's existing employment relationship, as the receipt of a reference enquiry may provoke an employer judgement that the employee is disloyal or lacking in commitment. The second choice is whether it is **opinions** or **facts** that are sought. Valid opinions are highly dependent upon a sound knowledge of the applicant and also the specific job for which the individual has applied. The third choice relates to the **weight** given to reference information, bearing in mind that applicants choose their own personal referees and that employers of the applicant are bound by the duty of care in providing references. The duty, both in contract, through an implied term of mutual trust and confidence, and in tort, is to provide a fair and accurate reference. The duty extends to current employees and also to former employees. The employer is not obliged in law to give a comprehensive reference, except when not giving a comprehensive reference results in unlawful discrimination or victimisation. However, it is not enough that the reference is accurate; the overall impression given must be fair and reasonable. This duty of care has been reasserted several times, in *Spring v Guardian Assurance*, 1994, IRLR 460; *Bartholomew v London Borough of Hackney*, 1999, IRLR 246; *Coote v Granada Hospitality*, 1999, IRLR 452; and *TSB v Harris*, 2000, IRLR 157.

All of this is making employers more cautious about expressing opinions, and some are instigating 'no talk' reference policies or confining a response to information about the position held and employment dates. There appears to be a growing gap between the information employers would like to receive and what they are willing to give. A sensible guideline for completing reference enquiries may be to restrict the response to facts, or where opinions are to be given they should be based on facts.

In the context of the provisions of the Data Protection Act, 1998, it can remain difficult for employees to see their references. The recipient of a confidential reference can disclose it only if the Act's confidentiality rules are complied with, basically meaning that the permission of the referee is required, and the referee can withhold a reference from disclosure where it is given in confidence. Where the reference is 'in confidence' the employer will need to have separate filing arrangements or will have to remove the reference from the employee's file each time subject access is requested.

The speed of return and the usefulness of a written reference can be improved by:

- using the job description and person specification as the basis for reference questions
- giving sufficient background information
- clearly indicating the nature of the response required
- user-friendliness and ease of completion, plus enclosing a stamped and addressed envelope
- specifying a response time which is reasonable
- sending the enquiry to a named individual.

Oral references are an alternative and some would argue that they are more likely to elicit a 'truthful' response. Providers of telephone references should be aware of the ease with which the conversations can be recorded, although reputable suppliers of telephone equipment include a warning signal to inform you that a recording is taking place, and there are ethical issues involved in seeking 'off the record' references. A further reference decision is whether the completion of reference enquiries should be devolved to line managers or administered by a personnel function. There is a legal and an ethical need for care, fairness, accuracy and consistency, and each organisation needs to have a policy to achieve this in practice.

The interview

An interview is a social encounter between an applicant and a representative, or representatives, of an employer and personalises the recruitment and selection process. It is subject to all the problems associated with social interaction, individual personality and perceptual processes. Locate this within a ritualistic framework, and a context which may be emotionally charged, and a cauldron of tensions is created, often inhibiting appropriate selection decision. This raises the question of why organisations continue to bother with the selection interview. There are a number of reasons. First, it is almost inconceivable that employment would be offered without the employer actually seeing the prospective employee, and potential employees would be unlikely to feel comfortable about joining an organisation without meeting some of the organisational members. Second, interviewers frequently feel that they do it well and are insulated against healthy self-doubt about their ability to make good selection decisions. Third, despite being subject to considerable criticism, the interview can be improved through planning, structuring and the development of interviewing skills.

The interview is more than a selection device. It is a mechanism which is capable of communicating information about the job and the organisation to the candidate, with the aim of giving a realistic job preview (RJP). The RJP enables the applicant to make a more informed judgement. The interview also provides a forum for agreeing a course of action with the applicant.

The structure of an interview is subject to many variations, but it contains four basic elements. There will be oscillation between points 2 and 3 and variations in emphasis and time allowed for each of the elements.

1 Initial contact and explanation of the interview programme.

2 The interviewer asks questions and the interviewee responds with answers, and other information.

3 The interviewee asks questions and the interviewer responds, and supplies additional information.

4 Closing the interview and agreement on what happens next.

Research evidence suggests that interviewers have a tendency to make up their minds within the first few minutes of the interview, and the remainder of the time is spent confirming these first impressions. This is referred to as 'confirmatory information-seeking bias' and describes the situation where an interviewer asks questions to actively seek information in confirmation of the initial judgement. Other perceptual problems frequently occur in interviews, including:

- the halo or horns effect – a single good or bad characteristic or piece of information carries disproportionate weight in the selection decision

- the projection of the interviewer's characteristics or preferences – treating candidates more favourably or unfavourably on the basis of either similarity or dissimilarity to the interviewer

- positive or negative expectancy – created prior to the interview through access to partial candidate information

- stereotypical assumptions – about behaviour, preferences and probable work performance

- the recency effect – the influence and contrast of previous candidates distorting the proper assessment of current candidate information

- personal liking bias – the interviewer is influenced by whether or not the candidate is likeable

- risk aversion – the interviewer guards against making a wrong decision, resulting in greater weight being given to negative indicators at the expense of focusing on the positive areas of candidate suitability.

This potential for perceptual distortion can be compounded by other problems relating to the subjectivity and lack of skills of the interviewer. These problems include having inaccurate information about the vacancy, having too much faith in the interview as a fair discriminator, unwarranted confidence in interviewing skills, and variations in interview structure. Interviewers should recognise that it is easy for them to spend too much time talking, and the figure of only 20 per cent of the time is a good target. Behavioural variations of the interviewer, caused by mood, time constraints or the importance or urgency of other work demands, should not be overlooked.

Poorly structured interviews and a lack of interviewing skills will neuter the validity and reliability of the interview as a predictor. Recognising the fallibility of the interview is a prerequisite to enhancing the contribution it can make to the selection decision. The interview should normally be structured to ensure a focus on job-relevant information, sufficient time should be allocated to prepare for each candidate, and interviewers need to develop and exhibit sound interview skills (Exhibit 7.5). Training and practice in interviewing can significantly improve effectiveness and increase predictive validity and reliability.

Interviews take different forms. These include the one-to-one, the panel and the group interview.

Exhibit 7.5   Selection interviewing skills

- Awareness of perceptual distortions
- Practice in multi-sensory perception – listening, observing, evaluating, thinking, speaking (sequentially and simultaneously)
- The ability to probe and gather relevant information through the use of appropriate questioning techniques, particularly open and probing questions
- The confidence and ability to control the interview structure
- Positive use of body language and facial expression
- Finely tuned listening skills and the ability to recall elicited information accurately
- Stamina and sensitivity
- The use of appropriate strategies, including formality or informality, information gathering or problem centred, real-life or hypothetical issues and so on.

The one-to-one interview relies on the interface between the candidate and the individual representative of the organisation. It is often less oppressive than a situation where a candidate is faced with several organisational representatives at the same time. It can take place on its own, which raises questions about the appropriateness of locating the responsibility for the appointment decision in one person alone, or as part of a sequential process where the candidate may meet organisational representatives successively. The sequential process of one-to-one interviews allows cross-referencing of information before the decision is made, but unless the roles of each interviewer are clearly defined the result is a duplication of questions.

Panel interviews may be more time-efficient than one-to-one interviews, unless there is a sequence of panel interviews. They enable more members of the organisation to be involved, but there is a consequent proliferation of opinions and agendas and variable expertise. The panel interview may be perceived as more oppressive by the interviewee and this needs to be taken into account. In a panel interview the roles and contributions of the participants need to be agreed and precisely defined, and unless there is a clear locus of decision-making there is potential for either internal disputes or consensus seeking and 'group thinking'. Properly structured and conducted panel interviews are considered appropriate by many organisations and are a defence against accusations of the personal bias which may be associated with a dependence on a single interviewer in a one-to-one interview.

A group interview enables a number of applicants to be interviewed simultaneously by one or more interviewers. Such interviews are probably more eliminative than selective, and purport to measure characteristics such as sociability, self-confidence, leadership, team working and competitiveness. Group interviews can be time-efficient. A significant advantage is the opportunity to present organisational information to a number of applicants, rather than having to repeat it for each individual, and questions raised by one candidate may be of interest and value to other candidates. Group interviews need sensitive and skilled handling to ensure equity of treatment and should not be used as the sole basis for decision making. Displaying personal characteristics in front of interviewers and competing candidates is a stressful and uncomfortable experience for the interviewee and may impact negatively on the quality of the information generated. Group interviews presuppose a relatively large pool of applicants and will need to be acceptable in the context of the job-seeking expectations of the labour market from which the applicants are being drawn, for example in graduate recruitment where there may be a small number of vacancies and a large number of applicants.

Buckley, Norris and Wiese (2000) usefully sum up 100 years of research into selection interviewing:

> Negative findings about the predictive power, reliability, or validity of the interview have little meaning to the employers and interviewers that depend on the interview as their primary selection tool. The interview provides the personal, face-to-face contact that humans seek and desire. Until another method is developed that allows employers the same benefits and freedoms as the interview, the interview will continue to be used as a primary hiring tool. After almost 100 years of research on the interview, few strides have been taken toward creating a new and better selection tool to replace the interview. Many scholars, including a number of recent meta-analytic researchers, have attempted to encourage the use of the structured interview, citing its higher validity and inter-rater agreement. Others have taken an opposite stance, promoting the group interview, with little or no structure or interviewer involvement. The answer lies, perhaps, in a combination of the two methods.

Research by Barclay (1999) found that structured interviews which may include using job and competence analysis to make questions relevant to the job, asking the same questions of all candidates, using systematic scoring procedures and deploying questioning strategies such as behavioural or situational questions, are increasing in popularity. She attributes this to three reasons. First, there are the social aspects of interviewing – it is flexible, it provides the opportunity to meet the 'whole' person face to face, it involves line managers and it allows some bargaining and influencing to take place. Second, other methods have limitations, such as the time and costs and specialist training required, the potentially adverse effects on candidates, and the monopoly of techniques by personnel specialists, leading to marginalisation of line management. Third, there are benefits of structure in interviewing – more focus on relevant criteria and candidates' competencies, hence an increased likelihood of better selection decisions, and more consistency and fairness in treatment of candidates. It would seem that the popularity of interviewing as a selection technique is undiminished and it will continue in parallel with efforts to improve its reliability and validity.

Psychometric testing

Expert and professional advice is a prerequisite to the design, choice, administration and interpretation of psychometric tests. The CIPD Code on Psychological Testing provides comprehensive practitioner guidance.

The aim in this section is not to instruct in the use of psychometric tests, but to stimulate awareness of some of the main issues and themes.

Psychometric testing is generally used as a term which encompasses all forms of psychological assessment. There are five broad categories:

- *Attainment tests* measure current levels of knowledge or skill, for example word-processing tests or examinations.
- *General intelligence tests* measure overall intellectual capacity for thinking and reasoning.
- *Specific cognitive ability tests* measure verbal reasoning or numerical reasoning or manual dexterity or spatial ability.
- *Trainability tests* measure responsiveness to instruction or training and seek to assess learning potential and rate of response in relation to specific tasks or activities.
- *Personality questionnaires* aim to infer relatively enduring individual characteristics and traits as a basis for predicting behaviour.

In the case of properly validated attainment, general intelligence, cognitive ability and trainability tests, there is a general acceptance that the measurement outputs can be related to specific jobs, and appropriately chosen and used, there is little contention that they are able to provide useful information for selection decisions. The assessment of personality provides much more fertile ground for controversy.

Psychometric tests proliferated in the 1980s and 1990s, with hundreds now being available. The use of psychometric tests increased from around 30 per cent of organisations in 1985 to around 70 per cent of organisations in 1995 (Aston Business School reported in Pickard, 1996 and McHenry, 1977), although Baker and Cooper (2000) put the figure nearer 50 per cent. The increased availability and use of psychometric tests gives rise to concern about the huge potential for poor test design, indiscriminate use and inappropriate interpretation of outcomes. Shackleton is quoted as saying that 'some of the stuff on the market is rubbish, I wouldn't use it to select a toothbrush' (Pickard, 1996). The dangers to potential users lie in two beguiling features. First, the 'scientific' nature of psychometric devices can create an exaggerated impression of their value and accuracy. Second, design features in the test may generate information which effectively takes responsibility for a selection decision by indicating a pass or fail outcome, satisfying the risk aversion needs of the selector. It is beyond the scope of this generalist text to advise on the specific application of tests, but it is essential that organisations are careful and discriminating in their use of psychometric instruments. The British Psychological Society and the CIPD provide a framework for regulating the use of psychometric tests through a voluntary 'licensing' mechanism based on codes of practice and the certification of user competence.

Personality questionnaires are the most contentious form of psychometric assessment and therefore it is useful to focus on these. Personality questionnaires produce either a profile or a descriptive narrative of an individual. This raises the question of which profile or description is the 'best type' for the job. It is the identification of this 'best type' that is elusive. The individual personality information is compared to the profile of a representative sample of an appropriate population, either produced by the questionnaire supplier or generated by the user on the basis of the personality characteristics of successful and less successful organisational performers. Popular examples of personality assessment include the Myers Briggs Type Indicator (MBTI), Cattell's Sixteen Personality Factors (16PF) and the Saville and Holdsworth Occupational Personality Questionnaire (OPQ). The MBTI reports individual preferences on four scales of two opposite preferences. The opposite scales are extraversion and introversion, sensing and intuition, thinking and feeling, and judging and perceiving. They respectively deal with where the individual likes to focus attention, the way the individual looks at things, the way that the individual makes decisions and how the individual relates to the outer world. The MBTI outcome is one of 16 personality types, and Myers Briggs publish a description of the characteristics and work preferences frequently associated with each 'type' for the purpose of helping either the individual or the organisation to make more informed choices about the appropriateness of different types of work. The 16PF profile infers personality using Cattell's 16 primary traits and produces a line profile for each individual which can be used for comparison with the perceived 'best type' for a job. The OPQ is based on 30 personality dimensions and has scoring norms derived from 4000 British managers who took part in development trials. These OPQ dimensions are used to construct a desired personality profile against which the profiles of job applicants are matched. These examples of personality assessment are introduced to illustrate different approaches and because of widespread use – any criticisms of personality assessment in selection are not directed specifically at these reputable psychometric instruments.

Personality assessment has its advocates and accusers. Amongst the accusers are Blinkhorn and Johnson who ask the question:

> Are personality tests serious measures of personal qualities which predict behaviour, or are they the stage-managed bits of flummery intended to lend an air of scientific rigour to personnel practice? We fear the flummers are winning.

(1991: 38)

Personality 'tests' have a propensity to produce disparate outcomes on the basis of race or gender (Wood and Baron, 1992; McHenry, 1997). Quoting Blinkhorn again,

> I regard using personality testing as a filter as an abuse. I'm fairly sure it will be the next thing to hit the tribunals.
>
> (in Welch, 1996)

Personality assessment which seeks to identify 'the one best personality type' can be charged with being 'Tayloristic' by not fully taking into account contingency factors and also being at odds with concepts of promoting and managing diversity. As Goss points out:

> Selecting only particular types of personality may, eventually, lead to an incestuous organisational profile where, weakened by inbreeding, the ability to think innovatively and challengingly is eroded in favour of slavish conformity to established norms.
>
> (1994: 47)

Goss also raises the question of whether selection on the basis of personality profiling is an ethically acceptable form of social engineering in pursuit of corporate conformity. There are also issues about the acceptability of the intrusive nature of some of the instruments used to assess personality. The arguments are similar to those being used to debate the acceptability of using genetic profiling in employment decisions. Finally, there is the fairly obvious, but often overlooked, factor that personality assessment tends to measure stated preferences rather than behaviour. Although it is generally accepted that preferences shape individual behaviour, the correlation between these two factors is not necessarily going to be strong and will certainly be moderated by other factors in the workplace.

Despite these accusations it is important not to discard a potentially useful selection device.

> The CIPD broadly supports the use of psychological testing and believes that, used appropriately, testing can enhance decision-making, thus enabling managers to develop more informed and accurate perceptions about the ability and potential of individuals. To achieve this it is essential to integrate testing into the decision-making process. Even the best tests available are only as good as the process of which they form a part, and flawed decisions can be made based on even sound and verifiable data. A well designed policy on testing is therefore essential to ensure best practice and that the maximum benefits accrue from its use. Particular care should also be taken to ensure that tests themselves do not indirectly discriminate unfairly between certain groups. Test use alone is no guarantee of objectivity despite their scientific background.
>
> (CIPD, 2001)

The arguments in favour of personality assessment are threefold. First, there is evidence to suggest that personality assessment, used appropriately, has fairly good predictive validity. Second, there are factors which enhance the potential contribution of personality assessment, including using only properly validated tests, the appropriate training of administrators of the tests and the interpreters of the information generated, the carrying out of tests in standard conditions, proper confidentiality, sensitivity in giving feedback on test and profile results, and validating the match between individual personality characteristics and job requirements and performance. Third, personality assessment should be restricted to providing additional information for the selection process and should not constitute the sole method or principal basis for decision making.

The CIPD is fully aware of limitations of personality assessment generally and does not support its use as the sole basis of decision-making. It can be useful as an added dimension to decision-making but only when practitioners generally use those instruments that have been rigorously developed and for which thoroughly researched validation evidence and norms are available.

(CIPD, 2001)

Although most of this section has focused on personality assessment, there are some general guidelines which are applicable to all psychometric measurement. These are as follows.

- Psychometric assessment may have a useful role in selection provided it is used properly and in conjunction with other methods.
- Careful consideration should be given to the costs of psychometric testing, in terms of purchase and the time and effort required to administer and interpret the tests, in relation to the added-value to the selection decision.
- The limitations of psychometric testing and the limits of individual professional expertise should be recognised.
- Only reputable suppliers should be used and all assessors need to be trained to approved professional standards.
- Psychometric testing should respect the dignity of the individual.

See also Fowler (1997), Sternberg (1998), Fletcher (1998) and Stairs, Kandola and Sandford-Smith (2000).

Work sampling

Work sampling as an employee selection technique provides opportunities for candidates to experience job tasks and for the employing organisation to observe and assess candidate competencies and performance. Work sampling is an ability test which is organisation and job specific in design. There are clearly links with more generic tests of ability. Work sampling opportunities may be real, where the candidate actually does the job under supervision for a limited period, or simulated, where the job tasks are performed through role play or management games (Fowler, 1996). Work sampling is valuable in giving the candidate a realistic job preview.

The technique is illustrated by providing examples:

- car mechanic – diagnosing and repairing vehicle faults
- NVQ assessor – the assessment of the assessor assessing a candidate
- chef – preparing a meal
- telephone sales – following up leads by telephone
- sales assistant – selling a product and demonstrating ability to make add-on sales
- chauffeur or chauffeuse – driving a vehicle and interacting with the passenger

- HR practitioner – interviewing a job applicant, advising line managers or conducting a training session
- store detective – identifying suspicious behaviour, detecting a 'planted' shoplifter or, as a role reversal, simulated shoplifting by the store detective applicant without being detected!

The success or otherwise of this selection method will depend on appropriate design and use. It has the potential for relatively high predictive validity and to be acceptable to candidates through good face validity. The design principles include:

1 Determine the essential abilities for the job in question through discussion with job-holders and line managers – competency analysis.

2 Construct a work sampling activity which provides a genuine opportunity for the demonstration of the critical abilities required.

3 Determine the performance standards and assessment criteria, together with a mechanism for rating or scoring individual candidate performance.

4 Train assessors, pilot the work sample, evaluate and refine.

5 Develop clear, fair and consistent instructions for work sample candidates which include common advance information and a briefing immediately prior to the work sampling activity.

6 Locate the work sample appropriately within the recruitment and selection system, either to supplement other selection techniques or integrated within an assessment centre approach.

This systematic approach to work sampling in selection can be a disincentive, because it presents design challenges, is demanding in terms of time, people and other resources and, being organisation and job specific, will need to be regularly updated. It is therefore under-used. A useful *caveat* is provided by Fowler (1998): 'Work simulations provide valuable indications of actual or potential expertise, not precise measurements'. Work sampling can also include job-related outputs that a candidate 'may have prepared earlier', for example (subject to authenticity) a fashion design portfolio, a piece of French polishing or photographic evidence.

Assessment centres

An assessment centre is a process rather than a place. Assessment centres attempt to improve validity and reliability through the integration of multiple selection techniques. They are founded on the identification and assessment of dimensions which are judged to be indicative of future job performance. They exhibit certain characteristics, including a variety of assessment methods to form a total assessment system, the bringing together of a number of candidates, multi-dimensional evaluation of candidate competencies, behaviours, motivation and personality, and the training and use of organisational members to perform the roles of facilitators, observers and assessors. The cost of an assessment centre, financially and in terms of time, effort and other resources, is considerable, and it is only a practical proposition where there are a number of candidates for critical positions. Assessment centres are frequently associated with management jobs and selection to graduate training schemes. Assessment centres which are properly developed, applied and validated will improve the effectiveness and credibility of the selection process. They are used not only for the selection of employees, but also for internal promotion decisions, the identification of individual development needs and, somewhat controversially, in redundancy selection.

It is not possible to be prescriptive about how to develop assessment centres because they are tailored to the specific needs of an organisation. The pitfalls are considerable, and those considering developing an assessment centre should seek experienced advice and assistance, but it is possible to outline a design process, to identify a range of selection techniques and to draw attention to some key issues.

Assessment centre design will include job and competency analysis, choosing and combining assessment techniques, assembling an integrated programme, choosing and training assessors, selecting and preparing candidates and post-event review. Proper job analysis is necessary to identify the principal competencies and characteristics required for successful job performance. The outputs of the job analysis are job descriptions (or accountability profiles) and person specifications which provide the criteria for assessment centre design and the choice of assessment techniques. Assessment techniques need to be chosen to reflect the competencies and characteristics identified. Assessment centres are useful in penetrating behaviours relating to interpersonal relationships, leadership, influencing ability, sociability, competitiveness, self-motivation, tolerance, persuasiveness, problem analysis and decisiveness, *inter alia*. In addition to the collection of behavioural information it is possible and practical to make assessments of skill and gather biographical data. The key issue is to be clear about what is being assessed and to exercise informed judgement about the choice of assessment techniques.

The range of techniques is wide and they can either be purchased from reputable suppliers or designed by the organisation. They include:

- group discussions
- group activities – with leaders or leaderless
- presentations
- in-tray exercises and analytical activities
- role plays
- work simulations
- interviews – individual and/or group
- personality questionnaires
- other forms of psychometric assessment.

The assessment techniques need to be used in appropriate combinations, and there should be a specific focus on analysing the extent to which they are complementary or in conflict, and whether they are scheduled at suitable times within the assessment centre programme. Assessment centres lasting one day are typical and a duration of two or three days is not uncommon. A typical assessment centre may assess eight to twelve candidates.

The assessment process needs to be structured to enable the identification of candidate behaviours and performance. This involves the development and provision of assessment criteria for the assessors and the design of forms which can be used to capture information accurately on individual candidates, and which also provide a means of summarising each activity to contribute to the overall judgement. There is research evidence which questions whether it is necessary to assess candidates at a detailed level. The alternative to seeking summative information under a range of competence or behaviour dimensions is to require assessors to make an overall judgement. Clearly this is less complex for the assessor and more intuitive, but it acts against the provision of detailed information for participants and makes it more difficult to justify decisions. Assessors need to be appointed and trained and require skills in the observation, recording and evaluation of behaviour and performance. The application of these skills can be focused by:

- the clear definition of the objectives of the assessment centre
- a specification of the assessment criteria
- active assessor participation in, and reflection upon, the assessment activities prior to the assessment centre.

The ratio of assessors to candidates is typically 1:2, demonstrating the labour-intensive nature of this selection method. A useful by-product of assessor training can be the development and transfer of appraising skills back to the workplace, together with a sharpened awareness of behaviour and its relationship to performance. There are clearly some ethical issues about the treatment of the candidates and these are briefly introduced in Exhibit 7.6.

The assessment centre arrangements are an important feature and although, like Herzberg's hygiene factors (1959), they may not improve candidate assessment, unsatisfactory arrangements will significantly inhibit the quality of assessment. Equal time and attention therefore need to be given to the factors of location, date, travel, coordination of material, administrative support, refreshments and accommodation.

Exhibit 7.6 Ethics and assessment centres

- Candidates are entitled to know what to expect in order to exercise their right to withdraw.
- Unreasonable surprises should be avoided, although assessor intervention in some activities may be positive and appropriate.
- Observation of behaviour at informal times, for example over dinner or in the bar, is questionable practice.
- The assessment centre should not be designed as a tortuous event or incorporate features of physiological or psychological deprivation, for example by depriving candidates of sleep through requiring all-night preparation for a presentation.
- Sensitivity, professionalism and care should be exercised in giving feedback on behaviour or performance.
- Facilitators of activities should be skilled, to reduce the probability of causing psychological 'damage' to the participants.

A post-event review of the assessment centre is necessary to validate the process, to check for racial, sex, disability or other bias, as a reflective activity in order to improve future events, to identify any assessor development needs, and to conduct a cost–benefit analysis. There is value in piloting or having a trial run of a new assessment centre. Assessment centres, because they are capable of combining selection methods in a structured way, represent a powerful diagnostic device. Their predictive validity is comparatively high, but there is a positive correlation between investment costs and benefits achieved.

> Assessment centres have been shown to be the most comprehensive and predictive assessment device. And so they are – when they conform to certain principles. Unfortunately, this does not mean that sundry exercises cobbled together and called an assessment centre will automatically confer on the user the same level of effectiveness.
>
> (Fletcher and Anderson, 1998)

Biodata

Biodata is shorthand for biographical data and involves the collection and analysis of detailed personal information about candidates for employment or promotion. This personal information may include, for example, job stability, family circumstances and relationships, interests, non-academic educational experiences, attitudes, accomplishments and disappointments. The use of biodata is predicated on two beliefs: first, that prior experiences and circumstances shape distinctive behaviour patterns, and therefore abilities; and second, that accessing the experiences and circumstances of the individual enables the prediction of future behaviour and consequent job performance. A considerable amount of biographical data is already available to organisations. It exists in letters of application, CVs and application forms and is gathered at interview, but its collection, analysis and use in decision making is normally *ad hoc* and arbitrary. The biodata approach is an opportunity to systematise and add method.

The biodata process typically involves the following steps.

1 For a particular type of work, identify employees who are effective performers (EPs) and less effective performers (LEPs).

2 Generate a pool of general biodata items through job analysis, the interrogation of job-holders and accessing published inventories.

3 Apply the pool of biodata items to the EPs and LEPs through interviews, questionnaires, appraisal records and application forms to establish correlations between biodata and performance.

4 Eliminate biodata items that do not discriminate between EPs and LEPs or because they attract socially acceptable 'right answers' or because they offend sensitivities.

5 Pilot the refined biodata items and use the information generated to seek commonality amongst EPs and contrast with LEPs. Weight each biodata item to reflect the power of the correlation with performance.

6 Systematically rate applicants against the weighted biodata items.

The design, development and use of a systematic biodata system is resource intensive. It is also organisation and job specific and to be feasible probably requires a design sample size of several hundred and a large applicant pool. Criterion or item decay means that it will need regular updating. Using biodata as the only means of selection is inappropriate; it should be limited to establishing a *prima facie* case that an applicant should proceed to the next stage of the selection process. A biodata system is not readily transferable to other jobs or organisations, which may be indicative of a lack of theoretical underpinning. It therefore has low construct validity and why it works is more mysterious than substantiated. Biodata may also have low face validity, particularly if questions do not appear to have a direct connection with the job. The argument in favour of biodata is that it has relatively high predictive validity, at a similar level to personality questionnaires and assessment centres (Gunter, Furnham and Drakely, 1993). Investment in biodata development is likely to be more worthwhile where the cost of training or the cost of employee failure is high. Systematic biodata in the UK is probably used by less than 10 per cent of employing organisations. Use by recruitment consultants may be higher, in the range 12–16 per cent, although the research which produced these figures 'seemed to doubt whether they (recruitment consultants) understood the term (biodata) as . . . intended' (Sisson, 1994).

The major charge levelled at biodata is that it is at odds with best practice in equal opportunities. The collection and use of data which relates to marital status, family circumstances, gender, ethnic origin and so on, not only has considerable potential to perpetuate stereotypical job assumptions, but will probably fall foul of unfair discrimination legislation, the Data Protection Act and the Human Rights Act, and conflict with diversity objectives. The absence of a theoretical underpinning makes it problematic to demonstrate that biodata methods are free from bias, and in the USA 'a number of questions fall into the Equal Employment Opportunities Commission's suspect group' (Sisson, 1994); the same may apply in the UK. For example, the Equal Opportunities Commission advises against including questions on types of school as there is potential to exclude candidates from ethnic minorities. Biodata can be accused of being personality assessment in disguise – '(biodata is) nothing more than ill defined personality tests' (Smith, Gregg and Andrews, 1989) – and there may be better, cheaper and more ethical ways of assessing personality characteristics in the selection process. A final biodata criticism is its potentially intrusive nature through the active penetration of intimate personality information – should the right of an employing organisation be ethically circumscribed in this respect? Examples of biodata use include salespersons, financial officials, officer cadets for the merchant navy and, interestingly, students applying for accounting degrees in the USA.

Graphology

Graphology consists of the analysis of handwriting features such as size, slope, space, connection and pressure in order to generate a graphological profile. The profile is used to infer personality, cognitive and social characteristics in order to contribute to a judgement about job suitability. The use of graphology for selection decisions in Britain is estimated to be very low indeed, but it is much more popular in continental European countries, particularly France and Switzerland where a significant number of organisations use it (Fowler, 1991). Advocates of graphology argue that it is relatively cheap and easy to use and provides a vehicle for the projection of personal characteristics and the garnering of insights into the applicant. These insights can focus subsequent discussions and thereby make a useful contribution as an additional, but not as a standalone, selection technique.

The absence of empirical research data to underpin the credibility or validity of graphology makes it difficult to create a supportive case for it as a useful predictor of job performance, and there remains considerable scepticism:

> In many respects . . . graphology raises similar issues to those associated with biodata, in terms of an intuitive appeal mixed with an all too easy potential for confirming social stereotypes and superficial judgements . . . the potential dangers are probably greater (than biodata) as the mysteries of interpretation tend to be more esoteric and less directly derived from work place experience.
>
> (Goss, 1994: 51)

The CIPD remains unconvinced about the efficacy of graphology: 'On the evidence to date the CIPD concludes that graphology does not provide a sufficient basis on which to make important (employment) decisions' (CIPD Quick facts – Graphology, 2001). The low predictive validity of graphology may not be attributable to an inability of the technique to measure personality, but may indicate that personality characteristics themselves are actually poor indicators of performance. Fowler's slightly more encouraging view is that 'there is positive evidence to justify more intensive and better planned research' (1991: 43).

COMPETENCE-BASED RECRUITMENT AND SELECTION

The use of competencies in recruitment and selection is introduced briefly because it has the potential to sharpen the focus upon the abilities which are necessary to perform a job successfully, rather than on factors like age, educational qualifications and traditional job types. The rationale for the use of competencies in recruitment and selection is predicated on the following.

- Changes in the workforce profile can be accommodated through seeking opportunities to recruit from a wider range of sources.
- They are compatible with equality of opportunity objectives by challenging stereotypical assumptions through the recognition that competencies may have been acquired in a variety of work and non-work roles.
- Competencies are used in performance appraisal, in reward and in training and there is a logic in extending their use to include recruitment and selection.
- There are potential links with national vocational qualifications.
- The use of competencies in recruitment and selection will give a very realistic job preview.

Competence-based recruitment and selection involves first, the definition of competencies and performance criteria, and second, the design of recruitment and selection methods which enable the recognition of candidate competence. Experience of traditional approaches to recruitment and selection can inhibit the development of competence based methods (*see also* Corbridge and Pilbeam in Adam-Smith and Peacock, 1994; Farnham and Stevens, 2000).

SUCCESSFUL TRANSITION THROUGH PRE-ENGAGEMENT AND INDUCTION

Transition, from applicant to employee, is the fourth sub-system in the recruitment and selection process and the beginning of successful retention. **Transition** warrants equal attention to **attraction, reduction** and **selection**. Transition begins when contact is established between employer and applicant and is shaped by the recruitment and selection system and also by the behaviour of the participants. The employer–employee relationship begins to be formalised through job offer and acceptance and through pre-engagement communication. The contract of employment is enacted through the employee being ready, willing and able to work on the agreed date and the employer having work and wages available. The psychological contract, consisting of the pre-conceptions and expectations created during recruitment and selection, is realised or not realised when the employee starts work. Proper induction is important in contributing to the successful transition from applicant to employee.

The pre-engagement process

An offer of employment should normally be in writing and include the main features of employment, for example job, hours, start date, pay and benefits and so on. The offer letter should specify any conditions to which the offer is subject and state a method and a timescale for candidate acceptance or rejection. The pre-engagement process is also important in providing necessary information to both parties and can usefully be viewed as a communication activity which develops the employment relationship. Pre-engagement checklists can be prepared to collect and provide information necessary to integrate the candidate as an employee. A health check may be a part of the pre-engagement process; this may consist of the completion of a medical questionnaire or a consultation with a general practitioner appointed by the employer or through seeking to access medical records held by the employee's medical practitioner. The requirements of the Access to Medical Records Act 1988 need to be observed and employee consent is required prior to the application for medical information. Any medical require-ments should relate specifically to the demands of the particular job being offered and should be compatible with employer obligations under legislation relating to equality of employment opportunity, including any reasonable adjustments expected under the Disability Discrimination Act 1995 and the Human Rights Act 1998 (*see* Chapter 8).

The dialogue developed up to the selection decision needs to be actively continued during the period between offer and employment, as the potential employee remains empowered to deselect the employer. Information expected or required by the new employee should be considered, together with the best way of communicating it. This information can be discovered by reflecting on several empathetic questions.

- What would I like to know if I was coming to work here?
- Are there particular characteristics of the job or organisation that ought to be communicated?
- Does the employee know where to come on the first day, what to bring, what to wear and what to expect?

Induction

Induction is best viewed holistically. Induction is activated during the pre-engagement process and is not complete until the employer and the employee are reasonably satisfied with the employment relationship. This view of induction distances it from the common misconception that it consists of a first-day induction course with a programme of 'information overload'. This holistic approach recognises that the transition from candidate to employee may commence several months prior to starting work and continue for 12 or even 24 months into employment. An event known as an induction crisis frequently occurs during employee transition. The induction crisis occurs when an employee questions and then reasserts or rejects the initial decision to accept the employment. The reassertion of the decision is achieved through a reconciliation of any doubts, and the rejection of the initial decision will typically result in the employee seeking alternative employment. The induction crisis is often triggered by a relatively small incident, but will result in consideration being given by the employee to an accumulation of concerns. The message for the manager seeking successful transition is to be alert to this potential for an induction crisis and to respond to it in an empathetic and conflict-resolving manner.

It is not practical to prescribe an induction programme or package, but it is possible to identify the potential elements as a basis for formal and informal managerial interventions. Induction is a multi-faceted and continuous activity and the elements include:

- the provision of organisational information, including sources of rules and regulations
- the provision of job and department information
- the communication of organisational values and beliefs
- the encouragement of effective organisational relationships
- the provision of opportunities for concern resolution
- the analysis of training needs and the consideration of short-, medium- and long-term development responses
- the formal and informal review of performance
- access to a mentoring system.

Induction demands compete with operational demands and there is considerable scope for employers to revisit pre-engagement and induction arrangements, as time and effort invested in sound recruitment and selection practices can be squandered by poor transition.

THE CONTRACT OF EMPLOYMENT AND THE WRITTEN PARTICULARS OF EMPLOYMENT

The Employment Rights Act, 1996, provides for employees to receive a written statement of the main terms and conditions of employment, but it is essential to recognise that this constitutes only one element of the contract of employment.

Other constituent elements of the contract are, typically, common law duties and obligations, statutory rights, expressed terms, implied terms, collective agreements, custom and practice, *inter alia* (Farnham and Pimlott, 1995; Selwyn, 1993). The written statement of particulars has no direct legal force. It is only a written record of what the employer believes to be the main terms and conditions of employment, although it can be used as evidence by an Employment Tribunal in deciding upon contractual terms. The recruitment and selection process may also generate terms which can be implied or incorporated into the contract; examples include job advertisements, the recruitment pack, the job description, the person specification, agreements entered into at interview, and letters of offer and acceptance. It is therefore important to seek accuracy, consistency and good faith in recruitment and selection because of the potential implications for the contract. The Data Protection Act, 1998, gives employees access to their records whether manual or computerised, including information and interview notes retained from the recruitment and selection process.

Employees have to be given a written statement of the particulars of employment within two months of starting work (Employment Rights Act, 1996), if they are employed for over eight hours a week and for a period of more than one month. It is good practice to issue a written statement to all employees as soon as practicable after starting work, as it is a basis for resolving any contractual misunderstandings or disagreements. Core employment information should be given in a single written statement, termed the 'principal statement'. The information to be given is detailed in Exhibit 7.7. Within the statement reference can be made to other sources of information such as organisational rules or policies on, for example, sickness, pensions or discipline. Reference can also be made to procedural agreements and general reference material incorporated into an employee handbook.

Changes to written particulars must be notified to employees individually and in writing, as early as possible and at the latest within one month of the change. The written notification can refer the employee to updated reference documents, collective agreements or the employee handbook. Prior to working overseas for more than one month an employee must be given additional written particulars relating to the length of the posting, the currency for payment, any additional benefits and the terms and conditions of employment on return to the UK.

Exhibit 7.7   The written particulars required by law

The written particulars required by law include:

- names of the employer and employee
- the date the employment started
- the date when continuous employment began
- place of work, or the required places of work, and the employer's address
- where the employment is not intended to be permanent, the expected length, or the end date if fixed term
- the particulars of collective agreements directly affecting individual terms and conditions
- rate of pay, method of calculation and payment interval
- hours of work and normal working hours
- holiday entitlement and holiday pay
- arrangements for sickness and sick pay
- pension arrangements
- length of notice periods, on both sides
- job title or brief description of the job
- disciplinary and grievance – rules, arrangements and procedures.

EXIT INTERVIEWS – THE INITIAL STAGE OF THE RECRUITMENT AND SELECTION PROCESS?

This may seem a strange place to introduce exit interviews. Exit interviews are an important aspect of employee release, but they can also generate useful information and be revealing about the nature of the job and the desirability of the terms and conditions from the perspective of the employee. It can be argued, therefore, that *the exit interview can be the initial stage in the recruitment and selection process.*

An exit interview is an information gathering exercise that attempts to excavate the reasons why an employee is leaving the organisation with a view to preventing or reducing dysfunctional attrition. It should normally be conducted at some point between the employee resigning and the employee's last day of work, although some organisations attempt to collect information retrospectively. There are two perspectives on how the information collected might be useful. First, in the case of a valued employee it may enable the employer to prevent the employee leaving. This may at its simplest be the removal of a barrier to continued employment, for example a minor adjustment to working hours, the provision of a particular type of training or reassurance about opportunities for advancement. In these cases it would clearly have been preferable if the line manager had detected employee concerns earlier. Where the reason for leaving is better financial rewards, the employer may be able to match what the departing employee is being offered, but this has implications in terms of the potential impact on the reward perceptions of other employees and also the integrity of the employer's financial rewards strategies and practices. Making an increased offer also impacts on the balance of the psychological contract by implicitly bestowing more power on the employee, and the employer would have to live with the consequences of this. An alternative employer philosophy is to recognise that once an employee has reached the decision to leave, and communicated formally that they wish to end the contract, the cause is a lost one and the best the employer can hope for is a professional parting of the ways that maintains the dignity of the employer and the employee. The second, and perhaps more realistic perspective on exit interviews is the collection and analysis of why employees leave in general. The information collected in this way can be used to evaluate HR practices such as financial and non-financial rewards, training and development opportunities, advancement and career prospects, style of supervision and performance management, job design and degree of empowerment, socialisation opportunities and team working. The exit interview information then becomes part of the process of refining HR strategy, particularly in relation to the retention of talented employees.

The practical issues relating to exit interviews are who should do them and what questions should be asked. There is a strong argument for exit interviews being done by the line manager who is closest to the employee and to the nature of the work. It is interesting to note that some studies indicate that employees leave managers and not organisations, and the underlying causes of attrition may therefore be in managerial behaviour rather than the organisation's HR practices. The line manager would therefore need to be objective and detached about the information being collected. However, even this may not reassure the employee who may be unwilling to confront the line manager with information that the line manager may find unpalatable – after all, what is in it for the employee (apart perhaps from revenge) who is moving on to pastures new? The employee may also harbour fears about critical comments at the exit interview having a negative impact on the reference being provided to the new, or subsequent, employers. This interface of employee and employer perspectives raises an important issue and that is the potential difference between 'a reason for leaving' and 'the result of a reason for leaving'. Although these two concepts can be synonymous, this is not necessarily the case. For example, the result of a reason for leaving might be that the departing employee has secured a job with a higher rate of pay, but the real reason for leaving might be dissatisfaction with the style of supervision. It is the latter that has prompted the employee to seek alternative employment, but the employee will only resign once they have obtained a job which offers not only an escape from the supervisory style, but also the prospect of increased financial rewards. In this scenario it would be quite natural for the employee to propose that the increased financial rewards are the reason for leaving and for the line manager to accept this, leaving the real reason for leaving submerged. There is also the potential for an embittered employee to exaggerate scenarios or make unfounded accusations. The aim of the employer is therefore to excavate the underlying reasons for leaving rather than the *prima facie* reasons. For this reason, some organisations prefer the exit interview data to be collected by HR specialists. There may also be advantages in terms of consistency in the exit interview activity, but conversely it may cast the HR specialist in the role of 'big brother'.

Exit interviews require particular skills. These include providing a non-threatening environment, establishing rapport and the professional use of probing questions. Kransdorff (1995) observes that:

> While an exit interview appears little more than a conversation between two people, its effective utility necessitates it being professionally researched, scripted and edited to ensure its content, clarity, continuity an readability. Alongside the employment of professional oral research techniques, this requires the skills of an expert interviewer with a keen understanding of management issues, human resource management and corporate culture.

It is essential to create a climate where departing employees can feel relaxed about providing information on their reasons for leaving. The aim of the employer is to collect genuine information in a potentially rich arena for spurious data; for example, an employee may inflate the financial rewards being offered by their new employer in order to maintain face and overtly rationalise their reason for leaving. Not only is successful exit interviewing about providing the right environment, it is also about asking the right questions. As Kransdorff (1995) puts it, 'an exiting individual is a teeming repository of all the experiences over his/her period of tenure'. Baumruk (1999) recommends addressing seven key issues at exit interviews:

1 Compensation: Was the employee fairly paid? Were the benefits satisfactory? Was she/he recognised for the work he did?

2 Quality of the workplace: Is it safe and secure? Is there a realistic work/life balance?

3 Relationships: Were there problems with managers, co-workers or customers?

4 Opportunities: Were there opportunities for advancement, training and career development?

5 Culture: How well did the employee fit in? Was the work environment too conservative or too radical?

6 Job description: Does it fit the position? Could it be modified?

7 Leadership: Were there doubts about the company's goals or direction?

Exhibit 7.8 provides an example of a pro-forma for an exit interview.

There are two key issues with which to finish this section. First, strenuous efforts to collect genuine data will be fruitless unless something is done with the data. It therefore needs to be analysed, disseminated, discussed and actioned. This leads to the second issue, which is that appropriate degrees of confidentiality will need to be maintained. As Pont and Pont (1998) put it, 'once the information has been collated, it may be necessary to make further enquiries elsewhere, which then raises the issue of confidentiality – a factor which may contribute to the success, or not, of receiving candid answers from the leaver'. It is in reconciling this potential tension between employer action and confidentiality that exit interview information can be used by the organisation to gain valuable insights into how HR practices are perceived and as a consequence potentially critical problems can be identified and addressed.

Exhibit 7.8   An example of an exit interview pro-forma

The individual

Name
Department
Position
Job title
Length of service

The job

Best aspects
Worst aspects
Satisfaction with the type of work
Adequacy of training
Provision of equipment
Working conditions
Levels of responsibilities
Workload
Promotion opportunities

Rewards and benefits

Pay
Benefits
Recognition
Hours of work
Other contractual terms

Reasons for leaving

What prompted the employee to consider leaving?
Could anything have been done to retain the employee?
Was internal redeployment offered?

Work environment

Appropriateness of supervision
Relationships with colleagues
Inter-departmental relationships
Morale
Communication
HR policies and procedures
Would the employee consider returning?
Overall comments on company

Interviewer's observations and points for further action

SUMMARY LEARNING POINTS

1 Mutual trust and mutual respect in the recruitment and selection process are desirable aims for the employer and the potential employee.

2 The **reduction** sub-system consists of filtering out and rejecting unsuitable candidates on the basis of predetermined job criteria. In this way the pool of applicants is fairly and systematically reduced to a manageable number.

3 Candidates are empowered to deselect the employer at any stage of the recruitment and selection process, and process design should take account of this factor.

4 Validity, reliability and popularity are important concepts in understanding the potential, the limitations and the use of the various selection methods.

5 A range of **selection** methods is available and a critical perspective is essential to the exercise of informed choice in deciding which methods to use.

6 The **transition** from applicant to employee is a vital element of the recruitment and selection process and is the beginning of successful retention. Effective transition consists of giving proper weight of attention to the pre-engagement process, to holistic induction and to the legal, economic and psychological contracts of employment.

7 An exit interview can be considered the *initial* stage of recruitment and selection activity, because it is potentially revealing about the nature of the job and the desirability of the terms and conditions from the perspective of the employee. Exit interviews can generate useful information on a range of HR practices, but obtaining good quality data from departing employees is a challenging activity.

REFERENCES AND FURTHER READING

Adam-Smith, D. and Peacock, A.. (eds) (1994) *Cases in Organisational Behaviour: Case 22.* London: Pitman Publishing.

Advisory, Conciliation and Arbitration Service (2000) *Employing People: Advisory Booklet* (periodically revised).

Aikin, O. (1996) 'Be prepared for a data remember', *People Management*, May, 38–40.

Anderson, N. and Shackleton, V. (1993) *Successful Selection Interviewing.* Oxford: Blackwell.

Anderson, N. and Shackleton, V. (1994) 'Informed choices', *Personnel Today*, November, 33–4.

Arnold, J., Cooper, C. and Robertson, I. (1998) *Work Psychology: Understanding human behaviour in the workplace*, 3rd edition. London: Pitman Publishing.

Baker, B. and Cooper, J. (2000) 'Occupational testing and psychometric instruments: an ethical perspective', in Winstanley, D. and Woodall, J. (eds) *Ethical Issues in Contemporary HRM.* Basingstoke: Macmillan Business.

Barclay, J. (1999) 'Employee selection: a question of structure', *Personnel Review*, 28(1/2), 134–51.

Baumruk, R. (1999) 'Questions for exiting employees', *Training*, 36(10), 28.

Blinkhorn, S. and Johnson, C. (1991) 'Personality tests: the great debate', *Personnel Management*, September, 38–43.

Brotherton, P. (1996) 'Exit interviews can provide a reality check', *HR Magazine*, Spring, 45–50.

Buckley, M., Norris, A. and Wiese, D. (2000) 'A brief history of the selection interview: may the next 100 years be more fruitful', *Journal of Management History*, 6(3), 113–26.

CIPD (2000) *Recruitment Survey*. London: CIPD.

CIPD (2001) *Quick Facts: Assessment Centres. Quick Facts: Graphology. Quick Facts: Induction. Quick Facts: Psychological Testing*. London: CIPD.

Conway, J., Jako, R. and Goodman, D. (1995) 'A meta-analysis of inter-rater internal consistency and reliability of selection interviews', *Journal of Applied Psychology*, 80(5), 565–79.

Courtis, J. (1995) 'When it's incompetent not to discriminate', *People Management*, May, 23.

Farnham, D. and Pimlott, J. (1995) *Understanding Industrial Relations*. London: Cassell. Chapter 9.

Farnham, D. and Stevens, A. (2000) 'Developing and implementing competence-based recruitment and selection in a social services department', *International Journal of Public Sector Management*, 13(4), 369–82.

Fletcher, C. (1992) 'Ethics and the job interview', *Personnel Management*, March, 36–9.

Fletcher, C. (1993) 'Testing time for the world of psychometrics', *Personnel Management*, December, 46–50.

Fletcher, C. (1998) 'A deciding factor', *People Management*, 26 November, 38–40.

Fletcher, C. and Anderson, N. (1998) 'A superficial assessment', *People Management*, 14 May, 44–6.

Fowler, A. (1991) 'An even handed approach to graphology', *Personnel Management*, March, 40–2.

Fowler, A. (1996) 'How to: use games and choose winners', *People Management*, June, 42–3.

Fowler, A. (1997) 'How to select and use psychometric tests', *People Management*, 25 September, 45–6.

Fowler, A. (1998) 'Role rehearsal', *People Management*, 11 June, 52–5.

Goss, D. (1994) *Principles of HRM*. London: Routledge.

Gunter, B., Furnham, A. and Drakely, R. (1993) *Biodata: Biographical indicators of business performance*. London: Routledge.

Hackney, M. and Kleiner, B. (1994) 'Conducting an effective selection interview', *Work Study*, 43(2), 8–13.

Herzberg, F. (1959) *The Motivation to Work*. New York: John Wiley.

IPD Code on Psychological Testing (1995). London: IPD.

Kransdorff, A. (1995) 'Exit interviews as an induction tool', *Management Development Review*, 8(2), 37–40.

Leighton, P. (2000) 'Don't ask don't tell', *People Management*, 8 May, 42–4.

Lord, W. (1994) 'The evolution of a revolution', *Personnel Management*, February, 65.

McHenry, R. (1997) 'Tried and tested', *People Management*, January, 32–7.

Pickard, J. (1996) 'The wrong turns to avoid with tests', *People Management*, August, 20–5.

Pont, T. and Pont, G. (1998) *Interviewing Skills for Managers*. London: Piatkus.

Selwyn, N. (1993) *Selwyn's Law of Employment*. London: Butterworths.

Shackleton, V.J. and Newell, S. (1991) 'Management selection: a comparative survey of methods used in top British and French companies', *Journal of Occupational Psychology*, 64, 23–36.

Sisson, K. (1994) *Personnel Management*. Oxford: Blackwell.

Smith, M. (1994) 'A theory of the validity of predictors in selection', *Journal of Occupational and Organisational Psychology*, 67, 13–31.

Smith, M., Gregg, M. and Andrews, D. (1989) *Selection and Assessment*. London: Pitman Publishing.

Smith, M. and Robertson, I.T. (1993) *The Theory and Practice of Systematic Staff Selection*. Basingstoke: Macmillan.

Stairs, M., Kandola, B. and Sandford-Smith, R. (2000) 'Slim picking', *People Management*, 28 December, 28–30.

Sternberg, R. (1998) 'Survival of the fit test', *People Management*, 10 December, 29–33.

Welch, J. (1996) 'Recruiters face up to the moral imperative', *People Management*, June, 16.

Wood, R. and Baron, H. (1992) 'Psychological testing free from prejudice', *Personnel Management*, April, 34–9.

ASSIGNMENTS AND DISCUSSION TOPICS

1 Argue the case for and against the removal of personal information, such as age, gender, ethnic origin and family or marital circumstances, prior to the screening and shortlisting of applicants for employment.

2 Consider the extent to which your organisation validates the selection methods used and make recommendations on improving the validation process.

3 Assemble and critically evaluate application forms for similar jobs from three organisations. Consider them in terms of the three issues raised in this chapter – duality of purpose, ease or difficulty of completion, and standard or flexible design.

4 Discuss the advantages and disadvantages of seeking references either before shortlisting or before the interview or after the offer of employment.

5 Identify and discuss ethical considerations which are applicable to:

(a) the selection interview

(b) the use of psychometric assessment for selection purposes.

6 Consider the extended application form statements illustrated in Exhibit 7.4. Consider jobs in your organisation and comment on the extent to which this type of approach could be used in the application form. Give examples of specific questions for a particular job.

7 Critically evaluate the components of the recruitment and selection system in your organisation with reference to Exhibit 6.1 and either justify their use or make recommendations for improvement.

8 Design, develop and pilot a work sampling selection technique for a job of your choice.

9 The selection interview is generally acknowledged to be a relatively poor predictor of employee performance. Why is this and why do organisations continue to use the interview as a selection method? How can interviews be made more effective in practice?

10 Here are examples of statements used in food retailing to test the suitability of applicants for employment as retail assistants. The work involves serving customers and replenishing stock, and employees are expected to be flexible about the areas in which they work and the hours that they do. Applicants are required to respond to each statement with a yes or a no.

  1 I find it easy to change from one routine to another.
  2 People say I am a very sociable person.
  3 I do not enjoy lots of detail in my work.
  4 People say I am organised.
  5 When I join a company, I like to stay for quite a few years.
  6 I sometimes find it hard to cope with new things.
  7 People say I have quite a temper.
  8 I give myself plenty of time to get to work, so there's never any chance of being late.
  9 Untidy rooms bother me.
10 I would rather do the same things in a job than swap around.
11 If the money is good, I would take just about any job.
12 When I am with bosses, I don't mind saying how I feel about something.
13 Sometimes I find it hard to keep smiling.
14 When I start something I always see it through to the end.
15 People have sometimes said I live in a world of my own.
16 I spend a lot of time going out with friends.
17 I enjoy work for its own sake, not just for the wages.
18 Quite often I leave things unfinished and move onto something else.
19 People have told me I'm thorough in my work.
20 I would prefer to work the same hours every day.

What qualities are being assessed and how legitimate and effective is the test? Critically evaluate this battery of test questions using the dimensions of face validity, construct validity, concurrent validity, predictive validity, reliability, the motivation to give the right answers and methods of assessing the results.

11 Review the pre-engagement process through brainstorming first, information which needs to be collected from employees and, second, information which needs to be given to prospective employees. How should this be communicated?

12 Consider the elements of induction outlined in this chapter. To what extent are they present in your organisation? How can your induction processes be improved?

13 Discuss why the transition from candidate to employee is frequently given insufficient attention.

14 Who should conduct exit interviews, what questions should be asked and what should be done with the information collected?

CHAPTER 8

Equality of opportunity

INTRODUCTION

Equality of opportunity needs to be considered by every organisation in order to achieve effective people resourcing. The reason for this assertion is not because it is a good thing to do, nor because it is a legal requirement, but because effective resourcing depends on getting the right people into the organisation whatever their race, colour, sex, marital status, age or disability. It is commonly declared that people are 'the major asset' in any organisation and that the need to employ 'the best' is the objective of good and successful employers. However, it is what happens in practice which determines whether this rhetoric is turned into reality.

CHAPTER OBJECTIVES

- To introduce the main UK legislation relating to equality of opportunity and employment.
- To advise on the development and implementation of equal opportunity policies.
- To present the business case for equality of opportunity.
- To expose differences between an equal opportunities approach and a managing diversity philosophy.
- To explore the nature and potential impact of harassment and bullying at work.
- To outline equal pay legislation and practice.

DEFINING EQUALITY OF OPPORTUNITY

It is insufficient to put equal opportunities policies in place and assume that attitudinal change automatically follows. Organisations need to look at what is meant by equal opportunity and honestly identify first, the reasons for implementing an equal opportunities policy and, second, the outcomes they are seeking. Outcomes may be qualitative, achieving business benefits from the acquisition of the best people for jobs, or quantitative, achieving numerical targets for the representation of previously under-represented groups, or both. Without clear policy aims and objectives, effectiveness is difficult to assess and the policy cannot be properly reviewed.

Equal opportunity means different things to different people and different organisations. Straw (1989) provides a useful model which considers equal opportunities at three levels.

Level 1 – Equal opportunities as equal chance: creating a level playing field.
Level 2 – Equal opportunities as equal access: quotas on shortlists.
Level 3 – Equal opportunities as equal share: equal outcomes.

Straw argues that this is a progressive model and that these three levels define a hierarchy of aims, from the provision of equal chance to all groups, to the ideal of equal share where all groups are represented proportionately at all organisational levels. This model provides an interesting starting point for any organisation seriously considering equal opportunity issues. The objectives and priorities of the equal opportunities policy and approach are determined by the way equal opportunity is defined.

The phrase 'equal opportunity' is extensively used inside and outside organisations and it is valuable to seek a common understanding of the terminology. In examining what is meant by equal opportunity it is useful to explore the concepts of fairness and consistency, because they do not necessarily mean the same thing. Fairness, in the context of equality of opportunity, may mean aiming to treat people with respect, to recognise differing needs and, in order to be fair, to take account of those different needs in the decisions that are made. It may mean that, in practice, different decisions are made in dealing with what on the face of it are similar situations. Conversely, consistency is more about treating everyone the same. Where the consistency concept fails, in relation to equality of opportunity, is that it does not acknowledge differing individual needs. From a managerial perspective there may be comfort in consistency but this may be at the expense of fairness. Bureaucratic organisations, which rely on clear policies and management 'by the book', may be uncomfortable with the exercise of managerial discretion, but in order to operate an equal opportunities policy fairly, managerial discretion needs to be allowed and may need to be positively encouraged.

THE LEGISLATIVE FRAMEWORK

The main thrust of legislation in the UK has been aimed at protecting identified groups against discrimination. Current primary legislation covers sex, marital status, race, ethnic origin, disability and ex-offenders where a conviction is legally spent. In addition, a Code of Practice on Age Diversity in Employment, which was published by the DfEE in 1999 and is not currently underpinned by legislation, aims to help employers by defining good practice in employment. In 2000 the UK and other member states of the European Union adopted the Employment and Race Directives of Article 13 of the EC Treaty. These Directives provide a common framework for protection against unlawful discrimination and harassment. The scope of these Directives extends to access to employment, in both the public and private sectors, self-employment and working conditions as well as vocational guidance and training. In 2001 the Department for Trade and Industry issued a consultative document, 'Towards Equality and Diversity', which outlined government proposals to implement these Directives; the consultative period ended in March 2002. Full implementation of the Directives will involve new legislation covering age, sexual orientation and religion as well as changes to the Race Relations Act and the Disability Discrimination Act. Under the Race Directive 00/43 and Equal Treatment Directive 00/78 there will be additional UK enactment focusing on the 'principle of equal treatment' in the context of race and ethnic origin, sexual orientation and religion or belief by 2003 and disability and age by 2006. Discrimination law is a dynamic area, particularly when considered alongside evolving case law, and the informed practitioner or manager needs to keep abreast of developments.

Definitions of discrimination

It is important to understand what is meant, in law, by the term discrimination. The race and sex legislation identifies unlawful discrimination as direct or indirect. There is rarely an employer defence against an act of direct discrimination, except where a genuine occupational qualification exists, but an employer may seek to objectively justify indirect discrimination. Unlawful discrimination can also occur through victimisation and harassment. Both actual and potential employees have protection in law from unlawful discrimination. The disability discrimination legislation is different in not currently incorporating the notions of direct and indirect discrimination, and the issue is whether the less favourable treatment of a disabled person can be justified because it is relevant to the individual's circumstances and the employer can demonstrate that it is for a 'substantial' reason. Nonetheless, it is useful briefly to address direct and indirect discrimination and also victimisation and harassment.

Direct discrimination occurs when a person is treated less favourably than another on any of the grounds covered by the legislation. It is relatively easy to identify direct discrimination as the action is explicit. An example of direct discrimination would be to specify that only men were to be considered for promotion or to use different selection criteria for male and female promotion candidates.

Indirect discrimination occurs when an apparently neutral provision, criterion or practice is applied which disproportionately affects one of the protected groups, unless that criterion or requirement can be objectively justified. The legislation therefore allows the employer to 'objectively justify' a condition or requirement, even where it is indirectly discriminatory, for a business or other reason not connected with the individual applicant or employee, but a tribunal would have be satisfied that it was a genuine and substantial reason. It is better practice not to apply indirectly discriminatory conditions in the first place. Indicative illustrations of potential indirect discrimination include the specification of a qualifying length of service for eligibility for promotion, requirements which cannot be justified in terms of job content, for example requiring a level of written or spoken English greater than that necessary to do the job effectively, and signalling intent to discriminate by asking questions of one group of applicants such as 'When do you intend to start a family?' or 'How long do you intend staying in this country?'

Victimisation occurs when a person is treated less favourably than another because in relation to relevant equal opportunity legislation that person asserts a statutory right or makes an allegation in good faith or brings proceedings or gives evidence in proceedings.

Harassment, under the 2000 Directives, is defined as behaviour which has the effect of creating an intimidating, hostile, offensive or disturbing environment and is deemed to be discrimination where it is based on any of the grounds covered.

According to the 2001 ACAS Annual Report, discrimination claims brought by individuals to the employment tribunals registered a 21 per cent increase compared to the previous year. The ACAS Chief Executive commented, 'While the number of complaints to tribunals for many types of cases has levelled off recently, there is still a significant rise in discrimination cases passed to ACAS. This is a worrying trend in today's increasingly diverse labour market.' One of the main problems seems to be a lack of knowledge on the part of employers, indicating that there is still much to do in the workplace to inform employers and ensure that fair policies, procedures and practices are implemented.

In summary, primary legislation against discrimination, amended by subsequent enactment, includes:

* Rehabilitation of Offenders Act, 1974
* Sex Discrimination Act, 1975
* Race Relations Act, 1976
* Disability Discrimination Act, 1995.

These founding Acts and their amendments provide the underpinning principles for managerial action, and all decision makers in organisations need to be familiar with the operation of this legislation. In addition to these Acts the following legislation has important considerations for managing people at work:

* Equal Pay Act, 1970 and Equal Value Amendment Regulations, 1983
* Asylum and Immigration Act, 1996
* Human Rights Act, 1998.

It is inappropriate in a text of this type to discuss in detail such comprehensive and complex legislation, but each Act is briefly introduced to highlight the main concerns for managers.

Rehabilitation of Offenders Act (ROA)

The societal acknowledgement that being convicted of a criminal offence, and in particular the serving of a prison sentence, makes it difficult to subsequently secure employment and therefore to be fully rehabilitated gave rise to the ROA. This legislation requires some convictions to be regarded as spent by employers after a prescribed rehabilitation period, determined by the length and type of sentence (Exhibit 8.1).

Exhibit 8.1   ROA 1974 – rehabilitation periods

Conviction	Rehabilitation period	
	age 17 and over	under 17
Imprisonment for over 6 months and less than 30 months	10 years	10 years
Imprisonment for up to and including 6 months	7 years	3.5 years
Conditional discharge or probation	1 year	1 year
Absolute discharge	6 months	6 months
For young offenders:		
Borstal		7 years
Detention for 6–30 months		5 years
Detention for up to 6 months		3 years

Except in special cases, applicants do not have to declare spent convictions on applying for employment. Refusal of employment or dismissal for reason of a spent conviction is unlawful (*see also* Chapter 6 – Criminal Certificates: Police Act, 1997). Some occupations are exempted from this legislation and in these occupations criminal convictions are never considered spent for employment purposes. Jobs exempted from the legislation normally demand exceptional levels of trust or involve working with vulnerable members of the community. Exempted occupations can include the legal profession, accountants, medical professionals, jobs involving the care and control of young people and work in social services.

Sex Discrimination Act (SDA)

The SDA makes it unlawful to discriminate in employment on the basis of sex or marital status, except in the few cases where sex is a genuine occupational qualification (GOQ). This legislation applies to both women and men. Section 7 of the Act defines GOQs:

- the job involves the provision of personal services promoting education and welfare
- the job is in a single-sex establishment
- the job is in a private home and involves close social or physical contact with the employer
- to preserve privacy and decency where people may object to the presence of someone of the opposite sex
- where the employee has to 'live in' and there are no provisions for separate facilities
- in the pursuit of authenticity (for example, in drama productions where someone of a specified sex is essential)
- where the job is one of a pair to be given to a couple
- where the job is carried out outside the UK and the local culture prevents the person being effective in the role.

The SDA set up the Equal Opportunities Commission (EOC) as an independent body with terms of reference that include:

- to promote the equal treatment of women and men at work
- to monitor the operation of the legislation
- to make recommendations to government for improvements to the legislation, including the power to draw up codes of practice.

Anyone alleging discrimination on the grounds of sex or marital status may take his or her case to an Employment Tribunal. The 1975 Act required the person alleging discrimination to prove that discrimination had taken place. This is extremely difficult for individuals to do because frequently they do not have access to relevant information. For example, following an unsuccessful job application an individual applicant may *feel* unlawfully discriminated against either by the interviewer's conduct or by impressions received on visiting the organisation. However, the individual is unlikely to have access to information on the qualifications and experience of the person appointed. If the employer states that the appointed applicant meets the person specification and is more suitable for the position, then it is difficult for the rejected applicant to 'prove' otherwise. This aspect of the legislation had been criticised for some time, and the EOC and CRE recommended a change to the legislation to place the burden of proof on the employer to demonstrate that unlawful discrimination did *not* take place, provided that the claimant first established a *prima facie* case of discrimination. The change of UK government in 1997 led to the adoption of the EU Social Charter and as a consequence the Burden of Proof Directive 97/80 was extended to the UK. Article 4 states that where claimants establish 'facts from which it may be presumed that there has been direct or indirect discrimination, it shall be for the respondent to prove that there has been no breach of the principle of equal treatment'. The burden of proof has now switched to the employer or potential employer, and if an allegation is brought to a tribunal it is for the employer to establish that discrimination has not taken place.

Race Relations Act (RRA)

The RRA has a similar framework to the SDA and makes it unlawful to discriminate unfairly on the grounds of race, colour, nationality or ethnic origin. It is lawful to employ a person from a particular racial or ethnic group when a genuine occupational qualification (GOQ) exists. GOQ examples include:

- for authenticity when a person of a particular ethnic group is essential to a dramatic role or for modelling particular clothes or styles
- workers in ethnic restaurants who are in contact with customers
- the provision of personal or welfare services when these can be provided more effectively by persons from a particular racial group.

The Commission for Racial Equality (CRE) was established by the RRA with terms of reference similar to the EOC – the promotion of equal opportunities for racial minority groups and to monitor the operation of the Act. Like the EOC, the CRE can issue codes of practice setting out 'good employment practice' to promote equality of opportunity.

The Race Relations (Amendment) Act, 2000 is the first enactment following EC Article 13 and relates solely to public authorities. It places on them a general duty to eliminate unlawful racial discrimination, promote equality of opportunity and promote good race relations between persons of different racial groups. The Commission for Racial Equality is to produce a number of sector-specific Codes of Practice to give practical guidance on how organisations should fulfil their general duties. The CRE has powers to ask institutions to demonstrate compliance, and the Code of Practice will be used to assess the extent of the compliance.

Disability Discrimination Act (DDA)

The DDA gives statutory rights and some limited protection against discrimination to people with disabilities. The Act defines disability as:

> A physical or mental impairment which has a substantial and long-term adverse effect on a person's ability to carry out normal day-to-day activities. People who have a disability, and people who have had a disability, are covered by the Act.

This definition covers physical impairment affecting mobility or the senses, such as sight and hearing, and mental impairment, such as learning difficulties and recognised mental illness. A 'substantial effect' may include an inability to see moving traffic clearly, an inability to turn knobs or handles, or difficulties in memory or recall. 'Long-term' effects need to have lasted for 12 months or be likely to last for at least 12 months or longer. 'Day-to-day' activities are normal human activities relating to mobility, dexterity, coordination, lifting and carrying ability, speech, hearing, eyesight and learning and concentration abilities. Severe disfigurements and progressive medical conditions, such as cancer, HIV/AIDS and MS, are also covered by the Act, whilst some genetic dispositions are excluded. It can be seen that the stereotypical assumption of disabled people as being only those in wheelchairs is effectively exploded and a much broader definition of disability has entered employment considerations. It is unlawful to treat disabled persons less favourably because of their disability, unless the differential treatment can be justified. Less favourable treatment is justified only where it is 'relevant to the circumstances of the individual case' and where 'the reason for the treatment is substantial'. Even where an employer considers there to be a relevant and substantial reason for less favourable treatment, it is still necessary to consider whether the reason can be overcome or made less substantial through making reasonable adjustments to premises or to employment arrangements.

The legislation therefore requires employers to make 'reasonable adjustments' to employment arrangements, or to the workplace, to compensate for practical problems faced by a disabled person. Reasonable adjustments are not precisely defined, but include not only physical workplace alterations but also the reallocation of some tasks to enable the disabled person to fulfil the job demands (Exhibit 8.2).

Exhibit 8.2   Illustrations of DDA 'reasonable adjustments'

- Physically alter premises
- Allocate some job duties to another employee
- Redeploy the disabled person to an existing vacancy or to another location
- Amend the working times or other contractual arrangements
- Accept absence from work for treatment or other assistance
- Provide additional training, instruction or supervision
- Provide a reader or interpreter.

Reasonableness is determined by factors such as the ease or difficulty of making the adjustment, the extent to which the adjustment will improve the situation, the cost of the adjustment in relation to the benefit, and the employer's resources. At a minimum an employer needs to be able to demonstrate that options have been seriously considered. Reasonable adjustments can only be made where the employer knows about a disability.

The DDA does not apply to employers who employ fewer than 15 employees or to occupations such as the armed services, police and prison officers, and fire fighters, but they are encouraged to adhere to good practice. From 2004 all businesses irrespective of size will have to comply with the DDA and occupational exemptions are under scrutiny, with changes very likely. The DDA applies to all employment matters including selection, training, pay, promotion and dismissal. The Disability Rights Commission (DRC) was established by the Disability Rights Commission Act 1999 to replace the National Disability Council, which had no powers of enforcement. The powers of the DRC are similar to those of the EOC and CRE. Individual claims for discrimination can be brought to an employment tribunal and there is no limit to compensation, which is assessed in accordance with principles for damages in tort. A disabled person who experiences unfair discrimination should first complain to the employer using the DDA Questions Procedure, which allows a written questioning of the employer to help decide whether or not to bring legal proceedings before an employment tribunal.

The *Labour Force Survey* (Office for National Statistics, 2001) identified that there were over 6.6 million disabled people of working age in Great Britain, nearly one-fifth of the working population, and disabled people are nearly seven times as likely as non-disabled people to be out of work and claiming benefit. The early years of operation of the DDA have highlighted the potential difficulties which employers have faced in relation to implementation, and the CIPD (2000) makes the following recommendations for good practice in the employment of people with disabilities:

- critically review all employment practices and procedures to determine how the provisions of the DDA affect them
- provide appropriate training to employees and contractors to enable them to consider the occurrence and avoidance of unlawful discrimination
- initiate programmes which encourage applications from people with disabilities

- check person specifications to ensure that they are neutral and non-discriminatory
- concentrate on abilities to do the job
- as the Disability Rights Commission would say, 'see the person'.

Monitoring figures from the operation of the DDA, Meager *et al.* (1999) identify that there were more tribunal cases brought under the DDA than under the SDA or RRA in the first year of operation and also that there remains some confusion among employers as to their responsibilities under the Act (Exhibit 8.3).

Exhibit 8.3   DDA monitoring: key findings, 1999

- There were more cases taken under the employment provisions of the DDA in its first year than there were under the employment provisions of the Sex Discrimination Act (SDA) or Race Relations Act (RRA) in their first years.
- In most cases, the DDA claim was identified and initiated by an advisor (e.g. trade union official or advice centre) or representative, rather than the applicant.
- At least half of case study respondents (employers) had prior awareness of the DDA's existence, although not of its detailed contents. This applied in particular to some duties under the Act such as the duty to make reasonable adjustments.
- ACAS played a significant role in the resolution of cases with 41 per cent of cases being settled through ACAS.
- There was concern by employers over how far they were obliged, under the Act, to find out about the (potential) employee's medical condition/disability and by employees over how far they were required to reveal their condition to a (potential) employer.
- Cases were more likely to be won by applicants who were legally represented and those whose disability included sensory disabilities or internal organ problems.

The practical implications of the DDA for people resourcing

All personnel and development policies should be kept under review to ensure that the potential for disability discrimination in employment is recognised and addressed and that procedures comply with the Act. It should be kept in mind that the legal protection for people with disabilities only applies to those who meet the definition of disability as prescribed by the Act. Indicative illustrations of the implications for people resourcing are as follows.

Recruitment and selection procedures – should ensure non-discriminatory practices at the point of entry to the organisation. Job descriptions and person specifications should focus on the essential requirements of the job and not contain discriminatory reference to physical or mental states which exclude applicants. Applicants' 'ability' should be assessed against job criteria, with reasonable adjustments made if necessary. Other actions may include the following.

- Reviewing job advertisements for inclusivity.
- Accepting applications on audiotape.
- Reviewing written tests, particularly where the writing element is not essential to the job.
- Allowing disabled applicants to be accompanied during the selection process.
- Making arrangements to enable disabled applicants to gain physical access to selectors; expensive alterations to premises are not needed 'just in case' an application is received from a person with limited mobility, but the recruitment process should be capable of adjustment so that disabled persons can be interviewed.
- Reference to 'registered disabled persons' should be removed from application forms as this categorisation no longer applies.
- Consideration should be given to the acquisition and assessment of information on the health and ability of applicants, and health screening procedures may need to be extended so that a legitimate and lawful assessment can be made of any candidate's ability to do the job.
- Managers making selection decisions should be trained so that they fully understand the legislation and so that they implement policy and procedural changes.
- The induction process should allow the individual to participate; for example, training sessions involving the visual presentation of information may be inappropriate for the visually impaired.

Ignorance and prejudice are the enemies of equality of opportunity for people with disabilities, and the recruitment and selection process should focus on 'ability' rather than just seeing 'disability' to ensure that all applicants are objectively assessed on merit.

Health and safety – policies and procedures should be scrutinised to ensure that work systems have been addressed. Health and safety legislation requires risk assessment in the workplace to identify, assess and reduce risks. Risks should be reassessed in the context of the needs of a disabled employee and reasonable adjustments made.

Training and development – are important to every employee's participation in work. Disabled people should have access to appropriate training and their individual training needs should be identified through normal appraisal procedures. Denying access to equal treatment in training, because of stereotypical assumptions about the abilities of a disabled employee, is likely to constitute unlawful discrimination.

Reward policy – should be reviewed to ensure that pay decisions and pay progression are transparent, based on objective criteria and not discriminatory.

Discipline, dismissal and performance management procedures – are potentially difficult areas. A disabled employee should be treated in the same way as any other employee when it comes to work performance. However, if a performance shortfall is due to a disability the employer should ensure appropriate adjustments are made and provide sufficient support, training and time for performance to improve. Dismissal of a disabled person for reason of incapability may be fair provided the employer can demonstrate that reasonable adjustments have been made and that the employee has been treated fairly and reasonably in all the circumstances (*see also* Chapter 18).

Grievance procedures – require review to facilitate the expression and resolution of employee grievances and dissatisfactions associated with disability.

Sick absence policy – needs to make reference to the DDA. Particular care is required in taking disciplinary action against an employee because of absence associated with a disability. It may be necessary to discount absences which are attributable to the disability to ensure that the disabled employee is not being treated less fairly than other employees.

Equal opportunity policies – should be reviewed to reflect the requirements of the DDA and adjusted to incorporate all of the legislative requirements.

Asylum and Immigration Act, 1996 (AIA)

The Asylum and Immigration Act, 1996 requires employers, when offering employment, to check that potential employees have the right to work in the UK. The law places the onus on the employer but applies only where there is a contract of employment and not where there is a contract for services. The applicant should be able to produce acceptable evidence, which might include a NI number, a work permit, a letter from the Home Office or other suitable documentation. All applicants should be treated the same and asked for evidence and not just those whom the employer thinks may not have the right to work. Unless the AIA requirements are applied to every applicant, there is the potential for unlawful discrimination because the employer may be making assumptions which have no basis in fact (*see also* Chapter 7).

Human Rights Act 1998 (HRA)

The European Convention on Human Rights was brought into UK legislation in 2000 through the Human Rights Act, 1998 and applies to public bodies. There are implications for employment, and employers need to be mindful of this legislation in the recruitment process and throughout the employment cycle. The HRA gives some protection to individuals in terms of the right to peaceful assembly, the right to respect for privacy and family life and the right to freedom of thought, conscience, religion and expression. Examples of the implications for employment may include dress codes, rights for religious observance, the right to fair disciplinary hearing, the right to collectivise and join a trade union, and the right to reject as unacceptable a long-hours culture which impinges on privacy or family life. Although the HRA only applies directly to public bodies, there is potential for its application to private organisations. UK courts are required to interpret existing UK legislation in terms of its compatibility with the HRA principles. Managers in both public and private sectors will need to track developments in the human rights area.

Code of Practice on Age Diversity in Employment

The Code of Practice on Age Diversity in Employment, launched in 1999, aims to provide guidance on good practice in employment with regard to age and complements the government's proposed Age Equality Commission which will advise on the implementation of the EC Discrimination Directive. The code is a key part of the strategy to raise awareness of age discrimination in employment and to promote the benefits of age diversity. The age profile of the UK is changing. By 2010 around 40 per cent of the workforce will be over 45 years old and the age group 16–24 years will constitute only 17 per cent of the workforce. In order to meet the need for a highly skilled and knowledgeable workforce, it makes no business sense to exclude such a large proportion from consideration on arbitrary criteria such as age. The Code of Practice covers good practice on six aspects of employment practice and gives key advice to employers. The six aspects are:

- recruitment – based on the skills and abilities to do the job
- selection – selected on merit
- promotion – based on ability or potential
- training and development – based on need and encouragement to take advantage of training opportunities
- redundancy – selection based on objective job-related criteria
- retirement – schemes fairly developed and fairly applied.

An evaluation of the impact of the Code of Practice undertaken by NOP for the Department of Work and Pensions in 2001 found that while a voluntary code is useful it has limited effect on its own, and it was expected that the code would lead to legislation. The research findings highlighted that attitudes are quite entrenched on stereotypical lines, with young workers seen as lacking loyalty and commitment, lacking in experience and knowledge and lacking a work ethic; while older workers were seen as having difficulty adapting to new skills, likely to have ill health and be unambitious and focused on job security. These stereotypical attitudes have changed little since the introduction of the Code of Practice. Despite this rather disappointing finding on attitude, the Code of Practice appears to be having a small but positive effect, and the personnel practitioner is well placed to influence approaches to age diversity within the organisation. A concerted effort to comply with the code and to modify the operation of relevant policies will mean that the organisation is in a strong position with regard to compliance with legislation due by 2006.

POSITIVE ACTION

The achievement of equality of opportunity should result in changes in the workforce composition, but the elimination of discrimination in the workplace may not on its own achieve this outcome. Life chances and access to opportunities result in different starting points for people in terms of experience and qualifications. This is recognised by the

SDA and RRA, which allow for positive action (not positive discrimination – which is unlawful in the UK) to be taken in specific circumstances to redress inequality. The Acts state that:

(i) where within the previous 12 months there were no persons of the sex (or race) in question doing that work; or
(ii) the number of persons of that sex (or race) doing that work is comparatively small,

the employer can provide:

(i) access to facilities for training which would help fit such persons for work;
(ii) encouragement to take advantage of opportunities for doing that work.

(S48, SDA and S37, RRA)

The legislation does not allow preference in selection; it is concerned only with enabling more people from under-represented groups to achieve training and experience that fit them for applying for positions.

The most persuasive argument for change in contemporary value-for-money and customer-facing organisations may be the business case for equal opportunities. This requires organisations to stop looking outwards and doing only the minimum to comply with legal requirements, and to start looking inwards to recognise the added-value of a diverse workforce.

EQUAL OPPORTUNITIES POLICIES

The statement 'we are an equal opportunity employer' is extensively used because employers are eager to demonstrate to potential employees, customers and employment tribunals that they have implemented an equal opportunity policy. The EOC, CRE and DRC codes of practice encourage the development and implementation of an equal opportunity policy as a public statement of an intention not to discriminate unfairly. A policy statement is a useful starting point in setting objectives and defining priorities, but the policy will, by itself, achieve nothing; it must be accompanied by a programme of action that converts intention into achievement.

Equal opportunity policy statements

The vast majority of organisations have an equal opportunity policy, and policy statements can range from a half-page statement of intent to a detailed policy of several stages. Each organisation should develop a unique policy which is complementary to other personnel policies, in terms of wording and approach, and reflects particular organisational circumstances and needs. There are a number of steps to be considered in developing policy.

The assignment of organisational responsibility – This is a crucial element because the lack of specific responsibility can become a reason for lack of action. Overall responsibility should be assigned to someone with seniority and with sufficient power to achieve action. Ideally, equal opportunities should be incorporated into employee performance objectives throughout the organisation.

Communication – It is essential that employees and potential employees know and understand the organisation's approach to equality of opportunity. It can be an emotive subject and careful handling and appropriate investment in time and effort in communication reaps rewards.

Consider the framework – Define and justify the scope of the policy, the 'who' and 'what' it will address.

Consultation – Where trade unions are recognised the policy development will be subject to consultation or negotiation. In non-union organisations a joint management and staff working party may provide an appropriate vehicle for policy development. Consultation is a positive opportunity to gain workforce support for the policy as well as for eliciting the views of all those who will be affected.

In the early stages of development and implementation the policy statement should avoid specific targets or numerical objectives, as there is likely to be limited information on which to base precise outcomes and subsequent failure to achieve targets may lead to the policy losing credibility. The early focus should be on audit and review to establish the current organisational position.

Equal opportunity audit

To ensure that a policy gets results the organisation should audit the existing situation to enable suitable equal opportunity objectives and timescales to be agreed. Auditing can be contentious, and if communication and planning have been ineffective the cooperation of staff may not be forthcoming. If the provision of audit data is voluntary, the data will be incomplete and of limited value. If the mandatory provision of data is likely to be unacceptable to employees, the reason should be identified and addressed before an audit is proposed.

It is important to decide in detail the data that is required from the audit in terms of both current employees and recruitment monitoring. The collection and analysis of the data can be a long and tedious process and timing is important, because a lag between the collection of data and the introduction of recruitment monitoring will produce gaps in the data. There is an argument for introducing recruitment and selection monitoring first so that there are no 'new starters' without equal opportunity data. The minimum audit data is sex, marital status, age, ethnic origin and disabilities. Compliance with the Data Protection Act, 1998 is required for the collection, use and storage of this sensitive data. An input or data collection form should be designed, distributed, completed, returned and input into the system (Exhibit 8.4). The initial analysis of data from the audit should identify potential areas for targeting or prioritising. The identification of specific action points enables targets to be set, and regular analysis enables progress to be assessed. Auditing and monitoring are time consuming and, in all but small organisations, unlikely to be achieved without the effective use of an HRIS (*see* Chapter 5).

The prospect of organisational change often brings uncertainty and the expression of concerns; action on equality of opportunity is no exception. An unclear policy, which has been poorly communicated, may be indicated when:

- managers complain that standards are being lowered
- managers complain that they can no longer take decisions, 'everything is illegal or politically incorrect'
- employees complain of 'reverse or positive discrimination' and resent the policy
- people of one particular gender, ethnic minorities and disabled people do not believe in the policy
- people of one particular gender, ethnic minorities and disabled people still do not apply for jobs or for promotion
- tensions between employees from different racial groups or complaints of inequality become major confrontations or end in tribunals
- the policy is mocked or trivialised
- results are not being achieved.

These problems are indicative of a need for more effective communication and training. Ineffective implementation and lack of action leads to the cynicism that these statements suggest.

Exhibit 8.4   Equal opportunity audit form

CONFIDENTIAL – for monitoring purposes only	
Name:	Date of birth:
Address:	Age:
	Ethnic origin (see codes):
	Disability:
Department:	– sensory:
Job Title:	– mental:
Grade:	– physical:
Pay:	Male/Female

Review of personnel policies

An equal opportunity policy should be considered as an umbrella policy that impacts on other personnel policies (Fig. 8.1). The introduction of an equal opportunity policy requires that all other policies are reviewed in the context of the organisation's equal opportunity statements and aspirations.

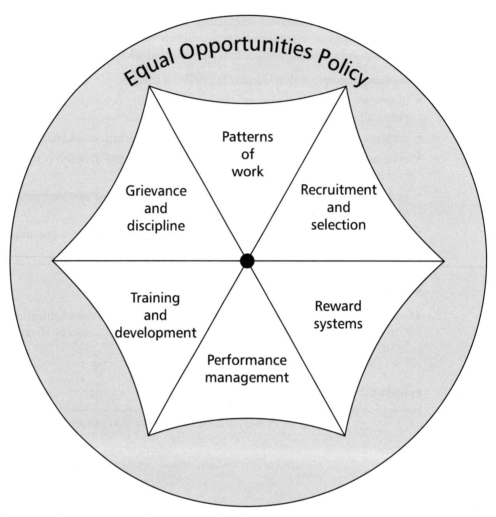

Fig. 8.1 Equal opportunities – an umbrella policy

Patterns of work – The implementation of an equal opportunity policy is a catalyst for reviewing the way that work is organised. Questions to be addressed include:

- Can there be more flexibility to meet the diverse needs of staff and the organisation?
- Are working hours and work patterns consistent with the policy statement?
- Have alternatives such as part-time, flexi-time or job-share been considered?

Recruitment and selection – Recruitment and selection policies and procedures should reflect equal opportunity legislation and the priorities of the organisation. Consideration should be given to:

- monitoring systems for applications
- the person specification and the potential for indirect discrimination

- recruitment advertising, including the use of neutral language and appropriate sources of recruitment
- the shortlisting process and who is involved
- the appropriateness of psychometric tests
- selection interviewing – process and training
- successful induction.

Reward systems – Reward systems must reflect the aims and objectives of the organisation in the context of the equality legislation and the equal opportunity policy. Questions to be considered are:

- Does the reward system 'feel fair'?
- Is there any obvious gender segregation of work?
- Are there any potential Equal Value claims?
- Do the benefits that are offered apply equally to all?
- Is there a place for flexibility in the provision of benefits?

Performance management – The systems for managing performance and the extent to which they are fair, equitable and reflect equal opportunity objectives require scrutiny:

- How are personal objectives set and measured, and by whom?
- Is there any element of the total system that gives cause for concern with regard to fairness and equity?
- How are promotion decisions made?
- Do issues such as length of service feature as unfair selection criteria?

Training and development – The nature of decisions about access to training opportunities requires critical evaluation. Apart from the obvious, such as restricted training opportunities for part-time staff, are there other areas of indirect discrimination?

- Who makes the decision on access to training and what criteria are applied?
- Is there a role for positive action?
- Are initiatives such as secondment and mentoring used and, if so, how are they used and who has access?

Grievance and discipline – Policies for the management of conflict need to be appraised to take full account of equal opportunity issues:

- How will issues of unfairness and inequity be raised and considered?
- Is the grievance procedure the most effective vehicle for dealing with employees' problems in this area or is there a need for other procedures to be agreed and implemented?
- How will proven discrimination be addressed within the disciplinary procedure?
- How will harassment and bullying be handled?

Family-friendly policies – A clear issue for further consideration is the development and implementation of family-friendly policies which contribute to creating a climate and culture where equal opportunities flourish. These may include:

- flexible working
- maternity and paternity leave
- career breaks
- the support of carers.

Without consideration of the *totality* of the impact of the equal opportunity policy on the way that people are managed, its effect will be diluted. The policy needs to be seen as central to the effective resourcing of the organisation.

Programme of action

The audit of the organisation and the review of personnel policies will reveal data on workforce composition, identify areas of concern and suggest priorities for action. The development of an action programme is not a one-off event, but a continuous activity which is constantly refocused by the ongoing collection of monitoring data. Initiatives need to be resourced and equality of opportunity objectives will not be achievable without a dedicated budget and investment in the programme. A defensive reaction to costs should be avoided and the focus should be on the benefits that can accrue where a positive equal opportunities climate prevails.

THE BUSINESS CASE FOR EQUAL OPPORTUNITY

Audit procedures provide information which can be used to identify priorities and action plans and this may enable the equal opportunity policy to become embedded within managerial activity. Concerns may be raised about the perceived costs of equal opportunity actions, and the HR practitioner should be seeking to devise an HR strategy which articulates the business benefits of effective equality of opportunity practices. This reduces the need to be defensive about equal opportunities or to pursue a minimalist response to the discrimination legislation. A more positive case can be constructed which focuses on the business benefits. Equality is not just about improving rights or remedying past discrimination; it can also make sound business sense. Inappropriate discrimination may deny an organisation access to skills, knowledge and experience that will enhance productivity. Unfair discrimination may lead to increased levels of employee stress, to higher absence levels or to lower quality work. Failure by management to deal with incidences of discrimination can lead to individuals taking action, making complaints or taking allegations to an employment tribunal. This may be costly in management time and may lead to tribunal decisions against the organisation with high levels of compensation being awarded.

Recruitment practices which are based on the best person for the job regardless of sex, race, disability and age are likely to lead to a more diverse workforce and this can bring business benefits. These benefits may include access to new markets, more creativity, a sharper client focus, and an improved public image because a good equality and diversity reputation may increase the ability of the organisation to compete for skilled and talented workers. Examples of employers with a positive business approach to equality of opportunity are B&Q and ASDA. B&Q value the contribution of the older or disabled employees who are perceived to be in tune with their customers' needs, and ASDA seek to recruit a cross-section of the local community in their stores in order to reflect their customer base. This can produce business benefits including cultural and religious awareness, as well as better communication with those whose first language is not English. There is, therefore, an added-value business case for equality of opportunity and for having a diverse workforce; it is not just about legal compliance.

MANAGING DIVERSITY

The managing diversity concept challenges the traditional equal opportunities approach by focusing on the *individual* rather than on disadvantaged or under-represented groups. The primary managerial concern is on harnessing the advantage to be gained from a diverse and multi-cultural workforce through maximising the achievement of all employees. It represents a very positive view of equality of opportunity and has the potential to challenge stereotypes.

> The basic concept of managing diversity accepts that the workforce consists of a diverse population of people. The diversity consists of visible and non-visible differences which will include factors such as sex, age, background, race, disability, personality, work style. It is founded on the premise that harnessing these differences will create a productive environment in which everybody feels valued, where their talents are being fully utilised and in which organisational goals are met.
>
> (Kandola and Fullerton, 1998)

Traditional equality of opportunity initiatives focus on disadvantaged groups, on target setting, on positive action, and on seeking to remedy past discrimination. This approach influences organisational strategy on equal opportunities, the policies introduced and the programmes of action developed. A managing diversity approach is much less concerned with target setting and positive action, and more focused on enabling individuals to achieve their potential within a supportive organisational culture which values people differences. A managing diversity philosophy is founded on the acceptance and recognition that individual differences are to be valued and actively used in the pursuit of organisational and individual goals. It asserts that embracing difference creates a culture which values the contribution of all employees and that this enhances performance and productivity (Exhibit 8.5).

A criticism of the equal opportunity approach is that the focus on disadvantaged groups fuels stereotypical images because the provision of support or development opportunities for a specified group reinforces stereotypical assumptions. For example,

Exhibit 8.5 A dichotomised illustration of equal opportunities and managing diversity

Equal opportunities	Managing diversity
Aimed at disadvantaged groups	Focuses on the individual
Seeks to remedy discrimination	Emphasises individual potential
Focuses on positive action for a few	Encourages all to achieve
A personnel department issue	Concerns all organisational members
Little emphasis on 'business needs'	Driven by 'business needs'
Sets targets	Develops an inclusive culture

assertiveness training for women can be perceived as reinforcing the idea that women are not assertive and that men, because (by implication) they are already assertive, do not need assertiveness training. A managing diversity approach would provide assertiveness training purely on the basis of identified training needs regardless of, and without acknowledging, gender issues. Another criticism is that the equal opportunities' concern with targets and with numbers can result in the best person not being selected if the decision maker is distracted by and gives priority to target achievement.

Although 'equal opportunities' and 'managing diversity' are often presented as dichotomous concepts, in reality the two are not mutually exclusive. Different approaches may be needed at different times to meet evolving organisational objectives. The most effective approach may be first to monitor the workforce profile and the operation of personnel policies, and second to promote the values and attitudes that enable the principles of managing diversity to be achieved. There is potential for the managing diversity concept to be used as an excuse for doing nothing. Rhetorical statements about valuing diversity and respecting the individual may disguise the absence of an equal opportunities policy, and it may even be argued that an equal opportunities policy is incompatible with and therefore detrimental to a managing diversity philosophy. Monitoring the profile of the workforce should still be part of a managing diversity approach and there should be evidence of change; if change does not occur then diversity benefits will not be accruing and a more proactive equal opportunities policy may be required.

Managing diversity offers a real chance to re-evaluate, review and, where necessary, revise what has been done in the name of equal opportunities. In order for this to be done effectively, managers are required to have a good grasp of what managing diversity means and how it differs from equal opportunities. Unless this is done and managers have the courage to change, managing diversity will be seen as an empty slogan and the latest short-lived management fad (Kandola and Fullerton, 1998).

HARASSMENT AT WORK

The EOC, CRE and DRC codes of practice provide guidelines for employers and employees, and the CIPD asserts that:

No-one should be worried about going to work because of the fear of harassment, bullying or abuse. An environment in which harassment occurs reflects as badly on the organisation as on any of the employees within it. The CIPD deplores any kind of harassment and urges employers to take steps to ensure that the dignity of employers and customers is not abused.

(*Source*: CIPD Statement on Harassment at Work, 1997)

Sexual harassment is defined in the European Commission Code of Practice as:

Unwanted conduct of a sexual nature, or other conduct based on sex, affecting the dignity of women and men at work. This can include unwelcome physical, verbal or non-verbal conduct.

Examples of harassing conduct include:

- unwelcome sexual attention
- insults or ridicule based on sex
- suggestions that sexual favours may enhance career prospects
- withholding career progression because of refusal of sexual favours
- environmental harassment, for example lewd or offensive jokes addressed to everyone in the room.

Similarly, racial harassment at work is unwelcome conduct based on race, racial insults or ridicule and other behaviour that undermines the employee.

Sexual and racial harassment at work are regarded as unlawful discrimination and are covered by the SDA and the RRA (*see* page 177). The Protection from Harassment Act, 1997, aimed primarily at criminalising 'stalking', makes it a criminal offence to behave in a way that causes harassment to another person or which causes that person to fear violence. The legislation is wide ranging and includes harassment on any grounds, real or threatened, and encompasses bullying at work.

Harassment should be eliminated from the workplace, not only because of legal and ethical requirements, but also because of the negative impact on the organisation. Harassment causes misery, increases absenteeism and staff turnover, and affects individual and team performance – it makes no business sense. Harassment is an exhibition of power. This power may be the power of status, the power of control or the power of a majority group. It is simplistic to perceive sexual harassment merely as an attempt to initiate sexual relations. It is also naive to think that it only happens to young, attractive women. It happens to both men and women and it is more rightly associated with the exertion of power and the exposure of vulnerability. Similarly, racial harassment, although most commonly based on skin colour, happens to a wide range of racial and ethnic groups.

Respecting the dignity of people at work means acknowledging that people can be subjected to humiliating behaviour on a number of grounds. Sexual and racial harassment are significant problems, but other grounds for intimidating behaviour include:

- TU membership or non-membership
- disability or impediment
- age
- health

193

- religion
- appearance
- personal beliefs
- sexual orientation.

Bullying at work

In addition to harassment based on difference, the issue of bullying at work, while not being a new phenomenon, is relatively recently defined. The Human Rights Act 1998 introduced into UK legislation the right not to be 'subjected to degrading treatment or punishment' and this will cover behaviour which constitutes bullying. The Manufacturing, Science and Finance union, or MSF, (2002) usefully defines bullying as 'persistent, offensive, abusive, intimidating, malicious or insulting behaviour, abuse of power or unfair penal sanctions, which make the recipient feel upset, threatened, humiliated or vulnerable, which undermines their self-confidence and which may cause them to suffer stress'. Bullying can be caused by many things, including pressure on managers to achieve targets, lack of management training or an aggressive or authoritarian organisational culture. Anyone may be a victim of bullying and it is important that there are organisational structures and procedures in place to enable the issue to be brought into the open and resolved. Like harassment, unresolved incidences of bullying may lead to a lack of motivation, increased staff turnover and higher levels of absence.

Policies to deal with harassment and bullying may be brought together in a 'Dignity at work' policy, which can encapsulate all of the issues around abuse of power and intimidation in the workplace.

Dignity at work policy

A dignity at work policy should be developed and implemented with one policy covering all types of harassment and bullying. The potential benefits are that it demonstrates managerial commitment, sets boundaries for employee behaviour and engenders a climate in which employees feel safe and not distracted from their work. The policy should have the public support of senior management. The policy needs an opening statement which asserts the importance of a work environment where everyone feels valued, where they can expect to be treated with respect and where harassment and bullying will not be tolerated. By undermining the dignity of people at work and affecting performance, both harassment and bullying are detrimental to the individual and to the organisation, and this managerial standpoint should be explicit in the policy. The policy should be positive, encourage victims and deter potential bullies and harassers. Indicative examples of unacceptable behaviour can be included to help define and clarify the boundaries; these might include verbal or physical threats, unjustified and persistent criticism, offensive or abusive personal remarks or belittling someone's contribution or opinion.

The policy should specify the procedure to be followed in cases of bullying and harassment. The procedures should be fair and consistent and provide formal and informal mechanisms for resolving problems quickly and effectively. Access to a confidential counselling, advice or support service, either internal or external, should be available. Each allegation should be quickly and thoroughly investigated and effective solutions implemented. The investigation process should be fair and objective and respect the confidentiality needs of all parties. The procedure should be clear and progressive and a victim should have options for action at each stage. The policy should make clear that behaviour at work is also an individual responsibility and that the organisation will not tolerate inappropriate behaviour.

Handling of incidents affecting the dignity of people at work

The loss of dignity at work is an important work-related issue and may lead to employees being fearful about coming to work and to stress and anxiety. It has the potential to result in poor performance, high levels of absence and the loss of good employees. Employers should not ignore allegations and managers should be trained to handle this sensitive, and often traumatic, workplace issue. Each report of bullying or harassment, formal or informal, should be taken seriously, as it often takes considerable courage for the employee to report an incident. A victim normally feels vulnerable and reluctant to complain. Insensitive comments or trivialisation of the issue at the reporting stage may result in the employee refusing to pursue the matter internally, choosing to resign and even alleging constructive dismissal. This is problematic for the employer, who is *prima facie* liable for the actions of employees, and it may be necessary to demonstrate to a tribunal that the managerial response to an allegation of bullying or harassment was adequate. Legal cases arising from an allegation can be expensive and time consuming, lead to adverse publicity and have a negative impact on employment relations generally.

The process of handling an allegation should include the following.

1 The reporting of the incident, either formally or informally, should be treated sensitively by the person to whom the incident is reported through attentive listening and the avoidance of apportioning blame.

2 The person making the allegation should be counselled and options for action explored. The options range from doing nothing to formally taking the complaint forward. The employee should be made aware of the range of support available, inside and outside the organisation.

3 The alleged harasser or bully should be confronted and told of the actions or words which are causing distress, that they are considered harmful and lacking respect and that they must stop. Natural justice principles normally demand that the harasser or bully should know the nature of any allegation and be given the opportunity to respond or change the behaviour. However, some behaviour is so serious that it contravenes criminal law, in which case they should be told that it is to be reported to the police.

4 The employee making the allegation should be advised to keep a diary or record of incidents and exchanges that occur. This is important if formal action subsequently arises. Incidents often take place in private – one person's word against another's. Documentary evidence in the form of diary notes with specific dates, times and

195

descriptions of the incident increase the credibility of the allegation and may increase the confidence of the victim to proceed.

5 If the harassment or bullying ceases, the employee may not want to take further action and this should normally be respected. If the employer has evidence that it is not an isolated case, a constructive discussion with the alleged harasser or bully may stimulate a change in behaviour.

6 If the unacceptable behaviour does not cease, the employee may seek remedy through the formal policy. This will require a full investigation, the interviewing of witnesses and the taking of statements from all parties. Confidentiality is important at this investigatory stage, as public discussions may lead to counter-allegations of unfair treatment from the harasser or bully.

7 The procedure should exist independently of the grievance procedure so that incidents can be reported to any appropriate manager and proceed through a suitable managerial chain.

8 'Proven' cases may result in advice but no punitive action, a disciplinary penalty, action short of dismissal, or dismissal. It may be appropriate to redeploy either of the parties, but the victim should not be disadvantaged. Redeployment of the harasser or bully may be a more acceptable course of action.

Grievance and disciplinary procedures will need to be reviewed to reflect the principles of the dignity at work policy, to refer to investigatory processes when allegations are made and to detail the disciplinary sanctions available. Introducing the policy requires a programme of communication so that all employees are fully aware of policy content and the procedures for dealing with allegations of unacceptable behaviour.

> An organisation's goal should be to develop a culture in which harassment is known to be unacceptable and where individuals are confident enough to bring complaints without fear of ridicule or reprisal. Everybody needs to feel responsible for challenging all forms of harassment and for upholding personal dignity. Developing and implementing policies and procedures creates a climate of greater confidence to challenge harassment. The right policies and procedures enable employers to tackle individual complaints quickly and effectively.
>
> (IPD, 1997)

EQUAL PAY

The Equal Pay Act, 1970, as amended by 1983 Equal Value Regulations, implies a pay equality clause into the contract of employment. Men and women are entitled to the same pay for the same work, and it is unlawful to differentiate between the terms and conditions of men and women where they are employed on:

- like work (work which is the same or broadly similar)
- work rated as equivalent under a non-discriminatory job evaluation scheme
- work of equal value even where the jobs are of a totally different nature (the equal value amendment).

The 1983 equal value amendment, which considerably broadened the scope of the Act, was implemented because the European Court judged the UK to be failing to apply fully the principle that men and women should receive equal pay for equal work as required by Article 119 of the Treaty of Rome. Therefore, in addition to similar work and jobs rated as equivalent, an employee is entitled to equal pay where a higher paid job being done by a member of the opposite sex is of equal value. Equal value is assessed using criteria such as job demands, skill, effort, responsibility and decision-making. Equal pay legislation and subsequent case law define pay very broadly and include all contractual terms. It may include basic pay, occupational pension, performance and profit related pay, sick pay, overtime and holiday pay.

For an equal pay claim to be legitimate, there must be a job comparator of the opposite sex, and the comparator must be employed by the same employer at the same place of work or at another place of work of the same or an associated employer where common terms and conditions are observed. The comparator can be a current employee or a predecessor or a successor. If the employer fails to respond to an equal pay claim, the employee has recourse to an employment tribunal.

An equal pay claim

The Equal Opportunities Commission has accused UK employers of being 'complacent on equal pay' (2000) with many employers still doing nothing to ensure that they are paying men and women fairly. In 30 years, since the Equal Pay Act, the gap between average hourly rates for men and women in full-time employment has reduced from 31 per cent in 1970 to 18 per cent in 2000, but the gap between the average hourly rates for full-time men and part-time women is still 39 per cent. The Equal Pay Task Force (2001), which was set up to look at the size of the problem, its causes and the barriers to progress, and to recommend practical action, states that the main reasons for the gap are:

- sex bias in payment systems
- concentration of women in low paid jobs
- women as primary carers.

Among other things, the Task Force recommends improvements to the employment tribunal system for equal pay claims, an update to the EOC Code of Practice on Equal Pay, and more openness and reporting on pay by employers. It is important to analyse and understand the reasons for pay differences in order to ensure that fair and lawful organisational policies, procedures and practices are put in place.

An employee can take a claim to an employment tribunal. If the tribunal decides that the work is 'like work', 'equivalent work' or 'work of equal value', and the employer does not have a genuine material defence, the claim will succeed. The claimant will be entitled to equal pay and to compensation. Compensation is currently limited to two years' back pay, but under proposals detailed in *Towards Equal Pay for Women* (DfEE, 2000) this could be increased to six years in England and Wales and five years in Scotland.

In an 'equal value' claim an employer will need to demonstrate that the work is not of equal value because of job differences that are of 'practical importance'. A tribunal will consider the size and nature of any differences as well as the frequency with which the differences occur. For example, in the case of physical strength being required for a particular job, the tribunal will take account of the degree of physical strength required and the frequency with which that strength is exercised. In reaching a judgement the tribunal can elect to rely on the documentary evidence provided by the parties or to visit the workplace and observe the work or to appoint an independent expert to evaluate the jobs of the claimant and the comparator. An independent expert, from a panel appointed by ACAS, does not make the decision about whether or not the jobs warrant equal pay; this is a matter of fact to be established by the tribunal.

If the tribunal decides that the jobs are not equal, the claim will fail. If a tribunal finds that the claimant is employed on like work or work rated as equivalent or on work of equal value, it does not necessarily end there, as the employer can resist the claim through providing a genuine material defence (GMD), which acknowledges that the jobs are equal but justifies the inequality in pay by a reason which is not related to sex. Indicative, but unreliable, GMDs include:

- geographical or cost of living differences
- labour market forces
- red circling – where an individual employee is on protected terms
- different collective bargaining arrangements
- differences in qualifications
- the value of other contractual terms.

The operation of employment tribunals in equal pay claims has been severely criticised in terms of time for resolution and complexity of operation; a simple case may take up to two years and more complex cases can take many years. The DfEE consultation paper *Towards Equal Pay for Women* has made six proposals for changes to the tribunal system to speed up equal pay claims:

- simplification of the rules on how tribunals deal with equal pay claims
- calling in an assessor to give expert advice and to help to speed up the process
- allowing groups of women with similar claims to bring a collective claim; this is currently not possible because all claims have to be individual claims
- reducing delays caused by different 'experts' giving evidence; only the independent expert will be allowed to give evidence
- removing the loophole which allowed tribunals to dismiss cases before they were properly investigated
- introducing a questionnaire procedure (similar to the DDA), which will allow the claimant to get key information from the employer prior to deciding whether or not to proceed with the claim.

The questionnaire procedure is included in the Employment Bill 2001 and may be introduced into law by 2003. Other changes may take longer.

The EOC Code of Practice on Equal Pay, issued in 1997, recommends that employers regularly review their pay systems for sex bias and provides advice on how this can be done. The European Court of Justice also states that it expects employers to be able to 'clearly and objectively justify their pay criteria where variable elements of pay are unequally distributed between the sexes'. In spite of this, very few employers monitor their pay systems and are therefore unable to report on gender pay differences. This indicates that reliance on a voluntary code is unlikely to affect the position of women's pay significantly in the short term. Through reporting and pay audit proposals the UK government is seeking to encourage employers through voluntary compliance, but this has met with a mixed response from employers and unions, with some organisations putting pressure on the government to legislate on this aspect of equal pay.

Achieving equal pay in practice

In addition to meeting the legal requirement, there are sound business reasons for ensuring equal pay.

> Pay systems which are transparent and value the entire workforce send positive messages about an organisation's values. Fair and non-discriminatory (pay) systems represent good management practice and contribute to the efficient achievement of business objectives by encouraging maximum productivity from all employees.
>
> (EOC Code of Practice on Equal Pay, 1997)

In order to achieve equal pay the Equal Pay Task Force (2001) has made strong and detailed recommendations to the EOC, and hence to government. They recognise the need for regular and thorough processes for equal pay review. They also identify the support that software companies could provide in developing effective equal pay management systems through having a series of sophisticated reports within commercial HR information systems. The task force also acknowledges that in some sectors there is a concern about the resource implications of too deep an investigation when this is only voluntary. There is not only a resource implication of undertaking the review but also a potential financial cost associated with rectifying any pay inequalities. The task force is recommending a two-stage review process to enable organisations to assess where they are in relation to pay equality. The first stage of the review focuses on the policy and asks the following questions:

1 Do you have an equal pay policy?

2 Is that policy communicated to all employees?

3 Is senior level responsibility for equal pay assigned?

4 Have your pay systems been reviewed to identify any gender gap?

5 Do you have a single job evaluation system?

If the answer is 'Yes' to all of these questions the organisation is making progress towards achieving equal pay. If the answer to questions 4 and 5 is 'No' the organisation can have no confidence that it is complying with equal pay legislation. The second stage of the process looks for more detailed and specific analysis such as:

- Comparisons of male and female average pay in each job within your organisation
- A clear statement of objective justification of any substantial difference in pay between men and women
- Need for targets to be set and regular monitoring to take place.

The Kingsmill report on women's employment and pay acknowledges that current equal pay legislation requires the employee to seek redress for a wrong committed by the employer, and consequently the solutions are limited to those available through a tribunal (Harper, 2002). The report therefore focused on the business case for employment equality and made a number of recommendations to government:

1 The creation of a centre of excellence to commission research on women's employment and pay.
2 A right for private-sector employees to request pay information to establish whether there is an equal pay case to be made.
3 The extension of the questionnaire procedure used in race and sex discrimination cases to equal pay claims.
4 Pay and employment reviews to be mandatory for public-sector organisations, and also organisations, which contract for public services be required to offer the same terms and conditions of employment where these have been established through a pay review or job evaluation.
5 Public sector managers to have diversity objectives in their appraisal.

Equal pay is a significant equal opportunities issue and will be on the HR agenda for the next few years. Government targets to halve the pay differential between men and women by 2006 are challenging.

SUMMARY LEARNING POINTS

1 Equality of opportunity is a complex concept attracting different interpretations. The interpretation will determine the organisational approach adopted.
2 UK anti-discrimination legislation is extensive and a knowledge of the law can guide principled managerial action. However, the law has had variable impact and may engender a minimalist approach to equality of opportunity.
3 Discrimination can be direct or indirect. Unintentional discrimination can be reduced through focusing only on objective and job-related criteria when making pay, selection or other people resourcing decisions.
4 Positive action can compensate for inequality of opportunity, but positive discrimination is unlawful in the UK.
5 The business case for equality of opportunity rather than the social, ethical, political or legal arguments may be the most persuasive to 'business focused' managers.
6 An equal opportunities policy frames managerial approach and actions and can positively impact on achieving equality of opportunity in practice. Managing diversity is

a contrasting equal opportunities philosophy which seeks to change the organisational culture to recognise that diversity and differences, if managed effectively, add value and increase competitive edge.

7 Harassment and bullying at work deny dignity to the individual and are dysfunctional to the organisation. A dignity at work policy and associated procedures are needed to deal with problems, to demonstrate that harassment and bullying are unacceptable and to create an environment where employees can feel secure and can be productive.

8 The equality agenda marches on, with potential for discrimination based on age, religion, sexual preference and other 'job-irrelevant factors' to be outlawed by emerging case law or statutory enactment.

9 Equal pay for equal work regardless of sex has the force of UK and European law. The huge number of variables in the pay and job equation make this a complex area and make employers vulnerable to employee claims.

10 The equal pay claims procedures through the employment tribunal system are not considered to have been effective. Changes are proposed which will streamline the system, provide the questionnaire procedure to claimants and encourage the monitoring and reporting of equal pay within the organisation.

REFERENCES AND FURTHER READING

Aitkenhead, M. and Liff, S. (1991) in Firth-Couzens, J. and West, M.A. *Women at Work*. Oxford: Oxford University Press.

CIPD (2000) *CIPD Quick Facts: Disability and employment*.

Commission of the European Community (1993) *How to Combat Sexual Harassment at Work*. EC Publications.

Coussey, M. and Jackson, H. (1991) *Equal Opportunities Practice*. London: Pitman Publishing.

Davidson, M.J. and Cooper, C.L. (1992) *Shattering the Glass Ceiling*. London: Paul Chapman Publishing.

DfEE (2000) *Towards Equal Pay for Women*. Consultation paper.

DL70 – Disability Discrimination Act – Employment (1996) DfEE.

EOC (1997) *Code of Practice on Equal Pay*. London: Equal Opportunities Commission.

Equal Opportunities Commission (2000) *Research Findings: Attitudes to equal pay*. London.

Equal Pay Task Force (2001) *Just Pay*.

Harper, D. (2002) 'Balancing the pay scales', *People Management*, 10 January, 17.

IPD (1996) *Managing Diversity – A position paper*.

IPD (1997) *Harassment at Work – Key facts*.

Kandola, R. and Fullerton, J. (1994) 'Diversity: more than just a slogan', *People Management*, November.

Kandola, R. and Fullerton, J. (1998) *Managing the Mosaic: Diversity in action*. London: CIPD.

Meager, N., Doyle, B., Evans, C., Kersley, B., Williams, M., O'Regan, S. and Tackey, N. (1999) 'Monitoring the DDA'. *DfEE Brief 119*, May.

MSF (2002) www.successunlimited.co.uk/bully/defns.htm

Office for National Statistics (2001) *Labour Force Survey*. London: HMSO.

Pitt, G. (2000) *Employment Law*. London: Sweet and Maxwell.

Ross, R. and Schneider, R. (1992) *From Equality to Diversity*. London: Pitman Publishing.

Selwyn, N. (2000) *Selwyn's Law of Employment*. London: Butterworth.

Stephens, T. (1999) *Bullying and Sexual Harassment*. London: CIPD.

Straw, J. (1989) *Equal Opportunities*. London: IPM.

Welch, J. (1996) 'The invisible minority', *People Management*, September.

ASSIGNMENTS AND DISCUSSION TOPICS

1 Consider the model of equal opportunity identified by Straw. What practical difference might these alternative views of equal opportunity make to the equal opportunities actions taken by your organisation?

2 Argue the case for and against positive discrimination to achieve equal opportunities.

3 How would you assess whether your organisation is 'an equal opportunity employer' in practice?

4 What data would you collect and what information would you produce to complete an equal opportunity audit? What workforce indicators are of importance with regard to equality of opportunity in your organisation?

5 Give a critical evaluation of the impact of the equal opportunities policy in your organisation on the achievement of business objectives.

6 'The business philosophy of managing diversity represents the way forward for equal opportunities' (*IPD Position Paper – Managing Diversity*). What is meant by the term 'managing diversity' and how does this differ in practice from the more traditional approach to achieving equality of opportunity in the workplace? How does the diversity approach add value and will it work?

7 Review a dignity at work policy. What factors are important in ensuring the effective operation of this policy?

8 What action would you take to reduce the chance of a successful equal pay claim in your organisation?

9 Identify gendered groups of jobs in your organisation. Compare them with regard to pay, and comment on whether any differences in pay are due to job demands or are objectively justifiable in terms of a genuine material defence.

10 The Age Diversity in Employment Code of Practice, 1999, covers good practice in six aspects of the employment cycle: recruitment, selection, promotion, training, redundancy and retirement. Discuss the **practical** ways in which these six areas of employment can be addressed. Are there any other HR areas that would need to be considered in order to achieve age diversity objectives?

CASE STUDY

Surfing the Internet

Marilyn Walker is a clerical officer with a large public sector organisation. She works full time in a busy office, doing mainly routine office work, and has been with the organisation for three years since leaving school at 17 years of age. The organisation is well equipped with information technology and Marilyn regularly uses the internal e-mail system and other internal software packages. She knows that the organisation is attached to the Internet, but she has had no training and has never used it.

One morning Marilyn arrived at work slightly earlier than usual to find that she could not get into her office as her supervisor had not yet arrived. Marilyn was not a key holder. She therefore sat in the corridor waiting for someone to arrive. While she was waiting, Gary White, a manager from another department, came along and saw Marilyn waiting and asked if she wanted to wait in his office. Not wanting to appear discourteous Marilyn agreed and went with him to wait for her co-workers.

When they entered his office he switched on his PC and logged in. They exchanged pleasantries about holidays and she felt quite at ease. After a few moments he asked her to come and look at his PC and on doing this Marilyn discovered that he had accessed screens that had mildly pornographic and titillating pictures and text. Marilyn felt very uncomfortable and embarrassed by this and did not know how to respond. She said very little to him, returned to her seat and hoped that someone would arrive soon so that she could start work. Two or three minutes later her manager, Sally Brown, arrived and Marilyn left Gary's office to start work without saying anything to either of them.

Marilyn became very anxious about work, she started arriving late and the quality of her work deteriorated. Sally Brown noticed the change in Marilyn's work but the department was very busy and she could not manage with staff who were not contributing 100 per cent. She talked to Marilyn briefly about her work and threatened her with 'the sack' unless she started to improve. One month later Marilyn resigned from the organisation.

1 Did Marilyn experience harassment?
2 What options should have been available to Marilyn to help her to handle the situation?
3 Comment on Sally's handling of the situation.
4 Is Marilyn likely to have any recourse to the law?

CHAPTER 9

Pay, reward and resourcing

INTRODUCTION

A prime objective of effective people resourcing is to have 'the right people, in the right place, at the right time, doing the right thing'. This cannot easily be achieved without the 'right' pay and reward strategies for the organisation. It is therefore appropriate to address some of the fundamentals of pay and reward, in this chapter and the next, whilst recognising that it is a turbulent area characterised by contextual complexity and tension. Universal pay solutions remain elusive and at best the choice is one of compromise between sometimes competing reward alternatives.

CHAPTER OBJECTIVES

- To introduce the concepts of 'old pay' and 'new pay', and to emphasise a contingent approach to reward management and strategy.
- To discuss the aims of a pay and reward policy and the structural elements of a pay system.
- To examine the purposes of job evaluation and the main formal job evaluation schemes.
- To explore graded pay, market-driven pay, performance-related pay and competence-based pay.

REWARD

The approach to paying people in the UK is undergoing considerable change, and the term 'reward' is increasingly being applied to contemporary remuneration strategies and policies. Reward encompasses pay, remuneration and compensation. It represents a portfolio of managerial practices where financial and non-financial elements are flexibly directed at enabling and rewarding employees who add value in the interests of competitive advantage. Reward is used as an holistic term to reflect a more dynamic and a more flexible approach. Reward is the total remuneration concept of pay and benefits together with non-financial recognition and motivation applied in a contemporary context.

NEW PAY AND OLD PAY

In addition to reward, the term 'new pay', originating in the USA, is in use in the UK (Lawler, 1995; Armstrong and Murlis, 1998; Lewis, 1998). 'New pay' and its juxtaposed 'stereotypical' opposite of 'old pay' are concepts which are used to distinguish between contemporary and traditional reward practices. Old pay is characterised by bureaucratic salary administration, organisational hierarchy, rigid job evaluation and grading systems, incremental progression, the lack of horizontal integration with other HR activities and the detachment of pay from the strategic objectives of the organisation. The primary concerns of old pay are fairness, consistency, equity and transparency. This is arguably more compatible with the traditional organisation structures and employment relationships of the 1970s and the 1980s. In the twenty-first century old pay, it is alleged, will inhibit organisational responsiveness and development in more turbulent organisational environments.

New pay can be viewed as a functional adaptation to changes in the external context and increasing competitive pressures. These external influences are demanding flatter, leaner and more flexible organisational forms, and this includes new forms of reward. The prime characteristics of new pay are first, the pursuit of the integration of pay with corporate strategy in order to achieve organisational objectives and commercial imperatives, and second, the use of pay and reward as a sophisticated lever to apply pressure to employee performance. New pay fits well with the 'people make the difference' doctrine by seeking to reward individuals in line with managerial perceptions of their worth to the organisation. Also at the heart of new pay and reward strategies is the need for integration with resourcing, development and relations strategies. This integration is necessary to avoid stimulating contradictory employee responses through conflicts in HR policies and practices.

New pay is focused on managing financial reward in order to send the right messages about performance and corporate values to employees. The emphasis is on rewarding contribution rather than seniority or status. New pay incorporates several reward themes:

- a connection between employee pay and employee performance as a variable incentive linked to corporate objectives through a performance management process
- a market-driven approach to pay and benefits to reflect the commercial worth of employees
- pay structures which are broadbanded to encourage flexible working and flexible deployment
- a flexible benefit approach which aims to provide individual choice within a diverse workforce

Employees are rewarded for assuming roles, displaying values, exhibiting behaviours (for example, in relation to customer orientation and quality initiatives) and pursuing performance objectives which are determined by management. An alternative title for new pay might therefore be 'business driven pay' (Armstrong and Brown, 2001). New pay is therefore overtly managerialistic and in the absence of any regulation through employee representation promotes a unitary employment relationship. This approach has to be squared with the possibility that employees and employers have different, and sometimes competing, objectives in terms of pay and reward. A process of listing respective employer and employee expectations of a pay policy will reveal that the overlap of objectives is never total, raising the ethical question about the extent to which managers are obligated to acknowledge the pay and reward expectations of employees (Heery, 1996).

In the new millennium, managerial concern for equity and fairness in differentials and relativities may be subordinated to the flexibility and uncertainty of new pay, with 'nimble reward systems' required for corporate survival (Ledford, 1995). However, in contrast to managerially driven new pay, skill or labour market shortages may empower employees to determine reward arrangements and this contextual factor clearly undermines any prescription in reward approaches. There is no escape from the contingencies of the reward context (*see* Chapter 10 on reward trends).

These dichotomised concepts of old and new pay are introduced here to provide a framework for analysis and investigation, rather than to prescribe new pay as the dominant or prevalent model. As with all contemporary developments new pay will have its critics and its champions, and this is best illustrated by two quotations:

> The year 2000 ... will see the beginning of relationships between employees and organisations that help us forget the labels of disenfranchised, adversarial and 'we versus them' that are presently too common. Although new pay is not likely to be the only factor that will help us move towards a more positive future, it is clearly the only way to make employee pay a constructive catalyst for this change.
>
> (Schuster and Zingheim, 1992)

> Literature on this subject (of new pay) seems riddled with imprecise cliches, generalisations, byzantine methodological accounts and evangelical reports using the latest buzz words.
>
> (Roberts, 1997)

Research by Poole and Jenkins, reported in Taylor (2000: 14), found substantial endorsement of new pay and human resource management approaches in a survey of 909 senior managers, but less evidence of their translation into reward practices, with the researchers concluding that 'in contrast with the policies of companies, many elements of new pay do not appear to have been widely adopted in practice in British companies'. In other words, whilst there is clearly a momentum to the strategic integration of reward and the pursuit of a 'new pay' philosophy, there is as yet no evidence to suggest that it is the dominant approach.

REWARD PHILOSOPHY, STRATEGY AND POLICY

Armstrong (1999) argues that the reward policy of an organisation flows from its philosophy and strategy, the philosophy being defined as '... the broad values and beliefs that an organisation holds about rewards ...' and the strategy as '... [indicating] the direction in which an organisation wants to go in developing its reward processes and structures'. Armstrong and Brown (2001) define reward strategy as:

A business focused statement of the intentions of the organisation concerning the development of future reward processes and practices, which are aligned to the business and human resource strategies of the organisation, its culture and the environment in which it operates.

The rationale for having a reward strategy is therefore to clarify organisational values, to provide a coherent sense of purpose and to promote a consistency between employee results and behaviour and key organisational goals. Organisations need a reward policy which ensures that the reward strategy is turned into action, and the policy 'provides guidelines for managers and personnel or pay specialists on how particular and recurring reward issues should be dealt with'. The reward policy will be contingent on sector, size and corporate culture. The CIPD research findings, discussed by Armstrong in *People Management* (2000), have 'squashed once and for all any idea that there is such a thing as best practice when applied to pay systems. It is best fit that matters, and a contingency approach is the one usually adopted'. For contingency theorists there is no such thing as 'best practice' in reward, only 'best fit'. Reward policy includes all components of the reward package, including the non-financial elements. However, as pay is the single largest element, the next section focuses on pay policy objectives and some of the issues that should be addressed in the development of policy.

Pay policy objectives

Pay is a fundamental part of the contract of employment and there are two parties to that contract. Therefore, in theory at least, both parties have to find acceptable the elements of the contract, including pay, in order to commit to it. However, the power of the parties is not equal and this can give rise to tension in the 'pay for work bargain' if this inherent conflict is not recognised. Pay policies need to be devised to meet the strategic organisational objectives and also to recognise employee expectations.

The employer's objectives – are ultimately to attract and retain the quality and quantity of staff to achieve strategic aims. This has to happen within the constraints of value for money, control of costs and the ability to pay. Pay policy decisions will have to be taken on organisational positioning in the competitive labour market and the image that the organisation wishes to portray. The employer may also be seeking to reward performance and commitment, to encourage employees to take on increased responsibility, to promote flexibility and to value the acquisition of skills and expertise. If the employer buys in services from contractors or consultants, the impact on the pay policy cannot be ignored, as higher or lower rates for contractors or consultants may distort or threaten the integrity of the pay policy objectives. In broader terms, the pay policy communicates the organisation's values and beliefs and sends clear signals about managerial expectations and the behaviour that will be rewarded.

The employee's expectations – in contrast, may include the maintenance of purchasing power in line with costs of living, or an increase in pay over time, and stability in pay. High variations in pay can make it difficult for employees to manage on a day-to-day basis. Employees normally expect pay that is 'felt fair'. People often have a good idea of their value in terms of the job, and if the pay they receive does not 'feel fair' their motivation and commitment may be adversely affected. Internal fairness is important: is my pay fair compared to others in the organisation? And external comparisons are made: am I paid a reasonable amount in comparison to the labour market? Employees expect to know the basis for the determination of the pay and therefore the structure and policy should be transparent.

There are tensions in meeting all of these employee and employer objectives and expectations, but employers who fail to recognise that employees have aspirations and expectations too may find that their overall objective of attracting and retaining high quality staff cannot be achieved.

Indicative pay policy issues

Value for money and control of costs – Value for money relates to getting the best employees within the organisation's financial constraints. Analysis of the organisation, the labour market and the competitors for employees will indicate the context in which the business is operating. Market intelligence will indicate the range of pay and benefits offered by labour market competitors and the pay policy will need to address exactly where the organisation wants to be placed within that range. A position at the top of the range will be costly and may mean paying more than is needed to resource the organisation. A position near the bottom may make it difficult to attract and retain staff.

Flexibility and the encouragement of multiskilling – If the organisation has a philosophy and strategy which seeks flexibility, teamworking and continuous staff development, then this should be reflected in the pay policy. What reward is given to those who acquire new skills and competence? If the pay system does not recognise this acquisition then tensions are created. Consideration of competence-based pay or team pay may complement flexibility and multiskilling objectives and ensure that employees know what is valued and what leads to increased reward.

Performance – Most organisations are now focused on improvements in performance and may have sophisticated performance appraisal and performance management systems. This performance objective needs to be addressed in pay policy development. What will be the nature of the performance measures and the rewards attached to the achievement of performance targets? Team versus individual performance pay may need to be examined.

Equity – Equity is important in the framing of policy, as differentials in pay should be transparent. How will decisions be taken about the 'value' of the job? The policy may need to include a job evaluation system that systematically reviews jobs, or job values may be determined by the market.

These are just examples of issues that may form part of the pay policy. There is clearly not one policy that can be developed and applied prescriptively. It will be determined by the organisation taking into account factors such as the sector, the size, the culture and the strategy. However, a policy should be developed and communicated so that employees know and understand the basis for the determination of pay and can judge for themselves the fairness, equity, consistency and transparency in operation.

Design of the pay structure

The pay policy provides what Armstrong (1999) calls the 'framework for action' and a pay structure that reflects the policy needs to be developed. Pay structures are needed to provide a logical framework for the monitoring and control of the reward system. There are five stages that need consideration whatever final structure is adopted.

1 Jobs within the organisation have to be ranked in terms of relative worth from the most simple to the most complex job in terms of the demands placed on the job-holder; this can be done by a system of job evaluation.

2 Jobs need to be grouped in a logical way. Jobs that are similar or that have attracted a similar value under a job evaluation scheme should be grouped together to reflect any natural clustering of jobs.

3 The size of the grouping has to be determined and a system of grades, broad bands or job families produced.

4 Cash values need to be allocated to the grades, broad bands or job families to reflect pay policy objectives.

5 Consideration should be given to employee pay progression – the way in which individual pay increases without promotion to a higher graded job. Common methods of progression are incremental, performance-related and competence-based systems.

ESTABLISHING AND INTERPRETING MARKET RATES

The identification of market rates for specified jobs is not an exact science. Collecting labour market information (market intelligence) does not produce a single pay figure which can be mechanistically relied upon as 'the market rate'. Market intelligence provides information which can be incorporated into reward decisions – market rates are more a question of judgement than a matter of fact. However, the tracking of labour market rates of pay is a fundamental activity where the objective is to recognise the external labour market in reward policy.

The collection of comparative pay data depends on comparing jobs on a like-for-like basis. The method of data collection is through surveys of like jobs in the external labour markets. In order to match jobs for survey purposes, a job title is normally inadequate and it is advisable to have a job description which summarises the main elements of the job, specifies the job context and also contains details of the reward package, including allowances, bonuses and other benefits. An individual market rate job profile should be produced prior to any survey (Exhibit 9.1). It is against this job profile that other jobs can be benchmarked for similarity, and hence give meaning to any pay comparison (Fowler, 1996a).

Exhibit 9.1   Market rate survey: illustrative job profile

1 Job title

2 Relative position in the organisation

3 Organisational context

4 Tasks, responsibilities and accountabilities

5 Competencies, qualifications and experience

6 Pay range

   Bonuses

   Benefits

7 Date of last review.

Comprehensive and accurate information will be difficult to acquire even with a job profile, but there are a number of sources which can be used for survey purposes. It is advisable to use a survey form in order to capture data more systematically (Exhibit 9.2). Survey sources include the following.

- Telephone or postal surveys of other organisations – many organisations will be prepared to exchange pay data for mutual advantage.

- Subscription to proprietary sources of data – produced either by specialist reward consultancies or by government, for example the Annual New Earnings Survey.

- Participation in local 'salary clubs' – networking with personnel practitioners with the aim of sharing market intelligence.

- Monitoring and analysing the pay information in job advertisements – although clearly the extent to which the advertisement data can be relied upon to reflect reality is uncertain.

- Surveying employment agencies and job centres – as these organisations are likely to have a 'finger on the pulse' of local and regional labour market rates.

- Collecting pay data at exit interviews – although this can be problematic to analyse; first, obtaining accurate data may be difficult because of either employee reluctance to disclose the new pay package or employee tendency to inflate it, and second, employees frequently only change employment when a better reward package is secured, which may skew this source of data.

These pay information sources are complementary rather than mutually exclusive and can be used to produce a more reliable labour market picture.

When the raw market data has been collected it needs to be analysed and presented in meaningful ways. The main techniques include the range of pay for a particular job, the mean average, the median or mid-point as this will compensate for extremes in the data set, upper and lower quartiles which define the market rate of the top 25 per cent and the bottom 25 per cent of the organisations in the survey, and deciles, which graduate the market rate in tenths. These statistical measures, as well as making comparison easier, will also enable decisions to be made about organisation positioning within the

Exhibit 9.2   Outline survey form for collecting market rate data

Organisation:

Job title:

(underpinned by a market rate survey: job profile)

Pay rate or range:

Incremental points and basis for progression:

Median pay rate:

Benefits:
- Performance-related pay
- Bonuses
- Allowances
- Weighting (e.g. London)
- Holidays
- Pensions
- Life/health insurance
- Discounts/employee purchase plan
- Car
- Other benefits

Next pay review date:

Date of survey:

Contact name, address, telephone no:

market rate range. For example, choices need to be made about whether pay and reward policy will reflect median rates, the upper or lower quartiles or, in the case of an organisation wishing to pay the best, the top decile. Market range positioning decisions will be based on beliefs about whether or not paying more for employees buys better performance and also, and often more pragmatically, about direct financial affordability. The market rate therefore provides an important external dimension to reward and resourcing strategies.

JOB EVALUATION

Job evaluation is a systematic way of determining the relative worth of jobs within an organisation. It is not a scientific process but a mechanism which produces a logical structure for defining jobs into a hierarchy. It is important to bear in mind that it is the job and not the job-holder that is being evaluated. The existence of a formal system of job evaluation provides transparency and increases the likelihood that pay decisions will be understood and generally accepted within the organisation. An analytical job evaluation scheme can also provide a defence in an equal pay claim.

However, job evaluation is not without criticism. First, a common feature of people resourcing is the need for flexibility, but formal job evaluation systems assess the jobs at one point in time and if change is rapid then any rank order of jobs produced may soon become outdated. A rigid job definition may discourage job-holders from constantly reviewing the job to assess what *needs* to be done; they may focus solely on the job that is described and evaluated, thus reducing the likelihood of job development. Second, the concentration on internal equity ignores market rates, and the introduction of a formal job evaluation system will need to address this issue and also decide how market disparities are handled. A system of premium payments may be introduced to offset this market problem, but it may distort the reward structure and needs to be kept under review to ensure that the premium is still required. Third, job evaluation is time consuming and costly to introduce and to maintain. To retain acceptance and credibility it must be regularly reviewed and formal systems of appeal introduced to consider any regrading claims. Finally, the formality of the process and the apparent 'accuracy' of the outcome belies the fact that job evaluation relies heavily on individual judgement, with all of the preconceptions of the value and importance of particular jobs. This leaves the system open to charges of distortion and subjectivity.

JOB EVALUATION SCHEMES

Job evaluation schemes can be divided into non-analytical and analytical schemes. Non-analytical schemes compare *whole jobs* with one another without breaking them down into separate parts. The most common non-analytical schemes are job ranking, paired comparison and job classification or job grading. Analytical schemes define or analyse the jobs in terms of a number of factors and score the jobs against these factors. The most common analytical schemes are points rating schemes which include named brand schemes like the Hay system. There is an increasing use of competency-based schemes which define, analyse and evaluate the jobs in terms of the competencies that are needed. This can shift the emphasis from the job to the person doing the job and therefore potentially conflicts with the fundamental precept of job evaluation, that it is the job which is evaluated and not the person doing the job.

Non-analytical schemes

Job ranking – is perhaps the most simple job evaluation method. It involves comparing whole jobs with one another and ranking them on the basis of whether one job is considered to be of more value than another. Job descriptions or accountability profiles are produced for all jobs within the organisation. Benchmark jobs are identified, which are representative of the range of jobs in the organisation; other jobs are compared to the

Job	A	B	C	D	E	F	G	Total	Rank
A	–	2	2	1	0	2	1	8	4
B	0	–	2	0	0	1	0	3	5
C	0	0	–	0	0	1	0	1	7
D	1	2	2	–	1	2	1	9	2
E	2	2	2	1	–	2	1	10	1
F	0	1	1	0	0	–	0	2	6
G	1	2	2	1	1	2	–	9	2

Fig. 9.1 Paired comparison score chart

benchmark job and are inserted into the hierarchy based on the perceived value of the job. The process is subjective and subject to stereotyping, preconceptions and misconceptions, lacks transparency and would not provide a defence in an equal pay claim. It may be relatively easy to decide between jobs where there is a significant difference in value, but it becomes increasingly difficult to deal with subtle or small differences and the rank order produced gives no indication of the size of the differences between the jobs. However, it is a low-cost scheme which can be undertaken quite quickly.

Paired comparisons – is an attempt to overcome some of the subjectivity of job ranking by systematically comparing each job with every other job and scoring 2, 1, or 0 in terms of whether the job is more, the same or less demanding. The output is a paired comparison score chart (Fig. 9.1) which produces total scores and a ranking of the jobs.

This scheme has advantages over the ranking method in reducing bias and inconsistency through scrutinising every job in the organisation. However, this increases the size of the job evaluation task and is clearly inappropriate for even relatively small organisations (the calculations needed for an organisation with 100 jobs would be 4950). A spreadsheet can be used to speed up the process of calculation, but the task of making the judgement on the scoring remains onerous.

Job classification – or job grading – is a job evaluation method which measures jobs against predetermined classifications or grade definitions. This in effect works in the reverse way to the other methods in that the first task is to define the jobs within the group that are to be evaluated. This method is most commonly used in large bureaucratic organisations with a fairly rigid hierarchy and where there are many jobs of a particular type. A significant problem with job classification is that it is difficult to devise meaningful definitions appropriate for very diverse jobs. For example, how easy is it to formulate a definition to meet the job requirements of a personnel officer, a cost controller or an IT systems support operator, all of which might fall within the same grade? Job classification works best where the jobs to be evaluated have some degree of commonality. A classic example of job classification is the nurse grading system used in the National Health Service. It works because it is restricted to one occupational group, there is a logic to it and there is a clear hierarchy of responsibility.

There are three stages to developing and implementing a job classification scheme:

1 The grade definitions have to be drawn up and agreed.
2 A job description must be produced for each job to be evaluated.
3 Each of the job descriptions is matched to the definition that most closely reflects the duties and responsibilities of the job and the appropriate grade is assigned.

This sounds relatively simple but the process is fraught with problems, the most notable being the agreement of the grade definition. As jobs become more complex the grading definitions become more generalised and the matching process more difficult. Anyone with involvement in the implementation of the job classification scheme for nurses in the NHS from 1988 will be aware of the considerable time it takes for all of the jobs to be graded and the extensive hours, even years, spent in hearing appeals.

Analytical schemes

A points rating scheme – is more complex to devise and operate, but being analytical it will provide a defence in an equal pay claim, provided that the factors chosen are free from gender bias. Tried and tested named brands are available which provide a relatively sound defence against equal value claims. Points rating schemes can be developed 'in house' to meet the needs of the organisation, but there is a requirement for specialist skills if they are to be successfully implemented and the expertise of specialist consultants may be necessary.

A points rating scheme starts with the definition of a number of factors that are common to all jobs. For example, responsibility for resources, skill and knowledge, decision making, level of education and job complexity. Care must be taken to ensure that the factors are gender neutral. The factors are normally weighted to reflect their importance to the job, but this is not mandatory as some schemes avoid weighting because of the potential for gender bias. Each factor is then divided into a number of factor levels. Not all of the factors need the same number of levels; for example, responsibility for resources could be divided into several levels indicating responsibility for people, responsibility for budgets and responsibility for physical resources. Each job factor is scored using the factor level, adjusted by the weighting, and the scores for each factor are totalled to produce a points score for the job and to position the job relative to the other jobs. Exhibit 9.3 represents an example of a points rating job evaluation scheme. It shows the factors and their respective weightings. Each job can be judged against these factors, with the resultant score out of 1000 establishing the rank position (*see* assignments). Points rating is a complex process to design, implement and maintain, and consequently a disadvantage of the points rating scheme is higher cost. The generation of a numerical job score also gives the impression of accuracy, but job evaluation is neither scientific nor completely accurate as subjective (human) decisions are taken at several stages of the process – at the factor stage, at the factor level stage and at the weighting stage. There are therefore several opportunities for bias and stereotyping to occur.

Exhibit 9.3   An example of the factors in a points rating scheme

Job evaluation factors and their weighting with a potential total score of 1000	
Factor	*Maximum rating*
Knowledge	163
Mental skills	78
Communication skills	78
Physical skills	65
Initiative and independence	104
Physical demands	50
Mental demand	50
Emotional demands	50
Responsibility for people (external)	78
Supervisory responsibility	78
Responsibility for finance	78
Responsibility for physical resources	78
Working conditions	50

Competence related – job evaluation is a contemporary method which analyses job roles and the competencies required to undertake the role. In operation it is similar to the points rating method except that it is competence-related factors that are identified, levels defined and weightings allocated. The selection of appropriate competencies is critical and should normally include both behavioural and job-related competencies. Again care should be taken to ensure gender neutrality.

The rank ordering of jobs is fundamental to the development of any reward system and while formal job evaluation undoubtedly has disadvantages it provides a framework for the structuring of jobs. Formal and traditional job evaluation schemes appear to be declining in some sectors while emerging in others. The link between analytical schemes and equal pay defence means that many employers are reluctant to disengage from them altogether.

GRADED PAY

Graded pay structures are developed following a process of formal or informal job evaluation. The output from this evaluation process is a distribution of jobs based upon their ranking or points rating (Fig. 9.2). Decisions need to be taken about how these jobs will be grouped. Traditional graded systems group jobs in quite narrow pay bands or scales with some overlapping of the grades; this type of pay structure occurs more in hierarchical structures with many and diverse jobs. The number of grades will depend on the organisational structure. A tall organisational structure will require more grades, whilst a flatter structure will require fewer grades.

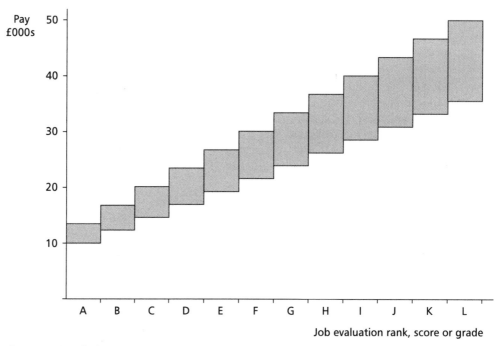

Fig. 9.2 Graded pay structure

Each job grade will have an associated pay scale and the width of the scale, normally expressed as a percentage, should be sufficient to allow for adequate incremental increases. It is usual for the percentage width of the pay scale to increase with more senior jobs to reflect greater responsibility. The width of each grade can vary from 20 per cent in the lower grade of a narrow grade structure, for example pay ranging from £10 000 to £12 000, to up to 50 per cent at the top of the structure, for example pay ranging from £30 000 to £45 000. The midpoint of the scale can represent the positioning in the labour market. A narrow banded graded pay system can produce a high number of grades and this can reduce organisational flexibility as there is little scope for pay enhancement, and there may be less scope for individual development. A narrow graded pay structure is unlikely to sit comfortably with a reward strategy of flexibility and continuous employee development.

Graded systems are traditionally based on the belief that individuals progress through the grade incrementally based on their length of service. Therefore each year the employee receives an annual increment until the top of the scale is reached; in some organisations this may be in as little as four years. If the job does not change or the job-holder does not move to a higher grade job there is no scope for further pay increases. Incremental pay progression is consistent with a strategy that rewards loyalty and commitment to the organisation but is less consistent with a strategy which focuses on flexibility and rewarding performance. Traditionally, graded pay has been the system used in the public sector, reflecting the bureaucratic structure. Increasingly organisations are using a hybrid model that has elements of graded incrementalism, but also includes elements of performance measurement.

Graded pay systems have the advantage of being transparent; everyone knows the grades and the monetary values assigned to the grades and in principle everyone on that grade will receive the same salary if they have been with the organisation for the same length of time. In recent times there has been a freeing up of the system to allow more managerial discretion, and increasingly new employees may start part way up the scale. However, this can lead to problems, as the person reaches the top of the scale sooner and may become demotivated by the lack of opportunity for progression in terms of both pay and personal development.

Control of the total pay bill is more straightforward with incremental progression, as the numbers in each grade are determined by the organisational structure and therefore the costs are known; there is no unknown performance element. Control is based on the assumption that people join the organisation and natural wastage or internal promotion will move people out of grades before they reach the top of the grade or shortly afterwards. This movement up and out of the grade provides a mechanism for controlling costs on or about the midpoint of the scale. This may happen in a dynamic labour market, but in a static labour market with lower staff turnover, costs increase as more employees reach the top of the scale. An example of this was the devolving of school budgets from Local Education Authorities. Staff budgets were devolved and normally funded on the basis of the midpoints of the approved grade distribution for the school and not on the basis of actual staff costs. Any school with a high number of long service staff, who were at or near the top of the grade, immediately had a funding problem as the devolved staff budget would not meet the actual pay bill.

There are disadvantages with graded pay systems and incremental progression. Grade boundaries may be rather arbitrary and it can be difficult to accurately grade jobs on the grade boundaries. Incremental progression may lead to a lack of motivation as every employee receives the annual increment, including the poor performer; but this issue is generally overstated because individuals work to achieve their objectives for a variety of reasons, pay being only one. A further disadvantage is the rigidity that narrowly graded systems place on an organisation. An organisation that is seeking change, more teamworking and increased flexibility may find that a graded pay system with incremental progression acts counter to these drives.

Graded pay systems with incremental progression are generally a declining trend, but there are still many workers in the UK who are employed in organisations which operate such a system. It is less likely that new graded systems with incremental progression will be developed. The privatisation of public utilities and the change to agency status of many public bodies results in greater freedom to make changes to existing graded payment systems. One change that seeks greater flexibility is broadbanding.

BROADBANDING

The CIPD guide to broadbanding of pay defines it as:

> the compression of a hierarchy of pay grades or salary ranges into a small number of wide bands, typically four or five. Each of the pay bands therefore spans the pay opportunities previously covered by several separate pay ranges. The focus is on lateral career movement within the bands and on competence growth and continuous development.

Broadbanding emerged in the USA in the early 1990s and although its application may be increasing it may be inappropriate for some organisational structures. Organisations most suited to the introduction of broadbanding are those that have 'delayered' and become 'leaner and flatter'. Organisations where promotion opportunities have declined and the need for flexibility and multiskilling have increased are more likely to benefit from broadbanding. This aligns the pay policy and structure with the reward philosophy and strategy and allows employers to develop a reward system which encourages lateral movement. Reward systems that focus on individual performance-related pay may limit the internal movement of staff. Job performance may increase with familiarity and expertise in doing the job and make staff reluctant to move if the performance element of pay is threatened. Limited opportunities for promotion may mean that staff are unlikely to move laterally if that has a detrimental effect on their pay, unless there is encouragement to do so. This could be through intrinsic rewards such as self-development or through financial rewards. The introduction of broadbanding may give the manager the freedom to reward the willingness to move and to acquire new skills. As Reissman (1995) commented,

> broadbanding helps to eliminate the obsession with grades and instead encourages employees to move to jobs where they can develop their career and add value to the organisation.

Broadbanding can be linked to job families, or different occupational groups, and appropriate monetary values assigned to the bands within the job family which allow market rates to be taken into account. The effective use of broadbanding can give more autonomy to the manager and therefore requires a better educated and more confident management. Armstrong and Brown (2001) summarise the potential benefits of broadbanded pay structures as:

- increasing flexibility in pay management
- reducing bureaucracy
- rewarding lateral development and continuous improvement
- clarifying career paths
- responding to the changing nature of work and employee expectations
- enabling greater line management involvement in pay determination.

A move from narrow grades to broad bands can lead to problems. Employees in the lower grades may be concerned that promotion opportunities have disappeared while those in the higher grades may feel that their job has been devalued. These concerns have to be identified and addressed. Changes to the pay system need to be communicated to staff and understood within the context of a changed organisational structure. Lateral moves need to be viewed by the employee as an opportunity for self-development and by the employer as a chance to enhance workforce skills. Broadbanded pay is therefore concerned with more than just pay:

> Broadbanded and job family structures are no longer treated simply as vehicles for delivering pay and are often seen as being complementary to competence and career development policies. The main aim is to provide information on development opportunities and career paths that, as part of a performance management process, can contribute to personal development planning.
>
> (Armstrong, 2000)

MARKET-DRIVEN PAY

Market-driven pay describes a reward approach where pay and benefits policy and practice is sharply responsive to the external labour market. It incorporates the philosophy of a particular job being 'worth' what the labour market commands at any one time – the concept of the market rate of pay. Market-driven pay is based on classical economic theory, where pay decisions are influenced by market supply and demand for labour. Buyers and sellers of labour, employers and employees respectively, engage in an employment and contractual relationship through the price mechanism of pay (Armstrong, 1999). Where supply of labour exceeds demand this will tend to suppress levels of pay; conversely, where the demand for work or skills of a particular kind exceeds supply there will be a tendency for upward pressure on pay. In order to secure the quality and quantity of employees required, employers, as the buyers of labour, need to adjust pay and reward packages to reflect the 'going rate'. Market-driven pay therefore focuses primarily on external relativities and is more concerned with 'commercial worth' than with establishing the 'relative worth' of jobs within an organisation. In a pure form market-driven pay gives primacy to the recruitment and retention objectives of reward strategy and implicitly subordinates concepts of fairness and equity.

A market-driven approach enables an employer to compete more effectively for the workers it requires and it is therefore an important consideration in developing reward strategy. However, as with other types of market there is no 'perfect labour market' and employers cannot simplistically rely on market-driven pay to deliver all pay policy objectives. Other factors to take into account include, for example, equity and fairness in the psychological and motivational equation, variations in individual performance which may need to be rewarded, the fact that as well as external labour market (ELM) relativities, there may be an internal labour market (ILM) which invokes reward considerations relating to promotion, progression and succession, and finally the organisation's 'ability to pay'. Market-driven pay is therefore a question of emphasis rather than the sole basis for making reward decisions. Establishing the market rate is probably best viewed as the identification of a range of pay for a particular type of work, within which decisions can be made about organisational positioning within the range, the impact of other elements of the reward package, the desired scope for reflecting individual performance and affordability. Identifying the market rate or range therefore serves to inform wider reward decisions within a market-driven policy.

PERFORMANCE-RELATED PAY

Although associated with 'new pay', performance-related pay (PRP) is not a new phenomenon, although in recent years PRP has received increased emphasis within reward strategies that seek integration with corporate strategies:

> Some attempt to relate pay to performance is the dominant feature of current reward strategies.
>
> (Torrington and Hall, 1996)

As the dominant contemporary feature in reward strategies PRP is given comprehensive treatment in this section which examines the motivational basis for PRP, places PRP within a wider context, explores some of PRP themes, conflicts and ambiguities and discusses the role of PRP within a performance management system. Individual PRP provides the principal focus, but there is increasing organisational interest in team-based PRP (team reward) and this is also given attention. The following PRP definition is proposed:

Individual PRP is the direct linkage of payment within the contract of employment to an assessment of performance based on the perceived contribution or value of the individual employee to the organisation at one point in time.

PRP has three sequential stages:

Stage 1 – the establishment of individual **performance criteria** by imposition, discussion or agreement.

Stage 2 – an **assessment of performance** against performance criteria, normally by the line manager.

Stage 3 – the **selective allocation of pay** to the assessment of performance, usually through the exercise of managerial prerogative.

The theoretical basis for PRP

The underlying theoretical basis for PRP is motivation theory. Content theories, such as those of Maslow (1943, 1987) and Herzberg (1959), draw attention to pay as one of many sources of human need. The satisfaction of this need can contribute to motivation at work, but the relative importance of pay as a motivator will vary with individual circumstances. More specific to PRP are the process theories of equity (Adams, 1965) and expectancy (Porter and Lawler, 1968; Lawler, 1973; Vroom, 1964) and it is useful to have an understanding of these.

Equity theory is founded on the psychological concept that humans have a need to be treated fairly at work in relation to other employees. Fairness is calculated by employees, primarily subconsciously, by making comparisons of the ratio of job inputs to job outputs. Inputs (*by the employee*) are effort, knowledge, skills, loyalty and flexibility, and outputs (*from the work*) are financial and non-financial rewards. Where rewards are perceived to be fair and equitable in relation to job inputs *in comparison* with other workers a state of equity exists, and according to equity theory this will contribute to and maintain motivation. Where inequity is perceived it has the potential to be demotivational. PRP in this equity context provides a mechanism for relating job outputs, in this case financial rewards, to inputs, thereby securing equity and employee motivation. Equity theory gives contemporary credence to the old concept of 'a fair day's pay for a fair day's work'.

Expectancy theory has many forms but all relate to the notion that employees will be motivated if direct relationships exist between effort, performance and reward (Kessler and Purcell, 1992). The summary expectancy model in Exhibit 9.4 is indicative of these relationships.

Exhibit 9.4   Expectancy theory of motivation

MOTIVATION

=

Effort to Performance relationship (E to P)

×

Performance to desired Outcomes linkage (P to O)

×

The Valence – personal perceived value of the desired rewards (V)

As with equity theory some form of individual 'cognitive calculus' (subconscious mental calculation) is assumed. First, the individual will make judgements about the probability (an expectancy) that increased effort, or decreased effort, will impact on performance levels (E to P relationship). Second, an assessment will be made of the likelihood (another expectancy) of certain levels of performance attracting desirable outcomes, including payment and rewards (P to O linkage). The third element is a measure of the perceived value of the desired outcome, the valence (or value to the individual) of the reward (V). The theoretical connection with PRP is made through an assumption that pay is a desired outcome, thereby creating a case for expressly linking pay to performance, in order to maintain or improve motivation. Implicit in this is the need to ensure that the reward has a high valence, which means that the PRP element of reward needs to be of sufficient value to the individual employee. In short, if pay depends on performance then employees will apply effort in pursuit of performance in order to secure the desired outcome of more pay.

There are several obvious problems with this pay and motivation equation. First, expectancy theory assumes that pay is a desired outcome, but other desired outcomes, both intrinsic and extrinsic, in a particular situation for a given individual, need to be identified in order to determine the weight of the pay element as a motivator. Second, expectancy theory suggests that the PRP element has to be meaningful and substantive in order to acquire a high valence, but organisations may not be able to afford meaningful amounts. If the PRP element is not significant or meaningful then, according to expectancy theory, it is unlikely to make a significant contribution to the motivation equation. Third, expectancy theory is silent on what amount of money motivates. Despite these difficulties expectancy theory does provide additional insights into the relationship between pay, performance and motivation.

The emergence of PRP

The competitive pressure in the external environments (*see* Chapter 1) has intensified interest in ensuring that employees add value through increased effort and focused performance. PRP is therefore a central tenet of 'new pay'. The aim is to 'put a performance message in the pay packet' and thereby induce a more performance conscious culture.

There are a number of drivers which have contributed to the emergence of PRP. First, the strategic (vertical) integration of reward is seen as an essential prerequisite for optimising organisational performance and, when explicitly linked to the achievement of organisational objectives, acts as a lever to direct individual performance to the pursuit of corporate goals. Second, the weakening of collectivism in the employment relationship, and a reduction in collective bargaining, have created a climate where it has been possible for organisations to individualise employment arrangements further through extending PRP (an alternative explanation is that PRP has been used as a managerial tool to weaken collectivism and trade union influence). Third, the Conservative government in the 1980s and 1990s was concerned with injecting enterprise values into the public sector, resulting in PRP being used as a mechanism for championing values associated with flexibility, efficiency and customer-orientation. This approach has continued with New Labour Governments. The factors contributing to the emergence of PRP are summarised in Fig. 9.3.

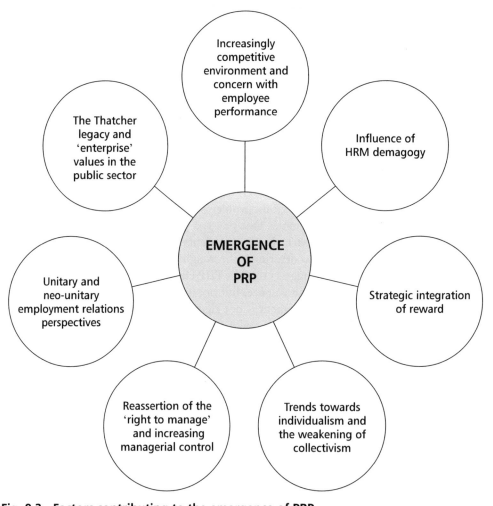

Fig. 9.3 Factors contributing to the emergence of PRP

PRP themes, conflicts and ambiguities

Several PRP themes are evident and these are exposed in order to enable more informed PRP decision making. They include:

- doubts about PRP as a motivator
- PRP and teamworking – facilitator or inhibitor?
- measuring and assessing performance – the challenges
- PRP and the potential for unfair discrimination
- compatibility of PRP and a professional ethos
- the perceptions of PRP recipients.

It is through an awareness of conflicts and ambiguities in these areas that attention can be paid to PRP design and practice.

Although in theory PRP has motivational potential, there is considerable research evidence which reveals doubts about the motivational effects in practice. The contrary argument is summarised by Kohn (1994): 'pay is not a motivator and all that money buys is temporary compliance'. Many managers, as well as researchers, are sceptical and have low expectations about the motivational abilities of pay. PRP may actually demotivate average performers because they receive small amounts of PRP (IDS 654, 1993). There appears to be some disparity between what it might be necessary to pay for PRP to be motivational and the actual amount of PRP awards. Evidence from the USA suggests that PRP payments need to be set at 30 per cent of basic pay in order to improve performance. Beaumont (1993) and Lawson (2000) are more modest, but still suggest that a merit based increase of the order of 10 to 15 per cent is needed to have any impact on motivation. Average pay awards in low single figures, the norm in low inflation economies, do not compare favourably with these research findings. The CIPD Survey (2000) reports a median figure of 4 per cent for PRP awards. Another aspect of the motivational properties of PRP relates to the potential for the displacement of objectives. The reduction of a whole job into a relatively easy to quantify collection of objectives may create an employee focus on achieving the objectives as determined, but not result in getting the whole job done effectively. The individual may focus on the specified objectives to secure enhanced payments, but may neglect other important features of the job. The motivational integrity of PRP may be more a matter of faith than fact, but Murlis (1996) argues that it is essential to distinguish between using PRP to manage performance (motivation) and using PRP to recognise performance (reward). If the PRP element is relatively small it is unrealistic for managers to expect PRP to offer much incentive and to motivate.

The individual performance focus of PRP has the potential to inhibit teamworking and fragment team behaviour. This is contrary to team cultures. Not only is there potential for individual performance and teamwork objectives to come into conflict, but also:

> the greater the individual dependency on other colleagues the less strong is the motivational potential of PRP because much of the achievement of performance is not within the control of the individual.

> (Robinson, 1992)

These concerns are prompting increasing interest in PRP based on team or group performance, although this practice is not yet widespread. Team- or group-based pay may solve some of the problems of individual PRP, but it does throw up some new ones (*see* page 227). An alternative strategy to team-based pay is to seek to reward individuals for teamwork and thereby reinforce the attitudes of individuals towards teamworking.

There are fundamental questions about Stages 1 and 2 of the PRP framework – establishing performance criteria and assessing performance effectively. It may be possible to do this where there is a direct and overt measurement available, as might be the case in some manual production work, but it is much more problematic for work which has less tangible and quantifiable outputs, as is likely in non-manual, managerial and professional occupations. In establishing and assessing performance against performance criteria there can be a tendency to measure what is easy to measure rather than what ought to be measured. An illustration of this is police effectiveness being assessed by the criteria of the incidence of crimes and of detection rates. In reality the ability of individual police officers to influence these measures is minimal, as levels of crime are attributable to much wider reasons than police performance. In any case, much police work is symbolic and therefore intangible – how is this element of performance assessed and measured (Savage, 1996)? Subjectivity is an inherent feature of PRP assessment, because the interactive process between assessor and assessee is vulnerable to a whole range of perceptual errors, including recency, the halo or horns effect, projection and other forms of distortion. In addition, workplace pressures will almost inevitably impact upon the assessment process. The pressures facing managers and the perceived intrusion of formal assessments, with associated form filling, may militate against managers taking the time and trouble to compensate for subjectivity.

The linkage of PRP decisions to an appraisal system produces a tension, because the dual managerial roles of 'coach' and 'judge' are potentially incompatible. On the one hand employees are being asked to expose weaknesses and areas for development so that they can be coached, and on the other hand a judgement of performance, with pay implications, will take place – hardly a scenario for a full and frank discussion about how an employee can develop in order to produce an even better performance. The solution is the separation of appraisal interviews from pay discussions, but although it is possible to seek to dissolve the link between performance appraisal and pay reviews to achieve more meaningful development discussions, it is probable that total 'divorce' is not realistic as some connection may remain in the minds of the assessor and the assessee.

PRP may discriminate unfairly against women as, in practice, it is primarily male managers who measure performance and they may tend to reward performance characterised by male values, with equal pay implications. There is concrete, if limited, evidence that the qualities associated with female workers tend to be downgraded in establishing performance criteria for PRP. The Equal Opportunities Commission (EOC) also suggests that discrimination may be occurring and recommends the monitoring of performance-related payments by gender. McColgan, from the Institute of Employment Rights (1994), attributes some inequalities in pay for men and women to PRP and presents a radical view by suggesting that if employers:

> wish to avoid such tiresome and expensive (equal value) litigation (they) would do well to place performance related pay on the scrapheap of unacceptable pay practices!

It is an anathema to many public servants, and others in professional occupations, to suggest that they might be motivated by pay linked to a judgement of their performance, but PRP has penetrated the health service, local authorities, the civil service, the police and education. The injection of enterprise values and governmental concern with organisational performance indicators is being translated into individual performance indicators and PRP. There is tension between the professional ethos of self-management and the managerialistic approach of PRP. Performance-related pay may fail to recognise that for professionals and public servants the psychological contract may have primacy over the economic contract – professionalism and ethics may matter more than money (Pilbeam, 1998).

The role of managers as 'the process controllers' of PRP arrangements tends to create positive perceptions of PRP, but where employee attitudes are examined the results are not encouraging. Employees have little trouble in identifying PRP tensions and contradictions. The views of employees of a major pharmaceutical group are revealing – 50 per cent did not think PRP was a fair system for all levels of staff, 50 per cent indicated that the PRP amount did not reflect performance, and 80 per cent felt that PRP did not encourage teamwork (Robinson, 1992). A survey of 20 000 telecommunications executives (reported in Goss, 1994) concluded that 50 per cent thought PRP was applied unfairly in practice, 70 per cent thought that bonuses were arbitrary, and 60 per cent *disagreed* that bonuses were paid for the achievement of objective measurable targets. A third survey (Pay and Benefits Bulletin 306, 1992) exposed the two most frequently expressed employee concerns as a lack of consistency in the assessment of performance between different assessors and the scope for individual bias to impact upon the assessment. Lawson (2000: 312) summarises recent research on employee perspectives towards PRP which indicate that employees are negative, or at best neutral, about PRP because they are not convinced that it motivates or that it is applied fairly.

Whether or not PRP is fair is a recurring theme and employees often suspect that some form of quota operates and that 'favouritism and unfairness is endemic' (Richardson and Marsden, 1991). Although PRP is rooted in equity theory, PRP practice may be different, attracting the 'rhetoric/reality' label – PRP being rhetorically fair but unfair in reality.

A number of these conflicts and ambiguities are presented as dichotomies in Exhibit 9.5 in order to stimulate a debate about the right balance between PRP belief and PRP scepticism.

Making PRP work and PRP within a wider performance management system

Although there are conflicts and ambiguities in PRP there is also widespread application of PRP schemes and it is useful to examine opportunities to contribute to success in PRP. Murlis (1994) refers to 'myths and legends' in PRP and constructively attempts to deflect and dismantle much of the criticism. This is helpful because it presents a concise overview of what is being said by proponents of PRP.

1 The 'bad press' and the executive reward debate are contributing to negative attitudes about PRP and need to be kept in perspective.

2 Assumptions that PRP can manage performance on its own are misguided.

Exhibit 9.5   Conflicts and ambiguities in PRP

Cautious PRP Believer – The Rhetoric?	Confirmed PRP Sceptic – The Reality?
• rewards performance at work	• pays for conformity to organisational norms
• allows individuals to be paid according to contribution	• divides teams and encourages individuals to pursue selfish goals
• complements performance management, empowerment and flexible working	• complements rhetorical trickery and fads
• is intrinsically fair – in theory	• creates feelings of unfairness and inequity – in practice
• motivates employees	• demotivates more employees than it motivates
• management view – performance improved	• recipients' view – performance not improved
• focuses effort on organisational goals	• has confused objectives which are difficult to evaluate
• amounts are meaningful	• amounts are not worth the effort
• is based on fair and objective performance measurement	• performance is assessed subjectively and only on what is easy to measure
• should be integrated with appraisal systems	• transforms the appraiser from a development coach to a judge and jury
• is central to the management of performance	• is marginal to the management of performance
• enables managers to reward employees	• significantly strengthens the right to manage/manipulate

3 There is potential for PRP to be used as a search and punish tool, particularly in a low trust environment, but it is an abuse of PRP to punish failure.

4 The perception that PRP needs quantifiable objectives is a 'management by objectives' hangover and should be replaced by focusing on what constitutes good performance. Armstrong and Brown (2001) prefer the term contribution-based pay – rewarding people for their outputs (results) *and* their inputs (competence); in other words, not only what they do but how they do it.

5 Potential for divisiveness can be counteracted by rewarding interdependency and teamworking, as PRP arrangements can be designed to send messages that teamwork values are important.

6 It is problematic to prove that PRP contributes to the bottom line, but PRP clarifies perceptions about performance and supports a performance culture.

7 Claims that PRP inhibits creativity and that it is an administrative nightmare are not necessarily valid, as these problems can be avoided.

8 The inflationary potential of PRP can be constrained by limiting overall budgets.

9 Rating drift and central tendency are endemic, but can be compensated for by revising rating schemes every few years.

Other learning points for the successful implementation of PRP include the following: realistic employee reward expectations as PRP is not a pay bonanza; PRP fits with an asset management approach to people; PRP is a continuous process, not a one-off introduction; and successful PRP is founded on effective overall performance management.

Critical success factors for PRP (Applebaum and Shapiro, 1991) include:

- sufficient individual differences in job performance and significant and meaningful breadth in pay ranges
- validity and reliability in the measurement of differences in individual job performance
- skilful appraisers and an organisational culture to support PRP
- equitable and competitive pay structures
- high trust environments and a willingness (toughness) to manage by managers.

The most encouraging aspect for PRP may be the potential role of PRP within an integrated performance management system (*see* Chapter 11).

Team-based PRP

Interest in team-based PRP is a reaction to the potential for individual PRP to prejudice teamworking and also reflects the significance being given to teamworking in contemporary organisations. 'It will take teamwork to cure cancer, maximise all students' learning, invent what comes after the television and create peace throughout the world – the truly committed, cooperative group is probably the most productive tool humans have' (Johnson and Johnson, 1997). Often referred to as 'team reward', team-based PRP incorporates the principle of linking the pay and non-financial benefits of the individual to the performance of a working group or team. The aim is to focus effort, encourage cooperative behaviour and send the cultural message that the organisation values teamworking. Whilst team-based PRP addresses some of the concerns about individual PRP, a number of different issues need to be appreciated. These include:

- the difficulty of identifying teams, particularly where they are transient
- the feasibility of establishing and measuring team performance through transparent criteria
- the frequency of team PRP, whether by time period or project, and the amount of payment in relation to other elements in the reward package
- the reliance of one team on another and whether this inhibits or facilitates team performance
- the potential for unhelpful inter-team competition, 'groupthink' and resistance to change
- the possibility of stifling individual creativity and motivation through pressure to conform to group norms
- contributions to the process of teamworking may need recognition as well as team results.

It can be seen from this list that many of the issues relate to disadvantages associated with very cohesive groups and therefore some theoretical appreciation of group development and the factors which influence group effectiveness is a necessary prerequisite to developing team reward systems.

There is limited take-up of team reward in the UK, but increasing interest. Brown (1996) reported a quarter of UK employers recognising teamworking in their pay systems with another 17 per cent actively panning its introduction. The IRS Survey (1998) reported only 6 per cent of organisations having team pay, although another 14 per cent were giving it active consideration. The CIPD Survey on PRP trends (2000) put the figure team for based PRP at 8 per cent of organisations. Team-based PRP is an opportunity, rather than a solution, and it is probably best suited to mature, stable and well-defined working groups. Other prerequisites include scope for autonomy, the interdependency of individuals, and teams composed of individuals who are flexible, multiskilled and good team players (Armstrong, 1999). It is unlikely to result in a 'team culture' on its own and requires underpinning with other teamworking initiatives. Team reward is another element in the search for 'perfect pay' and probably needs to be applied uniquely and in appropriate conditions. There is no reason why it cannot be integrated within a reward strategy which includes other forms of individual and market-related rewards – a 'blended' or hybrid strategy.

COMPETENCE-BASED PAY

The concept of competence is widely discussed in all areas of personnel and development, but is often characterised by mystique and muddle. Competence is defined in many ways, but it involves the appropriate combination of knowledge, skills and attitudes (KSAs) to achieve objectives. If competencies are used in other HR areas it is logical to include them in the reward system. Competence-based pay systems may focus on either:

- the acquisition of competencies
- the demonstration of competencies, or
- the extent to which competencies are used in the performance of the job.

The pay policy needs to be explicit about which of these is being rewarded. Payment for competence acquisition may be part of a strategy to increase flexibility and multiskilling, whereas rewarding the application of competence may stimulate better performance. Different competence categories may be used: behavioural competencies, managerial competencies, job competencies and even organisational competencies. The determination of competencies needs to recognise these different forms. Difficulties also arise out of what is to be rewarded, how it is to be assessed and by whom. Evidence from performance-related pay systems suggests that reliable judgement of performance by managers is not easy and the same is likely to be true of competencies.

A job described and evaluated in competencies offers the opportunity to use this framework for the appraisal and assessment of the job-holder, but it raises issues about the extent to which the job or the person is being evaluated. Performance-related pay systems have moved in recent years from a measure of inputs (how hard employees work) to a measure of outputs (how well employees have achieved their agreed objectives). Competence-based pay may be a return to the measurement of inputs, and the question then is what contribution does this make to achieving the objectives of the organisation? Sparrow (1996) offers a word of warning:

> There are four issues about which I . . . have some concern: the performance criteria on which competencies are based; the complex nature of what we are measuring; the relevance of the results to the organisation's future; the difficulty of making judgements about people's behaviour.

Competence is a fashionable concept, but should be applied discriminately, and competence-based pay needs to be complementary to the organisation's overall reward philosophy and strategy. The use of competencies in HR activities is further explored in Chapter 20.

PROFIT SHARING

Profit-related pay and employee share schemes are arrangements which enable employees to have a stake in the ups and downs of an enterprise; they represent financial participation by the employee. Profit-related pay involves the linkage of a proportion of employee reward to organisational profitability, whilst share ownership is a separate concept and involves financial investment by the employee with the prospect of dividend payment and increased share value. The aim of profit-sharing arrangements is to encourage employees to identify with and pursue the objectives of the organisation, and in return for this commitment employees share in corporate success. The effectiveness of profit sharing is difficult to evaluate because of the distance that exists between the effort of each individual employee and total corporate performance. The links between effort, performance and corporate outcomes, to use expectancy theory terms (*see* Exhibit 9.3), may be too uncertain to be motivational for the individual. However, profit sharing may engender a sense of commitment, ownership and esteem and contribute to corporate cohesiveness.

Although the idea that employees should have a financial stake in their employing organisation involves potential gain and potential loss, inevitably there is employee reluctance to jeopardise a portion of pay. In practice, profit-related pay schemes have tended either to reduce the risk of loss associated with salary substitution ('sacrifice') arrangements or to guarantee to make up any loss. The income tax advantages associated with Inland Revenue approved profit-related pay schemes were an added incentive to develop profit-related pay arrangements, but the phasing out of tax relief either increased costs for employers through compensating for employee loss of tax benefits, or alternatively reduced profit-related pay amounts for employees, making these schemes less attractive.

The 'employee stakeholder investing in the business' through profit sharing is the reciprocal concept of the 'business investing in people'; both are desirable in theory but more difficult to achieve in practice.

> Employees have complex sets of attitudes and desires, and financial participation schemes have to recognise these if they are to be successful. It is probably unrealistic to expect that any one participation scheme can have a transformational effect on employees or upon the firm in which it was introduced. They have to be used in conjunction with other human resource management instruments and, if well designed, may have mildly positive effects on firm performance.
>
> (Pendleton, 2000)

Profit sharing is another imaginative reward opportunity rather than a universal solution.

SUMMARY LEARNING POINTS

1 'New pay' is a label for contemporary reward practices which are strategically integrated with corporate goals and which use pay to lever up employee performance.

2 There is no 'one right way' to reward employees. The pay policy should provide a 'framework for action' which emanates from the reward philosophy and strategy of the organisation and takes account of the size, sector and corporate culture.

3 The market rate of pay is the 'going rate' for a job in the labour market and is a measurement of the commercial worth of employees. Market rate surveys gather labour market intelligence which informs reward decisions. The extent to which organisational pay policy reflects the market will be determined by reward philosophy and strategy.

4 Job evaluation is a systematic way of rank ordering jobs within an organisation. Non-analytical schemes consider whole jobs and analytical schemes factorise jobs. Only analytical schemes provide a defence in an equal pay claim.

5 A dominant feature of current reward strategies is to seek to relate pay to employee performance. Whilst performance-related pay is an attractive concept there are conflicts and ambiguities which need to be addressed in practice.

6 All pay policies tend to incorporate elements of job evaluation and labour market rates to a greater or lesser extent. In reality they may also be based on *ad hoc* decisions acknowledging the need to acquire a particular employee. The prevalent theme of the pay policy will generally reflect the corporate strategy of the organisation.

7 In relation to the employee market-driven pay reflects commercial worth, graded pay reflects relative worth, and performance-related pay reflects individual worth. These are sometimes competing reward strategies.

REFERENCES AND FURTHER READING

ACAS (1994) *Job Evaluation: An introduction.* Advisory Handbook.

Adams, J.S. (1965) 'Injustice in social exchange', *Advances in Experimental Social Psychology*, Vol. 2. New York: Academic Press.

Applebaum, S. and Shapiro, B. (1991) 'Pay for performance', *Journal of Management Development*, 10(8).

Armstrong, M. (1999) *Employee Reward.* London: CIPD.

Armstrong, M. (2000) 'Feel the width', *People Management*, 3 February, 34–8.

Armstrong, M. and Baron, A. (1995) *The Job Evaluation Handbook.* London: IPD.

Armstrong, M. and Brown, D. (2001) *New Dimensions in Pay Management.* London: CIPD.

Armstrong, M. and Murlis, H. (1994) *Reward Management.* London: Kogan Page and IPD.

Armstrong, M. and Murlis, H. (1998) *Reward Management: A handbook of remuneration strategy and practice.* London: Kogan Page.

Armstrong, M. and Ryden, O. (1997) *The IPD Guide to Broadbanding.* London: IPD.

Beaumont, P.B. (1993) *HRM: Key concepts and skills.* London: Sage.

Bradley-Hill, R. (1993) 'A two component approach to compensation', *Personnel Journal*, May.

Brown, D. (1996) 'Team rewards: lessons from the coal face', *Team Performance Management: an International Journal*, 2(2), 6–12.

CIPD Survey Report (2000) *Performance Pay Trends in the UK*.

Fowler, A. (1992) 'How to design a salary structure', *Personnel Management Plus*.

Fowler, A. (1996a) 'How to design and run salary surveys', *People Management*, September.

Fowler, A. (1996b) 'How to pick a job evaluation system', *People Management*, February.

Goss, D. (1994) *Principles of Human Resource Management*. London: Routledge.

Haslett, S. (1995) 'Broadbanding: a second generation approach', *Compensation and Benefits Review*, November/December, 27(6).

Heery, E. (1996) 'Risk, representation and the new pay', *Personnel Review*, 25(6). MCB University Press.

Herzberg, F. (1959) *The Motivation to Work*. New York: John Wiley.

IDS Management Pay Review 156: Policy and Analysis (1994) *More Doubts about Performance Pay*. February.

IDS Management Pay Review (1996) *New Evidence on Broadbanding*. IDS.

IDS Report 654 (1993) *Study Questions the Effectiveness of Performance-Related Pay*. December.

IDS Study 518 (1992) *Performance Management*. November.

Industrial Relations Services (1998) 'Pay prospects survey', *Pay and Benefits Bulletin 458*, 10–13.

IPD (1997) *Guide to Broadbanding of Pay*. London: IPD.

Johnson, D. and Johnson, F. (1997) *Joining Together: Group theory and group skills*. Boston, MA: Allyn and Bacon.

Kessler, I. and Purcell, J. (1992) 'Performance-related pay: objectives and applications', *Human Resource Management Journal*, 2(3), 16–33.

Kohn, H. (1994) 'PRP does not work', *Personnel Management Plus*, May, 3.

Lawler, E. (1973) *Motivation in Work Organisations*. Maidenhead: Brooks/Cole.

Lawler, E. (1995) 'The new pay: a strategic approach', *Compensation and Benefits Review*, July/August.

Lawson, P. (2000) 'Performance-related pay', in Thorpe, R. and Homan, G. (eds) *Strategic Reward Systems*. Harlow: FT Prentice Hall.

Ledford, G. (1995) 'Designing nimble reward systems', *Compensation and Benefits Review*, July/August.

Lewis, P. (1998) 'Exploring Lawler's new pay theory through the case of Finbank's reward strategy for managers', *Personnel Review*, 29(1), 10–31.

Maslow, A.H. (1943) 'A theory of human motivation', *Psychological Review*, 50, 370–96.

Maslow, A.H. (1987) *Motivation and Personality*. New York: Harper & Row.

McColgan, A. (1994) 'Time for equal merit', *Personnel Today*, March.

Murlis, H. (1994) 'The myth about performance pay', *Personnel Management*, August, 18.

Murlis, H. (ed.) (1996) *Pay at the Crossroads*. London: IPD.

Pay and Benefits Bulletin 306 (1992) 'Merit pay in the nineties', June, 3–7.

Pendleton, A. (2000) 'Profit sharing and employee share ownership', in Thorpe, R. and Homan, G. (eds) *Strategic Reward Systems*. Harlow: FT Prentice Hall.

Pilbeam, S. (1998) 'Individual performance related pay: believers and sceptics', *Employee Relations Review*. Croners.

Porter, L. and Lawler, E. (1968) *Managerial Attitudes and Performance*. New York: Irwin.

Reissman, L. (1995) 'Nine common myths about broadbands', *HR Magazine*, 40(8), 79–86.

Richardson, R. and Marsden, D. (1991) 'Does performance pay motivate?', *A Study of Inland Revenue Staff*. LSE.

Roberts, I. (1997) 'Remuneration and reward', in Beardwell, I. and Holden, L. (eds), *HRM: A contemporary perspective*. London: Pitman Publishing.

Robinson, S. (1992) 'The trouble with PRP', *Human Resources*, Spring.

Savage, S. (1996) in Farnham, D. and Horton, S. (eds) *Managing the New Public Services*. London: Macmillan.

Schuster, J. and Zingheim, P. (1992). *The New Pay: Linking employee and organisational performance*. New York: Lexington.

Sparrow, P. (1996) 'Too good to be true?' *People Management*, December.

Taylor, S. (2000) 'Debates in reward management', in Thorpe, R. and Homan, G. (eds) *Strategic Reward Systems*. Harlow: FT Prentice Hall.

Thorpe, R. and Homan, G. (2000) *Strategic Reward Systems*. Harlow: FT Prentice Hall.

Torrington, D. and Hall, L. (1996) Paper on Developments in the Personnel Management function: summary of research results.

Vroom, V.H. (1964) *Work and Motivation*. New York: John Wiley.

White, G. and Druker, J. (2000) *Reward Management: A critical text*. London: Routledge.

ASSIGNMENTS AND DISCUSSION TOPICS

1 In an organisation with which you are familiar, identify and discuss the reward philosophy and strategy. How is this communicated to employees?

2 Examine the reward policy and structure within your organisation to identify the ways in which it supports strategic aims and where there is potential conflict.

3 Assess the extent to which your organisation relates reward policy to external labour market rates and discuss how it gathers market intelligence.

4 What are the purposes of job evaluation systems? Discuss the advantages and disadvantages of formal job evaluation schemes.

5 Using Exhibit 9.3 discuss the benefits that may accrue from the illustrated points-rating scheme and identify the challenges that will need to be addressed in operationalising it. To what extent are the benefits and challenges indicative of points-rating job evaluation schemes in general?

6 What are the advantages and disadvantages of incremental payment systems?

7 Can a market-driven reward strategy also meet employee expectations of fairness and equity in pay and benefits?

8 Examine the part that team-based pay, competence-based pay and market-driven pay could play in the reward strategy of your organisation. What might inhibit the successful introduction of any of these initiatives?

9 What are the objectives of a performance-related pay strategy and why is it so managerially popular? What PRP challenges are faced by managers and what conditions are necessary for PRP to be an effective reward strategy?

10 Based on your *own personal experience and perceptions* of individual performance-related pay (PRP), complete the activity below, by circling a number for each statement. If practical, aggregate the results with a sample of students or work colleagues. In any event discuss your responses and findings in small groups.

PLEASE CIRCLE A NUMBER

Scoring System

Strongly disagree	=	1
Disagree	=	2
Neither disagree nor agree	=	3
Agree	=	4
Strongly agree	=	5

	strongly disagree				strongly agree
PRP is motivational	1	2	3	4	5
PRP is effective in rewarding good performance	1	2	3	4	5
PRP helps in recruitment	1	2	3	4	5
PRP assists in the retention of valuable people	1	2	3	4	5
PRP increases management control over individuals	1	2	3	4	5
PRP encourages a performance conscious culture	1	2	3	4	5
PRP is fair in principle	1	2	3	4	5
PRP is fair in practice	1	2	3	4	5
PRP incorporates valid and reliable measures of job performance	1	2	3	4	5
PRP inhibits teamworking	1	2	3	4	5
PRP only measures what is easy to measure	1	2	3	4	5
PRP is a good thing	1	2	3	4	5
PRP improves flexibility	1	2	3	4	5
PRP is inherently subjective	1	2	3	4	5
PRP makes financial control easier for organisations	1	2	3	4	5
PRP encourages common behaviours amongst employees	1	2	3	4	5
PRP enables employees to share in organisation success	1	2	3	4	5
PRP amounts are/have been meaningful to me	1	2	3	4	5
PRP improved my performance	1	2	3	4	5
PRP demotivates those who do not receive any	1	2	3	4	5
PRP performance measures were appropriate for me	1	2	3	4	5

CHAPTER 10

Reward, benefits and pensions

INTRODUCTION

To achieve the objective of resourcing the organisation effectively there has to be an understanding of the additional elements that make up the 'total package', or the total remuneration, for the employee, as the reward expectations of employees encompass more than just money. In addition to pay, the total remuneration package includes a range of other benefits. This chapter explores the nature of employee benefits, including flexible benefits, and exposes the basic principles of pensions. Combinations of base pay, variable pay and benefits, which are either employer prescribed or employee selected from the diet on offer, need to be developed to correspond with the overall reward strategy. The important concept of non-financial reward is also introduced. The search for 'perfect pay' continues enthusiastically and the external context and the internal organisational contingencies will drive this search for perfection in reward systems.

CHAPTER OBJECTIVES

- To explore the content of the employee benefit package and the notion of total remuneration.
- To examine the concept of flexible benefits.
- To expose the complexity of pensions, including state, occupational and personal pension arrangements.
- To identify developments in the harmonisation of terms and conditions of employment.
- To consider the Greenbury and Cadbury reports in the context of pay and reward.
- To identify a range of non-financial rewards.
- To consider emerging and declining trends in pay and reward.

TOTAL REMUNERATION AND BENEFITS

Reward strategy should be devised and developed to meet organisational and employee needs. The policy derived from the strategy has to determine not only the type of payment system and labour market positioning, but also the most appropriate combination of base pay, discretionary/variable pay and benefits. The total package should be sufficiently competitive to meet pay policy objectives. The concept of total remuneration includes all aspects of pay and benefits and creates a framework which allows the different elements of the package to be adjusted to meet the changing needs of the business and of the employee. The individual elements need to be assessed on the basis of cost to the employer and value to the employee and the most appropriate combination constructed for each grade of staff. The total remuneration concept can be applied to all staff, although the combination of the elements and the content of each element may be different. There are three elements of total remuneration.

1 *Base pay* is the basic salary, wage or hourly pay. It is 'the rate for the job'. Base pay can be derived from job evaluation to determine internal equity and from market intelligence.

2 *Discretionary/variable pay* is any additional element of financial reward which may or may not be consolidated. This can vary considerably from zero per cent where all pay is base pay, with no 'add-ons', to 100 per cent where all pay is variable pay and there is no element of 'rate for the job'. Variable pay of 100 per cent is sometimes associated with sales jobs and referred to as 'commission only' pay. Reward strategy and policy will determine the role that variable pay will play and the proportion of pay that is earned over and above base pay. Performance-related pay, team-based pay and competence-based pay, discussed in the previous chapter, are all examples of variable pay.

3 *Benefits* can be cash benefits or benefits which are not directly cash benefits, such as paid holidays, pension schemes, company cars or private health insurance.

It is difficult for the individual employee to assess the total value of the remuneration package as benefit items will vary in usage; for example, occupational sick pay will only be paid to those who are sick, pensions to those who retire, mortgage assistance to those who buy a house, and so on.

Employee benefits

Armstrong (1996) states that the main aims of any benefits system are:

> To contribute to the provision of a competitive total reward package, to provide for the needs of employees in terms of their security, and, sometimes, their requirements for special financial help, thus demonstrating to them that they are members of a caring organisation, to increase the commitment of employees to the organisation and to provide a tax-efficient method of remuneration.

Leopold (2002) describes benefits as 'the components of a reward package provided in addition to cash pay'. He goes on to look at the impact that benefits can have in 'employee attraction, retention and motivation' and to identify the three main types of employee benefits, namely welfare benefits which include pensions and health insurance, family-friendly benefits which might include family leave and child care vouchers, and job-related benefits which might include the company car or product discounts. The employer should benchmark benefits provision against those benefits provided by competitor organisations. Failure to do this may mean that the employer is providing benefits that the employee neither wants nor values. In this situation the reward strategy is not meeting its objectives and may indeed be costing the employer financially. Employers therefore need to understand what employees want. This can be established through regular employee attitude surveys of the value and importance of specific benefits. There is no 'one best' benefits package; it must be related to the other elements of the reward package and the culture of the organisation. Organisations with very high levels of base pay may provide fewer direct benefits, as employees are more able to provide these for themselves. A decision to provide limited benefits may be efficient for the employer, as there is little or no associated administrative cost. High base pay with limited benefit provision may attract recruits, but if the total reward package is not clearly understood retention difficulties may arise. Organisations therefore need to appreciate what other similar organisations are doing in order to remain competitive, and salary surveys (*see* Chapter 9) also need to provide information on benefits provision to inform decisions on market positioning.

Consideration has to be given to the contents of the benefits package and whether it is to be flexible or an employer-devised package. Benefit entitlement for different grades of staff and the circumstances of entitlement will need to be established; for example, will length of service criteria be required for some benefits and, if so, what might be the impact and how will it be managed? Finally, the tax implications of individual benefits should be determined and regularly reviewed so that employees can be fully informed. This is particularly important if the organisation is providing flexible benefits, as the employee should understand the tax implications of any combination of benefit choices.

Contents of the benefit package

Employee benefits are many and varied and there is no intention to review all of the options here. There is a focus on the most commonly provided benefits. Employers can be creative and there may be value in looking for inventiveness where there are cost pressures and also employees who are receptive to an innovative benefits approach.

The occupational pension is probably the most significant benefit provided by the organisation and valued by the employee. This is given more comprehensive treatment later in this chapter.

Private health care has increased in provision and importance in recent years. It has advantages to the employer and also to the employee who has access to medical provision when it is required, and is in greater control of treatment. It can reduce the amount of sick leave taken by addressing health issues early and enabling the employee to return to work. It may also be valued by the employee in providing access to care that may otherwise be out of reach. Health care provision can be offered on a different basis to different types of staff with options of additional family cover.

Life insurance cover may be provided as an element of the pension scheme or provided outside the scheme. Levels of cover may vary by grade from four times annual salary for senior staff to just annual salary for less senior positions.

Severance payments are increasingly valued by employees at a time of insecurity in employment. There is a statutory requirement to pay redundancy payments in certain circumstances. There are also examples of enhanced packages for some employees and these are supported by the tax system to a level of £30 000. Concerns about high levels of severance pay for senior executives are addressed below and the implications of redundancy are discussed in Chapter 19.

Financial assistance can range from low interest loans to mortgage benefits. These benefits are more commonly associated with the finance sector and may be considered to be 'product discounts' for employees. A mortgage benefit can be a problem for employees in making it difficult to leave a particular employer if it will impact on housing costs.

Company cars play an important role which appears to be unique to benefits in the UK. A company car may be provided solely as a 'perk' with no job use requirement and little 'business mileage' undertaken. In this case the income tax implications have changed in recent years to reduce the value of this benefit to the employee by increasing its cost. Tax disincentives appear to be having little impact and the company car remains a desirable benefit. A company car is also important in defining status and this is difficult to change. Company cars can be provided with private fuel, but this benefit has further tax implications.

Childcare can be important in the retention of women workers particularly, although access to childcare solely by female employees may be discriminatory. The rationing of childcare provision can be problematic. Other options include vouchers or enhanced payments for a period of time on return to work to fund childcare.

Leave entitlement is also a benefit. There are many types of leave, from emergency leave to annual holiday entitlement. Entitlement to these may be affected by length of service or level within the organisation.

Recognition awards can play a significant role in motivating individuals and in recognising individual or team achievement. An effective communication system is important to ensure employees know what has to be done to receive a recognition award. The announcement of the recipients may also be an important symbolic feature of this type of award. An example of a recognition award is a 'dinner for two', a small cash award of £50 to £100, paid to an employee in recognition of a particular task well done. The aim of this may be to reward the employee, and their partner, in a situation where perhaps the employee had to work longer hours than normal, therefore recognising the impact of work on family life. Team dinners may also be used to recognise achievement by rewarding the team. Privileged car parking for a determined period is another example. Recognition awards tend to be described as *honararia* in the public sector. The effectiveness of these types of rewards will be influenced by the valence attributed to them by the individual employee.

A variety of additional benefits, ranging from staff discounts and luncheon vouchers to subsidised meals and sports and social facilities, is available and all should be evaluated and considered in the context of the total reward package. Benefit cost will vary from organisation to organisation, but figures of 20–25 per cent of the total pay bill are not unusual. There is therefore a rationale for the active management of the benefits package to ensure that pay policy objectives are met and value for money is achieved. Each employee benefit should be costed and assessed for the contribution it makes to specific pay policy objectives to ensure that this element of reward is horizontally integrated with other HR strategies. An innovative approach is to offer flexible benefits.

FLEXIBLE BENEFITS

Flexible, cafeteria or 'pick and mix' benefits are terms given to benefit arrangements which allow the exercise of employee choice within a reward package. Flexible benefits are therefore more employee focused, rather than having the organisation focus inherent in prescribed benefit arrangements which are the same for all employees. Adding flexibility to traditional benefits packages can mean anything from allowing some choice in company car value to having different levels of pension contributions, but a truly flexible benefits scheme will allocate a benefits allowance and allow employees to trade part of the standard package for other benefits.

In essence flexible benefits involve the presentation of a menu or portfolio of benefits from which employees can select according to their needs, within manageable guidelines.

For example, pensions could be enhanced, life cover could be extended to dependants, extra holidays could be bought, a car benefit could be cashed-in or other 'benefit trading' could take place. The flexible benefit approach acknowledges diversity of need and circumstances in the workforce and can form part of a managing diversity policy. There are other potential advantages to the employer: first, through targeting the cost and value of employee benefits (and avoiding paying for what individuals do not want), and second, through linking available benefits with particular pay and reward objectives. Reward objectives include, amongst others, recruitment, retention, motivation, offering incentives, recognising performance, equity and cost reduction. A paired comparison exercise which rates elements of the benefits package as high, medium or low against the various pay and reward objectives will be revealing about the extent to which each benefit contributes to the achievement of particular objectives (*see* end-of-chapter assignments, pp. 256–7). Research by the Industrial Society (2000) and the *Gee Reward and Remuneration Strategies Survey* (1998) reported that the key reasons for introducing flexible benefits were staff retention, staff motivation, enhancing recruitment, competitive pressures in the labour market, not paying for benefits that employees do not want, and the ability to recognise diverse individual needs. Flexible benefits therefore provide an imaginative opportunity to integrate reward strategy with other HR strategies, and also with corporate strategy.

Flexible benefits empower employees by enabling them to recognise the value of their benefits and to exercise some control over their own rewards. This fits with a general shift in the UK towards individuals accepting greater responsibility for life management, not only in employment, but also in education, health and provision for old age. Taxation and other fiscal changes have also impacted on the value and cost of providing certain benefits, for example the increasing taxation liability of company cars. Flexible benefits are also compatible with any move to individualise the employment relationship, and with personal contracts. Employees have diverse economic, security and social needs, and several demographic trends have contributed to this. These trends include an increase in female participation in the labour market, an increase in single parents, those with caring responsibilities and others in the 'sandwich generation', an ageing workforce with increasing post-employment life expectancies, new career patterns, and dual-career families. Flexible benefits allow organisations to be responsive to the lifestyle needs of a more diverse workforce.

Whilst intrinsically attractive, flexible benefits present a number of complications and challenges, particularly in relation to the costs, time and effort associated with setup, implementation and on-going administration. The start of the process involves deciding upon which pay policy objectives are to be actively pursued. A benefits audit is needed to establish the relative costs to the organisation and the value to employees, or in expectancy theory terms (*see* Chapter 9) the valence, of particular benefits. Assessing employee benefit valence needs to be based on consultation and the surveying of preferences. The balance between core (for everyone) and flexible (choice) benefits also needs to be considered, along with the extent to which benefits can be exchanged for cash. Although paternalistic in tone, the employer clearly has an ethical responsibility to ensure that employees do not deny themselves, for example, sufficient holiday to prevent overwork and 'burnout', or sufficient provision for old age (which may receive less priority of attention from younger workers). The scope for benefit decision either '*between*' benefits or '*within*' benefits is also an important factor. For example, can life assurance cover be traded for extra holiday? Can different levels of health care provision be selected according to need, thereby releasing 'benefit credit' for other benefits or for cash? The research by the Industrial Society (2000) found that benefits most likely to be designated as core are basic pensions, life insurance for self and health care for self, and flexibility in benefits is most likely to be limited in the case of holiday, life insurance and medical insurance. Benefits most likely to be flexible are health care for spouse, company cars, additional holiday, childcare and other 'lifestyle features'.

The organisation needs to determine a method of allocating 'benefit credit' to employees. Is it a percentage of pay? Is it a fixed amount? Is it harmonised for every employee? Is it influenced by length of service or performance? One illustrative method is to calculate the total reward figure for each employee, combining the value of pay and benefits, and stipulate that at least 80 per cent must be retained as pay, 10 per cent must be used to buy core benefits and 10 per cent is available for selecting flexible benefits or exchanging for cash.

It is apparent that a system of flexible benefits involves considerable administrative complexity, but computerised systems are well equipped to deal with this. The extent to which employees can change their benefit decision also needs to be addressed; too short a review time will intensify administrative complexity, whilst too long a time between review may reduce the positive impact of flexible benefits that the employer is seeking. An annual review may therefore be an appropriate arrangement in some cases, although to meet employee needs it may be necessary to allow benefit adjustment in response to significant lifestyle changes such as getting married or divorced or having children. The advent of e-HR can potentially exploit the power of the Internet to facilitate the self-management of flexible benefits through enabling employees to go on-line to find out the value of their benefits package and model the impact of trading one benefit for another (Blackman, 1999). The French-owned telecommunications manufacturer, Alcatel Telecom, introduced flexible benefits for its 600 employees and installed electronic kiosks in the workplace to enable staff to monitor and modify their benefits (Mullen, 1998). Objective benefit advice also needs to be available for employees as choice for some may represent dilemmas for others. A change to flexible benefit arrangements may be viewed suspiciously by employees if the arrangements are not fully transparent and communicated effectively, as altering reward benefits goes to the heart of the employment relationship and employer motives may be questioned.

There are two final issues which need to be exposed. First, it is likely that professional taxation and actuarial advice will be necessary and this will have an associated cost. Second, an organisation can elect either an incremental or a 'big bang' approach to flexible benefit introduction. Ultimately the decision to pursue flexible benefit arrangements depends on a judgement about whether the advantages of recognising diversity, providing choice and focusing reward objectives outweigh the costs of complexity and administration – do flexible benefits gain competitive advantage? In 1997 there were fewer than 100 genuine flexible benefits schemes in the UK, but the number was increasing (Arkin, 1997). The *Gee Reward and Remuneration Strategies Survey* (1998) reported that flexible benefit schemes were not yet widespread. Only 16 per cent of respondents had flexible benefits arrangements, but another 30 per cent were considering implementation within three years.

PENSIONS

Employee pension arrangements and occupational pension schemes present a considerable challenge in terms of provision, administration and adherence to statutory and Inland Revenue requirements. Specialist actuarial and financial advice is normally needed for this complex benefit. In order to understand the advice, to be able to contribute to the development of pensions policy and to provide accurate information to employees, it is necessary to be familiar with broad pensions types and the specialist language that is used. Pension types can be categorised as follows:

- state pension arrangements
- occupational pensions – final salary (defined benefit), money purchase (defined contribution) and mixed benefit schemes
- personal pensions – group and individual.

Although addressed again later in this section, it is useful at this stage to distinguish between **final salary** and **money purchase** arrangements. Final salary schemes pay benefits which are determined by taking the number of years of employee service and applying them to final salary on retirement to produce a pensions entitlement.

Final salary arrangements therefore provide defined outputs or benefits.

In contrast, money purchase schemes pay benefits which are determined by the value of a pot of money which is accumulated through employee and employer contributions and investment decisions. The pot of money is ring-fenced to purchase a pension for the employee.

Money purchase arrangements therefore provide defined contributions, but do not provide defined or predictable outcomes.

State pension arrangements

A broad outline of state pension arrangements follows, but this is a dynamic area, first, because the Pensions Act, 1995, continues to impact significantly on state, and also on occupational pensions, and second, because the escalating cost of continuing to provide state pensions is of significant concern to government, and creative solutions to the 'pensions crisis' are being sought.

Subject to the payment or the receiving of credit for national insurance contributions (NICs) and age, pensioner citizens are entitled to a basic retirement pension termed the State Flat Rate Benefit (SFRB). It has become apparent that this cannot be relied upon by individuals to guarantee a continuation of their normal lifestyle in retirement. The uprating of basic state pension has for some time been linked to a general index of increases in prices rather than increases in pay. This has had the effect, because pay increases normally exceed price increases, of eroding the value of state pensions in relation to average earnings. Basic state pension stands at around 15 per cent of male median earnings. The basic state pension can be topped up through the State Earnings-Related Pension Scheme (SERPS) which provides an Additional Pension (AP) based on individual earnings and consequent national insurance contributions above the lower earnings limit. In effect higher earners pay higher national insurance contributions, currently subject to an upper limit, and therefore become entitled to additional state pension. SERPS may ultimately be superseded by a new state second pension.

Certain types of occupational pension schemes allow employees and employers to contract out of SERPS, but not the basic state pension. It is necessary for a contracted-out occupational pension scheme to provide benefits in place of SERPS and in return the employee and the employer will pay lower NICs. In order to contract out of SERPS it is necessary for employers to obtain a contracting-out certificate from the Contributions Agency. To obtain this certificate an employer will need to demonstrate that, in the case of final salary schemes (contracted-out salary-related – COSR), pension benefits are broadly equivalent to, or better than, those in a reference scheme – in effect passing a quality test. Alternatively, in the case of a contracted-out money purchase scheme (COMP) the employer will be obliged to make a minimum payment into the scheme that is equal to the reduction in the employer's and the reduction in the employee's NICs (currently around 3 per cent of pay in total). In order to make COMP schemes more attractive to older employees, the DSS will make extra payments into the scheme, through a NICs rebate, based on a sliding age scale up to a maximum of 9 per cent of pay at age 47 and over.

In order to draw state pension it is necessary to be of state pension age. This is being equalised at 65 years for men and women. Women born before 6 April 1950 will continue to be of state pension age at 60 years and women born between 6 April 1950 and 5 April 1955 will be of state pension age between 60 and 65 years depending upon their date of birth within this period.

The state pensions element of NICs is not invested in a fund for future pensioners, but is used to pay the pensions of current pensioners, and therefore NICs need to equal or exceed state pension payments at any one point in time, in a 'pay as you go' arrangement. There is considerable concern in the UK, and in the European Union generally, that the ageing population and increasing life expectancy post-employment effectively means that those in work will not be able or willing to finance the pensions of those in retirement. Effectively, as the dependency ratio, as it is known, increases so will the financial demands on those in active employment, pushing up the required levels of national insurance contribution. The current state pension arrangements may not be sustainable and this 'pensions crisis' may demand radical revision, including perhaps an increase in state pension age to 68 or 70 years, and a shifting of pensions responsibility to employers and employees.

Occupational pension schemes

An occupational pension scheme normally exhibits certain characteristics. These include the following.

- Pensions, or a lump sum to purchase a pension, are paid by employing organisations to employees on retirement.
- Deferred pensions, or pension transfers, are provided for employees who leave the organisation early.
- Pension benefits accrue to employee dependants.
- Pension funds are financed first, through a combination of employer contributions, tax relief and (usually) employee contributions and second, through investment by the pensions fund trustees.

In order to attract employee and employer tax relief on contributions, an occupational pension scheme must meet approved status criteria as determined by the Inland Revenue. The tax advantages are considerable and make it attractive for organisations to conform to the criteria. Briefly, the criteria include the setting up of the pension scheme as a trust, limiting maximum employee pension to two-thirds of final salary, allowing employees to commute a proportion of pension as a tax-free lump sum, conforming to rules governing the provision of life insurance and dependants' pensions benefits, and observing maxima for employee and employer contributions.

Many occupational pensions schemes require employee contributions and employer contributions, of the order of 5 per cent and 6 per cent of pay respectively. Where the scheme is non-contributory for the employee, a less frequent arrangement but an attractive employee benefit, an employer may need to contribute around 11 per cent of pay. These figures, based on a survey by the National Association of Pension Funds (Self, 1995), are only indicative, as clearly the level of employee and employer contributions will be determined actuarially through analysis of expected benefits in relation to the contributions and anticipated investment returns necessary to fund them. In effect it is the required '*funding rate*' which determines scheme contributions.

A final salary scheme (defined benefits) – This uses employee length of service and final salary in the calculation of pension entitlement. Typically, for each year of service final salary schemes accrue an employee entitlement to either 1/60 or 1/80 of final pay. Final pay may be defined as the salary on retirement or an average of the final three years' pay or the highest rate of pay during pensionable service. Forty years' service in a 1/60 scheme will produce a pension of two-thirds of final pay, the maximum allowable under Inland Revenue rules, and in a 1/80 scheme the same 40 years' service will produce a pension of one-half of final pay, plus a lump sum benefit, which in total equates to two-thirds of final pay. The scheme may allow employees to purchase extra years of pensionable service (past added years is the term used in the public sector) to com-pensate for service below a total of 40 years. The purchase of extra years will not benefit from employer contributions, but the employee contributions will qualify for income tax relief up to the maximum permitted by the Inland Revenue, currently 15 per cent of salary. Commutation of a proportion of salary, in order to release a tax-free lump sum for the employee, will normally be available in a final salary scheme. Early leavers from the scheme will normally qualify for a deferred pension, based on the number of years of pensionable service and salary on leaving, which is subject to statutory increases (*see* page 246). Alternatively the early leaver may request a transfer of the value of the pension fund to the new employer, but actuarial assumptions will often mean that the number of years of entitlement in the new scheme is less than the number of years in the old scheme. Therefore the early leaver will need to make predictions and judgements about expected salary increases, rates of inflation, value of the transfer and so on. If pensionable service on leaving is short, say under two years, the leaver may only receive a return of employee contributions. There are therefore potential disadvantages to early leavers and final salary schemes present portability problems.

Final salary schemes are attractive to employees because the higher the salary and the longer the pensionable service the greater the pension on retirement. In addition, the pension benefits have high predictability and reliability. Final salary schemes are less certain for the employer, because contributions will need to be made at whatever level is necessary to meet and sustain final salary pension commitments and therefore the invest-ment risk is primarily with the employer.

The cost of a final salary scheme rises as the number of pensioners and deferred pensioners increases. Around 50 per cent of occupational pension schemes are final salary types, but this figure looks set to decrease as employers seek less open-ended and more predictable contribution arrangements (Self, 1995).

The money purchase scheme (defined contributions) – This is an alternative to final salary arrangements and although it involves employee and employer contributions it has an entirely different basis for the calculation of employee benefits. The money pur-chase scheme has defined contributions and the investment risk is effectively transferred from the employer to the employee. The employee and employer contributions are paid into an investment fund to create 'a pot of money'. The pension entitlement on retirement will be the value of the fund and this is used to purchase a pension. The money purchase pension benefits depend, first, on investment growth, and second, on the pension conversion, or annuity, rates at the time the pension is purchased. The rules governing the time at which the pension has to be purchased have been relaxed to give the individual some flexibility in deciding precisely when to purchase the pensions product. Money purchase schemes may also present the employee with investment choices which may attract lower or higher returns in relation to the degree of investment risk. Money purchase schemes therefore give relative contribution certainty to the employer, but introduce unpredictability for the employee in terms of both making investment decisions and not having guaranteed pension benefits. Money purchase schemes have portability advantages over final salary arrangements, because the individual's fund can more easily be transferred to a new employer. There is no reason why with sufficient contributions and sound investment decisions a money purchase scheme cannot provide an adequate pension, but this relies on the employee entering a scheme relatively early in working life and sustaining adequate contributions. In order to expect a pension of one half of final salary an employee may need to invest 15 per cent of salary for 40 years (Self, 1995).

Money purchase schemes effectively enable a financial disengagement of the retiring employee, because the employer will not be paying the pension itself nor be responsible for any uprating. Therefore predictability in funding rate and relatively 'clean break' payment arrangements can make money purchase schemes more attractive to employers. Money purchase arrangements also provide employers with an opportunity to reduce the overall level of contribution made to pension benefits, but the likely effect will be that, on average, employees will retire with smaller pensions than if a final salary pension scheme had been maintained (Cooper, 2000). British Telecom, in 2001, notably closed its final salary scheme to new employees who will be offered money purchase arrangements. The BT scheme makes employer contributions relative to employee contributions subject to maxima. Although there is momentum for change a mass exit of employers from final salary schemes is not yet taking place, not least because of the unpopularity with employees of making such a change, but where pensions benefits are being offered for the first time the majority of employers are selecting money purchase arrangements in preference to a final salary scheme. The abolition by the Treasury in 1997 of the advanced corporation tax credit for pension fund dividends effectively reduces the dividend income of a fund by around 20 per cent. This will increase costs for employers or employees or for both. This may accelerate the move from defined benefit schemes linked to final salary to money purchase schemes where contributions are defined (*see* Exhibit 10.1).

A mixed benefit scheme – This is effectively a hybrid of final salary and money purchase principles and seeks to spread the investment risk between the employer and the employee, providing some predictability and allocating some risk to both parties. A minimum pension linked to final salary is guaranteed, whilst some pension entitlement will depend on investment returns.

A mixed benefit scheme therefore contains elements of defined benefits and defined contributions.

A CBI survey in 1994 predicted a substantial increase in these hybrid schemes and Taylor's research (1999) also detected this growing trend.

Exhibit 10.1 Comparison of final salary and money purchase pension schemes

Final salary	Money purchase
• Benefits are defined as a fraction of final pensionable pay, depending on length of service	• Benefits are purchased by the accumulation of contributions invested in a fund
• Benefits are not dependent on investment returns or annuity rates	• Benefits are dependent on contributions, investment returns and the cost of annuities
• Employer contributions are variable and made in excess of employee contributions	• Employer contributions are fixed
• Employer takes the financial risk	• Employee takes financial risk
• Certainty for the employee	• Certainty for the employer
• Early leavers' benefits are eroded because increases in deferred pension increases are linked to prices rather than earnings	• Early leavers do not lose because they effectively take their pensions fund with them
• Designed for long-serving employees with expectations of progressive increases in pensionable pay	• Designed for short-serving employees or those whose pensionable pay fluctuates
• Low portability	• High portability

Occupational pension schemes – rules and regulations

An occupational pension scheme needs rules which determine the type of scheme, eligibility for membership, contributions rate, range and type of benefits, method of calculating pensionable service and the normal pensionable age. In order to qualify as an Inland Revenue approved scheme the pension arrangements must be separated from the employing organisation and be set up as a trust. Trustees of the scheme are appointed to manage the investments, to ensure that employees receive proper entitlements and to ensure compliance with statutory obligations. The management of investments is normally achieved through the delegation of this role to investment and financial professionals. Trustees are obligated in law to act in the best financial interests of the scheme members and seek to maximise 'prudently' the investment returns.

Occupational pensions are subject to the provisions of the Pensions Act 1995, which set up the Occupational Pensions Regulatory Authority (OPRA). OPRA is funded by a levy on occupational schemes and has powers which can be likened to those of the Health and Safety Executive. The powers include prohibition or suspension of trustees, disqualification of auditors or trustees, and fines on individuals and corporate bodies for malpractice, with imprisonment for serious acts. Actuaries and auditors are statutorily obliged to report malpractice to OPRA. Trustees, and employees, may also 'complain' to OPRA and are provided with some protection against legal action for alleged breach of confidence. All occupational pension schemes pay a levy to OPRA to provide a fund to compensate pensions schemes which are 'victims' of theft and where the employer is not sufficiently solvent to make good the losses. Normally occupational pension scheme members, whether in employment or pensioners, are empowered to nominate at least one-third of the trustees to serve for a period of between three and six years. Trustees nominated by scheme members have a right to take time off work for pensions fund duties and training. Dismissal for asserting this statutory right will normally constitute unfair dismissal. Internal grievance procedures are required to enable scheme members and beneficiaries to express any concerns, and where dissatisfaction is not resolved recourse to the Occupational Pensions Advisory Service is available.

Pension earned after April 1997 is subject to a minimum annual increase in payment of either the increase in the retail price index or 5 per cent, whichever is the lower; deferred pensions have been protected by limited indexation for some time. However, if the inflation rate exceeds 5 per cent for several years the relative value of the pension will be eroded. Some schemes provide for additional triennial or quinquennial reviews which take account of inflation rates above 5 per cent, but action of this kind is voluntary. Pension entitlement is normally considered as pay and is therefore subject to European Directives on equality of treatment and equal pay, the consequence being that all occupational pension schemes must avoid direct and indirect discrimination, and scheme rules will need to ensure that men and women are treated equally. Since July 2000 employers have been obliged to provide access to their pension schemes to part-timers unless there is a genuine and objective reason for not doing so. Part-time workers no longer need to demonstrate indirect sex discrimination and must be given access on the same basis as full-time workers, and be provided with no less favourable benefits. There are constraints on the giving of pensions advice to employees. Factual information can be given by the employer in relation to scheme rules and employee pension entitlements, but financial and investment advice is the preserve of financial advisers and is regulated under the Financial Services Act 1986.

Why have an occupational pension scheme?

It is evident that associated with offering occupational pensions is complexity, regulation, administration and risk. Why is it that employers offer pensions arrangements? The answer lies in analysing the extent to which pensions provision achieves reward and other corporate objectives. Employer reasons for having a pension scheme may include:

- contributing to a competitive position in the labour market and enhancing recruitment and retention
- a genuine belief in the value of investing in people
- contributing to a positive customer image for the organisation
- because employees expect it and by sending signals that employee expectations are important there is potential for impact on motivation, commitment and performance
- providing management with the facility of flexing staff numbers through early retirement arrangements.

It needs to be recognised that whether or not these objectives are realisable, and also the extent to which employee behaviour is affected by pension arrangements, is dependent on labour market characteristics and this has implications for employers, and indeed for public policy. Research by Taylor (1999) identified groups of workers who appeared to value occupational pensions more highly – older employees, professional and higher paid staff, staff protected by trade unions and employees working in the financial sector. His research concludes that:

> Most firms perceive pensions to have a significant effect on the attraction and retention of some staff groups. It is questionable to assert that pension schemes continue to have a general effect on the attraction and retention of staff or that they are primarily provided to fulfil such objectives. Their significance in fact seems to vary considerably from labour market to labour market. Appropriately designed and communicated schemes continue to have an effect on the labour market behaviour of specific employee groups. Furthermore, there is evidence to suggest that this effect remains significant in spite of legislation designed to reduce the retentive power of occupational pensions.

Personal pensions

Personal pensions, whether individual or group, are not occupational pensions and are therefore not governed by the Pensions Act 1995. Personal pensions can only be taken out by individuals who are self-employed or who are not in an occupational scheme. A personal pension plan offers a defined contributions arrangement with the contributions being invested in a fund which is used to buy a pension on retirement. Personal pension benefits are therefore not guaranteed. As a general guide an investment fund of around £100 000 will need to be available to an individual on retirement to purchase a pension of £8 000–£10 000 per year. Contributions attract income tax relief and are subject to statutory maxima, but the relief available is more generous than on contributions to an occupational pension scheme. The percentage of salary which can attract tax relief also increases with age. Employers can contribute to an employee's personal pension, and although there is an organisational cost there is no involvement in risk or in benefit determination and the administrative burden is limited. Government concern for the substantial minority of people without adequate occupational or personal pension arrangements is focusing attention on improving private sector provision and also public/private partnering arrangements. 'Stakeholder' and 'citizen' pensions, for the lower paid and carers respectively, are ideas that are being developed in response to the 'pensions crisis'.

The Welfare Reform and Pensions Act 1999 gave legal identity to the concept of stakeholder pensions. Stakeholder pensions are effectively a rebranding of personal pensions and are principally targeted at workers with no pension provision other than state pension. The aim is to encourage more people to provide for retirement through early and regular saving and investment. Stakeholder pensions are intended to be accessible, flexible and value for money. Although originally designed for low- and middle-range earners, it is possible for individuals, other than controlling directors, who earn less than £30 000 per year to have concurrent membership of a defined benefit or defined contribution occupational pension scheme and a stakeholder scheme. From 2001 all employers with five or more employees are obliged to provide access to a stakeholder pension for all employees who have do not have access to a company scheme. There is no requirement to offer stakeholder arrangements where the employer either offers an occupational scheme which is open to *all* employees or has a group pension plan to which the employer makes contributions of at least 3 per cent of the employee's pay. Stakeholder contributions are normally made through automatic payroll deductions. Employees are not compelled to take out a stakeholder pension, nor are employers required to make a contribution to the employee's fund, although these two issues remain under governmental review. Stakeholder pensions are money purchase arrangements, are relatively low-cost because provider fees are capped at 1 per cent of the fund per year, and incorporate flexibility for increasing or decreasing employee contributions without penalty. Employees are entitled to annual benefit statements and must be allowed to change contribution levels at least once every six months. In choosing the stakeholder scheme, which must be registered with the Occupational Pensions Regulatory Authority, employers are required to consult with employees.

Group personal pensions are effectively a collection of individual personal pensions with the documentation and contributions being administered by the employer, or the employer's agent, on behalf of the employees. The employer will need to be clear about the distinction between the provision of pensions information and the giving of financial advice, not only because of the financial services regulation, but also in the context of public disquiet about the quality of pensions advice in recent years. In flexible and deregulated labour markets group personal pensions may be an appropriate employer provision for employees on non-standard contracts.

Although employees in occupational pension schemes are not able to subscribe to personal pensions, even if they may have access to concurrent stakeholder arrangements, they can top up their pension by paying additional voluntary contributions (AVCs) to an approved provider. The AVC arrangements may be linked to the occupational pension scheme and administered by the employer, or the individual may elect free-standing additional voluntary contributions (FSAVCs) with a provider who is not connected with the employing organisation. Tax relief is available on AVC/FSAVC contributions, subject to an overall maximum of 15 per cent of salary for *all* pension contributions.

Individuals should bear in mind that money paid into personal pensions or in the form of additional voluntary contributions is not available until retirement, or on death.

GREENBURY AND CADBURY

An important issue that continues to receive considerable attention is that of 'top people's pay'. The prevailing political situation during the 1980s favoured deregulation of the labour market and an increased focus on market-rate pay. There was opposition to interventions in the labour market, which included not just resistance to the minimum wage, but also an unwillingness to intervene in the contractual and reward arrangements for senior executives. This resulted in a significant widening of the gap between lower-paid workers and the pay of directors. An area of intense concern was, and continues to be, the pay of senior executives in the privatised utilities. The concepts of fairness, equity and transparency were perceived by many to have been violated. Senior executive pay was characterised not only by high levels of base pay, but also by service contracting and bonus schemes that led to high levels of reward. Many senior executives had three-year service contracts, and high levels of remuneration were defended by the high level of risk inherent in the lack of permanent contract. Consequently it was felt that there was a need to pay a market premium to appoint the right person. This was the cause of much concern as it also attracted high severance costs. Share options and share ownership schemes were common and the high performance in the stock market, particularly of the privatised utilities, led to large stock options being granted to the senior executives. This, at a time of cuts in staffing levels, led to accusations of 'fat cats' receiving unacceptably high levels of reward. Executive bonus schemes were routine and could lead to a substantial annual bonus.

These aspects of executive pay led in the 1990s to the establishment of two major government committees to look at 'top people's pay'. The Cadbury Committee on the Financial Aspects of Corporate Governance, which reported in 1993, was followed in 1995 by a committee chaired by Richard Greenbury which highlighted areas of concern about the remuneration of senior executives.

The Cadbury Committee recommendations included the following:

- Shareholders should have the right to restrict the period of a service contract.
- Directors' pay should be approved by a remuneration committee of non-executive directors.
- The elements of directors' pay should be itemised so that basic pay and other items are disclosed.
- Full disclosure of directors' and chief executive pay, including share options and pension contributions, should be made.

The focus of the Cadbury recommendations was clearly on disclosure and the provision of more information, but the impact on the level of pay was limited.

The report of the Greenbury Committee was more far-reaching and included:

- a tightening of the role of remuneration committees
- a recommendation that remuneration should 'be *sufficient* but *not excessive*'
- service contracts to be limited to one year
- an increase in the information to be included in the annual report.

This focus on the pay of special groups occurred because of concerns about equity, fairness and consistency which are fundamental to any reward system. As Littlefield points out in quoting Adrian Cadbury:

> What we want is a consistent policy on salaries, benefits and any other form of add-ons that run *'throughout'* the company. There has been a divorce between directors' salaries and what happens elsewhere in the company. Quite apart from not being good personnel practice it leads to dissatisfaction.
>
> (1995, emphasis added)

The Hampel Committee was set up in 1995 'to promote high standards of corporate governance' and to review Cadbury and Greenbury. In 1997 Hampel came down on the side of 'flexibility' rather than regulation. However, in 2001, following continuing public and shareholder concern with excessive salaries, up 16 per cent for the year and often bearing little relationship to corporate performance, the government announced proposals to give shareholders the right to approve executive pay packages. From 2003 quoted companies will be required to publish an annual report on directors' pay, including salary details for each director, and shareholders will then be able to vote on the report at the AGM.

HARMONISATION

The term harmonisation is used to describe the single status or staff status of employees, the removal of all differences in pay and conditions of employment, and the placing of all employees on a single pay and grading structure. These are ideal types, as generally harmonisation focuses on reducing the variations in pay and benefits between different groups of staff, allowing progression to be made towards the achievement of single status or staff status. Single status and staff status differ. Single status implies that all differences in conditions of employment are removed to give employees equal status, whereas staff status gives manual workers 'staff' terms and conditions of employment. Differences in pay and other conditions of employment are often due to outdated historical and social factors which reflected status distinctions in employment. Waged and salaried staff were not only paid by different methods, but also received a different range of benefits.

The creation of a single pay spine is relatively easy; it simply needs a sufficient range of pay to include all of the pay rates. The achievement of harmonisation is more complex. Benefits have developed differently for the groups of staff. In general, waged staff have longer contractual hours, receive overtime payments and may also have incentive bonus schemes to enhance the basic pay. Salaried staff tend to be contracted for fewer hours and have less entitlement to overtime, but pension, sick pay entitlement and other benefits may be substantially different. It is not only the financial benefits that are distinct. Access to development opportunities may also be different. Manual workers are traditionally 'trained for the job' to a level of job competence, while staff employees will more usually have their development needs acknowledged through the process of appraisal.

This unequal treatment of employees may conflict with the drive for greater flexibility, increased teamworking and a sharper business focus. Fowler (1997) in commenting on changes in local government states:

> Only when managers and employees stop dividing the workforce into separate categories, based on perceived status, will the process be complete. Only when all employees are genuinely considered to have potential to add value, and only when that potential is harnessed, can we say that we have succeeded.

The reasons for status differences and distinctions in terms and conditions of employment are often attitudinal and are therefore difficult to change. Farnham and Pimlott (1995) state:

> harmonisation . . . requires fundamental changes in employee attitudes and in managerial attitudes to the two groups, with sometimes radical changes in working methods.

Status has been protected not only by managerial action to retain distinctions between management and workers, but also by union action to retain distinctions between different craft workers and different unions. The development of greenfield sites and 'single-union' recognition has facilitated some change in practice.

Another obstacle to harmonisation is cost. The extension of staff status to all employees will place pressure on the total pay and benefits bill and may not be achievable without adversely affecting the total reward package of the existing 'staff' group. The timing of the introduction of harmonisation is critical and progress may only be made when there are sufficient funds available to enable all parties to benefit. Clearly a lack of harmony in employee treatment and rewards has the potential to conflict with or inhibit other HR strategies relating to unitary employment relations, functional flexibility, teamworking, collective commitment, customer satisfaction aspirations and responsiveness to change.

NON-FINANCIAL REWARD

The emphasis in reward strategy is understandably on the financial elements, but reward is a more holistic concept which includes extrinsic (external and including pay and benefits) and intrinsic (internal and non-financial) elements. Herzberg's hygiene and motivating factors (1959) now represent old theory and should not be applied without due care and attention, but the two-factor theory is useful in identifying extrinsic and intrinsic motivational factors at work. Extrinsic factors include pay, job security, working conditions, quality of supervision, organisational policies and administration and interpersonal relationships. Intrinsic factors include a sense of achievement, recognition, responsibility, interest in the work itself, potential for growth, self-actualisation and the quality of working life. Reward in a broad sense is therefore also concerned with these intrinsic or self-worth 'feelings' which require satisfaction. The extent to which extrinsic and intrinsic needs can be separated is problematic as there is some overlap, and the level of individual need satisfaction required will vary and be difficult to establish. As with other areas of reward strategy, the effectiveness and techniques of non-financial reward cannot be prescribed and need to be applied contingently. Non-financial reward illustrations that could stimulate a wider awareness of the reward concept include:

- redesigning work to provide greater variety, identity, significance, autonomy and feedback (Hackman and Oldham, 1980)
- providing symbolic rewards where appropriate; for example, the recognition aspects of 'employee of the month' designation, badges, citations
- creating a managerial culture of positive feedback, praise and recognition
- investing in people as a reward through facilitating access to training and development
- providing opportunities for increased responsibility through involvement in special projects
- encouraging career development aspirations
- responding positively to employee suggestions and criticisms
- facilitating a work/life balance.

The effectiveness of these rewards will be contingent on an employee's individual need for them at a particular time and general perceptions of their value. For example, being chosen as 'employee of the month' may be intensely satisfying for some, but abhorrent to others. Non-financial rewards cannot be applied indiscriminately or prescriptively.

CONTEMPORARY TRENDS IN REWARD

There are a number of internal and external shapers of reward strategy (Fig. 10.1) and these contextual factors give rise to emerging and declining trends (Exhibit 10.2).

Internal shapers – the culture of the organisation, including managerial beliefs about what motivates employees; integrated and strategic reward approaches associated with HRM; the reward expectations of the employee; employee consultation or negotiation arrangements; and the nature of the task.

External shapers – the economic climate; labour market shortages or surpluses; public policy on employment; pay legislation, for example tax breaks or the statutory minimum wage; the influence of EU directives; the changing structure of work and sectoral changes in types of work; and technological developments.

Therefore pay and reward is a highly contextual activity, and scanning and analysing the PESTEL environments (*see* Chapter 1) can reveal trends for the reward practitioner. General, but not universal, trends can be identified and an illustrative snapshot

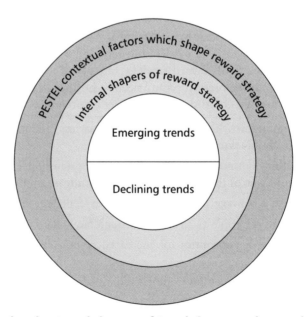

Fig. 10.1 Internal and external shapers of trends in pay and reward

Exhibit 10.2   Emerging and declining trends in reward

Declining reward trends	
Inflation linked increases	a low inflation climate is loosening the link between inflation and employee pay expectations
Annual pay reviews	longer term pay deals are not uncommon
Collective pay bargaining	not only because of a hostile political environment in the 1980s and 1990s, but also because of structural changes in employment; decline may be reversed if trade union recognition legislation bites; the balance between national and local bargaining is subject to change
Incremental pay systems	viewed as not responsive to the strategic integration of reward or to market pricing
Allowances and add-ons	reflecting movement to consolidate and simplify reward arrangements through 'clean pay'
Traditional job evaluation	inflexibility concerns when nimble reward strategies are needed in organic organisations
Emerging reward trends	
New pay	the strategic integration of reward with business objectives
Market-driven pay	labour market responsiveness
Performance-related pay	widespread application of individual PRP and increasing interest in team reward
Broadbanding	for increased flexibility in de-layered organisation structures
New patterns of work	creating demand for new patterns of reward
Competence-based pay	reflecting the spreading use of competencies in managing performance
Money purchase pensions	the escalating costs of final salary schemes and a transfer of the risk to employees; the pursuit of pensions portability in flexible labour markets
Harmonisation	to eliminate a source of division in unified organisations
Flexible benefits	to reflect the needs of a diverse workforce and to target benefits cost
Non-financial rewards	recognition of their power within a total reward strategy

is provided in Exhibit 10.2 as the basis for discussion and further development. Stredwick (2000) recognises the changing nature of pay through identifying the characteristics associated with treating pay as 'an expense' and treating pay as 'a means to competitive advantage'. In this context, his model identifies the characteristics of the new pay trend as encompassing:

- rewards for achieving desired results
- flexibility within a broadbanded structure
- variable pay where bonuses are added based on successful performance
- share options
- flexible benefit programme
- pay determined to meet local conditions
- wide variations from the boardroom to low-paid part-time staff
- pay for performance, skills or competence
- paying for employees' ideas, initiative and innovation
- incentives based on broad measures of organisational success.

Emerging and declining trends reflect the contextual and contingent nature of reward and in no way dampen enthusiasm for pursuing 'perfection' in reward systems. The search continues vigorously with reward systems increasingly characterised by sophistication and complexity. Figure 10.2 exposes for analysis a summary of the potential elements of contemporary reward strategies. Clearly, 'there are no quick fixes in reward, no perfect solutions, but there are genuine gains to be had' (Brown, 2000).

6	*Reinforcement through non-financial rewards*	Total reward strategy to include recognition, opportunities for self-actualisation, responsibility, job design and work/life balance
5	*A share in organisational success*	A variable pay element which is effectively a profit share in the private sector and an efficiency share in the public sector
4	*Team or group based PRP*	A variable pay element to reflect the perceived contribution of a team or unit
3	*Individual PRP*	A variable pay element related to a judgement about individual performance and/or contribution
2	*Flexible benefits*	A benefits package which allows choice and targets benefit cost in order to reflect diverse individual and organisational needs
1	*Base pay*	Market driven to reflect the commercial worth of employees; including incremental progression within broadbanded job grades or job families

Fig. 10.2   Towards a more sophisticated and complex reward strategy integrated horizontally with HR policies and vertically with corporate strategy

SUMMARY LEARNING POINTS

1 The benefits package is an important component of the reward policy. Benefits are costly to provide and should be linked to pay policy objectives to ensure value for money. Market comparisons are valuable and benefits should be surveyed and benchmarked.

2 Employees have diverse benefit needs. Flexible benefits provide an opportunity to respond to diversity in the workforce, to achieve equal opportunities objectives and to target benefit cost.

3 Employee pensions types consist of state, occupational and personal arrangements. Pensions are characterised by complexity, and knowledge of the specialist language is essential to understanding pensions legislation and options for provision. Defined contribution schemes are growing at the expense of defined benefit schemes.

4 The harmonisation of terms and conditions of employment may reduce dysfunctional status distinctions and divisions and increase flexibility and teamworking.

5 The Greenbury and Cadbury reports have been instrumental in regulating the rewards of senior executives and directors in response to public concerns about equity and fairness in relation to other workers. The government has now resorted to more prescriptive regulation.

6 Non-financial rewards have a significant value in satisfying the intrinsic needs of employees and provide managerial opportunities for increasing commitment, satisfaction and performance. Non-financial rewards are fundamental to a total reward strategy.

7 Internal and external factors shape reward strategies, and emerging and declining trends in reward can be tracked through scanning external organisational environments. The elusive search for 'perfect pay' continues unabated.

REFERENCES AND FURTHER READING

Allen, S. (1994) 'Sea change for pensions industry', *Personnel Management*, March, 44–8.

Arkin, A. (1997) 'Mutually inclusive', *People Management*, March.

Armstrong, M. (1996) *Employee Reward*. London: IPD.

Armstrong, M. and Brown, D. (2001) *New Dimensions in Pay Management*. London: CIPD.

Blackman, T. (1999) 'Trading in options', *People Management*, 6 May, 45–9.

Brown, D. (2000) 'Pay per view', *People Management*, 3 February, 41–2.

Conoley, M. (1995) 'Executive share options: a new dilemma for HR', *People Management*, August.

Cooper, D. (2000) 'A tale of two pension systems', *Employee Relations*, 22(3).

Farnham, D. and Pimlott, J. (1995) *Understanding Industrial Relations*. London: Cassell.

Fowler, A. (1997) 'Let's shed a tier', *People Management*, March.

Gee Reward and Remuneration Strategies Survey (1998) London: Gee Publishing.

Hackman, J. and Oldham, G. (1980) *Work Redesign*. Reading, MA: Addison-Wesley.

Herzberg, F. (1959) *The Motivation to Work*. New York: John Wiley.

Industrial Society (2000) *Managing Best Practice No. 75: Flexible Benefits*.

Leopold, J. (2002) *Human Resources in Organisations*. Harlow: FT Prentice Hall.

Littlefield, D. (1995) 'Personnel looks to pay role after Greenbury hint', *People Management*, August, 1(16), 15.

Merrick, N. (1994) 'Benefits to suit all tastes and lifestyles', *Personnel Management*, December.

Mullen, J. (1998) 'Booth opportunities', *People Management*, 16 April, 50–1.

Oldfield, M. (1994) *Understanding Occupational Pensions*. Croydon: Tolley.

Pensions Act (1995) London: HMSO.

Pensions Act – changes affecting occupational pensions contracted-out of SERPS (1996) Leaflet PECS-9/96. DSS.

Redman, T. and Wilkinson, A. (2001) *Contemporary Human Resource Management*. Harlow: FT Prentice Hall.

Report of the Committee on the Financial Aspects of Corporate Governance (1992). London: The Committee and Gee Publishing.

Roberts, C. (1985) *Harmonization: Whys and wherefores*. London: IPM.

Self, R. (1995) 'Changing roles for company pensions', *People Management*, October, 24–9.

Stredwick, J. (2000) 'Aligning rewards to organisational goals: a multinational's experience', *European Business Review*, 12(1). Bradford: MCB University Press.

Study Group on Directors' Remuneration (1995) Directors' remuneration: report of a study group chaired by Sir Richard Greenbury. London: Gee Publishing.

Taylor, S. (1999) 'Occupational pensions and the labour market', *Employee Relations Review*, issue 10, 25–32.

Taylor, S. and Earnshaw, J. (1995) 'The provision of occupational pensions in the 1990s: an exploration of employer objectives', *Employee Relations*, 17(2), 38–53.

The *Guardian* (1997) 'Shareholder power plan on top pay', 8 November, 26.

The *Guardian* (1997) 'Beckett hints at beefing up corporate governance', 12 November, 23.

Thompson, P. (2000) 'How to implement stakeholder pensions', *People Management*, 11 May, 46–8.

ASSIGNMENTS AND DISCUSSION TOPICS

1 List a range of employer pay policy objectives and list the range of benefits potentially available to employees. Undertake a paired comparison exercise in which you classify each benefit as high, medium or low in terms of the likelihood it will contribute to each pay policy objective. Aggregate your results and discuss your findings in small groups. How can this activity inform reward and benefit decisions?

2 Which benefits ought to be core (fixed and non-negotiable) and which benefits should be flexible (involving employee choice) within a flexible benefits package? Justify your decisions.

3 The directorate of your organisation is considering the introduction of flexible benefits for all employees and is seeking your advice. What advice would you give, first, about the added-value business advantages of flexible benefits, and second, about the feasibility, design and implementation of an appropriate flexible benefits scheme?

4 Occupational pensions are characterised by complexity, risk, regulation and administration. Why do organisations continue to offer employee pension arrangements?

5 Discuss the relative advantages and disadvantages of final salary (defined benefits) and money purchase (defined contributions) pension schemes.

6 Within a small group examine critically occupational pension arrangements in three different organisations.

7 Investigate an organisation where the terms and conditions of employment are not harmonised. Identify the pay elements, benefits and non-financial rewards available to different employee groups. What barriers to harmonisation exist and how can they be overcome?

8 In your organisation identify and assess the power of non-financial rewards. How can the power of non-financial rewards be maximised as part of a total reward strategy?

9 Which internal and external shapers of reward are currently influential and which emerging and declining trends are evident (*see* Fig. 10.2)?

CHAPTER 11

Managing and appraising performance

INTRODUCTION

Effective people resourcing includes not only the acquisition of the appropriate quantity and quality of people, but also the management of employees to ensure that performance is constantly reviewed and at a level which is consistent with the achievement of organisational objectives. Employees should know what is expected, not just in terms of duties and responsibilities but also in terms of standards of performance. Performance management is not just the appraisal of performance. It is an holistic process which requires the definition of organisational aims, the development of team and individual objectives, effective systems for measurement and assessment, reward systems that provide incentives, feedback that is constructive, and support for employees to develop and acquire the skills needed to contribute fully to organisational success. Managing employee absence is an important part of managing performance and is also addressed in this chapter.

CHAPTER OBJECTIVES

- To discuss the relationship between organisational objectives and performance management.
- To consider the performance management system and its potential role in the achievement of corporate objectives.
- To examine the role of appraisal and the variety of approaches to appraisal in the management of performance.
- To expose the reasons for employee absence and identify managerial interventions and controls.
- To focus on the complex nature of sick absence and suggest action at corporate and individual levels.

PERFORMANCE MANAGEMENT AND CORPORATE STRATEGY

Much is written and spoken about performance management and to understand this more fully it is important to be clear about what is meant by the term. Armstrong and Baron (2000) define performance management as:

> a strategic and integrated approach to delivering sustained success to organisations by improving the performance of the people who work in them and by developing the capabilities of teams and individual contributors.

Hendry *et al.* (1997) define performance management as:

> a systematic approach to improving individual and team performance in order to achieve organisational goals . . . the approach you take should depend on your organisation: its culture, its relationship with employees and the types of job that they do.

These definitions recognise that performance management systems need to be developed within the context of the organisational structure and culture. There are stages to be followed within the systematic performance management process, but there is no one right way. The performance management concept may be readily understood, 'feel fair' and be a suitable way of successfully managing people, but the problems lie in developing a performance management system that works. The introduction of a performance management system can be an important element in the development of a performance culture by requiring employees to take responsibility for the quality of their outputs and for identifying their development needs. Performance management sits comfortably with an HRM approach to the management of people through seeking to integrate HR and corporate strategies. The elements and linkages of a performance management system are exposed in Fig. 11.1.

THE PERFORMANCE MANAGEMENT SYSTEM

Performance management is a flexible process, not an annual event, and consists of the following stages:

- defining organisational goals
- setting objectives
- agreement of training and development plans
- performance appraisal
- regular feedback
- reward allocation
- development of individual career plans.

A systematic approach encourages the identification of objectives at all levels and the cascading of these objectives down through functional areas, departments and teams to individuals. It allows for the integration of team and individual objectives.

Fig. 11.1   Performance management

Defining organisational goals

Mission statements – Performance management starts with a clear exposition of the organisation's mission in a statement of values and beliefs. These define the organisational vision and are supportive of the corporate culture necessary to achieve business objectives. Mission statements have become increasingly popular and are considered an important component of corporate strategy in communicating consistently and succinctly to employees and customers. The publication of a mission statement is not an end in itself. Effective communication and enactment of the vision and the associated values is critical because employee acceptance is fundamental to the development of involvement and commitment. Success through people is often espoused and claimed, but it can only be achieved if the people 'buy-in' and cooperate. Mission statements that are merely fine words will fail.

Developing corporate strategy – Corporate strategy should reflect the mission with a focus on where the organisation is going and how it will get there. It is not a one-off activity, but a continuous process which is reviewed and adjusted in line with changes in the internal and external contexts. Consideration should be given to factors such as the stage in the economic cycle, labour markets and changing technology, *inter alia* (*see* Chapter 1). The strategy should be simple and focused and recognise the key factors for success, including the part that the management of performance plays in achieving corporate goals.

Developing HR strategy – The HR strategy should fully recognise the role the workforce plays in the achievement of organisational goals. An effective strategy can contribute to an environment where employees understand the culture of the organisation, the standards expected and the support available to achieve high levels of performance. A communication strategy is needed to win the 'hearts and minds' of employees. This somewhat evangelical perspective can attract the criticism that performance management is merely a mechanism for managerial control. This criticism can be exacerbated if employees neither understand nor accept the basis of the system. 'Warm words' can sound like empty words in the absence of a genuine managerial acknowledgement of the employees' contribution to corporate success or a failure to appreciate any employee concerns about the performance management system.

Research supported by the Institute of Employment Studies (IES) (Strebler *et al.*, 2001) questions the relevance and effectiveness of performance management systems in flatter and more flexible organisations, and also questions whether in many organisations the performance management system supports the needs of the business. This research shows that, in many organisations, the performance management system:

- lacks focus
- gives conflicting messages between encouragement and control
- has limited impact on business performance
- stretches managers who often lack the skills and motivation to operate it effectively.

It also illustrates the following:

- Participation in the review process, rather than the outcomes, matters most to employees.
- The importance of employee commitment is increasing.
- There is an emphasis on development but disillusion with the link.

This identifies the importance of constantly reviewing the systems and processes to ensure that they continue to meet the needs of the business.

Setting objectives

Objectives can be defined at the level of the unit, department, team or individual. At unit or departmental level they are closely aligned to organisational goals and specifically define the targets that the unit or department is expected to achieve to maximise its contribution. At team or individual level the objectives relate specifically to the role of the team or individual and the contribution that they are expected to make to the achievement of unit goals. Objectives are normally set by management, but to have legitimacy they should have the consent of or be agreed by the team or individual.

Setting objectives requires managers to be familiar with the skills and competencies of the employees and also with departmental objectives. Managers need to be able to describe the objectives in terms of tasks and behaviours and to allocate these tasks to the most appropriate individuals or teams. For the best results this should be done within a framework of equity and fairness, and should aim to provide motivating jobs which utilise skills and competencies whilst offering personal development opportunities.

Objectives can be SMART:

S	**Specific**	Define precisely what is required in clear language, so that it is understood by both employee and employer.
M	**Measurable**	Normally include numerical targets and qualitative outputs which can be assessed.
A	**Agreed**	Managers define objectives, but they are agreed with the employee. Management-imposed objectives that are not owned or accepted by the employee have less chance of being achieved.
R	**Realistic**	Objectives must be achievable and fairly allocated. Setting objectives which are easy to achieve for one employee while giving another objectives that are unlikely to be met is not only unfair but it may also be demotivational for both individuals.
T	**Time-related**	Incorporate clear target dates which are not open ended.

Exhibit 11.1 provides examples of a quantitative objective or target (1), a qualitative objective described in behavioural terms, but measured quantitatively (2), and also what is best described as a performance standard (3). Armstrong and Baron (2000) describe performance standards as 'a statement of the condition that exists when a job is being performed effectively'. These are more focused on the level of service provision and are a fundamental part of the job; although the detail of the objective may change, for example from two to three days if resources change, the task still has to be done to an agreed standard.

Exhibit 11.1   Examples of individual objectives

No.	Objective	Measure	Date	Rating
1	Make sales of £10 000 each quarter	Sales value	Year end	
2	Deal with customers promptly and politely, resolving problems quickly, ensuring that any delay is communicated to the customer	Customer complaints	Six monthly	
3	Respond to requests for recruitment details within two working days	Monitoring of records	Ongoing	

The two main criticisms of objective setting are:

1 *The difficulty of setting objectives.* This may result in setting objectives that can be measured at the expense of the less tangible elements of the job. The intangibles may still be fundamental to the achievement of a high level of performance and therefore not all parts of the job are covered.

2 *A loss of flexibility.* Organisational changes need to be incorporated into the objectives. If objectives are not constantly reviewed to retain currency, the individual may put effort into out-of-date objectives because they remain the basis for performance measurement and reward.

Rigid performance objectives can therefore become outdated in today's rapidly changing environments, and Rose (2000) examines the continuing role of SMART objectives. He contends that 'SMART objectives assume that organisations operate within a stable environment. But technology and globalisation have created a world in which winning organisations are those that can lead change, or can at least respond rapidly to market changes. The losers are those that are still driven by year-old objectives.' Consequently it is important that any performance management system is able to recognise and respond to the external and internal environments, and managers need to guard against the danger that rather than being a force for change the performance management system becomes an inhibitor of change.

Rose goes on to examine whether a process of 'continuous improvement' would not be more suited to organisations. The basis of continuous improvement is to identify key performance indicators and to strive to enhance these rather than setting targets which are based on past performance. This moves the organisation from being backward-looking to becoming more forward-looking and increases the flexibility in the systems. Rather than the rigidity of SMART objectives, CASE objectives may be more appropriate as a framework. CASE objectives are:

C **Conditions:** the environments within which the organisation operates; if these change then the objective should be reviewed.

A **Action:** describes what the employee or team should do.

S **Standards:** define the level of achievement expected.

E **Evaluation:** the process of regular review and adjustment.

Agreement of training and development plans

The setting and agreement of objectives should be accompanied by an assessment of the individual's competence to achieve them. Lack of skill is a major impediment to effective performance. Training and development needs should be analysed within the framework of the objectives, and plans should be put in place for the acquisition of the skills needed to achieve the required performance. It is unrealistic to expect improved levels of performance without continuously updated skills. Performance management can act as a catalyst in identifying and securing the most appropriate training and development activity for the organisation and for the individual. It promotes training in line with organisational objectives as well as training that individuals value for personal development.

Performance appraisal

Performance appraisal is a critical element in the performance management system. Performance appraisal is a sub-set of performance management and relates to the formal process of assessing and measuring employee performance against agreed objectives. Formal appraisal takes place regularly, usually annually, although it can occur more often. Performance appraisal invokes a variety of employee responses, from a feeling that it is 'a waste of time' to feelings that 'I want to know how well I am doing'. Neale (1991) observes:

> Appraisal is a compulsively fascinating subject, full of paradoxes and love–hate relationships. And appraisal schemes are really controversial . . . Some schemes are popular, with overtones of evangelical fervour, while others are at least equally detested and derided as 'the annual rain dance', 'the end of term report', etc.

A primary aim of performance appraisal can be to assess or measure the achievement of the individual against agreed objectives. This requires the exercise of managerial judgement in the review of quantitative and qualitative objectives, and with judgement comes the potential for subjectivity and bias. Measurement presents challenges, and the performance appraisal system needs to recognise the limitations of the process and endeavour to address these in the design of the system. Armstrong and Baron (2000) indicate that performance measures should relate to strategic goals, focus on outputs, indicate the evidence that is available as the basis for measurement and provide a sound basis for feedback. It follows, therefore, that in agreeing objectives the employee should know what evidence will be considered as the basis for measuring performance.

Types of appraisal schemes *Top-down schemes* are the most common, with the immediate line manager normally undertaking the formal appraisal of the employee. Criticisms of this include allegations about favouritism and lack of impartiality. Managers can be less than open and honest and respond differently to employees with whom they are friendly and employees who they dislike. To offset this tendency a 'grandparent' appraiser can be involved to act as moderator in the appraisal process by examining the reports and ratings and being an arbiter if there is disagreement between the appraising manager and the appraisee.

Self-appraisal is often incorporated informally in top-down schemes as a mechanism for encouraging openness and employee self-reflection. Self-appraisal is a logical dimension to formal appraisal processes and a system can be developed to include the views of the individual in the assessment. This can reduce the subjectivity of the sole appraising manager in the top-down system, as both reports and assessments are available to the grandparent appraiser.

Peer appraisal involves peers and colleagues in the assessment of performance. This introduces logistical difficulties as it is impractical to have one-to-one interviews with each member of the relevant peer group. An option is the introduction of an assessment questionnaire. Peer appraisal is also problematic in that first, it may be difficult to decide upon the appropriate peer group, and second, will the peer appraisers have sufficient skill and knowledge of the individual objectives and performance of the appraisee to undertake an objective assessment? Organisations structured in teams may be more able to introduce effective peer assessment and this can be formalised through an open discussion forum.

Upward appraisal includes the views of those who report to the appraisee and is a dimension of management development. It is normally limited to managers and operates by inviting assessment by the manager's staff. The assessment normally relates to managerial style and effectiveness, rather than the achievement of organisational objectives. It is most commonly undertaken through the completion and submission of documents which are analysed and returned to the manager. Views and comments may or may not be individually identifiable. The results of the appraisal can provide a forum for discussion within the department and may encourage a problem-solving approach to management development. Upward appraisal may be threatening for a manager and uncomfortable for 'subordinate appraisers'. Upward appraisal may also feature in employee opinion surveys.

Multi-rater appraisal or 360-degree feedback is a way of limiting the effect of the one-dimensional approach of the top-down schemes and building on the positive aspects of peer and upward appraisal. Multi-rater appraisers include peers, subordinates, internal and external customers and the manager. The aim is to achieve a broader view of employee performance. It can dilute subjectivity, increase customer focus, support team initiatives, decrease the hierarchical approach and provide greater employee involvement. The linkage of appraisal to pay is problematic in multi-rater appraisal in terms of consistency, consensus and fairness. Stakeholder appraisal is a form of multi-rater appraisal which provides a different group of appraisers. The stakeholding appraisers consist of those employees who are reliant on each other to get the job done. Discussion can be more open and less threatening in tone because of a philosophy of mutual support. It is more suited to public organisations and professional environments where plurality is acknowledged and where the stakeholders can come together to define objectives and develop ways of managing performance more effectively.

Problems associated with performance appraisal   There are problems associated with the implementation and management of performance appraisal schemes.

- Bureaucratisation – systems can be time consuming, not just in the time needed for the appraisal discussion, but also in the time needed to complete the appraisal documentation.

- Lack of commitment – a system has to deliver the objective of identifying and rewarding performance; if it is not seen to do this in practice it will fall into disrepute and both employees and managers will reduce their commitment to it.

- The tension between identifying development needs and allocating rewards can undermine the system (*see* page 267).

- Subjectivity and bias are inherent in one individual's assessment of another and there are real difficulties in developing objective measures. Managers require training to be able to identify and reduce personal bias.

- The recency effect – it is a human perceptual characteristic to be influenced by recent events, and employee achievement or lack of achievement close to the appraisal interview may distort the assessment. Skilled appraisees may capitalise on this by 'saving' achievements until just before the appraisal discussion.

- The appraisal system may be perceived by employees as a tool for managerial control which is used to reinforce managerially desired behaviours and to subdue the expression of dissatisfaction. In these circumstances the level of trust will be insufficient for the system to work effectively.

In order to reduce the effect of the problems associated with performance appraisal, it is important to set the policy and practice within an ethical framework. The framework should include reference to the trust, integrity and faith that management place in individual participation in the appraisal system. Winstanley and Stuart-Smith (1996) also state that there are four ethical principles, which should underpin the appraisal process: respect for the individual, mutual respect, procedural fairness and transparency of decision-making. An organisation which is open about the operation of its appraisal system, acknowledges what it can and cannot achieve and strives for employee involvement is more likely to have a higher level of managerial and employee support for performance management processes.

Regular feedback

Effective performance management is more than a once-a-year formal appraisal event. Continuous review of employee performance is needed together with effective feedback. Giving feedback can be challenging and managers need good communication skills to ensure that feedback is constructive and helpful. Feedback that is primarily focused on allocating blame damages employee self-confidence and acts as a negative influence on performance.

Fowler (1996) identifies key points for giving effective feedback.

- Be specific – it is insufficient to talk in general terms; to improve performance the employee needs evidence from actual occurrences to illustrate learning points.

- Be constructive – focus on what can be learnt from the specific events and how improvements can be made.

- Avoid comments about attitude or personality that cannot realistically be changed; concentrate on behaviour and the way that it affects performance.

- Give feedback regularly – do not leave feedback for the 'annual' review; it is important that it is timely and as close to the learning event as possible.

- Encourage self-reflection – feedback is not just about telling.

- Avoid argument – a practical discussion about differences of opinion on performance is much more helpful. It is also important to listen to the employee's point of view.

- Explain the reasons for any request for change that may be needed and encourage the development of an action plan.

- Take feedback yourself – the discussion should be two-way and there may be lessons to be learned about your own performance.

- Encourage the employee to seek regular feedback by being open and helpful.

Feedback is a critical element in the performance management system as it is the vehicle for reinforcing appropriate behaviour or for bringing about individual change. Objective setting and ensuring 'the right thing is done' is only one aspect; ensuring that 'it is done right' can be best achieved through open dialogue. One of the main purposes of feedback is to promote development and enable employees to achieve their potential. Success in improving performance reinforces constructive feedback and can increase employee confidence.

Reward allocation

Within a performance management system the linkage between employee performance and reward is self-evident and often necessary, but there is an argument for separating the formal appraisal process from pay decisions. The argument for separation is that the linkage with pay may affect the honesty of self-appraisal and interfere with the development objectives of the appraisal process by effectively transforming the manager from 'a coach' to 'a judge'. The employee is unlikely to be self-critical and expose weaknesses and development needs if it is going to impact on the allocation of monetary reward. However, in practice it is difficult to divorce the formal appraisal process from pay decisions (*see* Chapter 9 on performance-related pay). Employees expect increases in performance to be rewarded not just in monetary terms, but also intrinsically through the provision of opportunities for self-development and the reinforcement of a sense of achievement through positive feedback from the manager.

Development of personal development plans

An important output from the performance appraisal interview can be the development of performance development plans and organisational succession plans. The performance management system should enable individuals to reflect on and be realistic about personal development and work opportunities. A knowledge of individual strengths and weaknesses will facilitate this self-reflection and enlist the expertise and support of the manager. The manager can gain an improved understanding of the aspirations and ambitions of the employee. With openness and honesty these can be explored and plans developed to take into account individual aspirations, performance and potential, and this can be matched against the future needs of the organisation.

MANAGING SUB-STANDARD PERFORMANCE

As well as the development and reward elements of performance management, there is the issue of managing the individual whose performance is not meeting the required standard. Prior to managerial action it is necessary to have specified the performance standard, assessed the employee's current performance level and identified and communicated the performance gap. Clearly, employee acceptance of a problem is a prerequisite to effective action. There are three questions to be considered in managing sub-standard performance. Is the performance shortfall due to:

1 A lack of skill that could be remedied through training?
2 A lack of capability which is inherent and will not respond to training?
3 An unwillingness to perform?

The diagnosis of the cause of the problem determines the managerial response. If the performance shortfall is caused by a lack of skill then training, support and review is the response (*see* Chapter 12). If the sub-standard performance is due to an inherent lack of capability or an unwillingness to learn then redeployment, counselling or disciplinary action may be the answer (*see* Chapters 17 and 18).

MANAGING EMPLOYEE ABSENCE

If the purpose of employing people is to get work done in the pursuit of organisational objectives, it is a truism that employee absences, through impacting upon overall individual performance, have considerable potential to impede efficient and effective organisational performance. Absence from work cannot be eliminated, nor would this be a desirable aim, but employee absence can be proactively managed in the context of the needs of the organisation and the needs of the individual employees. Proactive absence management requires an understanding of the types of absence, a knowledge of the consequences of absence, and skill in applying techniques for monitoring and controlling absence. Employee absence which is sanctioned in advance, holiday leave for example, is less disruptive than absence which is unplanned, and a primary focus on the management of sick absence is therefore adopted in this section.

Types of absence

It is useful to identify the types of employee absence to illustrate the many reasons that employees have for not being present at work. Broad absence categories include:

- normal days off and flexitime
- holidays
- other sanctioned leave
- unauthorised absence
- sick absence.

The contract of employment should specify normal working hours, days off and any flexitime arrangements. It is through the determination of the contract, and through making any justifiable contractual changes, that management can seek to control the impact of normal employee absence by specifying when employees should be present at work. Effective human resource planning provides a means for managing normal days off and flexitime.

Holiday leave can also be managed through advance planning and through holiday controls which take account of patterns of organisational activity. These controls can include the extent of individual holiday entitlement, subject to statutory minima, the determination of 'holiday-free time zones', the specification of compulsory holiday periods, and limitations on the number and type of employees permitted to take leave at various times in the holiday year. These managerial controls are subject to legal, contractual and employee consent constraints, but the underlying principle is that holiday absence can be effectively managed through planning.

Other sanctioned employee leave can include maternity, parental, carers, 'time-off for dependants', jury service, public duties, domestic emergencies, sabbaticals, trade union duties, training and development, religious observance and so on. The potential for employee absence is huge and the development, definition and expression of the employer's attitude towards each of these types of sanctioned leave will achieve a balance between the needs of the individual and the needs of the organisation, and provide a means of reconciling the short-term disadvantages and long-term benefits to the organisation of these forms of employee absence. Formal written policies in these areas will make clear organisational values and guidelines for sanctioning leave other than normal days off and holidays. These leave policies should address issues of payment, or non-payment, in the context of any statutory requirements, the extent of the leave available and the process for sanctioning it. Written, agreed policies will promote equity, transparency and consistency in dealing with these inescapable leave issues.

Unauthorised absence, or absenteeism, can be defined as an occasion when an employee fails to report for work when contractually obliged to do so and without prior agreement for absence, or employee failure to notify the employer in line with sick absence procedures or sanctioned leave arrangements. Unauthorised absence threatens to breach the contract of employment because the employee is not ready, willing and able for work. It is normally treated as a disciplinary matter, being subject to proper investigation, the opportunity for the employee to explain, and a considered decision by a reasonable employer (*see* Chapters 17 and 18). The volume of this type of absenteeism is normally relatively small in comparison to other reasons for employee absence, and managerial control of absenteeism is available through the application of disciplinary procedures and the enforcement of the contract of employment. It is inevitable that some employees will conceal absenteeism as short-term sick absence and claims of being ill in these instances are difficult to disprove. However, if an employee exploits or abuses the sick absence rules or arrangements, there is the potential for gross misconduct leading to dismissal; for example, the dishonest claiming of sick pay or the wilful deceit of the employer will significantly undermine the mutual trust and confidence necessary to sustain the contract.

The management of sick absence not only presents a more complex set of issues and difficulties, but sick absence normally causes greater disruption to organisational activity. The management of sick absence therefore requires particular attention.

THE MANAGEMENT OF SICK ABSENCE

The principal reason for focusing on the management of sick absence is because of the cost to work organisations. Attempts are regularly made to measure and quantify sick absence volumes and costs, and surveys consistently reveal figures which provoke managerial concern (CBI, 1999; CBI/Percom, 1993; British Psychological Society, 1994; Industrial Relations Review and Report, 1993; ACAS, periodically; IDS, 1998; CIPD, 2001). Illustrative examples of these figures are as follows.

- In the UK approximately one million people are absent from work each day because of sickness or other unanticipated cause (ACAS, CBI).
- Each employee averages eight to nine days sick absence per year (CBI, CIPD).
- An average of 4 per cent of the potential working days available are lost because of sick absence, representing around 175–200 million days per year in the UK (IS, CBI).
- The annual direct financial cost is around £500 per employee (BPS, CIPD, ACAS), a total of approximately £12 billion for UK organisations (CBI, IDS, CIPD).

Financial figures are crude because they are predicated on the assumption that the calculation of sick absence payments equates to direct financial costs. Clearly this is not necessarily the case, but the figures serve to illustrate that sick absence justifies managerial intervention. In addition to any direct financial costs of covering the work of the absent employee, through temporary replacement or overtime working, there may be implications for productivity levels or the quality of customer service, the absence may be disruptive to the planning and organisation of work, and absent colleagues place extra demands on those who remain at work. High levels of sick absence may impact negatively on overall job satisfaction and morale:

> Because of these wide-ranging effects, not just on profitability but also on morale, high absence levels affect everyone in the organisation and cannot be regarded purely as a management problem. Employers and employees have an interest in ensuring that a few absent employees do not jeopardise their prosperity or job satisfaction. In working to establish and maintain ways of monitoring and controlling absence, managers and employee representatives not only control costs and increase productivity but also ensure the fair and consistent treatment of the whole workforce.

> (ACAS)

General sick absence patterns suggested by the research include the following.

- Workers in manual jobs tend to have higher levels of sick absence than non-manual employees.
- Public sector workers experience higher levels of sick absence than their private sector counterparts.
- Lack of job satisfaction and stress-related sickness are cited as significant causes of absence.
- Younger employees tend to have more frequent, short-term sick absence, whilst older employees tend to have less frequent but longer-term sick absence.
- Sick absence tends to be greater in larger working groups than in small groups where there is a heightened perception of interdependence.

In 1994 the 80 per cent reimbursement that most employers received for the payment of statutory sick pay (SSP) was abolished. This was intended to prompt employers to reduce costs arising from sick absence by providing an economic incentive. The direct cost of paying SSP was offset by a reduction in employers' national insurance contributions, although the compliance costs of SSP remain in terms of administering the scheme. This legislative change contributed to an upsurge in employer interest in the more proactive management of sick absence. Since 1997, and where occupational sick pay arrangements are more generous than SSP, it has been possible for employers to opt out of SSP arrangements, strengthening the economic incentive for employers to manage sick absence more effectively. Other drivers for more active absence management include the following (Bevan and Hayday, 1998).

- Maintaining competitiveness: as organisations reduce the number of staff they employ, the value of each remaining employee rises. Employers recognise that each day lost through absence represents lost production, disruption, reduced efficiency, compromised quality and lost opportunities.

- Employee expectations: employees have generally higher levels of health awareness and higher expectations of what a 'good' employer should provide in terms of working conditions and benefits. There is a growing body of case law where employees have sought, and obtained, legal redress for damage to their physical and mental health at work.

- Announcements by government: signalling that reducing sickness absence in the public sector is a high priority.

Although it is possible and practical to manage sick absence more actively in the pursuit of equity and organisational effectiveness, there is a danger of adopting a punitive managerial paradigm – the sending of a message to employees that management suspect that much of the sick absence lacks authenticity and validity. An over-zealous managerial approach may make genuinely committed employees feel guilty or at risk of retribution for being unwell and this will be detrimental to the employment relationship. There is a balance to be struck between the identification and resolution of employee attendance problems and the potential for the development of a destructive or dysfunctional organisational climate in relation to sick absence.

Causation

The root cause of sick absence is the fact that an employee is unwell, and where the employee is incapacitated there exists a state of being unfit for work. However, being unwell and being unfit for work are not necessarily synonymous. Research into causation (Steers and Porter, 1991) identifies scope for the exercise of employee judgement in deciding at which point 'being unwell' corresponds with 'being unfit for work' (see Exhibit 11.2). In effect, employee perceptions and decision-making impact upon levels of workplace sick absence. There are a number of influences on employee perceptions and decisions – first, the individual employee's attitudes and values; second, the level of job satisfaction and whether absence is considered as legitimate in remedying a perceived imbalance in the employee effort to reward relationship; third, discomfort or tensions at work may predispose an unwell individual to engage in pain-avoidance behaviour inducing a state of unfitness for work; fourth, the prevailing absence or attendance culture within the organisation; and, fifth, the nature of organisational policies, procedures and practices relating to sick absence. These causation influences, which need to be considered at individual, group and organisational levels, are introduced to demonstrate that an holistic approach to the management of sick absence is necessary and to suggest that the health of the psychological contract will be a factor in sick absence levels.

Exhibit 11.2   Being unwell, on a scale of 10, versus being unfit for work

10	**Very unwell**
9	
8	
7	
6	
5	**Moderately unwell**
4	
3	
2	
1	**Not very unwell**

At which point is an employee unfit for work and who decides?

Monitoring, measurement and control of sick absence

A systems approach to sick absence provides a useful framework for analysing the entry points for managerial intervention. The sick absence system (Fig. 11.2) consists of candidates for employment (the inputs), the managing of sick absence (the processing unit) and either a return to acceptable attendance levels or the exit of employees with unacceptable absence levels (the outputs or outcomes).

Controlling entry to the organisation is part of managing sick absence. Candidates for employment can be given pre-engagement screening through health questionnaires in the recruitment process. Checks by medical practitioners involve greater cost, and are subject to statutory restrictions (Access to Medical Records Act 1988), but provide a more informed opinion on fitness for employment. References relating to previous employment can include questions which solicit factual information about absence and attendance records. The objective of these activities is to establish capability for a particular job and to determine whether any reasonable adjustments to the work are necessary. The Data Protection Act, 1998 classes information on health as sensitive information requiring more overt employee consent to its collection, security and use. The employer also needs to be able to demonstrate that the health information is going to be used for a legitimate purpose. This poses some challenges for the employer.

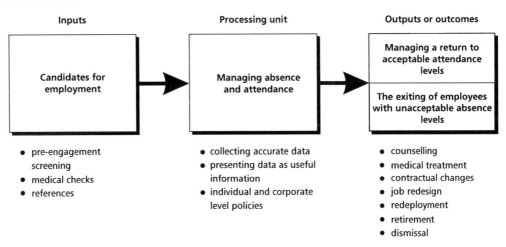

Inputs	Processing unit	Outputs or outcomes
Candidates for employment	Managing absence and attendance	Managing a return to acceptable attendance levels
		The exiting of employees with unacceptable absence levels

- pre-engagement screening
- medical checks
- references

- collecting accurate data
- presenting data as useful information
- individual and corporate level policies

- counselling
- medical treatment
- contractual changes
- job redesign
- redeployment
- retirement
- dismissal

Fig. 11.2   A systems approach to managing sick absence

A prerequisite to the management of sick absence is the collection of good quality data. Managerial attention needs to be directed at ensuring that absence data is timely, accurate and reliable. Without tight reporting and recording systems there is considerable potential for the under-reporting of sick absence, and without hard facts impressionistic and unsupported views will prevail and limit meaningful action. The employer needs to establish and communicate how sick absence should be reported, to whom it should be reported and when it should be reported. This involves consideration of whether absence should be reported to the line manager or to a personnel function. The argument for the former is not only that line managers should take responsibility for the effective management of their staff, but also that employee absence raises immediate operational issues. The argument for the direct reporting of sick absence to a personnel function is that the central collection of data is necessary for accurate adjustments to pay and for the coordination and analysis of organisation-wide sick absence data. Clearly, whichever arrangement applies, there needs to be reliable communication between the parties.

When should employees report absence from work? From an employer's perspective the sooner the better, and it may be reasonable to require employees to make contact before the contractual starting time, or soon after, so that operational decisions can be made expediently. The legitimate requirement for an employee to report sick within a constrained time period is dependent upon the employee's ability to make contact, either through being physically able and having a telephone or through having contact with someone who can call instead, and therefore any time requirement needs to be interpreted reasonably. Certification requirements need to be effectively communicated to employees and statutory obligations for the administration of statutory sick pay need to be observed.

Raw sick absence data need to be converted into managerial information and presented in a usable format. Basic absence measures such as the number of days for each employee and the total number of days in a given period are relatively easily available. A comparative measure known as the lost time rate or the potential working-days lost (PWL) rate is calculated by taking the number of days lost due to sick absence, for an individual or for a group of workers, as a percentage of the potential working days available in a period, of a month or a year.

$$PWL = \frac{\text{Number of days absence}}{\text{Potential working days available}} \times 100$$

For example, if a month (four weeks) is the given period, a department with ten employees who work five days a week will have 200 potential working days ($4 \times 10 \times 5$). If during that period eight days are lost, the PWL rate is 4 per cent. This calculation can be refined by using hours lost through sick absence, rather than whole days lost, to reflect more accurately the absence of part-time workers and the part-day absence of full-time workers. As long as a consistent measure is used, comparative information is generated. The PWL is a volume measure and does not reveal whether the sick absence in a period consists of the long-term absence of a small number of employees or whether it is made up of a high frequency of short-term sick absence. The frequency rate, sometimes called the inception rate, measures the number of instances or episodes of sick absence that occur in a given period.

$$\text{Frequency rate} = \frac{\text{Number of instances of sick absences}}{\text{Average number of employees}} \times 100$$

If, for example, a month is the given period, the average number of employees is 194 and the number of separate instances of sick absence, regardless of whether the same employee was absent more than once, is 35, the frequency rate is 18 per cent.

These measures provide valuable comparative information in terms of volume and frequency. Comparisons can be made between individuals, between departments or teams, on the basis of age, gender, job or working hours, and comparisons can be made over time. The measures can be benchmarked against those of other organisations. The objective is to determine the scale of any problem, to highlight any fluctuations and to focus attention on identified problems. The use of a computerised HR information system will be invaluable in generating comparative reports (*see* Chapter 5).

The frequency rate measure can be incorporated into an absence or attendance policy to provide 'triggers' for concern. This involves determining the frequency of individual employee absence which automatically stimulates managerial intervention and identifies an employee as an irregular attender. For example, concern may be triggered if an employee has four or more absences in a 12-month rolling period. Although attention may be drawn to a particular problem, the trigger point is a reason for scrutiny and **not** a reason for automatic warnings or other sanctions, as each case should be fairly and equitably considered on its merits. These triggers for concern send a powerful message to employees about what levels of absence are considered acceptable and also provide a consistent framework for managerial intervention. A disadvantage of these trigger points is that absence up to the trigger point level may be interpreted as an acceptable employee entitlement – the trigger point may legitimise a certain employee absence level (*see also* Exhibit 11.3).

In addition to considering volume and frequency, the proactive management of absence should seek to detect patterns of employee absence, perhaps relating to weekends, bank holidays, busy or slack periods, significant sporting events and so on. Detecting

Exhibit 11.3   Bradford Index

Frequent episodes of absence are disruptive. The Bradford Index is a mechanism for weighting frequency of sick absence.

$$\text{Bradford Index} = S^2 \times D$$

where S = spells of absence in the period

and D = total number of days absence in the period

For example, three employees all with a total of 10 days absence in a year, but with different spells, have a very different index:

Employee 1 with 1 spell – $1^2 \times 10$ days   =   10

Employee 2 with 2 spells – $2^2 \times 10$ days   =   40

Employee 3 with 10 spells – $10^2 \times 10$ days =   1000

The higher rating of frequency of absence produces a weighted comparative index and management can determine a points score to trigger scrutiny.

these patterns, exposing them to employees and having sufficient reasonable belief to take action are in fact based on concerns about the authenticity of any sick absence and raise issues about the mutual trust and confidence necessary to sustain a contract of employment rather than raising questions about the health and capability of the employee.

Corporate level action on sick absence

Although most employee sick absence is not within managerial control, action can be taken to reduce overall corporate absence. Corporate level action includes the improvement of working conditions, the provision of health services, attention to the motivation and satisfaction of employees, and having fair and consistent procedures for dealing with individual employees with sick absence problems. Ten specific areas are identified for possible managerial attention.

1 Examine the health of the psychological contract, measured by employee morale, perceptions of equity in treatment, intrinsic and extrinsic job satisfaction, levels of stress and the extent of reciprocal loyalty relationships.

2 Evaluate the prevailing corporate culture, sick absence custom and practice, organisational attendance norms and any perceptions of sick leave as an entitlement to identify whether the reorientation of employee values and beliefs is appropriate.

3 Audit organisational contributions, physical and psychological, to sick absence to reveal potential for work environment improvement, the redesign of jobs, the genuine empowerment of employees and the encouragement of team responsibility.

4 Review the provision of occupational health services and positive health programmes and design policies which address sensitive employment issues (*see* Chapter 14).

5 Increase the skill of line managers to deal fairly and consistently with sick absence problems and provide good absence information.

6 Use return to work interviews to establish the fitness of the employee to return and to express concern where appropriate – on a cautionary note there is potential for causing detriment to the employment relationship if the employee perceives that the purpose of the interview is to reach a verdict about whether or not the sick absence was genuine.

7 Consider the application of waiting days before the employee is entitled to company sick pay – in the short term this may act as a deterrent and can have a dramatic impact on absence levels, but there is the potential for it to be seen as a punitive measure with consequential harm to the employment relationship.

8 In contrast to point 7, consider offering incentives for attendance through rewarding, with extra payments, employees who have little or no sick absence in a period. Clearly there are cost implications and employees are being paid again for what they are contractually required to do. In addition, once a qualification for an attendance bonus is lost through an episode of sick absence, the incentive value is also lost for the remainder of the period. An attendance reward may convert sick absence into 'sickness presence' which may be detrimental to the employee, to other employees and to the organisation.

9 Review organisational policies critically in relation to flexibility in working times and the authorisation of reasonable absence for significant life events or emergencies. Flexibility in these areas can reduce sick absence.

10 Communicate corporate sick absence values. Transparent policies reassure employees that genuinely sick employees will be treated with fairness and consistency and that there are procedures in place to deal with excessive sick absence (because it increases the workload of others).

The CIPD Survey (2001) of over 1400 employers reports on the percentage of organisations using the following absence management practices:

82% Disciplinary procedure for unacceptable absences

81% Providing sickness absence information to line managers

78% Line management involvement in absence management

71% Leave for family circumstances

61% Return-to-work interviews for all absences

59% Occupational health professional involvement

48% Restricting sick pay

44% Managers trained in absence handling

43% Attendance record as a recruitment criterion

32% Stress counselling

28% Health promotion

20% Return-to-work interviews for longer-term absences only

18% Rehabilitation programme

17% Employee assistance programme

14% Attendance bonuses or incentives

12% Physiotherapy services

10% Disability leave not counted as sickness absence.

When asked to rate the effectiveness of these practices the users considered the most effective, in respect of short-term absence, to be return-to-work interviews, line management involvement, the provision of absence information to line managers, using the disciplinary procedure, restricting sick pay, and paying an attendance bonus. In respect of long-term absence, the most effective practices were considered to be the involvement of the occupational health professional, return-to-work interviews, rehabilitation programmes and line manager involvement. These figures and employer perceptions are introduced here not as some sort of definitive guide for managerial action but in order to stimulate debate about which practices might be most effective in particular organisational circumstances (see end-of-chapter assignment 11); there is no escape from contingency in HR practice.

Individual level action on sick absence

Managerial action in relation to an individual with an unacceptable absence record is problematic to prescribe, but there are a number of issues to consider. First, it is important to distinguish between frequent short-term absence and long-term ill health. The latter may best be pursued as ill-health termination of contract or retirement, depending upon organisational provision and the characteristics, circumstances and service of the employee concerned. Ill health which results in incapability is a potentially fair reason for dismissal (see Chapter 18). 'It is a commonly held view that to dismiss an employee because of ill health is unfair if the person is genuinely sick. This is not the case' (Stevens and Fitzgibbons, 2001). Where frequency of absence is the problem the employer may consider whether the validity of absence is in doubt. Where there are validity concerns it may be more appropriate to deal with the absence as a disciplinary issue. If there appears to be an underlying medical problem, a prognosis should be obtained from a medical practitioner to indicate whether and when the employee will be able to fulfil attendance expectations. A prognosis may also provide an opportunity for an employee to receive counselling or medical advice. The outcome of the prognosis will inform managerial action, but deciding on how to proceed remains a managerial and not a medical decision. It is not sensible or practical to define a point at which sick absence levels become unacceptable, as this depends on many factors such as the nature of the work, the consequences of the absence, the size and resources of the organisation, the length and quality of the employee's service and any mitigating circumstances. The employee has a duty to be ready, willing and able for work and it is for the employer to decide reasonably and fairly at which point 'enough is enough' and to take action against the employee. An interview or hearing with the individual employee will form part of any decision-making process, and factors relating to the sick absence encounter between the employee and the employer are exposed in Exhibit 11.4.

Exhibit 11.4   The sick absence encounter

- The encounter is potentially emotionally charged and there can be a clash of perspectives, with the employer, whilst being sympathetic, having a primary concern with organisational attendance needs and employees perceiving that they are being criticised for being sick.
- The facts from earlier discussions and the sick absence record are needed.
- The employee should receive notice of any interview, have the right to be accompanied and have the matter conducted in privacy and with confidentiality.
- The objective is to convey managerial concern and listen to and consider any employee response; this may involve an adjournment.
- Based on the information available, the managerial decision should be made and communicated, ensuring that the employee is clear on what is expected and on the consequences of an inability to meet the specified standard.
- It is normally appropriate to monitor attendance, provide support and instigate reviews.
- Even-handedness in the treatment of employees is an important principle of natural justice – employees with similar sick absence records should normally be treated similarly.

Alternative courses of action are available to managers following full consideration of the facts. These include managing a return to acceptable attendance levels through counselling, medical treatment, job redesign, redeployment (although there is no obligation on the employer to create a job) or contractual changes to accommodate the 'problem'. If these fail, or are inappropriate, then the employee may need to be released through either retirement or dismissal. In summary, three principles emerge for the management of long-term individual sick absence. First, the decision is not a medical decision but a managerial decision with a medical input; second, even-handedness of managerial action is desirable; third, being prepared to recognise the 'enough is enough' point, the point at which all alternatives have been exhausted and dismissal becomes a reasonable employer action in the circumstances.

Sick absence in relation to pregnancy, disability and stress requires particularly careful handling. Pregnancy sick absence is probably a no-go area for managerial action, although in certain circumstances it can trigger the start of maternity leave. For employees with a disability who qualify for protection under the Disability Discrimination Act 1995, the employer has a duty to consider reasonable adjustments to the work and may need to discount any absences related to the particular disability. Case law is beginning to suggest that the application of an attendance policy to disability-related absences may be discriminatory and therefore dismissal for disability-related absence may be unfair (Sage, 1998). The 'stress paradox' describes a situation in which a distressed employee may be fit for work as long as he or she is not at work, but the return to work, and the associated stress, provokes a recurrence of absence.

Some gains can be made in managing sick absence, but there is limited potential to reduce it and there is no quick fix. There is potential to create a punitive managerial paradigm which can be dysfunctional to the organisation. Perhaps there needs to be a shift away from the more punitive philosophy of absence control in favour of more enlightened 'attendance management' strategies which aim to provide a working environment which maximises and motivates employee attendance. McHugh (2001), although specific to local government in Northern Ireland, raises issues which have wider currency for the management of sick absence. In particular she identifies a failure 'to acknowledge the interdependence of individual and organisational well-being' and comments that 'high levels of ill health are indicative of ill health on the part of the organisation'. There is therefore a need for managers to recognise that absence levels will not be reduced purely by tightening controls on employees or setting targets (CIPD Survey, 2001); the organisation needs to be introspective about the contribution it makes to absence levels.

SUMMARY LEARNING POINTS

1 Performance management is an holistic process which aligns corporate, unit and individual objectives. It is supported by people management strategy and systems which encourage a performance culture with the aim of improving overall corporate performance.

2 SMART objectives may lead to rigidity in the system, and organisations may need to consider the process of continuous improvement or CASE objectives to remain a market leader.

3 Performance appraisal is a sub-set of performance management and includes the processes and procedures for the assessment of employee performance, the identification of training and development needs and the allocation of rewards.

4 Types of appraisal systems include top-down, self, peer, upward and 360-degree or multi-rater appraisal. The choice of appraisal system is influenced by the nature of the organisation and the external context.

5 Mechanisms for managing sub-standard performance include training and development, redeployment, counselling and disciplinary action. Diagnosis of the cause determines the managerial response.

6 Normal days off, holidays and other sanctioned leave can be managed through careful planning and through the application of clear and consistent organisational policies. Unauthorised absence (absenteeism) is effectively a disciplinary matter. Managing sick absence presents a more complex set of issues and difficulties.

7 Sick absence has a financial and an operational cost to the organisation and warrants managerial attention. An over-zealous approach to managing sick absence may lead to a punitive paradigm which is detrimental to the employment relationship.

8 Corporate sick absence levels are influenced by an array of individual and organisational factors. A systems approach to managing sick absence provides a framework for identifying entry points for managerial intervention.

9 Prerequisites to the effective management of sick absence are the collection, analysis and presentation of accurate and timely information. Managerial action needs to adopt a corporate approach as well as having firm and consistent policies for dealing with individuals.

REFERENCES AND FURTHER READING

Advisory, Conciliation and Arbitration Service (1999) *Absence: Advisory Booklet 5.*

Armstrong, M. (1994) *Performance Management.* London: Kogan Page.

Armstrong, M. (1996) *Employee Reward.* London: IPD.

Armstrong, M. and Baron, A. (2000) *Performance Management: The new realities.* London: CIPD.

Armstrong, M. and Murlis, H. (1991) *Reward Management.* London: Kogan Page.

Bevan, S. and Hayday, S. (1998) *Attendance Management: A review of good practice* (IES Report 353). Brighton: Institute of Employment Studies.

British Psychological Society (1994) *The Cost of Sick Absence.*

CBI (1999) *Absence and Labour Turnover Survey: Focus on absence.*

CBI/Percom (1993) *Survey of Absence.*

CIPD (2001) 'Employee absence: a survey of management policy and practice'. CIPD Survey Report.

Cole, A. (1994) 'Getting sick of ill nurses', *The Guardian*, 4 May.

Dibben, P., Philip, J. and Cunningham, I. (2001) 'Absence management in the public services: recent evidence from the UK', HRM Discussion Paper Series: No. 7, April.

Fowler, A. (1996) 'How to provide effective feedback', *People Management*, July, 2(14), 44–5.

Health at Work (1995) 'Managing attendance at work': HEA Annual Report (7).

Hegarty, S. (1995) 'The not-so-hidden cost that managers like to avoid', *Works Management*, 48(8), 78–81.

Hendry, C., Bradley, P. and Perkins, S. (1997) 'Missed a motivator', *People Management*, May.

IDS (1998) *Managing Absence.* London: Incomes Data Services Study 556.

Industrial Relations Review and Report (1993) *Employee Absence: Industrial Society and CBI chart patterns and policies*, Iss. 535, 3–7.

IRS Employment Review (1996) *Sickness Absence Monitoring 'Not Enough', says National Audit Office.* February, 2.

McHugh, M. (2001) 'Employee absence: an impediment to organisational health in local government', *The International Journal of Public Sector Management*, 14(1), 43–58.

Neale, F. (ed.) (1991) *The Handbook of Performance Management.* London: IPM.

Pringle, D. (1995) 'Tactics shift in the war of sick leave', *Personnel Today*, August.

Rose, M. (2000) 'Target practice', *People Management,* 23 November.

Sage, G. (1998) 'Health warning', *People Management*, 16 April, 23–4.

Steers, R. and Porter, L. (1991) *Motivation and Work Behaviour.* New York: McGraw-Hill.

Stevens, P. and Fitzgibbons, E. (2001) 'How to tackle long term sick leave', *People Management*, 12 July, 42–3.

Strebler, M.T., Robinson, D. and Bevan, S. (2001) *Performance Review: Balancing objectives and content.* Institute of Employment Studies.

Watkins, I. (1994) 'Sick excuses for swanning around', *Personnel Management*, April, 42–4.

Winstanley, D. and Stuart-Smith, K. (1996) 'Policing performance: the ethics of performance management', *Personnel Review*, 25(6), 66–84.

ASSIGNMENTS AND DISCUSSION TOPICS

1 Identify and then critically examine a performance management system. Discuss the extent to which it meets the requirements of the organisation for improved performance and the needs of the individual for recognition and reward.

2 Review the appraisal documentation in your organisation. What improvements would you recommend and why?

3 Role-play an interview with a colleague in which you discuss work performance. Consider how you would determine and set performance objectives, define performance standards and assess performance.

4 Critically evaluate the effectiveness of your organisation's holiday leave controls. Do they include 'holiday-free time zones', compulsory holiday periods and limits on the number and type of employees permitted to take leave at various times in the holiday year?

5 Critically examine the process for collecting sick absence information in your organisation. How effective is it in capturing accurate, timely and reliable data?

6 Find out the potential working-days lost (PWL) rate and the frequency rate in relation to sick absence, in percentage terms, in your organisation and benchmark it against those of other organisations. Comment on similarities and differences.

7 Argue the case for and against paying attendance bonuses.

8 What are the implications of the DDA, 1995 for managing sick absence?

9 What are the pros and cons of making monthly league tables of sick absence rates by department available to all employees?

10 What are the advantages and disadvantages of having waiting days for sick pay? What would be the implications of having one, three or five waiting days?

11 Examine the ten specific areas for managing sick absence at a corporate level, listed in this chapter, and comment on the effectiveness of each in relation to your own organisation.

12 The CIPD Survey (2001) of management practice in dealing with employee absence reported the finding that 'Respondents believe that, on average, one third of absence is not the result of ill health'. Clearly this is a perception and the reality is difficult to verify, but the implication is that a substantial proportion of sick absence is not genuine. Make your own assessment of this finding – is it the case that a third of absence involves dishonest intent? If so, what does this mean? What can be done about it?

13 High levels of sick absence are costly and disruptive to an employer. How would you, as the HR/personnel professional, respond to a demand from a line manager (your internal customer) to terminate the employment of an employee who has been absent from work with a legitimate illness for three months? How differently, if at all, would you respond to the demand if the employee in question had been absent from work for a total of two months in the past year, but this was made up of ten incidents of sick absence which averaged four days each?

CASE STUDY

Sick Susan and the Spice Girls

You are the personnel officer for a reputable high street retailer. A line manager has come to you for advice. He tells you that a member of his department, Susan, was absent from work yesterday and a friend had telephoned to report that Susan was sick with an 'upset stomach' and would not be attending work that day. Susan is 18 years old, is in her first job since leaving full-time education and has 11 months' full-time service. Her performance level is acceptable. On Susan's return to work today the line manager enquired about her health and was informed that she was feeling much better and perfectly able to undertake her duties.

The reason the line manager has come to see you is that there is something of a stir going on in the store because at lunchtime today the local newspaper had been printed and the front page contained a picture of a music concert featuring the Spice Girls. The concert had taken place the previous day. The reason for this being of interest is that the picture includes a clear and distinct image of Susan amongst the adoring fans. There is, therefore, a *prima facie* case (Susan has no known twin) that, instead of being ready, willing and able for work, Susan was attending the concert. You agree with the line manager that he should interview Susan to seek an explanation. It is difficult to do this with any degree of confidentiality because Susan is now infamous, the newspaper picture having gained very wide publicity amongst employees. A consequence of this is that 'the eyes and the ears' are on the store management to see what they will do, and what precedent will be established, in the case of Susan.

At the interview with the line manager Susan admits to being at the concert, but claims that the concert was in the afternoon. She qualifies this by stating that she had been genuinely ill with a 'stomach upset' in the morning, but she felt sufficiently recovered to attend the concert in the afternoon. She offers an apology for misinterpreting the rules as she thought that once she had reported sick she was not obliged to return to work that day even if she felt better. She asserts that she will know better in future. The line manager adjourns the hearing in order to consider the better in future. The line manager adjourns the hearing in order to consider the explanation. The line manager seeks your advice and it is agreed that you will check with the newspaper in the pursuit of 'further and better particulars'. On contacting the newspaper it is discovered that the photograph which captured Susan was actually taken before midday. This can be verified because the negative includes a record of the exact time of the photograph.

The line manager is in a quandary and your input to the decision is appropriate because of organisation-wide implications in terms of precedent. You have checked with the occupational health department who categorically state that there is no way that they can prove *or* disprove whether Susan had an upset stomach the day before. You therefore need to make a managerial decision.

Case study continued

1 What would be your decision and why?

2 What message would your decision send to other employees?

3 To what extent does natural justice allow us all (including Susan) to make a serious mistake?

4 Would your decision be any different if an extra piece of information is fed to the line manager by a senior member of his team to the effect that Susan had purchased her ticket for the concert two weeks previously and that this fact can be verified?

CHAPTER 12

Human resource development

by Amal El-Sawad

INTRODUCTION

Human resource development (HRD) is concerned with enhancing organisational performance through the effective development and deployment of organisational members. HRD activity has traditionally been classified under the headings of training, development and/or education. Training is a planned activity conducted over the short term to impart specific job-related knowledge, skills and attitudes (KSAs). Education is a much longer-term process developing broad and general KSAs, often not job-related at all. Both can contribute to individual development: 'the general enhancement and growth of an individual's skills and abilities through conscious and unconscious learning' (Buckley and Caple, 2000). However, sophisticated HRD strategies extend well beyond these activities. The focus is on individual (and hence organisational) 'learning', rather than training and education, which represent just a fraction of organisational learning opportunities. Viewed in this light, HRD can be seen to be inextricably linked to other resourcing functions. For example, reward strategies, work structure and design and the employee relations climate can be either conducive or obstructive to employee development, and can help create or destroy learning opportunities. The nature of HRD activity thus shapes and is shaped by people resourcing strategy as a whole.

CHAPTER OBJECTIVES

- To explore the concept of HRD together with its nature and scope and to outline the dualistic dimensions of HRD.
- To distinguish between the various HRD 'models in practice'.
- To differentiate 'organised learning' from 'organisational learning'.
- To consider the role of the HRD practitioner and consultant.
- To explain the use of the Training Cycle model for systematically identifying and responding to training and development needs.
- To understand the rationale for Continuous Development and to investigate the relationship between Total Quality Management and Continuous Development.
- To evaluate the impact of national training and development initiatives.
- To reflect on the contribution of HRD to effective people resourcing.

WHAT IS HUMAN RESOURCE DEVELOPMENT?

The way in which human resource development (HRD) is conceptualised by different theorists varies greatly, as does the way it is operationalised by different organisations. Though there is agreement on the broad objective of HRD, that is to enhance individual (and hence organisational) development and performance, disagreement centres on the means to this end. So, although a simple but comprehensive definition is often a useful starting point for exploring a particular concept, the breadth of the concept of HRD, and the resulting absence of a consensus definition, defies such treatment.

An alternative approach is to explore what HRD in practice involves in order to demonstrate its nature and scope. This can be done by considering the various organisational and individual needs which HRD attempts to respond to. For example, Bennett (1991) highlights the following:

- ensuring an adequate supply of properly trained personnel
- keeping present job performance levels at required standards
- developing skills, abilities and attitudes for future job requirements
- building greater job deployment flexibility
- coping with fast-changing technologies
- meeting statutory training requirements
- coping with reduced staffing levels and redundancy
- preparing staff for retirement.

Thompson and Mabey (1994) suggest that the constituent parts of an organisation's HRD strategy should involve:

- recruiting and inducting high quality people and deploying them effectively
- identifying and improving the skills and motivation of employees
- regular analyses of job content with regard to organisational objectives and individual skills
- reviewing technology and the potential for replacing routine tasks
- performance management and measurement
- identifying training needs
- providing training to improve current performance and enhance individual careers
- providing opportunities for individual self-development and personal growth
- helping employees to manage their own careers
- encouraging employees to accept change as the norm and as an opportunity.

From this, it is possible to highlight several key points and attempt to identify the main features of HRD. First, equating HRD with 'training' can be seen as far too narrow a conceptualisation. Developmental interventions come in many forms and are not the sole reserve of training courses. For example, changing the design of work to allow greater autonomy for employees or appointing an experienced and effective manager can all have developmental consequences for employees and hence organisations. Though training is undoubtedly an important aspect of HRD, it is only one aspect. Unfortunately, as will be demonstrated, much current 'HRD' practice is confined to training in its narrowest sense.

Second, despite the Training and Development Lead Body identifying the key aim of HRD as 'to develop human potential and assist organisations *and* individuals to achieve their objectives', it is nevertheless possible to detect a tension between organisational and individual needs and whether the former takes precedence over the latter. For example, from the organisation's perspective, developing the resources of the organisation includes discarding those that are no longer required. It is, however, doubtful whether those individuals being prepared for redundancy would perceive this as developmental or in line with their objectives! This leads on to a third feature, a less palatable side to HRD, akin to the 'soft' versus 'hard' elements of HRM, and depending on whether activities are concerned with '**human**' resource development, implying investment in people, or human '**resource**' development, suggesting cost and expendability. HRD in practice, it would seem, involves elements of both. Exhibit 12.1 highlights these and other dualistic (sometimes conflicting) dimensions of HRD, many of which will be referred to throughout the chapter.

Exhibit 12.1   The dualistic dimensions of HRD

Strategic	Operational
Organisation	Individual
Cultural	Structural
Change	Maintenance
Long-term	Short-term
Organic	Packaged
Proactive	Reactive
Future needs	Present needs
'Soft'	'Hard'
'Human' Resource Development	Human 'Resource' Development
Indirectly managed	Directly managed
Employee-driven	Employer-driven
Continuous development	*Ad hoc* development
Organisational learning	(No/dis-)organised learning
Double loop learning	Single loop learning
Investment	Cost
Enabled	Controlled
Structured	Unstructured
Facilitated	Directed

The first six dimensions listed are drawn directly from the work of Stewart and McGoldrick (1996) who view those on the right as *not* characteristic of (their conceptualisation of) HRD. Herein lies the source of problems of defining concisely what HRD is. If the **practice** of HRD encompasses those needs and activities listed above then, quite clearly, both ends of the spectrum can be, and frequently are, operating simultaneously and need not always be mutually exclusive. For example, the organisation can be proactively responding to long-term needs by undertaking succession planning activities, preparing high-potential staff for senior managerial posts. At the same time, the organisation may also be reactively delivering a packaged training programme in response to a recent change in legislation. Thus, HRD as a theoretical ideal – the 'how it should be' framework – does not appear to translate fully into the reality of practice – the 'how it currently is'. The justification for attempting to explore both ends of the spectrum in this chapter is, put simply, that practitioners striving to achieve the 'how it should be' need to first understand the 'how it is'.

THE DIFFERENT MODELS OF HRD

Parading under the label of HRD are a number of different 'models in practice' differentiated by the level of sophistication of HRD activity in terms of the nature and extent of learning activity. Figure 12.1 provides a framework for categorising four progressive levels of sophistication, four different HRD models.

Linking this framework to the broad patterns of HRD activities found evident within different organisations brings these models to life. Ashton *et al.* (1975) have identified three such patterns (intermittent, institutionalised and internalised), to which an extra one (investor) has been added for illustrative purposes.

The 'intermittent' pattern is characterised by low managerial commitment to HRD and consequently little visible HRD activity. Training and development interventions are infrequent, *ad hoc*, reactive and often in response to a crisis. There is, in effect, **no organised learning**.

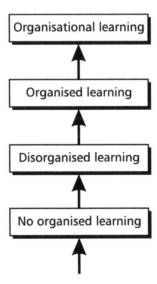

Fig. 12.1 HRD models in practice

The 'institutionalised' pattern is characterised by apparent managerial commitment to HRD and by a high level of visible HRD activity. Typically large HRD budgets are invested in extensive off-the-job training of a fixed menu format, often geared to assumed rather than actual development needs. Though the training on offer is well organised in administrative terms, **learning is disorganised**.

The 'investor' pattern is characterised by high managerial commitment to HRD and systematic, cyclical, organisationally managed approaches to identifying and responding to development needs. HRD expenditure, though substantial, is carefully managed, prioritised and targeted at actual business-defined development needs. This is **organised learning** rather than organisational learning.

The 'internalised' pattern is characterised by very high commitment to HRD, with managers demonstrating acceptance of a strong developmental ethos, but quietly so. The HRD activity is more invisible here, but only because the developmental philosophy is so strongly embedded within the culture of the organisation that learning is a day-to-day business-as-usual activity for managers and employees alike. This is **organisational learning** in practice.

The descriptions of different patterns of HRD activity serve to illustrate some of the dualistic dimensions of HRD in practice. The 'organised learning' pattern can be seen to serve a maintenance role, maintaining the organisational *status quo*. This can be linked to what is termed 'single loop learning', which involves the 'detection and correction of deviance in performance from established organisational norms' (Collin, 1994). 'Disorganised' and 'no organised' learning often fail to adequately achieve even this. In contrast, the 'organisational learning' pattern fosters organisational change and renewal on a continuous basis, encouraging creativity and innovation. This is linked to 'double loop learning' which consistently questions 'those very norms which define effective performance' (Collin, 1994) and appears consistent with Stewart and McGoldrick's (1996) conceptualisation of HRD.

The ease with which HRD practitioners can achieve this 'ideal', 'internalised' organisational learning model within their own organisations depends on the current position of the organisation. The lower the present level of sophistication, the further the distance to travel, the harder the task ahead. Which 'model' is in operation within an organisation is determined by a number of reciprocally determined factors, including managerial commitment to a developmental philosophy, the culture and climate of the organisation and whether this is conducive to development and learning, resources allocated to HRD, and employees' attitudes to learning and development. It is these factors which the HRD practitioner must tackle if HRD is to achieve its rather ambitious objectives of:

- enhancing quality, reducing costs and improving performance
- gaining competitive edge through the integration of business and strategic planning with wider organisational development and HR activities
- creating a learning climate
- engineering organisational change.

(Thomson and Mabey, 1994)

ROLE OF THE HRD PRACTITIONER AND CONSULTANT

Different conceptions of what constitutes effective HRD, as has been shown, leads to different patterns of HRD activity or models in practice. This in turn can be seen to result in differing definitions of effective HRD practitioners in terms of the role they play and the knowledge, skills and attitudes deemed necessary to succeed in these roles. There is, not surprisingly, as much variety here as in HRD practice itself.

Townsend (1985, cited in Rae, 1995), for example, focuses on practitioners' styles of delivery of training and education and identifies eight types: the Humble Expert, the Professional Trainer, the Oblivious Incompetent, the Arrogant Charlatan, the Boring Lecturer, the Directive Instructor, the Endearing Bumbler and the Shallow Persuader. (You may well be able to identify some of those who have taught and trained you amongst these types!) Gilley and Eggland (1989) have a much broader conception of the role of HRD practitioners, believing they need to be able to juggle a number of different roles simultaneously, attempting to balance and reconcile the needs of both the organisation and the individual by playing the part of strategist, marketer, individual development counsellor, needs analyst, task analyst, group facilitator, instructor, evaluator, and transfer agent. Bennett *et al.* (1984, cited in Rae, 1995) draw a contrast between HRD practitioners according to their orientation towards organisational change or organisational maintenance. 'Educators' and 'Innovators' share an organisational change orientation, while 'Caretakers' and 'Evangelists' strive to maintain the organisational *status quo*. Thus the dualistic dimensions of HRD can be seen to be reflected in the roles adopted by HRD practitioners, as can the various HRD models in practice, illustrated particularly well in the work of Pettigrew *et al.* (1982) who distinguish five different roles:

- *The 'Change Agent'* (which could be related to the 'internalised' HRD model) – champions change and organisational learning through cultural intervention (*see also* Chapter 21).
- *The 'Provider'* (akin to the 'Investor' model) – offers respected expertise aimed at maintenance of organisational performance.
- *The 'Passive Provider'* (a mixture of the 'institutionalised' and 'intermittent' models) – is also concerned with performance maintenance but is less skilled, less respected and the role is often little more than an administrative one.
- *The 'Training Manager'* – is responsible for the coordination of the training function.
- *The 'Role in Transition'* – attempting to move from 'Provider' to 'Change Agent' role.

Progressing an organisation's HRD model to the ideal 'internalised' one necessitates advancing the role of the HRD practitioner to a Change Agent or 'HRD Consultant' role and fostering what is variously referred to as a 'training ethos' or 'learning climate/culture' or indeed 'learning organisation'. However, such cultural change is notoriously difficult to achieve (this is covered in more detail in Chapter 21). Suffice it to say at this stage that what the HRD Consultant is striving to create is an organisation which:

- places high value on individual (and hence organisational) learning
- works towards full utilisation of all individual and group potential for learning and adapting to meet organisational objectives and in a way which fulfils the needs and aspirations of employees

- removes inhibitors to learning and replaces them with supportive systems for continuous learning

- creates a climate conducive to continuous learning and improvement.

(Burgoyne *et al.*, 1994)

Achieving these goals will involve HRD Consultants in:

1 Building up 'power bases' (Pettigrew *et al.*, 1982), using political awareness and skill to wield influence and win over key supporters at all levels of the organisation, especially line managers (and not least budget-holding senior managers) who will champion the 'learning' cause.

2 Exploring the whole personnel/HR policy package, ensuring that all disincentives to development and learning are removed. Thus work design, organisational structure, recruitment and selection policy, succession planning activities, equal opportunities, performance management and reward strategies must all be consistent with each other and conducive to a learning culture.

3 Promoting 'learning' in its broadest sense and not just job-related training.

4 Fostering a partnership approach to development which recognises and responds to (rather than ignores) the inevitable plurality of organisational and individual interests and objectives.

The receptiveness of the organisation to these activities will depend on the current level of sophistication of the organisation's HRD practices. It therefore may prove more fruitful to pursue 'organised learning' prior to 'organisational learning'.

THE TRAINING CYCLE – THE PATH TO ORGANISED LEARNING

The training cycle represents a planned, systematic and, as the name suggests, cyclical process for identifying and suitably responding to training and development needs. If utilised as intended – linking training and development interventions to business needs and systematically scanning the environment to track changes in these needs – it may be viewed as an approach similar in nature to the 'investor' pattern of HRD, striving to ensure training and development interventions are relevant to business objectives.

Figure 12.2 highlights the four major stages of the training cycle, and though it is not made explicit, the business needs of the organisation, both current and future, are considered to be the 'driving force' of the process (Bee and Bee, 1994).

Identifying training needs

Training and development needs can be assessed at an organisational, job/occupational, and/or individual level and this tripartite classification forms the framework for Training Needs Analysis (TNA). The methods and data sources used for assessing each level differ slightly, but since the process for identifying needs is broadly the same, they will be dealt with collectively here. Though TNA is often reactively triggered by a shortfall

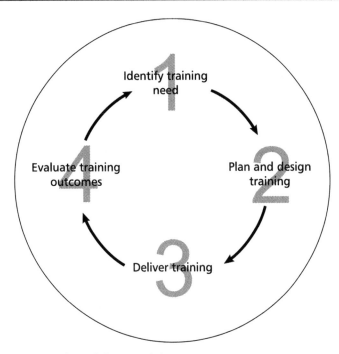

Fig. 12.2 The systematic training model

in expected performance, it can and should also be used to explore ways of improving performance in general, as well as proactively assessing future needs.

The first stage of TNA involves the collection of comprehensive data on:

- the external (political, economic, social, technological, legal) and competitive environment – drawn from environmental-scanning or 'horizon-watching' activities which should be conducted on an ongoing basis
- the organisation's internal environment – strategy, structure, technology, managerial style, culture, working conditions, as well as information on employees' aspirations, knowledge and skills, particularly in relation to their current roles.

Perhaps the richest source of data will come directly from employees themselves and observation, key informant interviews, group discussions and questionnaires are some of the methods which might be used to access this. In addition, much valuable data will already be available within the organisation, offering 'windows' (Bee and Bee, 1994) from which to view the current performance levels and capability of the organisation in relation to its present and future needs. These include business and strategic planning documents, including human resource and succession plans, and an array of data captured within management information systems – sales, labour turnover figures, sickness and absence records, number and nature of accidents, and quality measures such as customer complaints and wastage. Data from performance appraisal systems, probationary reviews and exit interviews can all alert the analyst to needs at an individual or group level. These figures are studied for trends and variances over time to detect 'deviances' in expected or desired performance.

These 'windows', combined with an assessment of the environment, offer measures of current and future business **performance needs** on the one hand and, on the other, the current performance and **capability levels** at an organisational, occupational/group and individual level. Comparing the two helps identify exactly where performance and capability gaps currently exist or are likely to arise and to define and specify the exact nature of these gaps. Once identified, the next stage is to assess whether training and development interventions might effectively address them – whether the performance gap is attributable to a deficiency in knowledge, skills or attitudes. This is not always the case and separating cause from effect is key at this stage. The root cause of performance problems may well lie in physical working conditions – equipment failure, social/psychological factors (such as adversarial manager–employee relationships), and/or the nature of the employment contract (such as employees having to work long hours for little pay, few holidays and/or on temporary contracts). In such cases, non-training solutions may offer eminently more suitable 'solutions'. Alternative options which can in themselves have developmental consequences and address performance gaps include, for example, work redesign, organisational restructuring, recruitment, and/or redeployment. Training interventions should only be considered when a genuine training need has been identified.

Training design and delivery

Having identified a training need, and the target population – those possessing the training need, whether select individuals, occupational/departmental groups or all employees within the organisation – the training solution needs to be designed. Identifying clear objectives of the training intervention is critical. Binsted's (1980) model offers a simple but useful framework. By clearly defining both the present state and the desired state of the target learners, the 'growth' required to get from the former to the latter will become apparent. This required growth, the gap between present and future states, forms the basis of the training design, informing other design and delivery decisions, including the:

- content of the training intervention (what is to be learned)
- sequence of learning activities (general then particular, concrete then abstract, doing then thinking)
- place (on- or off-the-job)
- trainers (tutors, line managers)
- time (when the training intervention will take place and how long it will last)
- media (computer-based training, video) and methods (lecture, group discussion).

Approaches to training delivery can be viewed as existing on a continuum. At one end of the spectrum is the 'packaged' traditional approach, where a body of knowledge and/or specific skills to be learned is carefully predetermined by the organisation and the training programme is delivered in a formal manner by 'experts', usually off-the-job, and often to a large number of employees. At the other end of the spectrum is an informal 'organic' experiential approach, with learning arising on-the-job or even 'through' the job, facilitated (often by a line manager or mentor) rather than directed by a tutor, with the individual negotiating and owning learning outcomes. Between the two extremes are a whole range of training delivery methods to choose from, including lectures, computer-based training, demonstration, individual or group projects and assignments, group discussions, role-playing, case studies, coaching, counselling and mentoring.

The objectives of the training intervention are the key considerations when selecting methods, as are related decisions such as whether the training intervention will occur on- or off-the-job, and whether internal or external HRD consultants will manage its design and/or delivery – so called 'make or buy' decisions. Numerous constraints will influence the selection, not least resource constraints in terms of time and money available, the urgency and importance of the training need, the availability of expertise within the organisation and, last but not least, the characteristics of the learners themselves: their motivation and willingness to learn and their preferred styles of learning.

Learning styles

To ensure that learning outcomes are achieved, HRD practitioners need an appreciation of 'how' people learn. There are a number of theories of learning; these are outlined elsewhere (see, for example, Harrison, 2000 or Reid and Barrington, 1999). One of the most influential comes from the work of Kolb (1996).

Kolb conceptualised the learning process as a four-stage cycle (Fig. 12.3) in which individuals first are exposed to new experiences, observe and reflect on these, integrate their observations into concepts and theories and then actively test these out in new

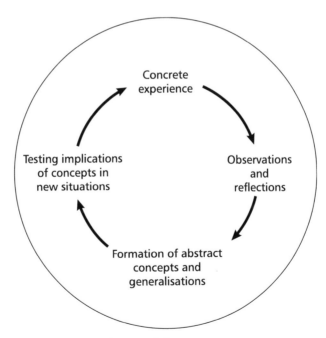

Fig. 12.3 The experiential learning model
Source: Organizational Psychology: Book of Readings (2nd edn) by Kolb *et al.,* © 1974. Reprinted by permission of Prentice-Hall, Inc. Upper Saddle River, NJ.

situations, leading to another new experience and kick-starting the whole learning cycle again. Many individuals have a preference for a particular stage in the cycle, corresponding with a particular learning ability or style. Honey and Mumford (1982), drawing on Kolb's learning cycle, identify the four styles and the learning preference associated with them:

- *Activists* learn best when they are actively involved in tasks.
- *Reflectors* learn best when they are given the opportunity to observe and reflect on activities.
- *Theorists* learn best when they can link new information or experiences to concepts and theories.
- *Pragmatists* learn best when they can apply new information to practical 'real-life' experiences.

The implications of these different learning styles are two-fold. First, from a training design perspective, an awareness of individual learning style preferences is an important consideration when deciding what training methods to adopt. For example, given a large class of learners with a diverse range of learning styles, the trainer must employ a diverse range of training methods to ensure all learning preferences are catered for. The downside to this is that the impact of the training programme on each individual is diluted in an attempt to accommodate all learning preferences.

Second, with much wider implications, and of particular interest for those intent on pursuing an 'organisational learning' model of HRD within their organisations, is the recognition that formal structured training represents just one small part of the myriad of learning opportunities presented to employees in their day-to-day work experiences. The most effective learners should involve themselves fully in all four stages of the cycle and yet the fact that individuals exercise strong learning preferences means these learning opportunities are frequently not fully capitalised on. Though pandering to their learning preferences and strengths may make sense in a one-off planned learning event, helping individuals to 'learn how to learn' by developing their learning weaknesses and least preferred learning styles is key if individual (and hence organisational) learning and development is to be maximised. As more and more individuals 'learn how to learn', HRD shifts along the continuum from organised learning (which is managerially controlled) towards organisational learning (which is individually directed).

Training and learning evaluation

Training and learning evaluation represents the final stage of a training cycle. Evaluation serves a number of different purposes, of which Easterby-Smith (1994) highlights four:

1 Proving – the worth or impact of a training programme.
2 Improving – ensuring that the learning intervention has improved performance.
3 Learning – evaluation viewed as part of the learning process itself, to be fed back into the preceding training cycle to foster continuous improvement.
4 Controlling – ensuring that individual trainees are performing to standard.

Reid and Barrington (1999) draw on the evaluation models suggested by other theorists and suggest five different levels at which training can be evaluated:

Level 1 – reactions of trainees to the training programme.

Level 2 – whether trainees learned what was intended.

Level 3 – whether the learning transfers back to the work environment.

Level 4 – whether the training has enhanced departmental performance.

Level 5 – the ultimate level: the extent to which the training has benefited the organisation.

Though not made explicit in this list, a major objective of evaluation is also to demonstrate the bottom-line impact of HRD investment – whether benefits derived warrant the financial costs incurred. This is often difficult to assess given that not all benefits can be easily translated into financial terms, that benefits may accrue over the long rather than the short term, and that consequently it is difficult to prove that changes, for better or worse, are directly attributable to the training intervention. However, such financial assessments are imperative to demonstrate the strategic impact of HRD and persuade organisations of the value of investing in HRD.

CONTINUOUS DEVELOPMENT – THE PATH TO ORGANISATIONAL LEARNING

What the training cycle is to would-be 'Providers' of **organised learning**, Continuous Development (CD) is to aspiring 'Change Agents' on a quest for **organisational learning**. Described as 'the ultimate intervention', CD is said to offer a unique approach to managing employee development which fosters a positive attitude to continuous learning and self-development and promotes the integration of learning with work (Reid and Barrington, 1999). This attitudinal dimension as the main feature (Stewart, 1999), distinguishing it from other HRD approaches, is also reflected in the CIPD's statement on Continuous Professional Development (CPD):

> CPD is an attitude as well as a process – the continual and conscious search for, and recognition of, learning in almost every activity and situation.

The CIPD identify the essential principles of CPD as follows:

- Development should be continuous, owned and managed by the individual learner.
- Learning objectives should be clear and should serve organisational needs as well as individual goals.
- Regular investment of time in learning should be seen as essential and not as an optional extra.

The fact that demonstrating evidence of CD is now a condition of CIPD membership may explain why the CIPD have relabelled their own CD programme as Continuous **Professional** Development. However, this runs the danger of suggesting that CD is the exclusive territory of 'professionals', the sole reserve of managerial/professional employees, as opposed to all employees. This goes against the learning ethos.

CD is not instead of but rather in addition to planned, off-the-job, formal training courses, though these make up only a small part of CD activity, which capitalises fully on experiential learning opportunities presented on-the-job and 'through' the job. Quite unlike other HRD approaches, CD recognises, values and positively encourages employees to take advantage of learning opportunities **outside** work. A much publicised 'best practice' example is Ford's 'Employee Development and Assistance Programme' (EDAP). Under the scheme, each employee is eligible to an annual grant of £200 towards the costs of personal development and training courses undertaken outside working hours, which need not be work-related at all. Take-up of the scheme has been described as phenomenal, with some 75 per cent of all staff benefiting. Rover's REAL programme (Rover Employee Assisted Learning) runs along similar lines. 'The ability of such schemes to trigger a previously inert enthusiasm for learning applies as much to . . . those at lower levels of the occupational hierarchy' (Maguire and Fuller, 1996), supporting the view that all employees should be included in CD-type initiatives. Indeed, car manufacturers appear to be the front-runners in such inclusive learning developments. Nissan too operates a CD programme for every employee (Wickens, 1991). Bosley *et al.* (2001) report details of Peugeot's 'Assisted Development Programme' which has been running since 1991. Every employee is entitled to apply for up to £250 each year to pay for vocational and/or non-vocational learning. Employees engage in a range of self-selected courses including, for example, sports coaching, public speaking, gardening, aromatherapy and more obvious computer skills and language programmes. It is estimated that at any one time some 25 per cent of employees are engaged in the scheme and thousands of employees have benefited.

In terms of process, instead of relying on an employer to identify training and development needs, individuals take responsibility for their own learning and development, continuously assess their own 'gaps' and seek learning opportunities to address these gaps. This may or may not involve formal training courses. Unlike traditional training approaches in which employees are passive recipients, with CD they transform (albeit gradually) from 'patients' to 'agents' of learning (Pedler *et al.*, 1988). Successive learning events allow the individual to develop confidence in their ability to learn – they in effect 'learn to learn' and to become autonomous continuous self-developers. Figure 12.4, from the work of Reid *et al.* (1992) graphically illustrates this process.

CD, in theory at least, represents a win–win situation with benefits accruing to both the individual and the organisation. For the individual, these can include improved (and improving) job performance, increasing individual learning capacity and the confidence to respond positively to change, leading, in turn, to enhanced employability, career prospects and general quality of working life. For the organisation, 'internalising' the CD philosophy and encouraging all employees to embrace it too can lead to enhanced organisational performance, the promotion of organisational change and development from within, and a route to organisational learning – and ultimately to a learning organisation. There are, however, only isolated and partial examples of CD in its fullest sense **in practice**. Structural, situational and dispositional factors all obstruct its successful implementation. Thus, for the time being at least, CD would appear to be more idealistic than realistic.

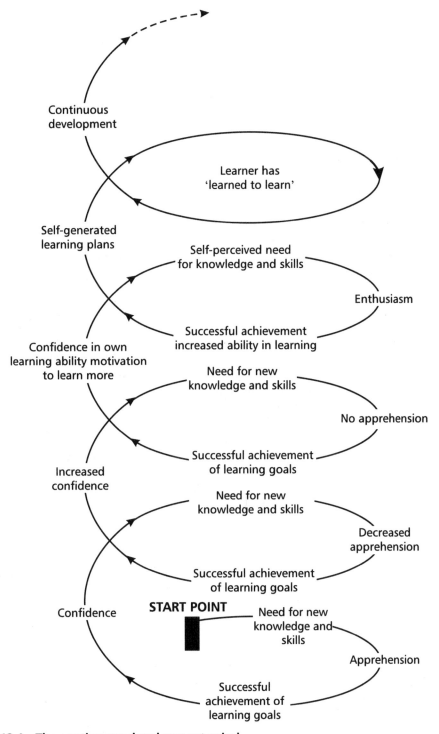

Fig. 12.4 The continuous development spiral

Source: *Training Interventions: Managing Employee Development* by Reid *et al*. (1992), Institute of Personnel Development.
Reproduced by permission of the publisher.

TOTAL QUALITY MANAGEMENT

The issue of quality has been on the organisational agenda for many years, but in the past it was restricted almost exclusively to the province of production. Here Quality Control departments typically concentrated their efforts on finding defective goods **after** they were manufactured – likened metaphorically to closing the stable door after the horse had bolted. Reactively attempting to correct deviance in performance after the event, rather than proactively seeking to **prevent** it in the first place and/or improve standards (an approach resembling the less sophisticated models of HRD), proved extremely costly. At one stage, typical costs of waste (non-quality) for Western companies such as IBM, Rank Xerox, Honeywell and ICI was estimated at 25 per cent of sales revenue, in sharp contrast to the corresponding figure of 5 per cent for Japanese organisations (MacDonald and Piggott, 1990).

As a result, interest in the Japanese-modelled Total Quality Management (TQM) grew. Conceptually at least, TQM has much in common with Continuous Development (CD) in that 'it is attitudinal, and aspires to endless improved performance'. Yet although 'TQM . . . supports the idea of learning within work, the main differences between TQM and CD lie in the absence of any commitment to promote "learning about learning" in TQM' (Reid *et al.*, 1992).

McGee and Tolchinsky (1993) identify continuous learning as an essential condition of continuous improvement and in turn of successful implementation of TQM. Indeed it would seem that a much closer relationship between TQM and the CD 'organisational learning' model of HRD might prove mutually beneficial. Quality, it is argued, offers one of the greatest incentives to organisations to improve employees' performance by investing in their training and development. Even the TQM guru, Deming, cites instituting training on-the-job and encouraging education as crucial elements. Thus, politically and strategically aware HRD consultants may profit from using TQM and its 'continuous improvement' philosophy as a lever for increasing managerial commitment to HRD and CD. Conversely, TQM, it seems, could equally 'use' HRD and CD since 'a crucial contribution to successful TQM must be the provision of (often extensive) training, both in terms of specific techniques linked to quality monitoring and by providing a basis for continuous development of skills appropriate to rapid change' (Goss, 1994).

The potentially rewarding relationship between HRD and TQM is illustrated neatly by the work of Masters (1996) who identifies from the literature the most frequently cited barriers to the successful implementation of TQM as:

- lack of managerial commitment
- inadequate knowledge or understanding of TQM
- inability to change organisational culture
- improper planning
- lack of continuous education and training
- failure to build a learning organisation that provides for continuous improvement
- incompatible organisational structure and isolated individuals and departments
- inappropriate reward system

- use of pre-packaged TQM programme not adapted to the organisation
- ineffective measurement techniques and lack of access to data and results
- short-term focus or using a 'Band-Aid' solution
- paying inadequate attention to internal and external customers
- inappropriate conditions for implementing TQM
- inadequate use of empowerment and teamwork.

But for the phrase 'TQM', one could be forgiven for thinking that the above list is actually referring to HRD. The coincidence of course is no accident. Given that HRD and TQM consultants broadly share ideologies, it makes sense that they also share many of the same problems in their attempts to put this ideology into practice. The good news is that HRD has, in theory, the solutions to its own problems and, along with other elements of the resourcing strategy, can be used to begin to tackle many of these barriers to implementing a developmental philosophy *and* TQM. The bad news is that some of these barriers are so deeply ingrained within organisational practices that the task is, at the very least, an uphill struggle.

Several factors in particular should be highlighted. First, since all other factors can usually be related back to this, is the 'inability to change organisational culture'. Culture is notoriously difficult, some say impossible, to manage (Chapter 21 picks up this discussion). Second, there is the issue of 'short-term focus' caused by the fact that 'companies attempting to introduce TQM are generally looking for immediate gains and therefore are likely to adopt a quick-fix approach rather than long-term cultural change' (Wilkinson *et al.*, 1992). TQM, and indeed HRD, is often viewed mistakenly as a panacea – a 'quick-fix' cure for all organisational ailments. This short-term mentality runs contrary to the principles of both TQM and the 'organisational learning' model of HRD. To give some idea of the time-frame involved in achieving what amounts to a cultural overhaul, two years after the launch of IBM's TQM programme (Market-Driven Quality) it was estimated that one-third of employees were demonstrating active commitment to the programme, one-third supported it in principle but their work regime remained unchanged, and the final third sceptically viewed the new initiative as just another managerial 'flavour of the month' and remained resolutely uncommitted. More alarmingly for 'short-termists' is the estimated 15 years taken for the Japanese quality revolution to occur, and the 20-year estimate given by Philips, the electrical giant, for their TQM programme to become woven into the organisational fabric. Short-termism and TQM clearly do not mix.

Finally, despite TQM being enshrined in the rhetoric of 'empowerment', far from experiencing TQM as empowering, emancipatory and developmental, research evidence suggests that managerial control is actually heightened through quality monitoring systems and 'surveillance' activities, whereby deviations from the prescribed standard of performance (again akin to the less sophisticated HRD models) are penalised both directly by management and indirectly through peer group pressure (Sewell and Wilkinson, 1992). Thus TQM in operation may actually discourage resourcefulness and creativity by encouraging homogeneity both in working practices and, more alarmingly, in employee profiles. A parallel can be drawn with the ideal model of TQM with employees being empowered through taking 'ownership' of their jobs, and with employees being encouraged to manage and own their learning in the CD model of HRD. As the practice of HRD illustrates, ideals do not always translate into practice. There is a great and very real tension between the rhetoric of enabling and empowerment on the one hand, and the reality of control and manipulation on the other, and until managers relinquish the latter, the progress of both the CD model of HRD and TQM will be severely hampered.

THE MACRO-HRD ENVIRONMENT

Appreciating the macro-HRD environment helps make sense of organisational HRD practices and activities. Evidence from the late 1980s showed that UK companies spent on average just 0.15 per cent of their annual turnover on training expenditure, in contrast with leading employers in the USA, West Germany and Japan who spent around 3 per cent – some 20 times as much (Keep, 1989). This low level of investment and the resulting low skills base was highlighted by a number of influential commentators as a major contributory factor to the UK's comparatively poor industrial performance and flagging economic fortunes, leaving it ill-equipped to contend with the high-skill, high-quality competitive strategies of its international competitors. Widespread belief that increased investment in training and development would prove an organisational (and economic) panacea, redressing the performance gap for which a lack of training was held responsible, elevated HRD to an issue of national strategic importance. As Gibb and Megginson (2001) point out, figures published by the National Advisory Council for Education and Training Targets (1999) confirm that companies that invest in HRD are more profitable than those that do not. There has consequently been a flurry of activity on the national scene and a series of National Learning Targets have been established. The current government's commitments include:

- To develop in everyone a commitment to lifelong learning, so as to enhance their lives, improve their employability in a changing labour market and create the skills that the economy and employers need.

- To encourage employers to invest in the training and development of their employees.

(DfEE, 2000)

Though grand and worthy aims, progress towards the targets is at best mixed. Scarce public resources mean that the government is in effect forced for the most part to maintain a voluntarist rather than interventionist stance, relying on employers to take the leading active and financial roles in delivering the training called for (Gibb and Megginson, 2001). The government's role is to attempt to stimulate the supply of training through a plethora of initiatives which are promoted and supervised by a number of government-sponsored agencies, both of which seem to be reinvented with 'bewildering frequency' (Gibb and Megginson, 2001). For example, the network of National Training Organisations was replaced in April 2002 by smaller Sector Skills Councils. Learning and Skills Councils replaced Training and Enterprise Councils in April 2001. The Department for Education and Employment was itself split into two departments in 2001 – the Department for Education and Skills, and the Department for Work and Pensions. Whatever the guise adopted, it is fair to say that a number of positive contributions have been made to the national training scene, notably N/SVQs, Investors in People, and Lifelong Learning initiatives.

National/Scottish Vocational Qualifications

National/Scottish Vocational Qualifications (NVQs) are nationally recognised standards of competence, 'expertly' defined by the National Training Organisation for each industry or occupational sector and based on National Occupational Standards, and consisting of five progressive levels of qualifications, from Level 1 covering basic skills to Level 5 covering professional and management skills. NVQs have been developed for a whole range of different occupations, for example full-time Trade Union officials, as well as for Training and Development professionals. There are now over 800 different NVQs available and by March 2000 2.8 million people in England and Wales alone had achieved an NVQ qualification.

NVQs have attracted some criticism. For example, it is suggested that 'employers (and many trainers) have seen NVQs as offering a simple answer to their training problems' (Reid *et al.*, 1992). Yet whilst the generic framework of NVQs may seem attractive, it neglects the fact that work roles differ greatly according to the characteristics of individuals who perform them and the organisations in which they work. The role of the HRD practitioner, for example, has diverse forms. The assumption is that what makes a good manager, or a good HRD practitioner, is known. Clearly it is much more complex than this. Whilst NVQs offer a template against which to assess and accredit employees' (and indeed non-employees') skills and competencies, there is some doubt as to whether they have developmental effects, since the competencies required to reach the standard may be those already possessed by an individual performing a specific job. In addition, although NVQs appear to offer individuals a clear qualifications ladder to climb, employers (particularly those favouring organised, single-loop learning) may well be reluctant to offer further training and development to individuals already judged competent and performing to standard in their current jobs. Furthermore, since NVQs are by definition exclusively job-related, any learning which is derived is narrowly focused. In terms of dualistic dimensions of HRD, NVQs would seem to serve to maintain the *status quo*, rather than contribute to organisational change, demanding conformance to predetermined employer-defined standards. However, companies that have used N/SVQs report improvements in staff motivation and product and service quality (Gibb and Megginson, 2001).

Learning and Skills Councils

The Learning and Skills Council was established in April 2001 and operates through 47 local offices (replacing the former Training and Enterprise Councils). It is responsible for all post-16 education and training, and works in concert with other agencies such as the Employment Service, Connexions and local colleges. The Council's remit includes:

- further education
- work-based training and workforce development
- adult and community learning
- adult information, advice and guidance
- education business links.

Each regional Learning and Skills Council draws representatives from the local community, including employers, community groups and learning providers. The aim is to generate education and training solutions which meet the priorities of the local community.

Investors in People

The 'Investors in People' (IiP) standard claims to encourage employers to raise organisational performance through the effective development of people. In terms of approaches to HRD, IiP can be seen to resemble a systematic, cyclical approach, similar to the 'investor' HRD model (which takes its name from IiP) and characterised by organised learning, as illustrated by the main parts of the standard requiring employers to commit to:

1 Making a public commitment from the top to develop all employees to achieve business objectives.
2 Regularly reviewing the training and development needs of all employees.
3 Taking action to train and develop individuals on recruitment and throughout their employment.
4 Evaluating investment in training and development to assess achievement and improve future effectiveness.

By October 1998 about 10 000 organisations had achieved the standard (Gibb and Megginson, 2001). By 2001 around 24 000 organisations had been recognised, with approximately 24 per cent of the UK workforce actively involved in the IiP programme (www.iipuk.co.uk). However, this is well below the original national target set by government – 50 per cent of organisations to have been awarded the standard by 1996 and 70 per cent by 2000 (DfEE, 1995). In fact, by 2000, some 68 per cent of medium and large organisations had disappointingly *not* been recognised. Interestingly, targets have since been apparently lowered considerably rather than efforts increased. The 2002 National Learning Targets for England are for 45 per cent of medium and large organisations to be recognised (latest figures for 2000 show 32 per cent had) and 10 000 small organisations to achieve the standard (6147 had by 2000). Though there is progress to report, clearly there is much more work to be done.

Of course, non-involvement in the standard should not necessarily be interpreted as an organisation's lack of commitment to employee training and development. Tellingly, research evidence has shown there to be 'no noticeable difference between recognised and non-involved employers on the percentage of the payroll spent on training' (Alberga *et al.*, 1997). What IiP does encourage, not least from its demand for evaluation systems to be put in place, is that expenditure is carefully targeted at meeting genuine training needs.

Criticisms of the IiP standard are those directed at systematic training approaches in general. For example, the advice that 'managers should be responsible for regularly agreeing needs with each employee in the context of business objectives' (Alberga *et al.*, 1997) assumes, somewhat naively, that individuals share managerial (and business) objectives, dismissing the inevitable tension between organisation and individual needs. In addition, the rather clinical approach advocated by IiP may mediate against, rather than capitalise fully on individual learning capacity, since:

> the spontaneous, experimental and often vivid experiences of learning which can be achieved by taking 'learning' as a way of life rather than as a consequence of the gap between what people currently know and what they ought to know according to the business plan are not covered in this [IiP] approach, which favours organised learning rather than organisational learning.
>
> (Alberga *et al.*, 1997)

Lifelong Learning

The concept of 'Lifelong Learning' has become central to government policy, and growing interest in its promotion is evidenced not least by the 1998 Green Paper entitled 'The Learning Age: A Renaissance of a New Britain' (Stewart, 1999) and the appointment in 1998 of the first Professor of Lifelong Learning at Warwick University (Reid and Barrington, 1999). The championing of 'Lifelong Learning' reflects:

> a recognition that basic schooling cannot meet an individual's continuing educational needs . . . that it is not sufficient merely to provide training to a certain number of individuals . . . rather that there has to be a more fundamental reappraisal of, and attitudinal shift towards, the value attached to learning by society as a whole.
>
> (Maguire and Fuller, 1996)

Linked to the concept of Continuous Development, the ideal of self-managed continuous learning is a well-defended one. Yet active commitment to self-managed continuous learning amongst individuals seems sparse, and it has been concluded that:

> We live in a culture that broadly understands the case for learning – but is not yet sufficiently motivated to turn that knowledge into action.
>
> (Ball, 1996)

To explore why this might be the case, the 'National Campaign for Learning', launched in April 1996, commissioned a poll of more than 5000 people to explore national attitudes to learning, discovering four broad groups. The first three groups – Improvers, Strivers, Drifters – all know and understand the value of learning. 'Improvers' are responding and taking action to better themselves. 'Strivers' are devoting some, although insufficient, effort to their own development. 'Drifters', however, are doing little or nothing and are (as a consequence, it is suggested) dissatisfied with their lives. The final group, 'Strugglers', neither value learning nor practise it.

In an attempt to change the national learning culture and encourage people back to learning, a number of initiatives have been launched of which Individual Learning

Accounts (ILAs) are arguably the most prominent. Following a number of regional pilot schemes, ILAs were launched nationally in 2000. Inspired by EDAP-style schemes noted earlier, individuals were eligible to receive a range of discounts and/or a government financial contribution to vocationally relevant learning activities (Bosley *et al.*, 2001). Encouragingly, ILAs proved far more popular than had been envisaged. Unfortunately, however, they have been suspended indefinitely since November 2001 amid allegations of training provider fraud. In any case, one of the concerns is that ILAs and other life-long learning initiatives may be taken up by those already committed to learning and fail to reach the 'Drifters' and 'Strugglers'. It is these groups which must be reached if real progress is to be made.

Structural, situational and dispositional factors which at best discourage and at worst deny individuals' learning opportunities are worth dwelling on since, for all the good intentions and encouraging developments on the HRD scene, both nationally and organisationally, opposing forces threaten to undo this work. For example,

• Evidence suggests:

> significant disparities in the proportions of certain groupings of individuals who participate in learning . . . factors such as social class, gender and ethnicity have been found significantly to affect the learning process.

> (Maguire and Fuller, 1996)

Access to educational and training opportunities favours higher social classes and full-time permanent professional and managerial staff (Reid and Barrington, 1999). These social inequalities are in danger of being reinforced and recreated within organisations.

• The government's deregulation and casualisation of the labour market is at odds with the stated aims of national training initiatives. Rises in part-time, casual, 'peripheral' and self-employment are characteristic of recent shifts in the labour market, with employers actively minimising rather than increasing their training commitment to these groups (Keep and Mayhew, 1995).

Pedler *et al.* (1988) have warned of the danger of 'self-development' being cynically 'hijacked' by those employers who see it as a justification for cutting training budgets, rather than investing in human resources. In this context, placing responsibility for learning and development onto the shoulders of individual learners may simultaneously serve to let employers (and government) off the hook, denying the part they have played in creating current conditions and abdicating some if not all responsibility for improving them. Whilst attempts to create a national learning culture are admirable, responsibility for achieving it must be shared, and this includes tackling some of the structural factors which mitigate against learning opportunities for all. Government, employers and individuals all have a part to play in shaping and sustaining it.

In many ways, the promotion of Lifelong Learning by the government is another manifestation of its voluntarist approach, attempting to stimulate demand for learning amongst individuals so as to put further pressure on employers to provide (and fund) more training and development. Their *faux pas* in this attempt is to fail to recognise that individuals' attitudes to learning do not develop in isolation. Employers must not fall into the same trap.

In pursuing a competitive strategy based on higher levels of skill, the need is not just for more skills within the workforce, but also for personnel management systems, and methods of work organisation and job design that will provide an environment in which those skills can be deployed to maximum productive effect.

(Keep and Mayhew, 1995)

Thus, HRD can play a central role in enhancing individual and organisational development and performance, though its contribution depends largely on the support of a consistent and integrated resourcing strategy.

SUMMARY LEARNING POINTS

1 Human resource development (HRD) is concerned with enhancing organisational performance through the effective development and deployment of employees. Though there is broad agreement on the objective of HRD, there is some disagreement on the means to achieving these ends.

2 Inherent within the practice of HRD are a series of dualistic and sometimes conflicting dimensions. These are reflected in the HRD activities of different organisations which can be seen to take on a number of different forms and possess varying degrees of sophistication. The role that HRD practitioners adopt mirrors the pattern of HRD activity within their organisation.

3 One of the most sophisticated approaches to HRD is embodied in the Training Cycle model which offers a systematic, planned approach to identifying and responding to training and development needs and a path to achieving 'organised learning'.

4 Continuous Development (CD), the route to 'organisational learning', is seen as the 'ultimate intervention' in which all employees become 'agents' rather than 'patients' of learning and in effect direct HRD activity themselves.

5 Total Quality Management can be seen to have much in common with the CD philosophy, not least sharing the same barriers to implementation. Merging the two approaches may have mutually beneficial results.

6 A number of national training and development initiatives have helped champion the cause of HRD. However, though there are pockets of promising activity, criticisms abound and progress has fallen far short of expectations. A number of deep-seated structural factors appear to be discouraging rather than encouraging HRD activity.

REFERENCES AND FURTHER READING

Alberga, T., Tyson, S. and Parsons, D. (1997) 'An evaluation of the Investors in People Standard', *Human Resource Management Journal*, 7(2), 47–59.

Ashton, D., Easterby-Smith, M. and Irvine, C. (1975) *Management Development: Theory and practice*. Bradford: MCB University Press.

Ball, C. (1996) 'You may say you're a drifter', *Times Higher Education Supplement*, 26 April.

Bee, F. and Bee, R. (1994) *Training Needs Analysis and Evaluation*. London: IPM.

Bennett, R. (1991) 'The effective trainer checklist', in Prior, J. (ed.) *Handbook of Training and Development*. Aldershot: Gower.

Binsted, D.S. (1980) 'Design for learning in management training and development: a view', *Journal of European Industrial Training*, 4(8).

Bosley, S., El-Sawad, A., Hughes, D., Jackson, C. and Watts, A.G. (2001) *Guidance and Individual Learning Accounts*. Derby: DfEE and CeGS.

Buckley, R. and Caple, J. (2000) *The Theory and Practice of Training*. London: Kogan Page.

Burgoyne, J., Pedler, M. and Boydell, T. (1994) *Towards the Learning Company: Concepts and practices*. London: McGraw-Hill.

Collin, A. (1994) 'Learning and development', in Beardwell, I. and Holden, L. (eds), *Human Resource Management*. London: Pitman Publishing.

Department for Education and Employment (1994) *Competitiveness: Helping businesses to win*. London: HMSO.

Department for Education and Employment (1995) *Competitiveness: Forging ahead*. London: HMSO.

Department for Education and Employment (2000) *National Learning Targets for England for 2002*. Sheffield: DfEE.

Easterby-Smith, M. (1994) *Evaluating Management Development, Training and Education*. Aldershot: Gower.

Gibb, S. and Megginson, D. (2001) 'Employee development', in Redman, T. and Wilkinson, A. (eds) *Contemporary Human Resource Management: Text and cases*. London: Financial Times/ Prentice Hall.

Gilley, J.W. and Eggland, S.A. (1989) *Principles of Human Resource Development*. Reading, MA: Addison-Wesley.

Goss, D. (1994) *Principles of Human Resource Management*. London: Routledge.

Harrison, R. (2000) *Employee Development*. London: CIPD.

Honey, P. and Mumford, A. (1982) *Manual of Learning Styles*. London: Peter Honey.

Keep, E. (1989) 'Corporate training strategies: the vital component?', in Storey, T. (ed.) *New Perspectives on Human Resource Management*. London: Routledge.

Keep, E. and Mayhew, K. (1995) 'Training policy for competitiveness: time for a new perspective?' in Metcalf, H. (ed.) *Future Skill Demand and Supply*. London: Policy Studies Institute.

Kolb, D.A. (1996) 'Management and the learning process', in Starkey, K. (ed.) *How Organisations Learn*. London: ITP.

MacDonald, J. and Piggott, J. (1990) *Global Quality: The new management culture*. London: Mercury.

Maguire, M. and Fuller, A. (1996) 'Lifelong learning and professional development', in Woodward, I. (ed.) *Continuing Professional Development: Issues in design and delivery*. London: Cassell.

Masters, R.J. (1996) 'Overcoming the barriers to TQM's success', *Quality Progress*, 29(5), 53–5.

McGee, E.C. and Tolchinsky, P.D. (1993) 'The convergence of total quality and work design', *Journal for Quality and Participation*, 16(2), 90–7.

Pedler, M., Burgoyne, J. and Boydell, T. (eds) (1988) *Applying Self-Development in Organisations*. Hemel Hempstead: Prentice Hall.

Pettigrew, A.M., Jones, G.R. and Reason, P.R. (1982) *Training and Development Roles in their Organisational Setting*. Sheffield: MSC.

Rae, L. (1995) *Techniques of Training*. Aldershot: Gower.

Reid, M.A., Barrington, H. and Kenney, J. (1992) *Training Interventions: Managing employee development*. London: IPM.

Reid, M.A. and Barrington, H. (1999) *Training Interventions*. London: CIPD.

Sewell, G. and Wilkinson, B. (1992) 'Empowerment or emasculation: shopfloor surveillance in a total quality organisation', in Blyton, P. and Turnbull, P. (eds) *Reassessing Human Resource Management*. London: Sage Publications.

Sloman, M. (1994) *A Handbook for Training Strategy*. Aldershot: Gower.

Stewart, J. (1999) *Employee Development Practice*. London: Financial Times/Pitman Publishing.

Stewart, J. and McGoldrick, J. (1996) *Human Resource Development: Perspectives, strategies and practice*. London: Pitman Publishing.

Thomson, R. and Mabey, C. (1994) *Developing Human Resources*. Oxford: Butterworth-Heinemann.

Truelove, S. (ed.) (1995) *The Handbook of Training and Development*. Oxford: Blackwell.

Wickens, P.D. (1991) 'Innovation in training creates a competitive edge', in Stevens, J. and Mackay, R. (eds) *Training and Competitiveness*. London: Kogan Page/National Economic Development Office.

Wilkinson, A., Marchington, M., Goodman, J. and Ackers, P. (1992) 'Total quality management and employee involvement', *Human Resource Management Journal*, 2(4), 1–20.

Woodruffe, C. (2000) *Development and Assessment Centres*. CIPD.

ASSIGNMENTS AND DISCUSSION TOPICS

1 Consider the organisation in which you are working (or one known to you). In what ways do you feel the following to be conducive and/or obstructive to your own development: the organisational structure; the design of your job; the organisational culture; your manager; the reward strategy? Could these features be improved? If so, how?

2 Which model does HRD activity in your organisation (or one known to you) reflect? What type of role do the organisation's HRD practitioners adopt?

3 Explain the major stages of the training cycle. What are the relative merits of a systematic, planned approach to identifying and responding to training and development needs?

4 How does 'organised learning' differ from 'organisational learning'? Why should organisations aspire towards the latter?

5 Organisations are often faced with barriers when attempting to implement Total Quality Management and Continuous Development. Identify these barriers. How might it be possible to overcome them?

6 Assess critically the impact the following national initiatives have had on redressing the UK's skills gap: the LSCs; NVQs (including the MCI initiative); the 'Investors in People' standard.

7 The National Campaign for Learning has hired you as an HRD consultant. Your task is to launch a national campaign to promote the case for Lifelong Learning. How would you approach this task?

8 'We live in a culture that broadly understands the case for learning – but is not yet sufficiently motivated to turn that knowledge into action' (Ball, 1996). Explain why this might be the case.

CHAPTER 13

Health and safety at work

INTRODUCTION

Each year approximately two million people suffer ill health caused or aggravated by work activities. This affects their quality of life, impairs work performance and gives rise to the loss of millions of working days. Effective people resourcing demands that managerial attention be given to health and safety at work, but despite the importance of health and safety matters they can be subordinated to immediate operational demands. There are three principal themes to this chapter. The first is the identification of a perceived tension between good health and safety practice and operational demands. The second is a practical overview of the legislative framework which informs health and safety practice and which is of relevance to the managers of people. The third is the promotion of the view that the effective management of health and safety is dependent not only on the legislative framework, but also on creating a positive health and safety culture.

CHAPTER OBJECTIVES

- To discuss the perceived tension between the performance imperative and employee health and safety at work.

- To recognise that prescriptive legislative approaches have been found wanting and the health and safety focus has shifted to ascribing employee and employer duties and responsibilities.

- To provide a practical overview of the legislative framework, in particular the Health and Safety at Work Act, 1974 and the Health and Safety Regulations, 1992 (consolidated in ERA: 1996) which implemented EU Directives.

- To offer guidance on the creation of an active and positive health and safety culture.

HEALTH AND SAFETY AT WORK AND THE PERFORMANCE IMPERATIVE

A concern in principle for the health and safety of employees and the encouragement of employee self-interest in health and safety are obvious prerequisites to the effective resourcing, management and satisfaction of people at work. Workplace reality can be different because of perceptions that health and safety constrains operational freedom and inhibits productivity. These perceptions may relegate health and safety attitudes and actions to a reluctant compliance to good practice and the law, or result in the avoidance of employee and employer obligations. The potential for conflict between the unfettered pursuit of operational efficiency and the protection of employees from hazards needs to be recognised in planning to manage health and safety successfully. The tension between 'the performance imperative' of organisations seeking survival in competitive environments, and health and safety responsibilities towards employees, is difficult for management to reconcile. The reconciliation is dependent on the belief that good health and safety equals good business.

Organisations have an ethical and social responsibility to give priority to workplace health and safety, but there are compelling business reasons why health and safety should be of significant interest to managers seeking quality employee performance. These include the following.

- Injuries, absence and ill health directly and seriously impact upon organisational efficiency and effectiveness (Exhibit 13.1).

- Mutual employer and employee interest in health and safety contributes to a healthy psychological contract (*see* Chapter 1).

- Health and safety concerns distract employees from quality concerns.

- Health and safety at work provides fertile ground for disciplinary breaches and grievance expression.

- Considerable obligations are placed on employers by an extensive legal framework and increasing European influence through directives and decisions.

- The development of an active health and safety culture requires attitudinal and behavioural change, with key roles for training, supervision and managerial standard setting.

Exhibit 13.1   The facts on work-related ill health and injury

- 30 million working days per year are lost due to accidents and ill health.
- 2 million people per year suffer from ill health caused or made worse by their jobs.
- 17 500 people per year are forced to give up work and 90 000 people per year have to change jobs because of illness or injury.
- Loss of potential output through absence from work, the cost of medical treatment and DSS administration costs are additional societal costs, bringing total costs to over £10 billion per year.

Source: *Good Health is Good Business*, HSE, 1996 and 1998.

High performance HR strategies recognise first, that people are a major source of competitive advantage, and second, that to contribute fully to organisational performance people need to feel valued. Creating an environment where people feel physically and psychologically safe seems to be a fairly fundamental demonstration that workers are valued. Effective health and safety therefore does make good business sense, and contributes to gaining the trust, commitment and involvement of employees, but health and safety will only receive priority of attention with top management commitment and an acceptance of responsibility throughout the organisation.

FROM PRESCRIPTION TO RESPONSIBILITY – STATUTORY REGULATION TO SELF-REGULATION

Contemporary health and safety concerns within the employment relationship have become more complex and include psychological as well as physical well-being. Health and safety legislation, until the Robens Report of 1972 and the Health and Safety at Work Act (HASAWA), 1974, was primarily focused on statutory regulation and on 'prescribing actions, behaviour and work processes'. This prescriptive approach was being defeated by accelerating technological development and the creative talents of employees who were finding new and innovative ways to damage themselves at work. The prescriptive legislation was onerous for employers, lacked clarity in wording and did not address the need to influence attitudes as well as constraining unsafe behaviour. Prescriptive legislation and statutory regulation are difficult to police and enforce. HASAWA heralded a new approach to health and safety by shifting the emphasis from buildings, machinery and prescribed employer actions to the establishment of the rights, responsibilities and duties of people at work. Shifting the emphasis from prescription to responsibility has not been entirely successful, and there remains a role for unambiguous guidance in many safety areas, but the philosophy of ascribing employer and employee responsibility and the promotion of self-regulation was maintained in the important Health and Safety Regulations, 1992 (*see* page 318).

Statutory provision aims:

> **to encourage the exercise of employer and employee judgement and responsibility, with decreased faith in legal prescription.**

This approach is more likely to engage the commitment of employees than the alternative of always being directed what to do. Active and positive health and safety cultures should be developed at work to replace a reliance on the legislation to predict and regulate every health and safety eventuality or to legitimise the punishing of employees who fail to comply with the law. Paradoxically, the 'responsibility and judgement approach' produces a tension between human desire for certainty, in this case the desire to know what is required in a particular health and safety situation, and the freedom to exercise discretion and judgement in a particular organisational context. To illustrate this point, the Display Screen Equipment Regulations (*see* page 324) allow employer discretion by not prescribing time threshold criteria for defining 'a display screen user'. This discretion can make it uncomfortable for those employees who have to decide upon the designation of users for the purposes of the regulations, with the result that prescriptive internal criteria are applied, for example the imposition of fixed time thresholds to define a display screen user. With discretion goes uncertainty.

> **Effectively there is a displacement of the tension between prescription and the exercise of judgement from the legislation to managerial decision makers.**

RECONCILING THE TWIN TENSIONS

The tensions between

1 the performance imperative and health and safety, and

2 the balance between legislative prescription and managerial judgement,

need to be reconciled if the management of health and safety at work is to be effective. A starting point for reconciliation is knowledge of health and safety law, codes of practice and Health and Safety Executive guidance, as these represent the body of knowledge associated with good health and safety practice. Health and safety is a detailed legislative area and the aim here is to provide sufficient information for managers and others responsible for health and safety to appreciate key principles and to know when expert advice is required. A basic understanding of health and safety law is useful regardless of whether specific organisational responsibility for health and safety is located with a personnel specialist, a health and safety officer or another 'competent person'. Whilst compliance with the law is an important concern, another perspective is to seek to deploy good practice in health and safety legislation to add value to organisational performance. All managers and employees have responsibility for health and safety at work, and a cascading of legislative knowledge will contribute to the development of an active and positive health and safety culture.

COMMON LAW DUTIES OF CARE

Employers have a common law duty **to take reasonable care** of each employee and are expected to safeguard employees against hazards which are reasonably foreseeable. The standard of care required is that of a 'prudent' employer. The duty of care includes operating safe premises, safe work systems and safe equipment, and ensuring that, through selection, training and supervision, employees are able to work safely and competently. Employees have common law duties **to cooperate** with the employer and **to exercise reasonable care** in the performance of work. These duties oblige an employee to make every effort to work safely, to abide by health and safety instructions and to contribute to achieving a safe working environment. Health and safety is therefore firmly rooted in the contract of employment through common law, making health and safety an employment issue. Statutory health and safety provision supports and extends these common law rights and duties.

THE HEALTH AND SAFETY AT WORK ACT (HASAWA) 1974

Prior to HASAWA the guiding statutes for employers were the Factories Act (FA), 1961 and the Offices, Shops and Railway Premises Act (OSRPA), 1963. These Acts applied to the premises indicated in the title of the Act, determined statutory employer and employee duties and set minimum standards in the working environment. FA and OSRPA regulate lighting, ventilation, working space, cleanliness, hygiene facilities, temperature and first aid arrangements. These Acts remain in force but their provisions are being replaced by health and safety regulations and codes of practice, and particularly by the Workplace Health, Safety and Welfare Regulations, 1992 and the health and safety provisions of the Employment Rights Act, 1996.

HASAWA represented a sea-change in the UK approach to health and safety legislation and was aimed at combating the endemic apathy towards health and safety provision, attributed to excessive, prescriptive and unintelligible law and compounded by ineffective policing and enforcement. HASAWA incorporated fundamental shifts in the approach to health and safety at work by:

1 Promoting a self-regulatory system in recognition that it is those who work with the risks who are most effective at recognising and responding to them.

2 Encouraging voluntary effort and personal responsibility for health and safety, rather than a reliance on prescriptive regulation.

3 Directing the statutory provision to cover people rather than just machinery and premises.

4 Extending the legislative scope to cover most employed persons, rather than specific places of work.

5 Enforcing the law through strengthened criminal sanctions.

6 Unifying the administration and enforcement through creating the Health and Safety Commission (HSC) and the Health and Safety Executive (HSE).

The provisions of health and safety law can be examined from the perspectives of duties (general duties and duties relating to safety policies, committees and representatives) and enforcement.

HASAWA – general duties

General statutory duties placed on the employer include providing:

- safe equipment, a safe workplace and a safe system of work
- safe arrangements for the use, handling, transport and storage of all articles and materials
- the information, training and supervision necessary for effective health and safety
- an adequate and safe means of entering and exiting the workplace
- adequate welfare; although welfare is not defined it is taken to mean the work environment features associated with FA and OSRPA, reflected more recently in the Workplace Health, Safety and Welfare Regulations (*see* page 324).

There are clearly similarities with common law duties, but HASAWA duties are more explicit and breaches of HASAWA duties are subject to criminal enforcement and sanction. A schedule of criminal penalties incorporates unlimited fines and imprisonment for employer failure to discharge a duty or failure to remedy a breach. Employers are not expected to exercise their duties without regard for the cost, difficulty and commercial implications, nor are they expected to predict unforeseen circumstances. The phrase which defines the extent and scope of the employer's duties is **as far as is reasonably practicable** (HASAWA, 1974). This permits employer judgement which weighs the health and safety risk against the burden of reducing or removing it. The statutory duty of care also applies in respect of non-employees legitimately on the premises and people outside the organisation who may be affected by the employer or employee acts or omissions.

There are further important duties placed on employers. These include:

- to prepare and update a written health and safety policy and to communicate it effectively and comprehensively to employees
- to recognise the appointment of safety representatives from recognised trade unions (or to consult directly with employees or with employee representatives – Consultation with Employees Regulations, 1996)
- to form a safety committee, where requested to do so in writing by at least two union safety representatives.

Employees also have HASAWA duties: first, to take reasonable care of their own safety, implying that a failure to do so will be a breach of duty punishable under HASAWA and therefore subject to legitimate managerial discipline, and also potentially subject to criminal proceedings; and second, to take reasonable care in respect of other people who may be affected by the employee's actions or omissions. Employees are therefore mutually responsible to each other for health and safety at work. Employees are also obligated to cooperate and not to interfere, whether by design or carelessness, with the employer, other people or any workplace provision which seeks to secure health and safety at work. These employee duties are made even more explicit in the Management of Health and Safety at Work Regulations and seek to engender the personal values and responsibility essential to achieving a positive safety culture.

Designers, manufacturers, suppliers and installers of articles, equipment and substances do not escape duties and responsibilities under the HASAWA. The responsibilities include, as far as is reasonably practicable, incorporating safety features in the design stage, testing for risks to health and seeking to minimise or eliminate them, and providing information, training and instruction for installation and use. HASAWA, along with more specific legislation (the Environmental Protection Act, 1990), makes reference to the emission of noxious and offensive substances and a higher standard of care is specified. Those responsible for premises are obligated to prevent noxious or offensive emissions by **the best practicable means**, which does not permit the costs and difficulty of eliminating pollution being weighed against the nature of the risk to health and safety (although a judgement about what constitutes the best practicable means still remains). This provides a contrast with the standard of care implied by 'as far as is reasonably practicable'.

The health and safety policy

A health and safety policy should include three sections – a positive statement of management attitude and commitment to health and safety, a specification of responsibilities and accountabilities for health and safety, and operational arrangements for health and safety. The content of the policy is not prescribed beyond these general sections, but guidance is available from the HSC (*Writing a Safety Policy Statement*: 1989 – peridically revised), the intention is that management should reflect upon their own particular hazards and risks and design an appropriate policy. Risk assessment outcomes, the designation of the safety competent persons (1992 Regulations) and emergency procedures should be included in the policy (Fowler, 1994).

Safety representatives and safety committees

HASAWA requires employers to recognise safety representatives appointed by trade unions, where trade unions are recognised. Union safety representatives have a right to be consulted about the full range of health and safety matters, including the appointment of the competent persons required by the 1992 Regulations, and have a wide range of functions which include:

- being consulted and making representations to employers
- investigating hazards and risks
- making safety inspections, having given reasonable notice
- considering employee complaints
- accessing and consulting with HSE inspectors
- being a member of the safety committee.

The Health and Safety (Consultation with Employees) Regulations, 1996 corrected the inconsistent position where only employers who recognised trade unions were required to recognise safety representatives. The 1996 Regulations require employers to consult employees where there is no appointed union representative. The consultation can either be directly with employees or through elected representatives of employment safety (ROES), and there is a duty to consult about:

- the introduction of measures substantially affecting health and safety
- the appointment of representatives
- the supply of statutory health and safety information
- health and safety training
- the health and safety consequences of introducing new technology.

There are similarities between the role of union safety representatives and ROES, but the investigatory functions are less evident in the latter. In order to perform their function adequately, all safety representatives are entitled to the information and training necessary to fulfil their duties, to reasonable time off work with pay during normal working hours, and to appropriate facilities. All safety representatives should be included in the updating and the communication of the safety policy. Union safety representatives and ROES have strengthened statutory protection against dismissal or action short of dismissal for duties associated with their legitimate role.

The statutory duty to create a safety committee relies on the appointment of union safety representatives, and consequently the duty is circumscribed, but where at least two safety representatives request it the employer is required to establish a safety committee. Apart from specifying a requirement for the committee to keep under review the measures taken to ensure the health and safety at work of employees, the composition and terms of reference of the committee are left to the discretion of the employer after consultation with employee representatives (Safety Representatives and Safety Committees Regulations, 1977).

Enforcement of health and safety law

The Health and Safety Commission (HSC) and the Health and Safety Executive (HSE) were established by HASAWA. The HSC is primarily an advisory body and the HSE is primarily the enforcement agency. The HSC consists of a chairperson, appointed by the Secretary of State, and nine other members; three each are chosen from employers' organisations, employee representatives' organisations and local authorities. The HSC is responsible for providing direction for national health and safety policy and proposing new law to secure the health, safety and welfare of the public and people at work. The HSC role incorporates research, approving codes of practice and providing information, training and advice. The HSE assists the HSC and is responsible for policing and enforcing health and safety law. Local authorities retain some responsibility for enforcement (Enforcing Authority Regulations, 1989) and along with the HSE appoint safety inspectors. Safety inspectors have wide-ranging powers, including the authority to:

- enter premises at any reasonable time
- be accompanied by authorised persons and a police officer, if obstructed
- use any equipment or materials necessary for investigation
- take samples, measurements and photographs
- direct that work areas be left undisturbed
- take possession of articles, substances or equipment, if reasonable cause is established
- take statements from appropriate persons
- examine organisational documents.

Safety inspectors have the power to issue improvement or prohibition notices. An improvement notice is used where the inspector is satisfied that there is a contravention of a statutory provision. An improvement notice identifies the statutory provision being contravened and requires that the contravention is remedied by a prescribed date. Where the inspector is of the opinion that an activity involves a risk of serious personal injury a prohibition notice, ordering the immediate or deferred cessation of the activity, can be issued. Failure to comply with an improvement or a prohibition notice is an offence. Appeals against these notices can be made to an Employment Tribunal (ET). In the case of an improvement notice, the appeal, which has to be lodged within 21 days of the date of the notice, has the effect of suspending the notice until the appeal is determined. In the case of a prohibition notice the appeal, also submitted to an ET within 21 days, does not suspend the notice. Approximately 10 000 improvement or prohibition notices are issued each year and they can be entered in a public register for at least three years, exposing 'transgressors' to public scrutiny and increasing the deterrent value of the notices (Environment and Safety Information Act, 1988).

The use of these notices and the willingness of inspectors to prosecute under the statutory provision are circumscribed by three factors. First, there are insufficient numbers of inspectors to police all employers and all employees; second, prosecution is time consuming for inspectors; and, third, there are difficulties in achieving successful prosecutions and therefore prosecutions only proceed where there is a real prospect of conviction. The number of prosecutions by the HSE in the UK averages around 2000 per year, of which around 80 per cent are successful, but the average penalty per conviction is only around £3000 (HSE Annual Reports). The HSE aims to secure compliance with the law through an educative and persuasive approach to discourage the displacement of health and safety responsibility to the inspectors. This is also intended to engender a view of the inspecting role as supportive and cooperative. The inspectorate is reasonably tolerant of employers who need time to respond to new health and safety regulation, and formal enforcement measures are unlikely unless risks to health and safety are obvious and imminent.

Regulations and approved codes of practice (ACOP)

HASAWA is an 'enabling Act'. It enables the Secretary of State to lay down legal standards in respect of health and safety through the simpler and more flexible process of making health and safety regulations. This regulation-making power is used widely, and regulations can be made in respect of almost anything related to health and safety at work. Examples include the Control of Substances Hazardous to Health Regulations (COSHH: 1988), which protect people at work from exposure to potentially hazardous substances through a process of risk assessment and responsible employer action; the Reporting of Injuries, Diseases and Dangerous Occurrences Regulations (RIDDOR: 1995) which impose reporting requirements for accidents and industrial diseases; and the 'six pack' of 1992 Regulations (consolidated in ERA: 1996) which implemented European Directives.

The Secretary of State is empowered to approve codes of practice drawn up by the HSC, the HSE or any other appropriate organisation. The purpose of the codes of practice is to provide practical guidance in interpreting and applying statutory provision. There is not a strict legal obligation on employers to observe the provisions of an approved health and safety code of practice, but a failure to do so may be taken into account by the courts. If an employer does not adhere to a code of practice it is open to them to demonstrate that a statutory health and safety obligation has been observed in some other way. It is sensible to follow the guidance in the codes as not only do they reflect good safety practice, but they also afford some protection against successful prosecution.

317

A PRACTICAL GUIDE TO THE 1992 HEALTH AND SAFETY REGULATIONS (CONSOLIDATED IN ERA, 1996)

The 1992 Regulations, known as the 'six-pack' (Fig. 13.1), are representative of contemporary thinking in health and safety at work, and managers will benefit from an appreciation of the content and approach of these regulations. The concept that employers are normally only obligated 'as far as is reasonably practicable' remains a core principle. Most of the requirements of the 1992 Regulations were already covered by existing UK legislation, but they express and make explicit a European standard for health and safety. Compliance with a more specific regulation, for example COSHH, is sufficient to comply with a corresponding duty in the 1992 Regulations, but where the 1992 Regulations exceed existing legislation it is necessary to consider additional

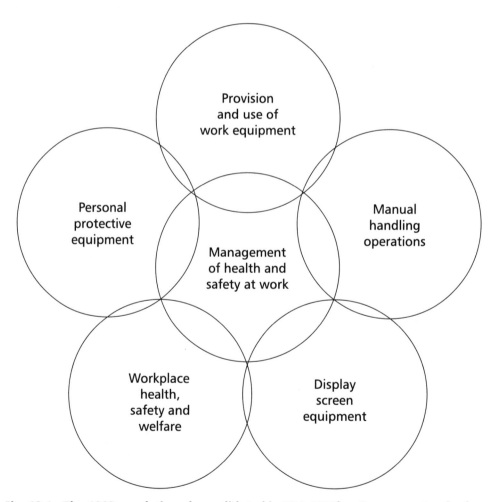

Fig. 13.1 The 1992 regulations (consolidated in ERA 1996): a European standard located in a UK health and safety philosophy

health and safety measures. The Management of Health and Safety at Work Regulations are largely a reflection of the HASAWA, but incorporating risk assessment. The Manual Handling Operations, the Display Screen Equipment and the Personal Protective Equipment Regulations were mostly new areas of regulation. The Provision and Use of Work Equipment Regulations were a combination of existing and new legislation. The Workplace Health, Safety and Welfare Regulations represent a contemporary version of the FA and OSRPA.

The Management of Health and Safety at Work Regulations emanated from the 'European Framework Directive' and provide a context for the other five sets of regulations (which emanated from 'Daughter Directives'). Health and safety is high on the European agenda for two reasons: first, because it is integral to the social dimension of the Single European Market, and second, because of the desire to contribute to a level (competitive) playing field through the harmonisation of health and safety standards across the European Union. The Single European Act (SEA, 1987) designated health and safety as an area of competence for qualified majority voting (QMV). This effectively removes the power of any one member state to veto health and safety proposals; and there has at times been contention between the UK and the European Commission over what should be included in health and safety QMV, for example in the case of the Working Time Directive which was designated as a health and safety measure.

The emphasis in the 1992 Regulations maintained by the HSC and the HSE, and in line with HASAWA, is away from prescription towards responsibility. The regulations were published to include approved codes of practice and guidance on regulations.

The underpinning philosophy is one of suitable and sufficient risk assessment, the exercise of informed judgement and a response that is reasonable in the circumstances.

Management of Health and Safety at Work (MHSW) regulations

These regulations provide a wide context for health and safety at work. The principal obligations include:

- risk assessment
- proper managerial arrangements for health and safety
- health surveillance
- appointment of 'competent persons' to assist with health and safety
- emergency procedures
- provision of information to employees and others
- coordination of health and safety in shared premises
- assessment of employee capability in relation to health and safety
- employee duties.

A critical MHSW requirement is:

To make a suitable and sufficient assessment of (the) risks to health and safety.

The objective is to assess the risks to health and safety of employees and others, in the workplace and outside, and the employer is therefore responsible for assessing risks within 'a responsibility zone'. Risk assessment may need to check the health and safety competence of contractors or the self-employed. Risk assessment should be documented and subject to regular review, with the significant findings and the managerial response recorded in writing and integrated into the safety policy. The MHSW code of practice advocates a commonsense approach to risk assessment. The initial assessment can be quick and simple and aimed at identifying whether there is a problem which warrants further investigation. Risk assessment is therefore concerned with recognising and responding to significant risks, not with bureaucracy or trivial risks. Risk assessment can take account of existing preventive measures and assessments undertaken for other purposes, under the COSHH Regulations for example, need not be repeated if they are considered to be 'suitable and sufficient'. Employers are required to undertake a systematic examination of work activity, and a five-step example of the process is provided in Exhibit 13.2.

A suitable and sufficient risk assessment will reflect what is reasonably practicable to expect employers to know about the hazards in their workplaces.

(MHSW ACOP, 1996)

Exhibit 13.2   A systematic approach to risk assessment

1 Identify the hazards – a hazard is the *potential* of a process, substance or activity to cause harm.

2 Assess and rank the risks associated with each hazard using three dimensions:
   - possible severity of harm
   - likelihood of harm
   - proportion of people at risk.

3 Identify the significant risks through the points rating of each hazard (Exhibit 11.3).

4 Prioritise the measures that need to be taken, obtaining expert assistance if necessary, to promote a safe and healthy working environment and to comply with statutory provision.

5 Plan and implement preventive and protective responses; monitor, evaluate, review and feed back into the risk assessment process.

An illustrative points-rating framework for the ranking of risks is provided in Exhibit 13.3, but each organisation should design an appropriate model to reflect their particular work environment and health and safety concerns. Risk assessment can be made more systematic, but a scoring framework only informs decision making – it is no substitute for the exercise of responsible judgement.

For each hazard the risk assessment rating model incorporates four dimensions.

Possible severity of harm – the seriousness of injury or illness that may occur, the length of the recovery time and the possibility and length of any absence.

Likelihood of harm – the probability that harm from a particular hazard will be realised, ranging from unlikely to inevitable.

Proportion of people at risk – the number of employees and others who may be exposed to the risk, ranging from several individuals to the total population of a responsibility zone.

Total hazard score – this is produced by multiplying the points ratings from which a total hazard score can be generated. The higher the score the more significant the risk. Finer graduations of four-, five- or six-point scales can be used.

Exhibit 13.3 Systematic risk assessment through points rating of each hazard

		Hazard description	
	Low	Medium	High
Severity of harm	1	2	3
Likelihood of harm	1	2	3
Proportion of population at risk	1	2	3

For a total hazard score from 1 to 27 circle a number for each of the three dimensions and multiply the three numbers.

Total Hazard Score (THS) =

The aim of risk assessment is to identify significant risks and not obscure those risks with an excess of information or by concentrating on trivial risks. The level of detail in the risk assessment should be broadly proportionate to risk. The risk assessment response should recognise the hierarchy of measures which focuses attention on eliminating risks rather than just compensating for them.

1 Avoid the risks altogether.
2 Combat the risks at source.
3 Reorganise the work or redesign the job.
4 Reduce the risk by training or protecting against the risk.

The effective planning, organisation, control, monitoring and review of preventive and protective measures for health and safety is required by the MHSW Regulations. This is largely what is expected under HASAWA and means that typical managerial skills and processes should also be applied to health and safety at work.

Health surveillance has the objective of detecting adverse health effects. Surveillance is necessary where there is a known adverse health condition and in other circumstances identified by risk assessment. Surveillance includes monitoring the workplace and the individual, and requires suitable equipment to measure physiological and psychological effects.

Employers are required *to appoint one or more competent persons who are able to assist . . . in undertaking the measures (necessary) to comply with* the regulations. Competent persons need training, experience and knowledge to be able to assist effectively. The key word is *assist*, because the responsibility for health and safety remains with all managers and employees; it is not abdicated to the competent health and safety person.

What constitutes competence is contingent on the organisational situation and at its simplest might include a basic knowledge of the work involved, an appreciation of the principles of risk assessment and an understanding of current health and safety applications. Complex and high risk activities will require specialist technical expertise. To be effective the competent person will need autonomy and authority.

Employers are required to establish *procedures to be followed in the event of serious and imminent danger*. The assessment of emergency procedures should focus on the adequacy of warning procedures, routes to places of safety, evacuation and mustering arrangements and first aid. Procedures for preventing or limiting access to dangerous areas are also necessary.

Employers have a responsibility to *provide comprehensible and relevant information* about the risks identified by the assessment, the preventive and protective measures being taken and the procedures for serious or imminent danger. Information can be provided on a need-to-know basis, but it must be comprehensible to those who do need to know. Information must also be made available to contractors and the self-employed, and the risk assessment should take account of specific risks to these groups.

It is necessary *to cooperate on health and safety measures* where workplaces are shared by different employers or by employers and the self-employed. At a minimum this should include the exchange of health and safety information, and it may extend to joint risk assessments and the appointment of a coordinator responsible for integrating health and safety activity.

Employers are required to assess *the health and safety capability* of employees as a continuous process and respond with adequate training. Health and safety training needs will be greatest on recruitment, job transfer, change of hours, new methods of working and the introduction of new technology.

Duties on employees are imposed by the MHSW Regulations and these extend HASAWA obligations. Employee duties are:

- to use and respect equipment, machinery and safety devices
- to cooperate with the employer and inform either the employer, or an employee with responsibility for health and safety, of any risk or threat to health and safety
- to inform the employer if health and safety arrangements, including training, are inadequate.

Manual Handling Operations (MHO) Regulations

Little manual handling regulation existed prior to the MHO Regulations. The rationale for a focus on manual handling in the workplace is the comparatively high risk of injury. More than a quarter of all reported accidents are associated with manual handling, the vast majority of manual handling injuries result in absences of three days or more, and almost one half of all manual handling injuries are sprains and strains of the back (HSE, 1992a). Many injuries could be avoided through an *ergonomic* approach to lifting and handling which takes account of the nature of the task, the characteristics of the load, constraints in the working environment and the capability of the individual. The MHO Regulations establish a hierarchy of safety measures:

1 *AVOID* hazardous manual handling as far as is reasonably practicable through eliminating the need to move the load or through automating the process.

2 *ASSESS* the risks to health and safety where manual handling cannot be avoided.

3 *REDUCE* the risk of injury by considering the size, shape and location of the load, the working environment, the need for further instruction and training in handling techniques, and the potential for provision of mechanical assistance.

An illustrative manual-handling risk assessment checklist is provided in Exhibit 13.4 and the risk profile informs managerial intervention (*see also* the flow diagram in 'How to follow the Manual Handling Regulations', HSE, 1992a).

Exhibit 13.4   An illustrative manual handling checklist

Is there a risk associated with	Please tick		
	Low	Medium	High
The task?			
– turning and twisting			
– bending			
– stretching			
– pushing or pulling			
– repetition			
– distance			
– handling equipment			
The environment?			
– space			
– lighting			
– temperature			
– obstacles			
The load?			
– shape			
– size			
– weight			
– special hazards			
The ability requirements?			
– skills and knowledge			
– information and training			
– physical or psychological capabilities			
Options for preventive and protective measures (avoid – assess – reduce):			

Display Screen Equipment (DSE) Regulations

The DSE Regulations cover three key areas:

- defining display screen users and display screen operators (these terms have specific meanings)
- risk assessment of display screen workstations
- eye test provision.

There is no clear-cut definition of a display screen user, as it depends on whether an employee 'habitually uses a display screen as significant part of normal work' (HSE, 1996; see also HSE, 1992b). The definition of a 'user' is therefore dependent on the frequency, continuity, pacing and intensity of display screen use. A display screen 'operator' is a self-employed person or a contractor working on an employer's premises who habitually uses a display screen as a significant part of normal work. Workstation risk assessment focuses on ergonomic factors and the potential for visual or musculo-skeletal fatigue (including RSI), but other display screen concerns include stress through pacing of work, epilepsy, facial dermatitis, radiation and threat to pregnancy.

There are three ways of responding to workstation risks: first, examine workstation design; second, consider the daily routine of users; and third, provide training. Work-station design requires consideration of posture, lighting, adjustability of equipment, space, heat, noise and software ergonomics. The daily routine of users or operators should be planned to include periodic interruptions of display screen work, through breaks or changes of activity which reduce the intensity of the display screen workload. Training of operators and users should include recognising hazards and risks, the need for rest or other activity breaks, the importance of posture, the use of equipment adjust-ment mechanisms and general ergonomics.

A user or operator can request an eye and eyesight test and the employer has a duty to make arrangements for an appropriate test, at the time of the initial request and at regular intervals. There is no conclusive evidence that display screen work causes per-manent damage to eyes or eyesight, but uncorrected vision defects contribute to visual fatigue. The rationale for testing and correcting vision is therefore to improve com-fort and performance. The employer is responsible for financing corrective appliances, but this liability only extends to providing adequate corrective appliances, normally spectacles, which correct vision at display screen viewing distance (measured by a keystone machine).

Workplace Health, Safety and Welfare (WHSW) Regulations

The WHSW Regulations replaced 38 pieces of existing legislation, including large parts of the Factories Act and the Offices, Shops and Railway Premises Act, and the standards are principally those of these Acts. General requirements can be categorised into four broad areas – the working environment, safety of movement, workplace facilities and housekeeping.

The working environment – should have a 'reasonable' indoor temperature; the code of practice recommends 16°C for sedentary work and 13°C for more active work. Ventilation should ensure a sufficient quantity of fresh or purified air, and lighting is required to be suitable, sufficient and, as far as is reasonably practicable, natural light. Personal space should be sufficient for health, safety and welfare purposes; the guideline is 11 cubic metres per person.

Safety of movement – focuses on safe traffic routes for people, including surfaces, slopes, obstructions, flooring construction, crossings, sensible speeds and signs. The safety and construction of doors, gates, stairways, lifts and escalators warrant special attention. The particular hazards associated with glazing require employers to assess glazing material and the arrangements for opening, cleaning and marking. Falls from heights, falls into substances and risks from falling objects also merit specific assessment.

Workplace facilities – include toilet, washing, changing, eating and resting arrangements; these are required to be 'suitable and sufficient'. Drinking water should be 'wholesome, accessible and marked'. Pregnant women and nursing mothers need to be provided with rest facilities near to sanitary facilities. People are entitled to protection from tobacco smoke discomfort.

Housekeeping – obligations require the efficient maintenance of the workplace, the equipment and the facilities, and emphasise the importance of cleanliness and the removal of waste material.

Provision and Use of Work Equipment (PUWE) Regulations

The PUWE Regulations reinforce the obligations of designers, manufacturers, suppliers, installers and employers specified in HASAWA. They consolidate the extensive legislation relating to work equipment, espouse general duties and list minimum requirements for work equipment. The principal obligations are that:

- selection of work equipment should consider safety integrity
- maintenance should be routine, preventive and logged
- information and instruction on the use of the equipment or machinery should be adequate, available in writing and comprehensible
- special protective measures are necessary for dangerous machine parts and where there is a risk of discharge, rupture, explosion, ejection and extreme temperatures
- the safety role of controls, control systems and isolation from power sources should receive special consideration.

Risk assessment is the key in deciding the level and complexity of the hazards, and frequently specialist and technical knowledge will be necessary in considering the safe provision and use of workplace equipment. For further guidance see HSE (1992c).

Personal Protective Equipment (PPE) regulations

Personal protective equipment includes clothing and is defined as 'all equipment . . . worn or held . . . at work which protects against risks to . . . (personal) health and safety' (HSE, 1992d). Detailed guidance and a specimen risk survey table are available in the PPE booklet (L25). The HSE also provides specific guidelines covering the head, the eyes, the arms and hands, the feet and the body. Hearing and respiratory protective equipment is covered under separate regulations. Employers have a duty to assess the need for personal protective equipment and provide equipment which is suitable for the purpose. This means ensuring that it offers adequate protection, it fits the employee, it is adequately maintained, storage is available and employees are appropriately trained and instructed. Employees have a duty to make full and proper use of PPE, to take care of it and report any defects or loss. PPE should be used as a 'last resort', as the hierarchy of responses principle demands that other health and safety measures should receive prior consideration.

PROTECTION AGAINST DISMISSAL – HEALTH AND SAFETY DUTIES AND CONCERNS

The influence of Europe in health and safety at work is also apparent in the Employment Rights Act (ERA), 1996, which consolidated health and safety measures stimulated by EU Directives. Employers are not lawfully able to dismiss, select for redundancy or subject employees to any other detriment for carrying out designated health and safety duties, alerting the employer to a reasonable health and safety concern, taking steps to protect themselves from danger which is reasonably believed to be serious and imminent, or leaving the workplace because of a reasonable fear of unavoidable danger. There is no service requirement for claims of unfair dismissal in relation to these actions.

SPECIAL GROUPS – YOUNG PEOPLE AND PREGNANT WOMEN

The Health and Safety (Young Persons) Regulations, 1997, implement the health and safety provisions of the European Directive on the Protection of Young People at Work and complement the risk assessment and information requirements of 1992 Regulations. Employers are required to:

- take particular account of young workers' lack of experience, absence of awareness of existing or potential risks and maturity when assessing risks to health and safety
- take account of the risk assessment in deciding whether a young person is prohibited from engaging in certain work
- inform parents (or those with parental responsibility) of school-age children of the outcome of the risk assessment and the health and safety measures introduced.

Pregnant employees regardless of length of service are also afforded greater protection (ERA: 1996). Risks to the health of the pregnant employee and the unborn child need to be assessed. This risk assessment needs to be undertaken by all organisations that employ, or potentially employ, women of childbearing age (which needs to be defined widely). The risk assessment cannot be left until pregnancy is declared, because damage to health may have already occurred. If risks are present, employers are obligated to redesign the work to make it safe or to transfer the employee to suitable alternative work, or if neither of these options is available to give paid leave.

THE WORKING TIME DIRECTIVE 1993

As a health and safety measure the Working Time Directive (WTD) was adopted by qualified majority voting. In the UK the Directive was implemented through the Working Time Regulations, 1998. The implications for organisations have been significant, because prior to this there was no generally applicable statutory provision which limited weekly working hours, regulated rest periods or gave entitlement to paid holiday. Exemptions, derogations and exclusions from the provisions of the WTD and the UK statutory response make this a complex area, and further legislation and case law will no doubt continue to be needed to clarify the position, but the main provisions, which apply to workers and not just employees, include:

- a maximum 48-hour working week, on average
- protection for workers against suffering a detriment for a refusal to work more than 48 hours
- a minimum of four weeks' paid annual leave
- a minimum of 11 consecutive hours' rest each working day and a minimum of 35 hours' uninterrupted rest each week
- night work restricted to eight hours' maximum in certain circumstances and health assessments are required for night workers
- in-work rest breaks of 20 minutes when working time is more than six hours.

It is clearly important that the Working Time Regulations are borne in mind when determining resourcing requirements. Employers are advised to conduct an impact assessment and develop an action plan. HSE inspectors are empowered to enforce the regulations and workers have recourse to employment tribunals.

The paid leave entitlement is relatively easy to implement, but the calculation of the 48-hour working week maximum, and the other provisions relating to working times, are more problematic, particularly as there is so much scope for individuals to opt out and for exemptions. The administration associated with monitoring and record keeping is perceived as burdensome by employer representative organisations. The Working Time Directive articulated an employer responsibility to adapt work to the worker and to seek ways to alleviate monotonous or repetitive work, but this was not given a high profile in the 1998 Regulations.

CREATING AN ACTIVE HEALTH AND SAFETY CULTURE

Health and safety legislation and regulation can only provide a framework, and it is the approach and actions of employers and employees that determine whether a safe and healthy work environment is a reality. In many low- or medium-risk environments compliance with the law is a rather blunt tool, and it is a belief in the added-value dimension of health and safety which is more likely to encourage an active and positive health and safety culture:

> The avoidance, prevention and reduction of risks at work needs to be an accepted part of the approach and attitudes at all levels of the organisation and apply to all of its activities. The existence of an active health and safety culture affecting the organisation as a whole needs to be ensured.
>
> (MHSW ACOP, 1992)

The commitment of top management, both articulated and enacted, is essential, as without this health and safety efforts will be undermined. A framework for organisational health and safety needs to be provided by a specific policy. The policy should be a working document which not only makes a statement of intent, but also clearly allocates health and safety resources and responsibility. Line managers have a critical role as standard setters. They need to be empowered and made responsible for health and safety in specific work areas, but this will not be sufficient if time and resources for health and safety are not made available. In addition, if managers are not judged on their health and safety performance, there is less chance of health and safety being given a business priority, and there is a case for appraising managers, or even offering them incentives, in relation to health and safety criteria. The appointment of competent persons with the expertise, status and influence to foster a positive health and safety culture will underpin managerial responsibility.

Those working with the risks, the employees, need to be involved in assessing and responding to the risks through effective communication processes and active consultation. One imaginative way of consulting with employees and engaging commitment is through creating safety focus groups as a channel for the expression of concerns and the examination of health and safety solutions. Disciplinary procedures should constructively reinforce health and safety rules, values and behaviours, and grievance procedures should encourage the expression of employee dissatisfaction with health and safety. The commitment of employees can be encouraged through appraising individuals on safe performance of the job and through safety training needs analysis. There may be advantages in integrating the reward strategy with the health safety policy in the pursuit of complementarity in the bundle of HR practices. A quality management approach of continuous improvement, individual responsibility and 'right first time' (TQM) can be adapted to health and safety management to create a 'total safety culture' (TSC), with safety values integrated with other organisational values (Exhibit 13.5, based on HSE guidelines).

Exhibit 13.5   Successful health and safety management

1 Determine the policy

- Create a clear, written policy which specifies responsibilities and arrangements for health and safety.
- Involve and inform employees, demonstrating top management support.

2 Organise for health and safety

- Recruit, induct, support and train for competence.
- Allocate health and safety responsibilities.
- Actively consult with and empower employees and their representatives.
- Communicate information about risks and preventive measures.

3 Set standards

- Promote knowledge of legal duties and good health and safety practice.
- Develop mechanisms for identifying and responding to risks.
- Establish performance standards for health and safety.

4 Measure performance

- Monitor performance against the established health and safety standards (active monitoring).
- Record accidents, injuries and ill health accurately, and monitor health and safety incidents and trends (reactive monitoring).

5 Audit

- Audit health and safety arrangements and use this information, together with active and reactive monitoring information, to promote a continuous improvement philosophy towards health and safety.
- Review all the above actions and arrangements regularly.

'Instead of thinking of health and safety management as an extra cost, see it as part of the normal approach to quality control, incident reduction and better productivity.'

(Bacon, J. Director General HSE, 1996)

HEALTH AND SAFETY – PRINCIPLE AND REALITY

The principle that health and safety at work makes good business sense can be promoted, but current employment trends produce a different operational perspective.

- The devolution of greater responsibility for people management to line managers may intensify the tension between the performance imperative and concern with health and safety at work.

- Financial and resource constraints may relegate health and safety in organisational priorities.

- There is increasing incidence of peripheral or atypical workers and this group may not attract the same health and safety attention as core workers.

- Employee job security concerns may inhibit the expression of genuine health and safety concerns.

- Managers continue to experience a renewed confidence in the right to manage and unless they are appraised on health and safety performance it may not receive priority of attention.

- The legislative framework is under challenge from a business-friendly government and the deregulatory pressures associated with creating freer competitive markets and more flexible labour markets.

There is a conundrum associated with the personnel management role in connection with health and safety at work. The personnel profession is seeking to demonstrate a sharper business focus and become 'a business partner'. This requires a detachment from welfare origins and a dumping of 'the fluffy bunny personnel role'. However, embracing an active health and safety role may result in HR practitioners straddling a tension between the operational preoccupation of some line managers and the added-value concern for the health and safety of employees.

A FRAMEWORK FOR ANALYSIS

This chapter provides opportunities for knowledge and understanding in the complex field of health and safety at work. The treatment of the subject is necessarily restricted, but tensions are exposed and managerial guidance is provided. Prescriptive assertions have been avoided, because an assertive approach will founder on organisational contingencies. A framework for analysis is proposed in Fig. 13.2 and this will help the critically evaluative student or practitioner to examine and respond to the health and safety at issues at work.

Competitive and economic pressures raise questions about the effectiveness of a self-regulatory approach to health and safety. Where responsibility for health and safety is primarily allocated to employers and employees, the strengthening of the right to manage allows managers who are anxious about maximising performance, to subordinate

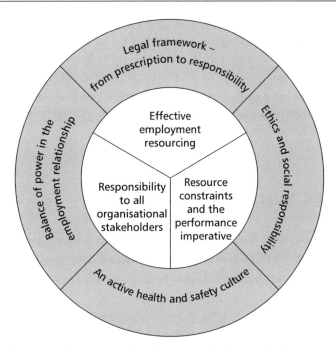

Fig. 13.2   Health and safety at work: a framework for analysis

health and safety concerns. Delayered, lean organisations, the intensification of work and employee feelings of insecurity do not provide a conducive environment for health and safety at work, but good health and safety remains good business and personal well-being remains a prime concern of individuals at work. In any case, if managers do not convincingly appear to value the safety and health of employees, how can any claims that 'we value our people' be believed? This may then undermine the whole HR strategy.

SUMMARY LEARNING POINTS

1 There is a tension between the performance imperative and a concern for the health and safety of employees. Although this tension is perceived rather than real, it needs to be reconciled as good health and safety is good business.

2 The legislative emphasis since 1974 has shifted from prescription and statutory regulation to employer responsibility and self-regulation. There is no escape from health and safety as employers, and employees, have extensive duties of care under common law, HASAWA and specific health and safety regulations.

3 A general knowledge of the law, particularly HASAWA and the 1992 Regulations (consolidated in ERA: 1996), is a prerequisite to effective health and safety management, but the law is insufficient on its own, as it is the development of an active and positive health and safety culture which creates a safe and healthy working environment.

331

4 The European Union is driving the health and safety agenda, but the prescriptive tone of the European approach is contrary to the self-regulatory philosophy of the UK. Some employment trends, including the balance of power in the employment relationship, may also threaten the effectiveness of a self-regulatory approach.

5 If managers do not convincingly appear to value the safety and health of employees, how can any claims that 'we value our people' be believed? This may then undermine the whole HR strategy.

REFERENCES AND FURTHER READING

Aikin, O. (1995) 'Taking care of pregnant workers', *People Management*, February.

DTI (1998) *A Guide to the Working Time Regulations*. Department of Trade and Industry.

Eves, D. (1995) 'Health and safety beyond the millennium', *Safety and Health Practitioner*, 13(4), 13–17.

Fairman, R. (1994) 'Robens: 20 years on', *Industrial Relations Review and Report 559*, May.

Fowler, A. (1994) 'How to produce a health and safety policy', *Personnel Management Plus*, January.

Fowler, A. (1995) 'How to make the workplace safer', *People Management*, January.

Goss, D. (1994) *Principles of Human Resource Management*. London: Routledge.

Health and Safety at Work etc. Act 1974 (1975). Chapter 37. London: HMSO.

HSC (1977) *Safety Representatives and Safety Committees*. London: HMSO.

HSC (1989) *Writing a Safety Policy Statement*. London: HMSO.

HSC (1992) *Management of Health and Safety at Work: Approved Code of Practice*. L21. London: HMSO.

HSC (1992) *Workplace Health, Safety and Welfare: Approved Code of Practice and Guidance*. L24. London: HMSO.

HSE (1988) *Introduction to COSHH*. London: HMSO.

HSE (1991) *Successful Health and Safety Management*. London: HMSO.

HSE (1992a) *Manual Handling: Guidance on Regulations*. L23. London: HMSO.

HSE (1992b) *Display Screen Equipment Work: Guidance on Regulations*. L26. London: HMSO.

HSE (1992c) *Work Equipment: Guidance on Regulations*. L22. London: HMSO.

HSE (1992d) *Personal Protective Equipment at Work: Guidance on Regulations*. L25. London: HMSO.

HSE (1996) *Good Health is Good Business*. Published in association with Works Management.

Institute of Personnel and Development (1995) *Personnel and Europe: Executive brief*.

IPD (1999) *Key Facts: The Working Time Regulations*.

IRS Employment Review 581 (1995) *Employers Back TUC Safety Strategy*, April.

James, P. (1990) 'Holding managers to account for health and safety', *Personnel Management*, April.

James, P. (1994) 'Worker representation and consultation: the impact of European requirements', *Employee Relations*, 16(7), 33–42.

Robens Report (1972) *Safety and Health at Work*. Cmnd 5034. London: HMSO.

Stranks, J. (2001) *A Manager's Guide to Health and Safety*. London: Kogan Page.

Thatcher, M. (1998) 'Clock wise', *People Management*, 3 September, 34–41.

Wright, M. (1998) 'Why do we manage health and safety?', *Occupational Health and Safety*, October, 34–7.

ASSIGNMENTS AND DISCUSSION TOPICS

1 Make suggestions on how the tension between health and safety at work and the performance imperative can be addressed within your organisation. How would you convince business-focused managers that the tension needs to be reconciled?

2 How can you quantify the economic and social costs of accidents and injuries at work?

3 Regulation and a legal framework are unlikely to be sufficient to create a healthy and safe working environment; this will require the commitment and cooperation of all those who manage the risks and of all those who create the risks. Make practical and convincing proposals on how an organisation can seek to create and maintain an active health and safety culture. What added value is there in creating and sustaining such a culture?

4 What characteristics are required for 'competent persons', in the context of the Management of Health and Safety at Work Regulations, in your organisation? Draw up a person specification and consider the selection process.

5 Design a presentation which will provide guidance to managers on how they can identify and respond to the health and safety training needs of their staff.

6 Health and safety policies are often written to meet legislative requirements rather than encourage an active health and safety culture. Defend your organisation's policy against this charge and make recommendations on how it can contribute more effectively to an active health and safety culture.

7 What are the employer obligations under the Control of Substances Hazardous to Health Regulations? Discuss the suitability and sufficiency of your employer's response to the COSHH Regulations and the associated code of practice.

8 Discuss the distinction between a hazard and a risk. Illustrate your discussion with examples of hazards and risks in your own organisation.

9 Use the model framework for risk assessment (Exhibit 13.2) to assess hazards in your workplace. Evaluate the framework critically and create a model for your organisation.

10 Present an argument to your managing director that line managers and employees ought to be appraised and rewarded on health and safety performance.

CASE STUDY

Health and safety in Cobras Department Store

A year ago you were appointed by the store director as the competent person responsible for assisting with health and safety in the Cobras department store. The store has a turnover of £30 million per annum and a staffing establishment of around 400. This case relates to the general services, warehousing and maintenance (GSWM) department. There are 50 staff in the GSWM department who undertake work associated with cleaning, general maintenance and repairs, transport and storage of goods and store security. The GSWM working environment contains many hazards and is characterised by significant risks to health and safety.

The GSWM department has traditionally had a poor health and safety record. The demands of supporting customer-focused sales departments have resulted in health and safety concerns being subordinated to operational demands. There is a carefree and fatalistic attitude towards health and safety amongst the staff, which is evident from high accident, injury and absence rates. Other problems include:

- unsafe manual handling
- irregular use of personal protective equipment
- untidy working areas
- poor storage of goods.

In a cooperative and supportive way you pointed out these health and safety problems to the GSWM department manager some months ago. Although being a bit 'put out' by what he perceived as something of an encroachment on his responsibilities, he reluctantly agreed to do something about your concerns. He stated, however, that his primary focus was on operational efficiency in a climate of tight resources and incessant demands from sales departments where the 'customer was king'. The GSWM manager prided himself on his direct management style and his ability to 'knock problems on the head' first time round. In his view it would be pointless to try to train and educate his staff and he had no time for presentations from occupational health professionals, video tapes or poster initiatives. He decided on a strategy of dealing immediately and severely with any incidents of unsafe practice, as he believed in the 'red hot stove' approach to the punishment of undesirable behaviour. He briefed his supervisors accordingly and they began a campaign of warnings and punishments in relation to unsafe practices, injuries and accidents. The punishments and sanctions included giving out unpleasant jobs, restricting access to desirable overtime, and causing embarrassment to health and safety transgressors by dressing them down in front of their co-workers.

A monitoring of accident and injury statistics revealed a downward trend in the first few months. This had to be offset by some deterioration in the relationship between GSWM and the sales departments. Sales department managers reported that GSWM staff were more concerned with health and comfort than they were with keeping the business alive.

Case study continued

It also became apparent that the decrease in accidents and injuries was illusory, as informal discussion with GSWM staff revealed that accidents and injuries were being under-reported because of a fear of being punished. It was also clear that the staff and the supervisors were uncomfortable about the adversarial relationship that was being created by the GSWM manager's policy on health and safety.

You had little alternative but to discuss this unsatisfactory picture with the GSWM manager. He was distressed by his apparent failure to resolve the problem and admitted that he appeared to have made things worse. You agreed that you would work together to put things right.

1 Comment on the style and approach of the GSWM manager in attempting to resolve the health and safety problems in his department. Why did his approach fail?

2 What strategy would you adopt to resolve the problems?

3 How can an active and positive health and safety culture be developed and what organisational processes or mechanisms will be required?

CHAPTER 14

Sensitive employment issues

INTRODUCTION

UK organisations are recognising the importance of health and welfare issues in enabling and encouraging employees to attend work regularly and productively. The importance of these issues is not driven solely by legislation or by altruism, but by the recognition that a fit and healthy workforce positively affects business performance through low levels of absence and through a healthy approach to work. Smoking, alcohol misuse, drug abuse, HIV/AIDS, violence and stress are sensitive employment issues and it could be argued that they are of no concern to the employer. However, organisations which recognise these issues and have a positive programme to address them through occupational health provision and policy guidelines can anticipate higher levels of performance. This chapter addresses relevant issues within each area and provides practical guidance on policy formulation and development.

CHAPTER OBJECTIVES

- To consider sensitive employment issues and recognise the importance of managing them to the benefit of the employer and the employee.
- To discuss smoking at work.
- To examine alcohol misuse and drug abuse in the workplace.
- To review issues relating to HIV/AIDS and employment.
- To explore the nature, extent and response to violence at work.
- To expose the causes of pressure and responses to stress.
- To give practical guidance on the development of policies in sensitive employment areas.

HEALTH AND WELFARE AT WORK

Organisations seeking to achieve a competitive edge recognise that investment in the health and well-being of the workforce can have a positive payback. CIPD figures from a 1996 survey of 97 organisations revealed that employers who have 'wellness' programmes incurred annual employment costs of between £1335 and £2910 less per employee than employers who do not. It should therefore be possible to convince business-focused managers that consideration of health issues has a quantifiable benefit. The law requires the employer to provide a safe and a *healthy* work environment (*see* Chapter 13), but it is not only the legal framework that levers up employer concern for health issues, it is also changing social attitudes and increasing employee expectations. A more educated and informed workforce expects the employer to take note of emerging medical evidence and changing lifestyles and to reflect these in the workplace. Employee expectations create pressure for the increased social responsibility of organisations across a range of personal and environmental matters. Many issues can be identified under the broad heading of health and welfare, but consideration is given to the sensitive employment areas of smoking, alcohol, drugs, HIV/AIDS, violence and stress.

POSITIVE HEALTH POLICIES

The law requires that an employer takes responsibility for *employee health and welfare* as well as for safety, and positive health policies can demonstrate employer concern with health. There is a logic to the view that if employees are the most valuable asset, investing in them through being proactive and recognising the value of education and information about health-related issues has to be worthwhile. Health policies provide a mechanism for managing health-related issues and are evidence of health issues being taken seriously. Health screening, health education and employee assistance programmes are complementary to proactive health policies.

Health screening can be provided to monitor the health of the workforce and to identify health difficulties before they develop into serious problems which result in long periods of absence. Health screening also presents an opportunity to encourage healthy lifestyles. Screening, as a form of health surveillance, can identify workplace contributions to ill-health and put in place mechanisms to address the workplace issues.

Health education on specific topics, such as diet and exercise, can be provided to inform the workforce about health issues and the associated benefits and risks. This identifies the organisation as an employer who values employees and enhances its reputation as an employer of choice, which may have a positive impact on recruitment and retention.

Employee assistance programmes (EAP) are confidential counselling services, often provided by an external supplier, which support employees in difficult personal circumstances. EAPs provide access to counsellors trained in handling potentially sensitive issues such as alcohol misuse, bereavement, financial difficulties, ill health and job loss. The advantage of an external EAP is that contact with the counsellor is semi-detached from the organisation and the employee may feel more reassured about confidentiality. The employer is provided with an annual aggregated statistical return by the EAP provider which analyses service use. This secures anonymity for the employee, but provides the employer with useful information about the issues that are challenging employees.

SMOKING AT WORK

Tobacco smoking dangers, such as heart disease, lung cancer and respiratory infections, and the hazards from passive smoking are well documented and known. This has implications for the employer's obligation to provide a safe and healthy work environment. Might an employer be in breach of the law by continuing to allow smoking in the workplace? The cost of smoking-related absence and concern over possible legal action related to passive smoking have put smoking at work on the business agenda. This makes it necessary to have a policy which identifies the issues and creates a framework for the management of smoking at work.

In 2000 the Health and Safety Commission (HSC) proposed the introduction of an Approved Code of Practice for passive smoking at work. The Code provides authoritative guidance on employer obligations under the 1974 Health and Safety at Work Act and the 1992 Management of Health and Safety at Work Regulations regarding passive smoking. This Code has special legal status, as employers will be assured that if they follow the guidance issued to support the Code they will be doing sufficient to comply with the law. The Code brings together existing good practice and requires all employers to:

- develop and implement a smoking at work policy
- undertake a risk analysis to inform the policy development
- consult with employees in devising the policy
- take into consideration the health of their employees, especially recognising the needs of those who have existing medical conditions such as asthma, which is covered by the DDA.

The HSC recognise the special circumstances surrounding those who work in a social environment, for example licensed premises and hotels, and has indicated that these employers should comply with the hospitality industry voluntary code on smoking contained in the Public Places Charter. This will constitute compliance with the Code in the short term. The HSC proposals send to employers even clearer signals of the dangers of passive smoking and the need to have in place an appropriate policy to manage smoking proactively in the workplace.

Smoking policy considerations

According to the Approved Code of Practice the aims of a smoking policy are to minimise employees' exposure to tobacco smoke, to minimise the risks to staff who work away from the workplace, and to ensure the health and welfare of smokers and non-smokers. In addition, the employer has to take into account the needs of employees with respiratory problems who, as a consequence of their health condition, may be 'treated less favourably' than other employees in being exposed to smoke in the air. Careful preparation and comprehensive investigation should be undertaken prior to smoking policy implementation, and extensive communication of the policy content will ease the introduction or the extension of the policy. The imposition of a unilateral smoking ban can lead to resentment, conflict and loss of trust, with consequent problems of enforcement.

Workforce attitudes towards smoking at work should be considered, and it is essential to seek the opinions of the employees in developing policy. A joint working party is a useful way of examining the policy options. The composition of this group should include representatives of management and employees who are smokers and non-smokers. The group needs clear terms of reference to enable it to draw conclusions and make recommendations to management, and therefore needs information such as:

- the forces for change – legal, social and organisational
- current smoking practice
- an assessment of employee opinion
- the policy options
- the support mechanisms available to smokers to assist with compliance.

The forces for change include:

1 Case law which provides legal precedents and principles based on the medical evidence that passive smoking is harmful to health. Employers will wish to avoid legal action from passive smoking 'victims'.

2 Social pressures which are raising the expectations of employees, customers and visitors about the quality of the work environment.

3 Organisational pressures which come from staff asserting a perceived right to a smoke-free work environment.

An examination of current smoking practice is needed to reveal the extent of smoking restriction and smoking freedom and to determine the current smoking status of the organisation. The analysis of existing practice, and the current restrictions in areas such as food handling or chemical handling, can be educative and highlight what does and does not work. The assessment of employee attitudes must be carefully framed, as the managerial decision to introduce a policy is based on the legal requirement for the employer to provide a safe work environment – the question is not whether to have a policy, but what kind of policy to have. A questionnaire to all employees, or a representative sample of smokers and non-smokers, will contribute to the assessment of policy options and enable conclusions to be drawn and recommendations to be made.

Various policy options can be investigated:

- smoking in designated areas
- smoking at designated times
- freedom for individual work areas to decide
- a total ban on smoking.

Smoking in designated areas can be an effective option, particularly when a policy is first introduced. It allows for a pragmatic and progressive approach which, coupled with health education, can enable the organisation to work towards more extensive coverage. Specific issues are associated with this option.

- What is meant by designated areas? If smoking is allowed in enclosed personal space, for example individual offices, this may be seen as unfair and divisive because only more senior employees are likely to have their own enclosed space.

- Designated areas may be distant from the individual's place of work and taking time off for smoking may adversely affect productivity. Employee relations' tensions may be created, with non-smokers feeling aggrieved about the perceived preferential treatment of smokers.
- Designated areas need ventilation to avoid the recirculation of air to non-smoking areas. Designated areas can magnify the problems of litter, a polluted atmosphere and fire risk.

Smoking at designated times allows for a relatively smoke-free work environment during specific periods of the day. Core times can be identified and agreed with the non-smoking population, and with tolerance and education this may be workable. However, it concentrates the problem and can be stressful for non-smokers if smokers all smoke at the same time. It is very much a compromise option and may provide an interim solution while working towards a more appropriate and acceptable option.

Freedom for individual work areas to decide may appear to be a fair and reasonable option, but the organisational status of the smoker may put non-smokers under pressure to accept a smoking environment, or vice versa. Employment relationships are characterised by inequality and it is difficult for the organisation to guarantee freedom of choice. The basis for decision needs to be specified and can present difficulties – will it be a simple majority, a certain percentage of the employees affected or consensual? This is unlikely to conform to the Approved Code of Practice but may also provide an interim option while developing a more appropriate solution.

A total ban creates problems for smokers who find it difficult to curtail or cease smoking. Smoking is an addiction and the reasonableness of the speedy introduction of a total ban could be challenged because of a 'custom and practice' right to smoke at work. Therefore a reasonable period of notice, of perhaps three months or more, may be needed to allow smokers to adjust to the new working arrangements. Failure to give reasonable notice may lead to allegations of unfairness and ultimately to constructive dismissal if the employee feels unable to continue working. A total ban raises enforcement issues and consideration should be given to how infringements of the policy will be dealt with as disciplinary action may be necessary. Smokers are innovative in creating refuge areas when faced with smoking bans, and the risk of fire and litter pollution increases if employees congregate and smoke in remote or obscure places. Some smokers would prefer not to smoke but, because of the addictive properties of nicotine, find it difficult or even impossible to cease. A reasonable employer will acknowledge this and offer support. Support mechanisms that can help smokers to adjust and to change behaviour include:

- health education
- counselling or self-help groups
- assistance in reducing nicotine dependence, through the provision of patches or chewing gum.

Regular and well-publicised support sessions for smokers send a strong message to the workforce that the organisation is committed to a healthy, smoke-free environment and also that it is supportive of employees who are adjusting to the new policy.

A smoking policy, whatever options are selected, will need to cover customer and visitor smoking behaviour and how to communicate the policy to them. Also, it may be inappropriate to sell or dispense tobacco products in the workplace, whilst banning or restricting smoking.

Smoking policy content

The policy should:

- be clear, unequivocal and communicated to all staff
- include a positive preamble which sets out the reasons for the policy and the position of the employer
- apply to all employees and include clear guidelines on customer, client and visitor smoking behaviour
- make a named person responsible for overall implementation and monitoring, but ensure that day-to-day responsibility for policy operation is with line managers
- ensure that explicit information is given to employees about smoking restrictions and the penalties for breaking the rules.

A policy implementation plan should be determined which should normally include a trial period to test out the working of the policy and to 'iron out' operational problems. The notice period should be stated together with a precise start date for policy introduction. The smoking policy should be regularly reviewed to take account of the Approved Code of Practice on passive smoking, to keep up with changes in legislation and to address any operational issues that arise.

ALCOHOL MISUSE

Alcohol misuse is an employment issue because of the effect it can have on safety and performance at work. The cost of alcohol misuse relates to sick absence, accidents at work, labour turnover, disruptions to working relationships and the adverse impact on the organisation's image. HSE figures (2000) indicate that each year in the UK up to 14 million working days are lost because of alcohol-related issues. Costs are difficult to estimate but are thought to be in the region of £3 billion per year. These levels of absence and the other costs make alcohol misuse an employer concern. A way of managing this sensitive employment issue is through the implementation of an alcohol policy. According to figures from the CIPD (2001), nearly half of UK employers do not have policies on tackling alcohol and drug misuse, and many of those that do have policies have developed them in response to a need to deal with absence and disciplinary matters. There is clearly a need for more formal and well thought-out policies. A policy enables the employer to manage occurrences in a responsible and positive way, rather than just reacting to circumstances as they arise.

Alcohol-related employment problems fall broadly into two categories: first, the employee who *occasionally* drinks inappropriately and may be unable to work for the odd day; and second, the employee who *often* drinks inappropriately, who may have an alcohol dependency and whose ability to attend work regularly or to perform effectively is severely affected. The first category can be treated as misconduct and dealt with through counselling and through the disciplinary procedure (*see* Chapters 17 and 18). The second category may indicate alcohol dependency and require treatment as an ill-health issue (*see also* Chapters 11 and 18). The treatment of alcohol dependence as an illness can be disputed, and alcohol dependency is specifically excluded from the list of disabilities covered by the DDA. However, employment tribunals classify addiction as an illness and as such would expect a reasonable employer to treat employees with an alcohol addiction fairly and reasonably and in the same way as employees with other health concerns.

Alcohol policy considerations

The policy should focus on establishing and articulating the managerial attitude towards alcohol use and misuse. A precise statement of the rules is required to govern alcohol consumption in the workplace and attendance at work when unfit due to the effects of alcohol. Work arrangements which encourage alcohol consumption, such as access to lunchtime drinking, customer hospitality and availability of alcohol on the premises, are powerful influences on employee 'norms' of behaviour, and the implementation of an alcohol policy without addressing these arrangements is less likely to succeed. An effective policy can lead to a safer, healthier and more motivated workforce through early identification of problems, dealing fairly with employees and offering assistance to treat and rehabilitate where appropriate.

A controversial development in recent years has been the introduction of alcohol-testing programmes. Random testing of employees for alcohol may contravene Article 8 of the Human Rights Act, 1998. The difficulty experienced by the Prison Service in drafting a policy proposing pre-employment testing and random testing of officers shows the potential dilemma faced by employers in seeking to implement a policy in this area (Donovan, 2000). The introduction of an alcohol-testing programme should therefore be treated with extreme caution. The culture of the organisation and the nature of the work will clearly influence whether testing should be introduced. The Transport and Works Act, 1992 allocates joint responsibility to employer and employee for alcohol-related driving incidents and places a duty on drivers not to allow their performance at work to be impaired by alcohol or drug consumption, but does not require testing for those employed as drivers.

Alcohol policy content

The policy statement should identify policy objectives:

- to promote a healthy and safe work environment
- to encourage employees with an alcohol dependency to feel that it can be discussed with their manager or with occupational health staff and that genuine and reasonable help will be forthcoming.

The coverage of the policy should be clear and relate to employees, contractors, customers and other visitors. The policy should spell out the dangers to the employee, and to colleagues, of working under the influence of alcohol. Reference should also be made to:

- organisational rules governing alcohol on the premises
- the effects of alcohol consumption outside work on safety and performance at work
- the importance of early identification of alcohol-related problems
- the benefits of effective treatment
- an acknowledgement that addiction is a health issue.

Explicit reference to alcohol addiction being treated similarly to other long-term health issues will put the issue into an ill-health context. Reference should be made to the support given for treatment and to other forms of employee assistance available. Where possible, sick pay entitlement should be maintained for the duration of agreed treatment and reassurance given that employment will not be in jeopardy if treatment is successful. The policy should contain assurances of confidentiality and sensitive handling. A reference to counselling and to possible disciplinary action for misuse which results in absence, performance or conduct problems should be included so that employees understand the distinction between alcohol misuse and alcohol addiction. There is a clear role for the education of employees in the hazards of alcohol and the education of managers in identifying and managing difficult situations in a sensitive and positive way. Fear of repercussions, loss of employment or employee vilification can be removed from alcohol situations and remedies found which benefit the employer and the employee. The policy needs regular review to examine whether it is working (Exhibit 14.1).

Exhibit 14.1   Indicative illustration of an alcohol policy

This policy has been developed in consultation with employee representatives and has the full support of management. This policy applies to all employees and to contractors working on organisational premises. Alcohol consumption or possession in the workplace is prohibited. The breaking of this rule will result in disciplinary action.

The organisation has a duty to protect all employees, and others, and alcohol misuse or addiction may affect employee health, safety and performance. The purpose of this policy is to protect employees from the dangers of inappropriate or excessive alcohol consumption and to encourage those with a problem to seek help. The organisation recognises that alcohol addiction may be an illness and can be treated in the same way as any other long-term illness.

The organisation is committed to support and assist in the treatment of those with an alcohol problem. Help is available from your manager, the occupational health department or through the Employee Assistance Programme. The employee has a right to confidentiality in all aspects of health care.

The employee is entitled to occupational sick pay while undergoing recognised and agreed treatment and has the right to return to work following effective treatment, subject to the approval of the occupational health practitioner. Employees will be supported during treatment. However, where treatment is unsuccessful and the employee is not able to return to his/her job, suitable alternative employment will be sought, but if it is not available termination of employment on the grounds of ill health will need to be considered.

DRUG ABUSE

Drug use and abuse is an increasing social problem. A report by the Royal College of Physicians (2000) claims that drug addiction has increased fourfold in the past ten years. It also estimates that 25 per cent of those who seek help for drug-related problems are in employment. Many drug users are therefore in work and when use or abuse affects workplace safety, employee performance or the reputation of the employer, drugs become an employment issue. For the purposes of policy making it is sensible to include *any* substance taken by the employee which adversely affects the ability to perform the job to the required standard. This may include prescribed as well as controlled drugs. There are two related issues associated with controlled drugs:

- It is illegal knowingly to have controlled drugs on the premises and take no action (Misuse of Drugs Act, 1971).
- The organisation will need a stance on police involvement.

The possession or taking of controlled drugs at work, as well as being likely to impact on workplace performance, potentially places the employer in an unlawful situation. The possession of controlled drugs should normally constitute gross misconduct and be dealt with under the disciplinary procedure. Whether the organisation chooses to involve the police is a managerial decision, but the organisational attitude to the involvement of the police should be known by employees and action should be consistent. An employee who takes controlled drugs outside the workplace and whose performance is not affected is unlikely to come to the attention of the employer, but where employees are convicted for drug taking or possession the employer is legitimately entitled to consider the consequences for employment. Publicity which damages organisational reputation, or convictions which damage employer confidence in the employee, may warrant disciplinary action.

Increasingly, employers are developing a single policy to cover both alcohol and drugs, with the focus being on the effect on work performance and the emphasis on health and safety, confidentiality and training (Pawsey, 2000). Whether the employer implements a single policy or two specific policies will depend on the nature of the organisation and the approach to be taken. However, the employer should be seeking a fair and consistent managerial response to those employees who declare an addiction to drugs and whose ability to attend regularly or perform satisfactorily is affected. Positive employee attempts to eliminate dependence on drugs can be supported through counselling, treatment and occupational sick pay with the aim of enabling a return to effective working.

Prescribed drugs present a different scenario – the drugs may be legitimate and necessary for the health of the employee, but employee work performance may be adversely affected. Policy development should recognise this problem, and prescribed drug taking which adversely affects performance should normally be dealt with under the sickness procedures. Action should be taken to:

- obtain a prognosis which includes the length of time for which the employee will need to take the prescribed drug and the work performance consequences of continued prescription
- identify and discuss with the employee the performance issues giving concern

- consider reasonable adjustments to the work, such as changing the contractual arrangements, allowing more flexible working or revising the job to accommodate the time needed for the employee to return to full health.

HIV AND AIDS IN THE WORKPLACE

Acquired Immune Deficiency Syndrome (AIDS) and Human Immuno-deficiency Virus (HIV), the precursor to full-blown AIDS, are features of modern society. HIV is transmitted through blood products, unprotected sexual activity and by an infected mother to her unborn child. HIV cannot be contracted through normal social contact and most workplace situations present no risk of cross-infection. An individual with the virus (HIV+) is normally able to attend work regularly and work performance is unaffected. A person living with full-blown AIDS may develop AIDS-related complex (ARC) and contract various illnesses and infections which will seriously impact on attendance and performance. This distinction between the two conditions was recognised in 1986 when the government issued the booklet *AIDS and Employment* to all employers. This advised employers that an HIV+ person should be able to work normally and that dismissal because of pressure from co-workers would expose the employer to claims of unfair dismissal. The 1980s concern of a UK epidemic of HIV and AIDS appears to have been unfounded and, although the number of infected people has increased, the very high number predicted has not materialised.

Ignoring the HIV and AIDS issues until a case arises is not a sensible managerial option as decisions taken under pressure may be inappropriate. Cases of HIV and AIDS raise issues which are different from those associated with other life-threatening illnesses. Distinctive HIV and AIDS issues include:

- prejudice which leads to discrimination
- anxiety and fear among employees about contracting the disease
- a lack of knowledge about the disease
- a lack of sympathy towards AIDS sufferers because of stereotypical assumptions and inaccurate perceptions about HIV transmission.

The advantage of investigating and addressing HIV and AIDS issues at work is in objectively defining the managerial approach prior to a case occurring in order to facilitate the handling of a case when it does. HIV and AIDS are emotive and emotional subjects which are characterised by misinformation and stereotypical assumptions, and this may test the ability of the most objective manager to handle a case fairly and consistently. Banas (1992), in a frank and readable account of the difficulties of actually *managing* the employment of staff who are living with AIDS, highlights the difficulties and the unpredictability of individual responses. HIV and AIDS are illnesses and an employee with an illness should be dealt with through the sickness and absence management policies and procedures. However, the distinctive issues relating to HIV and AIDS may justify further measures, including a specific policy, to ensure fair, reasonable and equitable treatment.

The language of the HIV and AIDS policy and the message it communicates are critical in setting the tone for the management of HIV and AIDS in the workplace. An analysis of AIDS policies by Goss and Adam-Smith (1994) identified the emergence of two distinct policy types:

The defensive policy – This may include a strong introductory statement that discrimination against people affected will not be tolerated, but further investigation of the policy detail identifies a shift which introduces a 'sense of uncertainty' about the differential treatment of people with HIV or AIDS. Statements are ostensibly written in language which conveys protection for the AIDS sufferer, but in practice are used for exclusion in order to 'defend' the organisation from AIDS sufferers.

The constructive policy – This is more focused on the normalisation of HIV and AIDS as a health matter. As a positive consequence it diverts attention from the stereotyping of and discrimination against the person living with AIDS.

HIV and AIDS policy issues

It is possible that an HIV and AIDS policy can be integrated into existing policies, but HIV and AIDS issues may need to be made explicit and clear direction given to managers and employees. The primary aim of the policy is to provide guidelines and actions which ensure fair and consistent treatment for all employees. Risk assessment will also inform policy development and should judge:

- the potential for transmission of the disease
- the likelihood and extent of any risks
- the necessary preventive and protective precautions against cross-transmission.

Employees have the right to confidentiality in health matters and this should be respected in the case of HIV and AIDS. There is no strict obligation for an infected person to tell the employer, HIV and AIDS are not notifiable diseases, and sufferers are advised by representative bodies not to reveal their illness. However, employees have a contractual duty of care and an infected employee in a 'sensitive' job has a responsibility to ensure that risks of transmission are assessed and minimised. The General Medical Council has ruled that HIV-infected doctors have an ethical duty to seek expert advice on any limits that should be placed on employment, to be determined by the nature of the work in which the doctor is engaged. By implication, this ethical duty could be extended to all health workers.

Employees required to work overseas, particularly in parts of the world where the incidence of HIV and AIDS is high and preventive measures less well developed, are exposed to increased risk and therefore need relevant advice and appropriate emergency medical equipment. Medical screening on recruitment which invites disclosure of medical history, including HIV and AIDS, should not be used to discriminate unfairly against the individual at the point of selection. In any case, HIV testing is unreliable and expensive and cannot predict future exposure to the virus. Although the Disability Discrimination

Act identifies HIV infection as outside the definition of disability, it expressly includes it as a progressive condition which has some effect on the infected individual but which does not, as yet, affect day-to-day activity. Consequently applicants for employment, and employees, are afforded some statutory protection against discrimination. However, the Terrence Higgins Trust in its report *Prejudice, Discrimination and HIV* (2001) recommends to government the extension of the DDA to cover these medical conditions from the *point of diagnosis*, rather than the *onset of the illness*. This is to give additional protection from discrimination to those who are diagnosed with HIV, regardless of whether the condition affects their ability to do the job.

Education is a key issue. All employees should receive accurate information about the issues and risks associated with HIV and AIDS as this will help to minimise problems when a case arises. The Terrence Higgins Trust report (2001) contends that one in five people with HIV has experienced discrimination in the past year. This discrimination occurs in all aspects of their lives, not just in employment, but the findings indicate that the level of public knowledge of HIV may be a factor. Education therefore needs to address common anxieties and fears, the nature of prejudice and discrimination, and should include facts about the disease. The limited potential for transmission of the disease through normal workplace activity should be made clear, whilst any risk situation should be identified.

HIV and AIDS policy content

A policy should:

1 Address HIV and AIDS as separate conditions because different issues are associated with each.

2 Make an opening statement to specify the organisational attitude to HIV and AIDS and state that as illnesses any cases will be dealt with through the sickness procedures.

3 Make clear that HIV-infected employees are able to work normally, and that employees with full-blown AIDS who are no longer able to work normally, in line with all employees with long-term illness, will be considered for redeployment, retraining, flexible working, home working, reduced hours or compassionate leave. Ideally the policy should extend these options to the carers of AIDS sufferers.

4 Assert that discrimination against employees with HIV and AIDS is unlawful and will not be tolerated.

5 State that applicants for employment will be assessed on their ability to do the job and that, in the spirit of the DDA, reasonable adjustments will be made where appropriate.

6 Reassure infected employees of confidentiality and provide guidance on support and counselling services.

7 Nominate organisational support workers so that the employee can elect to talk to the most appropriate person and not be forced to talk to the immediate manager.

8 Commit to the HIV and AIDS education of employees and managers.

The HIV and AIDS policy needs to be integrated with other personnel policies, particularly the disciplinary and grievance policies. The formal grievance procedure needs to be receptive to good-faith allegations of bullying or unfair treatment and the disciplinary procedure used if unfair treatment occurs.

Many of these issues are ones that would be addressed within a general ill-health policy and are relevant to any person with a long-term illness; it is interesting that they require separate expression in the context of HIV and AIDS and is indicative of the perceived 'special' nature of the disease. Does treating HIV and AIDS as something different perpetuate a myth?

VIOLENCE AT WORK

Violence appears to be an increasing part of everyday life and is also seen, more than ever, to be impacting on working life. The British Crime Survey figures (HSE, 1999) show that there were more than 1.2 million incidents of violence at work in 1997. Those most at risk are the police, followed by social workers, health care professionals, transport workers, retail staff and national and local government officials. Employers have a duty to look after the safety, health and welfare needs of their employees as well as customers and visitors to their premises. In order to meet this obligation, employers have to acknowledge the presence of violence within their workplace and put in place policies and procedures to deal with it. Violence is not just limited to physical attacks but should be defined more widely to reflect the role that verbal attacks and threats can have on the health and welfare of employees. The HSE (2001) define work-related violence as:

> **any incident in which a person is abused, threatened or assaulted in circumstances related to their work.**

The 1997 revision of the 1995 Reporting of Injuries, Diseases and Dangerous Occurrences Regulations requires incidents of non-consensual workplace violence to be recorded and, in some cases, reported to the HSE. This is limited to acts of physical violence and has been criticised by the TUC and by public service unions as being limited in scope through excluding physical threats and verbal assaults. This change in reporting does, however, enable a more complete picture of the nature and extent of physical violence in the workplace to be established. It is not only a legal requirement to provide a safe work environment, the protection of employees from violence at work can contribute to effectiveness and productivity. Investment in recruitment and training which is undermined by a lack of managerial action to protect employees from exposure to violence is wasted and likely to be repaid with low performance, high labour turnover and recruitment difficulties. Violence between employees normally constitutes serious or gross misconduct and is a disciplinary matter (*see* Chapters 17 and 18). The review of workplace violence in this section is primarily focused on violence which occurs to employees from sources external to the organisation.

There are a number of issues to be taken into consideration when reviewing the broader work environment where violence is likely to occur. These include the following.

The work environment – Both internal and external factors contribute to the risk of violence at work. The internal environment needs to be assessed for the availability of 'weapons', such as handy items of equipment, and also the need for protective devices such as screens and alarms. The assessment of the external environment includes the geographical location of the employer's premises and the incidence of local crime. If the location is a problem then systems for the safety of employees entering and leaving the building may be required, together with building security itself to combat unauthorised access.

The nature of the work – As discussed above, there are types of work that are more at risk from external violence. Those who provide services to the public, by the very nature of their work, come into contact with the clients and customers in sometimes frustrating and confrontational situations. The combination of frustration, anger and an inability of the employee to meet the customer demands can lead to 'customer rage' and increase the likelihood of a violent incident. Jobs that involve cash handling also carry increased risks, with bank staff, post office staff and retail staff being at higher risk from theft and associated violence.

The work situation itself – The high profile case of Suzy Lamplugh, the estate agent who was abducted when showing a client around a vacant property, highlights the risks to staff of working alone. Occupations where staff necessarily work alone, such as community nurses, some transport workers and social workers, present particular challenges and therefore need special consideration. An employee who works outside normal hours and after others have left the premises may be at greater risk, and work systems should ensure that employees are not permitted to work alone without adequate security arrangements.

The personal characteristics of the individual – Some employees are better equipped to deal with confrontational and potentially violent situations, but all staff should be trained to recognise potentially difficult situations and to respond accordingly. A survey of interactions between staff and customers can indicate triggers for frustration and anger and causes of violent exchanges. An analysis of these incidents informs managerial action, which may include changes in systems of work, the reduction of waiting time or the provision of a more amenable customer environment. Employees who are adequately trained to assess and control violent situations are less likely to be the victims of attack than employees who are unable to manage emotional exchanges, or cannot provide relevant information, or lack skills and confidence in difficult encounters with customers.

Causes of violence

It is difficult to prescribe the causes of violence, but it is useful to recognise the range of situations and circumstances to be considered. Examples are as follows.

- Waiting and delays can increase customer frustration, lead to anger and increase the potential for violence.
- Alcohol consumption can increase aggressive behaviour and contribute to a more threatening environment.
- Criminal intent, such as theft.
- People with a predisposition towards violence.

Record keeping and careful analysis will enable the causes of violence to be identified and assessed.

The effective management of violence

The Health and Safety Executive has published *Violence at Work – a guide for employers* (2001) which sets out a four-stage process for the effective management of violence in the workplace:

1 Do you have a problem?

2 Decide what action to take.

3 Take action.

4 Evaluate what you have done.

This is an iterative process because the evaluation will indicate which problems remain and the process will need to be worked through again.

1. Do you have a problem? – This is the first step in risk assessment and the advice to the employer is to talk to employees and register their concerns. All incidents of violence need to be recorded, including verbal abuse and threatening behaviour as well as physical attacks, in order that the triggers for violence can be identified. Employees may be reluctant to report everything as they may see the acceptance of aggressive behaviour as part of the job. Employees should be encouraged to report everything and to recognise the role this plays in the development of safe systems of work. Complete reporting and good records will enable appropriate procedures to be developed and appropriate action to be taken. Coding and classifying incidents, including place, time, trigger situation, nature of injury and the experiences of staff, will allow for useful reporting and analysis.

2. Decide what action to take – Following the consultation and the analysis, the employer will need to identify which staff are at risk and the nature of the risk. It is useful also to examine existing security arrangements and procedures and whether these are working effectively. Consideration can be given to job redesign to make jobs safer and provide a safer environment, for example better lighting or a more customer-friendly waiting area. Roberts (2001) identifies open plan offices and an appointment system as factors which reduced violent incidents from 5 per cent to 1 per cent in Australia. The UK Department for Work and Pensions is examining the impact of making changes to office layout and systems in an effort to reduce violent incidents. This has not met with an entirely positive reaction from employee representatives, highlighting the need to talk to staff and take on board their concerns. It is important to record the results of assessments and the subsequent decisions and to provide first, clear frameworks for action, and second, the information for evaluation and review.

3. *Take action* – This involves developing a detailed and precise policy for dealing with violence in the particular place of work based on the views of staff, the evidence of incidents and the work situation. The policy should include:

- the legal responsibilities of both the employer in providing a safe working environment and the employees in taking reasonable care of themselves and following safe procedures
- details of specific risks emanating from the risk assessment together with the organisational response, precautions and procedures
- what constitutes an incident, how it is reported and to whom
- education and training arrangements
- the availability of counselling services either through in-house trained counsellors or through an employee assistance programme.

A clear policy will help employees to understand what the employer is trying to achieve, and to enable them to cooperate in achieving it and to follow the correct procedures.

4. *Evaluate what you have done* – This policy, like all HR policies, should be regularly reviewed. A system of regular reporting of incidents, either through the Health and Safety Committee or through some other appropriate forum, will enable the continuous assessment of workplace violence and ensure that the action being taken is appropriate.

Roberts (2001) indicates that the HSE is supporting the development of draft occupational national standards for tackling workplace violence which are aimed at cutting the number of incidents by 10 per cent by 2003. The draft guidelines are included in Exhibit 14.2.

Exhibit 14.2 Employment NTO draft national occupational guidelines for tackling workplace violence

> The draft national occupational guidelines for tackling workplace violence are aimed at:
>
> - The development of policies and practices for particular organisations
> - The formation of a basis for national qualifications
> - The formation of the syllabus for training courses
> - The development of a grading system for training providers.

The legal requirement for risk assessment means that employers cannot ignore the intrusion of violence into the workplace. Open discussion of the issues, recruitment of staff who understand the nature of the work and the risks attached to it, and a well-designed and well-communicated policy will enable violence at work to be managed more effectively. Provided that employers know the causes of violence, assess the hazards to staff and seek to minimise the risk, they are fulfilling the statutory obligation and giving credence to the dictum of people being their most valuable resource.

STRESS AND DISTRESS

What is the extent of the stress problem? The CIPD (2001) report estimated that stress accounted for 40 million lost working days per year, at a cost to employers of around £7 billion. Midgely (1997) estimates that stress costs the UK between £3.7 and £11 billion per year and reported that the International Labour Organisation estimates that inefficiencies arising from stress can cost up to 10 per cent of a country's gross national product. Stuart (2001) comments on CBI research which puts stress-related absence at 187 million working days per year and costs the UK £12 billion. The HSE (White and Hamer, 2001) put the figure for lost working days at six and a half million. There is no consensus on the precise cost of stress, because of the difficulty of measuring it accurately, but despite these contrasting 'take your pick' figures there appears to be a general agreement that the potential costs are substantial. A TUC survey of 7000 health and safety officers found that stress at work was their biggest organisational concern (Littlefield, 1996), and a joint survey by the CIPD and the Institute of Occupational Health (Midgely, 1997) found that the 2000 personnel managers surveyed placed stress at the top of their list for occupational health research priorities. Smith *et al.* (2000), reported by the CIPD, suggest that one in five workers feel extremely stressed at work – in excess of 5 million workers in the UK. The CIPD (2001) state that 'stress is likely to become the most dangerous risk to business in the early part of the 21st century'. Briner (1999) urges a note of caution in the interpretation of findings like those above and questions whether stress is the modern epidemic that some people claim it is:

> A survey conducted by the Industrial Society in 1996 revealed that, while 53 per cent of respondents agreed that stress had increased, 76 per cent admitted that it had never been measured in their organisation. Similarly, 76 per cent thought that absenteeism was the most damaging effect of stress, while only 7 per cent measured the amount of absence caused by stress. It seems that many of us, HR managers and employees alike, simply assume that stress levels are high and having detrimental effects on people's well being and performance.

Whilst warning us against the 'stress bandwagon', Briner acknowledges that identifying and acting upon dysfunctional stress warrants further research and managerial attention. Acting knowledgeably on employee stress with the incentive of reducing costs, avoiding litigation, valuing people and protecting the investment in human capital would seem to be a prime area for managerial intervention, but effective intervention is not easy and the search for magic solutions is likely to be frustrating.

The power of the employer and the employee to act on stress effectively is constrained, because common reasons for stress are at least partially attributable to a conjunction of social, political, economic and global factors. These factors include the intensification of work, feelings of job insecurity, and employer demand for 'emotional labour'. The intensification of work, where employees are required to work harder, smarter and more flexibly, is a product of increasingly competitive organisational environments. Levels of unemployment, a strengthening of the right to manage, deregulated and 'flexible' labour markets, right-sizing and process re-engineering programmes, together with a proliferation of non-standard contracts of employment contribute to feelings of insecurity at work. Customer-focused cultures require 'emotional labour', as well as physical and intellectual labour, from employees, and HRM practices which seek to engage the hearts and minds of employees through involvement and through seeking behavioural commitment invite a psychological relationship between employer and employee which is more stressful than a simple wage for work bargain. Add to this the disappearance of a job for life, continuous organisational change and an emphasis on taking personal responsibility for lifetime learning, and the turbulence and potential stress of the job context become even more evident.

Simplistic stress solutions, often individually focused, fail to recognise the complex interplay of these contextual factors. As an example, assertiveness, including the ability to say 'No', and the effective management of time often feature in stress management programmes and are valuable management skills, but the contribution of these individual coping strategies to stress reduction is circumscribed by the wider societal and organisational context. Briner (1999) also challenges the efficacy of stress management courses:

> Does this (stress) training work? We need only to consider what is required in any course for it to have a reasonable chance of success. As a minimum the criteria would include an initial assessment of training needs; training design that can change behaviour that is linked to the outcomes of interest; an environment which allows the transfer of the newly learnt skill; and, evaluation. With stress management training it is often the case that none of these elements is in place. So, even in principle it is unlikely that stress management training can achieve its aims.

The effective management of stress at work therefore requires a corporate approach as well as the promotion of individual coping strategies.

The nature and sources of stress

In order to seek stress solutions it is important to understand the nature of stress, the potential sources of stress, the potential implications for the individual and for the organisation and the range of responses available. A stress audit and a stress policy help to target individual and organisational action. A framework for analysing stress is exposed in Fig. 14.1, but before discussing the elements of the framework two general points need to be made. First, an appropriate level of stress or pressure can be stimulating, healthy and desirable. It is when the perceived level of pressure becomes sub-optimal that human dysfunctionality can occur. Second, textbooks and articles on stress often expose a large menu of potential stressors and a huge range of negative implications, and this text is no different, but this gives the impression that stress is super-endemic and will inevitably produce all of the undesirable consequences. This encourages an exaggerated perception of the stress problems, which is unhelpful either by giving succour to stress sceptics or in inhibiting the development of focused and targeted managerial action.

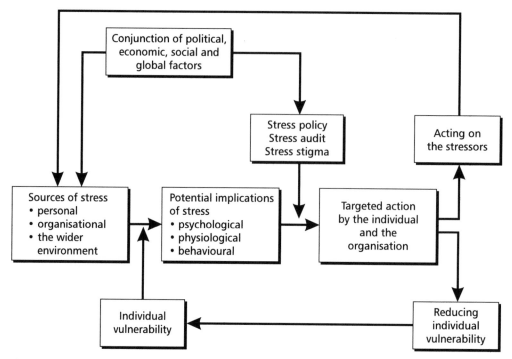

Fig. 14.1   A framework for analysing stress at work

Stress is about pressure on the individual and may be physical, intellectual, emotional or social. Pressure becomes distressing when the individual perceives it to be either excessive and beyond their ability to cope, or alternatively insufficient to provide stimulation. It is therefore distress which is potentially harmful and 'distress' that ought to be the focus of attention. Using the term distress distinguishes it from positive pressure at work (termed eustress). Whereas distress is about an imbalance between the level of pressure and individual ability to cope, eustress represents the 'goldilocks' pressure point, where the level of pressure on an individual is neither too much, nor too little, but just right.

Figure 14.2 illustrates a general relationship between pressure and performance and incorporates the idea that insufficient pressure as well as too much pressure causes distress. Identifying the eustress point for an individual is problematic. It will vary over time because the whole individual needs to be considered, and the level of pressure will be determined by a combination of work stress, life stress and event stress. Work stress includes workload, deadlines, work relationships, the nature and extent of change, the degree of control, working conditions and levels of security. Life stress describes the pressures of day-to-day living and will include personal finance, emotional relationships, family responsibilities and personal health. Event stress describes significant events such as getting married, buying a house, the birth of a child or coping with bereavement. Organisational, personal and wider environmental stressors are exposed in Exhibit 14.3.

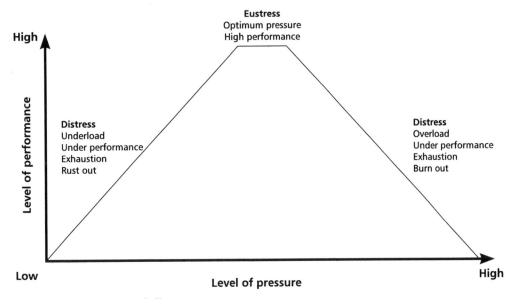

Fig. 14.2 Eustress and distress

Individual vulnerability to distress is influenced by many factors, including:

- individual personality differences, for example whether type A or type B (*see* below)
- internal or external locus of control – the extent to which individuals feel able to influence their own destiny
- the extent of personal support networks
- the capacity of personal coping strategies
- the ability to act on own perceptions of stress
- the compatibility of job experience, knowledge and skills with current job demands.

Type A behaviour is characterised by:

> an aggressive involvement in a chronic, incessant struggle to achieve more and more in less and less time and, if necessary, against the opposing efforts of other things or other people.
>
> (Robbins, 1993)

Type B behaviour is characterised by being:

> rarely harried by the desire to obtain a widely increasing number of things or to participate in an endlessly growing series of events in an ever decreasing amount of time.
>
> (Robbins, 1993)

Type A people may be more vulnerable to stress and more susceptible to ill health because of feelings of mistrust, hostility and anger generated by personality characteristics.

Exhibit 14.3 A menu of the potential sources of stress

Organisational stressors

- Work overload or underload – repetitive work, unrewarding work
- Poor job design – ergonomically, environmentally, lacking autonomy or variety
- Role ambiguity or role conflict
- Poor quality leadership or supervision
- Lack of participation in decision making
- Poor quality of relationships – horizontally, vertically or externally
- Responsibility for people or for achieving targets and objectives
- Organisational change
- The organisational climate
- Being subjected to bullying or harassment
- Pay, conditions and job insecurity.

Personal stressors

- Unhealthy eating, sleeping or exercise
- General health and whether it is abused
- Family and social relationships
- Significant life events
- Conflicting personal and organisational demands.

Wider environmental stressors

- The general economic situation
- Political uncertainty
- Social change and threats to personal values and standards
- Concern with the natural environment
- The pace of technological change
- Changing male and female role perceptions.

The general adaptation syndrome consists of the phases of alarm, resistance and exhaustion and maps the human response to stressful situations. The initial phase of 'alarm' produces physiological reactions, referred to as the 'fight or flight' response. This prepares the individual either to confront the challenge or to run away. The physiological reactions include increased heart rate, decreased blood flow to the digestive system and increased flow to the brain and muscles, release of adrenalin, rapid breathing and a sharpening of the senses. Unless the individual takes flight, the second general adaptation phase will be a heightening of the individual's 'resistance' to confront the stressful situation and to deal with it. Where the stressful situation persists without being resolved, individual resistance may be worn down, ultimately resulting in the third phase of 'exhaustion' and breakdown. There is therefore a limited human capacity to resist or adapt to stressful situations.

The potential implications of distress and a range of responses

Harmful pressure, or distress, manifests itself in a wide range of psychological, physiological and behavioural consequences.

Psychological implications include:

- anxiety, irritability, frustration, depression
- inability to concentrate, procrastination, decision paralysis, inaccurate recall, feelings of unreality
- job dissatisfaction, suppressed motivation
- disturbed sleep patterns.

Physiological implications include:

- muscular tension, headaches, palpitations
- heart disease, high blood pressure
- digestive problems, irritable bowel
- increased susceptibility to colds, influenza and respiratory infection.

Behavioural implications include:

- sub-optimum performance and productivity
- higher levels of absence, labour turnover and accident rates, and poor timekeeping
- tobacco, alcohol, caffeine and other substance abuse
- negative personal appearance and hygiene changes, weight loss or gain
- less effective personal and professional relationships.

These three areas are not mutually exclusive as some of the consequences overlap and feed each other. An important caveat that needs to be borne in mind is the fact that it is unlikely that one individual will suffer all of these potential implications of stress. They are reproduced here to highlight the range and extent of possible consequences and to enable recognition and targeted action.

A major hurdle to the effective management of distress at work is the social and professional stigma often associated with an admission of being a stress sufferer and not coping. It may be acceptable to admit to being pressurised, but less acceptable to admit to an inability to cope with work pressure. Macho-cultures will label a stress admission as a sign of weakness and inadequacy. Addressing the stress stigma is fundamental to the encouragement of 'coming out' by stress sufferers. An awareness of this stigma can help direct the organisation towards creating a climate, or at least a mechanism, where it is relatively safe for an employee to declare distress. Only through accessing stress information can employers begin to measure and assess the existence and the extent of the problem. An assessment of the sources and the implications of stress, 'a stress audit', is a prerequisite to targeted organisational and individual action. Positive stress action has two elements, both of which can be enacted by the individual and the organisation:

1 Reducing individual vulnerability to pressure.
2 Acting on the sources of stress – the stressors.

The strategies for reducing individual vulnerability normally receive priority of attention in stress management programmes at the expense of acting on the stressors. This risks a focus on the symptoms of stress rather than on the underlying causes, and tends to shift the stress burden and responsibility from the organisation to the individual.

> The role of the organisation in producing unhealthy systems and conditions of work is in danger of being ignored. In its place we get systems reinforcing the self-attribution of stress and anxiety as personal problems to be coped with rather than structural issues to be contested.
>
> (Thompson and McHugh in Clark, Chandler and Barry, 1997)

Strategies to reduce individual vulnerability include:

- counselling services, referral systems and the development of support networks
- the encouragement of healthy habits – diet, sleep, exercise
- the development of coping techniques – assertiveness, time management, the creation of safety zones, allowing time for leisure
- the use of relaxation techniques – massage, aromatherapy, yoga
- the displacement or ventilation of negative feelings through legitimate means – rigorous physical exercise, catharsis, a 'bug' list
- the development of skills, knowledge and competencies in line with job demands.

Strategies for acting on the stressors include:

- workload re-balancing, role clarification, job redesign
- critical evaluation of communication and change processes
- critical evaluation of the quality of leadership, management and supervision
- critical evaluation of intrinsic and extrinsic rewards
- provision of training and development opportunities to enhance job skills
- evaluating the physical work environment
- educating managers to recognise and respond to distress.

Briner (1999) provides a framework for a more strategic and targeted approach to managing stress based on a healthy scepticism about the extent of the problem, a search for specific problems, an evidence-based assessment of the nature of the problem, focused stress management interventions (SMIs), SMIs which integrate with other HR practices, and an evaluation of the effectiveness of the SMIs. In short, effective diagnosis is a prerequisite to focused stress solutions.

A further individual strategy for dealing with stress is the self-management of beliefs and the reframing of perceptions (Honey, 1993). There are three necessary beliefs:

1 Stress is not instinctive, but a 'learned reaction' to stimuli.

2 External stimuli do not automatically cause distress, it is the individual who 'chooses' to be stressed.

3 It is preferable to 'prevent' unwanted stress rather than suppressing it or expressing it.

The individual preventive response, based on these three beliefs, is to reframe the perceptions of pressure by challenging the thoughts themselves. This is done through making the thoughts more reliable, more rational, less exaggerated and less dogmatic, thus preventing 'feelings' of distress.

Stress policy

There are a number of reasons for having a stress policy, although less than 10 per cent of organisations have a formal stress policy (Littlefield, 1996). Stress issues may be subsumed within general health or well-being policies (CIPD, 2001). The reasons for a policy include focusing managerial attention on reducing the direct and indirect costs of stress, employer responsibility for the physical and mental health and safety of employees, the increasing threat of expensive litigation from distressed employees (*see* Walker *v* Northumberland County Council [1995] IRLR 35 and Cross *v* Highlands and Islands Enterprise [2001] IRLR 336), protecting the organisational image in relation to the customer base and the labour market, and underpinning a belief that people are a source of competitive advantage. Indicative stress policy content is listed in Exhibit 14.4.

Exhibit 14.4   Indicative content of a formal stress policy

1 A positive statement about the organisational attitude towards harmful stress.

2 A recognition of the need to de-stigmatise an admission of stress by an employee and the provision of stress-reporting channels.

3 Confidential counselling and referral services.

4 Stress education and awareness training.

5 Stress audit arrangements, risk assessment, use of well-being indicators and a commitment to act upon the stressors as well as support individual coping strategies.

6 A process of stress monitoring and policy review and integration with other HR practices.

Why do so few organisations have a formal stress policy? The answer may lie in where this section on stress started. The conjunction of external factors may inevitably produce levels of employee distress which are beyond managerial capacity to resolve. In this scenario a stress policy may merely be the key to a 'Pandora's box', a box which the organisation may pragmatically prefer to keep closed; but this does not resolve the fundamental issue that harmful stress is bad for the employee and bad for the organisation because it threatens to burn out the workforce.

Humans are not robots . . . Most cannot sustain the pace required by ever-more demanding performance targets in the long term, particularly if they have inadequate rest periods and work long hours. People must feel that they are sharing in the gains of lean (organisational) systems, not paying for it with their health.

(Baron in Littlefield, 1996)

In the UK we do not yet have a word for death from overwork, but the Japanese do – *karoshi*!

SUMMARY LEARNING POINTS

1 Investment in positive health policies can benefit the employer through higher levels of performance, lower levels of absence and improved recruitment and retention of staff.

2 Medical evidence, social attitudes and legal requirements make smoking at work an employment issue, and a range of smoking control options are available to the employer. Employee opinion is important, but managerial care is needed to avoid polarising smokers and non-smokers into opposing camps. A policy provides a framework for managing smoking at work.

3 Alcohol misuse and drug abuse may impact on employee attendance and work performance. As a consequence the organisational attitude towards alcohol and drugs, the counselling and support available to employees and the training and backing available to managers should be articulated in clear policies.

4 HIV and AIDS are features of life which are plagued by misinformation and arouse feelings of fear and uncertainty among the workforce. Employees who are HIV positive can work normally. People with HIV/AIDS may have some protection against discrimination under the Disability Discrimination Act. A policy on HIV and AIDS provides a fair and consistent framework for the management of difficult situations that arise.

5 The nature of the work determines the likelihood of violence at work. Violence may be threatened or actual, and verbal or physical, but whatever form it takes the employer has a statutory duty to assess the risks and implement strategies to reduce or eliminate the risk. As well as adversely impacting upon employee performance and effectiveness, employer failure to address violence at work can result in the constructive dismissal of employees.

6 Pressure is stimulating and motivating and a state of 'eustress' is a desirable aim, but inappropriate levels of pressure result in 'distress' which is harmful to the individual and to the organisation. The costs of distress are potentially substantial and warrant managerial attention. Managing harmful pressure involves acting upon the stressors as well as promoting individual coping strategies. A stress policy needs to address the stigma associated with admitting distress and also provide for a stress audit, an action plan, monitoring and review. Managerial efforts to combat stress are circumscribed by the conjunction of social, political, economic and global factors which tend to increase pressure at work.

REFERENCES AND FURTHER READING

Advisory, Conciliation and Arbitration Service. *Health and Employment – Advisory Booklet 15*.

Banas, G. (1992) 'Nothing prepared me to manage AIDS', *Harvard Business Review*, July/August.

Briner, R. (1999) 'Against the grain: stress', *People Management*, 30 September, 32–41.

Charlesworth, K. (1996) 'Are managers under stress? – a survey of management morale', *Institute of Management Research Report*.

CIPD (1998) *Information Note: Stress audits*.

CIPD (2001) *Quick Facts: Stress*.

Clark, H., Chandler, J. and Barry, J. (1997) 'Gender and work stress: experience, accommodation and resistance', *Occasional Papers in Organisational Analysis*. University of Portsmouth.

Cranwell-Ward, J. (1990) *Thriving on Stress*. London: Routledge.

DL70 – Disability Discrimination Act – Employment (1996) DfEE.

Donovan, P. (2000) 'Prison service violates privacy with substance abuse proposal', *People Management*, 12 October, 8.

Dunn, C. (1996) 'Preventing stress from harming the business', *People Management*, October.

Fingret, A. and Smith, A. (1995) *Occupational Health: a practical guide for managers*. London: Routledge.

Goss, D. and Adam-Smith, D. (1994) 'Empowerment or disempowerment? The limits and possibilities of workplace AIDS policy', in Aggleton, P. *et al.* (eds) *AIDS: foundations for the future*. London: Taylor and Francis.

Goss, D. and Adam-Smith, D. (1995) *Organizing AIDS: workplace and organizational responses to the HIV epidemic*. London: Taylor and Francis.

HSE (1996) *An Employers' Guide to Good Health is Good Business*.

HSE (1999) *Violence at Work: Findings from the British Crime Survey*.

HSE (2000) *Help on Work-related Stress*.

HSE (2001) *Violence at Work: A guide for employers*.

Health Education Authority (1991) *Aids and You*.

Honey, P. (1993) 'Managing unwanted stress', *Seminar Paper*, Wessex: IPD.

Incomes Data Services (1991) *Smoking at Work*. Study 474.

Incomes Data Services (1993) *AIDS Returns to the Agenda*. Study 528. April.

IPD (1996) *Occupational Health and Organisational Effectiveness – key facts*.

Jones, T. and Kleiner, B. (1990) 'Smoking and the work environment', *Employee Relations*, 12(4), 29–31.

Judge, L. (1996) 'What safety practitioners think about stress', *Safety and Health Practitioner*, 14(4), 8–20.

Littlefield, D. (1996) 'Stress epidemic hits modern workforces', *People Management*, October.

McKee, V. (1996) 'Working to a frenzy', *The Guardian*, 1 October.

Midgely, S. (1997) 'Pressure', *People Management*, 10 July, 36–9.

National AIDS Trust (1992) *Equitable AIDS Policy*.

Newell, S. (1995) *The Healthy Organisation: fairness, ethics and effective management*. London: Routledge.

Painter, R. (1990) 'Smoking policies: the legal implications', *Employee Relations*, 12(4), 17–21.

Pawsey, V. (2000) 'High time for action', *People Management*, 11 May, 24–32.

Robbins, S. (1993) *Organizational Behaviour*. Upper Saddle River, NJ: Prentice-Hall.

Roberts, Z. (2001) 'A rough guide to harmony', *People Management*, December 2001.

Royal College of Physicians (2000) Increases in drug addiction: report. London.

Smith, A., Johal, S. and Wadsworth, E. (2000) *Bristol Stress and Health at Work Study*. HSE Books.

Stuart, L. (2001) 'All stressed up and no place to go', *The Guardian*, 17 March.

Terrence Higgins Trust (2001) 'Prejudice, discrimination and HIV: a report', Policy Campaigns and Research Division, November, 1–26.

White, P. and Hamer, C. (2001) 'No time for relaxing over stress at work', *Personnel Today*, 30 October, 13.

ASSIGNMENTS AND DISCUSSION TOPICS

1 Critically review the smoking policy of your organisation (or one with which you are familiar) to ensure compliance with the HSE Approved Code of Practice on passive smoking. How is this policy monitored and how are infringements handled?

2 Why are issues such as smoking and alcohol, which are social activities, of any concern to the employer?

3 Make a case to your management team for introducing a specific policy on HIV and AIDS into your organisation. What should the policy include?

4 What should be done in your organisation to address the potential for violence against employees? Assess and respond to the training needs of a group of staff who may face violence in the workplace.

5 For your organisation (or an organisation where you are able to get access) use the HSE four-stage process to critically review the management of violence in the workplace. What conclusions can you draw from your review and what recommendations would you make to ensure compliance with the legislative responsibilities?

6 What are the main sources of stress in your organisation? What are the implications of these organisational stressors for the individual and for organisational effectiveness and how can management respond effectively?

7 To what extent do you think an individual can combat harmful pressure by managing beliefs about stress, by reframing personal perceptions and thereby preventing feelings of distress?

8 Select any of the sensitive employment issues and discuss the rationale for having an organisational policy to deal with it. What would you include in the policy and why?

CHAPTER 15

Employment relations in context

by Derek Adam-Smith

INTRODUCTION

Effective people resourcing is not achieved without an understanding and appreciation of the employment relationship. This chapter and the next expose the contextual nature of the employment relationship and the associated processes. Over the past two decades, the subject area of employment relations has undergone significant change. Conservative governments between 1979 and 1997 initiated a series of policies designed to weaken the power of trade unions, and the post-1997 labour governments have introduced a National Minimum Wage and a statutory right for union recognition. In response to increased competition for goods and services, many organisations introduced employment strategies devised to produce a closer fit with their business objectives. Such strategies were often accompanied by an emphasis on individualising the employment relationship. As a result of these developments, the reliance on collective bargaining between employers and trade unions to determine employees' terms and conditions of employment has been called into question. Consequently, trade unions themselves have been forced to re-examine the way in which they express their traditional role as the formal representative of employees.

CHAPTER OBJECTIVES

- To promote an awareness of the ways in which aspects of the employment relationship are changing.
- To encourage an understanding of the role of the state in employment relations and how public policy has changed since 1979.
- To make an assessment of the impact of European Union initiatives on employment practice.
- To consider the options for management in developing an employment relations strategy.
- To review the purpose of trade unions and to examine how they are responding to changes prompted by public policy and employer initiatives.

EMPLOYMENT RELATIONS AND PEOPLE RESOURCING

An understanding of the field of employment relations (or employee relations or industrial relations, as the subject may be titled – *see* page 378) remains an important one for those concerned with the management of people at work. Blyton and Turnbull (1998) maintain that its relevance is fourfold. First, the world of work remains central to the lives of most people, provoking interest in the settlement of terms and conditions of employment and the way in which people are treated at work. Second, employees are vital to an organisation's ability to achieve its business strategy, whether in the manufacturing or service sectors of the economy. Unless employees deliver the required skill and attention to their work, an organisation's potential for success will not be realised. Third, while managers and employees may share a common interest in ensuring a continuing successful enterprise, a tension exists between an employer's need for profit (or, in the case of the public sector, to remain within budget) and the workers' needs for wages and employment security. Fourth, the decline in the collective dimension to employment and the emergence of individualism (often under the banner of Human Resource Management) do not signal the end of the need to study collective employment relationships. Blyton and Turnbull go on to argue that:

> At first sight these 'position' statements, reflecting the basic importance, problematic nature and contemporary significance of employee relations, may appear almost too simple to warrant re-stating . . . (however) the tendency for them to be discarded or overlooked in some of the recent management literature may have led to a misconception about the continuing significance of collective employee relations in contemporary work organisations.

> (Blyton and Turnbull, 1998: 4)

Thus decisions over the wage for work bargain between employers and employees remain central to the achievement of effective resourcing of organisations. This will necessitate managers formulating answers to the following sorts of questions. Is a representative role for trade unions acceptable to the organisation and required by the employees? If so, how will this collective relationship be structured? What knowledge and skills are needed by managers involved in dealing with trade unions? If the employment relationship is to be conducted on an individualised basis, how will terms and conditions of employment be determined? To what extent is it important for employees, individually or collectively, to be involved in wider decisions outside their immediate work requirements? How do economic and political changes influence these relationships?

As Chapter 1 stressed, there is no one best way to structure the employment relationship. Providing answers to this question will involve making decisions that take account of the contexts and sector within which the organisation operates, the preferred style of key managers, and the organisation's size, ownership and business objectives. This chapter aims to provide an initial opportunity to examine those factors which have a bearing on the answers to these questions through a consideration of some key contextual changes in employment relations.

THE CHANGING NATURE OF EMPLOYMENT

Chapter 4 explored the way in which labour markets and patterns of work have changed in recent years. These changes have particular significance for the structuring of the employment relationship and the interests of the key parties in employment relations – employers, employees, trade unions and the state. A number of key trends can be discerned from a consideration of statistics drawn from official publications.

First, the level of unemployment has risen and fallen dramatically since the late 1970s when it stood at around 5 per cent. It rose to over 10 per cent in 1987 before declining to below 7 per cent in 1990. During the recession of the early 1990s unemployment climbed to almost 10 per cent again before falling to its current rate of around 4 per cent. Thus, although the level of unemployment is broadly the same as it was 20 years ago, these wide swings in its rate suggest that workers are more likely to move in and out of employment, leading to feelings of job insecurity. As Gregg *et al.* (2000: 54) point out, 'For nearly three-quarters of the workforce, job instability as measured by job tenure has increased in the last ten years or so.'

Second, although the number of people working full-time has declined, part-time employment grew from under six million in 1980 to around eight million by the mid-1990s, some three-quarters of this increase being accounted for by women taking part-time jobs. Self-employment increased by some 1.2 million between 1979 and 1990 before levelling off. At the same time there has been a modest increase in those employed on temporary contracts. Whilst recognising that some people choose such forms of employment, the primary drive for more flexible working time arrangements comes from employers:

> the most important reason is the fit between these types of work and specific business needs (such as part-time jobs which cover extended opening hours).
>
> (Beatson, 1995: 57)

Third, data from the Workplace Industrial Relations Survey (Millward *et al.*, 2000) shows that the proportion of employees working in private-sector manufacturing declined from 38 per cent in 1980 to 25 per cent in 1998. Over the same period, however, employment in private-sector services grew from 26 per cent to 44 per cent.

The combination of these trends suggests that the nature of employment has undergone significant changes in a relatively short period of time. It is possible to conclude that there has been a shift away from full-time, male employment in the manufacturing sector. There are substantially more women in employment, often working on a part-time or temporary basis. The use of sub-contracting by employers, utilising the growing numbers of the self-employed, provides greater flexibility because the employer enters into a contract for services rather than a contract of employment with its attendant legal protection (*see* Chapters 4, 18 and 19). For every two people working in manufacturing there are seven employed in services. As a result of these trends in the nature of employment, some commentators have suggested that 'employment relations' provides a more adequate description of the subject area (Sisson, 1991; Hartley and Stephenson, 1992). For many, the term 'industrial relations' is characteristic of a previous era of high trade union membership amongst predominately manual workers in extraction, heavy engineering and manufacturing industries. Even the more 'modern' employee relations does not always reflect the fact that many of those working in organisations are not employees but self-employed, and the nature of temporary work means that many staff know that they will spend little time employed in a particular organisation.

THE ROLE OF THE STATE

Employment relations does not exist in a vacuum but is affected by, and in turn affects, the political, economic and social contexts within which it operates. In order to understand the changes that have taken place, it is therefore necessary to examine the way in which governments have sought to influence British employment relations, since 'it is the only actor in the situation which can change the rules of the system' (Crouch, 1982: 146).

To aid this analysis it is possible to identify four interrelated roles that the state plays. First, as its elected custodian, governments develop a range of policies aimed at developing a stable and competitive economy, controlling inflationary pressures and seeking to maintain a healthy balance of payments. Second, to support some of its policy objectives governments can introduce legislation to parliament. Of particular interest here is the law governing employment and trade unions. Third, where conflict between employers and trade unions is viewed as having a detrimental impact on economic performance or the achievement of social objectives, the government can, either through its own ministers or through specially created agencies, intervene in industrial disputes. Finally, since a substantial number of people are employed in the public sector, actions by the government in its role as an employer (either directly in the case of the Civil Service or indirectly in local authorities, for example) will have significant consequences for employment relations. Each of these roles – policy maker, legislator, intervenor and employer – will be considered in turn.

Policy maker

In order to understand the contemporary relevance of the interrelationship between employment relations and economic policy, it is helpful to briefly review the way in which public policy has developed since 1945. The period from 1945 to 1979 is generally characterised as one of consensus between the two main political parties in the management of the economy and in the role trade unions and collective bargaining were to play in employment. According to Farnham and Pimlott (1995: 214), this consensus involved:

> the maintenance of full employment and the welfare state; continuing state ownership of industries nationalised between 1945 and 1951; high levels of public expenditure; the continuation of the legal-abstentionist or voluntarist tradition of industrial relations; and the involvement of the Trades Union Congress (TUC) in government decisions affecting the welfare state and the management of the national economy.

Of these, 'a commitment to the maintenance of full employment had been the centre-piece of the . . . consensus' (Kessler and Bayliss, 1995: 53). This policy was philosophic-ally underpinned by an adherence to Keynesian demand management economics which offered a strategy for managing the economy so that full employment could be maintained. However, this commitment, combined with a reliance on 'free' collective bargaining as the preferred method for determining pay and terms and conditions for employees, began to produce significant difficulties for employers. In the private sector powerful trade unions were able to bargain for increased earnings (over and above the 'market rate') and, with limited alternative labour available, employers were forced to raise pay rates to attract and retain employees, particularly where there were skill shortages. Employers in the public sector were unable to attract sufficient staff unless they were able to offer comparable pay rates, which led to increased demands on the public borrowing requirement to fund these pay awards. The result of these pressures in the economy was an increase in inflation. Faced with this problem, governments throughout the 1960s and 1970s searched repeatedly for an incomes policy which would limit the increase in earning levels without abandoning the commitment to full employment. Despite some limited success, the search for an effective incomes policy came to an end in the 'winter of discontent' in 1978–79. However, it has been observed that the policy of full employment also hindered any fundamental adjustment of the economy to the increasingly competitive international pressures:

> So, not only did governments find it increasingly difficult to prevent unemployment rising but productivity, unit labour costs, investment and profitability were getting increasingly out of line with Britain's major competitors in Europe and the rising economies of the Far East.
>
> (Kessler and Bayliss, 1995: 54)

The election of the Conservative government led by Margaret Thatcher in 1979 marked a 'sea-change' in economic policy and fundamental changes in the relationship between government and trade unions, in part driven by the need to make the economy more competitive. The tenets of the incoming administration are succinctly summed up by Crouch (1995) thus:

> The post-1979 Conservative governments have had a strong neo-liberal ideology. This has pre-disposed them: to reject Keynesian demand management and the search for full employment; to oppose policy deals with trade unions that would involve taking action incompatible with neo-liberal principles; and to reject relations with organisations of interests – on both sides of business but especially on the labour side – that interfered with neo-liberal policy priorities.
>
> (Crouch, 1995: 238)

Demand management strategies pursued under Keynesian economics, complemented by incomes policies, were replaced by an adherence to monetarist policies. The control of inflation was to be achieved through tight control of the money supply and use of interest rates, leaving the market mechanism to prevail. Not only did this mean that ailing industries and organisations would not receive public subsidies (if there was no market for its products at the price demanded, the organisation would have to rationalise its operations or close), but also that the labour market should be subject to these same disciplines. If unemployment rose, the cause was that the cost of labour (wages) was too high. As employees adjusted their expectations in this new economic reality, jobs would be accepted for lower pay. The resultant profitability of companies would encourage them to take on more staff (assuming demand remained) and lead to a consequent fall in unemployment. Since trade unions were a major factor in distorting the working of the labour market through their ability to bargain collectively on behalf of employees, the achievement of this policy required that the pervasiveness of collective bargaining would need to be tackled. Primarily this objective was achieved through the use of legal measures designed to curtail what was seen as the excessive power of the trade unions (*see* page 380).

In addition, as Crouch (1995) has noted, government policy between 1979 and 1997 also removed the elements of tripartism (cooperation between government, unions and employers) which had become a key element of public policy. In part this was achieved through *ad hoc* measures such as the exclusion of union leaders from government inquiries, commissions and the like, and a reduction in meetings between ministers and unions. In particular, tripartite channels such as the National Economic Development Council (NEDC) (a regular forum bringing together representatives of unions, employers and government to discuss economic issues) and the Manpower Services Commission (MSC) (which involved employers and workers' organisations in discussions concerning the working of the labour market and industrial relations) were gradually marginalised and eventually abolished (Crouch, 1995).

Thus public policy on employment relations under these Conservative governments can be seen to be one seeking to remove barriers to the working of the free labour market, and in particular, reducing the power and influence of trade unions both in their negotiations with employers and in the management of the economy.

The election of a Labour government in 1997 (and its subsequent re-election in 2001) heralded a further change in public policy. The approach of 'New Labour' to employment policy has been characterised as a 'Third Way'. Although its precise meaning remains elusive and open to debate (Giddens, 1998; Nuti, 1999), this is perhaps best understood to involve a rejection of both the voluntarist, consensus period from 1945 to 1979 and the monetarist, free-market policies of Conservative governments up to 1997, hence the '*Third* Way'. As the Prime Minister has defined it: 'not *laissez-faire* nor state control and rigidity; but an active Government role linked to improving the employability of the workforce' (Blair, 1998, cited in Undy, 1999: 316).

Four main components of Labour's employment policy can be identified. The first is a more active labour market policy. This can be seen, for example, in the development of the 'New Deal', the broad aim of which is to improve the skill base of the workforce. Initially targeted at young people without jobs and funded by a 'windfall tax' on the privatised utilities, the scheme has been extended to include older people who have difficulty finding employment where jobs require increasing levels of skill. Second, the Government introduced a National Minimum Wage in 1999 which provided statutorily backed minimum hourly pay for all workers in the country. Third, legislation has been passed which provides trade unions with a legal route to gain recognition where an employer has refused to grant it voluntarily. Fourth, the Labour Government has taken a more pro-European stance than that of its immediate predecessors, including the signing of the 'Social Chapter' of the Maastricht Treaty. Each of these last three components is dealt with in later sections of this chapter.

Legislator

The law that applies to employment can be divided broadly into two parts: that concerned with an individual employee's contract of employment with the employer, and the law governing the relationship between employers and trade unions. The position of individual employment protection rights is discussed elsewhere in this book (*see* Chapters 6, 7, 8, 13, 17, 18 and 19). This section will concentrate on the development of collective labour law and, in addition, will outline the provisions related to statutory union recognition and the National Minimum Wage.

Collective labour law

Turning first to the changes in collective labour law, significant changes were made to the legal status of action taken by trade unions in pursuit of their objectives by the Conservative governments between 1979 and 1997. Although the Labour governments since 1997 have made some minor changes, the overwhelming majority of the legislation remains in place. In order to meet its policy objectives of deregulating the labour market, Conservative governments in the 1980s and 1990s abandoned the 'abstentionist role' that the law played in employment relations. British industrial relations up to this time had been characterised as a voluntary process in which the law 'stood apart' from the determination of terms and conditions of employment. This, it was believed, was best left to employers and trade unions to decide through the medium of free collective bargaining. Legislation that was enacted had the aim of supporting and complementing collective bargaining (in areas such as health and safety, employment protection and regulating employment in Wages Councils industries) and of providing trade unions with the ability to call for industrial action without being subject to legal claims by employers for common law liabilities. Although some commentators have noted that the voluntary system was under pressure through the 1960s and 1970s (Hyman, 1995; Crouch, 1995), it was the election of the Thatcher government which initiated a series of acts of parliament which have made far-reaching changes to the collective labour law framework. 'The period has seen the final death of voluntarism, under which law was essentially an adjunct to an autonomous self-regulated system of industrial relations' (Dickens and Hall, 1995: 256). The aims of this legislation have been characterised by these authors as follows:

> The major thrust of the legislation since 1979 is clear: to weaken trade union power, to assert individualist rather than collective values and reassert employer prerogative.
>
> (Dickens and Hall, 1995)

As the previous section has indicated, the bargaining strategies of trade unions were seen to distort the operation of the labour market, and thus the immunities granted to them in relation to industrial action became the prime focus of the legal measures adopted by the government. In Britain, there is no 'right to strike' – employees who do so are in breach of their contracts of employment and thus liable to dismissal by their employer. Although legislation passed in the 1970s prevented selective dismissal of strikers, these provisions were amended to give employers greater freedom to lawfully dismiss those on strike. However, since coming to power the Labour government has passed legislation so that workers undertaking official industrial action cannot be sacked during the first eight weeks of the dispute. For trade unions the freedom to take industrial action is derived from the granting of statutory immunities from claims under common law where such action would be judged otherwise to be 'in restraint of trade'. Trade union power was weakened through a series of acts of parliament designed to limit these immunities. It is not possible to provide a detailed exposition of the changes in this chapter, but Exhibit 15.1 provides, by way of illustration, a summary of the transformation in key areas of collective labour law.

Exhibit 15.1   Summary of key changes to collective employment law, 1979 to 2002

Area	*1979*	*2002*
Dismissal of strikers	Employment tribunals barred from hearing unfair dismissal claims from employees dismissed while on strike, unless the employer selectively dismisses employees. If the employer subsequently selectively re-employs dismissed employees then all those not re-employed have a claim for unfair dismissal	Provided there is no selective dismissal, tribunals are barred from hearing claims of unfair dismissal, provided no strikers are dismissed in the first eight weeks of the dispute. After three months an employer may selectively re-employ dismissed strikers with no liability for unfair dismissal from those not re-employed. However, in the case of *unofficial industrial action* (not authorised by the trade union) the employer may selectively dismiss those on strike without any legal redress being available to the dismissed employees
Definition of a trade dispute	The definition of a trade dispute covered *any* dispute between employers and workers or between workers and workers which was connected with terms and conditions of employment of any person	Defined now under the Trade Union and Labour Relations (Consolidation) Act 1992 as a dispute between *workers and their employer* which relates *wholly or mainly* to terms and conditions of employment
Trade union immunity	Trade unions which organised industrial action were granted protection from civil liability for inducing workers to break their contracts of employment – subject to their actions being in 'contemplation or furtherance of a trade dispute'. Trade unions (as organisations) had wide-ranging civil immunity for acts committed by their members or officials irrespective of whether or not they	All secondary action, such as 'sympathy' strikes, is unlawful even if this involves employees of the same employer who are not involved in the primary dispute

Political strikes, i.e. those designed to change government policy (such as on privatisation), are also unlawful |

continued

Exhibit 15.1   continued

Area	1979	2002
	were carried out in contemplation or furtherance of a trade dispute. Unions were provided also with immunity for actions which resulted in a breach of a commercial contract, thus making *secondary action* by trade unions lawful	
Picketing	One or more persons were allowed to attend at, or near, any place (other than a person's home) to peacefully obtain or communicate information or persuade any person to work or not to work, provided the picketing was in contemplation or furtherance of a trade dispute	Picketing is now only lawful where the person attends at or near his or her place of work, or in the case of a trade union official, at or near the place or work of a member whom they represent. The Code of Practice on Picketing provides more detailed guidance, including the recommendation that the number of pickets should be limited to six at any one workplace entrance
Ballots	No legal requirements to hold secret ballots	Detailed provisions now exist over the requirements for a secret ballot if any resulting industrial action is to attract immunity from civil action. In principle the law requires a secret postal ballot to be conducted and notice to be given to the employer of the holding of a ballot, its result and those employees likely to be involved in the industrial action
Damages for unlawful industrial action	Because of the immunity granted to trade unions, they could not be sued for damages as a result of any loss suffered through industrial action	Industrial action which falls outside the detailed legal requirements, such as definition of dispute, ballots, picketing or secondary action, makes the union liable for damages, up to a specified maximum depending on membership size, to be paid to the employer who has suffered a loss. Ordinary citizens have the right to seek court orders to restrain unlawful industrial action
Closed shop	Dismissal of an employee because of a refusal to join, or because of resignation from, a trade union where a Union Membership Agreement (UMA) exists was fair unless the person could show a 'deeply held religious conviction' against being a member of a trade union	Dismissal of an employee for resigning from a union or failing to employ a person because of their refusal to join a union can be the basis for a claim at an employment tribunal. Any industrial action organised by a trade union to seek to enforce a UMA on an employer is specifically ruled to be outside the protection offered for civil action.

According to Auerbach (1990), the approach of successive conservative governments can be seen as a 'dual track' policy – a policy of restriction and a policy of regulation. The former concentrated on the immunities enjoyed by unions. The circumstances under which these immunities were applicable were substantially narrowed, making industrial action outside the employees' workplace generally unlawful. Sympathy strikes (where employees not in dispute with their employer go on strike to support others), picketing not at the employees' own place of work and industrial action for political purposes were all made unlawful.

The policy of regulation sought to place specific legal requirements on trade unions engaged in industrial action. Complex, detailed requirements on secret postal ballots needed before lawful action can be embarked upon were put in place. In addition, unions who are found to be involved in unlawful industrial action can be sued. In the case of employers who suffer as a result of unlawful action, limited damages, to be paid by the union, are available. In addition, any individual deprived of goods or services because of unlawful industrial action may seek a court order restraining the organisation of such action.

Legislation over the past 20 years has reduced the power of trade unions in relation to both their bargaining relationship with employers and their ability to pursue political objectives. How employers and unions have responded to these new circumstances will be considered later in the chapter. It is clear, however, that as a result of these changes, the balance of power has swung in favour of employers. The Labour government has been at pains to point out that there is no intention to significantly alter this body of law beyond those relatively minor changes made already.

Statutory union recognition

Despite maintaining much of the legislation passed under its Conservative predecessors, in June 2000 as part of the Employment Relations Act, 1999 the Labour government introduced a statutory right for trade unions to gain recognition from a reluctant employer. Although the procedures are designed to encourage voluntary agreement between the trade union and an employer, they are supported by mandatory provisions which can be activated if no agreement is reached and, according to one commentator, '. . . could change the face of employee relations in the UK' (Younson, 2000: 44). The legislation does not apply to firms with fewer than 21 employees, and the union must be able to show that it has at least 10 per cent of employees already in membership if it is to be able to use the mandatory provisions. Where voluntary agreement is not reached the union is required to apply to the Central Arbitration Committee (CAC), a long-standing body in UK employment relations. The CAC will oversee the operation of the statutory procedure, including the conduct of a ballot of all workers for whom the union is claiming recognition. Where a union is granted recognition under these provisions, the employer is required to negotiate with it on, at least, matters concerned with pay, hours of work and holidays.

The first decision that the CAC needs to make is the 'bargaining unit' (see Chapter 16). This is a definable group of employees, for example hourly paid staff, for which the union will be recognised as the negotiating body. Since it is a majority of these employees who will need to vote in favour, employers may be tempted to argue that the unit should be as large as possible as this may dilute the union's influence. Similarly, the union is likely to seek a small unit where it believes it has strong support. Thus the definition of the bargaining unit is a key step in the procedure. Under the legislation, the CAC is required to take account of a number of factors in addition to employer and union views when determining the size of the unit. These include the compatibility of the unit with effective management, the avoidance of small, fragmented bargaining units, the physical location of the employees, and any existing bargaining arrangements.

Once the bargaining unit is defined, if at least 50 per cent of the employees in the unit are union members then the CAC will declare that the union should be recognised. If membership is less than this figure, the CAC will call a secret ballot of employees. However, even if the 50 per cent threshold is achieved, the CAC may require a ballot in two circumstances: first, if it believes that this would be in the interests of good employment relations, and second, if it feels that membership evidence, for example a snap recruitment campaign, suggests that employees may not wish union representation. Where a secret ballot is undertaken, recognition will be granted if it is supported by a majority of those voting *and* that this majority amounts to at least 40 per cent of those in the bargaining unit. For example, suppose that there are 100 employees in the bargaining unit and 45 take part in the vote, with 36 in favour of union recognition. While a majority of those voting want the union to be recognised (36 out of 45 = 80 per cent in favour), this result does not meet the threshold under the second test since fewer than 40 per cent of those in the unit voted in favour. This second condition appears to have been included to ensure that a small number of union members cannot impose recognition on a group of workers. The questionable assumption behind this provision is that employees not voting were against union recognition, though it is equally valid to suggest that those not voting had no strong views either way.

A number of claims for statutory union recognition have been received by the CAC, but the overwhelming majority of claims have been settled voluntarily and without recourse to the full procedure. This perhaps suggests that employers view a protracted battle over union recognition where there is support from the workforce is unlikely to engender good employment relations in the longer term. As Brown *et al.* (2001: 192) conclude: 'Statutory intervention to enforce the enhancement of that [employment] relationship may have as little likelihood of success as compulsory marriage has of achieving domestic stability.'

The National Minimum Wage

The second major legislative change introduced by the Labour government has been the establishment of a National Minimum Wage (NMW). Soon after its 1997 election victory the government established a Low Pay Commission (LPC) comprised of employer, trade union and independent members to consider the scope and level of the potential minimum wage. The LPC recommended that the hourly rates for the NMW should be defined for three different groups: a full adult rate; a development rate for adults in receipt of formal accredited training; and a young person's rate. The government accepted these principles, although with some amendments to the rates proposed by the LPC. The

NMW was introduced in April 1999, giving the UK, for the first time, a legally enforceable minimum hourly rate of pay for all workers with no sector or regional variations. The original rates set in 1999 were an adult rate of £3.60 per hour, a development rate of £3.20 per hour and a youth rate for those under 22 years of age of £3.00 per hour. Since the NMW came into effect the minimum rates have been adjusted. The adult rate was raised to £3.70 per hour in October 2000 and to £4.10 a year later. In June 2000 the youth rate was raised to £3.20 per hour, bringing it in line with the adult development rate; these were both increased, to £3.50 per hour, in October 2001. The government has also indicated that the adult rate will rise to £4.20 per hour in October 2002 if economic conditions permit.

The introduction of the NMW attracted a significant amount of criticism, mainly from employers and their representatives who argued that it would cause significant job losses, as employers in low-paying industries would not be able to afford the increases. However, the evidence available suggests that this has not been the case in general, although some small businesses have found the impact on their wage bills difficult to manage (LPC, 2001; Adam-Smith *et al.*, 2001a). In a study of the hospitality sector, a traditionally low-paying industry, Adam-Smith *et al.* (2001b) found that most employers had coped with the impact of the NMW with little difficulty. The evidence from this study shows that employers had had significant notice of the rates and were able to plan for its introduction. In addition, the strong economy and the resulting pressure on firms to attract and retain staff had forced up wage rates anyway, often beyond that required by minimum wage requirements. Thus the NMW appears to have been introduced into UK employment practice with limited difficulty, although a significant downturn in the economy may subsequently sharpen its impact, perhaps explaining the government's caution in attaching conditions to any further increase in October 2002.

Intervenor

That industrial action, particularly strikes, can have a damaging impact on the economy and society has been recognised by governments and leads to the identification of a third role of the state in employment relations, that of 'industrial peacekeeper' or intervenor. Here the government accepts some responsibility for seeking a speedy and satisfactory resolution to the dispute. This aim can be achieved by both formal and informal mechanisms. In the former case it involves the establishment of either permanent or *ad hoc* agencies or bodies to intervene in the dispute. Informal means include the direct involvement of government ministers in the dispute – an approach which has declined in significance in recent years.

Although formal mechanisms for the settlement of industrial disputes can be traced back to the passing of the Conciliation Act in 1896 and the Industrial Courts Act, 1919, the current publicly funded agency primarily having these responsibilities is the Advisory, Conciliation and Arbitration Service (ACAS). Established in 1974, ACAS has four main functions related to its overall aim of improving industrial relations:

- conciliation between an employer and an individual employee in cases which may lead to a claim at an employment tribunal, including unfair dismissal and unlawful deductions from pay

- collective conciliation between employers and trade unions where an employment dispute exists
- making arrangements for arbitration where conciliation has proved unsuccessful
- providing free advice to employers, trade unions and employees on a range of employment matters.

The nature of conciliation and arbitration is elaborated upon in the next chapter.

The development of ACAS policy and operational matters are determined by a nine-member council (plus chair) which includes equal representatives of trade unions and employers, and three independent members. It is one of the few tripartite organisations which have survived the changes to British employment relations.

Employer

The state is a major employer and it is not surprising, therefore, to find that its view of employment practice should be reflected in the way in which it manages its own workforce. Given the sharp dichotomy that exists between public policy before and after 1979, significant differences in the role of the state as an employer can be observed in the periods preceding and following this date (Farnham and Horton, 1993). Although the size of public sector employment has declined, it remains significant, with a substantial proportion of the workforce employed directly or indirectly by the state. The areas of employment under government control include the Civil Service, HM forces, local government, the National Health Service, police, education, and public corporations such as the Post Office.

Since the First World War, governments have attempted to act as a 'model' employer. Central to this approach had been the recognition of trade unions and the extensive use of collective bargaining, following the recommendations of the Whitley Committee in 1919, as the mechanism for determining pay and terms and conditions of employment. Organisations in the public sector encouraged their employees to join appropriate, recognised trade unions so that decisions over wages and other matters of employment should receive broad support amongst their workforces. Public sector employees, who enjoyed relatively high job security, were among the first to have pension and sick pay schemes and to have in place procedures covering such matters as discipline and grievances. This is not to say that employment relations in this sector were without criticism:

> This approach was not universally or evenly applied and the long standing concerns of public-sector trade unions with problems of low pay indicate that some groups fared better than others. Nonetheless, the idea of the good employer remained an aspiration of government policy even when not translated fully into practice.
>
> (Winchester and Bach, 1995: 308)

As well as adopting this specific employer role as a model of best practice for the private sector to follow, as Fredman and Morris (1989) point out, the government went beyond mere encouragement by requiring private-sector contractors from whom it purchased goods and services to pay fair wages when engaged on government work.

The changes to the state's role as an employer since 1979 can be seen in many parts of the public sector. First, it became an employer of fewer staff. Primarily this was through the privatisation of the utility companies (gas, water and electricity) and the nationalised industries and corporations such as British Steel, British Shipbuilders, British Airways, British Telecom and the Royal Ordnance Factories. In all, this removed some 1.5 million employees from the public sector. Second, in the National Health Service, which employs over one million people, the creation of the 'internal market', the appointment of general managers and the development of trust status for health authorities has attempted to bring the 'disciplines' of the market into the service and to direct management attention to the need for cost savings (which include those to be made in labour costs). Thus:

> In the 1990s the NHS has evolved from an integrated, professionally dominated bureaucracy into a plethora of separate organisations where managers hold the purse strings and increasingly make decisions using financial criteria. These reforms have undermined employees' job security and challenged traditional employment practices.
>
> (Winchester and Bach, 1995: 314)

Similar changes have been observed in local government where more than two and a half million people work. The government encouraged the adoption of local-level determination of pay in contrast to the centralised Whitley Council structure. In addition, significant changes have resulted from the introduction of Compulsory Competitive Tendering (CCT) for both manual and white-collar services. Jobs have been lost and employees' terms and conditions altered significantly.

In reviewing the current role of the state as an employer, Farnham and Pimlott (1995) argue that a 'new model' is emerging where public sector employment relations *follow* rather than lead the private sector. Thus this new model asserts the authority of management, rejects an employee role in the decision-making process beyond a consultative one, expects the unquestioning adoption of new working practices, and seeks to link pay with individual performance. Although faced with some possible re-nationalisation of Railtrack, the Labour government has broadly maintained a similar stance in respect of the rest of the public sector.

EUROPEAN SOCIAL POLICY

As a member of the European Union (EU) employment relations in the UK are subject to the Union's supra-national policy-making processes, although there is considerable controversy over the extent to which standardisation across the Union is desirable (Hall, 1994). Two features distinguish the formulation and implementation of European policy from that in the UK. First, the EU approach to the development of policy rests heavily on the active participation of the 'social partners', representatives of employers and employees, in the process. Second, unlike the tradition of voluntarism, the EU decisions are implemented through the passage of law, typically in the form of directives.

Perhaps the most controversial element of EU employment policy is the Social Chapter of the Maastricht Treaty. The Labour government has signed the chapter, thus reversing the decision of the Conservative government, which opted out because it believed the provisions were detrimental to the free-market approach to employment. However, before considering its implications it is important to note that employment relations are affected by EU decisions irrespective of the Social Chapter's contents. This may be seen in the following ways. First, the UK had already signed up to a number of directives passed before the Maastricht Treaty was agreed, including equal pay and equal treatment at work, and health and safety at work. Under the latter, changes to maternity leave and payments were introduced in the Trade Union Reform and Employment Rights Act, 1993. Similarly, this directive was used by the EU to propose a maximum 48-hour working week and minimum periods of daily rest and paid holidays (*see* Chapter 13). Second, decisions by the European Court of Justice, which acts as a final appeal court on matters covered by directives, can force the UK government to amend existing employment laws. For example, the adjudged failure of the UK to conform to the requirements of the Collective Redundancies and Transfer of Undertakings Directives forced the government to amend the law with regard to consultation with employee representatives (*see* Chapter 19).

Once the UK had signed the Social Chapter, it was required to implement any Directives introduced under Social Chapter authority. Four Directives have so far been passed which have an impact on UK employment relations. First, the European Works Council (EWC) Directive requires multinational companies with 1000 or more employees within the member countries of the EU, including at least 150 employees in at least two of these countries, to establish an information and consultation body covering the whole of its workforce. Each EWC must meet at least once a year to allow managers and elected employee representatives to discuss company plans and prospects. The inclusion of the UK within the Social Chapter means that an organisation's UK workforce will count towards these numerical thresholds. Second, the Parental Leave Directive requires employers to provide 13 weeks of leave for each parent up to the child's fifth birthday. The key elements of the Directive were included in the Employment Relations Act, 1999 which provided for employers and employees to agree their own scheme to implement these key elements, through either a collective agreement with recognised trade unions or a workforce agreement, the latter being an agreement made between an employer and the employees or their representatives. If such an agreement is not made then the Act contains a model scheme that will apply. Third, the Part-time Work Directive aims to remove discrimination against part-time workers, improve the quality of part-time work and facilitate the development of part-time work on a voluntary basis. Again, the UK law giving effect to the Directive is the Employment Relations Act, 1999. The first two aims of the Directive recognise that traditionally part-time workers have not necessarily enjoyed the same benefits as their full-time counterparts, for example in terms of sick pay provision and access to training. The third aim is designed to contribute to the flexible organisation of working time by making part-time work more attractive to workers, thereby easing employers' operation of a more flexible workforce. Finally, the Fixed-term Work Directive has similar aims to that on part-time work for those employed on fixed-term contracts. In addition, legislation will have to provide one or more of the following: objective reasons for the renewal of fixed-term contracts; a limit on the number of renewals; and/or a limit on the total duration of successive fixed-term employment contracts.

The impact of each Directive or decision will vary depending upon the employment characteristics of the individual business. It is clear, however, that European social policy will continue to have a significant impact on UK employment relations and that managers responsible for making people resourcing decisions in organisations will need to take account of its increasing influence on these matters.

MANAGEMENT STRATEGIES AND EMPLOYMENT RELATIONS

The previous section has indicated how public policy can influence the conduct of employment relations. Nonetheless, employers still retain significant scope in deciding how the employment relationship will be managed. In what can be seen as a seminal work on approaches to employment relations, Fox (1966) drew a distinction between two 'frames of reference' which underpin managerial action – the unitary and the pluralistic. The unitary view supposes an identity of interests between employer and employee with a single source of authority (managerial) and a sole focus of loyalty (the organisation's goals). Drawing on the team analogy, the unitary view perceives conflict to be irrational, the result of misunderstandings or poor communication. Trade unions are seen as an intrusion into the organisation which competes with management for the loyalty of employees. Pluralism, on the other hand, assumes that the organisation is composed of groups of individuals who have legitimate, competing interests. Conflict is seen as an inevitable result of these groups seeking to further their own interests. Trade unions exist as the legitimate representative agent of employees, expressing the inherent conflict in their relationship with management. The role of management is therefore one of seeking to reconcile these inevitable conflicts in their decision making.

Influential as these theories remain, the 'debate has moved on' (Edwards, 1995: 11). In particular, some writers claim to have identified a 'neo-unitary' (Farnham and Pimlott, 1995) or 'sophisticated unitary' (Scott, 1994) perspective. Here the loyalty of employees cannot be assumed as implied by the traditional unitary view, but commitment needs to be fostered by employers, typically through the adoption of what have become known as Human Resource Management (HRM) techniques (Storey, 1992a). Characterising neo-unitary theory, Farnham and Pimlott argue that:

> Its main aim seems to be to integrate employees, as individuals, into the companies in which they work. Its orientation is distinctly market centred, managerialistic and individualistic. By gaining employee commitment to quality production, customer needs and job flexibility, employers embracing this frame of reference have expectations of employee loyalty, customer satisfaction and product security in increasingly competitive market conditions.
>
> (Farnham and Pimlott, 1995: 46)

One key feature that emerges from this approach is a focus on the individual employee rather than concern with the collective relationship. This would seem to be compatible with the rise of HRM and the direction of public policy throughout the 1980s and into the 1990s. However, there is evidence that the collective relationship remains significant in many organisations (Millward *et al.*, 2000). Thus:

> The consequence of these changes is that the handling of '*both*' collective and individual issues (in unison) is likely to be the essential management requirement during the forthcoming period.
>
> (Storey and Sisson, 1993: 4)

Building on the implications of this view for management style, Purcell and Ahlstrand (1994) argue that individualism and collectivism are not necessarily polar opposites but rather two dimensions, which when combined, can illustrate ideal types of employee relations management style. According to these authors, individualism refers to:

> the extent to which the enterprise views its employees either as individuals with needs, aspirations, competencies and particular skills of their own, or treats them as homogeneous blocks of people, with personnel and payment policies unable to distinguish between individuals and individual performance.
>
> (Purcell and Ahlstrand, 1994: 179)

Collectivism, on the other hand, is closely related to the pluralist perspective and the question for management is:

> whether to oppose, condone, or encourage the emergence of the collective labour organisation, and to ask what sort of relationship should be developed with it. Pluralism in this sense is about power sources and power sharing.
>
> (Purcell and Ahlstrand, 1994: 183)

Individualism, they suggest, has three distinct points on its dimension. At the lowest level the cost of labour is to be minimised: employees simply have commodity status, to be bought from the external labour market when demand requires and to be shed if demand for services declines. At the top of the scale, employees are regarded as a resource, to be trained and developed accordingly, since greater emphasis is placed on the internal labour market. In between these, Purcell and Ahlstrand suggest a paternalist approach where companies have a tradition of welfare-based policies which seek to elicit loyalty from the employees.

Similarly, the collectivism dimension has three points on its scale. At its lowest point it refers to the classic unitary position of resisting union involvement, with (active) discouragement of employees to form any independent collective grouping. The centre position is characterised as an adversarial one. In the negotiating sense it implies a distributive form of bargaining (*see* Chapter 16) where compromise agreement between exaggerated positions is reached. A cooperative relationship implies a partnership between management and unions where joint, formal and informal approaches are taken to resolve problems between employees and employers. Combining these two dimensions produces a matrix with resulting management styles as shown in Fig. 15.1.

Each of the boxes is given a short title which seeks to capture the essence of the resulting management style. Two of the boxes, however, contain question marks, since Purcell and Ahlstrand argue that these approaches are 'inherently unstable'. In the bottom right-hand corner a situation is posited of collective cooperation but exploitation of the individual – a position that is unlikely to remain viable for any period of time. Similarly, treating employees as a resource (as portrayed in the top middle box) while collective relations are adversarial is likely to be untenable in the long term. Although this model has been criticised, particularly in relation to the stages on the individual dimension (Marchington and Parker, 1990; Storey, 1992b), it does offer a useful analytical framework for understanding the complexity (and possible tensions) of managerial style in employment relations. In particular, Purcell and Ahlstrand recognise the dynamic

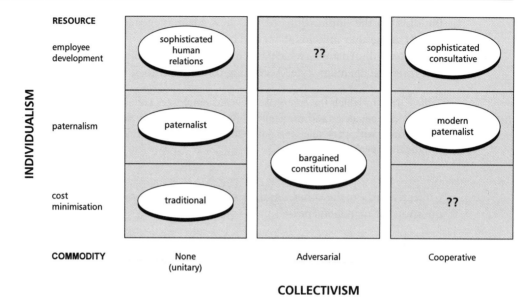

Fig. 15.1   The management style matrix

Source: HRM in the Multi-divisional Company by Purcell and Ahlstrand (1994). Reproduced by permission of Oxford University Press.

nature of the process and suggest that it is possible to use the matrix to trace changes in managerial style. For example, an organisation which de-recognises trade unions and adopts strategies typical of HRM may be seen to be moving from, say, an adversarial to a sophisticated human relations style. On the other hand, the adoption of practices designed to develop the existing workforce while seeking a more cooperative relationship with recognised unions may suggest a move from an adversarial to a sophisticated consultative style.

TRADE UNIONS

The changes evident in the field of employment relations have had far-reaching implications for trade unions. In 1979 some 55 per cent of the workforce were in union membership, collective bargaining was the primary method of determining terms and conditions of employment, and unions were a key party in the development of public policy on economic and social matters as well as on industrial relations itself. Two decades later, union membership had fallen to under one-third of the workforce, collective bargaining covered fewer than half of all employees (Cully *et al.*, 1999) and trade unions had been excluded from the determination of public policy. In part, the reduction in union membership can be attributed to the decline of the UK's manufacturing base where membership was traditionally high (Kessler and Bayliss, 1995). Significantly also, there has been evidence of employers de-recognising trade unions, although the actual extent remains debatable (Gall and McKay, 1994; Beaumont and Harris, 1995). The combination of these factors has led to questions being asked about the future role of trade unions in Britain. However, not all commentators share the view of the inevitability of union decline:

> Given . . . an easing of the hostile political climate and the efforts they themselves are making to expand their organizational capabilities, it seems clear that the trade unions will continue to maintain a presence in the future and may well even expand their influence.
>
> (Bradley *et al.*, 2000: 168)

In this section some of the prescriptions for overcoming the malaise in which unions find themselves will be explored.

Union mergers

Although union membership had been on a generally upward trend throughout the twentieth century until 1979, the number of trade unions had steadily declined, primarily through a process of merger and amalgamation. Since 1979 this has continued and there are now around 250 trade unions recorded by the Certification Officer for Trade Unions and Employers' Associations. This offers one long-term solution for the unions, that is, the creation of a small number of very large, and potentially powerful, unions covering a range of occupations and industries able to negotiate with employers from a position of numerical strength. However, the process to date has been generally *ad hoc* and thus some form of strategic basis, perhaps emanating from the Trades Union Congress, would be needed. As the TUC (1991) notes:

> the underlying motives of most contemporary mergers are defensive, or consolidatory, rather than expansionist . . . the merger process will continue and grow over the next ten years . . . Yet it will not lead to any discernible ideal 'model' or optimum union size . . . [the structure of] British unions will look as illogical and unplanned as before [although] . . . they will be much leaner and fitter; with more effective and improved services. . . .
>
> (in Kessler and Bayliss, 1995: 160)

Willman and Cave (1994) share similar concerns regarding the effectiveness of the merger process and suggest that some significant benefits might be gained through closer collaboration between existing trade unions. However, the trend towards larger unions seems set to continue and it is perhaps within this context that trade unions need to consider their representative role on behalf of workers.

New partnerships

A number of variants of this approach can be discerned (Guest, 1995; Hyman, 1994). This strategy accordingly:

> rests on the belief that economically, politically and socially Britain has, since 1979, gone through a period of fundamental and irreversible historical change. The unions must adjust to it or be marginalised from power and influence. By this view, unions need to accept the changes as permanent and shape their organisations and policies to meet them.
>
> (Farnham and Pimlott, 1995: 115)

This view suggests that unions will need to accept the shift in power towards employers and engage in new forms of relationships with them. In its guise of 'new realism' this might include the acceptance of single-union, no-strike agreements or partnership agreements (*see* Chapter 16).

As organisations adopt HRM techniques (with or without a strategic focus) Guest (1995) argues that unions should champion the cause rather than oppose it. Many of the core elements of HRM, at least in its 'soft' formulation, are compatible with the objectives of trade unions and offer fertile ground for unions, thus:

> By seeking partnership at the company level, unions may work to their own strengths and influence policy at the level where the important issues still seem to be decided. HRM may provide unions with one of their best chances of survival.
>
> (Guest, 1995: 136)

Certainly there is growing evidence that the initial hostility of unions towards HRM is softening and it is being seen as offering new grounds for bargaining.

Friendly society benefits

This strategy requires unions to develop a range of services to their members which may partly reflect the decline in the collectivist dimension in employment. Acceptance of the individualisation of the employment relationship may provide opportunities for unions to offer assistance on individual grievances, disciplinary and dismissal cases, as well as advice to those working on individual contracts. However, services can be offered beyond the immediate workplace:

> The type of facilities that might be provided and which have been discussed at recent union conferences range from banking and insurance, legal advice and travel facilities to social welfare, educational and creche facilities.
>
> (Guest, 1995: 133)

Although the contemporary nature of some services (travel and banking, for instance) may reflect growing affluence, the adoption of the principles of friendly societies is not new to unions. Indeed Webb and Webb (1896) identified the provision of such benefits of 'mutual insurance' as one method used by unions to protect their members' interests. While recognising the wider aspirations of workers, Hyman (1994) suggests caution is needed in terms of the primary function of unions:

> an organisation whose sole or dominant identity is to provide commercial services to discrete customers is not easily recognizable as a trade union.
>
> (Hyman, 1994: 134)

New markets

One further strategy that remains open to trade unions as their traditional membership amongst manual, full-time employees in the manufacturing sector declines, is to seek new membership from amongst new groups of employees. If there is some compatibility between union objectives and 'soft' HRM, then equally there are grounds for arguing that those workers exposed to its 'hard' variant or those treated as 'commodity' status could benefit from union membership. Wrench and Virdee (1996) report the findings of two case studies where trade unions had sought to recruit predominately female ethnic minority workers in low paid, insecure employment. They report limited success and support the argument that:

> the trade union movement has no hope of bringing unionisation to these workers unless it works in co-operation with communities and links unionisation to broader issues such as workplace discrimination, sexual and racial harassment at the workplace, health and safety, cultural, linguistic and religious rights, harassment by the police and immigration authorities and so on.
>
> (Wrench and Virdee, 1996: 273)

Some evidence that these lessons are being recognised by the union movement is shown in the analysis of the Transport and General Workers Union 'Link Up' campaign of the early 1990s (Snape, 1994). This was designed to recruit into membership those groups, including part-time and contract workers, who were traditionally unorganised. Although limited in its success, the campaign had a clearly articulated aim which was:

> to present a positive image to the wider community, playing down the view of unions as representatives of a narrow sectional interest group, linking recruitment with the social aims of the union, and emphasising community as well as workplace involvement.
>
> (Snape, 1994: 231)

The limited success of these initiatives suggests that trade unions have some distance to travel before these elements of the 'peripheral workforce' see any benefits in union membership. In addition, maintaining membership amongst such workers can be difficult for the unions because of the transient nature of these forms of employment. Furthermore, the cost of recruitment and servicing membership is higher where employment is to be found in small firms. Clearly these strategies of structural adjustment, new partnerships, benefits and new membership markets are not mutually exclusive. What they have in common is the need for unions to become more proactive in their approach to recruitment and to demonstrate positively the benefits that unions offer workers and employers.

SUMMARY LEARNING POINTS

1 The past two decades have witnessed radical changes to British employment relations. A series of governments hostile to trade unions and the principle of collective relations have, through legislation and economic and social policy, dramatically weakened trade unions and shifted the power in the employment relationship in favour of management.

2 Following the election of New Labour governments in 1997 and 2001, employment relations have witnessed further changes. It remains unlikely, however, that these will lead to a return to the corporatist approach characteristic of the 1970s.

3 Those managers within organisations responsible for people resourcing decisions will need to consider the impact of legislation providing a national minimum wage and statutory provisions for union recognition.

4 The signing of the Social Chapter by the UK government, together with further directives from Europe, mean that developments in European Social Policy will continue to affect resourcing decisions.

5 Faced with greater choice resulting from the shift in bargaining power in the employment relationship, organisations have been able to adopt an employee relations style which may retain a role for trade unions or signal a move towards a more individualistic relationship.

6 In these circumstances trade unions have been forced to seek new directions for their role as the representative of workers.

REFERENCES AND FURTHER READING

Adam-Smith, D., Goss, D. and Bairstow, S. (2001a) 'Coming to terms with New Labour('s) laws', *Employee Relations Review*, Issue 12, 3–9.

Adam-Smith, D., Norris, G. and Williams, S. (2001b) *The Impact of the National Minimum Wage in the Hospitality Sector: A case study investigation*, a report prepared for the Low Pay Commission, Employment Relations Research Group, Portsmouth Business School.

Auerbach, S. (1990) *Legislating for Conflict*. Oxford: Clarendon Press.

Beatson, M. (1995) 'Progress towards a flexible labour market', *Employment Gazette*, February, 55–66.

Beaumont, P.B. and Harris, R.I.D. (1995) 'Union de-recognition and declining union density in Britain', *Industrial and Labour Relations Review*, 48(3), 389–401.

Blyton, P. and Turnbull, P. (1998) *The Dynamics of Employee Relations*. Basingstoke: Macmillan.

Bradley, H., Erickson, M., Stephenson, C. and Williams, S. (2000) *Myths at Work*. Cambridge: Polity.

Brown, W., Deakin, S., Hudson, M. and Pratten, C. (2001) 'The limits of statutory union recognition', *Industrial Relations Journal*, 32(3), 180–94.

Crouch, C. (1982) *The Politics of Industrial Relations*. London: Fontana.

Crouch, C. (1995) 'The State: economic management and incomes policy' in Edwards, P. (ed.) *Industrial Relations: Theory and practice in Britain*. Oxford: Blackwell.

Cully, M., Woodland, S., O'Reilly, A. and Dix, G. (1999) *Britain at Work: As depicted by the 1998 Workplace Employee Relations Survey*. London: Routledge.

DE (1994) *Employment Gazette*, Historical Supplement (4). London.

Dickens, L. and Hall, M. (1995) 'The State: labour law and industrial relations' in Edwards, P. (ed.) *Industrial Relations: Theory and practice in Britain*. Oxford: Blackwell.

Edwards, P. (1995) 'The employment relationship' in Edwards, P. (ed.) *Industrial Relations: Theory and practice in Britain*. Oxford: Blackwell.

Farnham, D. and Horton, S. (eds) (1993) *Managing the New Public Services*. Basingstoke: Macmillan.

Farnham, D. and Pimlott, J. (1995) *Understanding Industrial Relations*. London: Cassell.

Fox, A. (1966) 'Industrial sociology and industrial relations', *Royal Commission Research Paper No. 3*. London: HMSO.

Fredman, S. and Morris, G. (1989) 'The state as employer: setting a new example', *Personnel Management*, August, 25–9.

Gall, G. and McKay, S. (1994) 'Trade union derecognition in Britain, 1984–1994', *British Journal of Industrial Relations*, 32(3), 433–48.

Giddens, A. (1998) *The Third Way*. Cambridge: Polity.

Gregg, P., Knight, G. and Wadsworth, J. (2000) 'Heaven knows I'm miserable now: job insecurity in the British labour market' in Heery, E. and Salmon, J. (eds) *The Insecure Workforce*. London: Routledge.

Guest, D. (1995) 'Human resource management, trade unions and industrial relations' in Storey, J. (ed.) *Human Resource Management: A critical text*. London: Routledge.

Hall, M. (1994) 'Industrial relations and the social dimension of European integration: before and after Maastricht' in Hyman, R. and Fenner, A. (eds) *New Frontiers in Industrial Relations*. Oxford: Blackwell.

Hartley, J.F. and Stephenson, G.M. (1992) *Employment Relations*. Oxford: Blackwell.

Hyman, R. (1994) 'Changing trade union identities and strategies' in Hyman, R. and Fenner, A. (eds) *New Frontiers in Industrial Relations*. Oxford: Blackwell.

Hyman, R. (1995) 'The historical evolution of British industrial relations' in Edwards, P. (ed.) *Industrial Relations: Theory and practice in Britain*. Oxford: Blackwell.

Kessler, S. and Bayliss, F. (1995) *Contemporary British Industrial Relations*. Basingstoke. Macmillan.

LPC (2001) *The National Minimum Wage: Making a difference*. Third report, volume 1 of the Low Pay Commission. London: HMSO.

Marchington, M. and Parker, P. (1990) *Changing Patterns of Employee Relations*. Hemel Hempstead: Harvester Wheatsheaf.

Millward, N., Bryson, A. and Forth, J. (2000) *All Change at Work? British employment relations 1980–1998, as depicted by the Workplace Industrial Relations Survey series*. London: Routledge.

Nuti, D. (1999) 'Making sense of the third way', *British Strategy Review*, 10(3).

Purcell, J. and Ahlstrand, B. (1994) *Human Resource Management in the Multi-divisional Company*. Oxford: Oxford University Press.

Salamon, M. (1998) *Industrial Relations: Theory and Practice* (3rd edn). Hemel Hempstead: Prentice Hall.

Scott, A. (1994) *Willing Slaves? British Workers Under Human Resource Management*. Cambridge: Cambridge University Press.

Sisson, K. (1991) 'Industrial relations', *Employee Relations*, 13(6), 3–10.

Snape, E. (1994) 'Reversing the decline? the TGWU's link up campaign', *Industrial Relations Journal*, 25(3), 222–33.

Storey, J. (1992a) *Developments in the Management of Human Resources*. Oxford: Blackwell.

Storey, J. (1992b) 'HRM in action: the truth is out at last', *Personnel Management*, April, 28–31.

Storey, J. and Sisson, K. (1993) *Managing Human Resources and Industrial Relations*. Buckingham: Open University Press.

Trades Union Congress (1991) *Unions in Europe in the 1990s*. London: TUC.

Undy, R. (1999) 'Annual review article: New Labour's "Industrial Relations Settlement": the Third Way?', *British Journal of Industrial Relations*, 37(2), 315–36.

Webb, S. and Webb, B. (1896) *The History of Trade Unions*. London: Longman.

Willman, P. and Cave, A. (1994) 'The union of the future: super-unions or joint ventures?', *British Journal of Industrial Relations*, 32(3), 395–412.

Winchester, D. and Bach, S. (1995) 'The state: the public sector' in Edwards, P. (ed.) *Industrial Relations: Theory and practice in Britain*. Oxford: Blackwell.

Wrench, J. and Virdee, S. (1996) 'Organising the unorganised: race, poor work and trade unions' in Ackers, P., Smith, C. and Smith, P. (eds) *The New Workplace and Trade Unionism*. London: Routledge.

Younson, F. (2000) 'How to handle a union recognition claim', *People Management*, 20 July, 44–6.

ASSIGNMENTS AND DISCUSSION TOPICS

1 Choose an organisation (or organisations) with which you are familiar or whose employment matters have been documented in the press, and assess what style of employment relations management (*see* Fig. 15.1) has been adopted. You should identify specific illustrations for both the collective and individual dimensions. Is there any evidence that management are attempting to change their style? If so, how are they changing and for what reasons?

2 Do trade unions still have a role in contemporary employment relations or are they an institution which is past its 'sell by date'? Why?

3 What benefits do employers gain from recognising trade unions as the representative of employees?

4 Has the balance of power in the employment relationship swung too far in favour of management?

5 Has the current role of the state reached an appropriate level of involvement in employment relations? If not, how and why should it change?

6 Is the statutory trade union recognition procedure a defence of the human rights of workers or an unnecessary and intrusive interference of managers' right to manage?

7 Should workers be given a legal right to strike?

8 Assess the advantages and disadvantages for employers, trade unions and employees of the National Minimum Wage.

9 To what extent, and for what reasons, is it now more appropriate to talk about *European* employment relations rather than British employment relations?

CHAPTER 16

Employment relations processes

by Derek Adam-Smith

INTRODUCTION

The previous chapter explored some of the ways in which the British context of employment relations has changed over the past two decades and the responses of both employers and trade unions to the new environment within which they operate. As a result of these developments the processes of employment relations, particularly the structure of collective bargaining, have been modified to meet new organisational circumstances and objectives. At the same time new approaches to managing the employment relationship have been introduced. Nonetheless it is possible to detect some continuity in the way in which decisions over the wage for work bargain are made.

CHAPTER OBJECTIVES

- To raise awareness of the role of employment relations procedures in the effective resourcing of the organisation.

- To develop an understanding of the structure of collective bargaining in Britain and the ways in which it is changing.

- To consider some recent initiatives in both individual and collective employment relations.

- To explore the nature and process of employment relations negotiations.

EMPLOYMENT RELATIONS POLICIES AND PEOPLE RESOURCING

Employment relations issues can be viewed as one particular aspect of the broader decisions that relate to the effective resourcing of organisations with people. Decisions regarding the recognition of trade unions and the way in which that relationship is structured, how non-union employees' terms and conditions will be determined, and the relevance and choice of forms of communication and involvement should logically flow from the broader human resourcing policies pursued by the organisation. The clear message is that in order to provide for consistency there needs to be a framework of general principles within the organisation to aid managers in day-to-day decision making. At the same time, a codified employment relations policy can be evaluated continuously to ensure its appropriateness as internal and external circumstances change.

However, employment policies do not operate in isolation from other parts of the business. Almost 30 years ago the Commission on Industrial Relations argued that an organisation's strategy for the management of people at work should flow from and be closely allied to its overall business strategy (CIR, 1973). The advent of Human Resource Management (HRM) as an alternative conceptualisation of the employment relationship proposes a greater emphasis on the need for organisations to integrate employment and business policies. Commenting upon the movement from formalisation and collectivism to flexibility and individualism implicit within the HRM model, Salamon notes that:

> this shift . . . has been the product of a strategic review by management of its industrial relations system to meet external pressures and constraints (in particular its economic environment) and, not least, to support and integrate more closely with its business objectives.

(Salamon, 1998: 455)

However, there is a substantial body of research which suggests that the approach of many organisations to the management of people remains pragmatic and opportunistic (Marginson *et al.*, 1988; Legge, 1995).

Where there is some form of proactive organisational policy for employment relations Salamon (1998) suggests that the issues requiring consideration can be grouped under five headings.

Managerial principles – Primary importance here is the issue of the managerial prerogative, that is, the extent to which management seeks freedom of action to make operational decisions. If there is a policy not to recognise trade unions then the only constraint affecting management is that contained in legal provisions. Even if unions are recognised then management may seek to limit formally the matters which will be subject to collective bargaining. In addition, employers may seek to ensure that they retain the right for managers to communicate directly with employees rather than through trade union channels.

The relationship between management and employees – The second group of issues is concerned with the extent to which employees are valued as an asset of the organisation, their right to be treated fairly in grievance and disciplinary matters, and their right to join a trade union. The basis on which trade unions will be recognised may form part of such considerations.

The determination of terms and conditions of employment – Issues to be addressed here include the development of equitable payment systems, the relationship between productivity and terms of employment, the use of collective bargaining, consultation and other mechanisms for dealing with employment matters.

Meeting mutual expectations – The application of appropriate methods of human resource planning, recruitment, training, motivation, promotion and termination which will achieve an appropriate balance between organisational requirements for a trained and experienced workforce with employees' needs for employment security.

The role of procedures – The use of procedures, perhaps developed with employee and/or trade union involvement, to resolve effectively employment differences between the parties.

Clearly the content of any organisation's employment relations policy will vary depending upon a number of factors. These include technological and economic circumstances, ownership (public service or private profit-making), organisation size amd market and business objectives.

It is of some significance that, while noting their belief that improvements had been made in employment relations in the 1980s, the Institute of Personnel and Development argued that:

> evidence can be found of a rising sense of grievance amongst people at work ... [it] shows that the level of confidence in top management and their handling of relations with employees particularly in generating trust has suffered, and the extent to which people feel involved in decisions that matter to them has lessened ... insecurity has damaged people's commitment.
>
> (IPD, 1996; *see also* Chapter 1)

Thus, according to this account, the changes evident in employment relations have not, of themselves, produced a more harmonious working environment. However, the processes which are utilised to meet policy objectives and the way in which they are operated may still be influential. An understanding of the choices open to organisations is consequently of importance to managers responsible for people resourcing decisions.

COLLECTIVE BARGAINING STRUCTURE

Collective bargaining may be defined as the method of determining terms and conditions of employment through the process of negotiation between representatives of employers (normally management) and employees (typically trade union officials). It is thus a method of 'joint' decision making which implies a need for agreement to be reached between the two negotiating parties. The outcomes of such negotiations are termed collective agreements. While there is little doubt that collective bargaining has declined over the past two decades, around a third of all employees working in establishments with 25 or more employees still have their terms and conditions of employment determined in this way (in 1984 the figure was over 70 per cent) (Cully *et al.*, 1999: 106). As Millward *et al.* (2000: 185) point out:

> ... collective bargaining covers fewer employees within workplaces where it exists and ... collective bargaining has ceased to be the dominant form of pay determination in the economy as a whole.

Beneath this overall decline, however, lie some important changes in the way in which employers have sought to tailor their collective bargaining arrangements more closely to their business objectives. How organisations have restructured their employment relations can be usefully explored through the changes that have occurred in bargaining structure. The term bargaining structure comprises a number of interrelated elements (Parker *et al.*, 1971) which help explain the different arrangements which may be found in organisations – 'bargaining levels', 'units' and 'agents' and 'scope'.

The first element is the 'level', or levels, at which bargaining takes place. This may involve multi-employer bargaining between employers' associations and trade unions at industry level and produce national collective agreements. While still common in much of the public sector, the use of multi-employer bargaining in the private sector has declined in importance. Bargaining may also take place at the company level or at the level of the establishment (in multi-plant organisations). Of course, an employer's choice is not confined to only one level. An employee's terms of employment may be made up of elements from national, company and establishment agreements. For example, the national agreement may set minimum rates of pay but these may be enhanced as a result of bargaining at the establishment level for employees working at that particular plant. Where a firm does not belong to an employers' organisation, bargaining may take place at either company level or at establishment level or both. Where establishment level negotiations take place these may be conducted within limits set by the organisation's head office.

The second element is the bargaining 'unit' or units and the bargaining 'agent'. The bargaining unit refers to the group of employees covered by a particular agreement or set of agreements and may vary in number from industry to industry and from company to company. There may be one set of agreements for skilled and craft workers, one for operative staff, another covering clerical and administrative employees and a further unit for supervisory staff. The bargaining agent identifies the trade union or unions that represent employees in the bargaining unit. Where only one union is recognised by the employer for a particular category of staff there will be a single bargaining agent within the unit; in multi-union companies there may be a greater number of agents for each unit. A firm's bargaining arrangements may be more complex where negotiations take place at both company and establishment level. For example, in a multi-plant firm if holiday entitlement is negotiated for all employees then there is only one bargaining unit within the company for that matter. However, if a bonus scheme is negotiated at plant level there may be a large number of bargaining units covering each group of workers.

The final element in the bargaining structure concerns the 'scope' of collective bargaining. This refers to the subject matter covered by the collective agreements. Again, the content of collective agreements will vary from organisation to organisation and, perhaps, within different bargaining units. While pay rates are common items covered by negotiation, a wide range of other topics may also be the subject of collective bargaining. These include hours of work, staffing levels, physical working conditions, the introduction of new technology and redundancy matters. The broad strategy of trade unions is to extend the scope of collective bargaining by seeking to negotiate over an increased range of topics, while management may wish to limit the matters which are subject to joint regulation. Where the scope of collective bargaining ends, the right to manage, or the managerial prerogative, begins. Thus the degree of managerial resistance to the extension of collective bargaining will depend upon the wish to make decisions without obtaining trade union agreement.

TRENDS IN COLLECTIVE BARGAINING

As a dynamic process it is likely that the arrangements for collective bargaining will change over time to take account of new circumstances. As bargaining power has swung in favour of management there have been managerial initiatives to tailor bargaining structures more closely to business objectives. As far as the scope of non-pay-related matters is concerned, there appears to be little major change in the topics over which bargaining took place during the 1990s. Although there was a slight fall in the number of workplaces where recruitment and working hours appeared on the bargaining agenda, there was an increase in the proportion that bargained with unions over the size of redundancy payments (Millward *et al.*, 2000: 168). However, given the importance of pay rates to employers operating in a competitive environment, the level at which pay is determined provides a good indication of employers' policy on collective bargaining arrangements, bargaining levels being the feature of bargaining structure most amenable to managerial influence.

The trends in the decline of collective bargaining as the source of employees' pay rates and in the level at which these are set are clearly shown in data drawn from the Workplace Industrial Relations Survey series (Millward *et al.*, 2000: 185–96). The data covers workplaces with 25 or more employees and identifies collective bargaining as the most common method of pay determination if at least 50 per cent of workers at a workplace were covered by this method. The overall pattern for the years in which the surveys have been conducted, 1984, 1990 and 1998, is shown in Exhibit 16.1.

Exhibit 16.1 Main method or level of pay determination in workplaces, 1984–1998
(rounded percentages – excludes small number of 'don't knows')

	1984	1990	1998
Not collective bargaining	40	58	71
Result of collective bargaining	60	42	29
Of which most important level:			
Multi-employer	41	23	13
Multi-site, single employer	12	14	12
Workplace	5	4	3

Source: Millward *et al.* (2000).

The most notable conclusion to be drawn is the decline in collective bargaining as the primary method of pay determination. Over the 14-year period it has fallen by a half, from 60 per cent in 1984 to just 29 per cent in 1998. Where collective bargaining remains the dominant method of pay determination it is significant that multi-employer bargaining has shown a similar dramatic decline, from 41 per cent in 1984 through 23 per cent in 1990 to only 13 per cent in the most recent survey. It would appear, then, that joint determination as a means of settling pay rates is likely to remain a minority method and that where it continues it is subject to much greater autonomy at the level of the employer.

In order to explore in more detail the factors affecting this decline, it is instructive to consider the changes that have occurred in each of the three main sectors of the economy: private-sector manufacturing and extraction, private-sector services, and the public sector. Comparable data for each is shown in Exhibits 16.2, 16.3 and 16.4.

Exhibit 16.2   Main method or level of pay determination in private-sector manufacturing workplaces, 1984–1998
(rounded percentages – excludes small number of 'don't knows')

	1984	1990	1998
Not collective bargaining	50	67	77
Result of collective bargaining	50	33	23
Of which most important level:			
Multi-employer	21	12	6
Multi-site, single employer	11	6	5
Workplace	17	14	12

Source: Millward *et al.* (2000).

As Exhibit 16.2 shows, in private-sector manufacturing the decline in collective bargaining followed a similar pattern to that experienced throughout the economy as a whole. In 1984 it was the dominant form of pay determination in one-half of all workplaces. By 1990 its incidence had fallen to one-third, and to under one-quarter by the time of the 1998 survey. Of those workplaces that continued to use collective bargaining to determine pay, significant changes can be seen in the level at which negotiations took place. In 1984 multi-employer bargaining accounted for over 40 per cent of these agreements but by 1998 this had fallen to 27 per cent. According to Millward *et al.* (2000: 188):

> The decline in the importance of multi-employer bargaining over this period reflects the demise of national agreements in industries such as engineering, textiles and cement manufacture; it represents the continuation of trends that began soon after the Second World War . . .

During the same period, however, there was a similar *increase* in importance of workplace or establishment level bargaining. In 1984 this accounted for around one-third of workplaces that utilised collective bargaining to determine pay, but by 1998 this proportion had grown to over one-half (53 per cent).

The picture in private-sector services (Exhibit 16.3) shows that collective bargaining has always been a minority method for pay determination and, reflecting the general trend, has continued to decline in importance.

Exhibit 16.3 Main method or level of pay determination in private-sector service workplaces, 1984–1998

(rounded percentages – excludes small number of 'don't knows')

	1984	1990	1998
Not collective bargaining	64	71	86
Result of collective bargaining	36	29	14
Of which most important level:			
Multi-employer	17	8	3
Multi-site, single employer	14	19	10
Workplace	3	2	1

Source: Millward *et al*. (2000).

In 1984 it was the dominant method in a little over one-third of workplaces and had shown a slight fall in the following six years to 29 per cent, a figure not dissimilar to that for private-sector manufacturing. However, by the time of the most recent survey only 14 per cent of workplaces jointly determined pay for the majority of employees, marking a significant decline in this method. According to Millward *et al*. (2000: 192) this decline was particularly pronounced in two sectors, retail and banking. Where collective bargaining remained the dominant method this is increasingly at the organisational level, rising from around 40 per cent of workplaces in 1984 to 70 per cent in 1998.

Compared to the private sector, collective bargaining remains the primary method of pay determination in the public sector as Exhibit 16.4 shows. Even here, however, some notable changes have occurred.

Exhibit 16.4 Main method or level of pay determination in public-sector workplaces, 1984–1998

(rounded percentages – excludes small number of 'don't knows')

	1984	1990	1998
Not collective bargaining	6	29	37
Result of collective bargaining	94	71	63
Of which most important level:			
Multi-employer	82	58	39
Multi-site, single employer	11	12	23
Workplace	0	0	1

Source: Millward *et al*. (2000).

For the majority of employees in 1984 collective bargaining was almost the sole means of pay determination, being the main method in 94 per cent of workplaces. During the following 14 years this proportion declined to 71 per cent in 1990 and to 63 per cent in the 1998 survey. This fall is largely accounted for by the establishment of pay review bodies for many health professionals and schoolteachers, which removed the determination of these workers' pay (but not other terms and conditions of employment) by collective bargaining (Millward *et al.*, 2000: 194). Unlike the private sector, where pay negotiations with trade unions remains dominant, the use of multi-employer bargaining continues to be the most common level, albeit of declining importance. Nonetheless, there is evidence of a rise in organisational level bargaining, trebling in importance from around 11 per cent in 1984 to over one-third in 1998. The main factors accounting for this shift appear to be the moves to decentralise negotiations to trust-level in the National Health Service and the reorganisation of many civil service functions into semi-autonomous agencies (Millward *et al.*, 2000: 195).

The ability of employers to shift the level of collective bargaining much closer to operational decision making has been facilitated by the declining power of trade unions discussed in the previous chapter. The main driving force behind the move to decentralised bargaining appears to be the need for management to tailor their pay policies and decisions more closely to wider organisational considerations which are themselves influenced by contextual factors (IRRR, 1989; Brown and Walsh, 1991). Thus where decisions over production, marketing and budgets have been decentralised, it is likely that managers at the business unit will take some responsibility for pay negotiations and other employment relations issues, albeit within limits set by higher management (Purcell, 1989). Where bargaining has been located at lower levels in the organisations, unit managers are able to relate pay decisions to particular business circumstances, including the performance of the unit, productivity improvements and local labour market characteristics.

Multi-employer versus decentralised bargaining

An explanation for the continuation of multi-employer bargaining in the private sector and the criteria that may influence multi-plant organisations in deciding whether to choose company or plant-level collective bargaining is offered by Towers (1992) who suggests that the maintenance of national agreements may be beneficial in industries that have the following characteristics:

- a large number of relatively small companies which are geographically concentrated
- strong competitive pressures
- high trade union membership and labour costs.

In these circumstances he suggests that:

> Small employers with limited time, resources and expertise are attracted by bargaining arrangements which secure negotiating skills, limit the influence of unions in the workplace, reduce vulnerability to competitive pay pressures in circumstances of labour intensity and set industry-wide standards.

(Towers, 1992: 5)

In those cases where (typically large) employers have withdrawn from national agreements, they face a choice over whether each plant should bargain separately with trade unions or whether to locate bargaining at the corporate level. Towers (1992) suggested criteria for this decision and these are shown in Exhibit 16.5.

Exhibit 16.5 Organisational criteria favouring company and plant-level bargaining

Criterion	Company-level bargaining	Plant-level bargaining
Company product/service	single product/service	multi-product/service
Product market	stable	unstable
Organisation structure	centralised	multi-divisional
Organisational functions	preference for centralised functions	preference for decentralised functions
Terms and conditions of employment	standardised across operations	decentralised across operations
Negotiating parties	preference for national trade union officials	preference for shop stewards

Source: 'Choosing bargaining levels: UK experience and implications' by Towers (1992), *Issues in People Management*. Reproduced by permission of the Chartered Institute of Personnel and Development.

While these criteria provide a useful guide to decision making, it must be remembered that the features identified may not simply fall under one of the headings. For example, an organisation may have a single product or service but be operating in an unstable market. Equally, the operation of two-tier organisational bargaining, where some subjects may be negotiated at the company level while others may be dealt with at the unit or plant level, has also been noted (Millward *et al.*, 2000). Nonetheless, it does provide a useful initial guide for managers in deciding the appropriate level for collective bargaining. What emerges from this overview of bargaining levels is that of a highly heterogeneous pattern where different employers make policy decisions based upon their assessment of a multiple and complex range of internal and external variables. The recent changes apparent in Britain suggest that employers are more carefully considering the relationship between collective bargaining and employment and business policies.

Single-table bargaining

Movements in the level of collective bargaining to a point closer to where other operational decisions are made are one illustration of managerial attempts to regain control over employment relations' processes. However, collective bargaining arrangements are more complex where a number of bargaining units exist within an organisation. In these cases managers may find themselves having to negotiate separate pay increases with several different bargaining agents. Not only does this take time and involve repetitive meetings, but it may also be difficult for managers to coordinate the outcomes of a series of negotiations. In part these difficulties have been eased by the continuing process of merger and amalgamation of unions, but there is evidence that managers have sought additional ways to reduce the number of bargaining groups with which they have to deal (Millward *et al.*, 2000).

One managerial initiative aimed at securing simplified bargaining structures in multi-union firms is to introduce a single negotiating forum for all employees, manual and non-manual, covered by collective bargaining – an arrangement that has been called 'single-table bargaining' (STB). Although potentially strengthening the bargaining position of recognised trade unions and making the consequences of any industrial action far more serious, it appears that the advantages resulting from simplified bargaining arrangements and the prevention of 'leapfrogging' claims – as one bargaining group seeks to maintain its differential over another – outweigh these disadvantages. In a review of a number of companies that had introduced single-table bargaining, Incomes Data Services (IDS, 1995) found that, although often linked to major organisational change, there was no one specific reason for their introduction. Among those cited by companies were:

- a move to decentralised pay bargaining providing the impetus to simplify the negotiating process
- the breakdown of national bargaining arrangements creating a vacuum which allowed employers to establish STB
- a need to survive in increasingly competitive markets prompting a review of working practices and STB being seen as a means to facilitate their introduction
- a blurring in the distinction first, between many manual jobs, and second, between white collar and manual work
- the move to STB being part of a policy to harmonise terms and conditions of employment (*see* Chapter 10).

There is strong evidence of an increase in the move to STB amongst many employers as part of a strategy to simplify bargaining arrangements:

> This type of arrangement became much more common between 1990 and 1998. Amongst workplaces where collective bargaining was the dominant form of pay setting, the proportion with single-table bargaining rose from 40 per cent in 1990 to 77 per cent in 1998. This shift, most marked in the public sector, but still very apparent in the private sector, *possibly represents one of the most striking changes in the nature of British industrial relations in the 1990s.*

> (Millward *et al.*, 2000: 203, emphasis added)

Trade unions appear broadly in favour of single-table bargaining, certainly in preference to single-union deals, since it may offer opportunities to widen the scope of collective bargaining. However, the process requires the unions to reach a consensus on their claim before meeting management, and this may prove difficult if each union has different priorities for the negotiations.

New-style collective agreements

A further attempt by managers to recast collective employment relationships has been through the introduction of 'new style agreements' (NSAs). Sometimes called 'no-strike' or 'single-union' agreements after two of their more controversial elements, NSAs emerged during the 1980s, particularly on 'greenfield' sites. They have been heralded as the prototype for the 'New Industrial Relations' which would replace the conflict-ridden era of the 1960s and 1970s (*see* Bassett, 1986; Wickens, 1987). For supporters of these agreements, the single-union deal:

> conjures up an image of modern and progressive industrial relations, allowing for responsible trade unionism within an institutional framework conducive to efficiency and profitability.
>
> (Lewis, 1990)

Part of the reason for the optimism such agreements attract can be seen in the features that typically go to make up the agreement. These are:

- the granting by an employer of sole bargaining rights to one trade union for all employees who wish representation
- a clause in the agreement which bans strikes (and other industrial action) where agreement on substantive issues cannot be reached, thus offering the tantalising possibility of 'strike free' employment relations
- the use of pendulum arbitration to resolve issues where there has been a failure to agree (*see* page 399)
- single-status for manual and non-manual employees where all terms and conditions except pay are common to all staff
- a comprehensive communication and consultation system with a company or works council as the key forum
- labour flexibility with traditional demarcation between jobs abolished, supported by clear training and retraining programmes and with pay linked to skills.

In a survey of 37 organisations which had concluded a new style agreement, IRS (1993) report that the most common motive amongst employers for introducing such an agreement was the avoidance of multi-unionism within the enterprise. It was anticipated that the adoption of a non-union stance would lead to recognition claims and that concluding an NSA at the outset would allow an agreement to be made on more favourable terms for management. Other reasons cited included consistency with single-status arrangements, securing greater flexibility and higher commitment from employees, a simplified bargaining process, and the maintenance of competitive advantage in the marketplace.

However, Gall (1993) points out that of the 194 agreements that he was able to identify, 180 had been signed before 1990. In assessing the reasons for their more recent decline, he suggests the following as significant factors:

- the reduction in investment as a result of the world recession, meaning that there were few 'greenfield' sites being constructed
- a major group of employers introducing NSAs being Japanese companies who had completed their inward investment in the UK in advance of the Single European Market established in 1992
- the growth in single-table bargaining and its attendant advantages having obviated the need for NSAs in 'brownfield' sites
- dissatisfaction over the results amongst some unions who were prominent signatories of NSAs.

What then of the significance of NSAs in terms of their impact on employers and trade unions? While much attention has been given to the first three features of the package (single-union representation and the no-strike and pendulum arbitration clauses), it is perhaps 'the comprehensive nature of the new style agreements which accounts for their claimed success' (Burrows, 1986: 68). Implicit here is the need for employers to invest in their employees, provide effective channels of communication and consultation, and offer 'good' terms and conditions of employment. To this extent they reflect a style of management consistent with a sophisticated consultative approach (*see* Chapter 15). Gall's (1993) research suggests that the NSAs signed by the time of his research covered some 220 000 employees. This amounts to only about 1 per cent of the total British workforce and less than 3 per cent of all trade union members. Numerically NSAs are not particularly significant. What must be recognised is that, through them, some major British trade unions have accepted the principle of 'no-strike' deals and have been prepared to sign an agreement which excludes from the company other unions that may have a legitimate claim to recruit workers in the firm. Thus their significance may lie in the political importance of their key features.

Partnership agreements

In the past few years another development in the collective relationship between employers and trade unions has emerged – that of partnership agreements. Although there is considerable debate over the precise meaning of partnership in this context (Tailby and Winchester, 2000), the key elements appear to be a commitment from employees and unions to greater flexibility in working practices in return for improved employment security. Three main drivers for the development of this approach can be identified. First, the Labour government's attempt to find a formulation of its 'Third Way' (*see* Chapter 15) appropriate to workplace relations. Second, the need of trade unions to demonstrate to employers that they continue to have a valuable role to play in the changed world of employment. Third, where employers had chosen to maintain a relationship with recognised trade unions, they have sought ways in which this relationship could assist in enhancing their competitiveness.

An understanding of the principles of partnership at work can be gleaned from the views of the Trades Union Congress (Monks, 1998) and the Involvement and Participation Association (Guest and Pecci, 1998), an organisation with a long history of promoting partnership and involvement at work. Although there are some differences in emphasis between the two bodies, the key principles can be summarised as follows: employment security for workers and workforce flexibility, appropriate training, informing and consulting employees, employee representation, and sharing of organisational success. In assessing the evidence so far on partnership agreements in practice, Tailby and Winchester (2000) point out that while their content is not radically different from existing employment relations and HRM practices, the process of negotiating such agreements contains some atypical features. These include joint management and union presentations to employees and workplace representatives, the use of outside consultants to assist in developing the framework of the agreement, and a focus on longer-term horizons. They go on to state:

In combination, these features of different phases of the negotiation process amount to the most distinctive characteristic of recent partnership agreements. In many cases, the language and rhetoric of agreements, and the close involvement of trade union officials in the management and legitimation of organizational culture-change programmes, imply an ideological break with past practice.

(Tailby and Winchester, 2000: 383–4)

Whether partnership agreements herald a new permanent basis for collective relationships or are merely the latest 'fad' will require the judgement of time. It is important to note, however, that embarking on such an approach requires significant senior management commitment and a change in management style. As one full-time union officer, involved in developing a partnership approach at a company, commented: 'I don't think our members should fear it, but, I mean, you can't have 150 years of the gaffer putting the boot in and then all of a sudden expect everybody to flip over' (Marks *et al.*, 1998: 218).

CONCILIATION, MEDIATION AND ARBITRATION

A key assumption of the negotiating process is that the two parties will reach an agreement to resolve the differences between them. However, it must be recognised that there will be circumstances where management and trade union representatives will not find a mutually acceptable solution and will register 'a failure to agree'. In these cases, conciliation, mediation and arbitration can be used as an alternative to industrial action. Each involves the introduction of a third party to assist in the resolution of the dispute. The differences in the three processes are shown in Exhibit 16.6.

The key distinction is between conciliation and arbitration. In the former the conciliator seeks to help the parties negotiate their solution to the dispute, while the use of arbitration suggests that the negotiators are unable to resolve the matter themselves and request a third party to decide on the issue. Mediation can be seen to be something of a 'halfway house' between the other two.

Pendulum arbitration

As interest has grown in NSAs attention has focused on the role that pendulum arbitration can play in the resolution of disputes. In conventional arbitration the arbitrator may make an award anywhere between the management offer and union claim at the point at which the negotiations broke down. However, in pendulum arbitration the arbitrator is required to find in favour of either the company or the trade union: a compromise solution is not allowed. Such a process, it is claimed, provides a strong incentive for both parties to reach a negotiated settlement rather than lose their case at arbitration: at least their respective final positions will be reasonable and equitable. In addition, should pendulum arbitration be used, the parties' final offer and final claim are likely to be fairly close so that neither is substantially dissatisfied with the award made (Burrows, 1986).

Exhibit 16.6   Third party dispute resolution

	Role	Approach to dispute resolution	How settlement reached
CONCILIATOR	'A CATALYST' seeking to narrow disagreements	Support negotiating process: help parties clarify objectives, extent of differences, identify possible solutions and find formulae to settle dispute; keep the parties talking	Responsibility for settlement rests jointly with the parties to the dispute
MEDIATOR	'A PROPOSER' of recommendations	More proactive approach than conciliation; from assessment of parties' written cases mediator makes proposals which may resolve dispute or provide basis for further negotiation	Responsibility with parties but mediator's views may be influential
ARBITRATOR	'An AWARD-MAKER' to end a dispute	Arbitrator (or panel of arbitrators) have agreed terms of reference from parties; take written and oral evidence and make an award based on the issues	Arbitrator decides on resolution of dispute; award usually binding on both parties

There are, however, some difficulties associated with the process, including the following.

- If bargaining has not proceeded in 'good faith' then the arbitrator may be forced to choose between two unreasonable positions.

- There may be some difficulty in clarifying the precise final positions of the two parties – can these be changed between the breakdown of negotiations and submission of the reference to the arbitrator?

- Where a dispute concerns a group of items, deciding on one package may mean that the merits of each individual item are ignored. However, allowing the arbitrator to deal with each issue would mean that the arbitrator is producing his or her own package, thus undermining the key principle of pendulum arbitration.

There seems to be little evidence of the widespread adoption of pendulum arbitration in Britain. It can be argued, however, that pendulum arbitration forces a more realistic view to be taken by both management and unions and provides an alternative to industrial action in dispute resolution.

Exhibit 16.7   Back to the future?

In an engineering company in the north-east of Britain that signed a New Style Agreement with the General, Municipal and Boilermakers Union, pendulum arbitration had been used on five occasions to determine the annual pay awards when no negotiated settlement could be reached. Four of the five arbitrators' decisions had gone in favour of the trade union. Dissatisfied with this position management gave notice of their intention to end the agreement. The union's response was to threaten industrial action to protect the 'no-strike' agreement!

Source: The Independent, 30 August 1991.

THE NON-UNION ORGANISATION

While collective bargaining remains an important method of conducting employment relations in the public sector and much of private manufacturing industry, its relative decline has led to attention being focused on the way in which relations are conducted in non-union organisations. A number of these organisations are small, independent companies in which employment terms and working conditions are often poor: what Sisson (1993) characterised as 'bleak houses' (*see also* Goss, 1991). However, growing interest has been shown in what Beaumont (1987) has called the 'household name' group of companies. These organisations, held up as examples of an alternative model for the conduct of employment relations, include IBM, Marks and Spencer, Hewlett Packard and Mars. Although recognising the possibility of over-generalisation, according to Blyton and Turnbull (1998) the characteristics of these non-union firms tend:

> to be a sense of caring, carefully chosen plant locations and working environments, market leadership, high growth and healthy profits, employment security, single status, promotion from within, an influential personnel department (and a high ratio of personnel staff to employees), competitive pay and benefit packages, profit sharing, open communications, and the careful selection and training of management, particularly at the supervisory level.
>
> (Blyton and Turnbull, 1998: 252)

In such firms there would appear to be evidence that the techniques associated with HRM are not only present but provide a clear guide to the development of employment policy and practice. It would seem, therefore, that each stage of Purcell and Ahlstrand's (1994) individualism axis – traditional unitary, paternalism and sophisticated human relations (*see* Chapter 15) – can be found in the non-union organisation.

In an attempt to expand on the nature of employment relations in the non-union firm, Guest and Hoque (1994) characterise such organisations as 'good', 'bad', 'ugly' and 'lucky' employers. Their distinction is based on whether the firm has a clear strategy for managing its human resources or not and the extent to which it operates a range of human resource policies, such as employee involvement schemes, performance related pay and sophisticated recruitment, selection and socialisation practices. 'Good' firms both have a clear human resources (HR) strategy and make extensive use of HR policies designed to provide employees with an alternative to trade union membership: in this sense HRM is used as a substitute for trade unions. Such companies would be typified by the 'household names' identified by Beaumont (1987) above. Neither 'bad' nor 'ugly' organisations would provide much, if anything, by way of HR policies. Such firms are often suppliers to larger businesses and typically compete on price and thus would consider the cost of such practices to be not viable. Their non-union status would thus derive from the belief that unions would limit flexibility and seek to push up wages, so threatening their survival. The distinction between them is that 'ugly' firms, unlike 'bad' ones, would have an HR strategy based on treating labour as a commodity, perhaps indicative of the 'hard' Human Resource Management approach. 'Lucky' firms are those without a strategy that may well have some practices that have been introduced on a piecemeal basis. There is therefore little by way of sophisticated HR management but equally no attempt to manage by fear. Thus their non-union position arises through luck rather than by deliberate management practice.

It would seem, then, that the picture of employment relations in non-union organisations is complex. While some companies appear to be following 'best practice' and have utilised HRM approaches as a means of investing in their employees as a resource, in others the more negative connotations of 'resource exploitation' seem more appropriate (*see also* Chapter 1).

PERSONAL CONTRACTS

All employees have an individual contract of employment, but where trade unions are recognised by the employer pay and some other terms of employment may be determined through collective bargaining. In such cases the terms of the collective agreement or agreements are incorporated into the employee's contract of employment. However, in keeping with the growing 'individualisation' of the employment relationship, greater use is being made of what have become known as 'personal contracts' to replace collectively determined contractual terms. Although most commonly used for managers and professional staff, they are also being applied to clerical and manual workers, for example in oil refining and distribution, and the docks. According to a report by Incomes Data Services:

> A personal contract is usually understood to be a contract that bypasses one or more elements of an existing union agreement. All future terms and conditions are expected to be settled on an individual basis between the employee and employer.
>
> (IDS, 1992: 20)

Where a personal contract has been accepted by a manager in return for giving up collective representation rights, it is usually accompanied by an improved benefits package and any future pay increases are normally linked to a performance review scheme.

Incomes Data Services note that, although the use of such contracts has expanded into the private sector, the main impact has been in the public sector and the newly privatised utilities, where managerial unionism has been traditionally strongest. The primary motive for their introduction is to provide management with greater flexibility and control in the employment relationship. For British Telecom the objective of introducing personal contracts to middle managers was:

> to identify them more fully with the management team and provide flexibility in remuneration which would facilitate the recruitment, retention and motivation of good quality people. [Collective bargaining] does not provide the flexibility to relate each individual's package to performance and/or marketplace.

> (IDS, 1992: 22)

While there may be some benefits for those who sign personal contracts, there are a number of disadvantages. These include the loss of trade union representation in employment matters, the need to work more flexible (often longer and more elastic) hours, a tighter monitoring of performance and the loss of influence over pay and conditions.

CONTEMPORARY APPROACHES TO EMPLOYEE INVOLVEMENT

As an employee relations process, employee involvement (EI) differs from collective bargaining in that the latter is a joint power-sharing strategy in which trade unions are incorporated into the organisational decision-making process. EI practices, on the other hand, are rarely trade union-based, are primarily concerned with building employee commitment to the organisation and offer little by way of shared decision-making. Thus

> the last decade has seen a renaissance of business interest in improving communications with and the involvement of employees at work. These 'new' employee involvement initiatives have been much more management sponsored than in the past, and as a result they have been more concerned with employee motivation and commitment to organisational objectives and performance than with issues of joint job regulation and power-sharing at enterprise level.

> (Marchington et al., 1992: 1)

Although serious doubts have been raised concerning the ability of EI techniques to deliver increased employee commitment to the organisation (Goss, 1994) and the extent to which employee expectations and business objectives are being met through such initiatives (Kessler and Undy, 1996), there is evidence to suggest that techniques associated with employee involvement have grown in both importance and scope over recent years (Millward et al., 2000). While employee involvement takes a variety of forms it can, according to Marchington (1995), be categorised into five groups: downward communication, upward problem-solving, task participation, consultation and representative participation, and financial participation.

Downward communication

In this form EI is characterised as a means by which management provides information to employees in order to develop their understanding of managerial plans and objectives. Such means include formal and informal communications between managers and their staff, employee reports, company newspapers, videos and annual presentations to employees by senior executives. Team briefings, used by many organisations, are regular meetings between supervisors and their work group at which primarily local but also wider organisational information is communicated to employees.

Upward problem-solving

This group of techniques is designed to utilise the knowledge and opinions of employees, either as individuals or in small groups. Marchington (1995) suggests that:

> These techniques have several objectives, such as to increase the stock of ideas within an organisation, to encourage cooperative relations at work, and to legitimise change.
>
> (Marchington, 1995: 283)

Suggestion schemes have a long history in Britain but they have seen a resurgence in recent years. Here, employees who have made a suggestion for improved performance or cost savings may receive a financial reward from the organisation. Total Quality Management (*see* Chapter 21) and quality circles are strategies which Japanese experience suggested might assist British companies in their search for improved quality and competitive advantage. Attitude surveys are a structured means to explore the opinions and views of employees on work and employment issues. Employee willingness to participate is likely to be conditional upon whether management are expected to act upon the feedback received.

Task participation

This third approach focuses upon schemes designed to encourage employees to expand the range of tasks they undertake. It has close links with the 'quality of working life' movement and may involve job rotation, job enrichment and teamworking practices. In these forms it contrasts with the Tayloristic approach to job design and underpins such initiatives as empowerment and semi-autonomous work groups. Here employees are granted greater authority to make decisions and accept responsibility for such matters as adherence to quality standards.

Consultation and representative participation

Unlike previous forms, this approach to EI is an indirect form of involvement in that processes such as joint consultation are based upon discussions between management and representatives of employees drawn from amongst them. Representatives are usually elected for a fixed period of time. Joint consultation differs from collective bargaining, since the final decision on any matter rests with management and is not the subject of a joint decision-making process. From a managerial perspective it can operate as a forum for grievances to be raised (particularly where unions are not recognised) and as a way of 'sounding out' employee representatives on managerial plans and proposed organisational change. According to the Workplace Industrial Relations Survey (WIRS), formal systems of consultation have declined, mainly due to the decline in the number of large workplaces where such arrangements are more common (Millward *et al.*, 2000).

Financial participation

The final category of EI techniques are those designed to relate the employee's overall pay to the success of the organisation and include profit-sharing schemes and employee share ownership plans. These schemes are discussed in Chapter 9, but the assumption behind them is that employees will work harder if they receive a personal financial reward from the organisation's success.

Clearly the types of EI outlined here are not mutually exclusive. In a case study research of 25 organisations, Marchington *et al.* (1992) found a wide range of different schemes being utilised. The choice of techniques needs to be made upon an assessment of their ability to assist in the meeting of business and employment relations objectives and the organisation's individual circumstances. Ackers *et al.* (1992) have sought to assess these circumstances and identify managerial purposes behind the introduction of employee involvement schemes. Three are worthy of particular note in terms of this chapter's objectives. The first they call Human Resource Management participation and note that two versions may exist. Version 1 is where trade unions are recognised but in their current weakened position. Here some form of direct communication with employees is used to bypass union communication channels. Version 2 is seen in non-union firms as part of a 'union avoidance' strategy, typified perhaps by practice in 'good' companies noted above. The second set of circumstances they define as Market Participation and, again, two versions can be identified. The circumstances associated with version 1 relate to competitive product market pressures, and EI schemes are designed to enhance the quality of the product or service offered with the aim of inducing customer loyalty. These would include such techniques as quality circles or customer care programmes. The second version is most often seen where the external labour market is tight and firms need to retain and recruit workers but where there is little scope to achieve this through major pay rises. The aim here is to enhance the quality of employees' working life and thus increase employee loyalty to the firm.

However, Ackers *et al.* also note the possibility of 'Faddish' Participation where managers introduce EI schemes as a result of following fashion or 'being seen to be doing something'. Some evidence that this may be happening can be seen in the assessment by Cully *et al.* (1999) of teamworking. This is often portrayed as a key element of task participation. In the Workplace Employee Relations Survey (WERS), managers claimed that in 65 per cent of workplaces most employees worked in teams. However, in 3 per cent of these, team members did not work with each other! Eight per cent of those remaining did not have responsibility for a specific product or service, and a further 19 per cent did not decide jointly how work was to be done. Thus the original 65 per cent claiming to have employees working in teams is whittled down to 35 per cent. Only 3 per cent actually appointed their own team leaders. This illustration would suggest that in some cases the rhetoric of EI is somewhat removed from the reality.

THE NEGOTIATION PROCESS

Negotiation is a process that is used by managers in a variety of workplace circumstances where there is some degree of conflict between a manager and another party. It occurs in discussions with suppliers or customers over the price, quality and timing of delivery of a product or service. Managers may regularly find themselves in negotiations with other managers over the allocation of responsibilities within an organisation. Where trade unions are recognised, negotiations with their representatives over pay, work allocation and other terms of employment are a feature of organisational life. While there are a number of common features in these different types of negotiation, the focus here is on negotiations over aspects of the wage for work bargain.

Contrasting approaches to conflict resolution

Negotiation takes place in those circumstances where there is a degree of conflict between the parties over the allocation of a resource. The aim of the process is to persuade the other party to move from their original position to one which is acceptable to both parties. It thus implies a need for compromise. This can most clearly be seen over pay negotiations, where employee representatives wish to maximise the return for the labour employed while managers will seek to limit the impact of additional cost to the provision of goods or services.

Two broad approaches to the resolution of conflict can be identified: competitive and collaborative bargaining. Competitive bargaining is characterised by 'I win – You lose, I lose – You win' where gains by one party will be at the expense of the other. The power or energy generated by the conflict is used to advance one particular sectional interest: management or employees. Collaborative bargaining, on the other hand, is characterised by 'I win – You win, I lose – You lose', suggesting that it is possible for both parties to benefit from the resolution of the differences. Here the energy is moulded to seek mutually satisfactory solutions in changing circumstances. Which approach will be chosen depends upon a number of factors which are summarised in Exhibit 16.8.

Exhibit 16.8   Key factors determining the approach to negotiation

- The issue
  - conflict of interest
  - common interest
- Stage of negotiations
- Quality of existing relations
  - trust
  - actions of others
- Preferred style and values
- Impact of external influences

Where there is a greater commonality of interest, for example over a health and safety matter, it may be more appropriate to employ a collaborative approach than where there is a more obvious conflict of interests. The latter might include managerial attempts to impose redundancies while the union is seeking security of employment. Different approaches may be more appropriate at different stages of the negotiations. Where productivity improvements are being sought as part of pay negotiations, a collaborative model may be more suitable for identifying sources of cost savings, but the actual distribution of the savings between the organisation and pay increases for employees may call for competitive tactics. Where there is a high level of trust between management and employees, it may be possible to treat matters as problems requiring a joint problem-solving approach rather than to view them as divisive issues. Clearly the personal values and the preferred style of the negotiating members are influential – some people may view all issues as competitive irrespective of the actual merits of the case. Finally, external influences such as technological and economic contexts may determine which approach is used.

Phases of negotiation

A useful framework for analysing the negotiating process is to identify that it passes through five related phases.

1 Preparation.

2 Opening presentation.

3 Development and bargaining.

4 Closing.

5 Implementation and review.

Preparation – Thorough and thoughtful preparation by both parties is the key to ensuring that negotiations provide an effective and mutually satisfying agreement for both employees and managers. In this phase a number of important activities take place in advance of any meetings with the other party. For the management team the identification and clarification of the issue or issues to be dealt with during the negotiations needs to be undertaken before any detailed consideration can be made. This may involve the collection and evaluation of relevant information. Importantly, managers should be aware of the organisation's policy and any constraints this places on the negotiations. Once these activities have been completed, it is possible for the negotiating team to set their objectives for the meetings that are to follow. Since negotiating implies an element of compromise, these objectives can be thought of as a range – from the preferred or ideal solution to a fallback position. The latter may represent, for example, the limits of a manager's authority. Setting a range of objectives is important to effective negotiations, since the union team will be undertaking a similar exercise and the settlement will be found within the area where the two sets of objectives overlap. This is portrayed in Fig. 16.1. The settlement of the issue will lie in the area between points B and C where the parties' negotiating objectives overlap. Where precisely the agreement will be

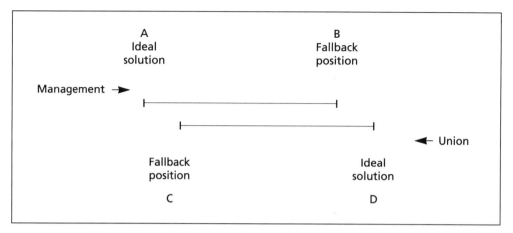

Fig. 16.1 Negotiating objectives: conditions for a settlement

reached will depend, in part, on the skills of the negotiators and the balance of power between management and the trade union.

Once objectives have been set, it is possible to develop arguments which support management's view of the case. At the same time, if there is some indication of the union's objectives and view of the case (perhaps because a formal claim has been submitted in advance of the meeting) then counter-arguments can be developed. Finally, particular responsibilities amongst the management negotiating team can be allocated. This may involve a consideration of the following questions: Who will lead the negotiations? Is there a need for a separate chair for the meeting? Are any managers with specialist expertise (such as health and safety, sales) needed? Will one member be responsible for note taking? It is important that all members are agreed on the objectives and strategy to be followed, since a lack of consensus may lead to weaknesses in management's case being exposed during the negotiations.

Opening presentation – Depending upon the nature and degree of formality of the negotiations, there may be a formal presentation of the respective management and union cases. Here, it is expected that each side will focus on their preferred solution. In the presentation of management's case the focus should be on why this objective is justified and there may be an attempt to set the context for the negotiations. In pay bargaining the performance of the company over the previous year may be explained in order to set the scene for the initial offer. The presentation should be relatively short and the key arguments that support management's case should be identified. If the union negotiators open the negotiations, their case should be listened to without interruption. Once this is completed, questions may be put to clarify points raised and to probe the strength of the arguments put forward. Once these presentations are completed and both parties are clear on each other's case, it may be appropriate to take an adjournment so that more detailed consideration can be given.

Development and bargaining – The third phase of the negotiations typically takes the greatest period of time as each party develops their case and assesses the merits of the arguments being placed before them. The main activity here is to seek to persuade the other party to move from their ideal solution. In general, one party should not move from their position unless there is some movement from the other. However, this can lead to stalemate, since neither is prepared to give ground for fear of making concessions without achieving some mutual shift by the other. This potential impasse can be overcome through the use of 'conditional proposals'. Management may suggest an area where they are prepared to move provided there is similar movement from the union on a matter which is of importance to the management team. For example, management may indicate that they are prepared to consider a reduction in the working week *if* the trade union representatives will reduce the size of their pay claim. If there is no movement in the latter then management have not committed themselves to shortening hours. It is important to 'signal' such proposals in advance by using such phrases as 'what if . . . then perhaps'.

Negotiations induce considerable stress on the negotiators. Opportunities for adjournments should be taken appropriately, to provide not only a chance to review progress but also a break from the meeting. It is vital that the negotiations do not degenerate into personal attacks, nor that emotionally charged phrases are used: one wrong word can set the meeting back.

Closing – At this phase of the negotiations the aim is to secure the best agreement possible. This may involve a complex package of details covering a wide range of matters. It is important that this phase is not rushed, no 'loose ends' are left and that both parties are clear on what has been agreed, otherwise there may be a 'secondary dispute' over some details, necessitating another set of negotiations which may be somewhat acrimonious since the anticipated agreement has not been forthcoming. In some cases the union may wish to ballot its members on whether they are prepared to accept the negotiated settlement. Of course, the possibility of agreement supposes that there is an overlap in the respective negotiating objectives. If there is not, then there will be a need to re-examine the solutions and establish new objectives. If that is beyond the ability or the authority of the negotiating parties then a failure to agree may be recorded and the use of third party intervention, such as conciliation or arbitration, considered.

Implementation and review – Negotiation is not an activity undertaken for its own sake, but is a process by which employees can have a voice in the decisions that affect their working lives and by which these decisions may be made more acceptable to them. Thus the effective implementation of the agreements reached is vital to the success of the process.

> This action has two aspects. The first is the effective communication with and dissemination of information to those affected by the agreement. The second is the devising of a programme of implementation which includes allocating responsibility and setting time-scales.

> (Corbridge and Pilbeam, 1993: 141–2)

The implications of the agreement need to be communicated to other managers and supervisors not involved in the negotiations, and the impact of the agreement on employees will have to be explained. How this latter responsibility will be apportioned between managers and union representatives will need to be decided and consideration given to what action employees can take if they are unclear or unsure of its impact.

SUMMARY LEARNING POINTS

1 The effective resourcing of organisations requires careful consideration of the range of employment relations processes which need to be tailored to the organisational objectives and its broader resourcing strategies.

2 Where trade unions are recognised management are faced with a number of choices regarding the structure of collective bargaining. Whether bargaining should be centralised or decentralised is likely to be determined by reference to the size and geographical spread of its business units, and its product and labour markets.

3 New forms of collective relationships such as single-table bargaining, new style agreements and partnership agreements are being adopted by employers who are seeking greater control over work processes.

4 In the non-union firm, or for categories of employees for whom unions are not recognised, management have greater freedom in determining the shape of the employment relationship, although employment practices in non-union firms are highly variable.

5 The growth in personal contracts reflects a desire by some organisations to remove managers (and other key workers) from the scope of collective bargaining.

6 The adoption of employee involvement techniques is evident in both unionised and non-union firms. These techniques are designed to elicit a greater level of employee performance and commitment to organisational objectives.

7 Reaching mutually acceptable agreements with trade union representatives requires managers to develop an understanding of the complexity of the negotiating process and the relevant problem-solving and communication skills.

REFERENCES AND FURTHER READING

Ackers, P., Marchington, M., Wilkinson, A. and Goodman, J. (1992) 'The use of cycles: explaining employee involvement in the 1990s', *Industrial Relations Journal*, 23(4), 268–83.

Bassett, P. (1986) *Strike Free: New Industrial Relations in Britain*. London: Macmillan.

Beaumont, P. (1987) *The Decline of Trade Union Organisation*. London: Croom Helm.

Blyton, P. and Turnbull, P. (1998) *The Dynamics of Employee Relations*. Basingstoke: Macmillan.

Brown, W. and Walsh, J. (1991) 'Pay determination in Britain in the 1980s; the anatomy of decentralisation', *Oxford Review of Economic Policy*, (1), 44–59.

Burrows, G. (1986) *'No-Strike' Agreements and Pendulum Arbitration*. London: IPM.

CIR (1973) 'The role of management in industrial relations', *CIR Report 34*. London: HMSO.

Corbridge, M. and Pilbeam, S. (1993) 'Negotiation, grievances, discipline and redundancy', in Farnham, D. (ed.) *Employee Relations*. London: IPM.

Cully, M., Woodland, S., O'Reilly, A. and Dix, G. (1999) *Britain at Work: As depicted by the 1998 Workplace Employee Relations Survey*. London: Routledge.

Gall, G. (1993) 'What ever happened to single union deals? A research note', *Industrial Relations Journal*, 24(1), 71–5.

Goss, D. (1991) 'In search of small firm industrial relations', in Burrows, R. (ed.) *Deciphering the Enterprise Culture: Entrepreneurship, petty capitalism and the restructuring of Britain*. London: Routledge, 152–75.

Goss, D. (1994) *Principles of Human Resource Management*. London: Routledge.

Guest, D. and Hoque, K. (1994) 'The good, the bad and the ugly: employment relations in the new non-union workplace', *Human Resource Management Journal*, 5(1), 1–14.

Guest, D. and Pecci, R. (1998) *The Partnership Company: Benchmarks for the future*. London: Involvement and Participation Association.

IDS (1992) 'Moving to personal contracts', *Top Pay Unit Review (139)*, Incomes Data Services.

IDS (1995) *Introducing Single Table Bargaining*, Study 584, August.

IPD (1996) *IPD Statement on Employment Relations*. London: IPD.

IRRR (1989) 'Decentralised bargaining in perspective', *Industrial Relations Review and Report* (451), IRS, 11–14.

IRS (1993) 'Single-union deals survey 1', *Industrial Relations Services Employment Trends*, (528), 3–15.

Kennedy, G., Benson, J. and McMillan, J. (1980) *Managing Negotiations*. London: Business Books.

Kessler, I. and Undy, R. (1996) 'The new employment relationship: examining the psychological contract', *Issues in People Management* (12). London: IPD.

Legge, K. (1995) *Human Resource Management: Rhetorics and realities*. Basingstoke: Macmillan.

Lewis, R. (1990) 'Strike free deals and pendulum arbitration', *British Journal of Industrial Relations*, 28(1), 32–56.

Marchington, M. (1995) 'Involvement and participation', in Storey, J. (ed.) *Human Resource Management: A critical text*. London: Routledge.

Marchington, M., Goodman, J., Wilkinson, A. and Ackers, P. (1992) 'Recent developments in employee involvement', *Employment Department Research Series No. 1*. London: HMSO.

Marginson, P., Edwards, P., Martin, R., Purcell, J. and Sisson, K. (1988) *Beyond the Workplace: Managing industrial relations in multi-plant enterprises*. Oxford: Blackwell.

Marks, A., Findlay, P., Hine, J., McKinlay, A. and Thompson, P. (1998) 'The politics of partnership? Innovation in employment relations in the Scottish spirits industry', *British Journal of Industrial Relations*, 36(2), 209–26.

Millward, N., Bryson, A. and Forth, J. (2000) *All Change at Work? British employment relations 1980–1998, as depicted by the Workplace Industrial Relations Survey series*. London: Routledge.

Monks, J. (1998) 'Trade unions, enterprise and the future', in Sparrow, P. and Marchington, M. (eds) *Human Resource Management: The new agenda*. Oxford: Blackwell.

Parker, P., Hawes, W. and Lumb, A. (1971) 'The reform of collective bargaining at plant and company level', *Department of Employment Manpower Papers* (5). London: HMSO.

Purcell, J. (1989) 'How to manage decentralised bargaining', *Personnel Management*, May, 53–5.

Purcell, J. and Ahlstrand, B. (1994) *Human Resource Management in the Multi-divisional Company*. Oxford: Oxford University Press.

Salamon, M. (1998) *Industrial Relations: Theory and Practice* (3rd edn). Hemel Hempstead: Prentice Hall.

Sisson, K. (1993) 'In search of human resource management', *British Journal of Industrial Relations*, 31(2), 201–10.

Tailby, S. and Winchester, D. (2000) 'Management and trade unions: towards social partnership', in Bach, S. and Sisson, K. (eds) *Personnel Management: A comprehensive guide to theory and practice*. Oxford: Blackwell.

Towers, B. (1992) 'Choosing bargaining levels: UK experience and implications', *Issues in People Management* (2). London: Institute of Personnel Management.

Wickens, P. (1987) *The Road to Nissan: Flexibility, quality, teamwork*. London: Macmillan.

ASSIGNMENTS AND DISCUSSION TOPICS

1 Undertake an analysis of the way in which pay increases are determined within your organisation. If trade unions are recognised, the analysis should cover the levels at which agreements are made, the different bargaining units and agents that are involved, and how the pay of non-union employees is determined. If the organisation is non-union, the analysis should focus on the criteria and means that are used to decide the level of pay increases and the extent to which employees are able to individually negotiate their pay increases.

2 Identify the employee involvement practices used in your organisation. For what reasons do you believe they have been introduced? Are they effective?

3 Discuss the contention that pendulum arbitration offers a civilised solution to resolving disputes without the use of industrial action.

4 Should there be a legal requirement for employers to recognise a trade union if a majority of employees are in favour?

5 Discuss the view that employee involvement techniques are simply a means by which an employer manipulates employees into believing they have a say in the organisation's decisions when the reality is that power remains with management.

6 Observe an employment relations negotiation within an organisation. What skills were used by the parties involved? Did the negotiations appear to be of a competitive or collaborative nature and what factors lead you to this view?

CHAPTER 17

Conflict resolution: discipline and grievance

INTRODUCTION

It is unrealistic to expect that relations between employers and employees will always be harmonious and inevitably there will be conflict within employment relationships. Either the employer will be dissatisfied with the employee or the employee will be dissatisfied with the employer, or both parties can be dissatisfied at the same time. The informal resolution of dissatisfaction is an essential and natural part of good day-to-day management, but more formal arrangements are necessary when dissatisfaction becomes unresolved conflict. Disciplinary and grievance procedures are formal mechanisms for resolving individual conflict and represent positive opportunities for corrective action and concern resolution. Fairness and consistency in disciplinary and grievance matters are fundamental features of sound employment relationships.

CHAPTER OBJECTIVES

- To recognise that unresolved conflict can be dysfunctional to the employment relationship.
- To examine the nature of discipline at work, the role of rules and the operation of disciplinary procedures.
- To analyse the disciplinary hearing and the interviewing skills required.
- To explore the value of a positive approach to the resolution of employee grievances.
- To examine the structure and operation of a grievance procedure and the nature of the grievance hearing.

INDIVIDUAL CONFLICT-RESOLVING MECHANISMS

Employer dissatisfaction may relate to employee performance, conduct, attendance or any other unfulfilled elements of the contract of employment. If the employee is not meeting the employer's legitimate expectations in the performance of the contract, there is potential for conflict between the two parties and it is reasonable for the employer to seek corrective action to resolve an unsatisfactory situation. Formalised corrective action is embodied in a disciplinary policy and procedure.

Employee dissatisfaction may relate to employer treatment, demands, expectations or any other enactment of the contractual relationship which is perceived to be unreasonable, inequitable or illegitimate. Employee dissatisfaction may impact negatively upon motivation, commitment and work performance. Unresolved conflict rooted in employee dissatisfaction can also destroy the contract of employment, either through the employee regarding it as being terminated or through employee resignation. The formal opportunity to remedy employee dissatisfaction and resolve the consequential conflict is provided by an effective grievance procedure.

Unresolved conflict is therefore likely to be dysfunctional to an employment relationship. Disciplinary and grievance procedures have the potential to remedy dissatisfaction, resolve conflict, promote organisational equity and facilitate mutual adjustment within the contract of employment.

A positive approach to resolving conflict is possible if discipline is viewed as an opportunity for corrective action and a grievance is viewed as an opportunity for the resolution of employee concerns. This approach will not exclude the application of managerial penalties and sanctions when necessary and appropriate.

THE NATURE OF DISCIPLINE AT WORK

Discipline at work means different things to different people and incorporates the concepts of self-discipline, peer discipline and managerial discipline. Self-discipline can be encouraged and developed through employment relations practices which seek to secure the commitment of employees to organisational objectives. Peer discipline, pressure from work colleagues, can be an effective remedy to sub-standard performance or conduct where team spirit prevails. Managerial discipline is the exercise of control over employee performance and behaviour based on legitimate organisational authority. Managerial dissatisfaction with employee performance or conduct potentially produces conflict in the employment relationship. The formal disciplinary process is a procedural way of managing this conflict, through emphasising managerial values and standards, and seeking employee consent within the employment relationship. The primary concern in this section is with managerial discipline.

Discipline at work can have the different objectives of retribution, deterrence and rehabilitation. Retribution implies some form of punishment, deterrence infers dissuading the employee, and other employees, from repeating the unsatisfactory conduct or performance, and rehabilitation suggests the pursuit of improvement and reconciliation between the parties to the employment relationship. Managerial behaviour in disciplinary matters is influenced by perceptions of what is meant by discipline. If it is perceived as punishment or the application of sanctions then a predisposition to a punitive approach is probable. If discipline is perceived as an opportunity to correct constructively an unsatisfactory situation then a predisposition to positive managerial interventions, including problem solving, support, training and clarification of employer expectation, is more likely.

Managerial discipline is a constructive process instigated by management against an employee who fails to meet reasonable employer expectations in terms of behaviour, conduct or adherence to rules.

Managerial disciplinary action can be constructive and rehabilitative and need not necessarily be retributive or punitive, although when encouragement, guidance or development do not resolve management dissatisfaction then sanctions against the employee may be necessary and legitimate.

> Disciplinary procedures should not be viewed primarily as a means of imposing sanctions. Rather they should be seen as a way of helping and encouraging improvement amongst workers whose conduct or standard of work is unsatisfactory. Some organisations may prefer to have separate procedures for dealing with issues of conduct and capability, but it is important to remember that any hearing which might result in a formal warning or some other action will be covered by the provisions on accompaniment set out in the Employment Relations Act, 1999.
>
> (ACAS Code of Practice)

Fairness, equity and consistency in the approach to discipline will minimise disagreements and benefit employment relations. A professional and ethical approach to discipline is neatly summed up in the statement, 'problem-solving to be the first resolve and punishment the last resort'. This approach maximises the opportunity for acceptance and correction of the problem and provides a sound foundation for managerial policy on discipline. In summary, effective managerial practice argues for an emphasis on prevention, problem solving and constructive approaches to discipline, because this is more likely to generate a positive response from employees and is more likely to protect the organisation's investment in human capital.

ORGANISATIONAL RULES

A prerequisite to effective managerial discipline is the existence of organisational rules. Rules set standards of conduct and define acceptable and unacceptable behaviour. Rules are necessary to let employees know where they stand and provide a framework for the employment relationship. Rules underpin managerial prerogative and aim to secure employee compliance to instructions which are deemed necessary to achieve organisational objectives. Rules are normally initiated, defined and communicated by management, although where the right to manage is circumscribed by individual or collective employee representation the rule-making process will be shared to some extent. If rule-making is subject to consultation, negotiation or codetermination, the rules may have greater acceptance and authority through having solicited a degree of employee consent. Rules should be designed with the aim of voluntary compliance rather than a reliance on retribution for non-compliance. If rules are to be effective they need to be perceived as reasonable by employees and accepted as workable by line managers who have to enforce them. The managerial expectation that rules will be observed is legitimised by the common law duties of the employee which are implied into the contract of employment; these duties include being ready, willing and able for work, the exercise of care and competence in the performance of the work and obedience to reasonable instructions. In all probability the contract of employment will also include express terms relating to the expected standards of employee conduct and performance. The employer is therefore contractually entitled to specify performance, attendance, timekeeping and conduct standards. Management cannot just rely on those rules which are overtly expressed, as rules evolve and become legitimised through custom and practice. For example, an unwritten but tacitly agreed arrangement where staff who work at a faster pace than the generally accepted norm are permitted to leave work an hour early on a Friday may become a contractual entitlement, through custom and practice. This may override management's written rule that employees should remain at their place of work until the contractual finishing time.

In addition to rules which are determined principally by management, and those arising out of custom and practice, rules emerge out of legal enactment and precedents. Examples of this include the statutory and case law associated with health and safety at work, unlawful discrimination and harassment. Societal standards, in so far as they can be defined, are also incorporated within the rules of the organisation. This incorporation is based on the concept that as a microcosm of society, work organisations will reflect generally accepted standards. These may include, for example, societal values associated with violence, drunkenness, dishonesty and sexual impropriety (Fig. 17.1).

Recognising that organisational rules are generated from several sources encourages a flexible and dynamic interpretation of the rules and this is more compatible with a problem-solving approach to any employee failure. As suggested earlier, for rules to be

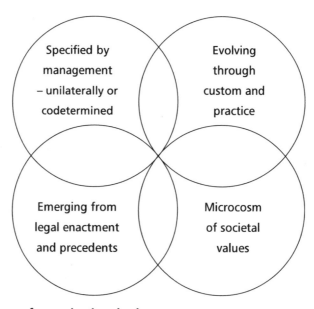

Fig. 17.1   Sources of organisational rules

effective they must be understood and accepted as reasonable by those who are to be covered by them and they also need to be acceptable as reasonable and workable to the managers who have to operate them. Disreputable rules will be difficult to operate and enforce. Whilst it is not possible to specify a rule for every eventuality:

> the aim should be to specify clearly and concisely those that are necessary for the efficient and safe performance of work and for the maintenance of satisfactory relations within the work-force and between workers and management. It is unlikely that any set of disciplinary rules can cover all circumstances that may arise. However, it is usual that rules would cover issues such as misconduct, sub-standard performance (where not covered by a separate capability procedure), harassment or victimisation, misuse of company facilities including computer facilities, poor timekeeping and unauthorised absences. The rules required will necessarily vary according to particular circumstances, such as the type of work, working conditions and size and location of the workplace. Whatever set of rules are eventually drawn up they should not be so general as to be meaningless.
>
> (ACAS Code of Practice 1, 2000)

Rules need to be available to employees through induction, notification and explanation, and the consequences of not conforming to rules should be clearly communicated to employees, particularly where the breaking of a rule will threaten continued employment.

DISCIPLINARY PROCEDURES

Whilst rules set the standards, disciplinary procedures provide a means for ensuring that standards are met and a method for dealing with a failure to meet them. Disciplinary problems can frequently be resolved by the team leader, supervisor or first line manager through counselling or through informal corrective action, and it is desirable to resolve any conflict at the lowest possible level. It is only when this managerial intervention fails that it becomes necessary to escalate the disciplinary matter and to enter a formal disciplinary procedure. A preamble in a disciplinary procedure to the effect that management will aim to resolve issues through counselling and other action outside the formal process will underpin this low level approach, and this is complementary to a policy of devolving people management responsibility to line managers.

There are a number of compelling reasons why organisations should be concerned with producing and operating sound and effective disciplinary procedures. First, approximately 4 per cent of employees, around one million cases annually, are subject to disciplinary procedures (Salamon, 1998), so the magnitude of the problem makes it worth tackling. Second, the importance of procedural fairness has been firmly established as a principle by employment tribunals. Third, the Employment Rights Act, 1996, specifies that the principal statement of employment conditions should make reference to disciplinary rules, procedures and appeal mechanisms. Fourth, the consistent application of fair and effective disciplinary procedures will minimise the potential for disagreements and misunderstandings in matters of discipline and reduce the probability of employee dismissal.

Principles of natural justice

There are advantages in disciplinary procedures conforming to the principles of natural justice. These principles have evolved from societal norms and case law and are universally associated with fairness and equity in the treatment of people. Disciplinary procedures which include the principles of natural justice will benefit from increased moral authority and will command more respect. Natural justice in discipline will enhance perceived equity and foster a voluntary compliance to organisational rules.

> These principles of natural justice have emerged from ideas of equity, due process and model legal practice and are therefore associated with citizen consent to the rule of law within civilised societies. In the employee relations context the advantage is in the employee, as a corporate citizen, consenting to abide by managerial rules because justice will be dispensed fairly.
>
> (Pilbeam and Corbridge, 2000)

Procedures which incorporate the principles of natural justice, and which are applied correctly, will significantly contribute to a demonstration of reasonableness, should an employer need to defend an allegation of unfair dismissal or unreasonable treatment at an employment tribunal. The principles of natural justice are understood rather than specified, and a useful way of viewing them is as 'the way I would like to be treated if I were the subject of managerial discipline'. An expression of the principles, in the context of employment, is included in Exhibit 17.1 and organisational disciplinary procedures should be tested against them.

Exhibit 17.1 Principles of natural justice in employment

In employment these incorporate:

- a knowledge of the standards or behaviour expected
- a knowledge of the alleged failure and the nature of the allegation
- an investigation to establish a *prima facie* case, which should normally precede any allegation
- the opportunity to offer an explanation and for this explanation to be fairly heard and considered
- the opportunity to be accompanied or represented
- the penalty should be appropriate in relation to the offence and take mitigating factors into account
- the opportunity and support to improve, except when misconduct goes to the root of the contract
- a right of appeal to a higher authority.

ACAS code of practice and advisory handbook

The ACAS advisory handbook and code of practice on disciplinary practice and procedures in employment provides practical guidance on handling disciplinary matters, and there is a strong case for disciplinary procedures to conform to this respected code. The

Exhibit 17.2   Essential features of disciplinary procedures (ACAS)

Good disciplinary procedures should:

- Be in writing
- Specify to whom they apply
- *Be non-discriminatory*
- Provide for matters to be dealt with *without undue delay*
- *Provide for proceedings, witness statements and records to be kept confidential*
- Indicate the disciplinary actions which may be taken
- Specify the levels of management which have the authority to take the various forms of disciplinary action
- Provide for *workers* to be informed of the complaints against them and where possible all relevant evidence before any hearing
- Provide *workers* with an opportunity to state their case before decisions are reached
- *Provide workers* with the right to be accompanied by a *fellow worker or a trade union official*
- Ensure that, except for gross misconduct, no *worker* is dismissed for a first breach of discipline
- Ensure that disciplinary action is not taken until the case has been carefully investigated
- Ensure that *workers* are given an explanation for any penalty imposed
- Provide a right of appeal – *normally to a more senior manager* – and specify the procedure to be followed.

The italicised text draws attention to the changes made in the year 2000 version of the code of practice.

Source: ACAS Code of Practice 1, paragraph 9.

provisions of the code are not legally binding and a failure to observe any provision will not render an employer liable to any proceedings, but provisions in the code which are considered relevant will be admissible in evidence at an employment tribunal and can be taken into account in reaching a decision. The code has stood the test of time and scrutiny, existing now for over 25 years, and it contains a checklist of the essential features of disciplinary procedures (Exhibit 17.2). Many of the essential features are related to the principles of natural justice.

The code of practice has been incorporated into the ACAS advisory handbook on discipline at work, first published in 1987 and revised in 2000. The handbook is intended to complement the code by providing more comprehensive guidance to employers by reflecting developments in good practice and emerging case law principles in the areas of discipline, absence and sub-standard work. Whilst recognising that each organisation must decide on the most appropriate procedures and practices, the handbook pinpoints issues to be considered in the handling of disciplinary matters and provides models of procedures (Exhibit 17.3).

Exhibit 17.3   Indicative model of a disciplinary procedure (ACAS)

Purpose and scope

This procedure is designed to help and encourage all employees to achieve and maintain standards of conduct, attendance and job performance. The company rules (a copy of which is displayed in the office) and this procedure apply to all employees. The aim is to ensure consistent and fair treatment for all.

Principles

a No disciplinary action will be taken against an employee until the case has been fully investigated.

b At every stage in the procedure the employee will be advised of the nature of the complaint against him or her and will be given the opportunity to state his or her case before any decision is made.

c At all stages the employee will have the right to be accompanied by a trade union representative, employee representative or work colleague during the disciplinary interview.

d No employee will be dismissed for a first breach of discipline except in the case of gross misconduct when the penalty will be dismissal without notice or payment in lieu of notice.

e An employee will have the right to appeal against any disciplinary penalty imposed.

f The procedure may be implemented at any stage if the employee's alleged misconduct warrants such action.

The Procedure

Stage 1 – First warning

Oral warning   If conduct or performance does not meet acceptable standards the worker will normally be given a formal oral warning. The individual will be advised of the reason for the warning and that it constitutes the first stage of the disciplinary procedure. A note of the oral warning will be kept but it will be spent after . . . months, subject to satisfactory conduct and performance.

Written warning   If the misconduct or performance is more serious the worker will receive a first formal written warning from their supervisor. This will give details of the complaint, the improvement or change in behaviour required, the timescale allowed for this and the right of appeal. A copy of this written warning will be kept by the supervisor but it will be disregarded for disciplinary purposes after . . . months subject to satisfactory conduct and performance.

The warning should also inform the worker of the right of appeal and that a final written warning may be considered if there is no sustained improvement or change.

Stage 2 – Final written warning

If the offence is serious, or there is a failure to improve during the currency of a prior warning, a *final written warning* may be given to the worker. This will give details of the complaint, the

Continued

Exhibit 17.3   continued

improvement required and the timescale. It will also warn that failure to improve may lead to action under stage 3 (dismissal or other action short of dismissal), and will refer to the right of appeal. A copy of this written warning will be kept by the supervisor but it will be disregarded for disciplinary purposes after . . . months subject to satisfactory conduct and performance.

Stage 3 – Dismissal or other sanction

If there is still a failure to improve the final step in the procedure may be *dismissal or some other action short of dismissal* such as demotion or disciplinary suspension or transfer (as allowed in the contract of employment). Dismissal decisions can only be taken by the appropriate Senior Manager, and the worker will be provided, as soon as is reasonably practicable, with written reasons for dismissal, the date on which the employment will terminate, and the right of appeal. The decision to dismiss will be confirmed in writing.

If some sanction short of dismissal is imposed, the worker will receive details of the complaint, will be warned that dismissal could result if there is no satisfactory improvement and will be advised of the right of appeal. A copy of this warning will be kept by the supervisor but will be disregarded for disciplinary purposes after . . . months subject to satisfactory conduct and performance.

Gross misconduct

The following list provides examples of offences which are normally regarded as gross misconduct:

- theft, fraud, deliberate falsification of records
- fighting, assault on another person
- deliberate damage to company property
- serious incapability through alcohol or being under the influence of illegal drugs
- serious negligence which causes unacceptable loss, damage or injury
- serious act of insubordination
- unauthorised entry to computer records.

If you are accused of an act of gross misconduct, you may be suspended from work on full pay, normally for no more than five working days, while the company investigates the alleged offence. If, on completion of the investigation and the full disciplinary procedure, the company is satisfied that gross misconduct has occurred, the result will normally be summary dismissal without notice or payment in lieu of notice.

Appeals

An employee who wishes to appeal against a disciplinary decision should inform . . . within two working days. The Senior Manager will hear all appeals and his/her decision is final. At the appeal any disciplinary penalty imposed will be reviewed, but it cannot be increased.

Source: Discipline at Work – ACAS Advisory Handbook 2000, Appendix 3.

The structure of a disciplinary procedure

The ACAS model of a procedure incorporates the notion of three incremental disciplinary stages based upon the nature and seriousness of the conduct or performance of the employee. If a disciplinary issue is not resolved at an informal level, it may become necessary to enter the formal disciplinary procedure. The first stage of the formal procedure may be a recorded oral warning or a formal written warning. Warnings should always make clear the consequences of a failure to improve or a repetition of the offence. The next stage of the procedure may be a final written warning. The final stage may be either 'ASOD' (action short of dismissal, including disciplinary transfer, or reduction in status and responsibility) or termination of employment. These stages are represented in Fig. 17.2.

Nature of the disciplinary matter and the procedural stage		Management response and action	Level of management (with advice from personnel specialist as required)
1	**Misconduct** which is not serious	**Oral warning**	**Team leader** or **Supervisor**
	More serious misconduct	**Written warning**	**Supervisor** or **Line manager**
2	**Serious misconduct** or repeated misconduct for which a written or oral warning has been received	**Final written warning**	**Line manager** and/or **Senior manager**
3	**Gross misconduct** or further misconduct for which a final written warning has been received	**Dismissal** or **Action short of dismissal** • Transfer • Demotion • Reward decrement • Suspension	**Senior manager**

Fig. 17.2 The principal incremental stages of a disciplinary procedure

Whilst providing a useful guide to employer action, the stages should not be viewed as a strict sequence as it is reasonable for an employer to have the flexibility to enter the procedure at any stage, depending upon the seriousness of the disciplinary matter. The earlier stages will normally be executed by team leaders, supervisors and first line managers, with more senior management becoming involved as the disciplinary matter escalates. The participation and role of a specialist personnel function will be contingent on organisational circumstances and senior management policy and attitude towards the devolution of HR responsibilities to line managers. There are examples of organisations in retailing and catering where an active personnel presence occurs at a very early stage in the disciplinary process, and in contrast there are examples of blue-chip organisations where the role of the personnel function is advisory and remote from the application of the disciplinary procedure.

Disciplinary procedures – operational issues

Case law has established the importance of thorough investigation in disciplinary matters. The initial aim of an investigation is to gather factual information which establishes whether or not there is a *prima facie* case for making an allegation. The disciplinary interview or hearing provides an opportunity for the employee to explain or respond to an allegation. Further investigation may be necessary following the hearing. Proper and objective investigation is an important element in establishing employer reasonableness at an employment tribunal, should this be necessary. The disciplinary matter should be dropped if investigation fails to establish a *prima facie* case to answer or if the employee's explanation is satisfactory. The employer does not have to prove beyond reasonable doubt that an employee has committed an offence or that the employee is 'guilty' of sub-standard performance; the burden of proof is one of 'establishing reasonable belief' based on the balance of probabilities taking into account the information available at the time (*see* Chapter 18).

It may be appropriate to suspend the employee from work during an investigation, particularly in cases of alleged gross misconduct. Suspension should normally be on the basis of paid leave unless the contract specifies unpaid suspension. Even where unpaid suspension is contractually legitimate, suspending an employee prior to providing an opportunity to explain may be perceived as premature punishment through loss of pay. Unpaid suspension in these circumstances may not only be perceived as unfair, but also be to the detriment of a workable employment relationship, if there is no case to answer or the employee provides a satisfactory explanation. Suspension, whether paid or unpaid, needs to be used judiciously. Sometimes it will be essential to use suspension in the interests of the employee or other employees or customers, clients and members of the public, or to protect the objectives of the organisation.

The reasonableness of employer action, more specifically addressed in the next chapter, is a guiding principle in the operation of disciplinary procedures and involves the assessment of whether disciplinary action falls within the range of responses of a reasonable employer. The concept of even-handedness, meaning that employers are normally expected to treat employees similarly in similar disciplinary matters, unless differences in treatment can be objectively justified, is also a well-established disciplinary principle. In order to be able to demonstrate reasonableness and even-handedness, it is important for employers to document disciplinary matters fully in terms of records of investigation, disciplinary hearings, warnings, monitoring and support.

In operating disciplinary procedures, are managers required to be impartial or objective? This is a problematic question. Impartiality suggests a lack of bias towards or against any particular side, but can management ever do anything but ultimately make decisions from a managerial perspective, and even if managers are impartial will employees believe it? The disciplinary procedure is a quasi-judicial process where, contrary to normal practice, the prosecution and judiciary are not separated and effectively the employer is acting as both prosecutor and judge; this militates against impartiality. Objectivity, in contrast, implies an interpretation of the facts and a decision-making process not distorted by emotion or personal bias. Objectivity acknowledges managerial prerogative but affords some protection to the employee against managerial whim, and in practice it is objectivity rather than impartiality which is normally incorporated into good disciplinary procedures.

Warnings and warning letters should normally spell out the nature of the offence or behaviour, the remedy or improvement required, and the support, guidance and monitoring to be provided, and should specify a review timescale (see the ACAS Handbook for examples of letters). The objective of a warning is to ensure that the employee not only understands and accepts the problem but is able to commit to resolving it by appreciating exactly what is required by management. The employee should be left in no doubt about the potential consequences of failure to resolve the problem, and such consequences should be specified as well. The seriousness of a warning is indicated to some extent by whether it is given orally, in writing or as a final warning. It is good practice to disregard warnings, or to consider them as spent, after a specified period of satisfactory conduct or performance. This is in the interests of natural justice so that the employee, having made a mistake and paid the appropriate penalty, has the opportunity to 'wipe the slate clean' in due course. The period for which the warning is to remain 'live' should be reasonable and determined by the particular merits of the case. There is an inherent tension in deciding upon the warning time limit between the desire to encourage employees to put the matter behind them, in the interests of re-establishing a positive employment relationship, and the provision of the opportunity for the 'repeat offender' to exploit the expiry of a warning by quickly lapsing into the unsatisfactory conduct or performance. Although the ACAS code provides guidance on time limits, suggesting six- and twelve-month periods for minor and serious matters respectively, these are only for general guidance. The employer is entitled to set a time limit which is reasonable in the particular circumstances and, exceptionally, the nature of any problem may be so serious that the warning cannot be disregarded in any future disciplinary matter and consequently cannot become spent.

In endeavouring to ensure that an employee fully understands a warning, it is useful to ask for a copy of the warning letter to be signed. This does not preclude the employee from responding to a warning in writing. This opens up a debate about whether the employee is being asked to sign a letter in order to:

(a) acknowledge receipt, *or*

(b) indicate that the content of the letter has been read and understood, *or*

(c) signify agreement with the content of the warning.

From a managerial perspective, achieving (a), (b) and (c) may be desirable, but unrealistic. There is no obligation on the employer to achieve (a), (b) or (c), but a reasonable employer will be expected to make every demonstrable effort to ensure that a warning letter is received and that it is capable of being understood by the recipient.

To avoid automatically attaching the disciplinary label to a managerial concern about the work performance of an individual, a distinction can be created between misconduct and work performance concerns through having separate disciplinary and capability procedures. This distinction is intended to encourage an even more positive approach to performance problems by focusing on managing a return to acceptable standards of performance. This incorporates a recognition that sub-standard performance may not be wilful or the result of irremedial incompetence and, as a consequence, warnings may be inappropriate. There are, for example, restoring-efficiency procedures in the civil service, in order to communicate a more positive, problem-solving and partnership approach to managing the return to effective performance, although ultimately the disciplinary procedure may need to be invoked. The positive approach to managerial concern about employee performance involves:

- identifying a performance gap through the objective specification of performance standards and the measurement of current performance
- an analysis of the reasons for the performance gap and deciding upon a suitable response which may include training, supervision, greater or lesser empowerment, clearer definition of objectives, re-balancing of the psychological or economic contracts, or indeed warnings and disciplinary action (*see also* Chapter 11).

Disciplinary interviews

When a *prima facie* case for the expression of a concern or an allegation has been reasonably established, a disciplinary interview or hearing should take place. The employee should be informed about the nature of the allegation or concern, be forewarned about the disciplinary status of the interview and where it fits into the procedure, be told of the right to be accompanied or represented, and given the time, date and place of attendance, ensuring that there is sufficient, but not excessive, time for preparation. As well as the right to a companion at a grievance hearing, section 10 of the ERA 1999 gives workers (not just employees) the right to make a reasonable request to be accompanied at a formal disciplinary hearing. The worker chooses the companion, who can be a fellow worker or a certified trade union official (who need not be employed by the same organisation). Non-unionised organisations have to accept a trade union official as a worker's companion, whether they like it or not. Even where a trade union is recognised, the companion does not have to be an official of that union and could come from a trade union of the worker's choice. The statutory role is one of companion rather than representative. The companion can confer with the worker during the hearing and is permitted to address the hearing but has no legal right to answer questions on behalf of the worker. The worker may propose an alternative date for the hearing if the chosen companion is not available on the date proposed for the hearing. In this case the employer is required to postpone the hearing to the date proposed by the worker, provided that the alternative date is reasonable, has regard for the availability of the manager and falls before the end of five working days of the date proposed by the employer. The companion is entitled to reasonable time off during working hours in order to fulfil his or her responsibilities (Temperton, 2000; Lewis and Sargeant, 2000; Aikin, 1999).

Interviews will rarely progress in neat, orderly stages, but a systematic framework can be helpful in contributing to fairness and in encouraging constructive discussion. At the interview the employer should normally:

- introduce those present and clarify their respective roles
- explain the purpose and process of the interview
- state the allegation or concern unambiguously, support it with any relevant facts or evidence, and allow the employee to clarify the allegation through questions
- offer the employee the opportunity to respond or to offer an explanation, to which the employer should listen attentively and sensitively, and allow the employee to consult with the companion
- question the employee in order to gather further particulars and confirm factual information
- consider carefully the employee's response or explanation
- make the decision, normally in adjournment, to ensure and demonstrate that proper consideration is being given to all the circumstances, including mitigating factors and previous work record
- accept that there is no case to answer or that it has been answered, in which case the disciplinary process ceases, or alternatively, decide that disciplinary action is necessary and inform the employee of the decision, and also of the right to appeal should there be dissatisfaction with the decision
- ensure that the employee knows what is now expected and by when, confirming written warnings by letter
- agree to provide reasonable support, training and feedback and to review the matter within the specified timescale.

These relatively straightforward guidelines disguise the fact that the interview is potentially a highly emotional encounter. The interviewer can be confronted with a range of responses, from aggression or distress on the one hand to passiveness and disinterest on the other; the employee may exhibit devious ingenuity or engage in self-denial behaviour. Professionalism, objectivity based on facts and rationality need to be demonstrated. The skills to be utilised include open and probing questioning, active listening, summarising, managing angry responses, sensitivity to feelings of devastation and the ability to focus on the facts in order to progress the meeting to a logical conclusion. All of this means that the disciplinary interview can be as challenging for the manager as it is for an employee. The interview should not be treated merely as a means of confirming suspicions or concerns, but as an opportunity to resolve any conflict in the employment relationship through improving conduct or performance on both sides. Fairness and consistency at the disciplinary hearing and in individual matters of discipline generally will ultimately contribute to good employment relations. Perhaps a corrective action procedure is a more appropriate name for a disciplinary procedure.

Disciplinary procedures and employment tribunals

UMIST research (Earnshaw, 1997) found that the main cause of employment tribunal claims being found in favour of the applicant is procedural defect. Where employees were successful in their claim for unfair dismissal, the success, almost without exception, was related to procedural shortcomings by the employer. Common procedural defects include:

- employees not being made fully aware of the allegation and any supporting evidence
- employees not being given the opportunity to respond to the allegation or the absence of a disciplinary hearing
- warnings not being sufficiently explicit
- insufficient time being given to the employee to remedy a problem
- insufficient investigation
- a concern with speed of action rather than proper consideration of the facts
- dismissal occurring in the course of an argument
- a failure to apply the disciplinary procedure in full
- the decision not to have or to use a formal disciplinary procedure.

Despite well-documented good practice, and the legitimacy of the principles of natural justice, there remains scope for education and advice to employers in relation to procedural fairness. A dismissal process need not necessarily be slow, or paper bound, but remedying procedural defects is a way to reduce claims for unfair dismissal and for making dismissals legally safe. Good disciplinary procedures will not eliminate all claims, but will make them easier to defend.

GRIEVANCES – EMPLOYEE CONCERN RESOLUTION

It is important to recognise, acknowledge and resolve concerns and issues that leave employees feeling unfairly treated. Failure to do this can result in employees deciding to take action to redress the perceived unfair treatment. This action may range from poor attendance or poor quality work, to leaving the organisation, which is costly and also unsatisfactory as the problem is unrecognised and unresolved. Good employee relations and good communication will encourage the informal resolution of problems, but the climate of the organisation will affect the presentation of problems to management. No formal presentation of problems does not necessarily mean that there are no problems; it may mean that employees feel their concerns will not be taken seriously or that they are afraid of repercussions. A grievance is the formal expression of dissatisfaction or injustice that an employee feels towards the employer. It is based on the legal and procedural right of individuals at work to formally express dissatisfaction with elements of the work situation and to have that dissatisfaction acknowledged and heard and an attempt made to resolve the situation. In expressing a grievance the employee is highlighting an issue of dissatisfaction which is considered sufficiently serious to present formally to management. The expression of a formal grievance is often triggered by a particular event which has left the employee feeling unfairly treated.

The terms dissatisfaction, complaint, grievance and dispute represent a hierarchy of the strength of employee feeling and willingness to present the issue formally to management. Dissatisfaction is felt, complaints are expressed informally, grievances are presented formally, and disputes may be internal or external and collective or individual. Not every employee dissatisfaction or complaint results in a grievance or a dispute. Whether it does or does not depends on the willingness of the employee to present the issue, the managerial response and whether it is resolved to the employee's satisfaction. The progression from the informal to the formal machinery may be seen in some organisations as a failure to address the issue at the informal level, resulting in the employee feeling that 'enough is enough' and there is no alternative but to use the formal procedure.

The culture of an organisation has a major effect on the way in which grievances are received and handled. In a unitary or neo-unitary organisation (*see* Chapter 15) there are assumptions that common values and common objectives are held by all employees and that the 'right to manage' is accepted by all (Farnham, 2000). In these organisations internal conflict is seen as dysfunctional and individuals may feel inhibited about raising a formal grievance because of the effect it may have on their career prospects and for fear of being labelled a 'deviant'. In a pluralist organisation, conflict is seen as inevitable and it is accepted that employees have a right to question managerial policies, procedures and decisions. The formal grievance procedure is more likely to be used, and the need for a formal mechanism for resolving conflict is taken for granted, in pluralistic employment relationships.

Employers are not yet required by law to have a grievance procedure, but under the Employment Rights Act, 1996 the employer must provide the name or job title of the person to whom individual employees should present the grievance. As yet, there is no statutory requirement for a staged procedure or for the grievance to be resolved to the satisfaction of the employee. The grievance procedure therefore forms a part of the written terms and conditions of employment. In addition, the ERA 1999 gives employees the right to be accompanied at a grievance hearing where 'a grievance hearing is related to the performance of a duty by an employer in relation to the worker'. This means a legal duty arising from statute or common law, for example contractual commitments. As with disciplinary hearings a companion, who may be a fellow worker or a trade union official, has the right to address the hearing. In practice this means that the employer has to consider each grievance carefully to ensure that this requirement is met and that the employee is not being denied a statutory right. Alternatively the employer may decide to give the employee the right to be accompanied, or to be represented, at *all* grievance hearings. The Public Interest Disclosure Act, 1998 obligates employers to provide, within the grievance procedure, the opportunity for workers to present concerns about malpractice, concerns about health and safety, suspicions of criminal acts or miscarriages of justice. Workers who have an 'honest and reasonable' belief about the existence of any of these issues should be able to raise concerns without fear of victimisation.

Employee concerns and grievance subjects vary. They can range from issues affecting one individual with no organisational implications, to issues affecting a group of workers which challenge management decisions and with the potential to escalate to a collective dispute before being settled. There are common issues that give rise to formal grievances.

Monetary issues – Job evaluation outcomes; disagreements over performance assessment that impacts on pay; additional allowances, such as unsocial hours or on-call allowances, that are unclear or where the employee disagrees over interpretation and application of policies.

Work-related issues – Allocation of work where the employee feels that decisions are not made fairly; the inequitable allocation of highly desirable or unpleasant tasks; unfairness in the distribution of overtime; unfairness in the allocation of holiday or other leave – are decisions equitable and transparent?

Challenges to authority – Employees may challenge management's right to make a decision or the manner of the decision, for example whether it was taken in line with the procedure. When the organisation is undergoing change and increased managerial discretion is encouraged, there may be increased incidence of this type of grievance.

Grievance procedures

Grievance procedures provide a formal mechanism for the presentation and resolution of employee dissatisfaction. Exhibit 17.4 indicates the basic elements to be considered in developing this formal mechanism.

Exhibit 17.4   The basic elements of a grievance procedure

- There should be a formal procedure.
- The procedure should be in writing.
- Management should agree with employee representatives the procedure for raising grievances and for settling them promptly and effectively.
- If there are separate procedures for grievances and disputes these should be linked.
- An individual grievance should be settled as close to the point of origin and as quickly as possible.

Grievance procedures should set out the stages through which a grievance progresses within the organisational hierarchy. This recognises the authority and responsibility of the parties at the different organisational levels and allows for a structured approach. The stages should also define the timescale for the resolution of the problem. This allows for a review of the decision by both parties at each stage. The number of stages in a procedure is largely determined by the organisation structure, but in practical terms no more than three to four stages are workable. More than this can lead to a procedure that is unwieldy, slow and potentially confusing in the way it operates. There are normally three levels for hearing grievances – departmental, functional and senior level.

1 The departmental level provides the first hearing of the grievance through the line manager of the aggrieved person.

2 The functional level conducts the next hearing of an unresolved grievance and involves the line manager's manager or the functional manager.

3 The senior level conducts the third (usually final) hearing of an unresolved grievance and involves a member of the senior management team or the managing director or the chief executive.

There can be provision for an external review of the grievance or dispute, but this is uncommon in individual grievances, although an employee can complain to an employment tribunal. External review is more common in a collective disputes procedure, with many organisations providing for third-party intervention through ACAS or an employers' association. Exhibit 17.5 illustrates a grievance hearing structure.

Exhibit 17.5   Hearing structure for grievance or dispute

Stage Four – disputes only (external)	ACAS or employers' association
Stage Three (internal)	Senior manager or managing director or chief executive
Stage Two	Functional manager or manager's manager
Stage One	Line manager

The timescale for resolution, from receipt of the written grievance to its settlement, should be clearly defined and the aim should be to settle the grievance in the shortest possible time. The outcome of the grievance must be notified to the aggrieved person in writing, stating their right to take the grievance to the next stage of the procedure if there is dissatisfaction with the decision of the reviewing manager. The grievance procedure should identify the type of issues that can be raised, but this should not be used as a means of restricting the use of the procedure. There are problems, personality clashes for example, that cannot usually be resolved using a grievance procedure but only through effective communication and management. An example of a grievance procedure is shown in Exhibit 17.6.

Exhibit 17.6   Example of a grievance procedure

If you feel unhappy about any aspect of the application of agreements, procedures or terms and conditions of your employment and its impact on you, you have the right to raise this issue formally through the grievance procedure. You may raise issues informally with your line manager at any time. If a situation is not dealt with to your satisfaction informally you should take it up immediately through the grievance procedure. You have the right to be accompanied at any of these meetings by a trade union representative or by an employee of your choice.

Stage 1   You should inform your line manager immediately in writing of any situation you feel is unfair. Your manager will meet with you within three working days.

Stage 2   If the issue remains unresolved, you may progress the matter to your functional manager or your manager's manager. A meeting will be held within a further five working days.

Stage 3   If the situation remains unresolved to your satisfaction a further meeting will be held with a member of the senior management team or a director as appropriate. This meeting will be held within a further ten working days.

Situations of a sensitive nature such as discrimination or harassment or which directly involve your line manager may be raised in the first instance with the personnel manager.

Discrimination and harassment are highly sensitive issues, needing particularly careful handling, and may require a different procedure. The person doing the harassing or discriminating may be someone from within the aggrieved person's line management structure and this would make it problematic for the issue to be raised and resolved through the standard grievance procedure. In these cases the grievance may need to be reported to a specially designated, and trained, person and there is therefore a strong argument for having a separate procedure to deal with these sensitive issues (*see* Chapter 8).

Grievance interviews

The importance of management taking any grievance seriously cannot be over-emphasised. If employees feel strongly enough to use the formal grievance procedure to raise complaints they have the right to a fair and respectful hearing. Dissatisfactions and complaints raised outside the formal procedure also need to be treated with priority to reduce the likelihood of formal processes being needed. Indicators of a potential problem with unresolved dissatisfaction are high levels of labour turnover, absenteeism and low morale. Failure to investigate or attempt to identify internal causes may result in unfair treatment being unreported and unresolved, and may lead to longer-term problems for the organisation. A number of skills and conditions are required for grievance interviewing.

Provide an appropriate physical environment. It is important to the employee that the situation is being taken seriously and therefore a room where the complaint can be heard in private, free from interruption, should be made available. The employee should be given notice of the date, time and venue and informed of the right to be accompanied.

Listen to, and hear, what is being said by the aggrieved individual. Any interview requires good active listening skills, appropriate body language and eye contact if the aggrieved employee is to feel that the issue is being listened to and heard.

Ask appropriate questions in a non-threatening way. Empathetic questioning is essential to understanding the nature of the grievance and how the aggrieved person feels. The complaint must be fully exposed and this may need careful probing and questioning so that all of the facts can be identified and clarified. Questions should be asked in a calm and non-threatening way to encourage the employee to speak openly without feeling that it will disadvantage the case. It is valuable to identify the outcome the aggrieved is looking for, because it is not uncommon for the situation to require a negotiated settlement – compromise may be the only way forward.

Prepare. A grievance is employee-initiated and, apart from reading the written grievance carefully and gathering the facts of the matter, there may be little the manager can do to prepare for the first interview. It is at the subsequent stages that managerial preparation is mainly undertaken.

Analyse the facts and take a decision. Having heard all the facts of the case, consulted the relevant policy and looked at similar situations that may have set precedents, the manager takes a decision. Whilst it may be necessary to seek advice from another manager or a personnel specialist, care must be taken not to jeopardise the fairness of treatment of the employee. A manager works within the framework of organisational policies and procedures and the decision may set another precedent, in effect contributing to 'organisational case law'; therefore any managerial interpretation must be one that the employer can live with. If further time is needed for investigation, employee agreement should be sought for extending the procedural timescale to avoid the further complaint of not adhering to the agreed procedure.

Communication and monitoring of decisions

An individual grievance ends with an outcome that is accepted by the individual or the procedure is exhausted, but the situation should not end there. It is important that the decision is communicated clearly to the employee within the procedural timescale and that both parties understand exactly what has been agreed. Communication with the employee should normally be face-to-face and followed up in writing. There is value in monitoring grievances in terms of issues raised and outcomes agreed. Some of the terms and conditions of employment may need to be rewritten in a format that is more easily understood by employees and managers, or training may be needed to explain the implementation of policies. Issues that constantly give rise to grievances may highlight a problem. All grievance decisions should be analysed for the impact on the organisation and the establishment of precedents and this requires a monitoring procedure with all decisions notified to a central point – frequently the personnel department. The decisions should be aggregated, evaluated and communicated anonymously to relevant managers. Grievance incidents can be used positively in management development.

There is potential for managers to feel threatened by employee use of the formal grievance procedure. If there is a manager with a high incidence of formal grievances it may be an indicator of a training need. Managers require support to develop a full knowledge of the application of policies and procedures and to have the confidence to take difficult decisions. Flatter organisational structures and managerial empowerment may result in managers increasingly being in decision-making situations which require discretion. Managerial discretion requires well-educated and well-trained managers who communicate well with staff, both informally and formally. Managers should not be made to feel that the expression of grievances is a failure on their part, and they need support and encouragement to deal with them in an open and positive way. Employee concerns will only be resolved if managers know about them.

The Employment Bill, 2001

The Employment Bill, 2001 proposes measures to improve dispute resolution. These include:

- introducing statutory dismissal, disciplinary and grievance procedures into all contracts of employment as an implied term

- preventing complaints from being presented to tribunals before all or part of the relevant statutory procedure has been completed

- a fixed period of conciliation in order to promote a settlement

- allowing tribunals to disregard procedural mistakes by employers, providing that the minimum standards under the disciplinary procedures have been met

- enabling tribunals to vary compensation awards by up to 50 per cent where the employer or employee has failed to use the statutory procedures.

SUMMARY LEARNING POINTS

1 Disciplinary and grievance procedures can be positively viewed as individual conflict-resolving mechanisms. They allow mutual adjustment within the contract of employment through corrective action and concern resolution.

2 Organisation rules relating to employee conduct and performance need to be clear, and disciplinary procedures should provide for fairness and consistency in dealing with employees who break the rules. Disciplinary procedures gain credibility and potential for effectiveness through the incorporation of the principles of natural justice and the ACAS essential features.

3 The ACAS advisory handbook on discipline at work, incorporating the code of practice, provides good practice guidance for the design and operation of disciplinary procedures.

4 Disciplinary interviewing is a highly skilled activity requiring resilience and professionalism. Although it is not typical for interviews to progress smoothly and through orderly stages, the elements and structure of a good practice interview can be identified.

5 The law requires that grievance reporting procedures are communicated to employees and employees have a right to be accompanied at a grievance hearing. Different levels of dissatisfaction are in evidence in organisations and not all result in the employee using a formal grievance procedure. The formal procedure should support the speedy resolution as close to the problem as possible, and the timescales for a hearing should be expressed and adhered to.

6 The grievance hearing must be carried out fairly and professionally, ensuring that appropriate time and conditions are provided. Managers need to be skilled to hear grievances in an open and positive way. Some sensitive issues require particularly careful handling and may need other mechanisms for reporting and hearing.

7 Managerial decisions emerging from grievances should be monitored for organisational impact and precedent. Communication is therefore very important both to the individual and to the organisation.

REFERENCES AND FURTHER READING

Advisory, Conciliation and Arbitration Service (2000) *Code of Practice 1: Disciplinary and grievance procedures.*

Advisory, Conciliation and Arbitration Service (2000) *Discipline at Work: ACAS advisory handbook 1.* Periodically revised.

Aikin, O. (1999) 'The differences the Employment Relations Bill will make to individual employees' rights in the workplace', *People Management*, 11 March, 27–8.

Earnshaw, J. (1997) 'Tribunals and tribulations', *People Management*, May, 34–6.

Employment Digest 270 (1989) *Preparing for a Disciplinary Interview*, June.

Employment Relations Act (1999) London: HMSO.

Employment Rights Act (1996) London: HMSO.

Farnham, D. (2000) *Employee Relations in Context.* London: CIPD.

Farnham, D. and Pimlott, J. (1995) *Understanding Industrial Relations.* London: Cassell.

Fowler, A. (1994) 'How to handle employee grievances', *People Management Plus*, October.

Fowler, A. (1996) 'How to conduct a disciplinary interview', *People Management*, November.

Lewis, D. and Sargeant, M. (2000) *Essentials of Employment Law.* London: CIPD.

Pilbeam, S. and Corbridge, M. (2000) 'The skills of employee relations', in Farnham, D. (ed.), *Employee Relations in Context.* London: CIPD.

Public Interest Disclosure Act (1998) London: HMSO.

Salamon, M. (1998) *Industrial Relations: Theory and practice* (3rd edn). Hemel Hempstead: Prentice Hall.

Temperton, E. (2000) 'Disciplinary procedures: the right to moral support', *People Management*, 16 March, 21–2.

ASSIGNMENTS AND DISCUSSION TOPICS

1 Discuss with student or work colleagues what they perceive to be the meaning of discipline at work; identify the retributive, deterrent and rehabilitative elements.

2 How can a positive and problem-solving approach to disciplinary matters be achieved in practice?

3 Critically evaluate the effectiveness of the communication of continuously evolving managerial rules to employees in your organisation.

4 Obtain one or more disciplinary procedures and test them against the principles of natural justice and the ACAS essential features.

5 Obtain copies of several disciplinary procedures and compare and contrast them in relation to:

- the number and specification of stages
- the managerial responsibilities at each stage
- the time limits on warnings
- the requirements to sign warning letters and the significance of the signature.

6 Discuss the view that managers can only be **objective** and never be **impartial** in disciplinary matters.

7 Critically evaluate the role of the personnel specialist in matters of employee discipline in several organisations and explain any similarities or differences.

8 Difficult cases – duty of care or disciplinary matter?

How would you respond to these employee statements at work and what are the issues you need to consider?

(a) *'My fingers are painful – I will be back next year!'*

(b) *'My doctor says I can't do that aspect of my job for health reasons.'*

9 One of your employees recently refused to leave the building when the fire alarm went off. Your task is to discuss how you would handle this incident, taking full account of the principles of natural justice and the features of a good disciplinary procedure. You can prepare for dealing with it by considering different responses from the employee in relation to the question *'Why did you refuse to leave the building?'* What would you do and what will be your decision?

10 What are the arguments for having a grievance procedure? What are the key professional and ethical characteristics of an effective grievance procedure?

11 Undertake a review of the grievance procedure in your organisation. Does it pass the test of a legal, workable and clear procedure?

12 What advice would you give to a newly appointed line manager who has been presented with a written formal grievance?

13 What skills or competencies do managers require to handle individual grievances fairly and equitably? Undertake a training needs analysis for grievance handling for a new manager in your organisation.

14 Investigate the number of formal grievances in your organisation over a specified period. Analyse the subjects of the grievances and the outcomes of the hearings. Write a brief report on your findings, paying particular attention to any organisational implications.

CASE STUDY

Discipline at work – Jobs for the Toys Limited

You are employed as the Personnel Officer at Jobs for the Toys Limited. It is a wholesale operation and supplies gifts, stationery and toys to the retail trade. There are approximately 120 employees.

You recently advertised for a Sales Office Manager and, as the successful applicant would be required to call on clients a couple of times each week, a pool car would be made available when required. In view of this driving requirement, the

Case study continued

job description and the person specification, and the application form, made it clear that applicants would need to have a current and clean driving licence.

The recruitment and selection process was successful and you appointed what you considered to be a good-grade candidate. Her name is Betty Garland. Betty has now been working for the organisation for several months and, although she is meeting the minimum job requirements, you do not feel that she is realising her potential as quickly as you had anticipated. In particular, her communication skills appear limited and at times she can give the impression of being either evasive or a little confused.

Since Betty started with the organisation there have been several occasions when a pool car has not been available. In these circumstances employees who need transport can hire a vehicle from The Self Drive Company, with whom you have a long-standing business relationship. On checking the invoices it became apparent to the Accounts Supervisor that the cost of hiring a car for Betty was greater than for other employees in the organisation. The Accounts Supervisor checked with The Self Drive Company, but did not receive a satisfactory explanation. She therefore drew it to your attention.

You contacted the car hire firm and discovered that the reason for Betty being charged a higher amount for the hire of a car was that, on inspecting her driving licence, The Self Drive Company noted that the licence contained a current endorsement for driving without insurance. This resulted in an additional premium being charged for the hiring of a car. Naturally this concerns you and you check Betty's personal file. The application form contains the following question: 'Do you hold a clean driving licence?' Betty has answered 'Yes'!

Questions and Activities

1 What impact does this situation have on the employment relationship between Jobs for the Toys and Betty, and what particular issues do you need to consider before embarking upon a course of action?

2 What alternative forms of action, or inaction, are available to you?

3 Taking account of the principles of natural justice, what will be your approach if you decide to hold a disciplinary hearing?

4 Be prepared to undertake the disciplinary hearing in a role-play situation with somebody taking the role of Betty.

5 Having undertaken the disciplinary hearing in which Betty confirms that she does have a current endorsement, which she failed to declare, what action will you take and why?

You can assume that Jobs for the Toys has a disciplinary policy and procedure which is based on ACAS guidelines.

CHAPTER 18

Termination of employment

INTRODUCTION

Employees who have been resourced into the organisation will at some stage disengage or be released from the contract of employment. Termination of employment, whether through dismissal, resignation or retirement, is a crucial function of the people resourcing aim of having the right people, in the right place, at the right time. It is necessary to understand the legal framework for dismissal, as it provides an effective practice guide and enables employers to act reasonably and fairly. In addition to statutory provision, case law establishes or redefines dismissal principles, and it is therefore necessary for managers to scan the legal environment. The effective management of termination of employment contributes to protecting an organisation's investment in people through ensuring that the right people remain in employment, and also avoids the financial and other costs associated with successful employee claims for unfair dismissal. Redundancy is given special consideration in the next chapter.

CHAPTER OBJECTIVES

- To examine the termination of the contract through dismissal.
- To consider relevant legislation, professionalism and good practice with a particular emphasis on fairness and reasonableness in the dismissal of employees.
- To offer practical guidance on fair reasons for dismissal and on avoiding successful claims for unfair dismissal.
- To introduce the structure and processes of employment tribunals.

INTRODUCTION TO DISMISSAL

The legal framework relating to dismissal is continuously evolving, not only through statute but also through principles which emerge from decisions in specific cases. The search for right and wrong answers in the management of employee dismissal is elusive, but this does not absolve practitioners from needing to know when more knowledgeable or expert advice is required. This is the rationale for a focus on dismissal in this chapter, because pitfalls await the unwary who may think a dismissal progresses smoothly and naturally. A more appropriate view is that:

> A dismissal consists of collecting relevant information, a sequence of decision points and informed judgement based on a knowledge of the legal framework, the principles of natural justice and considerable skill.

Dismissal cannot be divorced from the procedures for conflict resolution discussed in the previous chapter.

The legal environment should be continuously scanned for dismissal developments. This scanning provides guidance on current thinking in employment law, gives insights into how legislation is being interpreted, and identifies difficulties in which other employers have become entangled. A cautionary note is valid. Rather than searching for particular precedents, perhaps the domain of lawyers, it is advocated that dismissal decisions are guided by the general concepts of fairness, reasonableness and respect for the employee. This integrates an ethical dimension with the legal framework and contributes to good employment relations (Exhibit 18.1). Good dismissal practice and principles are preferable to mechanistic subservience to the law, and courts recognise that employers are not always perfect.

Exhibit 18.1   An ethical approach to dismissal within the legal framework

- Is the employee ready, willing and able?
- Is the employer able to provide work?
- Is the employee responding reasonably to the genuine needs and demands of the employer?
- Is the employee being treated with respect?
- Is the mutual trust and confidence necessary to the performance of the contract intact?

THE ORIGINS AND AIMS OF UNFAIR DISMISSAL LEGISLATION

Prior to the Industrial Relations Act (IRA), 1971, there was little constraint on employers who wished to dismiss employees and, with a few exceptions, dismissal could be for any reason or for no reason. The IRA created a limited job property right for employees and attributed a specific legal meaning to the concept of unfair dismissal. The main dismissal provisions are now consolidated in the Employment Rights Act (ERA), 1996. The law is intended to afford some protection to employees against unreasonable treatment by employers which ends in loss of employment. There is a debate about the extent to which the law was aimed at encouraging fair practice in dismissal, with the legal remedies as a backstop, and the extent to which the law had the objective of enabling unfairly dismissed employees to be reinstated in their jobs. Which of these two perspectives is adopted will influence a judgement about whether the law has been successful (*see* Summary learning points 2, 3, 5 and 6).

The right of employees not to be unfairly dismissed was feared by employers as a significant infringement of managerial prerogative. These fears are largely unrealised, because the legislation does not deprive employers of the freedom to dismiss employees, and employers cannot be required to re-employ dismissed employees. The legal protection provides for some financial sanctions against employers who dismiss employees unfairly and unreasonably. In reality:

The law actually legitimises dismissal by defining it as fair and reasonable in certain circumstances through providing a set of rules and guidelines which allow employers to dismiss employees without fear of adverse consequences – the right of managers to dismiss is effectively made legitimate.

TYPES OF DISMISSAL

Distinctions need to be drawn between different types of dismissal to avoid incorrect usage. Wrongful and unfair dismissal have different meanings. Wrongful dismissal relates to a fundamental breach of contract, normally because of improper notice periods or payments in lieu of notice. Wrongful dismissal claims were formerly heard by County Courts, but can now be adjudicated by an employment tribunal, by a chairperson sitting alone. The remedy for successful claims of wrongful dismissal is normally limited to an amount equal to the payment due from the date of the wrongful dismissal to the date when the employment would have been lawfully terminated.

Unfair dismissal, in contrast, has a distinct legal meaning and is a dismissal which is not for one of the potentially fair reasons, as defined by the ERA 1996, or is not reasonable in the circumstances.

Claims for unfair dismissals are heard by an employment tribunal.

Dismissal with notice, summary dismissal and instant dismissal also have different meanings. Employees are normally entitled to be given proper notice of termination of the contract by the employer; this is termed dismissal with notice. Frequently an employee will receive payment in lieu of notice, because the employer no longer wants the employee at work. Whether this payment in lieu of notice is contractually legitimate or whether it constitutes damages for failure to give proper notice is subject to legal debate, but in practical terms the employee faced with the prospect of being paid and not having to work for it frequently finds this an attractive option.

Summary dismissal is dismissal without notice and will be lawful when an employee breaches a fundamental term of the contract of employment. This will normally be the case if the employer establishes a reasonable belief that the employee has committed an act of gross misconduct or when there is a wilful refusal to obey a legitimate and reasonable instruction. Gross misconduct and refusals to obey instructions go to the root of the employment relationship and destroy the contract; in these circumstances the employer is not obligated by the contractual term to give contractual notice, and summary dismissal occurs. Instant dismissal, which is often confused with summary dismissal, describes an immediate dismissal *without* proper investigation and *without* incorporating the principles of natural justice. Instant dismissal, unlike summary dismissal, has no legal standing and is likely to be judged by an employment tribunal as procedurally unfair; it should therefore be avoided.

DISMISSAL DEFINED

There are three principal dismissal occurrences.

1 The employer terminates the contract of employment, with or without notice.
2 The employee terminates the contract of employment by reason of the employer's behaviour (commonly known as constructive dismissal).
3 A fixed-term contract expires and is not renewed.

Where there is unambiguous employer action to terminate employment, the fact of the dismissal may be relatively easy to establish. Employer intention to dismiss must be clear and the employee cannot unreasonably interpret as a dismissal an ambiguous statement, a dismissive comment or a dismissal attempt by an unauthorised person. The test is whether there is a genuine and legitimate intention to dismiss the employee. It is an obvious truism that dismissal needs to be established before any claim for unfair dismissal can proceed, but there is frequently debate on whether a dismissal has taken place and often a difficulty in identifying an effective date of termination with precision. Agreements to terminate the contract do not constitute dismissal, but are only valid if the employee agrees to terminate with full knowledge of all the implications. An invitation to resign, as a preferable alternative to being dismissed, or the persuasion to resign under duress, or the tricking of an employee into resigning, are likely to constitute dismissals.

If the employee resigns there is no dismissal, but employee intentions must be clear. A 'throw-away' comment by an employee, either in a provocative situation or when under pressure, cannot be snatched by the employer as a resignation. An unreasonable interpretation of employee words or actions will constitute a dismissal rather than a resignation, and proper investigation is needed to establish the real employee intention if 'reasonableness' is a managerial concern. Where the resignation is unambiguous the employer is not obliged to agree to a subsequent employee request to withdraw the resignation, although the employer can choose to do so. An employer can also choose to withdraw a dismissal if an error is made.

In the case of 'constructive dismissal' it is the employee who resigns, but claims that the contract of employment has been terminated by the employer's unreasonable treatment or behaviour. The elusive question is – under what circumstances can an employee resign and claim dismissal? This is explored later in this chapter. Dismissal can also occur through the expiry and non-renewal of a fixed-term contract. Dismissal at expiry will be lawful if there is a genuine employer need for a fixed-term contract, for example in the case of a project or a limited amount of work. Dismissal at the expiry of a fixed-term contract may be unreasonable if the contract is merely being used to limit statutory employment rights. To demonstrate reasonableness an employer may need to show that when a fixed-term contract expires the employee is fairly considered for other employment opportunities. An employer cannot lawfully avoid a continuous service requirement for statutory employee protection through a succession of fixed-term contracts. Attempts to avoid continuous employment through a succession of contracts which incorporate breaks in employment may be interpreted as 'a cessation of work within continuous employment'. It is the ratio of employment to unemployment with the same employer that will be significant in determining continuous employment. These complications are introduced because there is sometimes an uninformed view that fixed-term contracts, in supporting numerical flexibility, are largely free of legal constraint. Despite the generally positive mood of employment tribunals towards the employer's need to run enterprises flexibly and efficiently, employer freedom to use fixed-term contracts is circumscribed. First, it is no longer lawful for fixed-term workers to waive their rights to claim unfair dismissal (Employment Relations Act, 1999). Second, the European Union Fixed Term Work Directive gives fixed-term workers the same rights as those on unlimited contracts and seeks to control 'the abusive use of fixed-term contracts' (Aikin, 2001). Fixed-term contracts are an area where further and better advice may be desirable.

EMPLOYEE QUALIFICATION FOR UNFAIR DISMISSAL PROTECTION

To qualify for protection against unfair dismissal an individual must first be an employee, with a contract of employment. Currently, an individual with a contract for services will not qualify. The distinction between a contract of employment and a contract for services is becoming less easy to define, and specialist reading is necessary for those interested in the distinction. The courts tend to apply a 'multiple test' to determine employment or self-employment status (Selwyn, 2000). A mutual agreement for an employee to become self-employed is not conclusive and, in the context of this chapter, the 'self-employed' individual may retain statutory protection against unfair dismissal. Teleworking trends generate further complexity for employment status and protection.

Employees also need to be under 65 years of age or, where it is different, the normal retirement age for the organisation. The normal retirement age may be explicit or implied into the contract of employment. Where the normal retirement age varies within an organisation it is the relevant group of employees that is the reference point. Where there is flexibility of retirement age the upper age limit or the age at which employees can be compelled to retire will apply. Age limits on unfair dismissal protection are subject to challenge on the grounds of ageism.

Employees normally require one year's continuous service with the same employer, although some reasons for dismissal are inadmissible (*see* page 442) and do not have a service requirement, or in some cases an upper age limit. The continuous service qualification period for protection against unfair dismissal has been six months (in 1974) and two years (up to 1999), and sometimes up to five years for part-time workers. In striking a balance between equal treatment objectives, particularly concerns about the potential for indirect discrimination against female employees, and employer flexibility to run businesses efficiently through being able to dismiss employees during the first year, the government settled on the one-year qualification period. There is no reason why the one-year period should not be subject to further challenges.

INADMISSIBLE REASONS FOR DISMISSAL

Dismissal for an inadmissible reason will render it automatically unfair and the two-year service requirement will not normally apply. **Potentially** inadmissible reasons include dismissal on the grounds of:

- pregnancy or maternity
- sex or race or disability
- spent convictions
- refusal to work on a Sunday
- health and safety activities or actions
- asserting a statutory employment right
- trade union membership, activity or non-membership
- the relevant transfer of an undertaking
- making a protected public interest disclosure
- exercising rights under the Working Time Regulations, 1998
- *no* reason being given.

The scope of these inadmissible reasons may appear disproportionate in relation to the scope of the five potentially fair reasons (*see* below), but in practice the converse is the case. Inadmissible reasons are discussed briefly because managers need to recognise that special considerations apply. Good practice and an ethical approach will normally avert any problems.

Dismissal on the grounds of pregnancy, or for any reason connected to pregnancy, is effectively outlawed (ERA 1996: 599). This applies during pregnancy, during maternity leave or on return from maternity leave. It is unfair to select an employee for redundancy on the grounds of pregnancy or maternity leave. Attempts to construct a hypothetical 'pregnant-man' comparison to justify dismissal on the grounds of non-availability for work have failed (Webb *v* EMO [1995] IRLR 645 and Tele Danmark *v* Brandt-Neilsen [2001] IDS Brief 696, ECJ). By implication it may be unlawful to refuse to employ a pregnant woman or a woman of childbearing age because she may become pregnant. Dismissal on the grounds of sex, marital status, race or ethnic origin is effectively outlawed by the Sex Discrimination Act 1975 and the Race Relations Act 1976, as amended. The legislation covers acts of direct discrimination and also acts of indirect discrimination which are to the detriment of the employee and which cannot be objectively justified. Indirect discrimination may occur, for example, if employees are selected for redundancy on the basis that they work part-time hours, because this may have a disproportionate impact on women who make up the majority of part-time workers. Dismissal as a result of pressure from other employees on the grounds of sex, marital status, race or ethnic origin is not justifiable. The burden of proof is now on employers to demonstrate that unlawful sex or race discrimination did *not* take place. Dismissal on the grounds of a disability, as defined by the Disability Discrimination Act 1995, may be automatically unfair unless it is justifiable within the terms of the Act.

Under the Rehabilitation of Offenders Act 1974 a spent conviction is not a proper reason for dismissal, although certain occupations are exempted. Under the Sunday

Trading Act 1994, consolidated in ERA 1996, 'protected workers' who refuse to work on a Sunday cannot be fairly dismissed on the grounds of the refusal (New Employment Rights for Shop Workers – PL960 DfEE). Employers are not able to fairly dismiss employees for carrying out authorised health and safety duties or who alert the employer to a reasonable health and safety concern. It is normally unfair to dismiss an employee for ceasing work or taking other appropriate protective steps because of a genuine belief of being in serious and imminent danger. Employees will be unfairly dismissed if the principal reason is related to the assertion of a statutory employment right. This assertion may be an allegation that a right is being denied or other employee action, for example commencing employment tribunal proceedings, to enforce the right. The statutory right does not have to apply to the employee asserting the right. Also it is immaterial whether the asserting employee qualifies for the right; the test is whether the employee has a genuine belief of qualification and whether the allegation is made in good faith.

A dismissal will be unfair if it is for one of the following reasons:

- for becoming or proposing to become a member of an independent trade union
- for taking part or proposing to take part in the activities of an independent trade union at appropriate times
- for not being a member of a trade union or refusing to become a member or refusing to remain a member of a trade union.

Where a business or a part of a business, in legal terms an economic entity, is transferred from one employer to another, through sale or externalisation, a dismissal, by the old or the new employer, will be considered unfair if the reason for the dismissal is principally connected with the transfer of the undertaking. Dismissal relating to business transfers needs to be treated with considerable care, particularly as the guiding principles keep changing through case law. The Working Time Regulations (1998) provide workers with the right to paid leave and to rest periods, and also limit the number of hours they can be required to work on average in each week. Employees will be unfairly dismissed where they refuse to comply with an employer instruction which is in contravention of the regulations. The Public Interest Disclosure Act (1999) provides protection for 'whistleblowers' – workers who are dismissed or victimised for making a qualifying disclosure. Finally, a dismissal is automatically unfair where no reason is given.

FAIR REASONS FOR DISMISSAL

An employee can be lawfully dismissed for one of five potentially fair reasons:

- misconduct
- lack of capability
- redundancy
- statutory bar to employment
- some other substantial reason.

For a dismissal to be fair, not only must an employer have a fair reason but also the dismissal must pass the test of 'reasonableness in the circumstances'.

Misconduct dismissals lead to many complaints for unfair dismissal, and specific types of misconduct are explored later in this chapter. Lack of capability relates to the skill, aptitude, physical and mental abilities, health, flexibility and qualifications of the employee in relation to contractual duties. Redundancy will normally be fair and reasonable where selection for redundancy is based on an objective procedure, where consultation arrangements have been appropriate and where alternative employment options have been explored (Langston v University of Cranfield [1998] IRLB 591; EAT). A statutory bar applies where the continued employment of an employee would result in a contravention of a legal duty, and in these circumstances an employer may fairly dismiss. The fifth fair reason for dismissal is some other substantial reason (SOSR) of a kind that justifies dismissal, an acknowledgement that the previous four reasons are not exhaustive. These potentially fair reasons provide the employer with comprehensive scope for dismissal through legitimising it where:

- the employee's behaviour is unacceptable
- the employee cannot do the job
- there is no work for the employee
- the employee cannot legally be employed
- there are other substantial impediments to employment.

For a dismissal to be fair, an employer needs to show that it was for one of the five potentially fair reasons. This forms the basis for resisting any allegation of unfair dismissal. It is not always a simple matter to categorise correctly a dismissal and, although there should be a genuine effort to do so, an incorrect categorisation will not automatically invalidate the employer's argument that the dismissal was for a fair reason. As well as having a legal purpose, the five fair reasons for dismissal provide a useful framework for dealing with problems at work.

REASONABLENESS

Even where dismissal is for a fair reason, the substantive issue of whether the dismissal is fair rests on whether the action of the employer is 'reasonable in the circumstances'.

> The question of reasonableness will be determined in accordance with equity and the substantial merits of the case.
>
> (ERA, 1996)

Reasonableness is not determined by a judgement of whether the dismissal was correct, but 'whether the dismissal fell within the range of responses of a reasonable employer'. If the circumstances of the dismissal place it within this range, then it will be reasonable. Reasonableness in the circumstances is not an objective standard and the question of whether an employer acted reasonably involves consideration of the way in which the dismissal was carried out, in the context of the organisation's size and resources, and

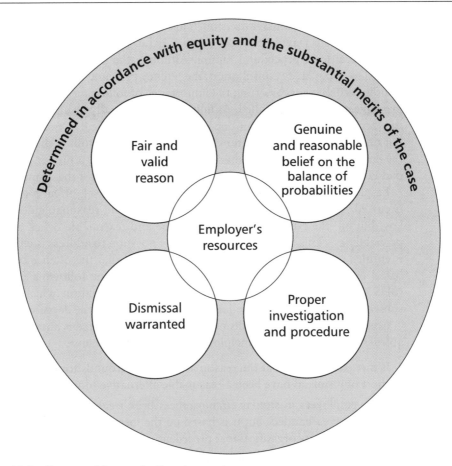

Fig. 18.1 Reasonableness in the circumstances

whether the reason for dismissing the employee was a sufficient reason. Figure 18.1 provides a framework for considering this concept of reasonableness.

The legal framework, the ACAS advisory handbook and tribunal decisions recognise that the size, the nature of the work activity and the resources of an organisation are material factors in determining reasonableness in the circumstances. A disciplinary procedure appropriate to a large organisation may be inappropriate for a much smaller one. The length of time and extent to which sub-standard employee performance can be accommodated will be influenced by the nature of the work and the impact of the individual performance on organisational effectiveness. Opportunities for redeployment, disciplinary transfer or other action short of dismissal will similarly be facilitated or limited by the employer's resources. Procedural fairness involves thorough investigation, a proper hearing, the opportunity for an employee to offer an explanation, accompaniment, and the right of appeal. Good documentation of the procedural steps in dismissal cases is important in establishing the reasonableness of employer action.

Until 1987 there existed a principle known as the 'no difference rule'. Even where a proper procedure had *not* been followed in a dismissal, it was open to an employer to argue that even if a proper procedure *had* been applied it would have made 'no difference' to the dismissal decision. This principle was effectively exploded in the case of Polkey *v* A E Dayton Services ([1987] IRLR 503), where dismissal was found to be unfair because of procedural failure. Although the procedural failure in that instance related to redundancy consultation, the 'Polkey principle' has been extended by tribunals to other dismissals, reasserting the importance of following a fair procedure. The Polkey principle needs to be qualified. Although it will normally be unreasonable to depart from the disciplinary procedure, a departure may be justified in exceptional circumstances, but only where a conscious and valid judgement not to follow the procedure is made by the employer prior to the dismissal. Failure to adhere to a proper procedure is not only bad HR practice, but may also impact on the legitimacy of the dismissal.

Employers do not have to '**prove**' that a dismissal offence or incident actually occurred. The burden of proof is not one of 'beyond reasonable doubt', as in criminal law, but on 'the establishment of a genuine and reasonable belief' and 'the balance of probabilities'. This is a vital distinction. The question to address is whether the employer is entitled to hold a genuine and reasonable belief that the offence or incident occurred based on the factual information available at the time following proper investigation (BHS *v* Burchell [1980] IRLR 379). Contrary information which becomes available subsequent to the dismissal will not normally invalidate the decision to dismiss.

Consideration of whether dismissal is actually warranted is another element of reasonableness. There are three principles to emerge from case law:

1 Is it reasonable to treat the reason as sufficient grounds for dismissal or would action short of dismissal have been a reasonable alternative (does the penalty fit the crime)?

2 Have employees in similar circumstances been treated similarly? This is the concept of being even-handed, but it is based on the merits of the case as the employer is not legally bound by organisational precedent.

3 Are there mitigating circumstances? Examples include previous good record, length of service, external pressures, aberration, or employer contribution to the circumstances of the dismissal.

FIVE FAIR REASONS EXPLORED

The five potentially fair reasons referred to on page 443 are now examined from a practical and managerial perspective. Prescriptive guidance is inappropriate, because each case will need to be considered on its substantial merits, but dismissal examples are explored and attention is drawn to related issues. The intention is to provide a focus for investigation when these issues arise at work.

Misconduct

It is necessary to differentiate between general misconduct, serious misconduct and gross misconduct. General and serious misconduct may not warrant dismissal until the disciplinary procedure has been exhausted and may be dealt with incrementally under that procedure. Gross misconduct may go to the root of the contract and warrant summary dismissal. The employer has a duty to determine and to communicate those types of misconduct that may lead to loss of employment.

> Employees should be made aware of the likely consequences of breaking rules and in particular they should be given a clear indication of the type of conduct which may warrant summary dismissal.

> (ACAS, Code of Practice 1, 2000)

It is good practice for employers to provide indicative examples of gross misconduct, without making them exclusive or exhaustive, as case law demonstrates that people are creative in identifying and enacting new forms of gross misconduct. Automatic dismissal for incidents of gross misconduct is not justified and natural justice principles should still apply. Seven examples of misconduct will be specifically addressed in the following sections:

- theft and dishonesty
- violence
- alcohol abuse
- breach of confidence
- refusal to obey instructions
- absenteeism
- misconduct outside the workplace.

These are potentially fair reasons for dismissal, but the focus of attention needs to be on the circumstances under which they warrant fair and reasonable dismissal. The crucial question will frequently be whether the mutual trust and confidence necessary for the performance of the contract has been destroyed by the conduct of the employee. If it has then dismissal will follow. An important consideration for employers is that action short of dismissal for very serious misconduct may send signals to the workforce that certain types of behaviour, although disapproved, do not result in loss of employment.

Theft and dishonesty. If an employee is suspected of theft or dishonesty the employer is not obliged to prove guilt beyond reasonable doubt. The employer's obligation is to establish a genuinely held and reasonable belief that the theft or dishonest act is attributable to the employee, following appropriate investigation. It is important to adhere to a proper procedure even where theft or dishonesty may appear to be an open and shut case. In a *prima facie* case of dishonesty the usual sequence of prior investigation, the opportunity for the employee to explain and the consideration of the explanation should still be followed. It is often appropriate to suspend the employee during the investigatory process.

Allegations of theft or dishonesty may result in criminal proceedings. There are several issues here. First, the employer may wish to establish a reasonable belief, depending on the nature of the offence, before involving the police, as simultaneous investigations with different burdens of proof may add complexity to the dismissal question. Second, once criminal investigations are initiated, freedom may be constrained because employer action may interfere with or prejudice judicial proceedings. Third, the employer is not obliged to await the outcome of a criminal trial before making a decision, although where a reasonable belief has not been established it may be appropriate to do so. Fourth, the employer can consider information not admissible in a criminal trial. Fifth, even if a dismissed employee is acquitted in a court of law the dismissal is not rendered unfair, provided the employer acted reasonably; in such circumstances the court proceedings are considered to be largely irrelevant. A serious breach of rules or regulations is normally associated with an act of dishonesty and it is this breach that may warrant dismissal, not an alleged criminal offence (see Exhibit 18.2).

Exhibit 18.2   An illustrative case of dishonesty dismissal and the burden of proof

Peter is a supervisor with Bright Lights, an electrical wholesaler, and has been employed for three years. Part of his job is to transfer electrical components to a sub-contractor, Tom, using official company documentation. Tom is a legitimate company sub-contractor who repairs faulty electrical appliances. On two occasions Peter, using official documentation, has transferred to Tom more electrical components than was justified. The surplus components have been sold to the trade and the money given to Peter by Tom. The estimated value of the surplus components is £300.

The employer discovers this arrangement. It is a breach of administrative procedures and clearly undermines the degree of trust and confidence the employer can have in Peter. A reasonable belief is established that the illegitimate transfers have taken place, in fact strong evidence exists. During the disciplinary hearing Peter realises that the employer can substantiate the allegation and he admits to it.

Peter's explanation is that he was merely responding to pressure from his friends in the trade to supply components at short notice, that he had no dishonest intention and he intended to arrange for the cost of the components to be charged to his employee account so that he could pay Bright Lights retrospectively. The employee account system enables employees to purchase electrical components by signing charging slips at the point of purchase and receiving a demand for payment at the end of each month. Bright Lights did not accept Peter's explanation as legitimate and after due consideration dismissed him summarily. Criminal proceedings were also instigated following a reporting of the matter to the police. At the same time Peter initiated a claim for unfair dismissal.

The decisions of the respective judicial bodies provide an interesting contrast. The employment tribunal was satisfied that the dismissal was fair and reasonable because the employer established a reasonable belief that a serious breach of rules had occurred and that the dismissal was justified because mutual trust and confidence in the contract of the employment had effectively been destroyed. In the criminal proceedings, Peter elected trial by jury and was acquitted on the charge of theft. The judge was influential in the verdict as he pointed out to the jury that Bright Lights may have contributed to the situation because the principle of retrospective employee payment was condoned by Bright Lights. The criminal issue was whether or not Peter intended to pay for the electrical components retrospectively, and it could not be established beyond all reasonable doubt that he did **not** intend to do so. He was therefore found 'not guilty'. This case brings into sharp relief the different issues and burdens of proof associated with Employment Law and Criminal Law. The 'not guilty' verdict does not invalidate the legitimacy of dismissal.

Under what circumstances is an act of theft or dishonesty not gross misconduct? This is problematic, but the question is posed because there may be an inclination to consider all acts of theft or dishonesty as gross misconduct – can such an inclination be justified? The seriousness of the act may be a determining factor, but how can the degree of seriousness be established? The following points need to be taken into account:

- the triviality or gravity of the offence, based on considerations of value, volume, frequency and impact on the business
- custom and practice relating to the offence and the extent to which rules are made clear and actually enforced
- the even-handedness with which offenders are treated; for example, it may be unreasonable to clamp down on a dishonest practice by making an example of one individual
- the organisational position of the offender; for example, responsibility for others, seniority and the level of trust necessary
- previous record, length of service and any substantive mitigating circumstances.

Some acts of theft or dishonesty will clearly be gross misconduct. However, depending upon the organisational circumstances, the use of telephones for personal calls, sending personal e-mail, using the Internet for non-business reasons, the freeloading of stationery, or the unauthorised removal of materials or equipment no longer required by the organisation may be less clear cut.

Violence. A very serious view is normally taken of violence by or between employees at work. Violence is not only a physical act, since threatening behaviour or harassment may constitute psychological violence. Although it is reasonable to rule that fighting will normally result in summary dismissal, this still needs to be communicated unambiguously. Even in the case of serious and overt violence, it remains necessary to investigate it thoroughly to establish reasons and motivation, but those involved should only be interviewed when they are in a fit state, emotionally and physically.

If it emerges that there is an aggressor and a victim, the latter only acting in self-defence, the employer can treat the aggressor and the victim differently. Where it is not possible to distinguish between an aggressor and a victim, and where the violent incident warrants summary dismissal, it may be reasonable for the employer to dismiss both parties. Although this may not appear to be fair, it is a demonstration of how an employer is entitled to protect the interests of the undertaking, if necessary to the detriment of the employee. Other issues which may be material to an investigation into violence include:

- the degree of violence
- the degree of provocation
- the location of the violent act
- custom and practice; for example, condoned horseplay or initiation rituals
- the position, length of service and record of those involved, together with any substantive mitigating circumstances
- implications for the standing or reputation of the organisation.

Consideration of these factors will enable a reasonable employer to reach a decision about whether dismissal or action short of dismissal is appropriate when dealing with violence at work.

Alcohol abuse. Merely being under the influence of alcohol at work may not be a sufficient reason for dismissal, unless some other act is committed whilst under the influence, such as an act of violence, damage, abuse or insubordination, or where there are serious safety implications or where the employee's position is such that the alcohol-related conduct goes to the root of the contract and destroys mutual trust and confidence. It is important to distinguish between the act of drinking, smelling of alcohol, being under the influence and being unfit for work, as they may warrant different managerial responses. The employee should always be asked to provide an explanation for any alcohol-related incidents, but only when in a fit state to do so.

An alcohol-related incident should be considered in the context of the organisational alcohol policy that defines the rules on alcohol consumption, which may range from a total ban, to drinking that is legitimate and socially acceptable (*see* Chapter 14). An aircraft pilot and a train driver have been fairly dismissed for relatively small amounts of alcohol consumption, but in contrast it may be entirely acceptable for employees in some occupations to entertain professional clients and consume alcohol as part of the hospitality activity. The provision of alcohol at authorised social functions may make an employer an accessory to alcohol-related misconduct. The alcohol rules should be clear and the employer is entitled to expect responsible behaviour from the employees even where the consumption is sanctioned.

Alcoholism and alcohol dependency may constitute a medical problem, with implications for support and treatment, and need to be treated differently from an incident of alcohol abuse. Failure by an employee to respond to alcohol counselling or treatment will be a fair reason for dismissal, probably on the grounds of incapability rather than misconduct. The test will be the reasonableness of the dismissal in the particular circumstances (*see* end-of-chapter assignment 4).

Breach of confidence. Employers are entitled to take a serious view of breaches of confidence by an employee, and the seriousness of these matters is recognised by tribunals. The employee owes a common law duty of fidelity to the employer. There are two principal ways in which confidence can be breached: first, by disclosing confidential information to a competitor or other unauthorised persons, and second, through seeking to bring the organisation into disrepute.

In a case of disclosing confidential information the factors to consider are the significance of the information itself, the means by which it was obtained, the motivation for disclosure, the position of the employee and the nature and extent of any potential or real damage to the organisation. Similarly, in bringing the organisation into disrepute, the issues will relate to significance, motivation, position and damage. Organisation culture and managerial values may influence the extent to which employees are 'permitted' to complain about or disparage the organisation, but it is unreasonable to expect employees not to express some discontent, and mutual trust and confidence will need to be destroyed before dismissal is reasonable.

Refusal to obey instructions.   An implicit obligation of the contract of employment is that an employee will obey the employer's instructions. A refusal to obey, enacted as either insubordination or disobedience, may amount to gross misconduct and be a fair reason for dismissal. The instructions must be legitimate and reasonable and there is no employee contractual obligation to conform to unlawful or unreasonable orders. Safety instructions can illustrate these points. Refusal by an employee to work safely, following proper instruction, may constitute gross misconduct, whilst refusal to work in an unsafe situation may be legitimate.

If an employee refuses to obey a managerial instruction, the issues to consider are the clarity and comprehensibility of the instruction, whether it is legitimate to insist that the instruction be carried out, and whether the employee is fully aware of the consequences of continued refusal.

The principle is that instructions have to be reasonable and refusals have to be unreasonable.

In cases of a refusal to obey instructions the employer needs to consider redeployment or other action short of dismissal as an alternative to terminating employment. Where the employee genuinely questions the legitimacy of instructions, a reasonable employer will take time to consider and explain, but the right to manage and the requirement to obey are fundamental features of the contract, and tribunal decisions tend to recognise that a refusal may result in loss of employment for the employee.

A contemporary question is the extent to which an employer can insist that an employee works 'beyond contract'. Is a refusal to work beyond contract legitimate or obstructive to the performance of the contract? The issue is again one of reasonableness – how much performance beyond contract is being required and what is normal practice? The position of one employee who refuses to work extra uncompensated hours or take on additional work may be undermined where the majority of employees conform to such an order.

Absenteeism.   Absenteeism in a misconduct context relates to unauthorised absence from work and not to ill-health absence which is a capability issue. Absenteeism is a difficult area as an employee may claim that the absence is due to sickness, and therefore implicitly authorised. The manager needs to establish the validity of sickness claims, but this is problematic. A false claim that absence is for reasons of sickness amounts to deception and, particularly where sick pay is concerned, can amount to dishonesty.

Unauthorised absence goes to the root of the contract because the employee is not ready, willing and able for work. The issues to consider include:

- the recorded level of absence
- whether the employee is aware of the standard expected and the consequences of a failure to meet an attendance standard
- whether the organisational implications of the absence are minor, serious or major
- whether employees are being treated similarly.

Monitoring systems are essential and lateness information should be integrated with absence data to provide a fuller picture (*see* Chapter 11). One incidence of wilful and unauthorised absence may effectively destroy the contract, but custom and practice are important. If, for example, the employer maintains a level of staffing to provide cover for absent employees and occasional unauthorised absence is implicitly accepted, dismissal for one incidence of absenteeism may be unreasonable. There remain occupations and patterns of work, perhaps involving early or late starts or unsociable hours or shift work, where absence is condoned to a limited extent and this is material to dismissal decisions.

Conduct outside the workplace. To what extent is employee conduct outside employment the legitimate concern of the employer? Tribunal decisions indicate that where employee conduct outside employment has adverse consequences for the employer it becomes of employer concern. Some guiding principles and examples are available. In principle, conduct outside employment has implications for the contract of employment if it significantly lowers confidence in the integrity of the employee, if the ability or work capacity of the employee is compromised, or if the conduct is substantially detrimental to organisational performance or reputation. A reasonable belief that the particular conduct has occurred needs to be established.

Illustrative examples of conduct outside employment which may, in certain circumstances, warrant dismissal include:

- conviction for a criminal offence, although an automatic dismissal rule would normally be unreasonable
- working for another employer, if that employment results in a reduction in the effectiveness of the individual or in a conflict of interest or where other employment is prohibited
- continuing to engage in legitimate activities which seriously spill over into employment, for example duties as a police special, territorial army service or political candidacy and activities
- membership of interest groups or pressure groups where the objectives are incompatible with those of the employer.

Those in the public eye, public servants and those working with vulnerable groups can legitimately anticipate a greater employer concern with conduct outside employment.

> It would seem, then, that employees may do what they like outside working hours, as long as it does not affect their ability to do the job under a contract of employment. It is therefore important . . . that the employer is able to make a convincing demonstration of the impact such behaviour will make.
>
> (Williams, 1996)

Lack of capability

This section deals with capability concerns relating to incompetence, lack of qualifications and ill health.

Incompetence. Competence encompasses skill, knowledge, flexibility and other attributes. The concern of the employer is whether competence is sufficient for the effective performance of the contract. Where incompetence results in sub-standard performance, it

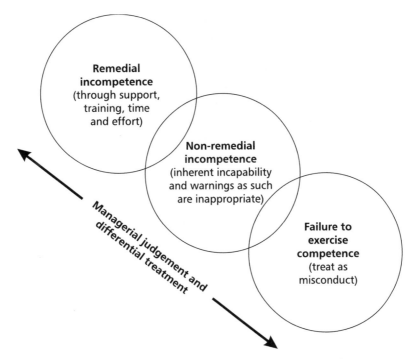

Fig. 18.2   Incapability or sub-standard work: incompetency typology

is useful to distinguish between remedial incompetence, non-remedial incompetence and a failure to exercise competence, because they need to be treated differently. Figure 18.2 displays these three types of incompetence as overlapping areas, and managerial judgement to determine which applies is necessary.

Remedial incompetence signifies that through genuine and joint action, competence can be developed and an acceptable standard of performance can be achieved. The following steps are required:

- ensure the employee understands the expected standard of work
- identify the gap between employee performance and the expected standard, focusing on the knowledge, skill and other attributes required
- provide sufficient time, opportunity, training and other support where practicable
- inform the employee of the consequences of a failure to achieve the required standards
- keep the matter under review and feed back on progress.

Non-remedial incompetence exists where, despite the best efforts of the employee and the employer, an acceptable standard of performance is not achievable. This is also termed inherent incapability. Warnings as such are not appropriate because they will not make any difference, but this does not negate the value of identifying a performance shortfall, pointing out the potential consequences and examining opportunities for contractual changes or redeployment, although there is no obligation to create a special job.

Failure to exercise competence, through carelessness, wilfulness or negligence, is a misconduct issue and needs to be treated accordingly.

Changing skill and knowledge demands may render incompetent an employee who was previously performing satisfactorily. This is no fault of the employee and significant changes in job demands may constitute job redundancy. Where job demands change but the identity of the job remains and the employee becomes incompetent, the employer is entitled to ensure that the business is not adversely affected. This may ultimately result in the fair dismissal of the employee for incapability. Employee competence can also be an issue when a newly appointed manager demands higher standards of competence and performance than had previously been the case, resulting in the redesignation of an employee as incompetent. To what degree is the new manager entitled to demand higher standards? The answer is 'to a reasonable degree', as the right to manage is respected in the contract of employment. These two illustrations demonstrate that competence is continuously redefined in response to reasonable managerial demands because organisations are not compelled to retain employees who are not competent to perform the contract.

Lack of qualifications. Academic, technical or professional qualifications may be deemed necessary for performance in the job and if qualifications are required prior to commencement of employment they should be checked out. Where they are required to be achieved within employment, a reasonable timescale and a reasonable number of attempts should be allowed. For dismissal to be reasonable the following points are also relevant:

- The qualifications required must be unambiguously determined by the employer.
- A contractual obligation to achieve the qualification must exist.
- The qualification must be essential to the performance of the contract.

Ill health. Lack of capability through ill health, because of unacceptable performance or absence levels, is difficult to manage and each case needs to be considered on its particular merits. The managerial judgement is objective and not emotive and treats the employee reasonably.

The ill-health process consists of a series of steps or decision points leading to a conclusion which frequently cannot be predicted early in the proceedings.

If there are doubts about the validity of absence, the matter should be dealt with as misconduct, not ill-health incapability. A common framework of ill-health dismissal principles can be utilised (Exhibit 18.3).

The managerial focus is not on diagnosing the ailment, but on the implications for the job. Warnings, in a conventional sense, are inappropriate because employees cannot be warned back to health, but employer concern, particularly where loss of employment is possible, must be conveyed. The purpose of the medical prognosis is predictive, and the aim is to establish the probability of improvement or deterioration in the health of the employee in so far as it may affect employment. Employer access to medical information needs employee consent under the Access to Medical Records Act, 1988 and the Data Protection Act, 1998 (*see* Chapters 5 and 11). Employee refusal to allow an employer access to relevant medical information or refusal to be consulted by an organisational medical practitioner presents a difficulty, but refusals to cooperate in these ways do not prohibit the employer from proceeding on the basis of the information that is available.

Exhibit 18.3   Principles for dealing with ill health

1 The employer's objective is fact-finding to establish capability, or otherwise, to perform the contract.
2 The employee, who has a duty to remain contactable, should know of any employer concern.
3 The employer should normally seek a medical prognosis.
4 The employee should know whether the job is at risk.
5 The employer should consider alternative work or contractual changes which provide continued employment, where practicable.
6 Employees with similar ill-health performance or absence records should receive parity of managerial attention, unless there is a valid reason for disparate attention.
7 Dismissal is not a medical decision, but a managerial decision with a medical input.
8 The decision to dismiss can be based on the 'enough is enough' principle.

A medical prognosis is more of an art than a science and involves uncertainty and sometimes conflicting predictions. The employee's medical practitioner, with legitimate claims to intimate professional knowledge of the employee, may provide one scenario, and the employer's medical practitioner, with legitimate claims to intimate professional knowledge of the work, may provide an alternative and contrasting scenario. In this situation the employer can seek a 'tie-break', which may only create a third alternative, or more pragmatically elect to follow the opinion of the practitioner who has been appointed by the organisation for the purpose. The decision to dismiss is always a managerial decision. The decision is informed by medical opinion, but takes account of the nature of the work, the impact on the organisation, the length or frequency of any absence, the resources and potential of the organisation to accommodate absence or reduced performance, and the employee's record and length of service.

An employee with ill-health problems may be able to return on reduced hours or with different responsibilities to facilitate rehabilitation to work. Unless transitional arrangements can be accommodated on a permanent basis, the employer is only expected to offer these contractual alterations for a limited and reasonable period. Whether an absent employee is receiving sick pay is largely irrelevant to the reasonableness of a dismissal. It is not necessary for an employer to await the expiry of any sick pay before dismissing where it is evident that the employee will not return to normal work, although it may be compassionate to do so. There is, however, potential for a wrongful dismissal claim where contractual sick pay terms are breached and this should be considered. Conversely, the expiry of sick pay is not a legitimate reason for dismissal; and paradoxically the expiry of sick pay in reducing the financial burden of absence on the employer may make lawful dismissal more difficult.

Frequent short-term sick absence is often more disruptive than a longer period of ill-health absence and in practice attracts less managerial and co-worker sympathy. Medical opinion is still valid in cases of frequent short-term absence in identifying underlying health issues which may respond to treatment. Medical certificates are not indisputable evidence of being unfit for work, although there is understandable hesitancy about challenging their legitimacy. There is a distinction between being unwell and being unfit for work (see Exhibit 11.2); the unwell but apparently fit employee brandishing a certificate of unfitness is provocative to other employees. There is a paradox here also, because in cases of psychological ill health the employee may be fit for work until actually returning to work.

Dismissal for incapability due to a disability will not automatically be unfair, but employers will need to justify a dismissal decision. Where an employee is unable to manage the essential elements of a job, even where reasonable adjustments have been made, and contractual changes and alternative employment are not practicable, then dismissal may be justified. In effect a more stringent test of reasonableness is applied to the ill-health dismissal of an employee classified as disabled under the Disability Discrimination Act, 1995.

The 'enough is enough' principle is the point at which the reasonable employer has exhausted alternatives to dismissal and is entitled to dismiss, however painful this may be for the employee or the employer. The principle applies equally to frequent absence and long-term ill health. In seeking to balance the need of the organisation to achieve its objectives efficiently and the need of the employee for further time to regain capability, the issue is whether 'the time has arrived when the employer can no longer reasonably be expected to keep the employee's post open for him' (Hart *v* Marshall [1977] IRLR 51). Effectively this is a test of whether the employee is able to give continuous and effective service.

Redundancy

Redundancy handling is given comprehensive treatment in Chapter 19. The purpose here is to demonstrate briefly that a framework exists to enable employers to dismiss fairly and legitimately for the reason of employee redundancy in the pursuit of organisational efficiency. When a business ceases, the result for the employee is termination of employment through redundancy and this will normally be a fair reason for dismissal. Redundancy through reorganisation and restructuring is also potentially fair. In addition to obligations to consult with employees and their representatives, to follow a fair procedure, to consider alternative work and to make statutory redundancy payments, employers are required to apply an objective and reasonable selection procedure if redundancy dismissal is to be fair. The training and enabling of the managers to handle individual redundancy situations is vital to ensuring procedural fairness.

Statutory bar to employment

A bar exists where employment contravenes a statutory duty or restriction and it would be unlawful to continue to employ the person in the position for which they are contracted. The loss of a driving licence by an employee employed in a driving capacity may constitute a fair reason for dismissal, but the dismissal still has to pass the test of reasonableness. This requires consideration of the seriousness of the driving offence, and whether it results in a loss of confidence and trust in the employee, the length of a driving ban, the extent of the driving required for the job, the viability of the employee making alternative transport arrangements and the practicability of redeployment. The loss of a driving licence is a serious matter but there are differences, for example, between a chauffeur who is banned for three years for drunken driving and a warehouse worker occasionally required to make deliveries who loses a driving licence for three months under the totting up of penalty points. Each case must be assessed on its merits.

The absence of a licence to practise in some positions in the legal, accountancy or medical professions, or the absence of a certificate of technical competence in, for example, occupations associated with electricity or power presses, may be a fair reason for dismissal, if it is reasonable in the circumstances. An employee failure to renew a work permit will normally be a statutory bar to continued employment.

Some Other Substantial Reason (SOSR)

This safety net reason for dismissal effectively recognises that the previous four reasons of misconduct, lack of capability, redundancy and statutory bar are not exhaustive. Sometimes referred to as an 'employers charter', it enables employers, and tribunals, to exercise discretion by identifying dismissal reasons which do not conveniently fall into other more specific categories. The essential consideration is that the reason must be substantial in nature and must warrant dismissal.

The most frequent 'other substantial reason' is dismissal of an employee because of their refusal to agree to a variation to contractual terms and conditions necessitated by organisational change, economic survival or other sound business reason. Although made some time age, the following statement by Aikin tends to epitomise the primacy given to business needs.

> The reasonableness (of the change) is to be considered from the employers' and not from the employees' point of view and is based on business needs.

> (Aikin, 1984)

The contract of employment is dynamic and if commercial imperatives demand changes in employment terms, even if disadvantageous to the employee, the changes may be reasonable and a refusal to accept them may warrant dismissal. For a dismissal to be reasonable an employer needs to demonstrate a sound reason for the change, consult with the employee, consider alternatives to dismissal, and facilitate any changes through timescale, training, compensation and other support as necessary and practicable. This gives considerable latitude to the employer, reinforces the right to manage and recognises that quite substantive changes in the contract can be made unilaterally. A majority of employees accepting a unilaterally imposed change in terms and conditions may undermine the reasonableness of a refusal to cooperate by a small number of individuals. There are many cases which uphold the employers' right to make unilateral changes in certain circumstances. The case of the chicken catcher in Exhibit 18.4 is illustrative of some of the considerations associated with changing terms and conditions of employment for operational reasons. The SOSR test is always whether the reason for dismissal is substantial, whether alternatives to dismissal have been exhausted and whether the dismissal falls within the range of responses of a reasonable employer.

Exhibit 18.4   The employer, the chickens and the chicken catcher and the balance of disadvantage – some other substantial reason (SOSR) for dismissal

Faccenda Chickens Ltd produced fresh chickens for large multiple suppliers. Mr Wilson was employed as a chicken catcher with normal working hours of 4 am to 12 noon from Monday to Friday. Three years after Mr Wilson was employed the growth of the business necessitated an extension to the number of hours during which chickens were caught. A commercial decision was made to vary the starting and finishing times of the chicken catchers. The organisation informed the employees of the proposed changes which would involve working an eight-hour shift, but with starting hours varying between 2 am and 10 am. The chicken catchers were given notice of the termination of their existing contracts and offered new contracts with revised terms. Employees were consulted individually about these changes.

Mr Wilson was not prepared to accept the new working arrangements. The employer listened to his objections, but ultimately he was given a week to make his decision about whether he would accept or reject the new contract. He clearly indicated that he was not prepared to accept it and he was dismissed. Mr Wilson lodged a claim for unfair dismissal and stated that he had two principal objections. First, his early shift from 4 am to 12 noon enabled him to spend time with his children, whereas the new contract would make it difficult for him to do this. Second, his existing hours enabled his wife to go out to work and this was an economic necessity.

At the employment tribunal it emerged that his wife had not worked for nearly a year and the tribunal did not consider this a substantial reason for objecting to the new working hours. The tribunal also examined the proposed working pattern under the new contract for a period of one month and concluded that it would not significantly reduce the number of times that Mr Wilson would be able to see his children.

The tribunal considered previous cases where an employee's dismissal for a refusal to accept new terms of employment necessitated by a reorganisation of a business was found to be for some other substantial reason and of a kind which justified dismissal in the circumstances. The tribunal declared that Mr Wilson's dismissal was for some other substantial reason because Faccenda Chickens faced rapid expansion and the reorganisation was necessary to improve efficiency. The dismissal was held to be fair.

Mr Wilson made an appeal to the Employment Appeal Tribunal on a point of law but the EAT did not support his view. The EAT was convinced that the employer had fully considered the pressures on the organisation, the needs of the chickens and the interests of the employee, and ultimately and on balance the employee would have to be inconvenienced.

Source: Wilson v Faccenda Chickens Ltd, EAT 98/86.

Other illustrative SOSR reasons judged to have been fair and reasonable in particular circumstances include:

- irreconcilable personality clashes
- customer complaints or pressure
- employee plans to join a competitor
- office affairs

- severe body odour and failure to improve personal hygiene
- failures to disclose a material fact or making false statements on application for employment.

CONSTRUCTIVE DISMISSAL

Under what circumstances can an employee resign and successfully claim constructive dismissal? There are two key words – 'conduct' and 'repudiation'. It is the conduct of the employer which is material, not whether there is an intention to cause the employee to resign, and the conduct must be such that it can be reasonably construed as repudiating the contract of employment. Employer conduct will only constitute repudiation if it is a significant breach of an express or implied term and it goes to the root of the contract, effectively destroying it. This inhibits employees from successfully claiming constructive dismissal merely on the grounds that they do not like something; the unreasonable treatment must be fundamental to the contract. Repudiation of the contract is accepted by the employee through the resignation, and where there is no resignation it can be inferred that the conduct of the employer has been tolerated and implicitly accepted. The employee is not excluded from registering an objection at the time and continuing to work. The registration of this objection reserves the right of the employee to subsequently claim constructive dismissal on the basis that the incident or behaviour was not on its own sufficient to warrant resignation, but when taken with other subsequent occurrences can be construed as destroying the contract. Therefore, in addition to a single repudiatory act resulting in constructive dismissal, for example failing to pay wages or a significant and unjustified change in terms and conditions, there can be cumulative constructive dismissal.

Indicative illustrations are provided in Exhibit 18.5 to give a flavour of constructive dismissal. In all cases the employee needs to demonstrate unambiguously that the employer's behaviour was not only unreasonable, but also that it forced a resignation. It is a question of degree in each case and ultimately whether mutual trust and confidence is fatally wounded.

Exhibit 18.5   Indicative examples of employer conduct which may be construed as constructive dismissal

- Issuing unjustified warnings or undermining authority or expressing unwarranted suspicions
- Using provocative or defamatory language or engaging in physical or psychological abuse
- Preventing access to pay increases, promotion or development opportunities
- Making unreasonable and substantial changes to job duties or terms and conditions
- Failing to respond effectively to genuine grievances
- Failing to provide effective support to victims of harassment, bullying or unfair discrimination
- Insisting on unsafe working practices
- Insisting on excessive workloads.

EMPLOYMENT TRIBUNALS

Employment tribunals (ETs) are independent judicial bodies intended to provide an accessible and non-legalistic process for dealing with individual employment disputes. It is debatable whether these intentions are being achieved, with legal representation the norm for employers and delays of many months in cases reaching tribunals because of caseloads. An ET consists of a legally qualified chairperson and two lay members. The appointment of lay members is to create a more impartial and practical approach, but there continues to be a trend of ET decisions being supportive of managerial prerogative. In some circumstances a chairperson may sit alone, although this is not normally the case in claims for unfair dismissal.

There is a continuing escalation of ET cases, with 30 000 applications in 1989 rising to 90 000 in 1995 and reaching almost 130 000 in 2001 (ACAS reports). This trend reflects the extension of individual employment rights and the greater willingness of individuals to seek redress for a grievance through the courts. Around 40 per cent of the complaints concern unfair dismissal allegations. Only around a third of all unfair dismissal cases actually reach a tribunal, with a third settled through ACAS intervention and a third withdrawn. Only 15 in every 100 unfair dismissal applications are found in favour of the employee, although in the large number of cases settled by ACAS or withdrawn by the applicant there will have been instances where a mutually acceptable agreement was reached. This is, however, a difficult area to penetrate because ACAS involvement is protected by confidentiality in conciliated settlements. The large number of ET cases is a matter of some concern, and alternative dispute resolution methods such as binding arbitration, a fixed period of conciliation to promote a timely settlement and a greater use of internal grievance procedures, are actively being considered (see below).

Measures introduced in 2001 (Employment Tribunals Regulations) to reduce the number of ET claims and to promote efficiency in the ET process included:

- an increase in the deposit, from £150 to £500, if a party continues to pursue or defend an action following a decision of 'no reasonable success' at a pre-hearing review

- an increase in the upper limit on costs for pursuing an unreasonable or misconceived case or for engaging in vexatious, abusive or disruptive behaviour, from £500 to £10 000

- an obligation on ETs to deal with cases expeditiously as well as fairly, allowing tribunal time which is proportionate to the significance of the case, and seeking to ensure that both parties are on an equal footing (does this mean that legal aid will need to be available?)

- a power to strike out a case for non-compliance with tribunal evidence directions, for example failure to comply with a witness order or a request for further and better particulars

- an obligation on the parties to assist the tribunal in dealing with cases justly.

Employment tribunal process

The parties to the process are the employee bringing the claim (the applicant) and the employer resisting the allegation (the respondent). To bring a claim of unfair dismissal the employee normally completes the application form ET1, obtainable from the Employment Service. The claim has to be made within three months of the effective date of termination or the date upon which the employee genuinely believes unfair dismissal took place. Where it was not reasonably practicable for the applicant to present the case within the three-month period, a tribunal may exceptionally exercise discretion to extend the time limit where it is considered just and equitable. The ET1 requires the applicant to state the complaint, identify the employer and indicate the remedy being sought. The remedy can be reinstatement or re-engagement or compensation. The ET1 will be registered and acknowledged on receipt by the Central Office of the Employment Tribunals. If the complaint falls outside those which may be considered or is out of time or the employee does not qualify for protection, then the case will not be heard and the applicant will be informed. If jurisdiction is established copies of the ET1 will be sent to the respondent and to an ACAS conciliation officer. The respondent is required to reply to the allegation of unfair dismissal, normally by completing a notice of appearance form ET3, within 14 days. The employer is required to confirm that dismissal took place, the dates of employment, salary details and whether there is an intention to resist the claim. The employer is also required to specify the grounds on which a claim is being resisted. A failure to respond to a notice of appearance may result in the right to take part in the tribunal proceedings being forfeited.

The ACAS role is characterised by impartiality and confidentiality. Conciliation officers have a duty to promote a settlement at the request of either party or on their own initiative. The promotion of a settlement will be the focus of concern for the conciliation officer, not the attribution of blame or guilt. Information given to a conciliation officer cannot be introduced at a tribunal hearing without the consent of the party who gave the information. Conciliated agreements reached through ACAS, or with the advice of independent legal representation, are binding and the applicant waives the right to continue with the claim.

The ET may instigate a preliminary hearing to establish whether it has the power to consider a complaint. Other preliminary hearings may be arranged to grant applications for 'further and better particulars' in relation to the claim or to make 'document discovery orders' or to make 'witness orders' compelling attendance at a hearing. This prior investigation aims to facilitate the process and avert surprises and courtroom antics at the hearing. A pre-hearing review may be arranged by the ET if it appears that either party has a weak case. This is intended to filter out any unmeritorious cases, and where the ET considers that a party has no reasonable prospect of success it can order that party to make a financial deposit of £500 as a condition of continuing to take part in the case. If the party against whom the order of a deposit is made decides to continue with proceedings, costs against that party may be awarded in certain circumstances and the deposit may be lost. Tribunals have the power to strike out an originating application or notice of appearance where the proceedings are conducted in a manner which is 'scandalous, frivolous or vexatious'. These rules in relation to costs, deposits and striking out of cases are intended to dissuade disaffected and dismissed employees from making claims which are devilish and have no chance of success. Costs can be awarded where a party acts abusively or disruptively either before or during a tribunal hearing.

The procedure at an ET hearing is informal and flexible and not bound by strict rules of evidence. The parties may give evidence, call witnesses to give evidence, question their own witnesses and those of the other party and address the tribunal. The tribunal members can question both parties and witnesses at any time. The case can be presented and defended by the parties involved or by named representatives. The tribunal decides upon the order of proceedings and the hearing will normally be in public, although there can be reporting restrictions in cases of sexual harassment or sexual misconduct.

Oral evidence plays a key part in establishing facts or refuting allegations and it is generally in the interests of both parties to attend the hearing. The oral evidence is heard under oath or affirmation and written documents in support of an argument should be available at the hearing. It is recommended that each party sends to the other party, and to the tribunal, a list or the 'bundle' of documents which are to be used at the hearing in order to simplify or shorten the hearing. Having heard the evidence the tribunal makes a decision, which may be unanimous or by majority vote, and the decision is usually announced at the end of the hearing. Written reasons for the decision, normally in summary form, are sent to the parties within a few weeks. There are certain circumstances in which a tribunal can be asked to review a decision, although this is exceptional, and a review will not be warranted merely because one party wants to reargue its case. Appeals against a decision can only be made on a point of law and are normally made to the Employment Appeal Tribunal (EAT). ET decisions are not binding on other tribunals, but tribunals are bound by precedents established by superior courts.

Remedies for unfair dismissal

If a tribunal finds that there has been no unfair dismissal the matter ends, subject to any appeal. Where the dismissal is found to be unfair the remedies are re-employment or compensation. The tribunal has the power to order reinstatement (re-employment in the same position with continuous service) or re-engagement (re-employment under a new contract in an alternative but similar and suitable position). In deciding whether to order re-employment the tribunal will consider:

• the wishes of the employee

• the practicability for the employer

• the extent of employee contribution to the dismissal.

The employer cannot be forced to re-employ a dismissed employee and re-employment occurs in less than 1 per cent of cases. A failure to comply with an order for reinstatement or re-engagement will normally result in the employee receiving additional compensation. If the tribunal decides that re-employment is not an appropriate remedy compensation will be awarded. The compensation may be reduced by any employee contribution to the dismissal or if the employee has failed to use an internal appeals procedure (maximum reduction in the award of 2 weeks pay) or if an employee unreasonably rejects a suitable offer of re-employment. The awards fall into three categories – a basic award, a compensatory award and an additional award.

The basic award is calculated on the basis of the number of years of continuous service and the age of the employee at dismissal, in the same way as redundancy payments. It is basic financial compensation for loss of employment and the maximum number of weeks' pay that can be awarded is 30. The statutory maxima used to calculate the basic award currently put the maximum award at around £7500.

A compensatory award is intended to take account of any financial loss which is a consequence of the dismissal. It embraces loss of pay, up to the date of the hearing and in the future, and loss of other employment benefits. The compensatory award is set at a level which the tribunal considers to be just and equitable in the circumstances. The employee is expected to make reasonable efforts, mainly through seeking other employment, to mitigate any loss, and part of the award may be recouped to offset any income support which has been paid. The limit on the compensatory awards was significantly increased in 1999 to £50 000 and this figure is index linked. In cases of unlawful discrimination there is no limit.

The additional award is payable when an employer refuses an ET order to re-employ and can be up to 52 weeks' pay.

Although the compensatory potential of these various awards may appear complex and extensive, the average employee compensation for dismissal is only around £3000, putting the job loss remedy in a rather different perspective. Awards in discrimination cases have been unlimited since 1993 and the average settlement is around £20 000. The tribunal decision includes a statement of the compensation awarded and specifies how it was calculated.

Arbitration for individual employment disputes and internal dispute resolution

As mentioned earlier, the escalating number of ET cases is provoking general concern, and arbitration for individual disputes as a binding alternative to an ET with the consent of both parties was made possible by the Employment Rights (Disputes Resolution) Act, 1998. Arbitration is potentially attractive through reducing the tribunal burden on employers and promoting a return to speedy and relatively informal responses to claims for employees. The scheme has been designed by ACAS and the features include:

- unfair dismissal claims only and where there are no jurisdictional issues
- arbitration as a binding alternative where both parties agree, with no right of appeal, except for arbitrator misconduct
- arbitrators appointed by ACAS and to follow the ACAS Code and Advisory Booklet on Discipline at Work
- arbitrator to fix the procedure and rules of evidence with the format being investigative rather than adversarial
- representatives permitted, but not necessarily, to be lawyers, and proceedings to be free from legal argument and case law
- arbitrator empowered to make the same awards as an ET
- proceedings to be in private and the decision not to be published.

Arbitration is potentially attractive because the process may save time and money and will avoid the formal and public tribunal proceedings. However, an arbitrator's approach is by definition more flexible, and the right to manage may not be respected to the same extent as has been customary at ETs, and also there are fears that the arbitration process may become as legalistic as the ET process. There is also the potential to generate even more unfair dismissal claims rather than reduce the number of ET hearings. Attention is also being given to promoting in-house dispute resolution through having more effective grievance procedures, based on the ACAS Code, and a requirement for employees to exhaust these before making a tribunal claim. This may have the advantage of postponing the breakdown in the employment relationship and of keeping the employee in employment whilst attempts are made to resolve the dispute, something which is not very practicable in the ET process.

SUMMARY LEARNING POINTS

1 There are no certainties in dismissal; statute law and case law provide principles but each case needs to be considered on its merits. Employers need sufficient understanding of dismissal law 'to know when more expert advice is necessary'. To be legitimate, dismissals need to be for a fair reason and reasonable in the circumstances. The existence of the contract is dependent on the continued existence of mutual trust and confidence between the employer and the employee. Employers are in no way deprived of the freedom to dismiss employees.

2 If the original intention of the legislation was for the primary remedy to be re-employment for the unfairly dismissed employee then the legislation has been an abject failure. Unfair dismissal legislation does not provide employment security, but only limited compensation for the loss of that security. The only way to provide employment security is to ensure that a dismissed employee is kept in employment until a claim is determined, hence the increasing interest in internal dispute resolution.

3 The retrospective nature of the process offers huge potential for the elimination of re-employment as a potential remedy because:

- the passage of time associated with the ET process and its adversarial nature provide considerable scope for attitudes to harden
- the tribunal hearing provides an opportunity for the parties to recognise that the employment relationship has irretrievably broken down
- the tribunal process can kill the desire of the employee to work for the employer because of perceived objectionable behaviour in resisting a claim
- the duty, and economic necessity, to mitigate any loss may result in the employee obtaining another job before the case is decided
- the employer may have covered the job by replacing the employee, making re-employment less practicable.

4 If an employer acts reasonably and follows a proper procedure, dismissal is legitim-ised and there is nothing to fear from unfair dismissal legislation. In general, the needs

of the undertaking will override the needs of the individual and tribunal decisions are very respectful of the right to manage.

5 The purpose of the legislative framework can be subjected to an alternative interpretation, that of encouraging good practice, and it is possible to be more optimistic in determining success. The principles applied by tribunals, the ACAS involvement and the publicity associated with unfair dismissal claims have combined to act as a conduit for disseminating good practice.

6 It is not the legal remedies available to employees that encourage employers to engage in fair and reasonable treatment. It is the pursuit of good employment relations, the undesirability of negative publicity, the time and costs involved in resisting unfair dismissal claims and, in some cases, a concern with ethics and professionalism in the management of people.

REFERENCES AND FURTHER READING

Advisory, Conciliation and Arbitration Service (2000) *Discipline at Work: The ACAS advisory handbook*. Periodically revised.

Aikin, O. (1984) 'Law at work: a need to reorganise', *Personnel Management*, February, 37–9.

Aikin, O. (1994a) 'Procedures for staff dismissal', *Personnel Management*, March, 55–6.

Aikin, O. (1994b) 'Law at work: unreasonable behaviour', *Personnel Management*, July, 51.

Aikin, O. (1999) 'The differences the employment relations bill will make to individual employees' rights in the workplace', *People Management*, 11 March, 27–8.

Aikin, O. (2001) *Employment Law Update*. Aikin Driver Partnership, June, 6–7.

Banerji, N. and Wareing, A. (1994) 'Unfair dismissal cases: 1987 and 1992 survey results compared', *Employment Gazette*, 102(10), 359–65.

Deeks, E. (2000) 'Lawyers plan in-house alternative disputes resolution (ADR) scheme', *People Management*, 3 August, 17.

Dickens, L. (1982) 'Unfair dismissal law: a decade of disillusion?', *Personnel Management*, February, 25–7.

DTI (2000) *Fair and Unfair Dismissal: A Guide for employers*. PL714. London: DTI.

Employment Department (1993) *Fair and Unfair Dismissal: A guide for employers*. PL 714 (Rev 2).

Employment Gazette (1994) 'Industrial and employment appeal tribunal statistics 1992–93 and 1993–94', 102(10), 367–71.

Employment Relations Act (1999) London: HMSO.

Employment Rights (Disputes Resolution) Act (1998) London: HMSO.

Equal Opportunities Review 55 (1994) *EOC Guidance on Part-Time Workers Decision*, May/June, 39–40.

Goodwyn, E. (1995) 'Will there be a flood of new claims for dismissal?', *People Management*, September, 53.

Industrial Relations Review and Report 555 (1994) 'Guidance on identifying reasons for dismissal', March, 11–14.

Industrial Relations Review and Report 556 (1994) 'EC equality law secures rights for part-timers', March, 2–4.

Industrial Relations Review and Report 566 (1994) 'Sunday Trading Act 1994: employment protection rights', August, 2–6.

Industrial Relations Review and Report 570 (1994) 'Inconsistent treatment not decisive in itself', October, 12–13.

Industrial Tribunals (1995) *Industrial Tribunals Procedures: England and Wales*. ITL 1.

IRS Employment Review 575 (1995) 'EAT addresses limits of "Polkey" reductions', January, 12–15.

Leadership and Organisation Development Journal (1995) 'Record year for ACAS: more solutions to more problems', 16(6), 41–2.

Lewis, D. and Sargeant, M. (2000) *Essentials of Employment Law*. London: CIPD.

Lewis, P. (1981) 'An analysis of why legislation has failed to provide employment protection for unfairly dismissed employees', *British Journal of Industrial Relations*, 19(3), 316–26.

Milne, S. (1995) 'Tribunals see a doubling of unfair firings', *The Guardian*, 16 August, 15.

Mordsley, B. (1998) 'Tribunals: system overhaul', *People Management*, 14 May, 23–4.

Muir, J. (1994) 'Alcohol and employment problems', *Work Study*, 43(7), 16–17.

Pilbeam, S. and Corbridge, M. (2000) 'The skills of employee relations', in Farnham, D., *Employee Relations in Context*. London: CIPD.

Salamon, M. (1998) *Industrial Relations: Theory and practice* (3rd edn). Hemel Hempstead: Prentice Hall.

Selwyn, N. (2000) *Selwyn's Law of Employment*. London: Butterworths.

Suter, E. (1997) *The Employment Law Checklist* (6th edn). London: IPD.

The Guardian (1997) 'Sex bias payouts reach record high', 20 June, 6.

Williams, A. (1995) 'Pregnant pause while Lords rethinks discrimination case', *People Management*, November, 45.

Williams, A. (1996) 'Coming to terms with extra-curricular sinners', *People Management*, January, 46.

ASSIGNMENTS AND DISCUSSION TOPICS

1 Read Exhibit 18.2 and discuss why the burden of proof is different under criminal and employment law. What implications does this have for the way that dismissals are handled by managers?

2 Are there any cases of condoned dishonest acts in your organisation? How did they come into being? Do they warrant dismissal? How could they be prevented or stopped?

3 In this chapter six potential areas for gross misconduct have been introduced – theft, violence, drunkenness, breach of confidence, refusal to obey legitimate instructions and misconduct outside the workplace. For the misconduct area you are allocated by

your tutor discuss in your sub-group the following two questions. What issues specific to your allocated area of misconduct normally need to be considered and invest-igated? Taking account of the principles of natural justice, at which point and under what circumstances does the misconduct become gross misconduct and therefore justify dismissal? Be prepared to report back briefly to the whole group.

4 Broken promise and high spirits – what is 'reasonable' in the context of dismissal is rarely a simple question and never reducible to an unequivocal response, so test your-self on this one. An employee had 11 years' unblemished service and no disciplinary record, and her performance was good. She got drunk at the 1995 Christmas party but promised it would never happen again. In the following July she concluded a successful deal and spent the rest of the afternoon entertaining the supplier at the bar on the employer's premises. She then slid down the first floor banisters but fell half way, breaking a tooth and fracturing her skull. It was agreed she did not have a drink problem and was only mildly drunk. The employer dismissed her and the Employment Tribunal decided that the dismissal was within *the band of reasonable responses*. An important factor was that they felt she could not be trusted after breaking her promise. The employee appealed. What would you have done in the circumstances, and why?

5 The number of employment tribunal cases has trebled in six years and this is creating a caseload for which the tribunal system is ill-equipped. Why is this the case and what can be done about it?

6 Attend an employment tribunal which is hearing a claim of unfair dismissal. Write up your experience with reference to the legal framework of dismissal, commenting upon whether:

(a) a proper procedure was followed;
(b) the employer acted reasonably in the circumstances;
(c) the employee contributed to the dismissal.

Present an executive summary of the main points to your class.

7 Some employees are excluded from protection against unfair dismissal. Should protec-tion be extended or reduced? Present arguments and counter-arguments.

8 Periodic surveys of unfair dismissal applications in 1987 and 1992 (Banerji and Wareing, 1994) identified the following characteristics of claims:

- The largest source of claims was in the distribution and hotel and catering industries.
- Most of the claims were from private-sector employees, although the public-sector share increased significantly between the surveys.
- Women are heavily under-represented in the number of claims.

Discuss the reasons for these findings.

9 Select and analyse two employment tribunal cases relating to unfair dismissal. Prepare a short paper which outlines the principles and arguments used in the cases and present it to your class.

CASE STUDY

Christmas spirit and the amorous kitchen porter

Is dismissal within the range of responses of a reasonable employer taking account of equity and the substantial merits of the case, or is action short of dismissal the response of a reasonable employer?

It is Christmas Eve in a department store and you are the personnel manager. You have had a busy Christmas trading period, having worked extremely long and unsocial hours, and you are looking forward to a few days' break, although you do have a management report to complete for your Diploma in Personnel Management course. At 3.00 pm the managing director (MD) storms into your office with a distressed catering manager in tow. The MD reports that he has just discovered the kitchen porter lying comatose on the staff staircase clutching a bottle of brandy, having reached this prone position only after trying to kiss and cuddle anyone in the proximity. These amorous advances were also made towards the MD himself, much to the merriment of a collection of other employees who observed the incident. Apparently this state of affairs had been going on for about an hour and was the talk of the store amongst the staff.

The kitchen porter has been employed for three years and normally works part-time hours, but has worked full time during the Christmas trading period. There is no other known incidence of alcohol abuse. His work is just satisfactory, although his performance gives cause for concern from time to time, and as a prank he recently barricaded himself in the washing-up area using cooking pots to construct a wall. He received an oral warning for this. There is a shortage of reliable and effective kitchen porters, both as direct employees and through employment agencies. The MD says he has matters of greater importance to deal with and makes it clear to you that he wants the matter sorted out before the end of the day.

1 What action would you take immediately?

2 What issues would you need to consider?

3 What would be your decision on disciplinary action?

4 Would it make any difference if it was the (female) catering colleagues of the kitchen porter who, with the knowledge and tacit agreement of the catering manager, presented the kitchen porter with the bottle of brandy at lunchtime as a Christmas present; the kitchen porter was then encouraged, probably enticed, by a couple of mischievous colleagues, spurred on by knowledge of his recent erratic behaviour with the potwash barricade, to have a drink from the brandy bottle?

CHAPTER 19

Redundancy and rebalancing the organisation

INTRODUCTION

Effectiveness in people resourcing means that from time to time there is a need to change the composition of the workforce. The pursuit of competitive advantage or the need for (or imposition of) efficiency gains may result in fewer workers being needed to do work of a particular type, causing some employees to be made redundant. This can take the form of a reduction in numbers or a change in the skill base of the workforce through the release of employees who do not have the required skills and the recruitment of employees who do. This can be a difficult time for any organisation and this chapter examines the way in which the process of redundancy can be managed through the development of appropriate policies and procedures. The rebalancing of the organisation following redundancies will also be considered as this requires managerial attention as well.

People can make the difference to organisational performance and be a source of competitive advantage, but a redundancy situation can unbalance the organisation and destroy the motivation, trust and commitment of the people upon whom the organisation relies for future success. In short, redundancy engenders fear and insecurity which damages the psychological contract between employers and employees, and this is detrimental to the organisation. From being told that they are 'the most valuable resource', people can perceive themselves as 'the most disposable resource'.

CHAPTER OBJECTIVES

- To define redundancy and identify the causes of redundancy.
- To examine relevant legislation and consider the rights and responsibilities of the employer and the employee.
- To outline alternative selection methods for compulsory redundancy.
- To suggest alternative measures which avoid redundancy.
- To discuss policies for the effective management of redundancy and expose the managerial skills needed to handle redundancy effectively.
- To introduce the concept of survivor syndrome and consider action necessary to rebalance the organisation post-redundancy.

DEFINITION OF REDUNDANCY

Redundancy is one of the potentially fair reasons for dismissal (*see* Chapter 18) and is defined by Salamon (1998) as occurring:

> In any situation where changes in an organisation's economic, operational or technological position results in a reduced workforce. That is irrespective of whether the reduction is achieved through compulsory dismissals, voluntary severance, natural wastage or employee transfers. It also applies whether it involves the loss of one job or a more significant reduction in part or all of the workforce.

An essential feature of a redundancy situation is that it stems from causes which are external to the individual. It involves conflict of interest between the managerial objective of maintaining an efficient and profitable organisation and the employee's objective of protecting their job.

A distinction can be drawn between 'job redundancy', where the job ceases and the employee is found alternative employment, and 'worker redundancy', where employees lose their jobs. In both of these scenarios a redundancy situation exists because the total number of jobs of a particular type within the organisation has reduced. More euphemistic terms are used to describe a redundancy situation, including deselection, downsizing, rightsizing and delayering, but job loss is a common characteristic. Entitlement to payment for losing a job through no fault of the individual is grounded in the idea of a job property right, but prior to the Redundancy Payments Act, 1965, the need to shed labour in a time of economic downturn was accepted as inevitable and absolutely embodied in the 'right to manage'. Consequently, the idea of payment to compensate for job loss, until 1965, was an alien concept.

CAUSES OF REDUNDANCY

A significant factor for modern businesses is the increasing pace of change. This can make human resource planning and accurate projections of the quantity and quality of workers more challenging. There are measures that can be taken by employers to increase worker flexibility, and a range of patterns of work are available that can enable the employer to respond effectively to the need for rapid change. However, there will be times when the employer will need to shed labour and restructure the organisation to accommodate internal or external pressures. In this scenario the requirement for employees decreases and a redundancy situation occurs. Redundancy is potentially a traumatic event and it is therefore important that the employer develops strategies which first, seek to avoid or reduce the need for compulsory redundancy, second, enable the redundancies to be handled fairly and lawfully, and third, reduce the negative consequences for those employees who remain and for subsequent organisational effectiveness.

There are four main causes of redundancy.

Structural decline in a sector or industry causes a decline in the demand for the product or service and leads to a reduced demand for labour. This will tend to affect all organisations within the sector. Examples are declines in the shipbuilding, steel and coal industries and more recently in the dot.com economy.

Decreases in the level of economic activity which affects sales or income. This may be either a general economic recession which impacts upon all sectors or it may be cyclical and specific to a particular area of economic activity, such as the building trade or the tourist industry.

Changing technology which can take place within a single organisation or across a sector. The introduction of new technology may reduce demand for the labour necessary to achieve the same level of output or it can change the skill requirements of the job and make some skills redundant. This can result in the redundancy of workers who do not have the required skills or the ability to acquire them.

Reorganisation or restructuring within the workforce in order to make more efficient and effective use of plant, machinery or the workforce to improve competitiveness, profitability or return on investment.

These causes of redundancy can be interrelated. A reduction in macro-economic activity may produce inflationary pressures, causing higher interest rates with upward pressure on domestic prices. This can contribute to an accelerated structural decline because imported goods and services become cheaper. In the face of foreign competition it may be necessary to seek to maintain viability through both restructuring the organisation and the introduction of new technology. A redundancy situation is often complex. Management may see the redundancy of employees as a managerial failure in not foreseeing the situation and responding in a more timely way with appropriate action. Trade unions may see their role as resisting redundancies and as an opportunity for industrial action with the aim of reducing the number of redundancies, extending the redundancy schedule or enhancing the redundancy package. Redundancy is often characterised by tension and conflict, and to be handled effectively it requires a knowledge of the law, a fair redundancy policy and skilled managers.

REDUNDANCY AND THE LAW

Redundancy is one of the fair reasons for dismissal specified in the Employment Rights Act, 1996. It occurs when the dismissal of employees is wholly or mainly attributable to the fact that:

the employer has ceased or intends to cease to carry on the business for the purposes for which the employee was employed;

or

the employer has ceased or intends to cease to carry on that business in the place where the employee was so employed;

or

the requirements of that business for employees to carry out work of a particular kind, or for employees to carry out work of a particular kind in the place where the employee was employed by the employer, have ceased or diminished or are expected to cease or diminish.

ERA, s 139(1)

471

The key words are *cease* and *diminish* – and the statutory definition translates into any situation where the whole organisation or part of it closes down or where the organisation has a reduced need for particular jobs. The Trade Union Reform and Employment Rights Act, 1993, extended the definition of redundancy for consultation purposes to 'any dismissal for a reason not related to the individual concerned or for a number of reasons all of which are not so related'. Employers have a statutory duty to inform the DTI, within the timescales laid down for consultation, that they intend to make more than 20 employees redundant, even when all of the redundancies are voluntary. This is to allow the DTI to provide assistance in finding alternative employment or training opportunities for the affected employees.

The legal framework for redundancy can be considered in four parts:

1 The payment of compensation for job loss.
2 Protection against unfair selection for redundancy.
3 The requirement for consultation with employees.
4 Other statutory rights.

REDUNDANCY PAYMENTS

Redundancy legislation provides for payments for the loss of employment which is 'wholly or mainly' due to redundancy. Some employees are excluded from this legislation:

- employees under the age of 18
- employees who have reached normal retirement age.

The Employment Protection (part-time employees) Regulations, 1995 removed the differential qualifying threshold for redundancy payments for full and part-time employees, and full-time and part-time employees should have the same entitlement to redundancy payments. The two-year qualifying period for redundancy payments is also subject to challenge and may well be reduced.

Statutory redundancy payments are based on age and length of continuous service (Exhibit 19.1). Overall entitlement is reduced in the final year of service before retirement by one twelfth for every completed month of service in that final year. In calculating redundancy payments the statutory limit for a week's pay in 2002 is £250 (reviewed periodically), whilst the number of years' service is restricted to a maximum of 20. The maximum statutory entitlement is therefore only £7500. As compensation for job loss this figure is salutary and highlights the limitations of statutory protection. At best a statutory redundancy payment provides a bridgehead or temporary financial respite for an employee who is effectively between jobs. Where an employer fails to make a statutory redundancy payment, the employee can take a claim for payment to a tribunal. Proposed amendments in the 2001 Employment Bill will require employees to use the grievance procedure before taking a claim for non-payment of statutory redundancy payment to the employment tribunal. A redundant employee has a right to a written statement of how a redundancy payment has been calculated, and a dispute about the calculation of the payment can also be referred to a tribunal. An employer can elect to make redundancy payments above the statutory minima.

Exhibit 19.1 Statutory redundancy payments

Age	Number of weeks' pay
18–21 years	$1/2$ week's pay per completed year
22–40 years	1 week's pay per completed year
41–63 years	$1^1/2$ weeks' pay per completed year
over 64 years	overall redundancy entitlement reduced by $1/12$ per month

SELECTION FOR REDUNDANCY

The selection criteria to be used by an employer in a redundancy situation are not defined in law. However, the employer must follow customary arrangements or agreed procedures, or if there are no customary arrangements or procedures selection should be based on objective criteria and also be reasonable in the circumstances. Selection for redundancy gives rise to many claims for unfair dismissal and managers need to be fair, reasonable and objective, ensuring that selection criteria are stated in the redundancy policy and applied in an even-handed way.

Selection for redundancy must be on the basis of objective criteria which are carefully and precisely defined and which can be applied in an independent way. The reason for having objective criteria is to ensure that employees are not unfairly selected for redundancy. Some selection criteria will almost inevitably be considered to be unfair by an employment tribunal, including:

- trade union activity or membership
- age
- part-time working, unless it can be clearly demonstrated that the work cannot be done on a part-time basis
- employee action on reasonable health and safety issues
- asserting a statutory employment right
- maternity-related issues. It is unfair if the basis of the selection is that the employee is on maternity leave. The Maternity and Paternity Regulations, 1999 clarified the position regarding the nature of the contract of employment during the extended period of maternity leave, and as long as there is a genuine redundancy situation and the employee is consulted in accordance with legislation, there is nothing to stop that employee being selected for redundancy on the basis of the application of the agreed criteria.

Selection is also unfair if it is based on the sex, marital status, disability or race of an employee. An employee selected for redundancy has a statutory right to be fairly selected, and if the employee considers that selection is unfair or not in line with agreed criteria, or if the criteria lack objectivity, then a claim can be made to an employment tribunal.

Redundancy can be non-compulsory or compulsory. Non-compulsory redundancy is more widely acceptable because employees elect job loss rather than being forced out, although they may need to be enticed by attractive financial arrangements, and therefore the damaging and demotivating effects of redundancy can potentially be minimised. Clearly non-compulsory redundancy may increase the short-term financial cost, but it may also achieve the reprofiling of the workforce in a shorter time than where adversarial relationships develop because of compulsory redundancies.

Non-compulsory redundancy

Voluntary redundancy – This occurs when the employer seeks volunteers for redundancy from the workforce. In this situation it is effectively the employee rather than management who makes the redundancy decision. Problems can occur if there are more volunteers from the workforce than are required, because the employer will still need to select for redundancy. Objective criteria are needed in order to make an appropriate selection from the volunteers, as the probability of achieving the precise number of volunteers required is low.

The advantage of voluntary redundancy is a reduction in the potential for conflict between management and employees, and the negative impact of redundancies on the total workforce will be reduced. It may, however, be a costly option because of the need to offer an enhancement to statutory redundancy payments as an employee incentive to volunteer for redundancy. Another potential disadvantage is the lack of control over who volunteers; the most valuable and skilled employees may opt to go because they find it easier to secure new employment. Refusing voluntary redundancy to those who want to leave can have a negative impact on their morale and motivation, and allowing the weak performers, or lower-skilled employees, to go can be perceived as rewarding them through an attractive severance package. This can lead to resentment amongst remaining employees and as a consequence be detrimental to employment relationships. Handling voluntary redundancy requires as much managerial skill as that required for compulsory redundancy situations.

Early retirement – This can also constitute redundancy, and the redundant worker will be eligible for redundancy payments and occupational pension. Care must be taken to ensure that the reason for dismissal is 'purely' redundancy and not just early retirement, because there are income tax implications. Redundancy payments are tax free up to a maximum of £30 000, but if the Inland Revenue judge the termination of employment to be early retirement rather than redundancy then payments made to the employee may be liable to income tax. Offering redundancy to employees nearing normal retirement age can be less contentious within the workforce, but asking for volunteers who are subsequently rejected for voluntary redundancy is very disappointing for the employees concerned and has negative implications for the employment relationship.

Early retirement can lead to a skewed age profile and little natural retirement for several years, making career progression difficult for those who remain.

Compulsory redundancy

Last in first out (LIFO) – This is a selection method that is transparent, easy to apply and easy for the workforce to understand. Therefore selection on the basis of the length of time in the job has a 'felt fair' appeal. LIFO can be applied on an organisation-wide basis or to a particular occupational group. LIFO can give rise to skill-mix problems where the most recent recruits have the most up-to-date skills, and electing to lose those first may not be commercially sound. Employees who have changed jobs internally need special consideration where LIFO is used, as the total length of service in the organisation, rather than in a particular job, should be used. An assessment of whether unlawful indirect discrimination is taking place is necessary if there is a disproportionate representation of women in the final LIFO listing. Career breaks and the more fragmented employment pattern of women may result in LIFO criteria having a disproportionate impact on female workers, and if that is the case other non-discriminatory criteria need to be considered. LIFO has the advantage of being a quantifiable criterion and is resistant to a charge of favouritism or managerial bias. It is also a lower-cost option because long-service staff are retained. LIFO can lead to a skewed age profile where those employees with shorter service are the younger employees.

Employee efficiency and effectiveness criteria – Such criteria can be used and may include assessments of employees' work performance, absence records and time keeping. This is often referred to as a measured factors approach. The application of efficiency and effectiveness criteria relies on accurate employee records, and care must be taken to ensure that the reason for dismissal is redundancy because the job has ceased to exist. If the reason for dismissal is purely related to employee incapability, or other personal factors relating to the job holder, a tribunal may rule that the reason for dismissal is not redundancy. Performance criteria which are not precise and transparent can generate feelings of unfairness or inconsistency and lead to claims that the reason for dismissal is incapability or misconduct rather than redundancy. The employer response to this claim would need to be that the employee's capability or conduct would be acceptable if the organisation was not in a redundancy situation and that no dismissal would otherwise have taken place. Redundancy selection on the basis of employee performance can contribute to the development of a performance culture by retaining the higher-performing employees. It can also positively affect morale if the workforce accept and relate to the performance criteria which are used, because the reward of increased job security is linked to high performance.

Appraisal ratings should not be used as the sole basis for redundancy selection as this may intensify concerns over a lack of managerial objectivity. Efficiency and effectiveness should be assessed using a range of objective performance measures, and managerial guidelines are needed to ensure consistent scoring. For example, points can be attached to the number of incidents of sick or other absence. Key performance criteria need to be identified for each episode of redundancy and weighted in proportion to importance.

Key criteria should be capable of being scored objectively from employee records and assessments. Reliance on employee records requires there to have been regular and consistent measurement of performance. The redundancy criteria can be produced in matrix form, with appropriate weightings, and each employee is scored against the criteria. Exhibit 19.2 illustrates this approach and in this case the higher the score the higher the ranking and the more valuable the employee. The workers with the lowest scores are more likely to be selected for redundancy. This systematic ranking approach, as long as it is reasonably objective and non-discriminatory, has tended to find favour with tribunals and is relatively fair and transparent to employees who can see how they are being assessed. It is also open to employers to use psychological assessment in choosing workers for redundancy, on the basis that if it is used for entry to the organisation it can also be used for exit from the organisation; the usual caveats apply (*see* Chapter 7).

Exhibit 19.2   Performance criteria for redundancy selection

	Selection criteria and weighting	Worker 1	Worker 2	Worker 3
1	Absence record* 10%	(20) 2	(0) 0	(90) 9
2	Appraisal rating 15%	(30) 4.5	(20) 3	(50) 7.5
3	Timekeeping 10%	(40) 4	(40) 4	(50) 5
4	Responsiveness to customers 20%	(80) 16	(40) 8	(80) 16
5	Achievement of key objectives 25%	(60) 15	(60) 15	(72) 18
6	Team skills 20%	(80) 16	(30) 6	(50) 10
	Total	57.5	36	65.5

* Absence Incidents – the number of incidents attracts a points rating:
>10 = 0; 8–10 = 10; 6–7 = 20; 4–5 = 30; 2–3 = 50; 1 = 70; 0 = 90.

The application of skills and the acquisition of qualifications – This can form the basis of selection for redundancy. The retention of skilled employees is clearly a commercial priority in order that an efficient and effective workforce remains after the redundancies. The required skills profile should be decided prior to individual decisions being taken.

A skills matrix needs to be produced, in a similar format to the performance criteria in Exhibit 19.2, but using and weighting key competencies. These competencies should flow from the corporate plan which should specify the skills profile required following the restructuring of the organisation. This selection method therefore aims to match employee skills to the organisational objectives. It is, however, problematic to define skill requirements in sufficient detail for objective and systematic measurement, and sufficient data on individual employee skills may not be available. Where skill data is available it may just reflect competencies which are exhibited and used rather than competencies which are actually possessed, and some form of competency testing or an assessment centre may therefore be necessary.

These selection methods are not mutually exclusive or exhaustive. They can be combined in various ways and may even result in employees being required to compete for a smaller number of jobs through a sophisticated selection and assessment process. Whatever selection criteria are decided upon, they must be applied fairly and equitably. The employer who applies a measured factor approach using performance criteria or competencies combined with a weighting and scoring system should ensure that neither the criteria nor the weightings are themselves discriminatory. The tribunal will not normally require the scores to be disclosed to anyone other than the individual. The employer should provide an appeals procedure in line with the disciplinary procedure. The advantage of the appeals procedure is that it potentially allows for complaints about unfair selection to be resolved internally and therefore reduces the likelihood of complaints to an employment tribunal. However, the message is clear: employers need to identify and apply selection criteria for redundancy objectively.

CONSULTATION WITH EMPLOYEES

There is a requirement for consultation between the employer and the employee in a redundancy situation regardless of the number of employees to be made redundant. The aim of managerial consultation with the employee is to listen to what the employee has to say and provide an opportunity for the avoidance or minimisation of the redundancy effect. Consultation should occur when redundancy proposals are still in a formative stage, and employees will need adequate information and proper time to respond.

Collective redundancies – In 1994 the European Court of Justice ruled that in giving consultation rights only to recognised trade unions, the UK was in breach of the spirit of the EU directive on employer consultation with workers' representatives in situations of collective redundancy. The Collective Redundancy and Transfer of Undertakings (Protection of Employment) Regulations, 1995 corrected this situation and required employer consultation with 'appropriate representatives' when 20 or more employees are to be made redundant. Since 1999 where there are recognised trade unions the employer is obliged to consult with the union. Where trade unions are not recognised, employee representatives must be elected. The number of employees to be made redundant determines the timing of consultation with employee representatives:

- Where 20–99 employees are to be made redundant, consultation should take place at least 30 days prior to the first dismissal.
- Where 100 or more employees are to be made redundant, consultation should take place at least 90 days before the first dismissal.

In all cases the employer should provide, and is required to disclose in writing to the employee representatives, the following information:

- the reasons for the proposed redundancies
- the numbers and type of employees to be made redundant
- the total number of employees of this type employed
- the proposed selection criteria
- the proposed implementation procedure and the timing
- redundancy payments.

The Collective Redundancies and Transfer of Undertakings (Protection of Employment: Amendment) Regulations, 1999 require employers to consult with employee representatives not only about those being made redundant, but also about others who might be affected by the dismissals by, for example, taking on additional duties left over from the redundant positions. Under these regulations employers are required to take an active role in ensuring that proper elections take place and also in protecting representatives from detrimental treatment. There must be sufficient representatives to represent the interests of all affected employees, and the term of office of representatives must be sufficient to enable the effective dissemination of information and for proper consultation to take place.

The collective redundancy regulations do not detail how many representatives are to be elected or specify how they should be elected, but the DTI provides guidelines which include:

- appropriate cover for all types of employees, allowing for a reasonable balance between the different interests of the groups
- sufficient time to nominate and consider alternative candidates
- a free vote for employees in a secret ballot
- following custom and practice within the organisation for internal elections, where it exists.

The election of employee representatives should therefore be held within a timescale that allows sufficient time subsequently to meet the legal requirements for consultation periods. The aim of the collective consultation is to seek to avoid dismissals or to reduce the number of staff affected and also to minimise the impact of the dismissals. Elected representatives have rights in law to enable them to fulfil their duties. These rights are similar to those of TU representatives and include access to the employees who are affected by the redundancy proposals, reasonable time off with pay to carry out the duties and to undertake appropriate training, and a right not to be dismissed because of their status as employee representatives. A genuine attempt must be made to consult in a meaningful way and where possible with 'a view to reaching agreement'. Whilst collective consultation is a statutory requirement, case law makes it clear that employers are still obliged to consult individually with those affected by redundancy. Collective consultation is therefore in addition to, and not in place of, individual consultation.

Small scale redundancy – Where fewer than 20 employees are to be made redundant, case law has reinforced the importance of the employer's duty to consult individually with each employee, and the employer should use the consultation process as a means of explaining and considering the individual's situation. Redundancy is a 'potentially fair' reason for dismissal, but the employer is still statutorily obliged to follow a reasonable procedure and this includes consultation with the individual threatened with job loss. Failure to consult may result in the reasonableness of the dismissal being challenged at a tribunal. The individual consultation should discuss why and how the individual has been selected, examine ways of avoiding redundancy and explore the possibility of suitable alternative work within the organisation.

OTHER STATUTORY RIGHTS

An employee who qualifies for statutory redundancy payments is entitled to 'reasonable' time off with pay to look for future employment. The law does not define reasonable time off, but an employer refusing time off to an employee under notice of redundancy for seeking alternative employment would need to demonstrate to a tribunal that the time being taken was unreasonable. Redundant employees are entitled to their statutory notice period or to payment in lieu of notice when they are not required to attend work during their period of notice. Failure by the employer to honour the notice period may result in a claim for wrongful dismissal. The Employment Rights Act permits an employee who is under threat of redundancy to have a trial period in a job which is considered 'suitable alternative work', without forfeiting redundancy payments. Case law has established what, in principle, constitutes suitable alternative work and when it may be unreasonable for the employee to reject it. To be suitable, the alternative work should normally provide similar rewards, have similar status, be within the employee's capability and not involve excessive inconvenience. The reason for the trial period may be either for the employer to assess the employee's ability to do the job or for the employee to try the job to decide whether or not it is suitable for his or her skills and experience. If, at the end of the trial period, which can last up to four weeks, either the employer or the employee legitimately and reasonably considers the job unsuitable, the employee retains the right to redundancy payments based on the original job.

THE AVOIDANCE OF REDUNDANCY

The avoidance of redundancy is a commendable goal, but the idea of a full employment policy or a no compulsory redundancy agreement is no longer realistic. Organisations should strive through their strategic and human resource planning activities to put in place resourcing policies that reduce the need for compulsory redundancy. The human resource plan (*see* Chapter 4) should anticipate internal and external pressures for change and guide people resourcing decisions to ensure incremental adjustments to workforce composition which avoid the organisational 'shock' of redundancies. This may be difficult to achieve at a time of rapid change or economic recession when reduced labour mobility and low turnover rates may mean that numerical human resource targets cannot be achieved through natural wastage. Employers should also be mindful of ways to adjust workforce composition at no or low cost.

Options for avoiding redundancy include:

- seeking business solutions
- reviewing the position of temporary workers and contractors
- the freezing of recruitment
- reducing or eliminating overtime working
- the retraining and redeployment of employees
- short-time working or lay-offs.

Managers can pursue business solutions to a downturn in a requirement for employees, for example the accessing of new markets or the introduction of new products or services. These responses are likely to be longer-term measures and may not eliminate the need for redundancy in the short to medium term. The business solution is an option in a competitive environment, but adjustments to the workforce in terms of numbers and skills may be inevitable if the organisation cannot react to market pressures and make business changes sufficiently quickly. Organisations facing a redundancy situation should normally review the position of temporary employees and contractors first. There is no redundancy payment entitlement for workers who do not have a contract of employment and the feasibility of releasing these workers is a logical first consideration. The position of employees on temporary or fixed-term contracts should also be reviewed, as these workers may have less expectation of long-term job security.

Another managerial option is the freezing of recruitment. If the aim is a reduction in costs through reducing the workforce and if the problem is relatively short term, a recruitment freeze may be the solution. The dilemma that arises with this option is that the freezing of recruitment affects the organisation in an arbitrary way and its impact is very difficult to predict. It is dependent solely on who resigns and from which job, and is therefore not based directly on business needs. A compromise approach is to scrutinise each vacancy with the aim of limiting recruitment to posts that are vital to the achievement of organisational objectives. This may ultimately achieve the head count target, but the cost savings may not be achieved within an acceptable timescale.

The need for redundancy may be reduced through reducing or eliminating overtime working. Surplus labour in one part of the organisation can be utilised to eliminate overtime working in other parts. This common-sense approach, whilst being attractive through the retention of employees, is difficult to implement in practice. If the organisation has employees with specialised but not transferable skills this option may not be practical. An organisation making some employees redundant while operating a policy of significant overtime working needs to ensure that the situation is handled carefully. A strategy to avoid redundancy in this situation is to retrain employees. If employees with the ability to undertake the necessary training and to acquire the new skills needed can be identified, this can be a successful method of avoiding redundancies. Anticipating the skill change requirements is crucial and sufficient time must be allowed for the retraining and reskilling to take place.

The use of short-time working or lay-offs is also an option to avoid redundancy, but organisations have no automatic right to lay off employees without pay or impose short-time working even if there is no work for them to do. A lay-off is where there is no work for the employees and no payment of wages is made. Short-time working is defined as where less than half of a normal week's pay is earned. To use short-time working or lay-offs without repudiating the contract of employment, either there needs to be an express term in the contract, or a unilateral change to the working arrangements by the employer must not be for an unreasonably long period. If it is for an unreasonable period, which may be only four weeks, employees may justifiably consider themselves to be made redundant and claim redundancy payments. Lay-offs and short-time working are short-term responses to a temporary reduction in demand for a product or service which may be resolved by temporarily cutting the wage bill.

THE EFFECTIVE MANAGEMENT OF REDUNDANCY

Organisations should seek to manage any redundancy situation in a systematic way to minimise resentment, and to ensure that redundancies are handled fairly and reasonably within the statutory framework. This involves having a redundancy policy and thinking about the practicalities of handling redundancy. An analytical framework for systematically managing redundancy is exposed in Fig. 19.1 and consideration of these elements will direct managerial action at each stage of the process.

The redundancy policy

Management must plan ahead for redundancy, not only through human resource planning, but also through having an agreed redundancy policy in place. A policy defines the parameters for managerial action and enables redundancy to be dealt with in a more objective way. A redundancy policy which is agreed, regularly reviewed, effectively communicated and clearly understood by employees is essential to the successful management of redundancy. The following elements should be included in a redundancy policy.

- *An opening statement* – make a positive organisational statement about the commitment to maintaining employment levels and job security, whilst acknowledging that the organisational need for employees and for skills of a particular kind changes over time and management may need to take action from time to time to align employment levels and skills profiles with business needs and objectives.

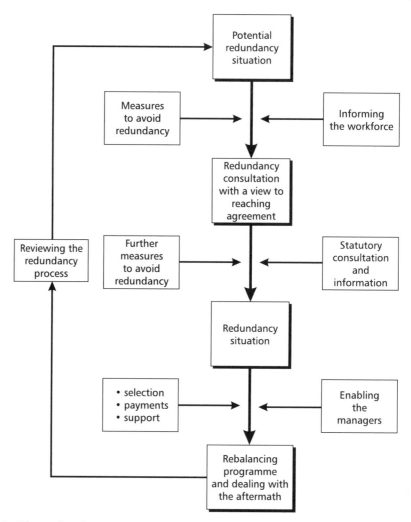

Fig. 19.1 The redundancy system

- *Consultation arrangements* – state the consultation arrangements to be used in individual and collective redundancy situations and specify the election arrangements for employee representatives in a collective redundancy situation.

- *Actions to be taken to reduce the need for redundancy* – refer to the alternative courses of managerial action that will be considered in order to avoid the need for employees to be made redundant.

- *Selection criteria* – define objective and transparent selection criteria to include the method and the process; specify any eligibility and the terms of voluntary severance, but acknowledge that an insufficient number of volunteers may mean that compulsory redundancies are necessary.

- *Redundancy payment arrangements* – specify statutory payments together with any enhancement to redundancy payments entitlement.

- *Redeployment procedures* – refer to organisational redeployment procedures and identify the process through which employees will be considered and selected.
- *Appeals procedure* – state the employee's right to appeal internally against the operation of the redundancy policy together with an outline of the appeals process and procedure.
- *Support systems* – specify organisational support such as outplacement services, counselling, training or time off for job search.

The handling of redundancy

Often the first indications of organisational difficulties result in the informal communications system, the grapevine, coming into operation, with rumour and misinformation exaggerating the redundancy threat and creating workforce tensions. The managerial fear of these tensions can result in attempts to keep things from employees. Organisations try to conceal a threat of redundancies for several reasons:

- the negative effect it may have on the business
- the decline in staff morale
- the adverse effect on the customers and shareholders
- the potential for decline in market share
- the loss of key workers.

The timing of an announcement to employees is important and needs to be carefully judged. Telling employees that their continued employment is threatened is a difficult thing to do. However, once the business decision to consider the redundancy option has been taken, employees should be informed in a sensitive and professional way. Employees will want answers to difficult questions and managers must be in a position to provide accurate information. Redundancy often occurs at a time of organisational change and redundancy itself can intensify the change required by the organisation, because those employees remaining will be doing jobs in different ways or be doing different jobs. It is important therefore that employees are persuaded of the need for change and that they accept the way in which redundancy fits into the change process. Individuals are, in general, resistant to change, but there can also be the desire for change and for new challenges. Change can be successfully managed (*see* Chapter 21) and the organisation can move to a position of strength. If change is not managed well, low morale and a decline in confidence can seriously and adversely affect the organisation and undermine the efforts of management to rebalance the organisation. A systematic approach to the management of a redundancy situation contributes to ensuring that appropriate actions are taken at the relevant time and that problems are minimised (Fig. 19.1).

The announcement to employees should be made at the same time as the communication of measures initiated to avoid redundancy and also the arrangements for preliminary consultation with employees. This initial consultation may lead to an exchange of information and then to the statutory consultation process. The outcome of the statutory period of consultation may be agreement on further avoidance measures or ideally for the redundancy requirement to be avoided, but this is uncommon and the organisation may have to acknowledge formally that a redundancy situation exists. An agreed redundancy policy will not only facilitate the redundancy selection process and provide information on redundancy payments, but it will also focus attention on:

- the enabling of managers to deal with the redundancy process
- the development of a communication strategy
- the arrangements needed for the counselling and support of redundant employees and also the survivors.

The training and enabling of managers – This is fundamental to the effective management of the sensitive and emotionally charged situation of redundancy. Many managers will not have dealt with this previously and may not be appropriately skilled. Managers need to be competent in handling the variety of employee responses and recognise the importance of treating each employee as an individual. A redundancy situation creates general concerns about security of employment and all employees will want to know if jobs are threatened. Common concerns and feelings are experienced by employees and awareness of these will help to predict reactions and allow for appropriate responses to be planned. However, individuals vary and stereotypical assumptions should not be made.

The financial implications of redundancy are normally significant to the individual, but work provides other rewards and satisfactions which are threatened by job loss. Employment may be central to an individual's social life, not only in providing opportunities for interactions at work, but also in providing access to social events. Job loss through redundancy or a change in hours or location through redeployment can significantly affect work/life balance. Extended travel, revised hours or a change to shift working may mean that the employee is too tired or is denied the opportunity for outside social activity. Individuals derive status and self-esteem from work and therefore any change in the working arrangements may affect individual morale. An employee may be afraid that job loss will result in a loss of status in the community, and there have been instances of redundant employees being afraid to inform family members and continuing to leave for work to give the impression of being employed. Another common employee concern is the fear of the unknown. The fear of change, or the anticipation, may have a more negative effect than the change itself, because many people are resistant to change, like familiarity and avoid situations that are threatening. Therefore managers, in dealing with redundancy, need to recognise this emotional dimension and have the sensitivity skills necessary to respond appropriately.

Managers should also recognise that individual circumstances and characteristics, such as age, gender and personality, affect individual responses. For example, young workers who suffer job loss may find it difficult to relate to their peers and be concerned about the effect on their social life, if the majority of their friends are in employment. Older workers may fear never working again and the real threat of age discrimination may demoralise the individual. Men (or women) may be concerned about the threat to their status as a 'bread winner' because this may be a source of recognition, security and self-esteem. Women (or men) may fear having to return to domesticity and the consequent loss of social and financial independence. An individual's financial situation, such as mortgage commitments, credit liabilities and family circumstances, will also have a significant impact on the individual response. Disproportionate publicity about large redundancy packages has contributed to the myth of large redundancy payments, but most redundant employees receive little more than the statutory minimum payment. Redundancy payments are therefore best viewed as a bridging arrangement to another job, rather than providing financial security for a long period.

Personality characteristics will influence individual responses to the threat of job loss. Some people will be resigned, some react angrily and others withdraw. Others may perceive redundancy as a challenge and an opportunity to do something new, or of being forced into accepting an opportunity that they have been afraid of previously. Those without external support, from the family or elsewhere, may find it helpful to have someone with whom to discuss the situation. There can be feelings of self-blame and these can be destructive. If other people are also being made redundant, the individual may be able to externalise the negative feelings and accept that the reason for job loss is attributable to circumstances beyond their control, and less stigma may occur or be perceived. The employee's length of service may influence feelings in a redundancy situation; those with a long period of employment may feel betrayed and have intensified feelings of anger, making it more difficult to adjust to what is happening.

Managers need to be able to recognise and to handle individual responses of anger, denial, fear and anxiety. There is rarely a place for humour in the redundancy encounters between management and employee. Good listening skills are necessary and employees should be allowed and encouraged to express their feelings. The redundancy consultation interview should not be hurried and sufficient time should be allotted for the manager to speak, listen and provide the information needed by the employee. Important information should be given in writing because the stressful circumstances of the interview may mean that information given orally is not accurately recalled by the employee. Information specific to the individual employee should be prepared prior to the interview, talked through during the interview and ideally handed to the employee soon after the interview. Line managers will often be anxious in a redundancy situation as they may also feel under threat. This needs to be recognised by those training the managers. In summary, training the managers involves developing the skills necessary to deal with the redundancy encounters with individual employees and providing information on the redundancy policy, the reasons for redundancies, the timing of redundancies and the individual entitlements in terms of payment, time off and support.

A communications strategy – This should guide managerial actions. Several steps are involved. The timing of the initial disclosure of the redundancy threat should be decided with care, and individual or group announcement strategies reviewed to determine which will work best. A senior management announcement is more likely to project an image of a concerned organisation that is not just 'passing the buck' to lower levels of management. The reasons for the redundancy threat should be communicated clearly and accurately, together with the alternative solutions being considered. Information on the prospect of any redundancy package should be outlined, be consistent with the policy and be communicated effectively. Opportunities to talk on an individual basis should be made available. Employees affected by redundancy decisions, both leavers and survivors, can perceive the process to be unethical if redundancy information is withheld, if inadequate advance notice is given, if redundancies are announced near or during holiday seasons, or if they learn about an impending downsizing from sources outside the organisation (Hopkins and Hopkins, 1999). In terms of practical implications managerial actions which are perceived to be unethical can lead to reduced productivity and morale and therefore to competitiveness and profitability problems.

Counselling and support – The organisation should consider the support that professional counselling can give to employees. There needs to be a system of employee access to staff who are trained and who know how to deal with individual responses to redundancy. Access to a counselling service should be communicated and should be sufficiently resourced to minimise waiting time. Counsellors can be either trained staff from within the organisation or specialist external consultants. If external consultants are chosen, the way in which they are deployed is important. Consultants should be placed with discretion, as there can be employee feelings of being 'taken over' by outsiders, which may lead to increased resentment. Having said this, the displacement of emotion and anger onto external consultants may be able to be used constructively by the organisation and allow managers and employees to relate to each other in an objective way, and without the emotional dimension. These external consultants (outplacement consultants) provide a wide range of services. Outplacement is 'the process whereby an individual or individuals, compelled to leave their employment, are given support and counselling to assist them in achieving the next stage of their career' (Eggert, 1991). The outplacement role is to facilitate the transition from the redundant job to the next employment or self-employment, and outplacement specialists have the skills, resources and contacts to assist in a variety of situations. The range of services include:

- financial planning and advice, which increases in importance if large redundancy packages are involved
- career counselling, including an appropriate battery of assessments to facilitate discussions and widen job options
- skills assessment and development
- job search skills, including application and CV advice, interview techniques and networking opportunities
- the setting up of a 'job shop'.

Outplacement services can help the redundant worker to progress through the stages of shock and disbelief towards success and hope in securing a new job.

Handling a redundancy situation which results in both those leaving and those remaining feeling reasonably positive presents a major challenge to the employer but can be pursued with careful preparation, effective communication and openness. In 1999, The Body Shop, whose reputation is built on its ethical approach to business and employment, needed to lose up to 200 jobs at its Littlehampton headquarters because of competitive pressures. Merrick (2000) reports that The Body Shop did not want to be seen as handing out redundancy notices without any regard for the people involved. The

Body Shop's challenge was to manage a major restructuring in a way that would sit well with the values of the business. A creative range of initiatives were developed, aimed at sending out a message that all staff were valued. These included:

- the setting up of an entrepreneurs' club to provide loans, coaching and mentoring, as well as opportunities for networking to those wanting to start their own business
- a £1000 training grant to those being made redundant (this was later expanded to all employees to recognise the needs of those remaining with the organisation)
- the opportunity for an additional redundancy payment to those over 50 who had still not found employment at the end of their redundancy period (this was claimed by only four out of 25 eligible)
- the development of an 'Alive in Body Shop' programme aimed at those employees who are suffering from 'survivor syndrome' (see below).

The effective management of redundancy is difficult and organisations do not get it right all the time, but a well-thought-out policy and procedure which recognises the business, legal, professional and ethical issues is more likely to be seen in a positive light and to contribute to organisational survival.

REBALANCING THE ORGANISATION AFTER REDUNDANCY

An important consideration, often not given sufficient attention, is the restructuring and rebalancing of the organisation following a redundancy programme. Whilst redundancy affects those being made redundant, it also affects those remaining, and the negative feeling associated with surviving redundancy through remaining in employment is termed 'survivor syndrome'. The surviving employees may experience relief at avoiding redundancy, but redundancies contribute to a destabilisation of the workforce as a whole, and concerns which remain after those made redundant have left the organisation need to be addressed if the organisation is to be successful.

Surviving employees will want to be reassured that those leaving are being supported because of their own fear of redundancy in the future, but at the same time surviving employees may feel neglected because of the managerial attention which is being directed at those being made redundant.

> The support for those leaving was excellent, but everyone was too busy to talk through the issues with the rest of us. I felt as if I no longer mattered very much.
>
> (a surviving employee, in Doherty and Horsted, 1995)

Managerial effort therefore needs to be focused not only on those leaving, but also on those remaining. Early consideration needs to be given to the shape, design and structure of the organisation post-redundancy. Strategic and human resource planning should anticipate how the organisation will be affected, not only in numbers of jobs but also in skills and structure. The development of a rebalancing plan and its communication to the workforce are vital if feelings of teamwork and confidence are to return. Uncertainty and lack of organisational direction may mean that those remaining will continue to experience insecurity and seek employment elsewhere, resulting in the loss of key skills and compromising the recovery of the organisation. Rebalancing the organisation and addressing survivor syndrome requires consideration of:

- communications strategies – to reduce uncertainties and develop survivor cohesiveness
- a human resource plan to reflect the business plan
- job redesign and work restructuring to reallocate work and to maximise the skills and experience of remaining staff in the context of business objectives
- skills analysis and training needs analysis in order to ensure that skills are utilised effectively and training needs are identified and addressed
- a focus on the training and development of surviving employees to ensure that the organisation moves forward – the cost-cutting philosophy of a redundancy exercise can mean that training and development are neglected.

A positive managerial response to the post-redundancy organisation sends the message that a planned and considered approach is being taken, contributes to the confidence of the remaining staff, builds commitment and ultimately helps the organisation to succeed.

SUMMARY LEARNING POINTS

1 A legislative framework exists to afford limited protection and compensation for employees who lose their job through no fault of their own. The legislation does not specify selection criteria for redundancy, but requires that fair and objective criteria are agreed and adhered to in any redundancy situation.

2 Organisations should strive to avoid the need for compulsory redundancy by careful consideration of a range of alternative actions. An agreed policy for the effective management of redundancy should be in place and communicated prior to a redundancy situation occurring. The policy should provide guidelines and information for managers to enable them to handle redundancy fairly, skilfully and consistently. The policy also lets employees know how they will be dealt with.

3 Employees display different responses to the threat of redundancy, making managing the process difficult and stressful for all concerned. Collective and individual consultation are key features of effective redundancy handling.

4 The timing of the communication of the threat of redundancy is vital. Poor managerial timing can adversely affect the organisation commercially and also reduce the confidence of employees in managerial effectiveness. It may also lead to the organisation losing key staff as they seek alternative employment.

5 A range of services can be provided to assist the employee in the transition to the next employer, or to retirement. Support or outplacement services for those leaving can also contribute to more positive feelings in those who remain with the organisation.

6 After redundancy the organisation needs to plan for the future. This strategic planning should occur prior to the redundancies and be communicated and implemented following redundancies. The organisation needs to be rebalanced, not only in terms of numbers but also in terms of structure, work allocation and skills. Survivors need as much consideration as these who leave.

7 Employees who remain with the organisation following a redundancy programme may have a reduced feeling of job security, and the fair treatment of those leaving and the effective communication of future plans and objectives are essential to building future organisational success.

8 Organisations which recognise the business, legal, professional and ethical considerations in handling redundancy situations are more likely to be seen in a positive light and achieve business success.

REFERENCES AND FURTHER READING

Advisory, Conciliation and Arbitration Service (2001) *Redundancy Handling: Advisory Booklet 12.*

CIPD (2002) *Redundancy: Quick Facts.*

Department of Employment (1987) *Redundancy, Consultation and Notification.*

Doherty, N. and Horsted, J. (1995) 'Helping survivors to stay on board', *People Management*, January, 26–31.

Eggert, M. (1991) *Outplacement*. London: IPM.

Farnham, D. and Pimlott, J. (1995) *Understanding Industrial Relations*. London: Cassell.

Hopkins, W. and Hopkins, S. (1999) 'The ethics of downsizing: perceptions of rights and responsibilities', *Journal of Business Ethics*, 18, 145–56.

Incomes Data Services (1992) *IDS Study 511 Managing Redundancy.*

Institute of Personnel Management (1991) *The IPM Redundancy Code.*

Lewis, P. (1993) *The Successful Management of Redundancy*. Oxford: Blackwell.

Merrick, N. (2000) 'A natural preparation', *People Management*, 26 October, 50–4.

Pilbeam, S. and Corbidge, M. (2000) 'The skills of employee relations', in Farnham, D. (ed.), *Employee Relations in Context*. London: CIPD.

Redefining Redundancy: Research Report 7 (2001) Penna, Sanders and Sidney Career Consulting, April, 1–12.

Rothwell, J. (2000) 'How to break the news of redundancies', *People Management*, November.

Salamon, M. (1998) *Industrial Relations: Theory and practice* (3rd edn). Hemel Hempstead: Prentice Hall.

Summerfield, J. (1996) 'Lean firms cannot afford to be mean', *People Management*, January, 30–2.

ASSIGNMENTS AND DISCUSSION TOPICS

1 Critically review the redundancy policy of your organisation or an organisation with which you are familiar. How fair, effective and workable are the selection criteria identified in the policy?

2 What employee data is needed to use competencies as credible and objective selection criteria? What difficulties might managers encounter?

3 Critically evaluate alternative measures that may be taken by an organisation in order to avoid compulsory redundancy.

4 Analyse the skills and competencies that managers need in order to manage the individual redundancy encounter effectively. How can the skills be acquired in this sensitive area of managerial action?

5 Evaluate the effectiveness of the support your organisation offers to employees who are being made redundant.

6 What advice would you give to a newly appointed line manager on the effective handling of redundancy?

7 Prepare a briefing paper in which you advise the management team on how to recognise and respond effectively to 'survivor syndrome'. Use the briefing paper as the basis for a short presentation to a small group of colleagues or fellow students.

CHAPTER 20

Competencies in people resourcing

by Sylvia Horton

INTRODUCTION

Competency management reflects a change from a job-based to a person-based approach to people resourcing. It grew, in the 1980s, out of an economic context of greater globalisation and increasing competitiveness in world markets, the emergence of a knowledge-based service economy, flatter organisational structures and greater decentralisation, more emphasis on teamworking, and the need for both functional and personal flexibility within organisations. The emergence of HRM, with its emphasis on people as the organisation's most important resource, also paved the way for the development of competency management. A growing number of organisations in both the private and public sectors are adopting competency frameworks which are designed to reflect the missions and goals of the organisation and to integrate organisational and HR strategies both horizontally and vertically. Competency management is not without its difficulties, although its benefits are widely acclaimed. This chapter examines the debates surrounding the concept and describes the ways in which it is currently used in people resourcing.

CHAPTER OBJECTIVES

- To identify the different meanings of competency.
- To trace the origins of the competency movement.
- To describe different ways of constructing competency frameworks.
- To illustrate the use of competency frameworks in the major activities of people resourcing.

DEFINITIONS AND CONCEPTS

What are competencies?

There are many different meanings, definitions and spellings and at least two distinct concepts to which the word competence is attached. There are also a range of foci which can be the basis for developing competency frameworks; these include jobs, tasks, roles, persons and organisations. Furthermore, competencies can relate to different levels within an organisation – strategic, supervisory and operational. As the Research Report on *Competency Frameworks in UK Organisations* (CIPD, 2001) states:

> The terms 'competence', 'competences', 'competency' and 'competencies' are used almost inter-changeably leading to some confusion not least regarding whether the term refers to an activity, a personality trait, a skill or even a task.

> (CIPD, 2001: 2)

Having given this 'health warning', we will begin by making a distinction (reflected in spelling) between **competency (ies)** which refers to

> *'the behavioural characteristic of an individual which is causally related to effective or superior performance in a job'* (Boyatzis, 1982)

and **competence(s)** which is

> *'the ability to perform activities within an occupation to a prescribed standard'* (Fletcher, 1991).

These two definitions reflect a difference in focus: the first relates to the inputs that help achieve successful performance at work and the second to the outcomes of competence. These are often described as 'behavioural competencies' and 'outcome-based compet-ences'. The simplest way to describe the difference is that competencies are about the people who do the work, while competence(s) are about the work and its achievement. These two approaches are sometimes identified as the American and British respectively.

What is competency management?

Competency management is an integrated set of activities concentrated on implementing and developing competencies of individuals, teams and organisations in order to realise the mission and the goals of the organisation and improve the performance of its staff. It is a particular approach to identifying, attracting, developing and rewarding the com-petencies necessary to realise the mission, goals, objectives and targets of the organisation.

What is a competency framework?

A competency framework is both a list of competencies but also a tool by which compet-encies are expressed, assessed and measured (Strebler *et al.*, 1997). Competency frame-works are generally based either on the 'behavioural' model, where competencies are expressed as the behaviours that individuals need to demonstrate their competency, and the 'minimum standards' model which relates to *the ability to perform activities within an occupation to a prescribed standard* (Fletcher, 1997).

Core competence

The term 'core' competence also has several meanings. Some use the concept to differentiate the essential (must have) from the subsidiary (might have) competencies that individuals need to do a job. A further use of the word is to refer to the common competencies that employees within an organisation need to have, irrespective of the role or the level at which they are operating. Hamel (1991) describes a core competence as 'a messy accumulation of learning', comprising tacit and explicit knowledge, skills and technologies, which gives an organisation a competitive advantage. Core competencies make a significant contribution to 'customer'-perceived value and 'customer' benefits. They are perceived as competitively unique and gateways to new markets. Organisations may have different types of core competencies. They may be market-access competencies (management of brand development, sales and marketing, technical support), integrity-related competencies (quality, cycle time management, just-in-time inventory management) that enable the organisation to do things quicker and more reliably than competitors, or functionally related competencies (skills which enable unique functionality). It is the 'core' competence that makes an organisation distinctive and gives it that competitive edge over its rivals. This idea of the 'core competency' has been central to academic and practitioner thinking on strategic management for the last decade.

To add to this complexity of competency lexicography, Strebler *et al.* (1997) highlight further terminological confusion as businesses adopt 'capabilities' or 'key success factors' to describe what are in effect competencies. Such variety alerts the reader to recognise that different terms may indicate differences about the focus (person versus job), the level of performance (competent versus effective or superior) and the object (role or organisation). To understand the subtle differences between the definitions and their use, one needs to trace the origins of the competency movement.

THE COMPETENCY MOVEMENT

The skills gap

By the late 1960s the economies of the USA and UK were experiencing pressures caused by globalisation, increased international competition and technological change. Both countries responded to these external forces in similar ways. First, there was a move to improve the standards and performance of the educational system, which was seen to be failing both business and individuals by not meeting the needs of the labour market or equipping young people with appropriate knowledge and skills to gain employment and do a good job. Reforms of the educational system occurred first in the USA and then in the UK. Both proceeded to reform their teacher training system and subsequently all three sectors of education. In the UK standard attainment tests (SATs) were introduced, along with a national curriculum and output assessment, in primary and secondary schools during the 1980s. In the 1990s league tables and quality ratings entered higher education.

Second, there was a move to raise the level of training in the workplace. Britain's worsening economic performance during the 1980s led the government to initiate a number of investigations and reports which emphasised the need for a flexible and adaptable workforce that could respond to economic change (Manpower Services Commission, 1981) and a comprehensive training programme based on new standards of occupational competence (MSC/NEDO, 1986). The British government put in place a system for setting standards across all sectors of industry. Industry Lead Bodies were created to develop the new standards and a National Council of Vocational Qualifications (NCVQ) was appointed to coordinate their work within a national framework. National Vocational Qualifications (NVQs) were seen as alternatives to the traditional educational qualifications conferred by academic examination bodies.

An NVQ comprises units of competence, each of which can be separately achieved and certificated. The NVQ process involved establishing the precise definition of the skills required to do particular jobs, assigning jobs to appropriate levels and evolving rigorous tests to assess whether people met the standards. It is not confined to manual and technical occupations but is fully comprehensive, covering all manual, clerical, technical, administrative, professional and managerial positions.

The NVQ Framework covers five levels from the basic competence required to undertake elementary, routine and predictable work activities (Level 1) through intermediate skills and competencies required for supervisory and work (Level 3) to competences involving the application of complex principles in unpredictable contexts associated with responsibility for substantive resources (Level 5).

(Winterton and Winterton, 1999)

Reports by Handy (1987) and Constable and McCormack (1987) indicated the particularly low standing and training of British management compared to its major competitors. The development of the chartered or professional manager, which began with the Management Charter Initiative (MCI, 1990) in 1987, was intended to encourage training and accreditation of recognised management skills that were subsequently developed within a NVQ framework.

During the 1990s the American government turned its attention to setting down national skills standards across all occupations and was clearly influenced by what had been happening in the UK. The Clinton Administration set up the National Skills Standards Board (NSSB) in 1994 to encourage the development of a voluntary national system of skill standards that may be assessed and certified. These standards can then be used:

by the nation to ensure the development of a high skill, high quality, high performance workforce, including the most skilled frontline workforce in the world.

(NSSB, 1998, sec. 502)

The NSSB's role is to establish occupational clusters that may share common skill standards and to establish Voluntary Partnerships (similar to the Lead Bodies or National

Training Organisations in the UK) which will be responsible for developing skill standards. The latter will relate to the level of knowledge and competence required to perform work-related functions successfully within an occupational cluster.

Managerial competencies

The second strand in the Anglo-American response to declining competitiveness was the investigation of management excellence. Some argue that the real father of the competency movement is McClelland (1973) who argued that traditional exams and tests were no good as predictors of whether people could do a job well and that there were other ways to look for competencies that would predict success. His approach to identifying competencies and his methodology of 'behavioural event interviewing' (*see* below) took off in a consultancy group, McBer Associates, which he founded in 1963. For the next decade McBer was busy developing competency models for many of America's top companies.

In 1982 the American Management Association commissioned Richard Boyatzis, of McBer Associates, to undertake research into 'successful' managers and to identify their attributes and features. Boyatzis (1982) concluded that there were 19 generic competencies that outstanding managers tend to have. These included personal traits, experience, motives and other attributes rather than specific skills. Boyatzis adopted the term 'competency', plural 'competencies', to describe an:

> underlying characteristic of an individual that is causally related to effective or superior performance in a job.

> (Boyatzis, 1982)

Boyatzis observed 2000 managers in 41 different management jobs and 12 organisations. He found a great deal of commonality but context was also important. He argued that it was necessary to construct a specific competency framework for each organisation even though the competencies are generic. His competency model, shown in Exhibit 20.1, groups managerial competencies into clusters which relate to the major functions of managers within any organisation. These are achieving the goals of the organisation, providing leadership, managing people and controlling and directing others. What is significant about this model is the emphasis on what managers *can do* and *how they do things*, in other words on how they behave rather than what skills or knowledge they have. Boyatzis showed what made some managers exceptional and others not.

Core competencies

During the 1970s and 1980s American academics turned their attention to strategic management as the key to competitive success. The work of Porter (1980, 1985) focused on the need to know and understand the market opportunities present in the fast-changing environment and how to select from options to diversify, decentralise, integrate or merge. Ideas on strategic management revolved particularly around PESTEL (political, economic, social, technological, environmental/ecological and legal contexts)

Exhibit 20.1 Boyatzis' competency model

Goal and action management cluster	Human resource management cluster
Concerned with impact: being concerned with symbols of power to have impact on others, concerned about status and reputation	*Use of socialised power:* ability to use influence to build alliances, networks, coalitions and teams
Diagnostic use of concepts: identifying and recognising patterns from an assortment of information by bringing a concept to the situation and attempting to interpret events through use of the concept	*Managing group process:* stimulating others to work effectively in groups
	Accurate self-assessment: seeing personal strengths and weaknesses and knowing one's own limitations (threshold competency)
Efficiency orientation: being concerned to do something better	*Positive regard:* having a belief in others, being optimistic and valuing others
Proactivity: being disposed to take action to achieve something	**Focus on others cluster**
Leadership cluster	*Perceptual objectivity:* avoiding bias or prejudice
Conceptualisation: ability to construct concepts out of data and information	*Self-control:* being able to subordinate self-interest in the interest of the organisation
Self-confidence: having presence and being decisive, knowing what you are doing, believing in it and doing it well	*Stamina and adaptability:* being able to maintain energy and commitment and showing flexibility and orientation to change
Oratorical skills: making articulate and well-communicated presentations to large and small groups	**Directing subordinates cluster**
Logical thought: placing events in causal sequence, being orderly and systematic (threshold competency)	Threshold competencies of developing others, spontaneity and use of unilateral power

Source: From *The Competent Manager* by Boyatzis, © 1982 John Wiley & Sons, Inc. This material is used by permission of John Wiley & Sons, Inc.

and SWOT (Strengths, Weaknesses, Opportunities, and Threats) analysis (Andrews, 1980). In an important article in the *Harvard Business Review* (1990), however, Prahalad and Hamel suggested that companies need to understand their core competencies and capabilities in order to successfully exploit their resources. All organisations have different types of resources that enable them to develop different strategies, but they have a distinctive advantage if they can develop strategies that their competitors are unable to imitate. The ability of managers to identify and exploit these special or 'core' competencies spells excellence. The competency movement in the US was greatly advanced by the work of Prahalad and Hamel's perception of core competencies:

Core competencies are the collective learning in the organisation especially how to co-ordinate diverse production skills and integrate multiple streams of technologies

(Prahalad and Hamel, 1990: 82)

and Hamel's view that real competition today is the competition over competencies:

conceiving of the firm as a portfolio of core competencies and disciplines suggests that inter-firm competition, as opposed to inter-product competition, is essentially concerned with the acquisition of skills.

(Hamel, 1991: 83)

Today, many organisations no longer define themselves as a collection of business units but as a portfolio of competencies.

The latest thinking on competencies is that an organisation's ability to learn and acquire new capabilities and competencies is a more important determinant of its competitive position than its current endowment of unique resources or the industry structure it currently faces. Sustainable competitive advantage in the long run is seen to arise from the superior ability to identify, build and leverage new competencies (Sanchez and Heene, 1996a, 1996b). The concept of the learning organisation, therefore, builds upon the ideas central to the competency movement outlined above.

Differences between American and British approaches to competencies

What therefore are the differences, if any, between the American and British approaches so often referred to in the HR literature? First, there are differences between the behavioural (American) and the standards (British) approach found in the opening definitions. Second, there is the difference between the emphasis on excellence or superior performance (American) and the benchmark standard performance (British). As Roberts (1997: 70) expresses it, 'It is the difference between drivers of performance and standards of work'. Although these distinctions are clear cut, in practice both approaches can be found in each country and within individual organisations. This is partly because the companies that first developed a competency approach in the UK were subsidiaries of American corporations. It is also because of criticisms of the UK's 'flawed model' and the need to combine both norm and criterion referenced approaches (Adams, 1998). From the outset there were serious criticisms of the NVQ system (Wilson, 1999) as it initially ignored explicit and tacit knowledge in favour of demonstrated skills, although some of those criticisms have been met and the concept has been widened and revised:

Occupational competence is defined as the ability to apply knowledge, understanding, practical and thinking skills to achieve effective performance to the standard required in employment. This includes solving problems and being sufficiently flexible to meet demands.

(NCVQ, 1997)

NVQs tend to be used for lower-level staff and less for strategic management development. There are, however, also criticisms of behavioural models of competency, in particular the difficulty of identifying and operationalising the concepts of competency, especially core competency, and of assessing and measuring it.

WHO USES COMPETENCY FRAMEWORKS?

Although no national surveys have been undertaken, there is widespread evidence that large private and public organisations in the service sector are developing and using competency frameworks and adopting competency management (Matthewman, 1995; Strebler and Bevan, 1996; Industrial Society, 1996; Winterton and Winterton, 1999; CIPD, 2001). There is less evidence that small and medium organisations (SMEs) are embracing competencies, although research in the civil service indicates that both small and large agencies are using competency approaches (Horton, 2000). Competencies have become one of the 'big ideas' in HRM on a par with management by objectives (MBO) and total quality management (TQM), and competency management is fast becoming a prominent HR strategy.

Many organisations have adopted the occupational standards developed by the NCVQ and the MCI, although their use is not as widespread as expected. Others have linked personal professional development to the standards set by lead bodies such as the CIPD, the BIM, RCN and CETSW. Gaining accredited Investors in People (IiP) status has been a major factor in adopting a structured competency-based training and development strategy, although this has been more important in the public than in the private sector because of a government commitment to IiP. There has also been pressure from the European Union and the British government to invest in human capital as the foundation for business success in the twenty-first century (DfEE, 1998). The emergence of an industry of private consultancy firms promoting competency management has been a further factor. A dedicated journal, *Competency and Emotional Intelligence*, published by Industrial Relations Services, is devoted entirely to the theory and practice of competencies and to disseminating information and good practice. It undertakes an annual survey on competency management, showing the increase in its uptake, and this is an important source of information on the growth and spread of its practice. The CIPD and British Institute of Management (BIM) have fully embraced the competency approach and as Lead Bodies also disseminate good practice and the latest ideas on personnel and management issues. Both Lead Bodies have been particularly active in promoting performance management, and competencies are clearly at the centre of performance.

WHY DO EMPLOYERS USE COMPETENCY FRAMEWORKS?

In various surveys carried out to establish why employers adopt a competency-based approach to management, the reasons given tend to be the same. One survey (Wustemann, 1999) revealed that employers introduce competencies because they think it will:

- improve individual performance (92%)
- support corporate values and objectives (82%)
- facilitate cultural change (60%)
- improve individuals' technical skills (44%)
- improve retention of staff (18%)
- improve recruitment and selection (6%).

Many employers cite the need to develop the future skills required by the business as the main reason (Strebler and Bevan, 1996), whilst others believe that competencies will provide a common language and facilitate cultural change (Strebler *et al.*, 1997).

Research carried out in the civil service (Horton and Farnham, 2000) demonstrated that over 80 per cent of the 134 civil service organisations in the survey used competency frameworks and a further 15 per cent were in the process of developing them. The reasons given for adopting competency management were that it

- enabled a common language and standard criteria to be applied across a range of personnel functions
- assisted both managers and employees in identifying training and development needs
- enabled the organisation to promote its values, goals and objectives
- assisted in the management of change
- enabled employees to know what was expected of them
- was a corollary of performance management.

This last point is important as it provides an explanation for the almost universal use of competency management in the civil service and its widespread use in other government organisations, including the NHS, local government, police and judicial system. Performance management has been imposed by central government on the public sector over the last 20 years (Horton and Farnham, 1999). All organisations now operate within clearly defined goals and objectives, performance targets and quality standards. This rationalistic and economistic approach requires that all resources, including human resources, are selected and used to ensure maximum performance. Competency frameworks are clearly an adjunct to performance management as they offer a means of identifying the skills, knowledge and attitudes required by staff to achieve the organisation's stated purpose.

The claims made for competency management are impressive and are often the reason why organisations in the private and voluntary sectors are adopting this fashionable idea. The claims, however, are often anecdotal with very little evidence to verify them or to measure their value added.

HOW TO CONSTRUCT A COMPETENCY FRAMEWORK

We have seen that a competency framework is a list of skills and competencies which identify and describe the behaviours necessary to perform a particular role or task at a particular level within an organisation. In the past organisations used very mechanistic approaches to job profiling by breaking jobs down into activities and processes, responsibilities and scope and identifying skills, experience or qualifications needed to do the job. Job analysis was in turn the basis for job descriptions and person specifications that would match the job profile, and for grading structures. Today the construction of job profiles and person specifications is more sophisticated. Emphasis is placed on ensuring they are organic rather than static, encompass 'soft' people skills and competencies and are future rather than backward oriented. Triangulation is also normally used in the information gathering stage.

Is constructing a competency framework any more than an aggregation of job profiles? The answer is *yes*. A competency framework defines the competency requirements relating to the tasks and roles within an organisation and puts them together into 'job families' and 'levels'. Job families refer to groups of jobs where the competencies are common irrespective of which part of the organisation the job is located in or, in the case of the MCI framework, which organisation. Such frameworks usually comprise 'generic competencies' that all people working within that occupation or type of job require. They may also include 'specific' competencies that are technical and relate to a particular role. Levels relate to the hierarchical position of the jobs and roles. For example, in the civil service there is a competency framework which covers only the Senior Civil Service – the top 3000 civil servants who are employed across departments. Hundreds of specific competency frameworks exist for levels below that in particular departments and agencies. The NVQ and MCI competency frameworks best illustrate levels.

Competencies are usually grouped into behavioural and technical categories. Behavioural competencies look at the way people behave or go about their work. They describe 'softer' attributes and traits and are therefore hard to observe and measure. Despite this, behavioural competencies are typically at the heart particularly of managerial competency frameworks. Technical competencies involve cognitive and practical skills that employees can demonstrate. These are frequently related to a specific role. They can only be used in a core framework, which covers similar workers, or they have to be added to core competencies for specific jobs. One way round this is to use *'competency to obtain technical knowledge'* which is often found in frameworks developed in the civil service, where a wide range of specialists and generalists work together in one organisation. In many organisations technical competencies are written into specific job descriptions and are kept separate from the competency framework.

Exhibit 20.2   Individual competencies

Knowledge	Expertise	Motivation	Values	Behaviour
To know		To want to know		To be able to
Technical competencies		Behavioural competencies		

A competency framework, then, can be based on behaviours or on substantive knowledge and skills or on a combination of the two (*see* Exhibit 20.2). The emphasis, however, is always on what needs to be done and how it should be done. The various components of competencies are identified by Sparrow and Hilltop (1993: 402) as follows.

- *Body of knowledge*: what an employee needs to know in order to be able to do the job and achieve the objectives the job specifies. This includes information in specific content areas.

- *Skills*: what an employee needs to possess in order to perform the tasks associated with the job; can be applied to a range of situations.

- *Attitudes, values and self-image*: what an employee needs to display in connection with achieving the tasks; attitudes that predict behaviour in the short or long term.
- *Traits*: characteristics or qualities that are associated with effectiveness. These may be physical characteristics or consistent responses to situations.
- *Motives*: drives or thoughts that are related to a particular goal; the things a person consistently thinks about or wants that cause him or her to act with commitment.
- *Self-image*: the understanding that a person has of themselves in the context of values held by others.
- *Social role*: the perception of social norms and behaviours that a person needs to adopt in order to fit in.

Many writers differentiate between 'threshold' and 'superior' competencies. Threshold competencies are those which are essential to performing a job, but are not causally related to superior job performance, while superior competencies are those which are causally linked to excellent performance. Boyatzis (1982) in his research into management competencies identified six threshold and 15 superior competencies (*see* Exhibit 20.1).

The 12 most common competencies found in competency frameworks (Wood and Payne, 1998: 27) are:

- communication
- achievement/results orientation
- customer focus
- teamwork
- leadership
- planning and organisation
- commercial/business awareness
- problem solving
- analytical thinking
- building relationships.

A close look at this list will reveal that they fall into three groups: thinking, feeling and acting.

TECHNIQUES FOR CONSTRUCTING COMPETENCY FRAMEWORKS

There are several techniques that can be used to identify competencies and construct competency maps, which fill in the details and describe all the different behaviours associated with specific and general competencies. These include repertory grids, critical incident analysis, skill questionnaires, diaries and benchmarking.

Repertory grids involve asking managers to divide their employees into 'good' and 'less good' performers. Two good and one less good performers are identified, and what makes the two good performers similar and distinguishes them from the poor performer is noted. This process is repeated several times until all the major differences have been identified. Managers are then asked questions to identify why the behaviours are different. The information is then categorised on a grid highlighting the range of behaviours in a variety of circumstances. This process results in a framework of behaviours that good performers might display.

Critical incident analysis involves collecting observed incidents that have proved to be very important or critical to performance. What emerge are the elements of job performance that make the difference between success and failure in a job. This process involves interviewing people who have observed or experienced at first hand the incidents being recorded. These anecdotal accounts are used to derive and build up a composite picture of job behaviour.

Skill questionnaires involve using a survey designed to find out, from a representative population, what are recognised as the requisite skills to perform a job well. Some involve the use of Likert scales to assess the relative importance attached to particular skills. Skills can range from cognitive through technical to interpersonal and personal skills.

Diaries involve asking people to keep a record of what they have done over a period of days to identify what tasks and what skills they needed to accomplish those tasks.

Benchmarking involves examining what other companies or organisations are doing and comparing your own practice against 'best practice' organisations. This can give an insight into what makes them successful or what is building success in your own organisation. Additionally it helps to see how a framework can work in practice. This is a very popular method either in isolation or combined with one or other of the methods identified above.

ASSESSING COMPETENCIES

A major criticism of the use of competencies is that they are not observable and measurable. Some mechanism, therefore, is essential for assessing competencies. One approach is to draw up clear descriptors of what is expected and give examples of desirable and undesirable behaviour. This is illustrated in the case study of the Senior Civil Service below. 'Softer' skills, such as teamworking and interpersonal skills, are notoriously difficult, however, to measure objectively. There are a number of ways that are increasingly used. These include

- assessment centres
- development centres
- field assessment (360-degree feedback)
- self-assessment
- computer aided simulation
- questionnaire predicting competencies.

The IDS study (1997a: 7) shows how British Sugar included a measure of team feedback within its competency assessment. 'Each team member rates their colleagues against the performance criteria for each competency.' A similar approach is adopted with 360-degree assessment. In Anglian Water employees and managers agree a number of objectives each year which will demonstrate achievement across the range of core competencies, including 'soft' ones (IDS, 1997a). Where assessing competencies remains a problem this leads to under-utilisation of the framework. Exhibit 20.3 provides an example of how a competency framework was created and assessment undertaken using effective and ineffective behavioural outputs.

Exhibit 20.3 Creating a new competency framework for the Senior Civil Service

In 1997 the new Labour government was committed to 'Modernising Government' (Cabinet Office, 1999a) and reforming the civil service (Cabinet Office, 1999b). As part of the reform agenda it was decided to construct a new competency framework for the SCS to reflect the competencies needed to carry through the government's modernisation programme. There was competitive tendering for the contract and Development Partnership, a small firm of ex-civil servants, won it. Their terms of reference were to work with the Cabinet Office to develop a new SCS competency framework, pilot and benchmark it, provide guidance on its implementation, assess training needs and assist in the integration of the new framework into the performance management process – all in 15 months. Phase 1 involved the research, survey and first drafting stage, Phase 2 the consultation, feedback and testing stage, and Phase 3 the final validation and implementation stages.

A variety of methods for constructing the framework were used. First, 14 top managers and stakeholders in the SCS were interviewed on their views of the Modernising Government agenda and the leadership role of the SCS in carrying it through. In particular, they were asked what competencies and behaviours SCSs need to be effective in the future. Second, detailed critical incident interviews were conducted with 20 SCS staff drawn from a wide range of departments and agencies. Third, four workshops were held, with 12 civil servants below the SCS in each, to discuss what they expect from people in the SCS. Fourth, interviews were held with top managers of six external organisations to get their ideas about what competencies were needed. Finally, they undertook an analysis of 360-degree feedback in the SCS. All these activities were completed within five weeks and a report was presented to the Civil Service Management Board (CSMB), identifying the key issues to emerge from the consultation process along with a draft framework.

Phase 2 involved a wide-ranging consultation process, as it was recognised that in order to get acceptance of the new framework all members of the SCS should be involved. It was also important to test its feasibility. The draft was presented and discussed at a number of steering meetings before being approved by the Civil Service Management Board (SCSMB). The framework was then piloted in 17 departments and agencies across a range of personnel functions including appraisal, coaching, training and 360-degree evaluation. Eleven validation workshops were held throughout the country and these included people from different departments and levels within the civil service. Finally, the new framework was put on line and all 3000 SCSs were invited to comment on it. Questionnaires were sent to staffs who were asked to say what competencies they thought they already had and what training would be needed.

continued

Exhibit 20.3   continued

The final draft of the competency framework was approved by the SCSMB in November. Between then and 1 April 2001, when the programme went live, departments and agencies had to prepare for its implementation. The Cabinet Office designed a just-in-time training programme for the implementation of a new performance management system incorporating the competency framework, which all SCSs had an opportunity to attend.

The new SCS framework is entirely behavioural and very simple. It consists of six core generic competencies and one level. Each competency has associated effective and ineffective behaviours and is linked to the aims and objectives of the government's modernising agenda. It illustrates the way that competency frameworks can be designed to bring about cultural change and the way people behave. It also may be a good practice model because of the intensively participative process involved and its transparency (Horton, 2000).

Senior Civil Service Competency Framework: Leadership for results

1. Giving purpose and direction: Creating and communicating a vision of the future

Effective behaviour	Ineffective behaviour
Is clear what needs to be achieved	Looks to others to provide direction
Involves people in deciding what has to be done	Takes an overly cautious approach
Communicates a compelling view of the future	Assumes people know what is required of them without being told
Sets clear short- and long-term objectives	Loses sight of the big picture
Creates practicable and achievable plans	Allows a culture which is intolerant of diversity
Establishes standards of behaviour which promote diversity	
Agrees clear responsibilities and objectives to deliver results	
Initiates change to make things happen	

2. Making a personal impact: Leading by example

Effective behaviour	Ineffective behaviour
Visible and approachable to all	Says one thing and does another
Acts with honesty and integrity	Takes contrary views as a personal criticism
Is valued for sound application of knowledge and expertise	Fights own corner, ignoring wider interests
Resilient and determined	Accepts the status quo
Challenges and is prepared to be challenged	Aloof and arrogant
Says what people may not want to hear	Aggressive, not assertive
Takes difficult decisions and measured risks	

continued

Exhibit 20.3   continued

Accepts responsibility for own decisions

Takes personal responsibility for making progress in equality and diversity

Implements corporate decisions with energy and commitment

3. Thinking strategically: Harnessing ideas and opportunities to achieve goals

Effective behaviour	Ineffective behaviour
Sensitive to wider political and organisational priorities	Works only from own perspective or assumptions about the world
Assimilates and makes sense of complex or conflicting data and different perspectives	Fails to make connections between ideas or people
Finds new ways of looking at issues	Focuses solely on the detail
Homes in on key issues and principles	Focuses on intellectual debate at the expense of action
Considers the potential and impact of technology	Fails to consider the needs of a diverse community
Identifies opportunities to improve delivery through partnership	
Anticipates and manages risks and consequences	
Gives objective advise based on sound evidence and analysis	
Communicates ideas clearly and persuasively	

4. Getting the best from people: Motivating and developing people to achieve high performance

Effective behaviour	Ineffective behaviour
Gets to know individuals and their aspirations	Works only with the most competent people
Adapts leadership style to different people, cultures and situations	Writes rather than speaks
Knows when to step in and when not to	Has a fixed management style
Listens and takes account of diverse views	Does not delegate challenging or interesting work
Gives and expects frequent constructive feedback	Is uncomfortable working with people from diverse backgrounds
Coaches individuals so they give of their best	Blames others
Tackles poor performance or inappropriate behaviour	Wields the red pen
Praises achievements and celebrates success	Avoids giving bad news

continued

505

Exhibit 20.3 continued

5. Learning and improving: Drawing on experience and new ideas to improve results

Effective behaviour	Ineffective behaviour
Aware of own strengths, weaknesses and motivation	Can't see things from other people's perspective
Applies learning from own and others' experience	Assumes at the outset different perspectives need not be taken on board
Builds productive relationships with people across and outside the organisation	Does not listen
Understands values and incorporates different perspectives	Sticks to outdated methods
Seeks new or different ideas and opportunities to learn	Unwilling to be exposed to risk and uncertainty
Readily shares ideas and information with others	
Encourages experimentation and adapts quickly and flexibly to change; tries innovative ways of working	
Works with partners to achieve the best practical outcome	
Adapts quickly and flexibly to change	

6. Focusing on delivery: Achieving value for money and results

Effective behaviour	Ineffective behaviour
Organises the work to deliver to time, budget and agreed quality standard	Commits to delivery regardless of impact on team or self
Negotiates for the resources to do the job	Focuses on the process rather than getting results
Rigorous in reviewing progress and performance	Avoids dealing with difficult problems
Puts customers first	Continually fire fighting
Is not deflected by obstacles or problems	Takes sole credit for achieving results
Shifts resources as priorities change	Does not manage risks
Seeks continuously to improve performance	
Makes best use of diverse talents, technology and resources to deliver results	

Crown copyright.

USING COMPETENCIES

The scope for using competency-based systems is wide ranging. Figure 20.1 demonstrates the areas of HRM where competency frameworks can be used. They can also be used to integrate and link an organisation's main HR processes to its business strategy. If used systematically, competencies tie together all HR processes from recruitment and induction to appraisal, training and development and rewards, so that they focus on the same key expectations and objectives and provide mutual reinforcement to each other (Matthewman, 1998). The ability to use competency frameworks in this holistic way depends on the degree of HR sophistication and the HR policies, processes and practices that are in place (Hefferman and Flood, 2000). The adoption of competency frameworks is generally associated with organisations possessing well-developed HRM processes rather than more basic personnel systems. The use of competency frameworks is also affected by organisational factors such as size, ownership and environment, as Hefferman and Flood (2000) found in their survey of 500 organisations in Ireland.

Most organisations tend to start using competency approaches in an *ad hoc* way in specific HR activities. Research indicates the most popular areas are training and development, staff appraisal and recruitment and selection (Horton, 2000; Rankin, 2001 – *see* Exhibit 20.4). There is less evidence of competency-based reward systems, although some organisations have sought to use them and the civil service is committed to doing so once their new performance and pay system, introduced in April 2001, is fully operational.

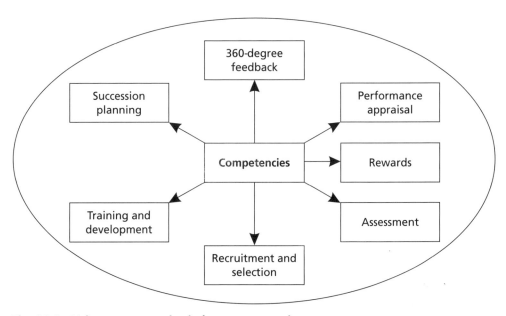

Fig. 20.1 Using competencies in human resourcing

Exhibit 20.4   Employers' use of competencies

Using competency frameworks	Percentage of employers
Training and development	87
Performance management	82
Personal development planning	82
Recruitment and selection	77
Job design	51
Cultural change	39
Grading design	33
Teamworking	31
Succession planning	26
Reward	24
Other	2

Recruitment and selection

The arguments for using competency-based approaches to recruitment and selection are first, that it focuses on the knowledge, skills and aptitudes which people require to do a job rather than their qualifications; second, that it permits more objective assessment of job candidates because it is based upon clear job profiles; and third, that it meets equity and diversity principles because the same criteria are applied in rating each candidate. Farnham and Stevens (2000) compare the traditional approach to recruitment in a local authority with a newly developed competency-based one and conclude that selection decisions are now more evidence-based and more objective and assessment of candidates is more rigorous.

In addition to developing more relevant selection criteria, improving interviewing and assessment techniques, the competency approach can provide a link through to post-entry training and development. A recent study reveals that when recruiting externally greater emphasis is placed on 'soft', transferable skills, whilst in internal selection the emphasis is more on technical competencies (IES, 1997a,b,c, 2000, 2001). There is also some evidence that using competency-based recruitment and selection can reduce labour turnover and recruit higher-performing staff (CIPD, 2000).

Wood and Payne (1998: 23) summarise the benefits as:

- improving accuracy in assessing people's suitability or potential for different jobs
- facilitating a closer match between a person's skills and interests and the demands of the job
- preventing assessors from making 'snap' decisions or basing decisions on factors irrelevant to the job

- underpinning the full range of assessment and development techniques – application forms, interviews, tests, assessment centres and appraisal ratings
- through disaggregating an individual's profile into specific skills and characteristics, development plans can more accurately be targeted to areas of true development need.

Performance management

Competencies are increasingly being used as a central factor in performance management systems, as the framework can provide a foundation for the whole performance cycle, from objective setting to appraisal and longer-term development (IDS, 1997a). Each competency identified in the framework at the appropriate level can be used as a basis of assessment in appraisals. Many organisations now expect employees to demonstrate their competency achievements. 'Soft' competencies that are very difficult to measure objectively can be assessed through 360-degree feedback. This is now being used increasingly in the civil service and in private organisations such as British Sugar (IDS, 1997b). Nevertheless, most organisations tend to use a balanced approach to performance assessment where competencies are only one element, along with other performance criteria including objectives.

Training and development

Amongst those organisations that have adopted competence-based management (CBM) it is almost universally applied in the area of training and development. The major reasons are that organisations see the importance of competency frameworks in identifying skill and ability gaps, training needs and designing training programmes. In most organisations competency-based training is business driven and aimed at immediate job needs (Strebler *et al.*, 1997) but in some it is oriented towards personal development. In the personal development review process competency frameworks are used to

- compare and identify
- discuss and agree
- undertake training and development
- review and evaluate.

Personal development in most organisations is still kept separate from performance management, although where competency management is holistic they are integrated. It is also kept separate from pay because it is felt it discourages people from admitting to development and training needs. Competency-based developmental approaches are more often used with managerial and white-collar staff than with technical and manual workers. A report by CIPD in 1999 found that most organisations in their survey preferred to develop their own frameworks for training and development rather than use the MCI or other occupational standards. However, other research (Loan-Clarke *et al.*, 2000) found SMEs using NVQs and MCI.

Appraisal

Competency frameworks are being used increasingly in the appraisal process, especially in performance and development appraisals. They are particularly useful in identifying the development needs of individuals and mapping out routes to career advancement and progression. Clear objectives in terms of developing and enhancing competencies can be set and strategies for achieving these objectives can be agreed. Today the emphasis is increasingly on personal development and employees are expecting to decide what development they need and how they could achieve it. Competency profiles help employees to see what is expected from them and how they can move up in the organisation. They also assist managers in planning for succession and ensuring that staff are prepared to fill senior roles.

Rewards

In 2000 one in eight companies was using competence-related pay and another 20 per cent were considering it (Pay and Benefits Bulletin, 2000). There is wide diversity in the ways that organisations link rewards to competencies. The most common method is to link individual performance-related pay to competencies, although this tends to be a subordinate factor compared to output targets. In a survey of competence-related award systems, Adams (1999) (cited in CIPD, 2001) identified four main ways in which employers made the link:

- 76 per cent used competencies in the design of grading structures
- 80 per cent used them in promotion
- 88 per cent used them to determine pay rises or cuts
- 56 per cent used them to determine how an overall pay rise should be divided into shares.

Employers give the main reasons for using competency-based rewards as:

- to motivate people and to encourage better performance
- to increase flexibility amongst the workforce
- to change employee behaviour
- to give employees access to job progression and to allow some form of job progression where no other form of promotion opportunities exists.

The CBI recorded similar reasons in their 1999 report.

Although there was a move in both the public and private sectors to link pay to competencies and performance during the 1990s, there is now some evidence of a reversal of that trend (*Competency and Emotional Intelligence Quarterly*, 1999). The reasons for the change of policy include first, the effect on other uses of the competency framework such as development and training; second, the effect of what is effectively individual performance-related pay on teamworking; and third, the potential for demotivating employees who are not rewarded.

THE PROS AND CONS OF COMPETENCY MANAGEMENT

The need for continuous improvement in performance has never been greater, whether it is in the NHS, Railtrack or Marks and Spencer. There are also pressures on organisations to obtain and retain the 'skilled' staff which are needed to achieve organisational 'success'. Competencies has caught on as a 'catch all' term to encompass what are a bundle of aptitudes, skills, abilities, orientations and behaviours which make up a 'good' or 'excellent' employee. Especially in the area of management, organisations no longer need stable, conscientious and reliable employees, although all those qualities are desirable. They want exceptional, enterprising, innovating and able people to lead the organisation in a highly competitive and fast-changing environment. Competency frameworks and competency management have been marketed as the latest good idea to take on board the need of organisations to identify good staff and to manage them effectively.

It is also acknowledged that a competency approach assists in the integration of corporate, business and human resource strategies, both horizontally and vertically, and provides a means of integrating human resource activities at every level too.

Horton and Farnham's (2000) research in the civil service found universal recognition benefits claimed for organisations, managers and individual staff by the human resource managers responding to the questionnaire. Specifically, competency frameworks clarify what is expected of staff, provide more objective measures of performance and can be constructed and used to carry through cultural an organisational change.

Competency management, however, is not without its critics. One of the major issues is the extent to which generalised, trans-organisational competency frameworks such as MCI have wrenched them from their context and hence the tacit knowledge that contributes so significantly to good performance. Further related concerns are as follows.

- Can competence or discrete competencies be identified from their contexts and inter-relationships and from tacit knowledge?

- Is it even meaningful to seek to identify competencies as common to a range of jobs, and if this can be done what are the most significant competencies in, say, a manager's job?

- Can competence be effectively measured and if so against what criteria?

- How meaningful are the frameworks produced, e.g. for the SCS?

- In these approaches to competence what assumptions are being made about the nature of reality and the appropriate ways to study it, e.g. epistemological and philosophical frameworks?

- How far does the concept of competence incorporate both tacit and formal knowledge 'know how' and 'know what'?

- Do they eliminate subjectivity and bias? Are the models gender biased?

Wood and Payne (1998) offer a further critique that competencies can be seen as living in the past, producing clones, highlighting irrelevancies and being in a time warp. Competency frameworks can get out of date quickly, may be difficult to change and have become an end in themselves rather than a means to an end! But what will take their place?

SUMMARY LEARNING POINTS

1 There are many definitions and spellings of competency and there are American and British approaches.

2 The competency movement developed because of increased competition from globalisation, changes in the structures and processes of organisations, work and HRM.

3 In the UK training and skills were seen as the key to competitive advantage, and a national vocational qualifications (NVQ) framework was created and occupational standards established.

4 In the USA managerial excellence was seen as the key to competitive advantage. This led to the development of competency frameworks based on behavioural characteristics of above-standard managers and later to the idea of core competencies of organisations.

5 Competency frameworks can be constructed in a number of ways using repertory grids, critical incident analysis, questionnaires, focus groups and job analysis.

6 A growing number of companies are convinced that using competency frameworks brings significant organisational benefits, although there is little empirical evidence to substantiate this.

7 Competency frameworks are used most frequently in training and development, appraisal and recruitment and selection.

8 There are criticisms of the competency approach, which include the difficulty of constructing frameworks, cost and time, a tendency to become over-bureaucratic, and the reduced ability of organisations to adapt to the future and innovate because of 'cloning'.

REFERENCES AND FURTHER READING

Adams, K. (1998) 'Peddling a flawed model', *Competency*, 5(3), 27–9.

Adams, K. (1999) 'Performance, development and reward at the Registers of Scotland', *Competency*, 6(3), 10–15.

Andrews, K. (1980) *The Concept of Corporate Strategy*. New York: Irvin.

Boyatzis, R. (1982) *The Competent Manager: A model for effective performance*. New York: Wiley.

Cabinet Office (1999a) *Modernising Government*. London: The Stationery Office.

Cabinet Office (1999b) *Reforming the Civil Service*. London: The Stationery Office.

CBI (1998) *Employment Trends Survey*. London: CBI.

CIPD (2001) *Competency Frameworks in UK Organisations* (Research Report). London: CIPD.

Competency and Emotional Intelligence Quarterly (1999) Vol. 6, no. 4.

Constable, J. and McCormack, R. (1987) *The Making of British Managers*. British Institute of Management and Confederation of British Industry.

Department for Education and Employment (1998) *The Learning Age: A renaissance for a new Britain* (Cm 3790). London: HMSO.

Farnham, D. and Stevens, A. (2000) 'Developing and implementing competence-based recruitment and selection in a social services department', *International Journal of Public Sector Management*, 13(4), 369–82.

Fletcher, S. (1991) *NVQs, Standards and Competence: A practical guide for employers, managers and trainers*. London: Kogan Page.

Fletcher, S. (1992) *Competence-based Assessment Techniques*. London: Kogan Page.

Fletcher, S. (1997) *Analysing Competencies*. London: Kogan Page.

Hamel, G. (1991) 'Competition for competence and inter-partner learning within international strategic alliances', *Strategic Management Journal*, 12, 83.

Handy, C. (1987) *The Making of Managers: A report on management education and training and development in the United States, West Germany, France, Japan and the UK*. London: Manpower Services Commission, National Economic Development Office and Confederation of British Industries.

Hefferman, M. and Flood, P. (2000) 'An exploration of the relationship between the adoption of managerial competencies, organisational characteristics and human resources sophistication and performance in Irish organisations', *Journal of European Industrial Training*, 24, 123–36.

Horton, S. (2000) 'Competency management in the British Civil Service', *International Journal of Public Sector Management*, 13(4), 354–68.

Horton, S. and Farnham, D. (1999) *Public Management in Britain*. London: Macmillan.

Horton, S. and Farnham, D. (2000) 'Competency-based approaches to human resources management in the British Civil Service: an initial analysis', paper given to the Personnel Policies Study Group at the EGPA Conference Caledonian University, Glasgow, August 2000.

Horton, S., Hondeghem, A. and Farnham, D. (2002) *International Perspectives on Competency-based Management in the Public Sector*. Brussels: IOS (forthcoming).

IES (1997a) *From Admin to Strategy: The changing face of the HR function* (IES Report 332). Brighton: Institute of Employment Studies.

IES (1997b) *Skills, Competencies and Gender: Issues for pay and training* (IES Report 333). Brighton: Institute of Employment Studies.

IES (1997c) *Getting the Best out of your Competencies* (IES Report 334). Brighton: Institute of Employment Studies.

IES (2000) *Employee Returns: Linking HR performance to business strategy* (IES Report 365). Brighton: Institute of Employment Studies.

IES (2001) *Performance Review: Balancing objectives and content* (IES Report 370). Brighton: Institute of Employment Studies.

Incomes Data Services (1997a) *Performance Management, Study No. 626*. London: IDS.

Incomes Data Services (1997b) *Developing Competency Frameworks, Study No. 639*. London: IDS.

Industrial Society (1996) *Management Competencies: Managing Best Practice Report 21*. London: Industrial Society.

Institute of Personnel and Development (2000) *Recruitment* (IPD Survey Report No. 14). London: IPD.

Loan-Clarke, J., Boocock, G., Smith, A. and Whittaker, J. (2000) 'Competence-based management development in small and medium sized enterprises: a multi-stakeholder analysis', *International Journal of Training and Development*, 4(3), 76–95.

Management Charter Initiative (1990) *Management Competencies: the Standards Project*. London: MCI.

Manpower Services Commission (1981) *A New Training Initiative: Agenda for action*. London: MSC.

Matthewman, T. (1995) 'Trends and developments in the use of competency frameworks', *Competency*, 2(4), 1–20.

Matthewman, J. (1998) 'Competencies in practice: the 5th HR-BC/IRS Annual Survey', *Journal of Performance through People*, 5(2), 2–10.

McClelland, D. (1973) 'Testing for competence rather than intelligence', *American Psychologist*, 28(1), 1–40.

MSC/NEDO (1986) *A Challenge to Complacency*. London: MSC/NEDO.

National Skills Standards Board (1998) www.ed.gov/legislation/GOALS2000/The Act/sec502.html.

NCVQ (1997) *Criteria for National Vocational Qualifications*. London: Qualifications and Curriculum Authority.

Pay and Benefits Bulletin (2000) 'Pay prospects for 2001: a survey of the public sector', *Pay and Benefits Bulletin*, 507, November, 4–13.

Porter, M. (1980) *Competitive Strategy*. New York: Free Press.

Porter, M. (1985) *Competitive Advantage*. New York: Free Press.

Prahalad, C. and Hamel, G. (1990) 'The core competence of the corporation', *Harvard Business Review*, 79–91.

Rankin, N. (2001) 'Raising performance through people: the eighth competency survey', *Competency and Emotional Intelligence – Annual Benchmarking Survey 2000/01*, 2–21.

Roberts, G. (1997) *Recruitment and Selection: A competency approach*. London: IPD.

Sanchez, R. and Heene, A. (1996a) *Dynamics of Competence-based Competition: Theory and practice in the new strategic management*. Oxford: Elsevier.

Sanchez, R. and Heene, A. (1996b) *Strategic Learning and Knowledge Management*. Chichester: Wiley.

Sparrow, P. and Hilltop, J.-M. (1993) *European Human Resource Management in Transition*. Cambridge: Cambridge University Press.

Strebler, M. and Bevan, S. (1996) *Competence-based Management Training*. Brighton: Institute of Employment Studies.

Strebler, M., Robinson, D. and Bevan, S. (1997) *Getting the Best out of Competencies* (IES Report 334). Brighton: Institute of Employment Studies.

Targett, S. (1997) 'NVQs poised for overseas sales push', *Financial Times*, 29 October.

Torrington, D. and Hall, L. (1991) *Personnel Management: A new approach*. Hemel Hempstead: Prentice Hall.

Wilson, D. (1999) 'The development of national standards in the USA', *Competence and Emotional Intelligence*, 6(3), 38–44.

Winterton, J. and Winterton, R. (1999) *Developing Managerial Competence*. London: Routledge.

Wood, R. and Payne, T. (1998) *Competency-based Recruitment and Selection*. Chichester: Wiley.

Wustemann, L. (1999) 'The way that UK employers are paying for competencies', *Competency and Emotional Intelligence – Annual Benchmarking Survey 1999/2000*, 46.

ASSIGNMENTS AND DISCUSSION TOPICS

1 What is the difference between the American and British approaches to competencies?

2 Describe and evaluate three ways in which a competency framework can be constructed.

3 Find out to what extent competency frameworks are used in your organisation or one you have researched. How effective are they?

4 What are the major problems in constructing a competency framework?

5 Why do you think competency-based management of rewards is the least popular area of use?

6 Can managers be trained to use competencies? If so, how would you design, deliver and evaluate a training programme?

7 Is competency management simply 'old wine in a new bottle'?

8 Critically evaluate the new Senior Civil Service Competency Framework.

CHAPTER 21

Organisation Development

by Amal El-Sawad

INTRODUCTION

The purpose of Organisation Development (OD) is to enhance the effectiveness of an organisation and the development and well-being of its members. OD is a practice-led discipline which adopts an integrative and holistic approach to the planning and management of organisational change. Its scope is therefore very broad. OD practitioners have been described as 'organisational doctors' (Morgan, 1986) and extending this medical metaphor helps illustrate the role they perform. OD practitioners assess the 'health' of the organisation, considering the nature of the organisation's internal and external environment and exploring the organisation's strategic, structural, technological, cultural and managerial characteristics. This thorough 'diagnosis' helps both to identify organisational 'ailments' and to suggest possible 'cures'. Aspects of the organisation can then be targeted for 'treatment' with planned change interventions aimed at restoring and maintaining organisational 'health' and preventing, as far as is possible, future 'illness'.

This chapter explores the concepts and theories underpinning OD, the stages of OD in terms of diagnosis, intervention and process maintenance activities as well as some of the difficulties and dilemmas facing OD practitioners. It does not, however, offer any prescriptive, straightforward or universal solutions. Organisations, like 'patients', are very different. Though they may display the same 'symptoms', the underlying causes may not be the same. Even if they are, 'treatments' suited to one may not be suited to another.

CHAPTER OBJECTIVES

- To define Organisation Development and the philosophies, values and assumptions underpinning the field.
- To evaluate the relationship between OD and more traditional strategic management methods.
- To understand the process of planning and managing change.
- To explore the concept of the Learning Organisation.
- To assess the impact of culture on change interventions.
- To outline the unique role of the OD consultant or 'change agent' and the skills and competencies required.
- To introduce the various OD intervention strategies and techniques.
- To appreciate the importance of evaluating the effectiveness of OD interventions.
- To consider the contribution that OD can make to the effective resourcing of the organisation.

WHAT IS ORGANISATION DEVELOPMENT?

Defining Organisation Development

Organisation Development (OD) has been defined in various ways by different authors. Porras and Robertson (1991) draw on a number of the definitions proffered by prominent OD theorists to explain OD in terms of its fundamental characteristics, purpose, scope, conceptual underpinnings, processes and targets:

> The purpose of OD is improvement in the organisation's effectiveness, its ability to adapt, its self-renewing processes or capacity, its health and its development of new and creative organisational solutions. Its scope is organisational or system-wide change. Its conceptual underpinnings derive from behavioural science theory, research and technology. Its process is planned, value-based, action-research oriented, technology-driven, consultant-aided, and directed or supported by top management. Its targets are the organisation's culture, structure, strategy, processes and congruence among the various key organisational factors.
>
> (Porras and Robertson, 1991)

It is curious that the many definitions of OD frequently fail to make explicit a pivotal aspect of the field, that is individual development. Yet successful organisation development is inextricably linked with and indeed largely depends on the effective individual development of the organisation's employees. It is a crucial (if implicit and therefore largely understated) assumption of OD. Therefore, the following OD definition is selected as the broadest and most apt for considering OD from an organisational resourcing perspective:

> Organisation Development is a set of behavioural science-based theories, values, strategies and techniques aimed at the planned change of the organisational work setting for the purpose of enhancing individual development and improving organisational performance.
>
> (Porras and Robertson, 1991)

OD philosophies, values and assumptions

OD has at its heart a set of guiding philosophies, values and assumptions. First and foremost are assumptions about people as individuals. Closely resembling McGregor's 'Theory Y', OD presumes that people, in general, strive towards personal growth and development and furthermore 'desire and are capable of making a higher contribution to the attainment of organisational goals than most organisational environments will permit' (French and Bell, 1990). This latter point can be illustrated by drawing on some illuminating research findings. For example, it is suggested that many people use less skill in their jobs than they do driving to work. It has also been estimated that managers on average operate at only 25 per cent of their full capacity, the 75 per cent of untapped potential being referred to as 'Personal Performance Headroom' (Wyatt, 1994). OD is concerned with finding ways to unleash this potential by 'modifying organisational constraints that are having a dampening and throttling effect' (French and Bell, 1990). The beneficiaries, it is assumed, are both the individual and the organisation. OD is thus

517

believed to represent a win–win situation, meeting individuals' personal development needs and the organisation's needs for improved effectiveness.

OD stresses the importance of organisational work groups, both formal and informal, and champions the values of openness and trust. It is concerned with the effect of the work group on individual members' feelings of satisfaction, inclusion and acceptance. It recognises that conflict may arise both within and between groups, and its concern with the adverse effects of suppressed feelings on group (and in turn organisational) functioning means it is committed to surfacing, confronting and dealing with conflict.

These assumptions, which unite OD practitioners, represent the philosophical foundations on which OD diagnosis, intervention and process maintenance activities are based. However, hampering the credibility of OD from a managerial viewpoint is the 'unwillingness of most managers to engage with high-level statements containing a sense of moral purpose, their lack of acceptance of the [OD] values . . . and an apparently overwhelming concern for personal development as the essential focus for organisational purpose' (Mumford, 1994). OD practitioners and managers, it seems, have differing fundamental assumptions. The notion of paradigms helps to explain why this is the case.

Organisational paradigms

A paradigm is the way in which individuals view the world around them, their assumptions about the nature of people, organisations and reality itself which, in an organisational context, shapes beliefs about how people and processes should be organised and managed. Four broad paradigms of organisational and social theory (Burrell and Morgan, 1979) have been outlined as:

- functionalist
- interpretive
- radical humanist
- radical structuralist.

Traditional organisation theory embodies many of the assumptions of the functionalist paradigm. This predominant managerial paradigm encourages managers to view their organisations as, for example, 'machines' (Morgan, 1986), interpreting them as possessing an objective reality from which they and their organisational members are separate. They are concerned with organisational efficiency and effectiveness and assess this in terms of objective, quantifiable data, for example profit, turnover and return on investment. Crucially, they identify their own goals as the goals of the organisation and assume others share these – a unitary frame of reference.

In contrast, OD recognises that the goals of individuals may be different from those of the organisation – a pluralist frame of reference. The assumptions of OD reflect much of that which is embodied in the 'interpretive' paradigm. Metaphorically, OD practitioners might view organisations as 'organisms', concerned with discovering and meeting the subjective development needs of organisational members and aware of the effect of the environment in shaping these needs. OD practitioners also recognise that organisations can become 'psychic prisons' trapping members into favoured ways of thinking and quashing creativity and potential (Morgan, 1986). For this reason they are interested in how individuals experience and make sense of their organisation and seek out subjective, qualitative data to understand the effectiveness of organisations in meeting individual needs. Yet though OD has a strong humanistic and developmental outlook, it also incorporates elements of the functionalist paradigm in terms of systems theory and contingency theory. OD in essence represents a shift from the favoured managerial 'hard S's of strategy and systems' to incorporate the 'soft S's of style and shared values' (Thompson and McHugh, 1995).

Thus OD may be viewed as 'challenging the legitimacy of what [managers] feel they already know about organisation, opening up a Pandora's box of new problems and issues that must be addressed' (Morgan, 1990). From this, we can see how threatening the OD paradigm may be to a functionalist manager who 'attempts to create a world characterised by certainty'. Yet new paradigms are also an opportunity to gain 'new insights and understanding' (Morgan, 1990). And increasingly, as orthodox management techniques on their own fail to deliver the expected results, managers are turning to OD for answers.

Stemming from an equal concern for organisation performance and employee well-being, OD adopts an 'anti-hierarchical and anti-authoritarian stance' (Beer and Walton, 1990). It is this aspect, representing a challenge to the predominant managerial paradigm, which perhaps explains why early OD initiatives of the 1960s and 1970s, which focused largely on managerial staff (to the neglect of other employees), conducted in essentially bureaucratic and hierarchical organisations, met with a mixed reception and led eventually to OD suffering a 'collapse of professional confidence'. However, in the post-bureaucratic, flatter, leaner organisations of the 1990s and beyond, OD is enjoying increased popularity. The advent of strategic HRM has put OD values (particularly its humanistic, developmental outlook) firmly on the managerial agenda.

> Companies still advertise for OD managers. This is the new ball game: OD as specific techniques within a broader organisational culture and Human Resource context ... targeted at workers as well as managers.
>
> (Thompson and McHugh, 1995)

CHANGING ORGANISATIONAL ENVIRONMENTS AND CORPORATE RENEWAL

Distinguished management analysts have over the years offered various (often contradictory) prescriptions for organisational and business success (see for instance the work of Lindblom, Mintzberg, Porter, Cyert and March, and Ansoff). Perhaps most infamous is the work of Peters and Waterman (1982) who analysed the practices of a number of 'excellent' companies and derived a success formula for other organisations to apply. Yet many of the original 'excellent' organisations, it is widely reported, have since fallen from grace, suggesting that these two 'organisational doctors' may have got it very wrong. However, though we must be wary of such success prescriptions, we must also be careful not to dismiss wholly their work or indeed that of other management gurus. From these apparent mistakes, there are valuable lessons to be learned.

The greatest lesson resides within an appreciation of the increasingly turbulent and dynamic environments within which organisations must operate. The last decade or so has witnessed increasingly fierce global competition coupled with dramatic changes in the political, legal, economic, socio-cultural and technological environments. These changes have had profound effects on organisations. Failing to be alert and responsive to such environmental changes can have dramatic consequences, putting the organisation's very existence at risk. Thus, whilst the success formulas in use by the organisations Peters and Waterman studied may well have been appropriate for those particular organisations in the early 1980s, dramatic environmental changes at a local, national and international level have subsequently rendered them increasingly inappropriate and ineffective for many, and disastrous for some. The experience of these organisations is far from unique. For example, Senge (1994) quotes a study conducted by Shell which found that of the 500 companies listed in the US Fortune 500 in 1970, only two-thirds still remained in 1983.

The work of Ansoff and Sullivan (1993) is illuminating in offering us answers to some of the questions which these examples throw up and a useful starting point for those who aspire to the role of OD practitioner or 'organisational doctor'. Could these organisations have been 'saved' and if so, how? It is imperative to understand, no more so than in the environment of the 1990s and beyond, that 'there is no single success formula which has universal validity' (Ansoff and Sullivan, 1993). This is not to write off the work of countless management scholars but more an attempt to qualify it. Work conducted by Ansoff over a period of 25 years involving a study of some 420 firms located in five countries across four different continents appears to achieve this. He has analysed the implications of different levels of environmental turbulence (a measure of the degree of changeability of an organisation's environment) on a scale of one (repetitive – no change) to five (surpriseful – discontinuous, unpredictable change) for organisational effectiveness. His work provides empirical support for the 'Contingent Strategic Success Formula' which 'identifies the environmental turbulence levels at which success prescriptions found in the management literature become valid'. To thrive, organisations must first assess the level of external environmental turbulence, and then align their organisational systems or internal environments accordingly in terms of strategy, technology, human resources, culture, and structure. Of course, though the theory is straightforward, putting it into practice is a much more complex task. Whilst Ansoff's functionalist perspective appears to succeed in imposing some certainty in an uncertain world, further dramatic shifts in the level of environmental turbulence can render 'solutions' which work today dysfunctional tomorrow.

The discussion thus far raises a key issue which will be returned to throughout this chapter. This relates to a contingency or, in simpler terms, an 'if-then' approach. An organisation's systems should be designed to 'fit' its particular environmental conditions (see Chapter 3 on best-fit HR strategy). If the environment is extremely turbulent then the systems should be tailored accordingly. There is nothing new in this. For example, the work of Lawrence and Lorsch showed how organisational integration (or centralisation) was appropriate for stable environments whereas differentiation was more effective in dynamic ones. Similarly, Burns and Stalker identified mechanistic (or bureaucratic) and organic (or flexible) structures as most apt for stable and changing environments respectively. The key point to note is that the impact of various environmental shifts is likely to be different for different organisations, contingent on a number of factors, for example the organisation's resource capabilities and/or the type of industry in which it is operating.

OD AND LINKS WITH STRATEGIC MANAGEMENT

There is much which unites OD with the field of strategic management though also aspects which divide the two. Both are concerned with improving organisational efficiency, effectiveness and performance. Both are concerned with exploring and dealing with many of the same issues, for example the environment, organisational systems and processes, organisational structure, and technology. What clearly sets the two fields apart are the approaches adopted. OD adopts an essentially humanist perspective and consequently focuses on both organisational performance and individual development in the belief that the two are interdependent.

Strategic management, on the other hand, traditionally adopting a functionalist/objective perspective, does not share OD's explicit commitment to individual development. In evidence, it is interesting to note that, in stark contrast to OD texts, many of the strategic management texts mention the human/people side of the organisation only briefly, if at all. Yet the view is supported that:

> organisational performance and personal development outcomes are interdependent. In the long-run, one cannot be achieved without the other and emphasising one at the expense of the other will yield neither.

> (Porras and Robertson, 1991)

This neglect of the people dimension is alarming. It may, however, explain why traditional approaches to strategic management have often failed to deliver expected outcomes in recent years.

There are great dangers in falling prey to the rationality and planning characteristic of traditional approaches to strategic management (Inns, 1996). Indeed, a survey conducted by Deloittes and reported in *The Economist* showed there to be no positive correlation between the performance of a company and whether or not it had a formal strategic planning operation (Pettigrew and Whipp, 1993), suggesting such activities add little value in terms of enhancing organisational effectiveness. In times of rapid change, even the most sophisticated strategic planning processes cannot accurately forecast the future. This perhaps explains why IBM, one of the original 'excellent' companies, drastically reduced its central planning function in the 1990s. It also further explains renewed interest in the practice of OD.

OD IN PRACTICE

'The organisation consists of interrelated sub-systems of a strategic, human, technological, structural and managerial nature which need to be internally consistent and adapted to [external] environmental conditions' (Morgan, 1986). OD, in simple terms, attempts to identify the nature of these internal sub-systems and to align them with the external environmental conditions. The OD process which achieves this consists of three main stages:

1 Diagnosis.
2 Intervention/action-taking.
3 Process maintenance.

Diagnosis, the first stage of OD, involves assessing the current circumstances under which the organisation is operating and the existing relationship between the organisation and its environment by exploring a number of diagnostic variables:

- external environment
- organisational vision
- organisational arrangements
- social factors
- technology
- physical setting
- individual behaviour
- outcomes in relation to organisational performance and individual development.

(Porras and Robertson, 1991)

OD consultants seek answers to a series of questions (Morgan, 1986). First, they investigate the nature of the organisation's environment: whether it is stable or turbulent; how economic, technological and socio-political changes are affecting it; the likelihood of future developments transforming the current state of affairs. Second, they explore current organisational strategy: the markets targeted; the product or service portfolio; the basis of competition (e.g. high quality or low cost); proactive or reactive. Third, they examine the kind of technology being used: the extent to which processes are standardised; the flexibility of technology; whether it allows scope for employee autonomy and responsibility. Fourth, the types of people employed and the organisational culture are explored: the core organisational values and beliefs; employees' work orientation, for example extrinsic or intrinsic. Fifth, the current organisational structure and managerial philosophy are analysed: bureaucratic or organic; authoritarian or democratic.

On completion of a thorough diagnosis, the OD consultant is then able to assess the 'fit' of the internal organisation to its external environment and identify any 'gaps' which exist between how the organisation is currently functioning and how it should be functioning to optimise organisational effectiveness and individual development. This assessment leads on to the second stage of the OD process: intervention/action-taking.

OD interventions can occur at a number of different levels – individual, group, departmental, organisational. The nature of intervention, or the actions taken and changes implemented, can be either incremental/evolutionary or transformational/revolutionary in nature. The different types of intervention available to the OD consultant are covered in more detail later in this chapter; suffice it to say at this stage that the choice of specific interventions is always contingent upon external environmental conditions and internal

Profile of organisational characteristics

Lines Ⓐ, Ⓑ and Ⓒ illustrate congruent, and line Ⓓ incongruent, relations between sub-systems

Fig. 21.1 Congruence and incongruence between organisational sub-systems
Source: From *Sociological Paradigms and Organisational Analysis* by Burrell and Morgan (1979), © Ashgate Publishing Limited.

organisational resource capabilities. Indeed, OD in practice operates under three key principles which can be referred to as the 'three Cs' of OD: *contingency, congruency* and *consistency*. These three principles hold for all stages of the OD process, not least the intervention stage. All interventions, whatever their level and nature, must achieve congruence between the internal and external environments of the organisation. For example, a mechanistic/bureaucratic structure would be incongruent with a turbulent, unpredictable environment, whereas an organic structure would be congruent. In addition, since changes intended to enhance performance in one part of the organisation can have negative if unintended consequences on another part, any changes implemented must be complemented by appropriate changes in interdependent processes and variables. That is, the sub-systems of the organisation must be 'internally consistent' (Morgan, 1986). For example, roles requiring high discretion and autonomy are inconsistent with an authoritarian managerial style. Figure 21.1 graphically depicts the desired congruence between organisational sub-systems contingent on the level of environmental turbulence for organisations A, B, and C. Organisation D, however, illustrates both incongruence and inconsistency – a situation to be avoided at all costs.

The third stage of OD is referred to as process maintenance. This should not be thought of as the final stage, since a number of feedback loops are built in which may in effect result in the whole OD process beginning again with further diagnosis. It is here that the action–research orientation of OD can be seen in operation. Process maintenance involves managing the change processes associated with interventions, researching and evaluating the effectiveness of these and taking further action where necessary. In essence, OD becomes an iterative process switching back and forth between diagnosis, decision, intervention/action and evaluation activities.

PLANNING AND MANAGING THE CHANGE PROCESS

Change management is a critical element of OD. However, those intent on becoming effective OD practitioners must be careful to distinguish one from the other. Although OD encompasses change management, the latter is only a part of effective OD – a frequently necessary condition, but never a sufficient one. It should not be assumed that all organisational change is developmental, from either the organisation's or the individual employee's perspective. In evidence of this, the success of many of the 'lean' initiatives (such as downsizing or TQM) introduced wholesale over recent years to make organisations more cost-effective and competitive is being questioned. Furthermore, some such schemes are now being relabelled 'mean' in terms of their regressive (as opposed to progressive) effects on the working lives of employees (Purcell and Hutchinson, 1996). This is not effective change management and it is certainly not OD.

Despite this, largely in response to increasingly turbulent business environments, a vast array of texts and articles have appeared offering prescriptions and promises of what effective change management might deliver in terms of improved organisational performance. The West's preoccupation with Japanese management techniques (despite serious doubts being raised about their transferability), alongside the earlier tale of the 'excellent' companies and those who attempted to emulate them, alerts us to the dangers of such prescriptions in lulling organisations into a false sense of security. Change based on the 'bandwagon effect' (Dawson, 1992), following the latest management fad with little thought for the fad's 'fit' with organisational and individual needs, is doomed to failure. The scale of the problem is indicated by estimates that an alarming 70 per cent of planned major organisational changes fail (Warrick, 1994). The suggested explanation is that change is poorly managed. However, it seems equally plausible that it is not simply a case of the right changes implemented wrongly, but also the wrong changes.

The objective of any change intervention should be enhanced organisational effectiveness and individual development. Managing change is merely the means to this end, not the end itself. Knowing how to manage change is simply not enough. Knowing what to change is of prime importance. Neither task is easy, compounded by the absence of a comprehensive, widely accepted, change-based model of organisations, although this deficiency should come as no surprise, since 'social systems with the complexity of organisations have been very difficult to model from a static perspective, much less a dynamic one' (Porras and Robertson, 1991). However, there are broad guidelines for planned change which offer the OD practitioner some direction. From an OD perspective, any change intervention should always be preceded by a comprehensive organisational diagnosis, should be designed on the basis of the three Cs of OD –

contingency, congruency and consistency, and implementation should be preceded by a thorough evaluation.

Planned change, which focuses on an organisation's general capabilities and arises from a deliberate decision to attempt to enhance effectiveness, can occur at the micro-level (involving anything from one individual to a whole group) or at the macro-level (involving the whole organisation). It is also possible to distinguish first-order, incremental, evolutionary change from second-order, transformational, revolutionary change. First-order change 'involves alterations in system characteristics without any shift either in fundamental assumptions or in the basic paradigm used by the system'. In contrast, second-order change is 'multidimensional, multilevel . . . radical organisational change involving a paradigm shift' (Porras and Robertson, 1991). First-order changes are 'traumatic' but 'in comparison to the sea-change implication of second-order changes, they are just storms in teacups. Sea-changes require mental shifts' (Dale, 1994). Clearly, then, the type of change profoundly affects the character and difficulty of the change management process. Organisational change is almost always a complex and messy process. 'Messy' describes the dynamic systems of problems facing those attempting to manage change. The higher the order of change, the more complex and messy the process.

There are unfortunately no 'cook-book solutions' (Dale, 1994) to help manage the 'mess', though there are a number of general change theories and models which offer insight into the nature and magnitude of the task in hand. The work of Lewin (1951) is probably the most renowned. The pressure for change can stem from any of a number of sources, for example technological, social, economic and/or political factors, creating driving forces for change. Lewin highlighted the way in which organisations exhibit a natural tendency to maintain a *status quo* by virtue of corresponding restraining forces within the organisation serving to obstruct change and preserve equilibrium. Only when the driving forces exceed the restraining forces can the current organisational equilibrium be challenged and change successfully achieved. Lewin therefore advocated 'force-field analysis', that is a comprehensive assessment of both driving and corresponding restraining forces, akin to the diagnosis phase of OD. Action can then be taken to respond to external pressures for change (the driving forces) by tackling internal resistance to it (the restraining forces).

Overcoming such restraining forces is arguably the hardest part of change management and should not be underestimated. For any particular driving force demanding change, restraining forces might stem from the threat of change to the current distribution of power and influence, individuals' fear of the unknown and the extent of their investment in the *status quo* or, in other words, how comfortable they are with current 'business as usual'. In general, the natural reaction of people subjected to change is one of resistance. The strength of this resistance can be very high. In fact, individual and organisational responses to change have been likened to that displayed by patients coming to terms with terminal illness. Fink *et al.* (1971) have summarised the stages of response to change as initial shock and disbelief, followed by a defensive retreat – clinging to the past, avoiding the reality of the present. With time comes an acknowledgement of the need to change, followed by a gradual adaptation to the new state and ultimately the required change. The speed with which individuals complete this process can vary enormously, since individuals respond to change very differently. As a general rule, however, the process of coming to terms with change, as with bereavement, is a long one and should not be unduly rushed. For second-order changes, the level of resistance is compounded and the timeframe involved in overcoming this is lengthened considerably. Effective change management should recognise and take account of this.

In addition to the necessity of employee acceptance of and involvement in the change programme, effective change management also demands the whole-hearted commitment of senior managers. Here, OD practitioners must beware of rhetorical commitment not matched by reality – of managerial lip-service substituting for genuine action. Managers are no more immune to experiencing change as threatening than their employees, and are just as likely to attempt to cling to the past they know than embrace the future they don't. Although the need for proactive mindsets is widely advocated in managerial circles, 'many organisations and their managers drive toward the future while looking in their rear view mirror' (Morgan, 1991). Organisational cultural peculiarities may also create restraining forces. Dale (1994) distinguishes three organisational types in terms of their approach to change. The ostrich type is characterised by a head-in-the-sand, 'it'll never happen here' attitude and is resistant to any change. The woodpecker approach is that of 'working harder'. In contrast, the owl approach aims to 'work smarter'. OD practitioners should be advocating and facilitating the owl approach to change management.

Addressing such restraining forces as those outlined above is the first of Lewin's (1951) three-stage change management model: unfreezing, changing (or movement) to the desired state, and refreezing. This first stage, unfreezing, effectively involves establishing disequilibrium within the organisational system by minimising the resistance. For this to be achieved, Lewin strongly emphasised the need for the involvement and consultation of all organisational members affected by the proposed change. Once this is completed, the proposed change can be implemented. The final stage, refreezing, is concerned with reinforcing and maintaining the change, perhaps by introducing new policies and procedures and/or new systems which reward desired behaviour in employees.

Lewin's model is a popular and widely used one and the framework, along with the call for participative approaches, is broadly echoed in much of the work of other change management theorists. For example, Beer *et al.* (1993) provide six steps to effective change:

1 Mobilise commitment to change through joint diagnosis of business problems.

2 Develop a shared vision of how to organise and manage for competitiveness.

3 Foster consensus for the new vision, competence to enact it and cohesion to move it along.

4 Spread revitalisation to all departments without pushing it from the top.

5 Institutionalise revitalisation through formal policies, systems and structures.

6 Monitor and adjust strategies in response to problems in the revitalisation process.

However, as King and Anderson (1995) point out, the pace of change in a rapidly developing business environment may mean that the refreezing stage of Lewin's model is never in fact reached before the next organisational change initiative has to be launched. In this respect, where the need for change on a continuous basis is a key feature, it may be more useful to view OD much less as a 'destination' and much more as a 'process-oriented journey' (Inns, 1996). In highly turbulent environments, change management, as an integral part of OD, should be viewed in much the same way.

THE LEARNING ORGANISATION

The Learning Organisation has been defined as 'an organisation which facilitates the learning of all its members and continuously transforms itself' (Pedler and Burgoyne, 1988). It is a 'vision for an organisational strategy to promote self-development amongst the membership and to harness this development corporately by continuously transforming itself as part of the same process' (Pedler, 1994). As a concept, the Learning Organisation has much to offer OD practitioners. The notion of continuous organisational transformation is particularly apt for the many organisations facing environments of extreme turbulence and dynamism where 'reacting and responding to change is no longer enough' (Dale, 1994). In such circumstances, traditional approaches to change management may be rendered inappropriate and unworkable, most notably when the pace of change is so great that the 'refreezing' dimension of Lewin's change model becomes obsolete. For these reasons, the Learning Organisation may be an eminently more suitable model for OD in the twenty-first century.

The ideas at the heart of the Learning Organisation have been around for some time. Its origins have been traced as far back as the 1920s and it was developed in particular in the 1960s, 1970s and 1980s with major contributions from theorists such as Argyris and Schon – also strongly influential in the OD field. It is therefore no accident that the Learning Organisation encapsulates many of the same basic values and philosophies of OD as well as many of the developments in the HRM field in general. For example, it shares OD's concern with 'bringing out the best in organisations and individuals' and it champions OD's cause in 'focusing attention on softer and underlying social, value and ethical issues which are emerging as important criteria in assessing the competence and capability of an organisation and its people' (Jones and Hendry, 1994). Furthermore, it attempts to meet three major objectives in line with those shared by OD practitioners:

> how to structure organisations to enhance performance; how to facilitate individual learning and development in a corporate setting; and how to ensure that organisations adapt quickly to changes in their external environment.
>
> (Coopey, 1996)

Coopey (1996) identifies some of the key characteristics of a Learning Organisation as:

- a learning climate – 'essentially a cultural template designed around a questioning frame of mind, tolerance of mistakes, the need for differences and the idea of continuous improvement'
- an ethos of self-responsibility
- self-development opportunities available to all
- a learning approach to strategy allowing continuous development and revision of policies and plans
- participative policy-making
- all boundary workers as environmental scanners (*see* Chapter 1)
- internal collaboration rather than competition

- reward flexibility – with reward systems made public and reviewed collectively
- inter-company learning – spreading the learning ethos to suppliers and customers
- temporary structures responsive to future changes in internal and external environments.

The Learning Organisation offers an extremely promising blueprint. However, at an applied level the idea has received minimal attention. Its advocates are criticised in respect of 'problems with the conceptual statements in terms of their ability to secure action' and for being 'longer on description of desirable states than they are for achieving those states' (Mumford, 1994). Thus, somewhat ironically, Learning Organisation theorists are clear about 'what' to change, but much less clear on 'how' to achieve these changes. Given the social and historical context which has framed the manner in which today's organisations function and operate, not least the political realities of them, it should come as no surprise that, in practice, 'there remains an elusive aspect to the Learning Organisation idea' (Jones and Hendry, 1994). In particular, the model's 'key feature' in terms of 'equality in the political sense of equal rights, responsibilities and privileges' amongst organisational members (Pedler and Burgoyne, 1988) is especially problematic in traditional, hierarchically structured organisations where 'direction from above is usual' (Pedler, 1994). Such structures 'do not easily lend themselves to members taking responsibility for their own development'. Self-development, as the foundation of the Learning Organisation, is 'first and foremost about learner power to act autonomously rather than trainer [or manager] power to direct and prescribe' (Pedler and Burgoyne, 1988). In this respect, it can be perceived as a challenge, or indeed a threat to, the current taken-for-granted power bases of many organisations.

The Learning Organisation in both theory and practice demands a paradigmatic shift away from current conceptions of organising and managing. Though such shifts cannot be achieved easily, painlessly or quickly, this is no reason to dismiss the vision. The Learning Organisation is the 'next frontier in development work'.

> Methodologies of group self-development, culture change, organisation change . . . offer some approaches from which we can at least extrapolate to postulate ways of developing the Learning [Organisation].

> (Pedler and Burgoyne, 1988)

For OD practitioners, the search is on for a facilitating structure or perhaps, more appropriately, a facilitating culture of self-development, self-responsibility, learning and knowledge management.

CULTURE MANAGEMENT

Organisational culture has been defined simply as 'the way we do things around here' (Deal and Kennedy, 1982). In essence, it represents the taken-for-granted beliefs and tacit laws which govern organisational behaviour. Culture is

> the pattern of basic assumptions that a given group has invented, discovered or developed in learning to cope with its problems of external adaptation and internal integration, and that have

worked well enough to be considered valid, and therefore, to be taught to new members as the correct way to perceive, think and feel in relation to these problems.

(Schein, 1984)

Watson (2002) defines culture as 'the set of meanings shared by members of a human grouping which defines what is good and bad, right and wrong and consequently defines the appropriate ways for members of that group to think and behave'.

Many factors shape culture. Some of the most strongly influential ones, such as the philosophy of the organisation's founders and the social and historical context in which the organisation has developed, cannot be changed. However, Robbins (1993), drawing on research findings, identifies a number of key characteristics offering a template to diagnose culture and to assess intervention options. Such characteristics include:

- the extent to which employees identify primarily with the organisation or their own job
- whether relations have an individualist or collectivist focus
- whether managerial style is people- or task-focused
- the extent of managerial control imposed
- the extent of risk tolerance
- conflict tolerance
- reward criteria
- the manner in which the organisation monitors and responds to changes in its environment.

Other clues to organisational culture lie in the selection criteria used to recruit new employees and the style and actions of senior management. It should be noted that whilst a dominant organisational culture may be identifiable, diverse sub-cultures may exist within the organisation, particularly if it is structurally organised on the basis of highly differentiated sub-units or departments. In such cases there is likely to be a 'mosaic of organisational realities rather than a uniform corporate culture' (Morgan, 1986). Whatever the case, these constituent elements or key characteristics of culture are the most likely targets for cultural change initiatives.

Culture change may in itself be selected as the primary OD intervention. However, an appreciation of cultural aspects is important for all other OD interventions as well. The predominant culture of an organisation (and/or the sub-cultures of the organisation's divisions) affects the extent to which other interventions (such as structural changes) can be successfully implemented. In this respect, given the need for congruency and consistency, culture may either become a secondary target for change intervention, or force the OD practitioner to consider alternative interventions more suited to the prevailing culture.

All of the activities that revolve around recruitment, selection, training, socialisation, the design of reward systems, the design and description of jobs and broader issues of organisational design require an understanding of how organisational culture influences present functioning. Many organisational change programmes that failed probably did so because they ignored cultural forces in the organisations in which they were to be installed.

(Schein, 1990)

At a national level as well as an organisational one, cultural characteristics can hamper the progress of change interventions. Indeed, the cultural peculiarities of UK organisations may mean that OD practitioners, in this country especially, have their work cut out for them. Pheysey (1993) contrasts 'US-style OD', for example 'an adaptive system is a good thing', with what he refers to as 'UK cultural blocks': 'we like to carry on as we always have done'. This latter exhibition of 'dynamic conservatism' (Dale, 1994) could explain why proposed change interventions, not least cultural ones, may meet with a very cool reception. Furthermore, adding to the discussion of how cultural differences impede the transferability of Japanese management techniques to Western organisations, Ali (1996) has explored the difficulties in attempting to transplant (essentially Western) OD perspectives directly to organisations in the Arab world, arguing that they should be remoulded to ensure they are 'relevant and effective in dealing with particular and peculiar cultural aspirations and problems'. This plea applies equally to all OD practitioners, not solely to those working across national boundaries, since organisations within the same sector operating in the same country may possess diverse cultures. Dale (1994) highlights the NHS Trusts as a prime example of this. These illustrative examples raise again the highly pertinent issue of the importance of contingency, congruency and consistency in OD interventions, drawing attention to the need for OD practitioners to tailor their approaches in line with the specific organisational cultural contexts, both internal and external.

The increasing preoccupation with culture has been attributed to the 'excellence' literature, including analyses of the Japanese economic miracle in the late twentieth century, both of which attributed much of the success of such organisations to 'strong' corporate cultures. As a result, a belief has developed that 'organisations with weak cultures may be less effective, less productive and less satisfying places in which to work' (Carnall, 1995). Such a view, however, warrants critical reflection. There are several classic examples of organisations whose strong organisational culture, once held up as being the key to their success, was subsequently identified as obstructing organisational responsiveness to environmental changes and blamed for a catastrophic downfall. The troubles faced by IBM in the early 1990s are a prime and much-quoted example. Criticised for being 'inward-looking, conformist, complacent . . . sunk into a morass of group-think and rigid rather than flexible in its outlook' (Legge, 1994), an organisation with a very strong culture may find it hard to survive in an environment characterised by extreme turbulence. This is because 'sharing meanings may have a positive integrative effect, but at the same time inhibit an organisation's ability to learn and adapt' (Legge, 1994). Thus, attempts to emulate the strong organisational cultures of 'exemplar' companies may be ill-advised. In addition, the feasibility of this type of culture management must also be questioned.

Several academic writers have engaged in the debate as to whether culture is something an organisation has or something an organisation is (for example, Legge, 1994; Meek, 1988; Smircich, 1983) or in Dawson's words (1992) 'can culture be "taught" or can it only be "caught"?' The distinction is an important one. The former view implies that culture lends itself to manipulation and management. In contrast, if culture is believed to be something an organisation is, borne from social interaction, enacted by organisational members, the extent to which it can be managed is highly questionable.

This latter perspective, of culture as 'emergent rather than prescribed', is gaining credence in the academic community (particularly in light of evidence of great difficulties experienced by those charged with engineering culture change) but is 'as one would expect from a view which denies the basis for deliberate manipulation, less popular with practitioners' (Dawson, 1992). A partial acceptance of both perspectives suggests that 'managers can influence the evolution of culture . . . by attempting to foster desired values, but they can never control culture in the sense that many management writers advocate' (Morgan, 1986). Therefore, 'it is more accurate to speak of the value dimensions of management systems than the vaguer and looser term "corporate cultures"' (Thompson and McHugh, 1995).

The feasibility of managing culture (or perhaps more appropriately organisational value systems) is contingent on the particular characteristics of an organisation. Dawson (1992) identifies a number of key aspects to consider: the degree of employee homogeneity; ethnic composition of wider social culture; size of the company; geographical dispersion; extent of consensus (or conflict) amongst stakeholders; and the timescale being considered. Clearly, if the employee population is large and heterogeneous, geographically dispersed across international boundaries, with a history of conflictual employee and shareholder relations, it is unrealistic to expect that a strong shared-value system can be nurtured within any timescale. In contrast, a small homogeneous employee population physically located in one place, characterised by consensual relationships, makes culture much more amenable to management in the medium if not short term.

Like all OD interventions, a decision to pursue cultural change should be based on a comprehensive organisational diagnosis taking fully into account feasibility considerations. The basic guidelines and models for change management in general apply equally to cultural change initiatives. The active (as opposed to merely rhetorical) support of managers and the involvement and participation of employees are crucial elements if genuine commitment and widespread adoption of the new values is to be secured rather than a superficial and temporary behavioural compliance.

Armstrong (2001) suggests that specific interventions could include communication programmes, training programmes (such as teamworking, customer care, quality) and complementary performance and reward management systems. In addition, recruitment and selection processes may be targeted to attract the type of people to fit the desired culture or indeed to reinforce the current culture. This latter intervention in particular raises important ethical considerations. An organisation interested in recruiting specific 'types' of people runs the danger of condoning either direct or indirect discriminatory practices. The ethical dilemma highlighted also by Watson (2002) is compounded when managers hold a monopoly in prescribing 'the correct way to perceive, think and feel'. A cynical observer might view this as a form of social engineering which sits ill at ease with OD practitioners' commitment to equal opportunities and flies in the face of the current vogue championing diversity as the route to 'help organisations to nurture creativity, innovation and thereby to tap hidden capacity for growth and improved competitiveness' (IPD, 1996). OD and HR professionals must grapple with and resolve this dilemma.

THE OD CONSULTANT AND CHANGE AGENT – ROLES AND SKILLS

The OD consultant

Effective relationships, so the theory goes, are based on trust, and the relationship between the OD consultant and their client organisation is no exception. To this end, OD consultants must possess a high level of self-awareness of their philosophies, values, beliefs and fundamental assumptions and must openly, honestly and explicitly express these to their prospective client. The rationale for this is straightforward.

OD consultant–client relationships are characterised by collaboration, 'relative equality' (French and Bell, 1990) and a shared, partnership approach to organisational problem-solving. The OD consultant's primary role is that of 'question-asker' with solutions to problems jointly generated and the locus of decision-making residing in the client. The OD consultant listens, offers help, facilitates the developmental process and continues the consultancy relationship for as long as the client organisation requires this assistance. OD consultants are likely to draw on qualitative data as much as quantitative data to diagnose the organisation.

In direct contrast to the OD consultant is the more traditional 'expert' consultant. The expert consultant takes ownership of the client's problem and adopts a primary role of 'answer-giver' relying almost exclusively on quantitative, 'rationalistic' approaches to diagnose the system. The expert consultant 'tells' the client what the problem is, 'sells' a solution and then terminates the client–consultant relationship. In contrast to the expert style, the OD approach to consultancy, coined by Schein as 'process consultation', is intended to allow organisational members to develop the key diagnostic and problem-solving skills to enable them to take the change management reins themselves – to become in-house process consultants. This is the critical distinguishing factor between the expert and OD consultant. French and Bell (1990) draw on an old Chinese proverb which illustrates the values underpinning OD and the rationale of OD consultancy approach: 'Give a man a fish and you have given him a meal; teach a man to fish and you have given him a livelihood.'

The change agent

Change agents are specialists in managing change and developing high-performance organisations, teams and individuals.

(Warrick, 1994)

The task of the change agent is an extremely challenging one demanding an array of skills and qualities. It is important, however, to distinguish between a change agent in the expert-consultant mode from an OD consultant. The two roles are quite clearly very different, demanding distinct skills and personal qualities.

Just how challenging the role of change agent is can be gleaned by studying the advertisements of organisations wishing to fill such vacancies (Exhibit 21.1 offers a somewhat daunting example). The range of skills and qualities required can be gauged by exploring those demanded by recruiting organisations' person specifications. For example, the person sought for the role in Exhibit 21.1 requires a 'strong, strategic and sharply commercial mind and a keen awareness of the impact of HR on the business plan'. Ernst and Young (*The Times*, 31 October 1996), advertising for consultants in 'Transformational Change' to assist 'FT350 and Fortune 500 companies to operate more efficiently, profitably and successfully', demand 'energetic, self-confident people with a strong commercial focus . . . bright, ambitious and dynamic . . . outstanding analytical and communication skills, combined with an understanding of making change happen in large organisations'.

Exhibit 21.1   The role of a change agent

'Our client wants change delivered in the UK. Very fast. Very competently. On a very large scale. A global group with newly acquired interests in the UK and Europe, they've launched a massive business re-engineering programme reaching into every aspect of their production and distribution operations. It demands change in processes, change in people and change in culture. The key to achieving that change will be you – the HR Director they wish to appoint on a 3–6 month contract

. . .

Your challenge: to accelerate the initiatives already started, bring fresh attitudes, approaches and procedures into the organisation, win hearts and minds and build highly motivated and committed teams which will deliver results. Quickly.'

Source: Price Waterhouse Executive Search and Selection, *Sunday Telegraph*, 12 January 1997.

The roles specified in Exhibit 21.1 stress organisational efficiency and 'bottom-line' performance as key objectives of the change process. Individual development is not mentioned and delivery times for solutions are predefined and tight. These are change agents in the expert-consultancy mode. OD theorists' shopping lists of competencies have a very different focus. For example, King and Anderson (1995) have identified six essential competencies required by a change agent. These are:

- knowledge of OD techniques
- commitment to high standards of professional and ethical integrity
- networking abilities
- elicitation skills to gather reliable information on organisational problems from organisational members
- evaluation and integration skills
- diagnostic and prognostic skills.

Porras and Robertson (1991) identify the characteristics of effective change agents as:

- interpersonal competence – listening and empathy; group process facilitation; sensitivity; ability to influence
- problem-solving capabilities – knowledge of theory and methods of change; ability to conceptualise and diagnose
- role as educator – create learning experiences; developing effective behaviour in others
- self-awareness – of own assumptions, needs and motivations.

They do, however, concede that, realistically, no one individual could hope to develop all the skills and qualities apparently demanded of change agents, and argue that they 'must know their capabilities and limitations and should carry out interventions that match their skills'. This is not to suggest that the selection of suitable OD interventions should be contingent on the change agent's competence (or lack of it). Indeed, such a situation poses great dangers. For example, the diagnosis stage may suggest that the organisation's information technology (IT) needs to be overhauled. A change agent lacking knowledge of IT may be tempted not to recommend such an intervention to 'save face' and plump instead for a restructuring programme with which she or he feels more confident to manage, despite the latter being in neither the organisation's nor its members' best interests. This is admittedly an extreme scenario, although in an uncollaborative client–consultant relationship, not an entirely unlikely one. It provides a solid rationale for a team of people from a range of organisational functions to take on the task of the change agent collectively, perhaps with the OD consultant designated as project coordinator. This would allow the skill weaknesses of each individual member to be offset by the strengths of others and also would ensure wide involvement in the change process through all three stages: diagnosis, intervention and process maintenance. This participative approach is likely to increase the likelihood of changes being implemented effectively. It carries with it further benefits. For example OD practitioners are criticised for their lack of organisational 'nous', failing to deal with the realities of organisational life, particularly in relation to power and politics (Hamlin and Davies, 1996). Involvement of a range of organisational members in debate, discussion, diagnosis and decision is likely to inform the OD consultant's assessment of the power games at work in the organisation. This involvement also facilitates the process of 'surfacing and testing mental models' or the prevalent and predominant organisational paradigm. Furthermore, by 'balancing inquiry and advocacy . . . distinguishing espoused theory from theory in use . . . recognising and defining defensive routines' (Senge, 1994), the current organisational blockages to change can be identified and addressed.

INTERVENTION STRATEGIES AND TECHNIQUES

A variety of OD intervention techniques exist, ranging from the simple to the highly complex, from a short-term to a long-term duration, from affecting one individual to affecting an entire organisation and from impacting on one organisational variable within one category (such as organising arrangements, social factors, technology, physical setting) to impacting on several variables across all categories.

(Porras and Robertson, 1991)

For example, Huse (1980) has identified ten different classifications of OD interventions as follows:

- individual consultation activities
- unstructured group training activities
- structured group training

- process consultation
- survey-guided development efforts
- job redesign
- personnel system methods
- management information and financial control systems
- organisational design
- integrated approaches.

French and Bell (1990) identify the major families of OD interventions as:

- diagnostic activities
- team-building activities
- intergroup activities
- survey feedback
- education and training
- techno-structural or structural activities
- process consultation
- grid OD (the Blake and Mouton model)
- third-party peacemaking, life and career planning
- planning and goal-setting
- strategic management activities.

Beer and Walton (1990) advocate two intervention approaches for improving both organisational effectiveness and individual well-being. The first, the 'Human-Process approach', 'involves employees in examining interpersonal, group and intergroup processes and planning changes in them which will improve effectiveness'. Given that employee motivation and behaviour are often assumed to be strongly influenced by factors such as job design, organisational structure, reward systems, and management control and information systems, they also recommend a 'techno-structural' approach to ensure that these organisational factors are congruent and consistent with desired behavioural outcomes.

OD theory does not prescribe which technique to use and when. Given the complexity of organisations, the differences in make-up which exist both within and between organisations and the key operating principles of the three Cs of OD – contingency, congruency and consistency, the absence of universal prescriptions or 'cook-book solutions' is to be expected and indeed welcomed. Instead, deciding which intervention to use is a two-stage process beginning with a thorough diagnosis of the organisation, assessing general problem areas in terms of incongruent organisational characteristics and gaps between current and desired organisational states.

The selection of specific interventions follows this assessment. Drawing on the collective knowledge and information provided by a diverse range of organisational members, OD consultants must assess which intervention technique is most likely to have the desired impact on the target organisational variable(s) whilst minimising or at least managing actively the 'domino effect' of negative consequences on other variables. Intervention technique selection choice is also contingent on resource constraints and the urgency with which change is required. It should not, however, be contingent, as some have suggested, on the skill set of the consultant. Additional expertise should be drafted in if the intervention required is beyond the OD consultant's range of competence.

Three major strategies in OD interventions have been identified as rational–empirical, normative–re-educative, and power–coercive (Chin and Benne, 1976). OD practitioners committed to the values of developmental humanism are likely to focus their primary attention on the normative–re-educative strategy, drawing on rational–empirical strategies to aid diagnosis, decision-making and evaluation of OD interventions. Power–coercive strategies sit ill at ease with a developmental philosophy and experience has shown that, of all three strategies, this is likely to be the least effective in securing genuine individual commitment to organisational goals.

Successful intervention is dependent on the validity of the information on which the decision is based and the internal commitment to the proposed change. However, even the best-laid plans can result in unintended consequences. This is why the third stage of OD, process maintenance, is so critical. All interventions, once implemented, must be carefully monitored and evaluated against intended outcomes.

EVALUATING THE EFFECTIVENESS OF OD INTERVENTIONS

'The problem of evaluation of strategies for change needs to be recognised as one of the most under-reported issues in British management literature' (Hamlin and Davies, 1996). Despite evaluation being recognised as a critical part of any change initiative, not least of OD interventions, it is nevertheless a much neglected activity. For example, cultural change initiatives have been widely publicised in recent years (such as within the NHS, British Airways and British Telecom) yet, as Legge (1994) points out, there are 'few if any systematic evaluations of them'. The problem is that evaluating the effectiveness of OD interventions is a complicated and difficult task. Comprehensive evaluation is nevertheless imperative. Without it, OD consultants lack credibility. It is one thing to promise enhanced organisational performance and individual well-being; proving it to be deliverable in practice is quite another.

The difficulties associated with evaluation arise for a number of reasons. For example, given the complexity and timeframe involved in major change initiatives, evaluative studies which are insufficiently longitudinal will not capture the long-term effects of the change, whether good, bad or indifferent. Similarly, a single study conducted too soon may not evaluate effectively the full long-term implications of the change. Thus, evaluation conducted, for instance, six months after changes have been implemented may show negative results. Employees may be in the process of coming to terms with the change and showing some signs of resistance, morale may be lowered as a result and this may have a knock-on effect on organisational profitability. However, an evaluation conducted say some three years after the change event may show great improvements in both organisational performance and employee well-being. The question raised at this time is whether these positive changes can genuinely be attributed to the OD intervention or caused by some other unrelated mediating factor which has occurred in the interim period, for example an improvement in environmental conditions.

The interdependency of organisational systems means that even a small-scale single intervention in one area can have large-scale knock-on effects on others. For example, following the overhaul of the reward system of a sales division, increased sales turnover and improved employee motivation may well be in evidence. But resentment of employees in other divisions may, paradoxically, adversely impact the performance of the organisation as a whole. Thus, although the intended outcomes of the intervention may be achieved at a divisional level, the overall effect is unintended and there will be detrimental outcomes at an organisational level. If the evaluation is only conducted at a divisional level, the wider impact of the changes will be missed and in this way, ironically, the ineffectiveness of the evaluation will actually be contributing to the overall ineffectiveness of the OD intervention.

How can these dilemmas be overcome? As with the other stages of the OD process there are unfortunately no simple, prescriptive solutions. However, the key principles remain, that is the three Cs of OD: contingency, congruency and consistency. The evaluation design must be contingent on the particular OD intervention being evaluated and the desired outcomes identified by the particular organisation. It must also contain measures to check that particular interventions are not creating incongruence and inconsistencies in the rest of the organisational system. If this is the case, steps must be taken to restore congruency, possibly by further interventions in the other areas. It is this point which demonstrates why OD should be thought of as a journey and not a destination in terms of the way in which the evaluation process feeds back into the first stage of the OD process – diagnosis.

Selecting an appropriate evaluation strategy calls for great skill and insight. It also calls for some political awareness in terms of what sorts of data are likely to be considered 'acceptable' evidence to different groups. The way in which the basic assumptions of OD practitioners and their 'humanistic' outlook differ from the predominant 'functionalist' managerial paradigm has already been noted. Where they exist, these differences have strong implications for evaluation in terms of the 'acceptability' of the approach to data collection adopted. Davies (1996) highlights two approaches to research and evaluation. One describes the effects of an intervention in a functional sense – the 'what' questions – which managers are likely to be predominantly interested in. The second approach analyses in detail the factors contributing to the effectiveness of an intervention – the 'what and why' questions. This latter approach informs future action and also contributes to OD's theoretical knowledge base. Both approaches are important. However, each demands different methodologies.

There are numerous evaluation methods available. These can be classified broadly under two headings: quantitative (or 'hard') approaches and qualitative (or 'soft') approaches. Quantitative methods, associated with the 'functionalist' paradigm, attempt to provide 'objective' measures of variables. In evaluation, measures of, for example, profit, turnover and return on investment would be used as organisational performance indicators. In addition, questionnaire methods surveying a representative sample of employees in an attempt to, for example, generalise the average feeling of well-being across the organisation might also be adopted. Quantitative methods are favoured by functionalists since they possess an objective scientific air. Yet it is precisely this air which can be illusory and it is recommended that such methods are combined with qualitative (or 'soft') approaches. Indeed, for OD consultants as committed to individual development and well-being as to organisational performance, qualitative approaches are essential to adequately assess the former, tapping into the subjective experiences and attitudes of individuals. Methods available include interviews, observation, focus or discussion groups, workshops, repertory grid technique and cognitive mapping, *inter alia*. It is widely recommended that multiple methods are used and that assessments are conducted both before and after the intervention. The specific choice of methods selected inevitably raises further issues of acceptability, given that quantitative approaches and methods are apparently strongly favoured by functionalist managers. However, OD consultants should not be daunted or deterred by the apparent ease with which qualitative data is dismissed by some if they are determined to discover both the 'what' and 'why' effects of OD interventions.

CONCLUSION AND CRITIQUE OF OD

OD is not without its critics. Several factors contributing to the scepticism surrounding OD can be identified. First, in contrast to many other business and management fields, OD is relatively new, having been in existence only for some 35 years. Its theoretical base is therefore still in its infancy. Second, there is a great paucity of OD research. That which has been conducted has been criticised as being methodologically flawed and, as a result, little is really known about the exact contribution of OD interventions to organisational improvement, and the utility of OD in the hard financial terms favoured by many managers has yet to be convincingly demonstrated. Third, the organisational processes which OD attempts to re-engineer are characterised by enormous complexity which cannot be easily managed and manipulated, nor as a result evaluated. Fourth, the long-range time perspective of many OD interventions 'combined with difficulties in demonstrating their contribution to organisational success criteria' (Legge, 1994) sits ill at ease with the financial short-termism characterising much of British industry. Fifth, the 'messianic rather than scientific flavour' of OD (Porras and Robertson, 1991) and its normative humanistic 'sweetness and light' values and assumptions are criticised for being at odds with the reality of those 'hard-nosed organisations that [operate] as bureaucracies and political jungles' (Legge, 1994). The pursuit of the 'democratisation of organisations' and 'power equalisation' is also criticised as being idealistic and 'naive in the sense of not seeing the real world' with a 'lack of attention to organisational realities' (French and Bell, 1990). In its defence, OD probably understands the use (and abuse) of power within organisations more than some commentators appreciate. Indeed, it is the 'anti-hierarchical and anti-authoritarian stance' (Beer and Walton, 1990) adopted by OD and the threat this poses to those in positions of power which may better explain much of their suspicion and scepticism.

It is perhaps little wonder that OD consultants have their work cut out for them in convincing their sceptics that OD can make a valuable and substantial contribution to improving organisational effectiveness, equipping organisations with the resources they require to thrive in turbulent and dynamic environments.

SUMMARY LEARNING POINTS

1 OD is concerned with improving organisational effectiveness and enhancing the development and well-being of organisational members through the planned management of change in organisational systems.

2 OD adopts a contingency approach to change management, ensuring that the internal strategic, human, cultural, technological, structural and managerial organisational systems are internally consistent and congruent with external environmental conditions.

3 These 'three Cs' of OD – contingency, congruency and consistency – underpin all activities in the three main stages of OD: diagnosis, intervention and process maintenance.

4 Planned change can occur at the individual, group, departmental and/or organisational level and can be incremental/evolutionary or transformational/revolutionary in nature. Models and theories of change offer broad guidelines on how to manage change, and top management commitment to and employee involvement in the change process is widely advocated. However, only a comprehensive organisational diagnosis can suggest what should be changed.

5 The concept of the Learning Organisation encapsulates many of the values of OD and may supersede traditional change management models which are inclined to be rendered obsolete in extremely turbulent environments. However, difficulties have been encountered in putting the theoretical concept into practice. There is currently a concern with how organisations can 'manage knowledge', and Knowledge Management as an HR intervention is on the contemporary OD agenda.

6 Culture has an important part to play in OD. Culture change, or more appropriately organisational value systems (given questions surrounding the feasibility of cultural change in the traditional sense), may be targeted as a primary intervention. Cultural peculiarities at a departmental, organisational, national and/or international level can also have a profound impact on the developmental process and must receive adequate consideration.

7 A variety of OD intervention techniques are available, the selection of which is contingent on the results of a thorough organisational diagnosis and assessment. Once implemented, all interventions must be comprehensively evaluated.

REFERENCES AND FURTHER READING

Ali, A.J. (1996) 'Organisational development in the Arab World', *Journal of Management Development*, 15(5), 4–21.

Ansoff, H.I. and Sullivan, P.A. (1993) 'Optimising profitability in turbulent environments: a formula for strategic success', *Long Range Planning*, 26(5), 11–23.

Armstrong, M. (2001) *A Handbook of Personnel Management Practice*. London: Kogan Page.

Beer, M., Eisenstat, R.A. and Spector, B. (1993) 'Why change programs don't produce change', in Mabey, C. and Mayon-White, B. (eds) *Managing Change*. London: Open University Press.

Beer, M. and Walton, E. (1990) 'Developing the competitive organisation: interventions and strategies', *American Psychologist*, February, 154–61.

Burrell, G. and Morgan, G. (1979) *Sociological Paradigms and Organisational Analysis*. London: Heinemann.

Carnall, C. (1995) *Managing Change in Organisations*. Hemel Hempstead: Prentice Hall.

Chin, R. and Benne, K. (1976) 'General strategies for effecting changes in human systems', in Bennis, W.G., Benne, K.D., Chin, R. and Corey, K.E. (eds) *The Planning of Change*. New York: Holt, Rinehart and Winston.

Coopey, J. (1996) 'Crucial gaps in the learning organisation: power, politics and ideology', in Starkey, K. (ed.) *How Organisations Learn*. London: International Thomson Business Press.

Dale, M. (1994) 'Learning organisations', in Mabey, C. and Iles, P. (eds) *Managing Learning*. London: Routledge.

Davies, G. (1996) 'Research methods and HRD', in Stewart, J. and McGoldrick, J. (eds) *Human Resource Development: Perspectives, strategies and practice*. London: Pitman Publishing.

Dawson, S. (1992) *Analysing Organisations*. Basingstoke: Macmillan.

Deal, T.E. and Kennedy, A. (1982) *Corporate Cultures*. Reading, MA: Addison-Wesley.

Fink, S.L., Beak, J. and Taddeo, K. (1971) 'Organisational crisis and change', *Journal of Applied Behavioural Science*, 7(1), 15–41.

French, W.L. and Bell, C.H. (1990) *Organisation Development: Behavioural science interventions for organisation improvement*. Engleword Cliffs, NJ: Prentice-Hall.

French, W.L., Bell, C.H. and Zawacki, R.A. (eds) (1994) *Organization Development and Transformation: Managing effective change*. Chicago: Irwin.

Hamlin, B. and Davies, G. (1996) 'The trainer as change agent: issues for practice', in Stewart, J. and McGoldrick, J. (eds) *Human Resource Development: Perspectives, strategies and practice*. London: Pitman Publishing.

Huse, E.F. (1980) *Organization Development and Change*. St Paul, MN: West Publishing.

Inns, D. (1996) 'Organisation development as a journey', in Oswick, C. and Grant, D. (eds) *Organisation Development: Metaphorical explorations*. London: Pitman Publishing.

IPD (1996) *Managing Diversity: An IPD position paper*. London: IPD.

Jones, A.M. and Hendry, C. (1994) 'The learning organisation: adult learning and organisational transformation', *British Journal of Management*, 5, 153–62.

King, N. and Anderson, N. (1995) *Innovation and Change in Organisations*. London: Routledge.

Legge, K. (1994) 'Managing culture: fact or fiction?', in Sisson, K. (ed.) *Personnel Management: A comprehensive guide to theory and practice in Britain*. Oxford: Blackwell.

Lewin, K. (1951) *Field Theory in Social Science*. New York: Harper & Row.

Meek, V.L. (1988) 'Organisational culture: origins and weaknesses', *Organisation Studies*, 9(4), 453–73.

Morgan, G. (1986) *Images of Organisation*. London: Sage.

Morgan, G. (1990) 'Paradigm diversity in organisational research', in Hassard, J. and Pym, D. (eds) *The Theory and Philosophy of Organisations: Critical issues and new perspectives*. London: Routledge.

Morgan, G. (1991) 'Emerging waves and challenges: the need for new competencies and mindsets', in Henry, J. (ed.) *Creative Management*. London: Sage.

Mumford, A. (1994) 'Individual and organisational learning: the pursuit of change', in Mabey, C. and Iles, P. (eds) *Managing Learning*. London: Routledge.

Pedler, M. (1994) 'Applying self-development in organisations', in Mabey, C. and Iles, P. (eds) *Managing Learning*. London: Routledge.

Pedler, M. and Burgoyne, J. (1988) 'Envisioning the learning company', in Pedler, M., Burgoyne, J. and Boydell, T. *Applying Self-Development in Organisations*. Hemel Hempstead: Prentice-Hall.

Peters, T.J. and Waterman, R.H. (1982) *In Search of Excellence: Lessons from America's companies*. New York: Harper & Row.

Pettigrew, A. and Whipp, R. (1993) 'Understanding the environment', in Mabey, C. and Mayon-White, B. (eds) *Managing Change*. London: Open University Press.

Pheysey, D.C. (1993) *Organisational Cultures: Types and transformations*. London: Routledge.

Porras, J.I. and Robertson, P.J. (1991) 'Organisation development: theory practice and research', in Dunnette, M.D. and Hough, L.M. (eds) *Handbook of Industrial and Organizational Psychology*. Palo Alto, CA: Consulting Psychologists Press.

Purcell, J. and Hutchinson, S. (1996) 'Lean and mean?', *People Management*, 2(20), 27–33.

Robbins, S.P. (1993) *Organizational Behaviour*. Englewood Cliffs, NJ: Prentice-Hall.

Schein, E. (1984) 'Coming to a new awareness of organisational culture', *Sloan Management Review*, Winter, 3–16.

Schein, E. (1990) 'Organizational culture', *American Psychologist*, 45(2), 109–19.

Senge, P. (1994) 'The leader's new work: building learning organisations', in Mabey, C. and Iles, P. (eds) *Managing Learning*. London: Routledge.

Smircich, L. (1983) 'Studying organisations as cultures', in Morgan, G. (ed.) *Beyond Method: Strategies for social research*. London: Sage.

Thompson, P. and McHugh, D. (1995) *Work Organisations: A critical introduction*. London: Macmillan Business.

Watson, T.J. (2002) *Organising and Managing Work*. London: Financial Times/Prentice-Hall.

Warrick, D.D. (1994) 'What executives, managers, and human resource professionals need to know about managing change', in French, W.L., Bell, C.H. and Zawacki, R.A. (eds) *Organization Development and Transformation: Managing effective change*. Chicago: Irwin.

Wyatt, S. (1994) 'Personal performance headroom', *Management Accounting*, 72(1), 44–5.

ASSIGNMENTS AND DISCUSSION TOPICS

1 Explain, drawing on the notion of paradigms, how and why the values and assumptions of OD practitioners may sometimes conflict with those of managers. Is it possible to resolve this conflict?

2 How does the role of OD-consultant and change agent differ from that of expert consultant?

3 You have been offered the position of HR Director/Change Agent outlined in Exhibit 21.1 on a contract lasting a maximum of six months. Drawing on your knowledge of the OD field, assess the extent to which the role's objectives are realistically achievable. What additional information (apart from salary!) would you need to know before deciding whether to accept the position?

4 Thinking about your own organisation (or one known to you):

- What are the major environmental changes (i.e. political, economic, social, technological, legal) which have impacted on its operation over the last decade?
- How has the organisation responded to these changes?
- What environmental changes do you foresee occurring in the next decade?
- How well equipped do you believe your organisation is to respond to these changes?

5 Examine the nature of the strategic, human, cultural, technological, structural and managerial systems of your organisational department. To what extent are these systems congruent with the external environment and consistent with each other? Recommend areas that might be targeted for change.

6 Conduct a 'force-field analysis' of your own organisation. What are the driving forces for change and the restraining forces likely to obstruct change? How might these restraining forces be overcome?

7 It is estimated that 70 per cent of planned major organisational change programmes fail. Explain why this is the case. What steps can be taken to improve the success of change management initiatives?

8 Identify the key characteristics of the Learning Organisation. Explain the difficulties which may be encountered when attempting to put the theoretical concept into practice.

9 Discuss the view that Knowledge Management is taking over from the pursuit of the Learning Organisation.

10 Analyse the key features of the culture of your organisation. Identify and describe the sub-cultures which exist within your organisation.

11 Assess the feasibility of a cultural change programme in your organisation.

12 In what ways do you think the culture of your organisation (a) contributes positively to and (b) hampers the effectiveness of the organisation and the development and well-being of its employees?

13 Evaluation is a critical part of any change initiative. Explain why this is the case. What factors would you take into consideration when designing an evaluation strategy?

NAME INDEX

SUBJECT INDEX

Note: **bold** page numbers indicate major references in long entries. Most references imply Britain, which is therefore omitted from the index.